To Gerlinde and Amélie,
for their love and inspiration

ANCIENT CHRISTIAN TEXTS

COMMENTARY ON ISAIAH

Eusebius of Caesarea

TRANSLATED WITH AN INTRODUCTION
AND NOTES BY
JONATHAN J. ARMSTRONG

EDITED BY
JOEL C. ELOWSKY

SERIES EDITORS
THOMAS C. ODEN AND GERALD L. BRAY

IVP Academic

An imprint of InterVarsity Press
Downers Grove, Illinois

InterVarsity Press
P.O. Box 1400, Downers Grove, IL 60515-1426
World Wide Web: www.ivpress.com
E-mail: email@ivpress.com

InterVarsity Press® is the book-publishing division of InterVarsity Christian Fellowship/USA®, a movement of students and faculty active on campus at hundreds of universities, colleges and schools of nursing in the United States of America, and a member movement of the International Fellowship of Evangelical Students. For information about local and regional activities, write Public Relations Dept., InterVarsity Christian Fellowship/USA, 6400 Schroeder Rd., P.O. Box 7895, Madison, WI 53707-7895, or visit the IVCF website at <www.intervarsity.org>.

Design: Cindy Kiple

Images: Saints Peter and Paul by Carlo Crivelli at Accademia, Venice/Art Resource, NY

Monogrammatic cross: Early Christian monogrammatic cross from Monastero, at Kunsthistorisches Museum, Vienna, Austria.
Erich Lessing/Art Resource, NY

ISBN 978-0-8308-2913-2

Printed in the United States of America ∞

Library of Congress Cataloging-in-Publication Data

Eusebius, of Caesarea, Bishop of Caesarea, approximately 260-approximately
340.
  [Commentaria in Hesaiam. English.]
  Commentary on Isaiah / Eusebius of Caesarea ; translated with an
introduction and notes by Jonathan J. Armstrong ; edited by Joel C.
Elowsky.
    pages cm.—(Ancient Christian texts)
  Includes bibliographical references and index.
  ISBN 978-0-8308-2913-2 (hardcover : alk. paper)
  1. Bible. Isaiah—Commentaries—Early works to 1800. I. Armstrong,
Jonathan J., 1980- II. Elowsky, Joel C., 1963- III. Title.
  BS1515.53.E9713 2013
  224'.107—dc23

                                                                           2013015283

P	24	23	22	21	20	19	18	17	16	15	14	13	12	11	10	9	8	7	6	5	4	3	2	1
Y	34	33	32	31	30	29	28	27	26	25	24	23	22	21	20	19	18	17	16	15	14	13

CONTENTS

GENERAL INTRODUCTION

Ancient Christian Texts (hereafter ACT) presents the full text of ancient Christian commentaries on Scripture that have remained so unnoticed that they have not yet been translated into English.

The patristic period (A.D. 95–750) is the time of the fathers of the church, when the exegesis of Scripture texts was in its primitive formation. This period spans from Clement of Rome to John of Damascus, embracing seven centuries of biblical interpretation, from the end of the New Testament to the mid-eighth century, including the Venerable Bede.

This series extends but does not reduplicate texts of the Ancient Christian Commentary on Scripture (ACCS). It presents full-length translations of texts that appear only as brief extracts in the ACCS. The ACCS began years ago authorizing full-length translations of key patristic texts on Scripture in order to provide fresh sources of valuable commentary that previously were not available in English. It is from these translations that the ACT series has emerged.

A multiyear project such as this requires a well-defined objective. The task is straightforward: *to introduce full-length translations of key texts of early Christian teaching, homilies and commentaries on a particular book of Scripture.* These are seminal documents that have decisively shaped the entire subsequent history of biblical exegesis, but in our time have been largely ignored.

To carry out this mission each volume of the Ancient Christian Texts series has four aspirations:

1. To show the approach of one of the early Christian writers in dealing with the problems of understanding, reading and conveying the meaning of a particular book of Scripture.

2. To make more fully available the whole argument of the ancient Christian interpreter of Scripture to all who wish to think with the early church about a particular canonical text.

3. To broaden the base of the biblical studies, Christian teaching and preaching to include classical Christian exegesis.

4. To stimulate Christian historical, biblical, theological and pastoral scholarship toward deeper inquiry into early classic practitioners of scriptural interpretation.

For Whom Is This Series Designed?

We have selected and translated these texts primarily for general and nonprofessional use by an audience of persons who study the Bible regularly.

In varied cultural settings around the world, contemporary readers are asking how they might grasp the meaning of sacred texts under the instruction of the great minds of the ancient church. They often study books of the Bible verse by verse, book by book, in groups and workshops, sometimes with a modern commentary in hand. But many who study the Bible intensively hunger to have available as well the thoughts of a reliable classic Christian commentator on this same text. This series will give the modern commentators a classical text for comparison and amplification. Readers will judge for themselves as to how valuable or complementary are their insights and guidance.

The classic texts we are translating were originally written for anyone (lay or clergy, believers or seekers) who wished to reflect and meditate with the great minds of the early church. They sought to illuminate the plain sense, theological wisdom, and moral and spiritual meaning of an individual book of Scripture. They were not written for an academic audience, but for a community of faith shaped by the sacred text.

Yet in serving this general audience, the editors remain determined not to neglect the rigorous requirements and needs of academic readers who until recently have had few full translations available to them in the history of exegesis. So this series is designed also to serve public libraries, universities, academic classes, homiletic preparation and historical interests worldwide in Christian scholarship and interpretation.

Hence our expected audience is not limited to the highly technical and specialized scholarly field of patristic studies, with its strong bent toward detailed word studies and explorations of cultural contexts. Though all of our editors and translators are patristic and linguistic scholars, they also are scholars who search for the meanings and implications of the texts. The audience is not primarily the university scholar concentrating on the study of the history of the transmission of the text or those with highly focused interests in textual morphology or historical-critical issues. If we succeed in serving our wider readers practically and well, we hope to serve as well college and seminary courses in Bible, church history, historical theology, hermeneutics and homiletics. These texts have not until now been available to these classes.

Readiness for Classic Spiritual Formation

Today global Christians are being steadily drawn toward these biblical and patristic sources for daily meditation and spiritual formation. They are on the outlook for primary classic sources of spiritual formation and biblical interpretation, presented in accessible form and grounded in reliable scholarship.

These crucial texts have had an extended epoch of sustained influence on Scripture interpretation, but virtually no influence in the modern period. They also deserve a hearing among modern readers and scholars. There is a growing awareness of the speculative excesses and spiritual and homiletic limitations of much post-Enlightenment criticism. Meanwhile the motifs, methods and approaches of ancient exegetes have remained unfamiliar not only to historians but to otherwise highly literate biblical scholars, trained exhaustively in the methods of historical and scientific criticism.

It is ironic that our times, which claim to be so fully furnished with historical insight and research methods, have neglected these texts more than scholars in previous centuries who could read them in their original languages.

This series provides indisputable evidence of the modern neglect of classic Christian exegesis: it remains a fact that extensive and once authoritative classic commentaries on Scripture still remain untranslated into any modern language. Even in China such a high level of neglect has not befallen classic Buddhist, Taoist and Confucian commentaries.

Ecumenical Scholarship

This series, like its two companion series, the ACCS and Ancient Christian Doctrine (ACD), is an expression of unceasing ecumenical efforts that have enjoyed the wide cooperation of distinguished scholars of many differing academic communities. Under this classic textual umbrella, it has brought together in common spirit Christians who have long distanced themselves from each other by competing church memories. But all of these traditions have an equal right to appeal to the early history of Christian exegesis. All of these traditions can, without a sacrifice of principle or intellect, come together to study texts common to them all. This is its ecumenical significance.

This series of translations is respectful of a distinctively theological reading of Scripture that cannot be reduced to historical, philosophical, scientific, or sociological insights or methods alone. It takes seriously the venerable tradition of ecumenical reflection concerning the premises of revelation, providence, apostolicity, canon and consensuality. A high respect is here granted, despite modern assumptions, to uniquely Christian theological forms of reasoning, such as classical consensual christological and triune reasoning, as distinguishing premises of classic Christian textual interpretation. These cannot be acquired by empirical methods alone. This approach does not pit theology against critical theory; instead, it incorporates critical historical methods and brings them into coordinate accountability within its larger purpose of listening to Scripture.

The internationally diverse character of our editors and translators corresponds with the global range of our audience, which bridges many major communions of Christianity. We have sought to bring together a distinguished international network of Protestant, Catholic and Orthodox scholars, editors and translators of the highest quality and reputation to accomplish this design.

But why just now at this historical moment is this need for patristic wisdom felt particularly by so many readers of Scripture? Part of the reason is that these readers have been longer deprived of significant contact with many of these vital sources of classic Christian exegesis.

The Ancient Commentary Tradition

This series focuses on texts that comment on Scripture and teach its meaning. We define a commentary in its plain-sense definition as a series of illustrative or explanatory notes on any work of enduring significance. The word *commentary* is an Anglicized form of the Latin *commentarius* (or "annotation" or "memoranda" on a subject, text or series of events). In its theological meaning it is a work that explains, analyzes or expounds a biblical book or portion of Scripture. Tertullian, Origen, John Chrysostom, Jerome, Augustine and Clement of Alexandria all revealed their familiarity with both the secular and religious commentators available to them as they unpacked the meanings of the sacred text at hand.

The commentary in ancient times typically began with a general introduction covering such questions as authorship, date, purpose and audience. It commented as needed on grammatical or lexical problems in the text and provided explanations of difficulties in the text. It typically moved verse by verse through a Scripture text, seeking to make its meaning clear and its import understood.

The general Western literary genre of commentary has been definitively shaped by the history of early Christian commentaries on Scripture. It is from Origen, Hilary, the *Opus imperfectum in Matthaeum*, John Chrysostom and Cyril of Alexandria that we learn what a commentary is—far more so than in the case of classic medical, philosophical or poetic commentaries. It leaves too much unsaid simply to assume that the Christian biblical commentary took a previously extant literary genre and reshaped it for Christian texts. Rather it is more accurate to say that *the Western literary genre of the commentary (and especially the biblical commentary) has patristic commentaries as its decisive pattern and prototype.*

It is only in the last two centuries, since the development of modern historicist methods of criticism, that modern writers have sought more strictly to delimit the definition of a commentary so as to include only certain limited interests focusing largely on historical-critical method, philological and grammatical observations, literary analysis, and socio-political or economic circumstances impinging on the text. While respecting all these approaches, the ACT editors do not hesitate to use the classic word *commentary* to define more broadly the genre of this series. These are commentaries in their classic sense.

The ACT editors freely take the assumption that the Christian canon is to be respected as the church's sacred text. The reading and preaching of Scripture are vital to religious life. The central hope of this endeavor is that it might contribute in some small way to the revitalization of religious faith and community through a renewed discovery of the earliest readings of the church's Scriptures.

An Appeal to Allow the Text to Speak for Itself

This prompts two appeals:

1. For those who begin by assuming as normative for a commentary only the norms considered typical for modern expressions of what a commentary is, we ask: Please allow the ancient commentators to define *commentarius* according to their own lights. Those who assume the preemptive authority and truthfulness of modern critical methods alone will always tend to view the classic Christian exegetes as dated, quaint, premodern, hence inadequate, and in some instances comic or even mean-spirited, prejudiced, unjust and oppressive. So in the interest of hermeneutical fairness, it is recommended that the modern reader not impose upon ancient Christian exegetes modern assumptions about valid readings of Scripture. The ancient Christian writers constantly challenge these unspoken, hidden and indeed often camouflaged assumptions that have become commonplace in our time.

We leave it to others to discuss the merits of ancient versus modern methods of exegesis. But even this cannot be done honestly without a serious examination of the texts of ancient exegesis. Ancient commentaries may be disqualified as commentaries by modern standards. But they remain commentaries by the standards of those who anteceded and formed the basis of the modern commentary.

The attempt to read a Scripture text while ruling out all theological and moral assumptions—as well as ecclesial, sacramental and dogmatic assumptions that have prevailed generally in the community of faith out of which it emerged—is a very thin enterprise indeed. Those who tendentiously may read a single page of patristic exegesis, gasp and toss it away because it does not conform adequately to the canons of modern exegesis and historicist commentary are surely not exhibiting a valid model for critical inquiry today.

2. In ancient Christian exegesis, chains of biblical references were often very important in thinking about the text in relation to the whole testimony of sacred Scripture, by the analogy of faith, comparing text with text, on the premise that *scripturam ex scriptura explicandam esse*. When ancient exegesis weaves many Scripture texts together, it does not limit its focus to a single text as much modern exegesis prefers, but constantly relates them to other texts, by analogy, intensively using typological reasoning, as did the rabbinic tradition.

Since the principle prevails in ancient Christian exegesis that each text is illumined by other texts and by the whole narrative of the history of revelation, we find in patristic comments on a given text many other subtexts interwoven in order to illumine that text. In these ways the models of exegesis often do not correspond with modern commentary assumptions, which tend to resist or rule out chains of scriptural reference. We implore the reader not to force the assumptions of twentieth-century hermeneutics upon the ancient Christian writers, who themselves knew nothing of what we now call hermeneutics.

The Complementarity of Research Methods in this Series

The Ancient Christian Texts series will employ several interrelated methods of research, which the editors and translators seek to bring together in a working integration. Principal among these methods are the following:

1. The editors, translators and annotators will bring to bear the best resources of *textual criticism* in preparation for their volumes. This series is not intended to produce a new critical edition of the original-language text. The best urtext in the original language will be used. Significant variants in the earliest manuscript sources of the text may be commented upon as needed in the annotations. But it will be assumed that the editors and translators will be familiar with the textual ambiguities of a particular text and be able to state their conclusions about significant differences among scholars. Since we are working with ancient texts that have, in some cases, problematic or ambiguous passages, we are obliged to employ all methods of historical, philological and textual inquiry appropriate to the study of ancient texts. To that end, we will appeal to the most reliable text-critical scholarship of both biblical and patristic studies. We will assume that our editors and translators have reviewed the international literature of textual critics regarding their text so as to provide the reader with a translation of the most authoritative and reliable form of the ancient text. We will leave it to the volume editors and translators, under the supervision of the general editors, to make these assessments. This will include the challenge of considering which variants within the biblical text itself might impinge upon the patristic text, and which forms or stemma of the biblical text the patristic writer was employing. The annotator will supply explanatory footnotes where these textual challenges may raise potential confusions for the reader.

2. Our editors and translators will seek to understand the *historical context* (including socioeconomic, political and psychological aspects as needed) of the text. These understandings are often vital to right discernment of the writer's intention. Yet we do not see our primary mission as that of discussing in detail these contexts. They are to be factored into the translation and commented on as needed in the annotations, but are not to become the primary focus of this series. Our central interest is less in the social location of the text or the philological history of particular words than in authorial intent and accurate translation. Assuming a proper social-historical contextualization of the text, the main focus of this series will be upon a dispassionate and fair translation and analysis of the text itself.

3. The main task is to set forth the meaning of the biblical text itself as understood by the patristic writer. The intention of our volume editors and translators is to help the reader see clearly into the meanings which patristic commentators have discovered in the biblical text. *Exegesis* in its classic sense implies an effort to explain, interpret and comment upon a text, its meaning, its sources and its connections with other texts. It implies

a close reading of the text, utilizing whatever linguistic, historical, literary or theological resources are available to explain the text. It is contrasted with *eisegesis*, which implies that interpreters have imposed their own personal opinions or assumptions upon the text. The patristic writers actively practiced intratextual exegesis, which seeks to define and identify the exact wording of the text, its grammatical structure and the interconnectedness of its parts. They also practiced extratextual exegesis, seeking to discern the geographical, historical or cultural context in which the text was written. Our editors and annotators will also be attentive as needed to the ways in which the ancient Christian writer described his own interpreting process or hermeneutic assumptions.

4. The underlying philosophy of translation that we employ in this series is, like the Ancient Christian Commentary on Scripture, termed *dynamic equivalency*. We wish to avoid the pitfalls of either too loose a paraphrase or too rigid a literal translation. We seek language that is literary but not purely literal. Whenever possible we have opted for the metaphors and terms that are normally in use in everyday English-speaking culture. Our purpose is to allow the ancient Christian writers to speak for themselves to ordinary readers in the present generation. We want to make it easier for the Bible reader to gain ready access to the deepest reflection of the ancient Christian community of faith on a particular book of Scripture. We seek a thought-for-thought translation rather than a formal equivalence or word-for-word style. This requires the words to be first translated accurately and then rendered in understandable idiom. We seek to present the same thoughts, feelings, connotations and effects of the original text in everyday English language. We have used vocabulary and language structures commonly used by the average person. We do not leave the quality of translation only to the primary translator, but pass it through several levels of editorial review before confirming it.

The Function of the ACT Introductions, Annotations and Translations

In writing the introduction for a particular volume of the ACT series, the translator or volume editor will discuss, where possible, the opinion of the writer regarding authorship of the text, the importance of the biblical book for other patristic interpreters, the availability or paucity of patristic comment, any salient points of debate between the Fathers, and any special challenges involved in translating and editing the particular volume. The introduction affords the opportunity to frame the entire commentary in a manner that will help the general reader understand the nature and significance of patristic comment on the biblical text under consideration and to help readers find their critical bearings so as to read and use the commentary in an informed way.

The footnotes will assist the reader with obscurities and potential confusions. In the annotations the volume editors have identified Scripture allusions and historical references embedded within the texts. Their purpose is to help the reader move easily from passage to passage without losing a sense of the whole.

The ACT general editors seek to be circumspect and meticulous in commissioning volume editors and translators. We strive for a high level of consistency and literary quality throughout the course of this series. We have sought out as volume editors and translators those patristic and biblical scholars who are thoroughly familiar with their original language sources, who are informed historically, and who are sympathetic to the needs of ordinary nonprofessional readers who may not have professional language skills.

Thomas C. Oden and Gerald L. Bray, Series Editors

ABBREVIATIONS

A.D.	anno domine
ca.	circa (about)
d.	died
ANF	Ante-Nicene Fathers
PL	Patrologia Latina

Eusebius of Caesarea

Comm. in Is.	*Commentarius in Isaiam (Commentary on Isaiah)*
Eccl. Hist.	*Historia Ecclesiastica (Ecclesiastical History)*
Vita Const.	*Vita Constantini (Life of Constantine)*

Jerome

De Vir. Ill.	*De Viris Illustribus (Illustrious Men)*

Origen

Princ.	*De Principiis (On First Principles)*

LXX	Septuagint
MT	Masoretic Text
NETS	New English Translation of the Septuagint
RSV	Revised Standard Version

TRANSLATOR'S ACKNOWLEDGMENTS

As with so many academic projects, this translation had a far longer history than I imagined it would when I first began. One morning, while walking from one campus building to another at Fordham University in New York City, my PhD adviser, Joseph T. Lienhard, S.J., mentioned to me that Eusebius of Caesarea's *Commentary on Isaiah* had not yet been translated into any modern language, although it represented the earliest Christian commentary on Isaiah to have survived antiquity and one of Eusebius's major exegetical works. As I remember that lovely spring morning now, I suspect that Father Lienhard was purposefully selling me on the project—especially as he frequently used to say that every young patristic scholar owes at least one new translation to the discipline. I had written my doctoral dissertation on Eusebius of Caesarea's role in the formation of the New Testament canon, and I was therefore intrigued that such a valuable ancient text from such a major church father had not yet appeared in translation.

During my first postdoctoral position at the Friedrich-Alexander-Universität Erlangen-Nürnberg in 2006–2007—a position for which I received a generous grant from the Deutscher Akademischer Austauschdienst—I researched under Professor Hanns Christof Brennecke as he and his team produced critical editions of the Greek texts of Athanasius. This was my first introduction to text-critical work, and the experience gave me the necessary courage to attempt a translation of Eusebius's commentary. Nevertheless, I knew that I would find the translation project extraordinarily challenging. Father Lienhard and Professor Brennecke had independently warned me about the impenetrability of Eusebius's Greek idiom. And then, there was the ominous rumor that not many years prior a French scholar had died trying to translate Eusebius's commentary for the *Sources Chrétiennes* series. It was in 2007–2008, during my second postdoctoral position at Wycliffe Hall, University of Oxford, that I began translating the commentary in earnest under the mentorship of the Rev. Dr. Peter W. L. Walker. Soon after arriving at Oxford, however, I was presented with the opportunity to lecture in New Testament and tutor in ancient Christian studies, an opportunity which I eagerly accepted as a brilliant step forward for my teaching career but which also significantly slowed progress on the translation. When I returned to the United States in 2009, now newly married and seeking employment amid the shattered economic conditions following the financial crisis, I felt I had no choice but to abandon the project. Had it not been for the persistent encouragement of my parents, Alan and Kathryn Armstrong, and my parents-in-law, Christoph and Sarah Jäschke, I would never have resumed translation.

After I joined the theological faculty of Moody Bible Institute – Spokane in 2010, the project took on new life. My deepest thanks go to Ms. Wendy Liddell and Dr. Jack Lewis, who have done so much as academic administrators to make MBI a remarkably welcoming scholarly community. Without their vision and support, the project would no doubt yet be years from completion. Dr. John McMath, my colleague at MBI and a formidable Isaiah scholar in his own right, spurred me on with his passionate interest and insightful queries. My thanks also go to my indefatigable research assistant, Collin Duff, and my gracious editor, Joel Elowsky, whose expertise improved the translation on innumerable points. I am indebted more than I can say or know to my wife, Gerlinde Armstrong, who has been a constant source of strength and confidence as I have pursued this project to completion.

Shortly after his conversion, Augustine wrote to Ambrose, the famous bishop of Milan, and asked him to recommend books that he should read in preparation for ordained ministry. Ambrose wrote back and advised Augustine to read Isaiah, citing as his reason the prophet's clear presentation of the gospel and call of the Gentiles. Augustine tells his reader in *Confessions* 9.5 that, although he endeavored to follow Ambrose's reading plan, he managed to work through only the first part of the prophecy before moving on to more perspicacious reading, never again to return to the study of Isaiah. "Fools rush in where angels and great saints fear to tread," I thought to myself many times as I struggled to untangle Eusebius's perverse grammar and strained to distill the intended meaning of his neologisms. I am acutely aware that future research will reveal many shortcomings in my translation. However, my hope is that this translation will contribute to our understanding of the early Christian interpretation of Isaiah, our understanding of the universality of God's call of salvation and ultimately our understanding of the gospel.

TRANSLATOR'S INTRODUCTION

Best known in modern times as the author of the *Historia Ecclesiastica*, Eusebius was better known in antiquity as an apologist and erudite biblical scholar.[1] And yet, despite his reputation in antiquity as a formidable student of Scripture, neither of Eusebius of Caesarea's magisterial works of exegesis—neither the *Commentary on Isaiah* nor the *Commentary on the Psalms*—has been available in complete form in any modern language until the publication of this translation. The fact that the *Commentary on Isaiah* has never before appeared in any modern language is all the more remarkable when one remembers that this commentary is the first Christian commentary on the prophet Isaiah to have survived to the present. Complete portraits of Eusebius of Caesarea's theology have been absent as a result of the inaccessibility of the *Commentary on Isaiah*. It is my hope that this translation will facilitate and encourage new scholarship on Eusebius of Caesarea's theology and the history of fourth-century Christian exegesis.

The Date of the Commentary

There has never been any dispute over the authorship of the commentary, but consensus has not yet been achieved concerning its date. The majority of scholars have been willing to venture only that the commentary was written after the Nicene Council in A.D. 325—reasoning that the optimism that permeates the commentary clearly reflects the Constantinian epoch. The discussion of the date of Eusebius's *Commentary on Isaiah* effectively has not developed since Adolf von Harnack, according to whose research the *terminus a quo* is to be set to 324 and the *terminus ad quem* cannot be set before the date of Eusebius's death in 339.[2] In setting the *terminus a quo* to 324, Harnack first notes that Eusebius speaks of persecution as a past reality, especially in

---

[1]D. S. Wallace-Hadrill writes in his classic study: "To the historian, Eusebius is the author of the *Chronicle* and the *Ecclesiastical History*. To the classical scholar, he is the author of the *Praeparatio Evangelica*, a storehouse of information about many centuries of Greek literature. The geographer knows him for his *Onomasticon*. The student of the biblical text looks to Eusebius as one who not only had himself a lively interest in matters concerning the text and canon of the scriptures, but who also quoted the scriptures copiously in almost every work he wrote. The theologian knows him for his part in the fourth century [*sic*] christological controversies following the rise of Arianism. Excavations of fourth-century churches in Palestine are made in the light of Eusebius' detailed descriptions of some of the great foundations of his time. From these and other view-points his work has been read, and an extensive bibliography of specialist studies in these different fields might be compiled" (*Eusebius of Caesarea* [London: A. R. Mowbray, 1960], 7).

[2]Adolf von Harnack, *Geschichte der altchristlichen Litteratur bis Eusebius* (Leipzig: J. C. Hinrichs, 1958), 2.2.123.

Comm. in Is. 44.5.[3] Harnack further notes that in *Comm. in Is.* 49.23, Eusebius exults in the conversion of Constantine and his programmatic privileging of the church. Although Eusebius does not specifically state that he is referring to Constantine, the allusion is unmistakable:

> He then states that *kings* will be the *foster fathers* of the church of God, and he says that the *women who rule* them will be her *nurses*. And we saw with our own eyes this literally fulfilled among them, for those who bear authority in the abovementioned position have carried the church of God as *foster fathers*. And the *women who rule* over them (here the text is clearly referring to those who are served as the "principalities and powers" over each nation and each district in the abovementioned kingdom) will provide for those of the church who are in need as *nurses*, supplying them with an abundant allowance by royal sanction [νεύματι βασιλικῷ τὰ σιτηρέσια χορηγοῦσαι].
> . . . And whoever has seen with his own eyes the aforementioned "principalities and powers" in the church of God bending their knees and pressing their foreheads to the ground, how could he not confess that he has witnessed the literal and historical fulfillment of this exact prophecy, which says: *On the face of the earth they shall bow down to you, and they shall lick the dust of your feet.*[4]

The above reference to the "abundant allowance by royal sanction" reads remarkably similarly to Eusebius's description from *Vita Constantini* of the charity Constantine bestowed on the church:

> But to the churches of God in particular he was exceptionally generous in his provision, in one place bestowing estates, and elsewhere grain allowances [σιτοδοσίας ἐπὶ χορηγίᾳ] to feed poor men, orphan children, and women in distress. Then with great concern he also provided huge quantities of clothing for the naked and unclad. He singled out as worthy of special honour those who had dedicated their lives to godly philosophy. He would all but worship God's choir of those sanctified in perpetual virginity, believing that in the souls of such as these dwelt the God to whom they had consecrated themselves.[5]

Scholarship after Harnack has produced no more decisive conclusions. Wallace-Hadrill avers: "We cannot be more definite about its date than placing it well after 324."[6] In his *Handbook of Patristic Exegesis*, Charles Kannengiesser offers only that the commentary "probably dates from the years following the Council of Nicaea, 325."[7] Michael J. Hollerich, whose *Eusebius of Caesarea's Commentary on Isaiah* has thus far been the only

---

[3]Wallace-Hadrill agrees: "The *Commentary on Isaiah* cannot be dated with certainty, but the references to the persecution which occur throughout the work make clear that it was composed after the persecution was ended" (*Eusebius of Caesarea*, 32).

[4]*Comm. in Is.* 49.23; Joseph Ziegler, ed., *Der Jesajakommentar* (Berlin: Akademie-Verlag, 1975), 316.

[5]*Vita Const.* 4.28; Eusebius, *Life of Constantine: Introduction, Translation and Commentary*, trans. Averil Cameron and Stuart G. Hall (Oxford: Clarendon Press, 1999), 163; Friedhelm Winkelmann, ed., *Über das Leben des Kaisers Konstantin* (Berlin: Akademie-Verlag, 1975), 130.

[6]*Eusebius of Caesarea*, 52. Wallace-Hadrill is willing to commit only to the conclusion that "the *Commentary on Isaiah* is unambiguously a post-Nicene work" (51).

[7]Charles Kannengiesser, *Handbook of Patristic Exegesis* (Leiden: Brill, 2004), 2:677.

monograph-length study of this work, deduces that the absence of direct references to the Arian controversy may indicate that the commentary "was written in the immediate wake of the Council of Nicaea."[8] Timothy D. Barns, who has conducted the most exhaustive study of the chronology of Eusebius's works, concludes that Eusebius was "at work" on the commentary around the year 330.[9]

In the process of translating the commentary, I came across a pair of previously un-noted paragraphs that I am convinced allude to the baptism of Constantine. If my thesis proves correct, we may advance the *terminus a quo* of the *Commentary on Isaiah* to 337, and we may therefore date the commentary to the very end of Eusebius's life. The first of the relevant passages comes in *Comm. in Is.* 60:3-4, in which Eusebius comments on the Septuagintal phrase "nations shall walk by your light, and kings by your brightness":

> For it was this *light* [φωτί] that you announced before, and it was by this *light* that the prophets and patriarchs and all those among the Jews who lived as citizens of the godly commonwealth had the eyes of their souls *enlightened* [ἐφωτίσθησαν], and it is by this *light* that the *Gentiles*, foreigners and people of other races will be *enlightened* [φωτισθήσεται]. The text also speaks of *brightness* [λαμπρότητι], for you announced that the city has been wiped [ἐσμηγμένη] and scrubbed [ἀποσμηχομένη] and brightened [λαμπρυνομένη] and cleansed [καθαιρομένη] from every filth [ῥύπον] and stain [κηλῖδα] by the divine words [λόγοις θείοις]. And foreign *kings* will be cleansed by this *brightness* and scrubbed in the power of the divine mysteries [θείων μυστηρίων]. One has to marvel and be amazed at the fulfillment of the oracle, how it was fulfilled during our times when the above *kings* were deemed worthy [καταξιουμένων] of the grace "by washing" [cf. Tit 3:5] [διὰ λουτροῦ].[10]

It is noteworthy that Eusebius has reversed the order of the terms *kings* and *nations* as they appear in the Septuagint, thus arriving upon the phrase "kings by your brightness." Eusebius's alteration of the text is not arbitrary but motivated by his conviction that the baptism of Constantine is to be seen as the fulfillment of biblical prophecy. When one compares the paragraph above with Eusebius's description of the baptism of Constantine in *Vita Constantini*, the allusion becomes clear:

> But when he became aware that his life was ending, he perceived that this was the time to purify [καθάρσεως] himself from the offences which he had at any time com-mitted [πεπλημμελημένων], trusting that whatever sins it had been his lot as a mortal to commit [διαμαρτεῖν], he could wash [ἀπορρύψασθαι] them from his soul by the power of the secret words [λόγων ἀπορρήτων] and the saving bath [σωτηρίῳ λουτρῷ]. . . . [The bishops] in their turn performing the customary rites fulfilled the divine laws and imparted the secret gifts [ἀπορρήτων], giving such preliminary instruc-tion as is required [ὅσα χρὴ προδιαστειλάμενοι]. Alone of all the Emperors from

---

[8]Michael J. Hollerich, *Eusebius of Caesarea's Commentary on Isaiah* (Oxford: Clarendon Press, 1999), 12.
[9]Timothy D. Barns, *Constantine and Eusebius* (Cambridge, MA: Harvard University Press, 1981), 278.
[10]Ziegler, *Der Jesajakommentar*, 370-71.

the beginning of time Constantine was initiated by rebirth [ἀναγεννώμενος] in the mysteries of Christ [Χριστοῦ μυστηρίοις], and exulted in the Spirit on being vouch-safed [ἀξιούμενος] the divine seal [θείας σφραγῖδος], and was renewed and filled with divine light [φωτὸς θείου], rejoicing in his soul because of his intense faith, awestruck at the manifestation of the divinely inspired power. When the due ceremonies were complete, he put on bright [λαμπροῖς] imperial clothes which shone [ἐκλάμπουσι] like light [φωτὸς], and rested on a pure white couch, being unwilling to touch a purple robe again. Then he lifted up his voice and offered up a prayer of thanksgiving to God, after which he went on to say, "I know that now I am in the true sense blessed, that now I have been shown worthy [πεφάνθαι ἄξιον] of immortal life, and now that I have received divine light [θείου φωτός]."[11]

The second relevant passage comes in *Comm. in Is.* 60:10-11, when Eusebius again appears to allude to the baptism of Constantine:

Therefore, it has been said: *And your gates shall always be opened—day and night they shall not be shut.* And who are the *gates* of the city of God except the teachers who instruct in elementary and introductory doctrine [αἱ στοιχειώδεις καὶ εἰσακτικαὶ διδασκαλίαι], whom the text says are *opened night and day* to all so as to admit all who have been elected from all the nations to serve God? Therefore, the text says: *To bring to you the power* [δύναμιν] *of nations,* and he promises to admit even the *kings* of their *nations* into the aforementioned *gates.* For, the *powers* [δυνάμεις] of *nations* are the ones who are able to say: "I can do all things in him who strengthens me," and their *kings* are the chosen ones who are worthy of the kingdom of heaven. And, since we have now seen literal *kings*—Roman emperors—run through the *gates* of the church of God and be deemed worthy [καταξιουμένους] of the mysteries [μυστηρίων] within these *gates,* how could anyone not testify to the truth of the prophecy?[12]

Why does Eusebius merely allude to the baptism of Constantine, speaking of the king who was "deemed worthy of the grace 'by washing'" and the Roman emperor who ran "through the *gates* of the church of God" and was "deemed worthy of the mysteries"? Why does Eusebius not name Constantine? It may be that doing so would have offended Eusebius's poetic sensibilities—at least, we can say that Eusebius does not even consistently supply names in his account of the baptism of Constantine in *Vita Constantini.*[13]

Setting the *terminus a quo* of the *Commentary on Isaiah* to the date of the baptism of

---

[11]*Vita Const.* 4.61.2, 4.62.4-4.63.1; *Life of Constantine,* 177-78; Winkelmann, *Über das Leben des Kaisers Konstantin,* 145-46. Additionally, further on in *Comm. in Is.* 60.4, Eusebius writes: "For, since they are tender souls and still infants, 'longing for the spiritual and pure milk like newborn babes,' and since they are *'children* of Abraham' through rebirth in Christ [ἐν Χριστῷ ἀναγεννήσεως], they are borne along and *carried on shoulders* and lifted up by their teachers who lead them by the hand [ὑπὸ τῶν χειραγωγούντων αὐτὰς διδασκάλων]" (Ziegler, *Der Jesajakommentar,* 371). These lines parallel Eusebius's description of the "preliminary instruction" that Constantine received before baptism (*Vita Const.* 4.62.4; *Life of Constantine,* 178).

[12]Ziegler, *Der Jesajakommentar,* 375. Eusebius's enthusiasm for interpreting the Constantinian revolution as the fulfillment of biblical prophecy continues in *Comm. in Is.* 60:16, when he perhaps again alludes to the catechetical instruction that Constantine received before baptism and definitely alludes to Constantine's lavish construction projects for the church.

[13]In explaining why Eusebius of Caesarea does not mention that it was Eusebius of Nicomedia who baptized Constantine, Cameron writes: "It is standard practice for Eusebius of Caesarea as for other panegyrists to leave even major figures unnamed" (*Life of Constantine,* 341).

Constantine, several days before the emperor's death on May 22, 337,[14] we therefore conclude that this work represents one of the final works of Eusebius's life. This was a time of intense literary activity for the aged bishop of Caesarea, for in these final months Eusebius finished not only the *Commentary on Isaiah* but also *Against Marcellus* and *Ecclesiastical Theology*. Because Eusebius celebrates the beauties of Constantine's Church of the Holy Sepulcher in his *Commentary on the Psalms*, and because it is known that this church was consecrated in 335, we may add this monumental work to the list of books that Eusebius completed in his final years.[15] Eusebius died on May 30, 339, as one of the best respected biblical scholars of his day and one whose ecclesiastical responsibilities had thrust him into some of the most controversial theological intrigues of the century.[16]

The Manuscript History of the Commentary

A critical edition of the *Commentary on Isaiah* has been available since 1975, when Joseph Ziegler published *Der Jesajakommentar* in the *Griechische Christliche Schriftsteller* (GCS) series. The fact that the commentary has been available in a critical edition for a relatively short time stands as the primary reason why the commentary has been so little studied thus far. Before the appearance of the GCS edition, scholars had access to the text of the commentary only in volume 24 of J. P. Migne's *Patrologia Graeca* series.[17] The text reproduced by Migne represents the work of the Maurist patristic scholar Bernard de Montfaucon.[18] Montfaucon collated his edition from four Medieval Greek manuscripts, all of which are housed at the Bibliothèque Nationale in Paris. Two of these Greek manuscripts date from the tenth century (codices 1891 and 2437), one dates from the twelfth century (codex 2438), and one dates from the thirteenth century (codex 1892). Three of the four manuscripts are disheveled and fragmentary, but the manuscripts are relatively unanimous in their testimony to the first sixteen chapters of the commentary. After chapter sixteen of the text, there are significant differences between the manuscripts, and careful research was required to reconstruct the text. In the preface to the GCS edition, Ziegler explains the most important of the editorial decisions necessary in preparing the critical edition of the Greek text for publication, and I must refer the interested reader to his expert introduction for further details.[19]

---

[14]*Life of Constantine*, 340.

[15]See *Comm. in Ps.* 87.10.

[16]See J. B. Lightfoot, "Eusebius of Caesarea," in *Dictionary of Christian Biography*, ed. William George Smith and Henry Wace (London: J. Murray, 1887), 2:318-34. This article remains one of the most complete accounts of Eusebius's biography available.

[17]ΕΥΣΕΒΙΟΥ ΤΟΥ ΠΑΜΦΙΛΟΥ ΥΠΟΜΝΗΜΑΤΑ ΕΙΣ ΤΟΝ ΕΣΑΙΑΝ, EUSEBII PAMPHILI COMMENTARIA IN HESAIAM (Paris, 1857), 77-526.

[18]*Collectio nova Patrum et Scriptorum Graecorum II* (Paris, 1706), 347-593.

[19]Ziegler, *Der Jesajakommentar*, x-xviii; see also Hollerich, *Eusebius of Caesarea's Commentary on Isaiah*, 15-18; Robert Devreesse, "L'édition du Commentaire d'Eusèbe de Césarée sur Isaïe. Interpolations et omissions," *Revue Biblique* 42 (1933): 540-55.

Early Christian Exegesis of Isaiah

Eusebius's work is the first Christian commentary on Isaiah to have survived antiquity. Nevertheless, Eusebius was not the first Christian to begin drafting a commentary on Isaiah, and it would certainly not be true to say that it fell to Eusebius alone to develop a Christian reading of Isaiah. Jesus quoted Isaiah often, and the apostolic community continued to explain Christian tradition in the language of the prophet Isaiah. Origen of Alexandria was the first to venture to commit a systematic interpretation of Isaiah to writing, but despite the fact that he dedicated thirty volumes to the monumental project, Origen's commentary extended only to Isaiah 30:6.[20] In his own commentary, Eusebius repeatedly refers to Origen's earlier work, informing the reader at which point several of the volumes of Origen's commentary ended.[21] It is therefore apparent that Eusebius worked with Origen's commentary open beside him, and we may conclude that many of Eusebius's observations found their source in Origen, although because Origen's commentary has been lost (except for a couple of fragments), there is no way to verify the exact percentage of Eusebius's commentary that was copied from Origen's.[22] Jerome provides conflicting accounts concerning whether Eusebius published his own commentary in ten or fifteen books,[23] and this has led some to speculate that Eusebius circulated the first ten books before completing the entire commentary.

Jerome records that Hippolytus of Rome (d. ca. A.D. 236) and Victorinus of Pettau (d. ca. A.D. 304) both composed commentaries on Isaiah before Eusebius.[24] However, Eusebius appears not to have been aware of Hippolytus's commentary on Isaiah, since he does not mention it in his list of Hippolytus's works,[25] and Eusebius never anywhere demonstrates knowledge of Victorinus's works, which were written in Latin. Only the briefest of fragments of Hippolytus's commentary survives, and nothing from Victorinus's is known to exist, rendering a comparison of these earlier works with Eusebius's *Commentary on Isaiah* impossible. After Eusebius, John Chrysostom, Jerome, Cyril of Alexandria, Theodoret of Cyrrhus and Procopius of Gaza each published commentaries on Isaiah. Jerome acknowledges that he had access to both Eusebius's commentary and to Origen's when he wrote his own. It appears that Jerome relied in places so completely on Eusebius that his citations of the text of Isaiah are drawn neither from the Septuagint nor from the Vulgate

---

[20]Eusebius mentions Origen's commentary on Isaiah among Origen's Caesarean works (*Eccl. Hist.* 6.32.1-3), not among Origen's earlier Alexandrian works (*Eccl. Hist.* 6.24.1-3). Eusebius attests: "Origen himself was busy at that time putting together his *Commentary on Isaiah.* . . . On the third section of Isaiah, as far as the vision of the beasts in the desert, thirty books have come into my hands" (*Eccl. Hist.* 6.32.1 [*The History of the Church*, trans. G. A. Williamson (London: Penguin, 1989), 269]).

[21]*Comm. in Is.* 7:5-9; 10:7-11, 22-23; 13:16; 14:4-7, 8-21; 16:7-8; 30:5.

[22]Origen's commentary on Isaiah has been lost, but nine of his homilies on Isaiah have been preserved in Jerome's translation (see PL 24:901-36).

[23]See Jerome *De Vir. Ill.,* 81.2; *Comm. in Is.* 1.1.

[24]*De Vir. Ill.* 61.2; 74.2.

[25]*Hist. Eccl.* 6.22.1-2.

but directly from Eusebius's commentary.[26] Inasmuch as it greatly informed Jerome's own interpretation of Isaiah, Eusebius's commentary enjoys a colossal legacy not only in Greek exegesis but in the Latin exegetical tradition as well.[27]

Eusebius's Theory of Interpretation

The first point of reference in any discussion of Eusebius's hermeneutics is Origen—whose protégé Eusebius proves himself to be in so many respects—and yet, one cannot explain Eusebius's exegesis by examining the theories of Origen alone. Wallace-Hadrill writes insightfully: "Eusebius was too devoted a disciple of Origen to be a good Antiochene in exegesis, too Palestinian to be a thorough-going Alexandrian."[28] One recalls that Origen maintained that the Scripture is tripartite and contains three levels of meaning: the literal sense, the moral sense and the spiritual or allegorical sense.[29] Whereas Origen expends by far his greatest energy and creativity in expounding the allegorical sense of the text, Eusebius demonstrates a commitment to the literal sense of the text and historical research that is not found in Origen's exegetical writings.[30]

In the preface to the commentary, Eusebius clearly articulates his theory of interpretation: the biblical text is bipartite and contains two levels of meaning—the literal sense and the deeper or allegorical sense. Eusebius thus streamlines Origen's system into what he must have perceived to be a more workable paradigm. The opening line of the commentary reads: "At times the Spirit delivered his revelation to the prophet plainly, so that there was no need of allegory to explain the message, but only an understanding of the actual words themselves. But at other times, the Spirit communicated through symbols and circumstances, placing other meanings in certain key words and even in names."[31] Eusebius then proceeds to advocate the legitimacy of allegorical interpretation by appealing to the story of Joseph and the words of Jesus. Eusebius first writes: "For example, in Joseph's dreams, the number of the 'eleven stars' that appeared 'to bown down' represents 'his brothers.' At another time, he saw his 'brothers' gathering 'ears of corn,' thus foreshadowing the famine. And so it is for the prophet Isaiah."[32] As the Holy Spirit inspired Joseph's dreams with an allegorical meaning, so we should learn to read the prophecies of Isaiah, Eusebius reasons. Eusebius then turns to the authority of Jesus in order to dem-

---

[26]Ziegler, *Der Jesajakommentar*, xlviii. The formulas that Jerome uses to introduce a particular citation of Scripture often even correspond to the formulas that Eusebius had used in the same passage (xlix).

[27]See Hollerich, *Eusebius of Caesarea's Commentary on Isaiah*, 13.

[28]*Eusebius of Caesarea*, 97.

[29]Origen writes: "For as man is said to consist of body, and soul, and spirit, so also does sacred Scripture" (ANF 4:359). See *Comm. in Is.* 49:11, where, very unusually, Eusebius interprets the word *Jerusalem* precisely according to Origen's tripartite interpretive scheme.

[30]Wallace-Hadrill continues: "Eusebius' association with the sites and peoples of the Bible and his interest in the biblical associations of his own region gave the humanity of Christ an importance for him that it never had for Origen, and centered his theology in the Incarnation" (*Eusebius of Caesarea*, 97).

[31]*Comm. in Is.*, preface.

[32]Ibid.

onstrate the undeniable admissibility of allegorical interpretation: "Such things are also found in the teachings of the Savior, in which it is recorded that he said: 'Do you not say, "There are four months, then comes the harvest"? Lift up your eyes, and see how the fields are already white for harvest.' It is clear what this verse is about, and yet one could find countless meanings. The same is true concerning writings of the prophet at hand."[33] This saying of Jesus clearly contains a figure of speech—the "fields" that are "white for harvest"—but the metaphor is so elementary to students of Gospel literature that the modern interpreter may not immediately understand that Eusebius claims this metaphor as an "allegory" and therefore as a precedent for his own allegorical reading of Isaiah. Equipped with these examples from the Old and New Testaments, Eusebius confidently enters the complexities of the Isaianic oracles.

One further note on Eusebius's theory of interpretation could be drawn from the preface to the commentary. In his use of the Joseph story, Eusebius subtly alters the biblical text in order to accommodate his allegorical exegesis. To be entirely accurate, Eusebius conflates two accounts from the life of Joseph: the story of Joseph's dream about the sheaves of his brothers from Genesis 37:5-8 and the story of Pharaoh's dream about seven ears of corn from Genesis 41:5-7. In the biblical narrative, Joseph's brothers are gathering sheaves, not ears of corn, and the dream signifies Joseph's future elevation, not a coming famine. One at first imagines that Eusebius failed to remember the precise details of the accounts from the life of Joseph, and this may indeed be the case. However, as Eusebius moves from the story of Joseph to the words of Jesus, one could also conclude that this rearrangement of the biblical text serves Eusebius's exegetical end, for the rearranged account from the Joseph narrative corresponds perfectly to Jesus' "allegory." We therefore witness Eusebius's conviction that the allegorical significance in some way represents the true structure of the text. We witness this conviction throughout the commentary as Eusebius attempts not only to indentify allegorical meanings for isolated words and concepts but in fact to weave a comprehensive allegorical subtext.

Sometimes Eusebius exhibits this conviction in the complexity that he is willing to see in a single allegory, as in the passage on the vineyard of the Lord from Isaiah 5. The vineyard represents the Jewish people; the hedge around the vineyard represents the prophets; the choice vine among the vineyard stands for the inspired Scriptures, or perhaps the people whom Moses led up from Egypt during the exodus or perhaps Jesus, who called himself the "true vine"; the tower in the midst of the vineyard represents the temple, and the wine vat represents the altar before the temple; the clouds that sent no rain represent the absence of the prophetic ministry after Jesus; and the thorns that the vineyard produced represent the Jews' rejection of the Christ.[34] More frequently, however, Eusebius

---

[33]Ibid.

[34]*Comm. in Is.* 5:2-7. This is the most carefully developed allegory in the entire commentary, and Eusebius cites this passage as the paradigmatic allegory in the preface and elsewhere.

demonstrates his conviction of the priority of the allegorical sense in his tendency to return to an allegorical precedent in order to explain the imagery of the current passage. For example, when Eusebius encounters the women who are enlightening the city (Is 27:11b), he is confident that these women are to be interpreted as the women who first witnessed the empty tomb, since several verses prior in Isaiah 27:2 the theme of the vineyard of the Lord reemerges, therefore establishing the spread of the apostolic preaching—the fruit that the master of the vineyard had always hoped to see—as the interpretive framework. Now and again Eusebius will even select the Greek translation on which he comments based on the criterion of which rendering most compellingly sustains the continued development of his allegorical interpretation.

In a curious turn of irony, Eusebius understands the very concept of biblical prophecy in a surprisingly literal way: prophecy is not purely moral exhortation but the foretelling of historical events. In *Comm. in Is.* 44:24–45:13, Eusebius exults in the dramatic fulfillment of the prophecy that Cyrus the Great would release the Jews from the Babylonian captivity.[35] For lesser known prophecies, too, Eusebius often finds a specific event from the historical record to be the most attractive reading. Eusebius interprets the story of Shebna's removal from the priesthood as a picture of the loss of the Jewish priesthood after the destruction of Jerusalem.[36] Eusebius avers that the phrase "he will blaze up and not be overwhelmed" should be read as a foreshadowing of the resurrection of Christ.[37] In scores of passages, especially the oracles of judgment, Eusebius presents interpretations that evidence careful historical research.[38] Jerome in fact even complains that Eusebius's commentary is unacceptably literal, conjecturing that Eusebius's method must have been to expound the literal sense of the text in so far as his command of the historical record allowed and only to retreat to an allegorical interpretation when his knowledge of history failed him![39]

Jerome's judgment of Eusebius is premature. Examples could be multiplied in which Eusebius prefers an allegorical interpretation over a literal one. In one passage, Eusebius

---

[35]Eusebius even calls on Josephus, *Jewish Antiquities* 11.1.3-4, in order to validate his historical claim (*Comm. in Is.* 45:8).

[36]*Comm. in Is.* 22:15-25.

[37]*Comm. in Is.* 42:4.

[38]Wallace-Hadrill notes: "Eusebius, for all his scorn of Jewish exegetical method, may have followed Origen in seeking information on historical points from the Jews. . . . If Eusebius is, in fact, seeking information from Jewish sources, it shows him as being very concerned to establish the most literal and historical meaning of his biblical texts. It was, perhaps, a course of action to which he turned only late in life, for in his early *Prophetic Eclogues* he writes derisively and often of the failure of Jewish attempts to make sense of their scriptures by such literal methods of exegesis without reference to Christ" (*Eusebius of Caesarea*, 79-80).

[39]Jerome, *Comm. in Is.* 18.1. Quasten notes that Jerome "adds that Eusebius promised in the title an historical exposition, but often forgets his promise and ends in the allegorism of Origen" (Johannes Quasten, *Patrology* [Westminster, MD: Newman Press, 1960], 3:338; see Jerome, *Comm. in Is.* 5.86 [Roger Gryson, ed., *Commentaires de Jerome sur Le Prophete Isaie* {Freiburg: Herder, 1993}, 611]). Wallace-Hadrill concludes against Jerome: "The proportion of the total number of verses of Isaiah which Eusebius allegorises is hardly sufficient cause for complaint that he deserts the literal sense" (*Eusebius of Caesarea*, 83). Perhaps Jerome is reflecting on Eusebius's statement: "And we already observed in the preface to this commentary, sometimes the prophetic message is to be rendered literally and not allegorically, and sometimes, when the people are unwilling to listen, the spirit is forced to express the prophecy as an allegory" (*Comm. in Is.* 11:15; see also 19:5-7).

interprets the "ox" and the "bear" as those boorish people who are able to understand only the literal sense. Eusebius's voice is here indistinguishable from Origen's: "There are savage and coarse people who understand only the literal interpretation of the graces of the divine Scripture. The divine Scripture is the nourishing word of souls, but its secrets escape the notice of our minds, for the meaning is surrounded by a husk."[40] In *Comm. in Is.* 19:18, Eusebius interprets the five cities of Egypt that swear allegiance to the Lord as standing allegorically for the five offices of the church: bishops, elders, deacons, the enlightened and those who merely attend services.[41] In passages where one would anticipate a more historical reading, Eusebius surprises his modern reader with an allegory: the "rock" on which Jesus promised to build his church in Matthew 16:18 is the gospel.[42] In passages where one would imagine an elaborate allegory as more appropriate, Eusebius restricts his comments to a historical scope: the "wine and milk" that Isaiah encourages one to buy without money reminds Eusebius that milk used to be administered alongside the wine of the Eucharist to newly baptized Christians.[43]

As has been noted previously by many scholars, as Caesarea lies somewhere between Alexandria and Antioch, so Eusebius's exegesis lies somewhere between the Alexandrian school of interpretation and the Antiochene school.[44] Perhaps Eusebius's first and last principle of interpretation is what Christian exegetes would come to call the *analogia fidei*, that Scripture is to interpret Scripture. Eusebius's most consistent hermeneutical principle is to introduce the reader to other passages of Scripture that share a common vocabulary and theological theme.[45] Robert Louis Wilken, who has investigated Eusebius's commentary on Isaiah extensively, writes enlighteningly: "In contrast to modern theological writings in which the Bible is cited in support of theological ideas, and hence

---

[40]*Comm. in Is.* 11:7; cf. Origen, *First Principles* 4.1.20; see also Eusebius, *Comm. in Is.* 59:10.

[41]See also *Comm. in Is.* 42:11-12.

[42]*Comm. in Is.* 28:16.

[43]"And you should not be ignorant of the fact that, in former times, mystical milk was administered to those who were born again in Christ along with the body and blood of the new covenant. And, they say that this custom is preserved in certain churches still even now. But, if this text is not interpreted according to the literal sense, the mystical blood of Christ is administered to those who are deemed worthy of regeneration in Christ instead of wine and instead of milk" (*Comm. in Is.* 55:1; cf. Tertullian, *De Corona* 3). Wallace-Hadrill remarks in reference to Eusebius's other treatises: "Allegorical reference to the Eucharist is conspicuously absent from these works" (*Eusebius of Caesarea*, 90).

[44]Hollerich articulates Eusebius's exegetical aim about as precisely as can be done: "We will see that for Eusebius the difference between 'literal' (historical) and 'spiritual' interpretation meant something like the difference between fact and interpretation. His blend of literal and spiritual interpretation was marked by a dedication to grammatical analysis of the text, an acceptance of the church's traditional apologetic exegesis, a belief in the supernatural inspiration of biblical prophecy, a moderate and cautious exploitation of figurative interpretation, and a vivid sense of the hand of God in the events of his own day" (*Eusebius of Caesarea's Commentary on Isaiah*, 67).

[45]This, too, may be read as a heritage from Origen, as Ronald E. Heine explains: "A third premise of Origen's hermeneutic is that the way one discovers the hidden meaning of a passage of Scripture is by searching for 'similar expressions . . . scattered about in the Scriptures' (*Princ.* 4.3.5). Origen expresses the principle in the language of the Hebrew teacher who told him the story about the house full of locked rooms whose keys lay scattered about" (*Origen: Scholarship in the Service of the Church* [Oxford: Oxford University Press, 2010], 135). Heine elaborates: "One way Origen enters this hidden world of Scripture is by using the principle that he had learned from 'the Hebrew' in his early days at Alexandria and which he labeled with the Pauline phrase of 'comparing spiritual things with spiritual.' He searches in Scripture for all the other occurrences of a key word in his text and uses these other contexts to suggest nuances of meaning for the target text" (ibid., 208).

usually relegated to the footnotes, in the early church words of the Bible were the linguistic skeleton for the exposition of ideas."[46] Eusebius's constant comparison of the Greek of the Septuagint with the translations of Symmachus, Aquila and Theodotion tells us that Eusebius searched for possible theological significance in even the minutest exchange of synonyms.[47] For Eusebius, the task of the text critic and the exegete—as well as the task of the historian, geographer and philosopher—is one and the same. Eusebius was a polymath, and precisely for this reason his theory of interpretation cannot be perfectly described according to professional standards of any one discipline. But, perhaps also precisely for this reason, Eusebius has something new to offer every reader. Sometimes breathtakingly brilliant, sometimes unspeakably mundane, Eusebius's commentary on Isaiah deserves fresh study today.

Eusebius works his way systematically through the entire text of Isaiah. Of course, the Scriptures were then not divided into chapter and verse, and the amount of text that Eusebius comments on per section in his commentary varies. The words in italics in this translation represent quotations from the passage on which Eusebius comments in the specific section. Where the Greek of Eusebius's Old Testament citations correspond exactly with the Greek of Alfred Rahlfs's Septuagint, I used NETS as a neutral translation for this project.[48] Where the Greek of Eusebius's New Testament citations correspond exactly with the Greek of the UBS4 New Testament, I used the RSV as a neutral translation of the text. Not infrequently, the full sense of Eusebius's comments cannot be understood without reference to the Septuagint text of the specific passage from Isaiah. In the text of this translation, boldface, bracketed numbers reflect Scripture passages or the page numbers in the critical text of Eusebius's commentary. It should be readily apparent which are chapter and verse numbers and which are page numbers.

Eusebius and the Jews

A word on Eusebius's attitude toward the Jews is necessary. Only a few months after beginning the translation of the text, I discovered that the commentary is littered with language that one would classify as anti-Semitic in the contemporary theological milieu. Alarmed by the prejudiced and disparaging statements that I encountered, I approached my mentor about the possibility of producing an abridged version of the commentary in which the anti-Semitic lines were expunged. In the course of our conversations, it became clear that such a version of the commentary would be neither fair nor serviceable to either

---

[46]Robert Louis Wilken, *The Spirit of Early Christian Thought: Seeking the Face of God* (New Haven, CT: Yale University Press, 2003), 43. Kannengieser echoes this conclusion in his analysis: "[Eusebius] also quotes other biblical books, literally or by paraphrasing them, in such a massive frequency that his own writing seems entirely permeated by Scripture" (*Handbook of Patristic Exegesis*, 2:677).

[47]It should be noted that Eusebius also appeals to the various Greek translations of the Old Testament in his other exegetical and apologetic works, and therefore this feature is not unique to Eusebius's exposition of Isaiah. See Wallace-Hadrill, *Eusebius of Caesarea*, 87.

[48]Benjamin G. Wright and Albert Pietersma, eds., *A New English Translation of the Septuagint* (Oxford: Oxford University Press, 2007).

the modern Christian or Jewish reader. I henceforth proceeded to translate the text as faithfully and clearly as possible, but I then decided that a candid discussion of Eusebius's attitude toward the Jews would be a mandatory part of the introduction.

At first it seems that Eusebius misses few opportunities to interpret the oracles of judgment as literal or allegorical condemnations of the Jews. At the beginning of the commentary, in his comments on Isaiah 1:1, Eusebius plainly states his understanding that Isaiah "informs the listener that the entire case of his prophecy is against the Jewish nation." One can imagine that Eusebius's statements perhaps read more innocently seventeen centuries ago, but today one can only read them as injurious: "The Holy Spirit convicts the Jewish nation and considers them miserable and the worst of all nations, since they derive profit neither from their adoption as sons, nor from the honor of which they were deemed worthy by God."[49] Egregiously, Eusebius blames the Jews for the crucifixion of the Christ,[50] frequently claiming that the destruction of Jerusalem in A.D. 70 was a direct punishment for the rejection of the Messiah. Eusebius blatantly advocates replacement theology—that is, Eusebius believes that God's chosen people are no longer the Jews but now Christian Gentiles. Speaking in reference to the "godly polity," the blessed rule of God among his people, Eusebius writes: "This government was organized by the Jewish people long ago, but it has since collapsed, and now from out of the whole world it has been raised up again in the church of Christ and has been 'founded on the rock.'"[51] Eusebius's enthusiasm for Constantine's favorable policies toward Christians is to be expected, but his appeal to this favor as an argument that God has abandoned the Jews is theologically indefensible and unchristian.

Eusebius's anti-Semitic statements are as obvious as they are painful, and I therefore will not reproduce them all here. However, lest I prejudice the reader against Eusebius as an anti-Semite and thereby preclude an opened and balanced analysis of Eusebius's theological legacy, it is appropriate that I not leave the statements in which Eusebius expresses hope and goodwill for the Jews unmentioned. Eusebius indeed blames the Jews for the crucifixion of Jesus, but he nevertheless also states that forgiveness can be granted even for this sin and that the Jews can receive salvation.[52] In his discussion of Isaiah 1:27, although Eusebius declares dogmatically that the Jews will never be regathered to the Holy Land, still he interprets the phrase "its captivity shall be saved with judgment and with

---

[49]*Comm. in Is.* 1:2-3.

[50]See also *Comm. in Is.* 1:31; 5:2-7, 11-17; 6:11-13; 22:2-3, 4-6; 27:12-13; 29:3; 33:3-4; 50:4-5, 9; 51:4, 17; 52:4-5; 59:3, 11-12, 14-18. At the same time, Eusebius can also say that the apostle Paul was "in all ways and all over stained with the blood of the Savior" in his persecution of the church (*Comm. in Is.* 4:4). After a particularly stinging passage in which Eusebius blames the Jews for the crucifixion of Christ, Eusebius yet adds, "one could apply these general principles and this generic threat to all who are wise in their own conceit" (*Comm. in Is.* 5:21-23), therefore indicating that his fervor was not always directed uniquely against the Jews.

[51]*Comm. in Is.* 1:25-26. Concerning Eusebius's theme of the "godly polity," see especially Hollerich, *Eusebius of Caesarea's Commentary on Isaiah*, 103.

[52]*Comm. in Is.* 53:9-10.

mercy" as a reference to the Jews who shall convert to Christianity and be saved.[53] In *Comm. in Is.* 7:21-25, although Eusebius can say that "since the captivity in Babylon and the uprising from that place, the Jews have been in the most extreme poverty regarding God," yet in the same paragraph Eusebius also says that the one who is nourished from the "one young cow and two sheep" represents the one "who after careful study may gain one or two lessons from the Jewish teachings."[54] In *Comm. in Is.* 25:6-8, in which context the Lord promises to prepare a feast for all nations, Eusebius notes that the feast of eternal salvation will be "neither for Israel nor the Jewish people exclusively but for all nations."[55] In his comments on Isaiah 41:9, Eusebius interprets those whom the Lord called from the ends of the earth as the Jews, adding: "For there were many Jews who welcomed the word of Christ during the apostolic times, not only in the land of Judea but also in the other nations."[56] Eusebius indeed blames the Jews for the destruction of Jerusalem, but he also can embrace the Jewish foundations of Christianity: "For just as the Jews were responsible for its destruction, so again they became the builders of the new structure—the apostles of our Savior and the disciples and evangelists, through whom the Church of God was raised up from the nations."[57] One final passage in which Eusebius appears to voice a ray of hope for the Jews should be reviewed:

> And he then says *there shall be a pure way, and it shall be called a holy way.* And one could say that this way leads to the thrice-blest destination "of the heavenly city of God," and the Savior spoke of this way when he said: "I am the *way.*" Therefore, the saving word directs those who go to the Father and into the kingdom of heaven through him. It is prophesied that only the saints will be permitted to travel the *way* established in the wilderness, and it is evident that *no one* who is *unclean shall pass* through this *way.* But he also says *those who have been dispersed shall walk on it.* And who are these ones if not those who were once scattered abroad by God and who had wandered far from the truth? For these ones shall run back again and, after finding the straight and steady *way, they shall walk in it.*[58]

Eusebius does not specifically mention the Jews, and therefore some scholars may not admit this as evidence to inform our understanding of Eusebius's attitude toward the Jews. In my judgment, the most reasonable conclusion is that Eusebius is speaking of the Jews when he says that the people "who were once scattered abroad by God and who had wandered far from the truth" shall be restored to the way of salvation.

---

[53]See also *Comm. in Is.* 60:1-2.

[54]In *Comm. in Is.* 32:20, too, Eusebius can affirm: "Therefore, because the apostles of our Savior cast the gospel seed 'to the Jews first and afterwards to the Greeks,' the text rightly says: *Happy is the one who sows beside every water, where ox and donkey tread.* In this context, *water* alludes to the inspired Scriptures, which were *treaded* out by the Jews and the people of the nations."

[55]See also *Comm. in Is.* 61:8.

[56]See also *Comm. in Is.* 43:13; 48:17-19.

[57]*Comm. in Is.* 49:17.

[58]*Comm. in Is.* 35:7-8.

Conclusion

Eusebius produced four monumental works during his life, the first pair apologetic in nature and the second pair exegetical: the *Praeparatio Evangelica*, the *Demonstratio Evangelica*, the *Commentary on the Psalms* and the *Commentary on Isaiah*. In his first apologetic work, Eusebius aims to demonstrate the religious superiority of the Judeo-Christian tradition, and in the second, he seeks to explain the parting of the ways between Judaism and Christianity. Eusebius's exegetical works are best set within the scope of his grander, apologetic project. In his *Commentary on Isaiah*, Eusebius advances his longstanding apologetic aim of demonstrating the superiority of Christianity—in this case, the superiority of the Christian reading of Scripture over the Jewish reading. But, as Brevard Childs writes, Eusebius understood that the message of Isaiah was neither for Gentile nor Jew alone but for all peoples: "The flow of the nations to Mount Zion in search of the law of Christ sounds the book's preeminent note: the revelation of a universal salvation culminating in the ingathering of all nations."[59] The reason for Eusebius's selection of Isaiah is clear—Isaiah inspired the apostolic vision of Jesus' messianic mission. Jesus communicated the purpose of his own ministry in the language of Isaiah, and therefore the prophecies of Isaiah are part of the very definition of the gospel. This is the message that Eusebius hoped to elucidate in his commentary, and this is the message that I hope will be conveyed in this translation.

---

[59]Brevard Childs, *The Struggle to Understand Isaiah as Christian Scripture* (Grand Rapids: Eerdmans, 2004), 85.

EUSEBIUS OF CAESAREA
Commentary on Isaiah

At times the Spirit delivered his revelation to the prophet plainly, so that there was no need of allegory to explain the message, but only an understanding of the actual words themselves. But at other times, the Spirit communicated through symbols and circumstances, placing other meanings in certain key words and even in names. For example, in Joseph's dreams, the number of the "eleven stars"[1] that appeared "to bow down" represents "his brothers." At another time, he saw his "brothers" gathering "ears of corn,"[2] thus foreshadowing the famine. And so it is for the prophet Isaiah. Many of the things that he prophesied he saw through symbols, and many of the things that he prophesied he spoke in a complicated fashion, weaving together a literal and a metaphorical sense. Such things are also found in the teachings of the Savior, in which it is recorded that he said: "Do you not say, 'There are four months, then comes the harvest'? Lift up your eyes, and see how the fields are already white for harvest."[3] It is clear what this verse is about, and yet one could find countless meanings. The same is true concerning writings of the prophet at hand. You find phrases that should be understood precisely as stated, such as: "What to me is the multitude of your sacrifices? says the Lord; I am full of whole burnt offerings,"[4] and so on. But there are also verses that concern only the allegorical sense, such as: "The beloved had a vineyard on a hill, on a fertile place,"[5] and so forth.

[1:1] The *vision*[6] was no ordinary vision, says Isaiah, and it did not befall bodily eyes. It was rather a prophetic and mysterious vision of what would happen afterward in the distant future. For imagine that someone were to watch the approach of an enemy army as reflected in a large silver platter, and he witnessed the ravaging and siege of the land as well as the selling into slavery of those in the bloom of youth. It seems that Isaiah saw the vision in the same way, not while asleep but awake, as the divine Spirit shone on his soul.

Isaiah set to prophesying neither as a pastime nor in order to give lessons for profit, but after leaving his field and livelihood (and very life, at least as it is known to many), he devoted himself to the quiet contemplation of the inspiration and wisdom he had received. We should mention here too that Isaiah was also an evangelist and that he performed the same duty as the evangelists did. For he preaches the Son of God surpassingly, here expounding divine truths and there [4] foretelling the angelic announcement in the heavens, and the "virgin"[7] birth (declaring beforehand that his name would be "Emmanuel") and the resurrection, and he even prophesied about the apostle Paul. For the same Scripture also states: "Then I heard the voice of the Lord saying, 'Whom shall I send, and who will go to this people?' And I said, 'Here am I! Send me.'"[8]

He informs the listener that the entire case of his prophecy is against the Jewish nation

---

Chapter 1 [1]Gen 37:9-10. [2]Gen 41:5-7, 22-24. [3]Jn 4:35. [4]Is 1:11. [5]Is 5:1. [6]The Hebrew word translated "word" in Is 1:1 is rendered "vision" in the LXX. [7]Cf. Is 7:14. [8]Is 6:8; Eusebius is here playing with the similar Greek words "apostle" (ἀπόστολος) and "to send" (ἀποστέλλω).

because he brings a case not only against the first king listed but also against the second and third, and against the fourth as well.[9] One will find this to be the case concerning the denouncements proclaimed against each *kingdom* of the Jewish nation: prophesies were made against them until the very end of the kingdom, whether one counts the end of the kingdom as the disbandment of the Jewish nation or as the destruction of the land and the city of Jerusalem. Why then did he begin to speak first *against Judea*, as it would seem, and then later on "against Babylon"[10] and "Egypt"[11]? He began with those who thought themselves to be dedicated to God, according to what has been said elsewhere: "Begin at my sanctuary"[12] and the "mighty men will be mightily tested."[13]

After the period of these four kings had been sealed, a new state of affairs for the Jewish people arrived, and it seems that neither the truths in the literal sense nor those in the underlying sense concerning these affairs failed to happen later, in times then still distant. The reader should notice that the book as a whole appears to have been joined together into a unity and that the message was delivered by the prophet in parts over several lengthy intervals of time, so that the book contains a great deal of precise information about future events. Isaiah wrote in this way in order that the interpretation of the prophecies recorded in it could be determined after a while and so that the prophecy would also be applicable to the events that occurred in each reign. After fifty years, the time of the appointed kings was completed, according to what was said and proclaimed throughout the whole book.

[1:2-3] The divine Spirit filled the soul of the prophet with the appropriate power and uttered through the prophetic mouth as through an

instrument what had been appointed and prepared in advance for the hearers of the words spoken by the Lord. It is for this reason that he says, *For the Lord has spoken*. The prophet then presents the word itself which *the Lord spoke* and which the text tells us was spoken from the very mouth of the Lord: *I begat sons and exalted them*. And so, in fact, the *Lord spoke* the word, and the prophetic Spirit listened to the voice of the Lord and delivered the word through the prophet as through an instrument before an audience of people. The prophet attended to what the Lord had said, and he calls the elements to council for the instruction of the reader. The *heaven* hears the divine powers and the *earth* is the dwelling place of mortals. He calls on *heaven* to *hear* and the *earth* to *give ear* either because they are animate (for the heavenly bodies and the elements of the earth also have souls, according to some theories); or he summons the unseen powers through those elements; or, since prophecies were supposed to happen much later, and the prophet was of a mortal and transient nature, he addressed the word to what would remain; or, he calls on the *heaven* and the *earth* because the Jewish people were not worthy. He in fact attributes *hearing* to *heaven* and the ability to *give ear* to the earth, and this is in essence the better reading, although it is all rather literal.

[5] He says *I begat sons* because people have rational souls and were created "according to his image,"[14] and because our first parents were created with a special prerogative.

The prophet speaks in riddles when he says, *The ox knows its owner*. Although the Gentiles—who formerly surpassed irrational animals in almost nothing—*will understand*, Israel *will not understand*. For he did not write that Israel *has not understood* but rather that Israel *will not understand*.[15] In the illustration

---

[9]As the first verse of Isaiah tells us, the ministry of Isaiah spanned the reigns of four kings of Judah: Uzziah, Jotham, Ahaz and Hezekiah. [10]Is 13:1. [11]Cf. Is 19:1. [12]Ezek 9:6 rsv. [13]Wis 6:6 rsv. [14]Gen 1:26-27. [15]Although the lxx clearly says συνῆκεν, Eusebius concludes the opposite and writes συνῆσει instead.

from the natural realm, of course, the *ox* and *donkey know* their keepers. But those who have been blessed with such providential care from God, and who not only have been created rational but who have even been deemed worthy to be called the people of God, have been honored with the appellation *sons*. And those whom the Lord *reared* and *educated* and honored and *brought up* are not like irrational creatures; they *know* the Lord. I suppose that he is prophetically alluding to the very Christ of God, who as Lord dwelled among those of absolutely every nation, according to the incarnation, but Israel would neither receive him nor *acknowledge* him, nor take notice of him, because, as the text says, *they will not understand.*

Therefore, the prophetic Spirit witnessed that the Son had spoken these words of introduction in his own person, and in the accusations brought one after another, it was no longer the Lord but the Spirit himself who was casting blame on the people, as when in another context he said to those being accused by the Lord, *Ah, sinful nation.*

Because of these things, then, the Holy Spirit convicts the Jewish nation and considers them miserable and the worst of all the nations since they derive profit neither from their adoption as sons, nor from the honor of which they were deemed worthy by God. Even though they were exalted and obtained the greatest privileges from him, they were not often struck with amazement by the extravagance of the love of God, and they were therefore punished and chastened because of their impiety: "For whom the Lord loves, he disciplines, and he punishes every son he accepts."[16]

We should note that those who call themselves Israel because they descend "from the stock of Abraham"[17] and who take pride in the fact that, "according to the flesh," they are "of the seed"[18] of people loved by God—those people the Holy Spirit calls a *sinful nation* and

a people laden with iniquity, an evil seed and *sons who deal corruptly.* He thus teaches that those who foolishly take pride in their race and "forefathers"[19] are deluded.

In another context, the prophet says that the Son is the *Lord.* It may be appropriate to identify the Son in the citation as the Son of God, the Word, who was of human nature and a rational soul as other humans, since the text says, *I begat sons and exalted them.* The text says in addition: *You have forsaken the Lord, and you provoked to anger the Holy One of Israel.* Who did they *abandon* but Christ, whom they caused to suffer through their *provoking to anger* and *abandoning* and the rest? [6] One should observe that, in the charges that he brings against all of the Jewish people, the rulers as well as the subjects, the prophet accuses them of nothing other than *abandoning the Lord.* For he does not censure them for idolatry but because *they abandoned the Lord,* whom *ox* and *donkey know,* but *Israel does not know.* For this reason he justly reckons them miserable and considers them as far worse than those who are irrational by nature.

[1:5-6] He claims that they have a certain untreatable and incurable disease, for he says, *Every head has become troubled, and every heart has become sad. From the feet to the head—there is no health in it.* Then the Word even despairs of their remedy, saying, *There is no emollient to put on, nor oil nor bandages.* Lest anyone think that he would have any standing, even after the time when one may take hold of the saving advent of Christ, the prophet then says: "God's wrath has come upon them at last!"[20] Although the reader might not arrive at the truth from what we have said over the last little while—since at times and in each generation there were men loved by God among them, and even during the captivity in Babylon—we reasonably deduce from the aforementioned

---

[16]Prov 3:12. [17]Acts 13:26. [18]Rom 1:3. [19]Rom 4:1. [20]1 Thess 2:16 RSV.

evidences the final deposition of the Jewish people. This happened because they did not understand the Christ of God who dwelt among them. Besieged by the Romans, they were no longer the *head* people. And so *they were alienated* at any rate, *in what came after, and every head of theirs*[21] (this clearly refers to the ruling authorities) *has become humbled in sickness, every heart has become sad; as (from the feet to the head) there is no health in it* (the author is clearly speaking here from the lesser to the greater),[22] and no one could come up with any saving medicine for them. For so it was that when they found wine or another efficacious medicine of health and salvation, they would deny the Lord, neither acknowledging him nor understanding that the only physician of their souls had lived among them and that he was able to cure every disease and every infirmity of their souls and bodies. But rather than salvation, *there is no health in it, whether a sore or a bruise,* and so on. Symmachus renders this verse this way: *There is nothing healthy in him, but only bruises and sores and stroke marks, and they have not been closed up or bound up or softened with oil.*

[1:7-8] The verse, *Your country lies desolate, your cities are burned with fire,* and other such statements had in fact not transpired at the point in time at which they were pronounced, but they were to happen later in far-off times that the prophet had seen in advance. Here, instead of *like a booth in a vineyard,* Symmachus writes: *like a hut in a vineyard, like a night watch in a cucumber field, like a plundered city.* It is quite clear from what follows that the *vineyard* in this context is the entire nation, for the prophet himself says, "For the vineyard of the Lord is the house of Israel, and the man of Judah is a beloved young plant."[23] Then [7] he

brings forward the grounds for their desertion: "I waited for it to produce justice, but it produced lawlessness—nor did it produce righteousness but a cry."[24]

In light of the statement above—"They have forsaken the Lord and provoked to anger the Holy One of Israel"[25]—it could also be said that *they will be abandoned.* The verse that says that *they have been abandoned like a booth in a vineyard* signifies their complete lack of fruitfulness. For until the promise of their good fruit has been fulfilled, the *vineyard* has been turned over to the guard, who after erecting a *booth,* looks down from the heights above and keeps watch over the *vineyard.* If the fruit of the vineyard should fail to appear, so that the keeper not labor in vain, he *leaves behind* the barren land and withdraws the *booth* from its present station. And so, the divine Spirit then prophesied that the same would be true of the temple. We should note that when the entire nation is understood to be the *vineyard,* then the booth that was set up in the middle of all would be the temple in Jerusalem. Thus the guard watches over the *vineyard* as from a lookout tower. But since "instead of a cluster of grapes it produced thorns,"[26] he then prophesies that the city and the temple *will be abandoned.* He says, *like a booth in a vineyard, and like a garden-watcher's hut in a cucumber field* because the practices they called virtuous did not yield quality bunches of grapes, but it was not quite late summer at that point. Such was the temporary and corporeal worship according to "the law of Moses." In appearance it was a bustling harvest, but it was temporary. For this reason the place where the late summer fruits were thriving is called a *garden-watcher's hut,* and it is this lodge that he says *will be abandoned.* But *abandoning* the *booth* and *lodge* of their very master has resulted in the guard and

---

[21]It is unclear which Scripture verse Eusebius intends to cite.   [22]Speaking "from the lesser to the greater" was an ancient rhetorical device and was employed by many New Testament authors as well. In this instance, the author begins by stating that the head and the heart are sick and then ends by saying that the entire body is diseased.   [23]Is 5:7.   [24]Is 5:7.   [25]Is 1:4.   [26]Is 5:4.

the entire *city* being *besieged*, and the area and the nation have become a wilderness.

[1:9] Later, the apostolic band, the *survivors* from among them, "came to know and acknowledge him."[27] They were rightly appointed from the multitude, and the word from the mouth of the prophet makes mention of them, saying: *If the Lord of Hosts had not left us a few surviving offspring, we would have become like Sodom and been made similar to Gomorrah.* For it would be absurd to suppose that the apostles were called an impious *seed;*[28] thus they are not the aforementioned "evil offspring, lawless sons."[29]

By the divine Spirit, therefore, the prophets foresaw this consolation for the people in the face of the destruction of the entire nation and went on to say: *If the Lord of Hosts had not left us offspring, we would have become like Sodom and made similar to Gomorrah.*

[1:10] The prophet compares them with the *rulers of Sodom* and *the people of Gomorrah* because catastrophe was about to overcome them, and because they burned with impiety, like the men who lived in *Sodom* [8] and *Gomorrah* and because of the similarity of their lifestyle. The prophet himself sets this forth, continuing on in the rest of the verse, saying: "They proclaim their lawlessness like Sodom; they exhibit it. Woe to their soul, because they resolved to take evil advice against themselves, saying: 'Let us enchain the just, for he is of no use to us.'"[30] Surely, it is now evident on what grounds he called them *rulers of Sodom.*

The children of the Jews held their heads high and took pride in the virtue of their ancestors—after all, they were "descendants of Abraham"[31] and the offspring of Israel. The Word then rightly humbles their boastfulness

and brings down their conceited opinions, calling the renowned *rulers* of Israel *rulers of Sodom* and stigmatizing those who style themselves to be the *people* of God as the *people of Gomorrah,* since their practices equaled the wickedness of long ago.

[1:11-15] The Word introduces a new law of instruction, one that dismisses the corporeal worship according to Moses. We are talking about those who were rulers of the nation during the times of the Savior, who dared to act against the Lord. They thought that God was placated with burnt offerings and drink offerings and other bodily acts of worship according to the law. The Word alludes to these things when he says: *What to me is the multitude of your sacrifices,* and so on. And the verse continues: *I have had enough,* and so forth. He brings the whole reason for such threats as he continues and says, *Your hands are full of blood,* "For they filled up the measure of the evil of their fathers."[32] In all this, he maintains nothing less than that they have been discredited with idolatry, because "They did not know the Lord,"[33] and because "They did not understand him," and finally, "They have forsaken the Lord and provoked to anger the Holy One of Israel."[34] And the Word alludes to all these things, for *their hands were full of blood* through the murder which they carried out against the Christ, in keeping with the slaughter of countless prophets. Yes, their hands were *full of blood.* Therefore, despite every *feast* and festival and all the rest by which they thought that they would secure the forgiveness of sins according to the law of Moses, he has separated from them after their provocation against Christ. And seeing what sort of threat was placed on them, he announces *I will no longer pardon your sins,*[35] and this very prophecy was fulfilled among

---

[27]Cf. Is 1:3. [28]Eusebius uses the Greek word σπέρμα to mean both "survivor" and "seed." [29]Is 1:4. [30]Is 3:9-10. [31]Jn 8:33, 37. [32]Mt 23:32. [33]Cf. Is 1:3. [34]Cf. Is 1:4. [35]Eusebius appears to believe that this statement is a quotation of Is 1:15a, although this reading is not supported by the Hebrew or LXX.

them after the plot against our Savior. For this reason he says the rest as well: *Your hands are full of blood*, and thus it is fair to say that their *hands* were *full of blood*. He then adds this verse: *I will no longer forgive your sins*, and *even if you make many petitions, I will not listen to you*.

[1:16] [9] After dealing with these introductory matters and the charges against those who were revealed to be "rulers of Sodom and the people of Gomorrah,"[36] the Lord most decidedly passes on to the good hope to which they are called. For if they would turn from wickedness and withdraw from their self-chosen worship according to the corporeal law, they could become subjects of his new covenant and of the new law and word. Now that the oversight of those under the old covenant is past, the mysteries of the new covenant and of the new law enter. He already delivered these mysteries in the Gospels, saying: "Unless one is born of water and the Spirit, he cannot enter the kingdom of God."[37] Well then, the benevolent Lord admonishes those who are held fast by such wickedness and defiled by the aforementioned blood to strive to take up the new covenant. It is held out to them as a promise, whereby the forgiveness of sins is procured even for those who have sinned exceedingly. For this reason the text says to them: *Wash yourselves; become clean*. The saving and purifying word which secures souls is not referring to the Mosaic laws but exhorts the reader to strive for the evangelical tradition: *Wash yourselves; become clean; remove the evil deeds from your souls*. And do this, he says, *before my eyes*. He does not tell them to turn away from their sins with some ostentatious show, as people would suppose, but in their very soul which only God sees: *remove your evil deeds*. He continues: *from before my eyes; cease from your evil deeds*.

[1:17] Then, after turning away from wickedness, do not stop until you have taken up the virtuous life, consulting the new teaching according to the Gospel where you learn of the good life. And so the text says, *Learn to do good; seek judgment*, and after setting these things right, *rescue the one who is wronged; defend the orphan, and do justice to plead for the widow*.

[1:18] Once you have followed through on all these things, gather up your courage. Come. *Let us argue it out* in a court of justice, you and me. Although I suffered much at your hands, you were shown much kindness and your considerations were taken into account. Even after such wicked trespasses of every kind, you received amnesty. I washed *your hands* so they were cleaner than *snow* after becoming red from the aforementioned *blood*. I established you through "the washing of regeneration."[38] And as far as concerns you, if any such plea for grace were possible, you should of course claim it.

[1:19] The text continues on: *And if you are willing and listen to me* when you *are washed*, and if you follow through on the remaining things according to the prescribed method, *You shall eat the good things of the land*. The Word here reasons with the Jewish people, [10] who were the very children of those whom he had exhorted through the corporeal promise in the desert places. It is said about the true word or the heavenly seed, according to the saving parable, that it is received and apprehended in the soil of the soul. Sometimes the word is cast and is "choked"[39] or destroyed in a variety of other ways, and other times it "yields"[40] delightful "fruit in thirty or sixty or a hundredfold." It follows that it is the good soil of the soul that takes up moral progress and virtuous perfection and apprehends the promises of the kingdom of heaven and the

---

[36]Cf. Is 1:10. [37]Jn 3:5 RSV. [38]Cf. Tit 3:5. [39]Mt 13:7. [40]Mt 13:8.

heavenly land, about which the Savior himself taught in the Gospels: "Blessed are the meek, for they shall inherit the earth."[41] And so the seeds that are good fall on this heavenly soil, "What no eye has seen, nor ear heard, nor the heart of man conceived."[42] Here too "heavenly"[43] is to be understood as "Jerusalem."

[1:20] Therefore, the Word promises these things to those who believe, but at the same time, he warns the disobedient, saying: *But if you are not willing nor listen to me, the dagger will devour you; for the mouth of the Lord has spoken.*[44] These predictions were in fact fulfilled right after they were delivered. Those among the aforementioned rulers and Jewish people who did not listen to the saving grace were immediately (not later!) delivered to the sword of the enemy—the Romans, who invaded them and conquered everywhere with the law of war. What is the *sword* if not the enemy?[45] And they were delivered to this fate because they were disobedient to the calling of the grace of Christ.

[1:21-22] Therefore, neither the Hebrew nor the other Greek translations[46] are to be interpreted in this context as referring to the *Zion* remembered. The Word teaches that faithful men of old built the city, and thus it was called a *faithful city* (one could also say it was a *city of the faithful*). At that time it was *full of justice* and *righteousness*, since it was then the dwelling place of virtuous souls. *Righteousness lodged in it.* This *righteousness* made its home and settled in it. Long ago the phrase *full of justice* was an apt description, perhaps around the time of David. He first conquered the city from the hands of another people and settled the ark of God and the tabernacle in it.[47] Once he had appointed his own royal court, the place was called the "city of David." For it is quite likely that it was then *faithful* and *full of justice and* [11] *righteousness*, but now it has become a *harlot* because of those committing fornication in her, and they are the ones whom the rest of the verse exposes when it states, *but now murderers.*

This verse could be interpreted in harmony with the above statements about the times of our Savior. For after the text refers to those who commit fornication against the Word, the bridegroom, as *murderers*, the Holy Spirit goes on to say to them, *Your silver has no value.* But in addition to committing fornication and being *murderers*, they feign to expound pious language and to search the divine Scriptures and to observe the Jewish apocryphal stories from the readings. But their *silver* has *no value.* This verse is obviously talking about the "Jewish myths,"[48] which are silly tales, and for this reason have been "cast aside."[49] Their teachers too, *peddling*[50] their doctrines as they do, are suitably called *peddlers, mixing wine with water.* They water down the pure, sharp, tonic sense of the inspired Scriptures through their silly Jewish apocryphal stories.

[1:23] Although they were called by the Savior, they did not listen. They were even *companions of thieves*, assembling with the thieving betrayer Judas and taking part in the betrayal of the teacher. They were themselves corrupt, and they sold the standards of justice for bribes. *They ran after a reward* in that they were not willing to receive correction, even though it would have profited them; on the contrary, they preferred to deal in wickedness. Thus Symmachus says *they run after retribution.* Those entrusted with the visitation of all who

---

[41]Mt 5:5 RSV. [42]1 Cor 2:9. [43]Heb 12:22. [44]Is 1:20. [45]The Greek word Eusebius chooses, διαβολικός, can mean "enemy" in a purely political sense or "devilish." Eusebius is implying that the political overthrow of Israel reflected a spiritual defeat as well. [46]The other Greek translations refer not to the LXX but the three other Greek versions Eusebius uses: Symmachus, Aquila and Theodotion. [47]2 Kings 5:6-12. [48]Tit 1:14; 1 Tim 4:7. [49]1 Tim 4:4. [50]Is 1:22b in the LXX reads: "your peddlers mix their wine with water"; cf. 2 Cor 2:17.

are impoverished neither *defend the orphan* nor assist *widows*. Those proclaimed as *murderers* are charged with all this, and it is possible to trace what they have done back to their forefathers, and so he says: "Those who were the murderers of the prophets of God long ago."[51]

[1:24] The phrase *Lord of Hosts* is interpreted as *Lord of divine powers* or *Lord of armies*. The word refers to our Savior and Lord, the only-begotten Word of God, who, because of the deeds of those accused of being *murderers*, warns: *Ah, mighty ones of Israel*.[52] The Gospel says something similar about them when it says, "Woe to you, scribes and Pharisees, hypocrites!"[53] All this was proclaimed to the rulers and the powerful of the nation accusing them of distortion. *The Sovereign, the Lord of Hosts* says that *woes* will be on them. Once the *wrath* of his avenging and punitive power has been revealed, it *will not abate*, neither will it cease, he tells us, until it has punished them.

[1:25-26] But the Word, who is benevolent and "does not will the death of the sinner but repentance,"[54] promises to supply a remedy [12] for those who do not require wrath. And what is this promised remedy but his *hand* which was present, saving and healing right alongside his *wrath*? For he says that his design was *to start burning away the dross* and to purify and to separate out the worthless from the precious. In Symmachus's translation, it reads: *And I will smelt away your dross until you are pure*. But in Theodotion's: *And I will filter out your grape skins until you are pure*. For just as those who refine copper or iron by fire remove *the dross* and those who squeeze clusters of grapes in a wine vat throw away the *grape skins* and the dregs after the grapes have been juiced,

so the divine author says: *I will filter out your grape skins until you are pure*. Aquila appeals to a similar metaphor in his translation: *And I will filter out your olive pulp until you are pure*.[55] What is the *dross*, and what are the *grape skins*? The metaphor in all cases is one of a refinement process: *I will remove from you all the lawless and all the arrogant*.[56] After *turning my hand against you*, I will separate *your dross* and *your grape skins*. The text then states that the survivors of the prophesied trials that were discussed above will be tested "as gold is tested with fire."[57] *I will set up your judges* and there will be such *counselors* as there were in ancient times, on whose account *the city* was then *faithful* and *full of justice* and *righteousness*. He promises that a "remnant, chosen by grace"[58] will be found among them, and the remnant in this context again signifies the disciples of our Savior in the new city when these things will be established—the city which is sometimes called the *city of righteousness* and the *faithful mother city Zion*, titles that speak of the administration of the divinely favored government. This government was organized by the Jewish people long ago, but it has since collapsed, and now from out of the whole world it has been raised up again in the church of Christ and has been "founded on the rock."[59] And those who preside as *judges* and *counselors from the beginning* of this beautiful city are in fact to be understood as the apostles and the disciples of our Savior. Those from the apostolic succession who were established as presiding officers of the church of God still shine through even now, for the seed of good trees bears good fruit.

[1:27] These prophecies are to be interpreted as concerning a remnant of the Jewish people, and the following prediction is parallel with

---

[51]Mt 23:31, 37; Acts 7:52. [52]In the LXX this phrase refers to those concerning whom judgment is pronounced; the RSV renders the Hebrew to refer to God. [53]Mt 23:13 RSV. [54]Cf. Ezek 18:23, 32; 33:11. [55]Aquila sees the metaphor as one of pressing olives in order to produce olive oil. The wide variety in the ancient translations of this verse reflects the ambiguity of the Hebrew, some of which has been passed into the Greek translations. [56]Is 1:25b LXX. [57]Cf. Zech 13:9; Prov 8:10; Sir 2:5. [58]Rom 11:5 RSV. [59]Cf. Mt 7:25.

hem: *for its captivity shall be saved with judgment and with mercy,* or, according to all the other translators, *and with righteousness.* If one takes the reading *for its captivity shall be saved with judgment,* it is clear that only those who are deemed worthy of salvation will be made part of the promise. The children of the Jews imagine in vain that there will be a reversal of the dispersion of their entire nation, but it is clear from what the Word **[13]** promises that not all will return but only those who are deemed worthy. One should understand the return from *captivity* as the conversion of souls from error to the true knowledge of God. The Savior presented this true knowledge when he took the scroll of Isaiah in the synagogue and, after reading the passage to which the scroll was open, he said, "The Spirit of the Lord is on me, because he has anointed me to preach good news to the poor."[60] "And he closed the book" and said, "Today this Scripture has been fulfilled in your hearing,"[61] thus teaching that he himself was the redeemer of human souls.

[1:28-29] The Word already taught who *those who forsake the Lord* are when he said, "Ah, sinful nation, a people full of sins, an evil seed, evil offspring, you have forsaken the Lord and provoked to anger the Holy One of Israel."[62] Therefore the Word threatens them with a final, absolute devastation and ruin. When they come to their senses, *they shall be ashamed,* he says, because their ancestors earlier had acted profanely and committed idolatry long ago. Since they were *ashamed,* the text says in addition, they will not make the same mistake as their predecessors: *they shall be ashamed of their idols, which they themselves wanted, and of their gardens, which they desired.*

The shame of what is reproachful springs up in them from their very consciousness, and it will lead to a transformation of their impudent and ruthless conduct.[63] The full completion of the prophecy has finally been worked out. Therefore the Jewish nation no longer commits idolatry as their ancestors did, but they were truly *ashamed.* They saw the demons of their ancestors, and there are those who have been converted from the nations through the teaching of Christ to the word of godliness. In this way the prophecy has been fulfilled, saying: *For they shall be ashamed of their idols, which they themselves wanted, and they were embarrassed because of their gardens, which they desired.* As concerns the *gardens,* their ancestors finished with these idolatrous practices for the most part.[64]

[1:30] He teaches that those who long ago were the "vineyard of the LORD of hosts"[65] and a "green olive tree"[66] and the "well-growing vine Israel"[67] will suffer in such a disastrous way that they will be comparable to *a Terebinth,* and not even one in bloom, but one *that has shed its leaves.* Then this sign will come: no one will ever be able to find anything lush at all or anything on which to procure strength to live. The only yield will be a multitude of withered souls, and for this reason the prophet compares it with the fruits of the *Terebinth,* which are the toughest and driest of all. If you have seen such things as were fulfilled in the present Jewish nation, then you know why the text says: *You shall be like a Terebinth that has shed its leaves,* or, according to Symmachus, *like a Terebinth whose leaves fell away.* They were also *like an orchard that has no water.* Therefore, if **[14]** anyone has seen the reports in the divine Scriptures (and which you will even read in the canonical[68] prophets) and read the historical and poetical books, and the various hymns

---

[60]Lk 4:18. [61]Lk 4:20-21. [62]Is 1:4. [63]In this elegant Greek sentence, Eusebius plays with several synonyms for the word *shame.* [64]Eusebius's comment would seem to reflect the fact that the practice of worshiping idols in groves died out relatively early in Israel's history. [65]Is 5:7 RSV. [66]Jer 11:16 RSV. [67]Hos 10:1. [68]νομικῶν.

and psalms, then he truly has seen the *garden* and the park filled with every kind of good thing. But if he seeks the vital and fertile and living Word among them—the Word of which it is said, "the one who drinks will have a spring of water welling up to eternal life"[69]— he will never find it. Therefore they are declared to be *like an orchard that has no water.*

[1:31] He says that *their strength shall be like a stalk*, and neither of grain nor of any other of the indispensable plants, but he says as *a stalk of flax*, for their "strong man and strong woman, their strength of bread and strength of water, their mighty one and strong one"[70] have been taken away from them. For this reason they are not able to say with Christ's disciples, "I can do all things in him who strengthens me,"[71] or, "Who shall separate us from the love of Christ? Shall tribulation, or distress?"[72] and so on. In this way their *strength* was *as a stalk of flax*. Not only was their freedom destroyed (though they used to plume themselves with their independence,[73] longing for a domestic kingdom), but also there were those to whom it fell to serve with the Roman military men. *Their works* are *like sparks*, in as much as their deeds are causes of fire, and "they built with neither gold, nor silver nor precious stones, but rather wood and hay and straw."[74] And so he says along with all these statements: *And the lawless and the sinners shall be burned together, and there shall be no one to quench them.* You see how the word threatens them with destruction by fire and burning; this is the end of the present prophecy against them. He uttered the prophecy and then, immediately (rather than much later!) after the impudence against our Savior, the mother city was consumed by flame. For those who had acted profanely in it, the "wrath of God"[75] and what is related to

sparks—the eternal "unquenchable fire"[76]—is "stored up for them on the day of wrath."[77]

[2:1-4] Following this, after the charges against the people of the circumcision and after the sentence against them had been carried out, he now passes over to address the calling of the Gentiles. The prophetic Spirit foretells the conversion of the Gentiles to God. Then, after these statements about the new *law* and *word*, he turns his thoughts towards the new *mountain* and *house of God*, to which God will come when those of foreign tribes (he says, Gentiles) who have abandoned the gods of their ancestors come to know the God of the prophets, the one whom the prophets call the *God of Jacob*. And he gives the clearest sign of the time when [15] these things will be accomplished. The sign will be that the gospel of peace will then be preached to every nation, and there will no longer be districts and governments, neither will nations form factions and rise up against each other, nor will the cities of various nation-states go to war and fight with one another. Everyone everywhere will live in harmony and peace. No longer will those who till the earth have any forethought for swords and instruments of war as in the old days, which they used to practice because of the frequent uprisings of their neighbors. These things were fulfilled right after the coming of our Savior Jesus Christ. And that no one could find the same stable and peaceful state of affairs as existed in prior times under the Roman rule following the times of our Savior, we may see with our own eyes. There were civil relations between nations. There was peace everywhere, in the country as well as in the cities, when the new *law* and the evangelical *word* ruled over the lands of the Jews and over *Zion* itself. And

---

[69]Jn 4:14. [70]Is 3:1-2. [71]Phil 4:13. [72]Rom 8:35 RSV. [73]Eusebius plays with this Greek word, which primarily means to allow one's hair to grow long, and by implication to be proud, but it can also refer to the full growth of stalks waving in the wind. [74]1 Cor 3:12. [75]Cf. Rom 2:5. [76]Cf. Mt 3:12. [77]Cf. Rom 2:5.

peace ruled the world without hindrance and filled all nations. Therefore, we may reasonably say that when the new situation was beginning to emerge, after the first accusation and sentence against the Jewish nation, and in fact when the gospel was beginning to emerge, the prophetic Spirit delivered a proclamation introducing the word of God that came to Isaiah. And this is also what the Gospel is talking about when it says, "In the beginning was the Word."[1] For, since the calling of the Gentiles had been prophesied, it was necessary for God to advance the word and the preaching of the aforementioned to the Gentiles.

In Symmachus's translation the prophecy reads: *for of Judea and Jerusalem*. Regarding the phrase and subject at hand, one could say that the word is *for* them because of the fact that the first preaching of the saving and evangelical grace took place in *Judea* and in *Jerusalem*. Thus the Christ of God walked about *Judea* and Galilee, and he was constantly in and out of *Jerusalem* "preaching the kingdom of God."[2] From our study of the preceding accusations, we have come to learn that the phrases and storyline and meaning of the text (in this case, *Judea* and *Jerusalem*) may result in something other than we would anticipate. We should thus note that according to Symmachus, this verse reads: *The word that came to the prophet was for Judea and Jerusalem.*

The kindest promise was made to the Jewish nation, and it is true that it was revealed that they would possess their own land, but now the calling in fact has been engaging the Gentiles. In this charge against the Jewish people, to which we have already referred, there is again this threat against *Judea* and *Jerusalem*. Therefore, in no way does he introduce the new *law* as parallel to the *law* of

Moses or as another *word* parallel to the old, but rather as a new *mountain*, unseen in times past but now *manifest*.[3] The *house of God* will be known to all *nations*, but, one should note, not to the Jewish people or *Judea* and *Jerusalem*. The promises to the *nations* are the very same, and the Word stands by these promises. And what should one say about the meaning of *Judea*, which is revealed in the verse that reads, "In Judah God is known"?[4] [16] The soul that has received the knowledge of God could truly be *Judea*, and then it would be true that "in Judah God is known." It is certain, however, that he does not call the Gentile knowledge of God *Judea*.[5] And the *house of God* which endures in *Judea* would probably be the church of the Gentiles (here under the name *house of God* or *mountain*), which has been "founded" on the saving and indestructible "rock" and which speaks of the *word* of God.[6] You should not imagine that this interpretation exceeds the truth, for in the account of the vision that the prophet *Daniel* saw, we read "a stone was cut out from the *mountain* without human hands."[7] Here, "stone" speaks of the humanity of the Savior and "mountain" speaks of God the Word.[8] He prophesies that these things will happen in *the last days*. You will understand that the phrase *the house of God shall be on the tops of the mountains* reminds us that our Savior hears the prayers of his church. "A city set on a hill cannot be hid."[9] *The mountain of God* may be understood in various ways. Like the Jewish people who read the Scriptures literally, one could assume that it is the land of Palestine. But according to the deeper meaning, according to the final *word*, the high and heavenly and angelic *word* of God and the divine apostle of the "heavenly" *Zion*[10] teaches that it is "the Jerusalem above, which is the

---

Chapter Two [1]Jn 1:1 RSV. [2]Cf. Lk 8:1. [3]The LXX reads "manifest," not "established," as in Is 2:2 RSV. [4]Ps 76:1 RSV. [5]Eusebius wants to make clear that even if the Jews do not possess the true knowledge of God, one should not assume that pagan theology therefore must be correct. [6]Cf. Mt 7:25. [7]Cf. Dan 2:34, 45. [8]Eusebius here finds an allegorical identification in Isaiah's prophecy of the humanity and divinity of Christ. [9]Mt 5:14 RSV. [10]Cf. Heb 12:22.

mother of us all."[11] This *mountain* was not *manifest* to the men of old, but the divine Spirit prophesies that it will be *manifest to all nations in the last days*, when Christ would "appear to put away sin."[12] Therefore *all nations*—"both Greeks and barbarians,"[13] which indeed turn from the error of polytheism and from the literal mountains which were in ancient times thought to be dedicated to demons or to the gods—will strive after the God who is proclaimed in revelation. For this reason, as though speaking one to another, he says: *Come, let us go up to the mountain of the Lord and to the house of the God of Jacob, and he will declare to us his way, and we will walk in it.* And so the Word promises to the *nations* that he will make *the mountain and the house of God manifest* in the heavens and known to all who are instructed.

The Christ could very well be this evangelical *law*, who relocated from the "heavenly" *Zion* above and set up shop[14] in the *Zion* on the earth, where the death of the Savior at the hands of men and his resurrection from the dead took place. For once the mysteries and precepts of the new covenant came to power, they advanced throughout the entire world. This same *law* and the new preaching of the evangelical word *to all nations* educated those who welcomed it in what concerns *the mountain and the house of God*, and it taught the nations, saying: *Come, let us go up to the mountain of the Lord and to the house of the God of Jacob.* He also *judged between the nations*, separating for himself the worthy and picking out those who are called from among those who are not called. The evangelical *Word judged between the nations*, for he convicted [17] many a people, here exposing the former error among those who have believed in him, there convicting those who have not believed in him, who perish along with their case. Those who have received him, who were set free from every inclination for war, spend the rest of their quiet lives recovering in peace, no longer inciting hostility from opposing powers nor living as subject to the demons who had mastery over them long ago. The Savior himself bestowed this "peace" to his disciples when he said: "Peace I leave with you; my peace I give to you."[15] This means literally that, in the end, after his theophany and after the preaching of the evangelical *law* to the *nations*, the *nations* were deemed worthy to partake of the deepest peace. It also speaks of the word that Christ gave that *they shall beat their daggers into plows* and *their spears into pruning hooks* and that war will no longer be taught, although training for war used to be compulsory and was practiced in the country as well as in the cities from the children on up because of the fear of hostile uprisings.

[2:5-9] Accordingly, after the prophet had dealt in detail with the calling of the Gentiles and the peace that had been dispersed among all people (and this peace was shown in what is related to peace—God's tender love in calling the people his own), he then spoke about the reception of the grace of Christ that was given to all nations. Thus he says: *And now, O house of Jacob, come, let us walk by the light of the Lord.* He recounts the vision for the exhortation and encouragement of the people and himself, pleading to be allotted a share in *the light of the Lord*, calling the *light of the Lord* the law of the new covenant that proceeded *from Zion* and the saving and evangelical *word*. And it is not *Jacob* who is called forth to come to the *light* of knowledge of the *Lord*, but his *house*, which happens to be in darkness. This, then, dovetails with the next verse, which says: *For he has abandoned his people, the house of Jacob.* Hurry up, then, you who are of the

---

[11]Cf. Gal 4:26. [12]Heb 9:26. [13]Cf. Rom 1:14. [14]ὁρμηθεὶς. Literally translated, this line would read: "who moved his *base of operations* or *headquarters* from the 'heavenly' Zion above to the Zion on the earth." [15]Jn 14:27 RSV.

forsaken house and come with me; for I am ready to walk by the light of the Lord with you. And he calls the Jewish people the house of Jacob, not because they were Jacob or because they were worthy to be called by their forefather's name. The only thing that was the same is that they were loitering in the house because it was empty. For this reason he has forsaken them, and, as if defending God, he also brings this charge against them: Because their country was filled with divinations [18] as it had been in the beginning, and the rest. And so he establishes that it was not for no reason that the light of the Lord that shone on every nation has abandoned them. According to the interpretation of the seventy, this verse reads: He has abandoned his people, and what follows this statement fits in with the second verse: Let us walk by the light of the Lord.

After advising the people thus, the prophet says: Come, let us walk by the light of the Lord. It stands true for the rest of what is said that it no longer pertains to the people, but the prophet is speaking to the Lord himself. Instead of he has abandoned his people, Aquila renders this verse: You let your people, the house of Jacob, alone, and Symmachus: you cast your people away. He then presents the next reason for the letting go of the people when he says that their land was filled up with "omens and divinations"[16] and every idolatry, just as in ancient times when foreign tribes such as the Amorrites, Hivites and Jebusites inhabited the place and practiced terrible things. And so he says that the land of the house of Jacob will be filled with inhabitants from foreign lands, and these people from foreign tribes will have children, and the land will be filled with them. The land that was once called the land of God will be filled with military men, which he foretells when he speaks of the multitude of horses and chariots in the next verse. Again he says that their land will be filled with those

who are preoccupied with gold and silver, and he says further that their land will be filled with the abominations, the works of their hands. And whose works are these but those of the inhabitants of foreign tribes, who bow down to the things their own fingers have made? All these symptoms of spiritual ill health were contracted from the nations of foreign tribes and idolaters who are supposed to have built Jerusalem itself and the land of Judea. And all of this was fulfilled after the coming of our Savior and after the delivery of the evangelical word that "enlightened every nation."[17] When they did not obey the prophet who had called them saying, Come, let us walk by the light of the Lord, the Jewish people were delivered over to the authority of the Romans. And so the prophet, pained in soul, cried aloud to the Lord himself: you have abandoned your people, the house of Jacob.

Afterwards, he presents evidence demonstrating that the people who were let go and abandoned by the Lord would be forced to surrender their land to nations of other races, whose iniquities will be counted up, the prophet says, as he cries aloud to the Lord himself: Will you not pardon them?[18] He replies: I certainly will not forgive them. Aquila renders this phrase: You will not remove them, will you? And Symmachus: You will not pardon them, will you? But he would never have said this in reference to the Jews. For the prophet did not entreat the Lord for his own people but prayed according to the interpretation expounded above. All these statements about those who attacked Jerusalem and occupied it with military forces and all the idolatry, the prophet adduces as arguments against the people.

[2:10-12] [19] And I think that the preceding prophecies were fulfilled in one sense when the Romans invaded the Jewish nation and the land was ravaged and everyone fled from the

---

[16]Cf. Deut 18:14.   [17]Cf. Jn 1:9.   [18]Eusebius's citations reflect a text tradition not preserved in the lxx.

face of the enemy and hid *in the rocks* and *caves* because of the wrath of God hanging over them. Then *the haughty were humbled*, and those who flaunt their wealth (though they were no one of importance before) were put to shame, overtaken by *the day of the Lord*. I speak of the avenging of the Christ, at which time *the day of the Lord* extracted justice not only from *the arrogant* and from prominent persons but even from the land, the splendor of which was ravaged and eradicated by the enemy when they struck down the *towers* and demolished the *walls* and trounced all *that is lofty*. We read in historical accounts that enemy armies captured their ships at sea, and so from all quarters the Jewish nation was then humbled and plundered—all because they did not listen to the prophet who exhorted them, saying: "Come, let us walk by the light of the Lord."[19] They handed themselves over willingly. Calling these things to witness, the prophet predicts that the "wrath to come"[20] will overtake them if they do not receive the "light of the Lord."[21] In the same way, he prophesies that there will be an overthrow of the idolatry among humankind and that *the Lord alone will be exalted* in the presence of all. Everything that is exalted and that rises up against the knowledge of God will be abased.

I think that the prophet ran out of patience, as discussed above, and so he prophesied concerning the foreign tribes that appear to have lived in the land of the Jewish nation and that occupied Jerusalem itself, and he beseeches God in prayer, saying: "Will you not pardon them?"[22] Accordingly, they were regarded as deserving "the righteous judgment of God."[23] The Lord showed him "the day of vengeance"[24] for all who will pursue iniquities, and having seen it in advance, he then advised them to keep watch already for "the wrath to come"[25] that will overtake all the wicked. For

this reason, concerning those who seem to have built the land, to whom we referred above, he says: *They will enter into the rock and hide in the earth from before the fear of the Lord and from the glory of his strength, when he rises to crush the earth. For the eyes of the Lord are lofty, but man is lowly, and the loftiness of humankind shall be brought low, and the Lord alone will be exalted in that day.* I think that these things were said concerning the day of judgment, and therefore the Word prophesies what is at hand not only for Judea but for all such people in general. And thus he says in addition: *For the day of the Lord of hosts will be against everyone who is insolent and haughty, against everyone who is lofty and high; and they shall be humbled.* For clearly through these prophecies he introduces a universal judgment [20] against all the wicked. For this very reason, neither in the Hebrew text nor in the other Greek translations are the words *and now* expressed, although they are represented in the reading among us, which reads: *and now, enter into the rocks and hide.* And so he did not prophesy these things concerning the present time but concerning the universal judgment of God.

[2:13-17] Then, as discussed above, when he remembered "the chariots and the horses"[26] that had been acquired and the "gold and silver," the wealth and treasures that had been amassed, he foreshadowed the coming judgment in the figure of an allegory, appealing to the images of what he calls *cedars of Lebanon and acorn trees and high mountains and hills and high towers and walls and ships.* He prophesies that there will be a destruction of everything "according to the awaited day of the Lord."[27] After speaking here in obscure riddles about the "the rulers of this age,"[28] the high and honorable things, "the principalities and powers and the world rulers in this life,"[29] and

---

[19]Is 2:5. [20]Cf. Mt 3:7. [21]Cf. Is 2:5. [22]Is 2:9; at this point too, Eusebius's reading does not correspond to the Hebrew or the LXX. [23]Cf. Rom 2:5. [24]Cf. Deut 32:35. [25]Cf. Mt 3:7. [26]Cf. Is 2:7. [27]Cf. 2 Pet 3:12. [28]See 1 Cor 2:6. [29]Cf. Eph 6:12.

"those who do not acknowledge God,"[30] the prophet prayed, saying: "Will you not pardon them?"[31] The Holy Spirit, who healed his soul, showed him the suffering that was about to befall his relatives.

[2:18-21] Afterwards, when he remembered, as discussed above, how "the land was filled with the abominations, the works of their hands, and they bowed down to the things their own fingers had made; and so a person bowed down, and a person was humbled,"[32] then he prophesies with these words: *And they will hide all the works of their hands carrying them into caves and into the clefts of the rocks and into the holes of the earth.* And again: *On that day a man will throw away his silver and gold abominations, which they made for themselves to bow down to.* At the moment when the day of God overtakes their *glories,* which formerly they had in their soul concerning the error of polytheism, *they will hide* their shattered delusions, and *they will throw away* and disown of their own will every false impression that they ever had about their idols. They will do this *from before the fear of the Lord.* But even at the time of the first coming of our Savior, these things began to be accomplished in part as the evangelical word was preached to all nations. Therefore, as far as we are concerned, the error of the gods of old (as the Gentiles imagined them to be) had already been refuted, since they were not able to come to their aid. For this reason, every idolater *has been humbled,* **[21]** and *only the Lord* of everything *will be exalted.* The error of those who once presumed their idols to be gods was refuted, and their wooden statues of costly materials were taken away from among them. According to the prophecy, *they will hide* their inanimate statues in *caves,* so that they might not be acquired by royal men for their costly

material. I suppose one is forced to come to the conclusion that these things did finally occur after the saving advent. Since Jerusalem was idolatrous, or rather, since the entirety of Judea had been deceived, the Babylonian army in effect occupied a certain area of Judea. After laying waste to everything, they killed many of those whom they had captured, carrying off the women and children to their own country. The invasion had been announced in advance and was expected to happen, but because the fear and anguish that had fallen on the Jewish people at this time was so great, they *hid themselves* in *caves* and in the clefts of the mountains, and they fled to the most inaccessible places. Their hand was altogether too feeble against those who opposed them.

[2:22[33]] And then comes the verse: *Turn away from man in whose nostrils is breath, for of what account is he?* This verse is attested in the supplement.[34] And so it seems that the word exhorts them not to pay attention to those events, neither to "put their hope in humanity"[35]—mortals whose very life is stored in their *nostrils.*

[3:1-3] With these prophecies concerning "the day of vengeance"[1] having been delivered, and with the preceding having been laid out, the prophet commences from a new starting point, threatening the removal of the graces from among the former people of God, which he says will be taken away from them neither because of their idolatries nor because of certain other practices but because of one truly godless, wicked and evil counsel against the Lord. Therefore, in view of all the threats against them, he brings on another accusation, saying: "They have proclaimed their sin like that of Sodom; and they have made it plain. Woe to their soul, because they have given evil

---

[30]Cf. Ps 78:6. [31]Is 2:9. [32]Is 2:8-9. [33]This passage does not exist in the LXX. [34]Eusebius is acknowledging that this text is not present in the Hebrew. [35]Cf. Ps 118:8-9. **Chapter Three** [1]Cf. Deut 32:35.

counsel against themselves, saying: 'Let us bind the just, for he is a nuisance to us.'"[2] This was the reason for all the threats. I suppose one is forced to come to the conclusion that these things did finally occur after the saving advent. For this reason the prophet says, *The Lord will take away from Jerusalem and from Judah a strong man and a strong woman*, or, as in Aquila's version, *the supports and pillars*, or, as in Symmachus's version, *the foundations and substructures*. You will perceive in these phrases the very apostolic word, which calls what suits the life according to God the "pillar and bulwark."[3] In every society as among the former people of God there were certain figures who were like "bulwarks" and *foundations* of the entire nation, whom the Word threatens will be taken away. For, later, there will be neither *bread* nor *water*, and the *strength of bread, and the strength of water* will be taken away. [22] This will sound familiar to you, because another prophet has said: "'Behold, the days are coming,' says the Lord, 'and I will send a famine on the land; not a famine of *bread*, nor a thirst for *water*, but a famine of hearing the word of the Lord.'"[4] The nourishing *bread* of the soul and likewise the spiritual drink is the word. The Jewish people also suppose that they partake in this *bread* and drink in their pursuit of the divine Scriptures and their elaboration of their thorough knowledge and scholarly endeavors, but you will not find the *stay* of the nourishing words and the refreshment of the life-giving fountain among them.

The prophet threatens that the *mighty one* and *strong one* and the *diviner will be taken away from them*. Neither the Hebrew version nor the other Greek translations have the word *mighty*. But instead, Aquila renders it as *powerful*, Symmachus as *courageous* and

Theodotion as *principal man*. He threatens that the *principal* and the *powerful*, and even the *soldier and the judge* (the other Greek translations read *arbiter*[5] instead) and every *prophet* and *diviner* will be taken away from them. I suppose one is forced to come to the conclusion that these things did finally occur after the saving advent. Therefore, if anyone should maintain that these things were said concerning the oppression during the time of the prophet Isaiah or concerning the besieging of the Babylonians, he will be refuted as one who entertains erroneous opinions.

For most of the prophets then, before and during the siege, lived among them in Jerusalem itself and around Babylon itself, and after the subsequent return there were also *judges*[6] among them *judging the people*. Therefore in Babylon itself Daniel judged "the elders,"[7] and after the return from exile, Jeshua the son of Jozadak and Zerubbabel the son of Shealtiel led some of the people down [to Judah], and later still, Ezra and Nehemiah and the elders who had been bestowed with sagacity and wisdom adorned their nation. Then you will find that there were even eminent *warriors* among them around the times of the Maccabeans, when at any rate there were *officers of fifty* in their military ranks. And it is probable that there were *wonderful counselors* among them, and those who were *skilled* with words, and *architects*. There were also *intelligent listeners* among them, who accepted the truth of the words of the prophet and, after scrutiny, rejected those of the false prophets, and they did this by the spirit of discernment. Therefore, in ancient times, all these things abounded in the Jewish nation, and suddenly it was deserted and "taken away."[8] And then, in accordance with the prophecy ("from Jerusalem and from Judea"), all these things trans-

---

[2]Is 3:9-10. [3]Cf. 1 Tim 3:15. [4]Amos 8:11. [5]Eusebius notes that the LXX reads δικαστής whereas Symmachus, Aquila and Theodotion all read κριτής. The words are essentially synonyms. [6]This is the same Greek word that is translated "avenger" above. [7]Cf. Sus 44-62. [8]Cf. Is 3:1.

pired all at once (and not sometime later!) because of their scheme against our Savior.

[3:4-11] That which had been predicted of all the prophet's predictions happened: the people were handed over to the *mockers* of the Lord and their *young rulers*. And the Word explains anew that the reason why he accuses them of all these things is not their idolatry but because *they have given evil counsel against* [23] *themselves, saying: "Let us bind the just, for he is a nuisance to us,"* and also because *their tongues are joined with lawlessness, being disobedient toward the things of the Lord.* But Symmachus has instead: *Their tongues and their practices provoked the Lord*; and Aquila: *Their tongue and practices provoked the Lord to anger.* You see the reason why the previously mentioned things *were taken away.* For their own *tongues* provoked[9] the Lord, at which point in time they vented their wicked voices, saying: *"Away with him, away with him,"*[10] *"His blood be on us and on our children!"*[11] For then truly *Their tongue and practices were against the Lord and provoked him.* For this reason he next makes the deeper meaning quite clear when he goes on to say: *They have proclaimed their lawlessness sin like that of Sodom; and they have made it plain. Woe to their soul, because they have given evil counsel against themselves, saying: "Let us bind the just, for he is a nuisance to us."* And this indeed was the reason for the removal of the gifts of God that shone in the old days.

And on seeing those who are called the *patriarchs*[12] of the Jewish people—for they were truly *youths*, not only concerning the age of their bodies but also concerning their incompletely developed souls and premature thinking—who would not say that the teachers who were left were *mockers*? Concerning them the prophet proclaimed: *And the people will fall together, man against man, and a man against his neighbor; the child will stumble against the elder, and the dishonored against the honorable.* No one in the army or any citizen (who did not have the word of God among them)—even if in poverty and thinking himself to be in need—would go so far as to say that he had neither *cloak* nor enough *bread* to eat. Indeed, the graceful *cloak* is a euphemism signifying what covers the disfigurement of their soul, and *bread* signifies the deeper meaning of the nourishing word. Therefore he says: *Because a man will seize his brother or his father's kinsman, saying: "You have a cloak; you be our leader, and let my food be under you"; but he will answer and say on that day: "I will not be your leader; for in my house there is neither bread nor cloak."* Then he indicates the desertion of the land and the absolute destruction of Jerusalem when he goes on to say next: *Jerusalem is abandoned, and Judah has fallen.* The reason has been stated above: because of *their tongues,* through which *they provoked* God, and because *they have given evil counsel* against their own soul, or rather, they suffered these things according to that which was resolved.[13] For this reason *they shall eat the fruit of their works*[14] and *woes* shall befall *the lawless one* [24], because *evil things will happen to him according to the works of his hands.* "For whatever a man sows, that he will also reap."[15]

[3:12] *Your exactors strip you clean.* Those who are overcome and those who offend someone, they indeed falter in their knowledge due to wickedness, since they have been pricked and injured in conscience by the things they do; those who go in the right way in ignorance are, so to speak, borne by fattened

---

[9]The Greek terms underlying the three words all translated as "provoked" above are synonyms, each offering a slightly different nuance. [10]Jn 19:15 RSV. [11]Mt 27:25 RSV. [12]Here Eusebius is not referring to the three patriarchs, Abraham, Isaac and Jacob, but to those who exercised leadership during the chaotic times both before and during the Babylonian captivity. [13]Eusebius is implying that the plans of these individuals could not thwart the plan that God had all along. [14]In the RSV, this line is one of comfort addressed to the righteous. [15]Gal 6:7 RSV.

beasts.[16] And these deceptive leaders are the last mentioned of the bad predictions. They lay down destruction for themselves and others through deception and other perversities. Accordingly, the Word of God, on seeing many among the Jewish people who fall into error, does away with the accusations that have been brought earlier. In what has been laid out above, he recommends to them the sorts of things that the tender-hearted Christ also calls out in an encouraging voice to his people, whom he makes his own and draws to the knowledge of himself. Therefore every person who goes in the right way, even he sins elsewhere. However, a lenient judgment is brought on him, since one deals out lenient judgments to those who offend in ignorance. For this reason he says: *My people*. He then refutes those charges among them which arise from a disbelief in him. He called these charges, as discussed above, "mockers."[17] For this reason he says: *My people, your exactors strip you clean.* For the rulers of the Jewish nation desire to amass profit from God because of the first-fruits and the tithes and the other things they offer as rulers and teachers, not committing the knowledge that they had acquired to Christ. He then presents this statement besides: *Your exactors strip you clean, and your creditors lord it over you.* And who are the *creditors*, and what is the above-mentioned profit, on which account the leaders were not correcting sinners but only flattering and congratulating those with whom they consorted? For this reason he convicts these leaders, saying: *My people, those who congratulate you mislead you and confuse the path of your feet.* For turning away from the straight path that leads to the saving word, they twisted the steps of their soul. And for those who are deceived by their congratulations, *the path of their feet is thrown into confusion.* Indeed, tribulation summons forth

self-abasement, but congratulations engender only our natural tendencies.

[3:13-15] And so, he next says to those who act in this way: *But now the Lord will stand up to judge*; and again: *The Lord himself will enter into judgment with the elders of the people and with their rulers.* Therefore, the *elders* and *rulers*, those who fail to watch the vineyard through sound teaching and the good example of one's own life, these will be called to account. Then, being present at the judgment seat of the Lord, he censures them to their face, convicting them saying: *But you, why have you burned my vineyard, and why is the spoil of the poor in your houses? Why do you wrong my people and shame the face of the poor?* If, *in our houses*, we have what has been given for the repose of day laborers, so to speak, then we defraud the indigent. The custom for those who do wrong and defraud is that [25] they are then called to account with violence and abuse by those who have been wronged. They shame them, disparage them and threaten blows. For this reason he says that they heard of the shame of the injustice among you; turn away from your tyranny over the *poor*. He even now calls his *people* his *vineyard set ablaze.* They have been cheated through robbery and the distortion of their teachings, but he summons them once again to himself and turns them away from the aforementioned perversion of their teachings. And so, in close alignment with all this, after he had prophesied the first advent of the Savior and the distortion *of the rulers* of the people, he delivers a prophecy about his second coming, saying: *The Lord himself will enter into judgment with the elders of the people and with their rulers.*

[3:16-23] Instead of *tassels*, Aquila translates it as *leather belts.* And instead of *crescents* Sym-

---

[16]Eusebius sets up his principle: Whether besieged by temptation from without or inspired to uncontrolled action by the passions within, these fail knowingly. And even those who go in the right way without God do so in ignorance.   [17]Is 3:4.

machus has *necklaces or collars*. Where Aquila has *weavings*, Symmachus has *ornamental chains*. And again, instead of *bracelets*, Symmachus has *aprons*. The prophecy and all the above appears to have been addressed to the men, and one should probably suppose that none of the above has been said to the women, but he places a threat against them when he describes their former lifestyle as reveling in "wanton pleasure"[18] and living in wealth. In their great abundance, they never thought about God. For this reason he threatens to *strip* them of those things that enable them to live in luxury.

[3:24] Instead of their former luxury, he indicates that they will get the short end of the exchange: *Instead of a pleasant scent there will be dust; instead of a girdle, you will gird yourself with a rope; and instead of a head adornment, you will have baldness because of your works; and instead of a tunic blended with purple, you will gird yourself about with sackcloth.* It is possible that these things were said not only concerning the women but also concerning frivolous souls that have become womanish. It is probable that these things were fulfilled after the controversy that the people of the circumcision had with our Savior and Lord. Those who then lived surrounded by wealth in *Zion* were the *daughters* who "lived wantonly"[19] and had no feeling for those enveloped in misery.

[3:25-26] Therefore, with these threats having been justly made against them, the prophecy states that they will be handed over to the *sword* of their enemies. He foreshadowed the Roman invasion when he said: *Your most beautiful son, whom you love, he shall fall by the dagger; and your strong men shall fall by dagger.* Instead of this, Symmachus renders this verse in this way: *Instead of beauty, the beautiful of your number will fall by the sword, and your powerful will fall*

in battle, when *the city will be emptied and mourn*. And so it has been said concerning it according to the Septuagint: *you shall be left alone and shall be dashed to the ground.*

[4:1] With the final destitution of the place being foretold through these signs, he next addresses [26] these things: since the men have departed and no longer live because of the slaughter of the *sword*, the prophet says that *seven women shall take hold of one man* and beseech him to allow them to take on his name and nothing more. They needed nothing else except his *name* and someone who would represent them socially,[1] so that they might not be forsaken or reproached by anyone because they did not have husbands. For this reason, when these women found this rare man among all those who had perished, they said to him: *Just let your name be called on us; take away our reproach.* This is indeed the literal meaning of the text, but as others have said before, the man is to be interpreted as the Savior, and *the seven women* are the seven powers of the Holy Spirit that came to the first man because they could find none other who would take them in. And these seven powers are the "spirit of wisdom and understanding, of counsel and might, of knowledge and godliness" and above all "the spirit of the fear of God."[2]

[4:2-3] *On that day God will shine forth.* Here he teaches that the horrors that we have formerly discussed will be at one and the same time accompanied by the radiant light of God; the former things were indeed gloomy, but the present things are more cheerful. How then can it be that the benevolent promises will be accomplished at the same time as the other things? For the phrase *in that day* has to do with his Christ, by whom also the aforementioned cheerful events will take place. And

[18]Cf. Jas 5:5. [19]Cf. Amos 6:4. **Chapter Four** [1]The Greek verb προΐστημι literally means "to stand before," and in this context means to "protect" or "represent socially." [2]Is 11:2-3.

thus he says: *God will gloriously shine on the earth with counsel.* But Symmachus here reads instead: *The Lord will be ascendant and eminent in the power and glory of the earth.*[3] He next brings forward the benevolent promises for all the people (even though it would seem that the word contradicts itself here), and now he proclaims not to the entire nation but only to the *remnant* from it: *God will shine forth over the earth gloriously in counsel, to uplift and glorify what remains of Jerusalem, and what is left behind in Jerusalem will be called holy.* These were the ones whom the former prophecy reveals as the "offspring" who *remain,* in which context we read: "And if the Lord of hosts had not *left* us a few offspring, we would have been like Sodom, and made similar to Gomorrah."[4] He here presents those from the Jewish people who have believed in Christ, among whom were the apostles who dispersed the spiritual and heavenly offspring among all nations. For this very reason the prophecy at hand foretells what we have discussed, saying: *On that day,* clearly referring to the time when they are cast aside, *God will gloriously shine on the earth with counsel, to uplift and glorify what remains of Israel, and those appointed to life in Jerusalem will be called holy.* And so the prophecy has been worked out, because those from Israel who first believed in Christ—the apostles and disciples and evangelists of the Savior—they were *uplifted* and *glorified,* for they were famous everywhere on earth and throughout the whole world. [27] And still, even now, before all the nations, "both Greeks and barbarians,"[5] they are *glorified*—their name as well as their teaching. These alone *will be called holy* who were deemed worthy and *were appointed* to eternal *life* "in the heavenly Jerusalem."[6] To these apostles the voice of our Savior was entrusted, who said: "rejoice that your names are written in heaven."[7]

[4:4] The prophet makes it clear how they will be worthy of these things when he says next: *The Lord will wash away the filth of the sons and daughters of Zion and will cleanse the blood from their midst by a spirit of judgment.* He here clearly alludes to the "washing of regeneration,"[8] which he also set forth, as we have discussed, when he said: "Wash yourselves; become clean."[9] Well, now the time of this washing is proclaimed. *By a spirit of judgment* does not differ at all from the phrase in the Gospels, "with the Holy Spirit and with fire."[10] He speaks of the *filth* of their souls, souls that had become defiled and stained from *blood,* and as we have discussed above, the Word remembered this blood when he said: "Your hands are full of blood."[11] He then calls this *blood* the blood in the midst of Jerusalem in the present prophecy when he says: *The Lord will wash away the filth of the sons and daughters of Zion and will cleanse the blood.* And the reason why the *daughters of Zion* are accused again in the passage we discussed above is provided in the next verse: "Because the daughters of Zion were lifted up and walked with an uplifted neck,"[12] and the rest. He says these things concerning those who had taken part in the murder against the Savior but who converted a little later and made his gospel known. Paul was one of these, who "indeed at first ravaged the church of God"[13] "and consented to the death"[14] of Stephen. Paul was in every which way stained with the blood of the Savior all over, but he later converted and was "baptized"[15] *by a spirit of judgment.* All these statements apply equally well to Paul—*they will be washed and they will be clean.* "For by judgment"[16] "they shall be saved" "and by righteousness,"[17] and *by a spirit of judgment.* One should note that the present word is totally harmonious with the evangelical witness concerning our Savior which in-

---

[3]This beautiful Greek line applies the imagery of a rising star to the glory that God will assume. [4]Is 1:9. [5]Rom 1:14. [6]Cf. Heb 12:22.
[7]Lk 10:20 RSV. [8]Tit 3:5. [9]Is 1:16. [10]Mt 3:11. [11]Is 1:15. [12]Is 3:16. [13]Acts 8:3. [14]Acts 8:1. [15]Acts 9:18. [16]Is 1:27. [17]Is 1:27.

structed us, saying: "He will baptize you with the Holy Spirit and with fire."[18] For the phrase *by a spirit of judgment and by a spirit of burning* differs not in the slightest from "with the Holy Spirit and with fire." For the fiery words that were addressed to them produced in them a cleansing from their sins. Likewise it is said of the Savior in the Gospel that he "baptized" not with water but "with the Holy Spirit and with fire." When John [28] taught concerning himself, he said, "I baptize you with water," but concerning the Savior, he said, "he will baptize you with the Holy Spirit and with fire."[19]

[4:5-6] Concerning these things he goes on to say: *Then he will come, and as for every place in Zion, and all that surrounds it, a cloud will overshadow it by day.* And who it is that *will come,* another prophet presents, saying: "the Deliverer will come from Zion,"[20] and he says again, "Yet a little while, the coming one shall come, and shall not tarry."[21] After he comes, he will fulfill all that has been prophesied. Instead of *he will come,* the Hebrew text and all the other Greek translations read: *The Lord will create over the whole site of Mount Zion.* The expression "new creation"[22] refers to the fact that the church of God has been founded in every place. Here the evangelical word is called *Mount Zion,* on which "the new creation" has been constructed, not by any human hand but by the Lord himself, who said: "On this rock I will build my church."[23] He is speaking of the church when he says *all that surrounds it, a cloud will overshadow and like a light of fire burning by night; with all glory will it be covered.* This all will sound rather familiar when we retrace the history of Moses, in which we read that Christ "went before them by a pillar of cloud by day" and "during the night by a pillar of fire"[24] to provide them with light. The present prophet predicts that it will be just like

this with the church of God. For he says that *a cloud will overshadow it by day* (in order that it might not be scorched by the fiery heat) and that there will be *a light by night, the splendor of fire* (in order that it might not be lost in the dark). And again he says that the *glory* of God *will overshadow* the entire church so that it will not be harmed by anything, neither by the *heat* of day nor by the *harshness* and *rains* of day. In these statements the Word of God teaches us that his right hand will *overshadow* the church, so that through all its journey nothing will harm it, neither while it experiences conditions of success and peace nor in times of persecution. He says that it will remain ever faultless and true and *overshadowed* by the *glory* of God, so that it will neither be scorched in the *heat by day* nor *even by the harshness and rains,* and it will not be harmed by the winter winds. For this reason it has been said: *With all glory it will be covered; and it will serve as shade from the heat and as a shelter and a hideout from the harshness and rain.*

[5:1] The prophetic Spirit adds on yet to those things which had already been predicted, and at this point the next part of the same "vision" happens which "Isaiah the son of Amoz saw against Judah and against Jerusalem."[1] Passing through the things delivered by the mouth of the Holy Spirit and already discussed above, he says: *I will now sing for the beloved a song of my loved one.* But instead of *concerning my vineyard,* the Hebrew text and the other Greek translations render the phrase: *concerning his vineyard.* It is for the beloved, he says, that *I will sing a song*—a song that is not mine nor composed by me, but by him who sang his beloved's song concerning a vineyard. It is *a song quite full of* lamentation and weeping. Aquila interpreted the verse in this way: *I will sing my uncle's ballad to my dear friend concerning his*

---

[18]Mt 3:11 rsv. [19]Mt 3:11 rsv. [20]Is 59:20; Rom 11:26. [21]Hab 2:3; Heb 10:37. [22]Cf. 2 Cor 5:17; Gal 6:15. [23]Mt 16:18 rsv. [24]Ex 13:21. **Chapter Five** [1]Is 1:1. The Greek text is defective at this point.

vineyard; and Symmachus: *I will sing for my beloved my beloved's song in his vineyard;* **[29]** and Theodotion: *I will sing for my beloved a song, my beloved's song, concerning his vineyard.* He does not say *mine* but *my beloved's* in regard to the song. When the verse is rendered as *concerning his vineyard* rather than *in his vineyard*, it makes it a ballad of lamentation. *He who was loved* was one and the same as the *beloved*,[2] for indeed *he who was loved* refers to God and his Father, and *beloved* refers to the Holy Spirit.[3] The prophetic spirit expresses this when he says: *I will now sing for the beloved a song of my beloved concerning my vineyard.* And in the ballad, his good deeds *in the vineyard* are recounted, and he rebukes the depravity *of the vineyard*, and so he also prophesies concerning the things that are about to happen to it. For this very reason, the *beloved* of God, who acquired the special people of the circumcision as his inheritance and portion, greatly laments their destruction which occurred because they cast aside human kindness. For he says: *The beloved had a vineyard on a hill, on a fertile place;* or according to Symmachus: *in an olive grove on a hill;* or according to Aquila: *on my son's olive hill.* In saying *fertile*, the prophet declares the land of Judea to be bountiful,[4] and he says *on a hill* because the royal mother city Jerusalem had been constructed in it. For the Scripture is accustomed to referring to kings as *horns*.[5]

[5:2-7] *He put a hedge* around the vineyard. Clearly this refers to the people as a whole. After he had fenced all around them in every way with his angels, *he fenced them in* with the prophets and supported them with holy men, and even *planted a choice vine* among them.

And what was this *choice vine* if not precisely the inspired Scripture and the godly word which has been delivered to every nation? And according to another traditional metaphor, the *vineyard of the Lord* is *the house of Israel.* He also says of the *vine:* "A *vine* you transferred from Egypt; you threw out nations and you planted its roots."[6] For the *vine* is revealed to be the people that proceeded out of Egypt, led by Moses. The *choice vine* (Symmachus translates it as *chosen vine*) which he *planted* in the midst of the people may possibly be something else. This vine is the Word of God himself who taught concerning himself in the Gospels, saying: "I am the true *vine*, and my Father is the vinedresser."[7] For the special people received the planting of the divine knowledge from him, and the spiritual planting was for this *chosen vine*, which he "grafted"[8] into the ancient Egyptian *vine.* The *tower* that *he built in the midst of* the **[30]** vineyard is clearly the temple, and the *wine vat* that he *dug out in it* would be the altar before the temple. And since the lord of the vineyard had done all these things himself, he expected to receive fruits worthy of such meticulous care. But instead of bunches of grapes *it produced thorns*, or according to Aquila, *rotten grapes*, or according to Symmachus, *unripe grapes.* After the Holy Spirit had said these things concerning the Lord of the vineyard, the Lord cut off the rest of the grapes, and referring to them as judged, he says: *And now, those who dwell in Jerusalem and man of Judah, judge between me and my vineyard.* For if anyone among you says that he belongs "to the chosen of the royal race"[9] or that he originates from the tribe of Judah, then he is indeed a citizen of Jerusalem, and every word applies to him. "You be the

---

[2]Eusebius employs here two synonyms, one translated in this sentence as the one "who was loved" and "beloved." [3]Here we have a fascinating precursor to Augustine's trinitarian theology based on the metaphor of the lover (the Father), the beloved (the Son) and the love that is shared between them (the Holy Spirit). [4]Literally translated, this word means "fatty" or "full of fat." [5]This is the same Greek word that is translated as "hill" above. The word primarily means "horn" but shares the meaning of "hill" in this passage. [6]Ps 80:8. [7]Jn 15:1 RSV. [8]Cf. Rom 11:17, 19, 23, 24. [9]Cf. 1 Pet 2:9.

udges of what I have said and of the *wicked-ness* of the vineyard," says the Lord. "Advise me: what should one *do* after such meticulous care, or what should there have been that was not provided?" And if you have nothing to say, listen to me foretell what I am about to do. You have probably learned that it would be advantageous to do such things, so that you might not suffer what is being threatened. Therefore, first of all the *hedge* of the vineyard was taken down, and he says *I will remove the wall* of my protection that fortified all around the vineyard. And when this happens, *it shall be plundered* and *trampled down* by anyone who decides to loot it and trample it. And never again will it achieve any produce, although it once had worthy fruits. *For a thorn shall come up into it as into a wasteland, and I will also command the clouds, that they send no rain to it.* The *clouds* represent the prophets because of the spotlessness and radiance[10] of their life.[11] For through the prophets, the heavenly Word ministered to those whom the Lord threatened to remove. He brings on a more penetrating charge, saying: *Thus I waited for him to produce justice, but he produced lawlessness, and he did not produce righteousness but a cry.* "Every mortal sin"[12] sends up a *cry*, "crying out" the fact that it was done. Therefore it was said: "The voice of the blood of Abel your brother is crying to me."[13]

Certain aspects from what was discussed above are believed to have been prophesied about the deeds of provocation that the people committed against the Savior. *Thorns* indeed they placed on him, and they sent up a godless *cry* against him. For this reason absolute ruin and final desolation overtook them, which is also called "wrath to the utmost."[14] For from

that time until now, they have not been deemed worthy of any oversight, and the fall of their *tower* remains (I am speaking concerning the temple), and every nation considers it to be neglected, untended and uncultivated. And neither do the *clouds* minister spiritual *rain* on them. In fact, the prophets of old attended them on enemy territory, as in Babylon and Egypt, and now, after the return journey from these places, the prophecy has in actuality been fulfilled among them: **[31]** *I will also command the clouds, that they send no rain to it.* Someone could say that there were intervals between the prophets even before the sojourn of the Savior, but the temple and the corporeal worship also endured until his coming.[15] After the last Roman siege, the present word finally proved to be true.

[5:8-10] It is indeed possible that these prophecies were general precepts against those who are plagued with greed toward others, and it is possible also to understand what has been recounted above in the deeper sense. For now he is about to prophesy the desertion of the land and the destruction of its people. He is correct when he deems as miserable those who do not foresee what is coming and who have given themselves completely over to wicked-ness and greed. They plunder neighboring houses and annex the fields adjoining their own. The divine Spirit calls them miserable and teaches that they are truly pitiable and wretched because, being absolutely senseless, their greed is insatiable. He then threatens the ruin not only of their houses but also of the land, since they were no longer to be granted a blessing from God; in fact they were under a curse because they yielded nothing worthy of

---

[10]Or "translucence." [11]The reader may associate "rain" and "lack of sunshine" with clouds rather than "spotlessness" or "radiance," but Eusebius's point is probably that clouds are free from dirt or stain, and in this way, clouds are a fitting metaphor for the lofty life of virtue modeled by the prophets. [12]1 Jn 5:16, 17. [13]Gen 4:10. [14]1 Thess 2:16. [15]Eusebius's logic seems to be that, because the temple then still stood, one could say that the "watch tower" in the Lord's vineyard also stood. However, now that the "watch tower" has toppled, we can be sure that the remainder of the prophecy will be fulfilled as well.

those who toiled in it and cultivated it. He says: *For where ten yoke of oxen shall work, that land shall produce one jarful, and he who sows six bushels shall produce three measures.* It is quite apparent that he said this concerning the *vineyard*, since, as he has already stated, "it produced thorns instead of a cluster of grapes,"[16] "nor righteousness but a cry for justice" and "lawlessness instead of justice."[17] And what are the "thorns," and what is the "cry" for justice, and what is the "lawlessness" but their greed and wickedness? He teaches this to be so when he states: *ten yoke of oxen will not produce* more *than one jarful,* and he may have developed this poetic sequence in the ballad that gave an account of the vineyard. That is to say, it will require a great many resources[18] and *ten yoke of oxen to produce one jarful.* He here adumbrates that those who will be found worthy of salvation among them will be rare, which was also revealed in much of what we have discussed above.

[5:11-17] The affair about the "thorns" that "the vine produced instead of a cluster of grapes"[19] has been this way from the beginning. There is no doubt that, after the daring deed against our Savior, they should have mourned because of the "wrath to come"[20] that will "overtake" them, but instead they squandered their leisure in "dissipation,"[21] "drunkenness"[22] and other wantonness. For this reason they are deemed miserable by the Word, since they are blind to the evils that will overtake them in a little while. Since they failed to profit from the opportunity to contemplate the starker meaning of those things that have already been laid out, he does not entrust them with an opportunity to contemplate higher things because they were only interested in inspecting the dimmer realities. Nevertheless, it seems as though the Word rebuked the

practices that had been uncovered, and he threatens them that famine, and death, and war, and even captivity will come. All these things happened after the generation of our Savior's times. [32] And all these things distinctly happened to them during the reign of the Roman emperors Vespasian and Hadrian. According to the deeper meaning of the text, they were deprived of the spiritual bread of life, and still even now their souls hunger and are in need of heavenly nourishment, as the Scripture has said concerning them: "Toward the evening they will return, and will be famished like a dog and encircle a city,"[23] who "denied"[24] "the author of life,"[25] falling on his soul and bringing him to death. But, unbelievably, they turned away the redeemer of the captivity of souls who had come "to proclaim release to the captives and recovering of sight to the blind."[26] Having been delivered over to an enemy mentality, they remained in the captivity of their souls. But instead of *Those who have been plundered shall graze like bulls,* Symmachus writes: *And the lambs will graze as they are led into captivity, and the sojourners will eat stolen refuse.* This was fulfilled to the letter. For concerning the rulers of the people, who were used to doing the leading, they were led away as a herd of bulls to a deserved captivity; and concerning those who were carried away by foreigners, *strangers* attacked them and settlers from abroad occupied their deserted lands. As we have discussed above, these things were revealed concerning whom it was said: "In your very presence foreigners devour your land, and it has been made desolate, overthrown by foreign people."[27]

[5:18-19] Here is what happened next. Although they heard much of the Savior's teachings, and of his apostles after him, it did not

---

[16]Cf. Is 5:4. [17]Cf. Is 5:7. [18]The word πληθοσπόρος does not occur elsewhere in recorded Greek literature. [19]Is 5:4. [20]Mt 3:7. [21]Lk 21:34. [22]1 Pet 4:3. [23]Ps 59:6, 14. [24]Cf. Acts 3:13, 14. [25]Cf. Acts 3:15. [26]Lk 4:18 RSV; cf. Is 61:1. [27]Is 1:7.

profit them at all. Entrenched in disbelief and perversion, they supplemented their sins, offending with a second sin on top of the first and a third on top of the second, and they entwined still other offenses with these. And so Symmachus's version reads: *Woe to those who draw lawlessness to themselves as with a rope of folly and sin as with the rein of a wagon.* They did not believe the threats that the prophets of old and the Savior himself delivered against them but rather only listened to them as pieces recited for pleasure. For this reason it reads: *Who say, "Let him quickly bring near the things he will do, that we may see them; and let the plan of the Holy One of Israel come, that we may know it."* In this context, *the Holy One of Israel* signifies the only-begotten Word of God.

[5:20] He applies these things to those who were accused at first. For those who distort the sound Word and blaspheme the *light* of the Savior's gospel, who claim that the *sweet* and nourishing words of our Savior are *bitter*, incorrectly believe that their fallacious and evil arguments are good. They placed the *darkness* of the error that encloses their **[33]** souls in the land of *light*. They produce the bitterness and poison of evil, even as they persecute the enjoyment of what is sweet. One can even now still find those such as the children of Israel who turn away from the truth of the gospel and instead pursue "silly myths"[28] and the *darkness* of ignorance. In this deliberate course of action, "they denied the Christ of God"[29] and they "asked for Barabbas,"[30] placing their portion among the "robbers"[31] and "criminals."[32] But joining in with the godless and pagan nations, they even approve idolatries, and they alienate themselves from the chaste and holy people of God and persecute them.

[5:21-23] One could apply these general principles and this generic threat to all who are wise in their own conceit, as these principles also convict those who have been accused throughout the prophecy. They did not attend to the stern[33] words of the Savior's teachings but acted as those who are *wise in themselves and knowledgeable in their own sight.* Later on we read that, as *strong ones* and party animals,[34] they abandoned their whole life to strong drink, stupefying themselves in the darkness of ignorance. Now they *mix drinks*[35] for others, such as the one called *liquor*, although the other Greek translations call it *an intoxicating drink*.[36] This was what they practiced as "peddlers of God's word."[37] For this reason, it is said above of them: "your peddlers, mixing wine with water."[38] These are they who accepted bribes, even declaring the wicked righteous and the guilty *not guilty*. And so the word threatens and brings charges against them when he says the rest of the things he said.

[5:24] The Word deliberately announced in advance the things that would happen "before they happen,"[39] preferring to check wickedness with the fear of a threat. The idea was that he would call back to their senses those who heard and learned ahead of time of the things that would come on them. For this reason he addresses those who incessantly sin. For it is not because of fortune, or physical necessity or destiny but because of the aforementioned perversions that are found among you that the "vineyard of the Lord"[40] will come suddenly on you here if you produce neither bunches of grapes nor good fruits but "wood, hay, straw"[41] and multiply "your thorns."[42] It is therefore quite reasonable for him to say concerning this grace:

---

[28]1 Tim 4:7. [29]Acts 3:13, 14. [30]Mt 27:20. [31]Mt 27: 38, 44. [32]Lk 23:32, 39. [33]The Greek word κακός primarily means "evil," "abusive" or "reproachful." [34]Literally translated, this phrase would read: "those who are able to do many things among the people." [35]For Eusebius, "mixing drinks" meant primarily to reconstitute wine. [36]We are unable to decipher the nuances of Eusebius's classifications of these alcoholic drinks. [37]2 Cor 2:17 RSV. [38]Is 1:22. [39]Is 46:10. [40]Is 5:7. [41]1 Cor 3:12. [42]Is 5:4.

as stubble will be burned by a coal of fire and burned up by a weakened flame, so the root of your wickedness will be like fine dust and as stubble in a fire. Even your youthful blossom [34] (it is clear that he is speaking about the body), the glory of wealth and the prestige of every nation will be scattered to the winds as a cloud of dust by an act of justice that is yet to come. He said that these things will occur among them because of what has already been said: They did not want the law of the Lord of hosts and have provoked the oracle of the Holy One of Israel. Here one can see that it was not their idolatry that he accuses but that they did not want the law of the Lord of hosts. And concerning this law it has been said above: "For out of Zion shall go forth a law, and the word of the Lord from Jerusalem."[43] Therefore, they were unwilling to receive the law of the New Testament, and they even provoked the living word of God. But in Aquila's version, this text reads: They cast aside the law of the Lord of armies, and they rent the word of the Holy One of Israel to pieces; and in Symmachus's version: They disqualified the law of the Lord of powers, and they provoked the word of the Holy One of Israel.

[5:25] Concerning this grace he also says: And the Lord of hosts was enraged with anger against his people. He willed that they should be his very own people and that they should be called as such, but they were not willing. And he laid his hand on them and struck them—all these things because of the reasons that have been considered. But he adds to these statements, saying: And the mountains were provoked, and their carcasses became like dung in the middle of the road. In all these things his wrath has not turned away, but his hand is still high. He thereby indicates that there will be an invasion of their enemies and a multitude of the slain, so that the mountains will be filled with the dead bodies and the whole land will be full of

their carcasses. The wrath of God evidently continued to be against them and has not turned away, as such things were exhibited among them, and the hand of God was still high against them because they continued to sin. Note exactly what the verse says: His hand is still high. It says that the wrath of God endures against them still, even now, which the apostle also states when he says: "But God's wrath has come on them at last."[44] He states next through these things that the mountains and the land were about to be filled with their carcasses.

He sketches out the military opposition and invasion of the Gentiles against the people because they did not receive the new law and the word of the Lord of hosts. He states that the mountains were provoked. In Aquila's version, this reads rather: violently agitated; and in Symmachus's version: greatly troubled. The statement their carcasses became like dung in the middle of the road informs us that all these things happened among them during the invasion of their enemies. They did not do this to themselves, [35] but God brought the siege on those who had been accused, and they were dragged and carted away in a single night.

[5:26-30] The Word indicates this when he says: Therefore he will raise a signal among the nations that are far away and whistle for them from the end of the earth. In these things he is speaking of the encampment of the Roman army that headed out from the western parts against Jerusalem. If he had wanted to refer to the Babylonians or the Assyrians, he would have mentioned them by name or called them the people "from the north,"[45] as he was accustomed to doing because they dwelled among the regions to the north of the land of Judea. But now, just as in the history of the Roman opposition, he calls the Gentile multitude those who stood far away and who dwelled at the end of the earth. Afterwards, he

---

[43]Is 2:3. [44]1 Thess 2:16. [45]Is 14:31; 45:21; Jer 4:6.

delineates the wrath of the military men, and he vividly describes the spears and swords and all the other weapons of war, the equipment of their *horses* and *chariots*. He says in addition concerning those who besiege them: *They rush like lions, but stand by like a lion's whelp, and he will seize and roar like the sound of a surging sea.* One can begin to imagine the vastness of the enemy army in the prophet's metaphor of *the sound of a surging sea.* For as someone could say these things about the *sea* that we experience every day, so from here we come to understand the testimony of the imagery. This has been said, therefore, concerning those who besiege them there, while concerning those who will be besieged the text says: *And they will look to the land, and behold, there will be harsh darkness in their dismay.* This is the end of the prophecy during the reign of Uzziah, which indeed began with the words "Hear, O heaven, and give ear, O earth, for the Lord has spoken."[46] It carried through until the present passage, in which the final war against them was threatened and darkness came on *those who provoked the oracle of the Lord and did not want the law* of his New Testament. And after the end of the reign of King Uzziah, the following were seen in a vision concerning the times of Jotham. For this is the account of the one who succeeded the throne of Uzziah.

[6:1] The same prophet saw with his own eyes[1] *the Lord of hosts* over his temple, in which the prophet often preached. And he relates in detail what transpired quite literally right before his eyes when he states next: "O wretched man that I am! I am stunned; for being a man and having unclean lips, I live among a people having unclean lips, and I have seen the King, the Lord of hosts, with my eyes!"[2] There is no doubt that it was the man who is described above who made this statement. He said that he saw *the Lord of hosts*, and the text records that he saw him with his own eyes. And he records the time of the vision when he says: *And it happened in the year that King Uzziah died I saw the Lord of hosts sitting on a throne, lofty and raised up.* I believe it is clearly stated who was revealed through the entire [36] prophecy as *the Lord of hosts*[3] (although the phrase is also translated *Lord of armies* or *Lord of powers*). He thus introduces God as he was seen. However, concerning the unbegotten divinity, it has been said: "No one has ever *seen* God; the only Son, who is in the bosom of the Father, he has made him known."[4] And the Savior himself taught: "Not that any one has seen the Father except him who is from God; he has *seen* the Father."[5] Surely then the *Lord of hosts* who appeared to the prophet was another than the unbegotten and invisible and incomprehensible divinity. And who could this be but "the only-begotten God, who is in the bosom of the Father,"[6] who stepped down from his own exalted position, and, lowering himself from that position, made himself visible and comprehensible to humanity? It was in this way that "he appeared to Abraham," at which time "he said to him, 'To your offspring I will give this land.'"[7]

The Scripture says further: "So he built there an altar to the Lord, who had appeared to him";[8] and again: "Abraham came to be ninety-nine years old, and the Lord appeared to him";[9] and once more: "The Lord appeared to him by the oak of Mamre."[10] And concerning Isaac it has been said: "He proceeded and went up to the well of the oath, and on that night the Lord appeared to him."[11] Further, it was said to Jacob: "I am the God who appeared to you at a divine place."[12] And also, when "he came to Bethel, and all the people who were with him, and there he built an altar, and called the name of the house[13]

---

[46]Is 1:2. **Chapter Six** [1]Or, "in a vision." [2]Is 6:5. [3]In the Greek text, the word *Lord* is written twice. This is probably a scribal error. [4]Jn 1:18 RSV. [5]Jn 6:46 RSV. [6]Jn 1:18. [7]Gen 12:7. [8]Gen 12:7. [9]Gen 17:1. [10]Gen 18:1. [11]Gen 26:23-24. [12]Gen 31:13. [13]Eusebius preserves a variant reading. The LXX reads: "the name of the place."

Bethel, because there God had revealed himself to him."[14] Again, it is said: "God appeared to Jacob again in Luza."[15] At another time it says that God appeared to him in the form of a man: "Your name shall no more be called Jacob, but Israel shall be your name, because you have prevailed with God and with men you are powerful."[16] And: "So he called the name of the place 'the face of God' saying, 'For I have seen God face to face, and my life has been preserved.'"[17] Moses also, to whom God listened when he beseeched him, saying: "If I have found favor before you, disclose yourself to me, let me see you recognizably."[18] And he answered him and said: "Even this word that you have spoken I will do for you, for you have found favor before me."[19]

Ezekiel also "saw a form that had the appearance of a man"[20] "who was seated on the cherubim,"[21] and "from his loins and all the way down was fire, and above his loins was the appearance of brightness."[22] Through all these statements we do not learn that the visions were similar to the above description but only that they were dissimilar.[23] For it has been said by Moses: "You shall not be able to see my face; for a person shall never see my face and live."[24] For the face of [37] God the Word and the divinity of the only-begotten Son of God could never be apprehensible to mortal nature. The glory of the Word was seen by Ezekiel through enigmas. He assumed a certain form before Abraham and was seen in the figure of a man when Abraham was "by the oak"[25] and "washed the feet"[26] and shared a table with the divine stranger. Likewise also in the case of Jacob. A man wrestled with him "until the breaking of day,"[27] whom the Scripture calls a "man," but he identified himself when he said: "Your name shall no more be called Jacob, but Israel shall

be your name, because you have prevailed with God."[28] And Jacob also said concerning this: "For I have seen God face to face, and my life has been preserved."[29] And the present prophet *saw* and also witnessed *glory*. Thus, as we discussed above, he saw the glory of our Savior Jesus Christ.

Thus it was for Moses, and for Ezekiel too, but the vision God revealed to each was not the same. The prophet assuredly did not see the glory of our Savior with his bodily eyes, but (we may infer from the deeper meaning of the text) with eyes enlightened by the Holy Spirit. For as the eyes of the body are aided in seeing objects of perception by an abundance of external beams of light, so in the same way the eyes of the soul, once cleared by spiritual light, are able to recognize the sights that have been illuminated. The Savior also taught this when he said: "Blessed are the pure in heart, for *they shall see* God,"[30] and Isaiah was one who, at the end of the reign of King Uzziah, *saw the Lord*. Why then did he not see the aforementioned apparition while still living but *in the year that he died?* Because Uzziah the king dared to attempt the unholy act of burning incense in the temple, the glory of God, which in ancient times had overshadowed the house, withdrew its presence for the remainder of his life, and he lived as a leper in Jerusalem. For as a king, he was allowed to live there. And so he expired, and Jotham his son succeeded him as king, concerning whom it has been written: "He was a son of twenty-five years when he became king, and he reigned sixteen years in Jerusalem. And he did what was right in the sight of the Lord."[31] It would be fair to say that he quit this life in the same year that he had been struck leprous. It was pleasing to God for Jotham to receive the

[14]Gen 35:6-7. [15]Gen 35:9. [16]Gen 32:28. [17]Gen 32:30. [18]Ex 33:13. [19]Ex 33:17. [20]Ezek 8:2. [21]Cf. e.g., 1 Sam 4:4. [22]Ezek 8:2. [23]This is a literal translation. Good systematic theological reasoning forces Eusebius to say that the descriptions do not teach positively but negatively. All that we may deduce from these descriptions is that God did not appear like a man, but this is the only way to begin to describe the vision that Moses experienced. [24]Ex 33:20. [25]Gen 18:1. [26]Gen 18:4. [27]Gen 32:24. [28]Gen 32:28. [29]Gen 32: 30. [30]Mt 5:8 rsv. [31]2 Kings 15:33-34.

kingdom, and once again the glory of God returned to the house (clearly that means over the temple). The prophet narrates: *And it happened in the year that King Uzziah died that I saw the Lord of hosts sitting on a throne, lofty and raised up, and the house was full of his glory.* Therefore the *house* [38] was filled with *glory*, and the prophet did not *see the Lord* within the house but rather *sitting on a throne, lofty and raised up.* And this was what the divine Scripture was talking about when it says: "The LORD is in his holy temple, the LORD's *throne* is in heaven."[32] The Lord himself revealed this when he said: "Heaven is my *throne* and the earth is the footstool of my feet; what kind of *house* will you build for me, says the Lord."[33] So then, the prophet saw the *Lord* enthroned in the kingdom of heaven with spiritual[34] eyes. He says that *the house was full of glory* on the earth, and there was a certain brilliant splendor from heaven above and a sparkling from the divine Word that shone on the house.

[6:2] There were certain incorporeal, divine and supramundane powers, whom Daniel revealed when he said: "A thousand thousands served him, and ten thousand times ten thousand stood before him."[35] Some people suppose that there are only two *seraphim*, but I believe in the deeper meaning of the Scripture which says that *the seraphim stand around him*, and I think that there are more. They attend the great and righteous King as a crown from all sides, the throne itself vigilant, enlightened and enlivened by him. And thus those who encircle the *Lord of hosts* are called *seraphim* (although this title is also translated *Lord of powers* or *Lord of armies*). It is said that each *one had six wings*, and they adorned themselves with their wings. With these *wings*, with this innate

excellence and these celestial[36] powers, they are borne, soaring through heaven and sky. They have been granted a certain spiritual function and influence over certain affairs that are not to be spoken to us. For just as the human body is equipped with the five physical faculties of seeing, hearing, smell, taste and touch, so the angels of God partake in the "superior gifts"[37] and prophesy future events and heal the sick and raise the dead and speak in tongues of wisdom and partake in knowledge. Thus, it is conceivable that the Word calls the divine powers and inexplicable abilities which the angelic beings have been granted and which are unknowable to us *wings*. It has been said concerning the winds:[38] "Who walks about on the wings of winds."[39] Their bodily form is not completely unimaginable to us, since the birds of course also spread their wings in the wind.

And concerning the *wings of the seraphim* (whether they are incredible powers or deeds they have done), we read that *with two they covered their face.* They did not cover the face of the Lord, [39] but their own face, not daring to look directly into the vision that was before them, because "no one knows the Son except the Father who begot him."[40] And *they covered* their own *feet.* One could say that the last step of their proper posture is protecting their steps and the actions of their lives, so that they do not stand in the presence of the King with uncovered feet. For this reason, they were *veiled* and concealed the course of their life, and they allowed only the middle of their constitution to be seen. And they admired his wisdom intensely—the wisdom of the middle of the foreknowledge and administration of the only-begotten. They dared neither to gaze into his divine face nor in the same manner to appear with exposed feet because of his

---

[32]Ps 11:4 RSV. [33]Is 66:1; Acts 7:49. [34]The word *spiritual* here is the same word Eusebius uses to refer to a "spiritual" reading of the text as opposed to the "literal" reading. [35]Dan 7:10. [36]The Greek adjective μετεωροπόλος literally means "busying oneself with high things." [37]Cf. 1 Cor 12:31. [38]The Greek term here is ἄνεμος ("wind"), but the context indicates he is talking about the wings of the seraphim. Perhaps Eusebius's point is that the seraphim's wings are like the wind. [39]Ps 104:3. [40]Mt 11:27.

immense, interminable and incomprehensible nature. They were amazed at the inexpressible divinity of the one who is seen.

Symmachus renders this verse in this way: *In the year that Uzziah the king died, I saw the Lord of hosts sitting on a throne, high and lifted up, and those before his feet filled the temple. Seraphim stood above, each with six wings.* He says *those before his feet filled the temple* because the temple had stood on the earth as the "footstool"[41] of God. "For heaven is his throne, and the earth is the footstool of his feet." And so he rightly says that those *before his feet filled* the house on earth which he had seen. *And seraphim stood above,* which means *above* the house and not *above* the Lord. The prophet pronounces himself wretched, and he *was silent,* neither crying out together with the *seraphim* nor heralding to them the hymn in praise of the holiness of the Lord. And he says that the reason that he was silent was that he had *unclean lips* and was from a society of ungodly people.

[6:3-4] *One* called *to another* and cried: *Holy, holy, Lord of hosts; the whole earth is full of his glory.* And they did not cry in one voice, nor did they call aloud everything collectively, but they expressed their wonder and the terror of the sight *one to another.* The descent of the glory of the Word of God from on high onto the humble most especially astonished them. Therefore this presented to them the greatest marvel: not only was heaven *full of his glory,* but it flooded even as far as the *earth,* so that *the whole earth was filled with his glory.* For the extravagance of the benevolence to humanity of *the one sitting on the highest throne* filled the earth, and in times of old the temple among the inhabitants of Jerusalem was filled with these sights, at least at that time. For this reason it was said above: "The house was full of his glory."[42] The *seraphim* were shouting in triumph because apparently *all* the *earth* would

be filled with *his glory.* For they were expressing great admiration in foreknowledge of what was to be subsequently accomplished in prophecies after the first advent of our Savior into **[40]** humanity. For truly his first advent was known among all the Gentiles and preached to the whole world—not only the knowledge of his first advent but also the *glory* of his praise. For then, on seeing his *glory* on the *earth* that was about to shine forth, with nothing from the earthly and mortal reality hindering it, they were rightly calling aloud: *Holy, holy, holy is the Lord of hosts.* His holiness was proclaimed not once but repeatedly, and they were indeed astonished beyond measure for a countless and infinite and eternal span of time. Therefore *one called to another,* each one expressing his wonder to his neighbor.

And the lintel was raised. The *lintel* of the temple was *raised* by this shout, *and the house was filled with smoke* (secretly adumbrating the Word), so that *the whole earth was full of his glory.* The temple in that place was about to be laid bare, and the wilderness *of the raised lintel* would be abandoned, and the temple that was *full of smoke* would be delivered over to fire. For *smoke* is the sign of fire. Accordingly, through these things the Word foreshadowed that the place would be abandoned and burned in the end, after which *the whole world would be filled with the glory* of the Lord—no longer filling only one house but myriads of houses established all over the whole world which would be much better than that one. Following the cry of the *seraphim,* the prophet, seeing these things, stood in agony, but not so as to perish along with the multitude of the people. For, after he saw what was described above, it was said that "the house was full of the glory of God,"[43] and after the shout there was no longer *glory* but *smoke.*

[6:5] He rightly ordains the change for the worse for the house, and it is thrown into

---

[41]Is 66:1; Acts 7:49. [42]Is 6:1. [43]Cf. Is 6:1.

disorder and anguish, and it is no accident that the place suffered these things. But he confesses that the *glory* of the revealed *Lord* prevailed, united in mortal nature. And he deems himself miserable when he says: "O wretched man that I am! I am stunned; for being a man and having unclean lips, I live among a people having unclean lips; and I have seen the King, the Lord of hosts."[44] And he confesses that he is *unclean*, not his soul but his entire body. He knew that he had committed no *unclean* deed, and so he says only that he had *unclean* lips. The rest of his body and soul was clean, according to the verse: "Blessed are the pure in heart, for they shall see God."[45] And he had *unclean lips*, not from another place but rather from his involvement with the *unclean*. For he was probably forced to speak with *unclean men*—the worthy associating with the depravity of those through whom he sullied his *lips*. And so the precise life of the prophet was perfect in the smallest details, but at the same time he calumniates [41] the mortal nature as ever corrupt, fulsome and unworthy. Therefore he says that he is a man. For the devil carries away the person who has been clothed in corrupt flesh.

[6:6] Indeed it has been said by Jeremiah the prophet: "You that are, Sovereign, Lord! Behold, I do not know how to speak, because I am rather young."[46] "The Lord stretched out his hand and touched my mouth; and the Lord said to me, 'Behold, I have given my words to your mouth.'"[47] For since the lips of Jeremiah were not in need of cleansing, the text says rightly that "the hand of the Lord touched his mouth"[48] and filled him with the prophetic grace. And here the Lord did not deliver the cleansing for which Isaiah beseeched him, but the Lord *sent one of the seraphim* bearing a *live coal*, and he approached *and cleansed his lips completely with the live coal*. And this is why *seraphim* translated into the Greek language means "those who set on fire" or "those that burn." To me they seem to be "those who purify" the ones who ask for purification, and for this reason *the seraphim* brought the purifying *coal* to the *lips* of the prophet, for one of these *seraphim* was exhorted to do this. This was the *coal from the altar* from which perhaps the benevolent Lord offered himself on an *altar* of such saving and purifying coals. Therefore it has been said somewhere: "coals were ignited by him."[49] And it is said that God himself appeared before Moses as a "consuming fire."[50] In the Gospels it is attested that the Savior will "baptize" the worthy "with the Holy Spirit and with fire."[51] All these things teach us about the Word, for no one is able to receive cleansing from sins except through the divine fire. "The fire will test what sort of work each one has done,"[52] and it says that "the one who is saved" "will be saved as through fire."[53]

[6:7] Therefore, it was right that the *lips* of even such a prophet *were purified* with a *coal of fire*. For this reason it is said of him: *Behold, this has touched your lips; your lawlessness is forgiven, and your sins are cleansed.* What sort of *lawlessnesses* and *sins* does he confess that his *lips* had committed?

[6:8] Subsequently, after the cleansing of his lips, he was deemed worthy to hear the voice of *the one sitting on the throne* saying: *Whom shall I send, and who will go to this people?* Then this voice which spoke in the middle voice approved the willingness of the prophet, so that he might obtain the reward of his good resolution.[54] For this reason he did not order him to

---

[44]Is 6:5. [45]Mt 5:8 RSV. [46]Jer 1:6. [47]Jer 1:9. [48]Jer 1:9. [49]Ps 18:8. [50]Cf. Deut 4:24, 9:3; Heb 12:29. [51]Mt 3:11 RSV. [52]1 Cor 3:13 RSV. [53]1 Cor 3:15. [54]The verb to which Eusebius is referring is πορεύσεται, translated above as "who will go." Greek grammarians today would call this verb deponent rather than middle. Eusebius, however, is observing that the divine voice is asking a question rather than stating a command.

depart in the imperative mood, but he spoke in the middle voice, asking him whether he might be ready to do this. And the one who answered with much courage, in as much as *his lips had been cleansed*, said: *Here am I; send me!*

[6:9-10] [42] And the voice came to him: *Go, and say to this people: "You will listen by listening, but you will not understand, and looking you will look, but you will not perceive."* And he does not state for us what they will look for while looking and whom they will listen to while listening, after they stopped paying attention and attending to the word, which is a discipline of the mind. For you saw the "Lord,"[55] O prophet, and "you saw" with your eyes, but this people will always be looking and never seeing. And as you listened to the voice at the present time, so he will listen at some time in the future. But the people will certainly neither understand nor know nor desire to receive his grace. And clearly he who said these things revealed his coming among people.

And how it was that they were *looking* but did not look, he expounds next when he says: *They have shut their eyes, so that they might not see with their eyes.* For indeed, in as much as the Savior is the light of everything that exists, he illuminated their souls, and "he bestowed sight to the blind."[56] But *their eyes were shut so that they might not see*, and so that though *looking they did not look.* For he who pays attention and carefully examines and then looks down on and thinks contemptuously of what was seen, or he who is deluded and *shuts* his eyes so that he does not see, is the one who *sees* but does not see. Therefore, they had the ability *to see* by the grace of the one who was seen, but they never saw because they *shut their own eyes* and deluded themselves into *not seeing.* And so also one may *listen by listening* but again *not listen* since *he does not understand*

what is said, or he may take no heed and think contemptuously of what is said. That is what happened, because their own *ears were heavy*, just as if they were stopped up and deaf. Therefore the voice of the Lord prophesied that these things would be about the people of the Jews, and they were fulfilled in what happened during the sojourn of the Savior. When he was present, they were "seeing with eyes but not seeing,"[57] and although he was teaching "the secrets of the kingdom"[58] they did not understand. And, although they saw the glory of the Lord filling all the earth through his churches, their hearts were not deeply moved, and in fact it produced unbelief in them. For this reason he says further: *they have shut their eyes, so that they might not see with their eyes, and hear with their ears, and understand with their hearts, and turn and I would heal them.*

[6:11-13] And after the prophet attended to these statements, he asked saying: *How long, O Lord?* What will be the end of such blindness as theirs? And he answered: *Until cities become desolate, because they are not inhabited.* Through these he signifies the onslaught of the first invasion of the Romans in their place after their provocation against the Savior, and many Jewish cities were then ravaged by Emperor **[43]** Vespasian and brought to utter ruin, so that neither their memory nor their name survived. And instead of saying: *And after these things, God will send people far away,* Symmachus renders the verse more clearly when he says: *And the Lord will make people to be far away.* And the word indicates that at that very time the captivity would endure for the majority of the Jewish nation, and the diaspora, when they were scattered while fleeing the circumstances pressing on them. Because of those things he says that the time of the diaspora might be prolonged at that

---

[55]Is 6:1. [56]Lk 7:21. [57]Mt 13:13. [58]Mt 13:11 RSV.

time; for he says *those who have been left will be multiplied on the land* (others being added to the earlier ones). And these forsaken places will be so vast that when the earlier ones are compared with them, they will be considered to be a fraction of the expanse of them. For he says that *a tenth will remain in it*. Next, he states what sort of end will happen for those who survive: *And again it will be plundered as a Terebinth tree or as an acorn tree when it falls from its station*. But in Symmachus's version we read: *And again it will be for fodder as an oak tree and as an acorn, which stands alone after it has shed its husk*. Thus the Word foretells how it would become an absolute desert. And this was fulfilled during the times of Hadrian, when the remaining Jews revolted for a second time in an unfortunate turn of events, and they were forbidden by the laws and imperial edicts to even see the desolation of their mother city.

And the Word used remarkably apt metaphors when it proclaimed of the Jewish people: *For they will be as a Terebinth tree or an oak tree or an acorn when it falls from its station*. For no longer are they called "vineyard of the Lord of hosts"[59] or "the garden of God"[60] or a "green olive tree"[61] or a "palm tree of the righteous,"[62] nor does he say that they will be as any other indispensable plant of those days. And it is not only that they are compared with an *acorn*, but one that has *fallen out of its husk*; and *as a Terebinth*, or, according to Symmachus's translation, *as an oak*. And the divine Scripture is accustomed to calling the *oak* and *acorn* and copse barren and the most uncultivated of wild trees. Afterwards the Scripture wishes to signify that they are comparable to the other Gentile tribes, and it says that the very people of the Jews are superior in nothing to the other Gentile tribes, neither in mode nor manner of life, but actually occupy a worse position. And on the one hand, they offer their own lands,

and they present their fruits according to nature, but on the other hand, they have fallen out from their own kind and do not act like them. For this reason they are compared with an *oak* (a plant of the field) and an *acorn* (a nourishing fruit for irrational animals), and one that *has fallen from its station*.

Next concerning these things with asterisks[63] he further mentions their *holy seed*, concerning whom he also said above: "If the Lord of hosts **[44]** had not left us offspring, we would have been like Sodom and been made similar to Gomorrah."[64] The phrase *holy seed, its pillar* is not present in our transcriptions, and for this reason it would seem to be noteworthy. Theodotion rendered it thus: *holy seed, its pillar*; and Aquila: *sanctified stump, its recording tablet*; and Symmachus: *the holy seed, its opposition*. What sort of *opposition* or *recording tablet* of the fallen people does he say it is, or how is their *holy seed* the thing that did not fall, or how is the same fall not for those who survived? But this could be those who have received the saving grace "who hear with their ears"[65] and who *see* with their eyes, whom the Savior congratulates when he says: "But blessed are your eyes, for they see, and your ears, for they hear."[66]

[7:1] Now that the earlier events of the prophecy were spoken about *Uzziah the King*, whom *Jotham* succeeded at the beginning of his "reign,"[1] we shall discuss the extended vision that the prophet saw, through which he presented the divinity of the only-begotten Son of God and prophesied these things until they came to pass. The prophecy did not lack many words concerning the time for the establishment of the godly king, whom the people were likely to follow also. And after the time of the vision he passed his "sixteen years."[2] It was during all these events that *Jotham* ruled, and

---

[59] Is 5:7. [60] Is 51:3; Gen 13:10; Ezek 28:13; 31:8. [61] Jer 11:16. [62] Ps 92:12. [63] The asterisk appears in the Hexapla and in early Christian manuscripts as a text-critical marker. [64] Is 1:9. [65] Mt 13:13. [66] Mt 13:16 rsv. **Chapter Seven** [1] Cf. Is 1:1. [2] 2 Chron 27:1.

then Ahaz, the most ungodly of men, began to reign. Above all else, those events already foretold concern the prophecy of the birth of the Son of God according to the flesh. And, after the word prophesies about his divinity, it has much to say about his birth among humanity. And the story of the word of prophecy is that *two kings* rose up against *Ahaz*, one of whom was named *Rezin*, the ruler of Syria, who took possession of the royal city Damascus and conquered multitudes of Jews in the city called Samaria. And the other was *Pekah the son of Remaliah*. And after they made an agreement, they went to war with *Ahaz*, who then ruled Jerusalem[3] and led the tribes of the Jewish nation. But indeed, God delivered *Ahaz* and the people under him to the aforementioned kings because of his many iniquities. "One hundred and twenty thousand"[4] of them were slain, and no fewer than "two hundred thousand"[5] were led away as captives. Such then were the circumstances of their first confrontation, and it was not long afterwards that the aforementioned kings (I mean of Damascus and Samaria) again prepared for war against *Ahaz*, planning to lay siege and capture Jerusalem, slay *Ahaz* and appoint another as king in his place—the one who was called the "son of Tabeel."[6]

[7:2-3] This did not escape the notice of *Ahaz* or of the people under him who were called the *house of David*. And thus those from the tribe of David and every ruler and every subject from his succession called out for aid. Therefore, when they learned the revelation that their enemies were about to attack them again, *their souls were agitated*, that is, *they were afraid*, or, in Symmachus's version, *they were driven into confusion*, or in Aquila's version, *their hearts quaked*. And not a little emotional turmoil seized not only those of royal ancestry, but everyone else as well, [45] for they remem-

bered the previous atrocities which they received from them, although few had attempted a siege before. One could compare their hearts which were *driven into confusion* and shaken from the report with *oak trees* blown about by the most extreme *wind*. But the good Lord had pity and showed them kindness and sent a prophet who advised *Ahaz* to keep himself fearless and calm. For indeed he would now gain the help of God, even if not at first, for the first time he delivered them over to their enemies because of their eccentric iniquities, and they suffered the aforementioned ordeals. And then he commanded the prophet to meet up and present himself to *Ahaz* at a certain specific place, and he ordered *his remaining son* to succeed him during his time, so that both he and his son and the prophet from among all the people (whose soul, it seems to me, succeeded him) might approach the king and say what had been ordered.

[7:4] For it was necessary also for the son of the prophet to be instructed by that father in the delivered teachings so that he not remain in and be destroyed along with the multitude. And the good courage present in him accepted and performed what had been ordered, and he met with *Ahaz* and told him what God had commanded: *take care to be at rest* (according to Aquila's version) or *take care and be at rest* (according to Theodotion's version). *Be attentive and quiet*. And being encouraged, he said by the word of God: be calm and *do not fear, nor let your soul be feeble because of these two logs*, because of those who have no light at all, because of those whom, it would seem, were only a quenched and *smoking firebrand*. For such are *the two kings* whom you have appointed in fear and anguish. For in as much as my didactic power informs me correctly, that which is customarily called "wrath" in prophetic oracles were the former

---

[3]There is a lacuna in the text at this point. [4]2 Chron 28:6. [5]2 Chron 28:8. [6]Is 7:6.

events which pursued after you to refute the things that you supposed to be gods, and you indeed were confident that they were gods, but they were proved to be nothing when your enemies drew you away into captivity. Nevertheless, it was not my wrath, the good and steadfast God himself says, but the former events that struck you in all that happened. And now again, I will heal every one of your diseases if you turn from your former deception and truly learn to live godly lives.

[7:5-9] *And therefore these are the two kings.* They are the king of Syria and the king of Samaria: Aram and also Syria. Samaria is the city that is now called Sebaste. And even though they boasted great things and, as we said above, made careful plans, they did not act according to judgment. For I am the very *Lord of hosts* (that is to say that he is the *Lord* of divine *powers* and of the *armies* of the angels of heaven); I will not overturn their *plans* but allow them to be carried out to the end, determining to save you then so that you might have the very clearest display of my beneficent and saving power. For it was enough to have *Damascus* as a *head* in Syria, over which Rezin was the king, and *Ephraim* in Samaria. And so the multitude of the nine and a half tribes of Israel was called *Ephraim* because their ruler was from *Ephraim*. And therefore it was sufficient [46] also for them to have Samaria and the son of *Remaliah* as ruler. And so, learn this, O *Ahaz*: the kingdom of Samaria will be demolished and its subjects will be prisoners of war for these same kings! They will be sent away to Assyria because of their outrageous and wicked deeds. And if you are curious to know the time, know that within *sixty-five years* the king of the Assyrians will come. And after he has shattered all resistance, he will take them as captives and resettle them in his own land.

God appointed the prophet to speak these things to Ahaz himself and to the people under him, urging them on to turn to God and to have faith and not to disbelieve what had been said. For this reason he goes on to say to them all: *If you do not believe, you will not understand.* Therefore the word of God indeed was fulfilled not in a time then far distant. The aforementioned time was completed, and Damascus and Samaria and their rulers were conquered by the king of Assyria. Therefore the prophecy was confirmed through the accomplishment of these events, and the *sixty-five years* that he spoke concerning the children of the Hebrews were exactly completed. (The years were completed in the twenty-fifth year of the reign of Uzziah, if anyone should care to count.) For in fact both the prophet Amos and Isaiah prophesied about this. For first Amos foretells the approaching captivity that is about to come on Israel when he says: "Israel shall be lead captive from his land."[7] And against Samaria this same prophet prophesies in the days of Uzziah the king of Judah, "two years before the earthquake."[8] And he says that this earthquake occurred when Uzziah entered into the sanctuary to sacrifice and was "struck with leprosy," and the fat from the altar spilled out during the earthquake. Therefore, it is proper to say that Amos prophesied against Samaria and against Jerusalem "two years before the earthquake"[9] and that one must count the *sixty-five years* from that point onward. And Uzziah lived twenty-seven additional years, since altogether "he reigned fifty-two years,"[10] and the events which were recounted transpired in his twenty-fifth year. First Amos prophesied concerning the captivity of Israel, and then "Jotham reigned sixteen years"[11] and "Ahaz" likewise for "sixteen years."[12] If the six years from the reign of Hezekiah are added together we have *sixty-five* years in all. And in the

---

[7]Amos 7:11. [8]Amos 1:1. [9]Amos 1:1. [10]2 Chron 26:3. [11]Cf. 2 Chron 27:1. [12]Cf. 2 Chron 28:1.

following year of Hezekiah's reign Israel endured the last captivity. In accordance with the prophecies he announced that he would *give* him a *sign*, through which he would know that he would be saved. But being hard of heart and immersed in demonic deception, he refused and *declined* a *sign* from God, and in this he proved himself to be unfaithful and unruly. One should know that, in Origen, the eighth volume of his exegetical works covers up to this point.

[7:10-13] **[47]** Instead of *in the depths or in the heights*, Symmachus says: *Ask for yourself a sign from the Lord your God, go down into Hades or up to heaven.* And Aquila says: *Request for yourself a sign from the Lord your God, go down into Hades or rise up above.* And Theodotion says: *Ask for yourself a sign from the Lord your God, go down into Hades or lift yourself up high.* We will recognize that the mention about the *sign in the depths or in the heights* is from the books of Moses. For it was said concerning the signs which were in Egypt by Moses: "He sent out signs and wonders in your midst, O Egypt."[13] From the earth came frogs and locust and lice and flies, and from heaven came hail and fire and the three days of darkness. And someone could also say that the *sign* to Hezekiah was a *sign* from heaven, "when the sun stepped backward and the shadow ran the other way ten steps."[14] And indeed a *sign from the depths* was given to Saul, when, after his death, Samuel foretold his fate. Likewise Jonah acted as a "sign"[15] *from the depths*, "from the belly of the fish,"[16] when he went along and preached to the Ninevites, people of another tribe. Therefore Ahaz was bidden to *ask for a sign*, through which he would be saved and the people with him. God gave him the opportunity to choose *the sign*, and if he had asked for a *sign from the depths*, it would have been given to him (*from the depths* is not different from

from Hades), or *from the heights*, and from the things raised up above them. And once he had heard, he refused, since he was irreligious and not obedient to the God who had charged him, for he did not want to set up a test for the power of the wonder-working God. Therefore he says: *I will not ask for a sign, for nor will I put the Lord to the test.* Then the prophet complained of the desperation of the man literally right before his face and continues on to say: *Hear now, O house of David. Is it a small thing for you to provoke a fight with mortals? How then will you provoke a fight with the Lord?* And earlier he called those who descended from the lineage of David the *house of David* when he said: "it was reported to the house of David saying 'Aram has made an agreement with Ephraim.'"[17] Therefore, he delivered the above statements to this same *house of David* because he no longer deemed Ahaz worthy of the word. And what did he answer to the *house of David?* He says: *Is it a small thing for you to provoke a fight with men? How then will you provoke a fight with the Lord?* Instead of this, Aquila translated this passage in this manner: *Listen then, O house of David. Is it not enough to weary men, that you also weary my God?* And in Symmachus's version: *Listen then, O house of David. Is it not sufficient for you to fatigue men, that you even fatigue* **[48]** *my God?* And in Theodotion's version: *And he said: Listen then, O house of David. Is it a small thing for you to provoke a fight with men, that you even provoke a fight with my God?* This is the sense of the above statements: When will you stop contending with the men of God? For I say that the prophets of God are surrounded by filth and hardship and strife for the sake of your salvation. But then you even vex and provoke a fight with *my God*, whom you do not know and whose promises you refuse to believe. For indeed, because of his abounding benevolence, God commands you *to ask for a sign* of salva-

---

[13]Ps 135:9. [14]Cf. Is 38:10; Sir 48:23; 2 Kings 20:11. [15]Mt 12:39. [16]Jon 2:1 RSV. [17]Is 7:2.

tion from him, through which it is to be proved that you will be saved and delivered from *the two kings* who are waging war against you. And you remain in your wickedness and *provoke a fight* with him and likewise cause trouble for his prophets as well as for him, and in your disbelief you repeatedly contrived schemes against them.

[7:14] But although you are such sinners, God again proves himself to be so merciful and does not let you fall to the side and perish, and even though you do not wish it, he will offer you a *sign* of salvation. And what is this *sign?* A certain paradoxical wonder will appear among humanity, such a *sign* as never before has been heard of from the beginning of time. A *virgin* will conceive, apart from relations with a man, and she will give birth to God, the Savior of the human race. Therefore, God is about to allow *himself* to undergo such a birth, and this is the *sign* of salvation that he offers you. Then what was *in the depths* will reach even *to the heights.* He says *in the depths* because he will go down to Hades, and *to the heights* because he will ascend to heaven.

For that very reason, O *house of David,* you surely remember the time when your enemies were assembling and you pronounced this one's name *Emmanuel.* The force of the word is present in the translation, for the name means *God with us.* But rather, believing in the *sign,* have courage and no longer summon the gods of Damascus or appeal to those who are no help at all, but call on *Emmanuel* (the name is here to be understood as *God among humanity*), having complete confidence and believing in the power of the name. And so we come to understand the matter accurately: the prophecy to the *house of David* prescribes that the one who will be born of *the virgin* be called *Emmanuel,* saying: *And you shall name him Emmanuel.* And the same is true for you, O

house of David, you who are present with the prophet and hearken to these words, *you shall name* the prophesied one *Emmanuel,* just as he very clearly instructed you. You invoked him who is your assistant, continually and repeatedly calling *Emmanuel,* appealing to this God who is present with you. For it will be after an extremely long time that the *virgin* will conceive and *bear* a son. The full completion of the prophecy will happen when the Savior will shine forth from [49] the race of all humanity; then among them he will proclaim another name and title of the Savior. But then you, O *house of David,* after you received a sign of a good omen from the Lord, you appealed to him and named him *Emmanuel.* For he who has such a surname will procure salvation for you: believe and obey what he commands.

Therefore because it had been said, *and they shall name him Emmanuel,* it appeared as though the entire prophecy would transpire in a time yet to come. And so controversy has always surrounded this verse, because the holy *virgin* who bore our Savior "called his name Jesus"[18] and not *Emmanuel,* in accordance with the divine injunction that the angel addressed to Joseph: "Do not fear to take Mary your wife, for that which is conceived in her is of the Holy Spirit; she will bear a son, and you shall call his *name* Jesus, for he will save his people from their sins."[19] If therefore our Savior and Lord who was born according to the prophecy received the appellation "Jesus" rather than *Emmanuel* from the *virgin,* how then was the verse proven true which reads: *And they shall name him Emmanuel?* For this very reason the prophecy has not been thus stated. For he was not about to be called by this designation by all people, and the prophetic word accurately embraces the phrase *you shall name.* For you, O *house of David,* because of whom these things are prophesied, you understood the sign of salvation (*he will be called Emmanuel*) to have

---

[18]Mt 1:21. [19]Mt 1:20-21 RSV.

appeared when your enemies joined forces against you and you were delivered from them. Make a note of this. Indeed, he will then be born from a *virgin*, and already God is *with us*, and therefore great things are given freely to you for your salvation. If one believes in the divine ordinance, you might unceasingly invoke the same aid, calling on *Emmanuel*. For you do not need a magic spell or to call on demons to assist you, but only call on *Emmanuel* and thus be saved. This is how he originally expressed these things through the prophet, but certain ones who did not perceive these things put down "and they will call"[20] in the Gospel according to Matthew instead of *you will call*, thus not preserving the precise prophetic diction. And it stands as such in the Hebrew version, and correspondingly it is rendered *and you will call* in all the Greek translations. But instead of the *virgin*, she is called a *maiden* according to the other translations. But if a *maiden* has never before conceived, then she is called a *virgin*. For probably the holy *virgin* conceived the Savior not as a prepubescent child, but when she was a *maiden* at a marriageable age and as a mature [50] young woman. Therefore, this is the wonder in time that he prophesies will take place, [. . .][21] and it is addressed in an exclusive sense to *the house of David*, which stands in need of the aid of the Savior. *And you shall name him Emmanuel.* Therefore he says to call on him who stands not far away, for he is always present and attends those who call on him.

[7:15-17] If you marvel when you hear that God was born, you should believe also that he will yearn after food fit for an infant. For it will not be as an apparition that he will appear among people, nor will it be that he merely seems to be present, but truly he will endure such a birth, as also to partake in baby food, I mean, *butter* and *honey* as other babies. This

indeed is perhaps indicative of his humanity and divinity: *Because before he knows or prefers evil things, he shall choose what is good. For before the child knows good or bad, he defies evil to choose what is good.* And the Word indicates that even at birth, *Emmanuel* would have a certain penetrating and ingenious sense of the good, acquiring from that time an ability to discern good from evil, indeed shaking off the *evil* and accepting only the *good*. For he says that *Emmanuel* will have such a nature and ability from his birth. Let us then delineate that the coming judgment of our Savior against the whole world will be as stated, when indeed he will reject every *evil* person after he tests him, and he will accept only the *good* as worthy of his grace. And this he will achieve from the period of infancy, even from his very birth.

Because of this, you ought to know *O Ahaz*, and you *O house of David*, and all you of the royal race, that the time will come when *God will bring on you and on your people* and on those in your keeping *and on your ancestral house* (clearly the *house* of David) *certain days* such as you have never experienced before. And especially those who lived in Samaria drew the invasion of the Assyrians onto themselves, for they indeed prevented and hindered an attack against you, since they invited the assault on themselves. For when the inhabitants of Jerusalem were thrown over into impiety, the principal men of the cities attempted to keep them out of the way of the attack against the house of David, which was to come in the predicted time in the coming days. He subsequently teaches that a certain event will occur then when he says: *And on that day the Lord will whistle*, and the rest.

[7:18-19] Through these statements the Word indicates the invasion of the Egyptian army, and he associates the uncleanness of idolatry with *flies* because blood and gore attract such

---

[20]Mt 1:23. [21]This theologically crucial sentence unfortunately has a lacuna.

pests. He says that all this will come on the *land* of the Jews, and not without God, but the mere nod of the Lord will set them to action, and with a whistle will incite them to come from *Egypt*. And they will not come from all Egypt, but rather from *parts* of Egypt. And not only does it say that *the Lord will whistle for flies* for those who were delivered over to the Egyptians but *also for the bee* that inhabits the land of the Assyrians **[51]** (clearly this refers to an enemy force). The Word represented the Assyrians as a *bee* because the people had suffered by the enemy spear and the Assyrians had conquered the rest of the people. And therefore he says that after *the bees* turn and are incited by the whistling of the Lord, *they will come* from the *country of the Assyrians*. Then they will come and *rest in the ravines* of the Jewish people *and in the clefts of the rocks and into the caves and into every crevice and on every tree*, and thus they will descend on all their cities. And therefore this anguish has come on you, concerning whom the word came to me, and on these your lands, in which one ought to have anticipated and dreaded the arrival of the said Egyptians and Assyrians, rather than these *two kings*, I mean of Samaria and of Damascus. For they are "smoldering firebrands"[22] that bear no flame, and their power has been quenched.

Therefore, this prophetic text and narrative was indeed fulfilled during the times of the first siege of Jerusalem by those who were in the service of the Babylonians—that is, the Egyptians, those who are called *flies*. This was fulfilled when Pharaoh Necho was in the land of the Jews and attacked Josiah, king of Jerusalem, and he slew this God-fearing man. Then, not long afterwards, the king of the Babylonians, Nebuchadnezzer, attacked with a great and powerful army and razed the city to its foundations and burned down the temple. He reduced every people to utter slavery, and

demolished the remaining cities and set up Assyrian residences in the land of the Jews. Therefore, the prophecies at hand were fulfilled at the time when the enemy *bees* from the *country of the Assyrians* forced them to emigrate to the furthest wilderness. They settled in the valleys and *ravines* and *caves* on the periphery of the land of the Jews when the destruction of the cities overtook them, as the text goes on to describe.

[7:20] Then the word predicted what would happen to every people in the land of the Jews during the prophesied *days* (for it had been said that *he will bring these days on* them): they will indeed be delivered over to the Egyptian *flies*, so that the most godly Josiah will be under the hand of the king of the Egyptians, and the *bees* of the Assyrians will prevail over the entire Jewish land, and they will occupy their deserts and the *ravines* and the *caves* and *every tree*. And they will settle there in leisure and be unafraid with absolute freedom from care. He then continues on to deliver a prediction of the overthrow of the ruler of these Assyrians and Chaldeans through the aforementioned statements.[23] For indeed the Assyrians continued to be in power over Asia and the entirety of Egypt and Libya and of large portions **[52]** of the whole world for about one thousand three hundred years. And the dominion of these unconquerable people was great and did not stop until they had abolished or "besieged"[24] everything in Jerusalem and set the temple of God "ablaze" and carried off the sacred vessels and all the ornaments in the temple to Babylon and dedicated them to their own idols. For not long after these things had been accomplished, the Medes did in fact clear out the rule of the Assyrians. And Cyrus, the first king of the Persians, freely gave liberty to the Jewish captives and allowed those who wished to

---

[22]Cf. Is 7:4. [23]The Greek word here literally means "voices." [24]Cf. 2 Kings 24:11; 25:8-21.

make their return journey to the land of the Jews and rebuild the temple in Jerusalem. He gave back the ornaments and the priestly vessels that had been taken in antiquity, and he ordered that they be dedicated in the temple that was then being prepared.

But these things were accomplished in this manner in the following era; through Isaiah, the prophetic Spirit provided a prediction of what would occur. In the text at hand, he prophesies what will happen at the hand of the ruler of the Assyrians after the invasion, what the aforementioned *bees* from their land would do when they set foot on the land of the Jews. Therefore he says: *On that day the Lord will shave with the great and hired razor of the king of the Assyrians*, not only *the head* that formerly had long hair, before the Assyrians seized control over the empire, but *even the hairs of the feet* (clearly an anthropomorphism) *and the beard*. This is the right natural order for men. The prophetic Word called the cruel race of the enemies a *razor hired* by the Lord, and God says that *he will shave* the king of the Assyrians (clearly their every kingdom and dominion), so that he will look humble, unmanly, disorderly and misshapen. The Medes later received the same end at the mere nod of God when in judgment they were overtaken. The rule of the Assyrians was dissolved and the dominion of the Persians over the entirety of Asia was divided.

[7:21-25] The Word foreshadows poverty and utter destitution through these things, and even a shortage and scarcity of grain for food. For there will be no herds of cattle or flocks of *sheep*; instead a man will own but one *young cow* and tend but *two sheep*. The fact that *every one left on the land* will eat *butter* and *honey* may be a token of the final destitution and famine of bread that will be present. Then the

Word shows forth yet more clearly when he continues on and says: *And it shall be in that day that every place where there used to be a thousand vines, worth a thousand shekels, will become barren ground and thorn*. And again: *For all the land will be barren ground and thorn*. Surely then *because the land will be barren and full of thorns*, no one will have any grain. *The one who is left* will not nourish himself with food suitable for men, and rather than wine [53] he will be sustained with *milk* and *butter and honey*. And these are acquired neither from multiple herds of cattle nor from flocks of sheep but from cheap and pitiable animals. For one will be nourished from the yield of one *young cow* and *two sheep*.[25] These events came about during the Babylonian captivity, when the prophecy was repeated that the people would soon be forced to leave.[26] The present story about those who departed into another place states: "But the captain of the guard left some of the poor from the land to be vinedressers in the land of Benjamin."[27] After a little while the text states again:[28] "And as for the people who were left behind in the land of Judah, whom Nebuchadnezzar the king of Babylon, had left behind—he also appointed over them Gedaliah."[29] It says further: "And Gedaliah swore to the men who were with him, saying, 'Fear not a passing of the Chaldeans; stay in the land, and be subject to the king of Babylon, and it shall be well with you.'"[30] They indeed remembered the present word, the prediction that alluded to the poor and the indigent in saying: *Everyone that is left on the land will eat butter and honey*. For *every one left on the land* was the people along with Gedaliah. Because of the shortage of grain for food, he predicts that they will be nourished *with milk and butter* (the food of the smallest of nurslings), since the entire land was turned into a *barren* desert *and thorns* through men.

---

[25]There is a lacuna in the text at this point. [26]There is another lacuna following this sentence. [27]2 Kings 25:12. [28]There is yet another lacuna in the text at this point. [29]2 Kings 25:22. [30]2 Kings 25:24.

Since the captivity in Babylon and the uprising from that place, the Jews have been in the most extreme poverty regarding God. Indeed, after these things, prophets failed to appear among them, and there was no one worthy of remembrance among them after the writing of Ezra, but the kingdom itself was demolished. No longer did anyone of the house of David rule among them, nor did anyone "rich toward God"[31] shine forth among them. But if there is anyone who says that there was a spiritual man worthy of renown among them, this one might seldom find one *young cow* or *two sheep* among them; the soul of the entire country had been laid waste. The man about whom it is revealed that he will have food fit for an infant in store—*milk and butter and honey*—will have nothing more for the aforesaid nurslings, so that the man *left* among them will enjoy these things. Again, *the one left* may even be among these, but the one who is saved from the destruction of the many and who preserves the spiritual image is indeed rare. He is the one who after careful study may gain one or two lessons from the Jewish teachings, just as there will be a *young cow from the cattle and two sheep* (indeed, today these are clean animals). But so too, he will scarcely find even these; all that will be left will be wolves and jackals, wild beasts and venomous reptiles. This is why he will scarcely find one *young cow or two sheep* among them; and although the *man who is left* among them *will tend* them, he will not receive any produce from them, nor will they yield any solid food or nourishment **[54]** suitable for men. But because they offer instruction only in childish things, they are able only to produce a certain milky food appropriate for infants and nothing better. He who scarcely found the *young cow and two sheep* tended them because of all that had befallen the souls of the multitude and their wilderness. The Word therefore was

present and said: *All the land shall be barren ground and thorn*. And again: *if there might be a thousand vines, they will become barren ground and thorn*. They suffered then from the invisible enemies that besieged their soul, concerning whom the text says next: *With dart and arrow they will enter there, for all the land will be barren ground and thorn*. And not only will *all* their *land be barren ground and thorns*, but even *every hill* that used to be *ploughed*, and the hill will cause no *fear* because its land is high and elevated. It *will be barren ground*, for *barren ground and thorns* offer no fruit or anything nourishing for people, but only useless brambles *a sheep can feed on and an ox can tread*.

[8:1-4] The Word will accomplish the things that will happen in the enumerated days; about these it was said: "God will bring on you and on your people and on your ancestral house such days as have not yet come."[1] The Word again takes up the meaning of the birth of *Emmanuel*. For the house of David was exhorted to call on the name of *Emmanuel* instead of a charm and to be confident and believe that through him they would be saved from those "two kings"[2] who press against them. And the Word of necessity again takes up this theme, for he taught that *Emmanuel* would have an unusual birth and one different from those of mortal nature. He will not be conceived from the union of a man and woman but will be born from a chaste "maiden," an unwedded "virgin."[3] It is of utmost importance to note that the Lord himself no longer addresses Ahaz or the house of Judah but unveils the mystery of the ineffable birth of *Emmanuel* for the prophet alone—the mystery of how "the virgin shall be with child and bear a son."[4] The Lord himself shows this plainly when he says: *And I went to the prophetess, and she conceived and bore a son.*[5] In order that rumors might not

---

[31]Cf. Lk 12:21. **Chapter Eight** [1]Is 7:17. [2]Cf. Is 7:16. [3]Is 7:14. [4]Is 7:14. [5]Is 8:3.

then spread in the hearing of everyone, it was to be kept in a secret writing. He exhorted the prophet *to take a large, fresh roll of papyrus* (or a scroll, or parchment or a codex,[6] according to the other Greek versions) *and to write in it with a man's pen*, that is, in the writing in common use and known among people. For there is another writing, that of God, not written with *a man's pen* but with the power of the Word of God, "registering the worthy in the book of the living."[7] **[55]** But now he enjoins the prophet *to write* in it with *a man's pen* about *the hasty plundering from spoils*. He it was who formerly "bound fast the strong man," the devil, "and plundered his goods."[8]

For through the power of *Emmanuel*, the time has already drawn near and in fact is present, the time in which the aforementioned "two kings"[9] *will be despoiled*, who are the king of Damascus and the king appointed over Samaria by the king of the Assyrians through the ineffable name of *Emmanuel*. And he orders the prophet *to write* on the *large, fresh roll of papyrus* the things that he was about to speak, and to do this in the presence of two witnesses, one of whom was a *priest* and the other a prophet. And the narrative mentions *the priest Uriah*,[10] who was consecrated to God during the times of Isaiah the prophet, as well as *Zechariah*, who served during the reign of King Hezekiah. And therefore the book of Chronicles says: "He set himself to seek the Lord in the days of Zechariah, who instructed him in the fear of God."[11] For this very reason he says about these two men: *Make for me witnesses; take a fresh roll of papyrus* and get ready *to write in it with a man's pen*, and the *witnesses who shall testify for me* shall be present. Thereupon *write* these words in the said *roll of papyrus: And I went to the prophetess, and she conceived and bore a son*. The Lord who administers justice says these things. For one must attend

carefully to the diction of the whole writing: *The Lord said to me* (as though entering into a personal conversation with him); *and I went to the prophetess, and she conceived and bore a son*. Then he who administers justice commanded the prophet to *write* these things in the *fresh roll of papyrus*, as it was said above: "Look, the virgin shall be with child and bear a son,"[12] and the rest. Now we must of necessity ask the present question: How could this possibly be? The Lord himself shows us plainly when he said: *And I went to the prophetess* instead of *I myself will go in with the prophetess*. He calls the prophetess "the virgin"[13] because it was the Holy Spirit who communed with her, just as the angel had said: "The Holy Spirit will come on you, and the power of the Most High will overshadow you."[14] Accordingly, this "power of the Most High" is that which said in the prophecy: *And I went to the prophetess*. According to a certain prophetic convention, he relates the things that are about to happen as though they had already happened.

I myself, says the prophet, *will go in with the prophetess*, and thus *conceiving she will bear a son*. And you are this one himself, O prophet. Thus call now: *seize the spoils in haste, plunder quickly*, for before his birth in the flesh he will bring about absolute ruin to these two **[56]** kings who are now attacking the house of David. For he *will receive the strength of Damascus, and* he will plunder *the spoils of Samaria*. And he will do this through the king of the Assyrians. But speak only what has been revealed and hand the writing over to the witnesses, so that it might be kept for the times after these, since the new covenant is about to achieve the full completion of what has been prophesied.

[8:5-6] The same theme comes up again in what is prophesied, and therefore it is said:

---

[6]The Greek word here (κεφαλίς) is another word for "scroll." [7]Ps 69:28. [8]Mt 12:29; Lk 11:22. [9]Cf. Is 7:16. [10]Cf. 2 Kings 16:10-16. [11]2 Chron 26:5. [12]Is 7:14. [13]Is 7:14. [14]Lk 1:35 RSV.

Then the Lord said to me. The Lord spoke again to the prophet as before, but this time he said not to instruct all the people, for the people were not doing what had been commanded. For he was commanded "not to fear" "the two smoldering sticks (or firebrands)"[15] or to be distressed about the aforesaid "two kings"[16] but only to call on *Emmanuel,* believing in the ordinance of God. But he was unwilling to do this and preferred to serve the aforementioned kings (who were his enemies, no less) rather than to believe in God and to call on *Emmanuel.* Therefore the prophet was told: *Because this people does not want the water of Siloam that flows gently.* What is the *water of Siloam* if not the promised *Emmanuel,* who was a "spring of living *water* welling up to eternal life"[17] and a spring *of water that flows gently?* For then again it *imperceptibly* and *gently held intercourse* with the people, irrigating them and desiring to watch over their souls, for not as yet had the message been "preached to every nation."[18] Therefore it has been aptly said that the *water flows gently* and that the spring "of Siloam is translated 'sent.'"[19] The people who are accused by the Lord for not being *willing* to believe in the ordinance and to call on *Emmanuel,* who is the *water of Siloam that flows gently*—they are a desert apart from him.

[8:7-8] Therefore since they were disbelieving, they preferred to subject themselves to the king of Damascus and the king of Samaria, who were their enemies, rather than to do what had been commanded. The word threatens that there will be no grace for those who subject themselves to *the king of the Assyrians,* whom he also calls the *waters of the mighty and abundant.* In opposition to the *water of Siloam that flows gently,* he contrasted *the waters of the river mighty and abundant.* And this one was *the king of the Assyrians.* For this reason he also says that Judea *will go up and walk on their* *every wall and he will take away from Judea any man who can lift his head or who is capable of accomplishing anything,* so that they will no longer have a *head* over the remaining people, that is, they will have no rulers or kings. **[57]** He prophesies that they will have such a great multitude of enemies that the entire *breadth of the Jewish country will be filled with them,* and in fact this very thing occurred in keeping with the narrative during the times of Jeremiah the prophet, when Nebuchadnezzar the last king of the Assyrians attacked and brought about everything that had been declared beforehand.

[8:9-10] And these things concerning *Emmanuel* are tied to this occasion. And therefore the text begins with the word *Emmanuel,* although it translates as *God with us.* Therefore the Hebrew text has *Emmanuel* instead of *God with us,* and again at the end it is said: *And whatever word you speak, it will not remain for you, because God is with us,* again which translates as *Emmanuel.* The prophet accordingly convicted those discussed above, because the people, although calling on *Emmanuel,* did not want to be better than their enemies. He calls on *Emmanuel,* setting up the accusations made beforehand against someone other than himself, that is, against those whom he also warned about the invasion of the Assyrians. On the one hand, therefore, he threatened the unbelieving with the aforementioned things, but on the other hand, the prophet calls on *Emmanuel* from his own mouth and from those of the people all around him saying: *God is with us.*

Then he turns the discussion to the calling of the Gentiles and prescribes that they too should acknowledge *Emmanuel* when he says: *Learn, you nations.* And what should *you nations* know? Emmanuel himself. For the people of the circumcision "neither know him nor understand,"[20] nor do they want to believe the prophecy, and neither did they yield, nor

---

[15]Is 7:4. [16]Is 7:16. [17]Jn 4:14. [18]Mt 28:19. [19]Jn 9:7. [20]Cf. Is 1:3.

were they obedient to the ordinance. Instead, the *nations* received the knowledge of what was prophesied and did understand him. Do not dare to stand against him or you will be conquered and *defeated*. *Listen* to the command, all of you who live at the *ends of the earth*. And to the strong and powerful among you I say, conquered and *defeated*, submit to the Word! And do this readily, knowing that even if you do not want to hear it, you will be overcome. And if, standing against the calling of God, you should concoct certain contrivances and schemes against the Word that calls you, you will be rebuked for toiling for empty things. Your every counsel, *whatever counsel you take, the Lord will scatter it, and whatever word you will speak*—threatening to do anything contrary to *Emmanuel*—*it will not remain for you*. And we say these things because *Emmanuel is with us*. On the one hand, these things are therefore spoken by the mouth of the prophet to the *Gentiles*, and on the other hand, the Word transitions here and again speaks concerning those who do not as of yet want to call on *Emmanuel*.

[8:11-13] **[58]** After the Word told the Gentiles to know *Emmanuel*, he moves on to the Jewish people, rebuking them as *ones who reject with a strong hand*. For, being called by this hand, they were bound to obey, but they were *rejecting* and gainsaying. Therefore he says: *Thus says the Lord, with a strong hand do they reject* and to those who *walk* not in the *straight* and "royal"[21] and beloved *way of God* but in the *course of the way of this people*. *Never say*, he says, that the command to keep out of the way *of the course of this people* is *hard*. For *this people* thinks it is *hard*, but you who keep out of the way *of the course of this people*, *do not say* that this is *hard*. And even if those of the unbelievers should plot against you as against runaways, you *are not to fear what they fear*,

and although plagued and persecuted, you are not to be *troubled* by them. Rather, *sanctifying* only *the Lord of powers*, impress his *fear* on yourselves. "The fear of the Lord is the beginning of wisdom."[22] And because of this, all fear is banished from humanity.

Symmachus rendered this phrase in this manner: *Here* he says *the Lord said to me that with a strong hand also he kept me from walking in the way of this people saying: "You will not say that everything that this people says is an insurrection."* The Lord says that such things are *in his own hand*. Receiving him, *he kept him from the way of this people* and reserved the prophet for himself, instructing him not to walk in the same *way* as *this* unbelieving *people*, who were not willing to call on *Emmanuel*. And *he kept me, saying: "You will not say that there is an insurrection."* For these are those who after pleading with you to call on *Emmanuel* were leading your *insurrection* while beating their own retreat, but *you will not say* this.

[8:14-15] And, if you only have this *fear* and *trust in him*, then take courage, knowing well that *he will become your holy precinct*, so that your bodily *holy precinct* will no longer be necessary. It was called the *holy precinct* by the ancient Hebrews who understood this as the temple and what is contained in its innermost part. This is what will happen to you who are carried away by them, *believing* in the Lord as your *holy precinct*, for it is not the bodily temple but the Lord himself who sanctifies you, *if you trust in him*. Therefore, no one should fear this people and withdraw himself, but believe and have courage even in your *fear*. For it will be *a holy precinct* for you, and you will not stumble over it *as a stumbling stone*, neither *will you encounter it as a rock of calamity*.[23] And so it will be in *the house of Jacob* because of their unbelief. For those who live in *Jerusalem* are as in *a trap and in a pit* "because they reject[24] the strong hand"

---

[21]Cf. Num 20:17; 21:22. [22]Ps 111:10. [23]The Greek word here means "calamity," "misfortune" or "trap." [24]Cf. Is 8:11.

of the Lord, instead considering it a *stone of stumbling* and a *rock* [59] *of calamity* although such does not exist in nature. For he is a *sanctuary* to those who believe in him. You see how the prophet calls the same Lord a *stone of stumbling* and a *rock of scandal*. On the one hand, he says that he will be such *to those sitting in Jerusalem and to the two houses of Israel*, while on the other hand, he teaches that he will be a *sanctuary* to those who have believed in him. How therefore was he a *stone of stumbling* and a *rock of scandal* to those who addressed him as *Emmanuel* through the conception of the virgin? Thus also the divine apostle taught these things when he said: "A stumbling block to Jews and folly to Gentiles."[25] But the *houses of Israel* were two. On the one hand, there was the house of the rulers among them, and on the other hand, there was the house of those who are ruled. But *to these two houses* (clearly referring collectively to the entire nation, the rulers as well as the ruled), he says that the same Lord will be for them *a trap and a scandal*.

[8:16-18] Instead of: *Then shall become manifest those who seal up the law so that they might not learn*, Symmachus translates this verse thus: *Bind a testimony, seal the law in my lessons*; and Theodotion: *Bind a testimony, seal the law for my doctrines*; and Aquila likewise: *Bind a testimony, seal the law for my doctrines*. And the Lord says these things after the prophecy had been delivered "concerning the two houses of Israel and concerning the inhabitants of Jerusalem,"[26] whenever the aforesaid events, he says, might happen to them. *Then bind the testimony, seal the law for my doctrines*. For then there will no longer be any need for the law of Moses or of testimonies about him, because the new teaching delivers his *doctrines* through the new covenant (clearly to all those who have been called from the Gentiles to his teaching, *then they shall become manifest who seal the law that they might not learn it*). For those who receive the gospel and who have been taught life according to the new covenant, it is just as if they placed seals on the law. They put it away since it is no longer of any use because something better is now available. And the same ones who wait for grace through Jesus Christ *will say*: "*I will wait for God, who has turned away his face from the house of Jacob, and I will trust in him*." Therefore he is also a *holy precinct* for them, according to the promise that was made when he said: "If you trust in him, he will become your holy precinct."[27] And according to Symmachus: *And they will say*: "*I will wait for the Lord who hides his face from the house of Jacob, and I will wait for him*." And certain ones *will say* these things, he teaches in addition: *Here am I and the children whom God has given me*. Therefore the Jewish children were fleshly, from men and women, but these children are from the same Lord who administers justice, "who were born not of blood or of the will of the flesh but of God,"[28] for such children have been given to him [60] from the Father. They no longer hold to the law through Moses but *wait for the Lord and trust in him*. And incredibly, he says that not only these *children have been given to him from God*, but even the *signs and portents* that will be *in the house of Israel* during the prophesied times. But according to the other Greek translations, it reads: *Here am I, and the children whom the Lord has given me are for signs and portents in Israel*. For he says God gave me these children in order to produce through them *signs and portents in Israel*. These things were fulfilled when the Savior "gave authority" to his *children* (clearly to the disciples and apostles) "to heal every disease and every infirmity."[29] And he exhorted them "to go" "to the lost sheep of the house of Jacob"[30] with *signs and portents*. Therefore he goes on: "Heal the sick, cleanse lepers."[31] And

---

[25]1 Cor 1:23 RSV. [26]Cf. Is 8:14. [27]Is 8:14. [28]Jn 1:13. [29]Mt 10:1. [30]Mt 10:6. [31]Mt 10:8.

all these things were *from the Lord of hosts who dwells on Mount Zion.* And they have been revealed through what we have discussed earlier. The sort of dwelling place he had was in the "heavenly"[32] *Mount Zion,* concerning which the apostle says: "You have come to Mount Zion and to the city of the living God, the heavenly Jerusalem."[33]

[8:19] The Word foretold what would happen concerning the children of Christ (I am talking about the apostles and his disciples) and concerning the *signs* and *portents* that were accomplished through them. It was through them also that the calling of the Gentiles occurred. He then teaches the things stated above (as though spoken to them) concerning the recent and new people, the people from the Gentiles who come to understand through Christ. Listen to these things, O my students, you who have repented of the error of the polytheism of the Gentiles. Certain of your long-time acquaintances and friends—whether your fathers or another of your relatives—must have urged you to leave behind your former delusions of marveling at the divinations and oracles and such things which were performed among you through demons. Do not believe in the counsel of these divinations and oracles, neither marvel at the demons who *utter sounds from the belly* of men who are called Pythons,[34] nor marvel at those who according to certain artificers, skilled in witchcraft, are supposed to levitate off the ground; rather, revere the Lord alone among yourselves. And further, they who have been deceived believe that each *nation* is protected by its own *god,* and they believe that they have received unerring knowledge. But why do they practice divination or *seek after* their own gods or meddle in the affairs of the *dead,* asking them about the activities of the *living,* while depriving everyone else of life? For this is stupid and foolish.

[8:20-22] Therefore, since you have the word of God and the evangelical *law,* which *has been given* to you *as a help,* learn whatever you need from them and submit to them, since they *are* not the kind of *gifts* that stand apart from the truth. [61] For it is not natural to turn away from the law of God for money, but these sorts of people love to practice divination for those who have superstitious fears, and many from among them cunningly practice sorcery and often sell the oracles that they make up for the deception of those who consult oracles. But the *law* of God is not like this. It is true: "he will teach you the truth concerning everything."[35]

And if you do not pay attention to the *law* of God, *a harsh famine shall come on you, and it shall be that when you become hungry, you will be distressed, and you will vilify your ruler and the fathers. And they will look up to heaven above, and they will observe the earth below. And behold, there will be dire straits, affliction, and distress and darkness, so that they cannot see. And the one who is in distress will not be perplexed for a time.* These things have been said to those who have no desire to examine the *law* of God and to submit to it and to revere it alone. For he said this once. Listen because *he has given the law as a help,* an impartial and incorruptible *law,* and when submitting to this law, it is necessary to turn away from every deception of demonic operation and to be deceived neither by oracles nor by divinations. For the *law* of God is sufficient and has been given to you in place of everything else. And if anyone should fall away from it, he will be delivered over to *famine,* "neither to a *famine* of bread nor to a lack of water, but to a *famine* of hearing the word of the Lord."[36] For whether one is vigilant[37] about the divine *law* or is a deserter who is offended by the law because of the fake oracles and demonic divinations, there will be *a famine* of spiritual

---

[32]Heb 12:22. [33]Heb 12:22 RSV. [34]"Pytho" was the name for the spirit of divination. [35]Cf. Lk 12:12; Jn 14:26; 16:13. [36]Amos 8:11.
[37]The Greek word here refers to the guard who would stand beside the charioteer.

nourishment, and displacement and exasperation will follow, so that they will fall away even into blasphemies and arguments, *calling down curses on his own* former *king*, whom also *God himself* called. But according to the Septuagint, they were delivered over to the said *famine*, inasmuch as they did not turn their souls to the life-giving nourishment of the *law. They will be grieved, and they will vilify your ruler and the fathers,* so that they hold nothing of the fathers as revered (clearly referring to the ordinances of the churches which were delivered to us from our fathers). *They will vilify* also *the ruler,* blaspheming the leader of the inspired readings and even the Word himself, the Christ of God, *the ruler* of the evangelical *law.* Therefore their souls will be encompassed with *darkness,* inasmuch as they will then be apostates of the divine *law* and given over to the deceit outside. And they will be confined in *affliction* and *distress,* so that everyone *looking up to heaven above and down to earth below,* although looking intently, will no longer see light but only *affliction and anguish.* And whereas the Septuagint has *the one who is in distress shall not be perplexed for a time,* Symmachus translates this phrase as follows: *faintness and anguish and darkness and displacement. For there will be no faintness to whom there is no affliction.* And he says that these things will be for those who abandon the divine *law* and doubt after receiving the first grace and who are again dragged down into the error of the polytheism of the Gentiles.

[9:1] [62] We say that the preceding passage of the prophecy has been bound up with the words concerning Emmanuel. On the one hand, he went through previously the forewarnings for those who did not believe in him, but on the other hand, in close alignment with all this, the prophecies at hand were spoken about those who received him. And that there were certain people who received the Christ of God first one learns from the evangelical Scriptures, in which it has been said: "Now when Jesus heard that John had been arrested, he withdrew into Galilee; and leaving Nazareth he went and dwelt in Capernaum by the sea, in the territory of Zebulun and Naphtali, that what was spoken by the prophet Isaiah might be fulfilled: 'The land of Zebulun and the land of Naphtali, toward the sea, across the Jordan, Galilee of the Gentiles—the people who sat in darkness have seen a great light, and for those who sat in the region and shadow of death light has dawned.' From that time Jesus began to preach, saying, 'The kingdom of heaven is at hand.'"[1] And therefore the holy Gospel records where the first apostles landed,[2] and the prophecy foretells all that was about to happen. And therefore he preached the gospel *first* to those in *Galilee.* For when Emmanuel was revealed and about to spend his time among humanity, it was necessary that the country not keep silent. And the country was *Galilee,* in which the Word preached the saving drink, saying: *Drink this first, do it quickly, O country of Zebulun and land of Naphtali.*

And the tribe of *Zebulun* and the tribe of *Naphtali* were the two tribes which were allotted *Galilee* in the distribution of the land administered by Joshua son of Nun. But it happened that Greeks lived in this land in the midst of the two tribes (for not only Jews but also other races were inhabiting the land at this time). The word must have remembered this when it said: *And the rest by the sea beyond the Jordan.* And being exceedingly accurate, it brings forward even another *Galilee* when it says: *Those by the sea and beyond the Jordan.* It says *by the sea* concerning every harbor around the lake of Gennesaret, which has been remembered in the Gospel as the "sea." Therefore it says: "As he passed by the Sea of Galilee, he saw two brothers."[3] And from there the

---

Chapter Nine [1]Mt 4:12-17. [2]There is unfortunately a lacuna at this point in the text. [3]Mt 4:18.

disciples of our Savior started out. And Capernaum and Bethsaida and Chorazin and the other villages, which the evangelical Scriptures mention around the harbor of Tiberias, are still even now to be found there. And this *Galilee* lies *beyond the Jordan*, where the Christ of God spent the majority of his time. Therefore he *first* announced the saving drink and the *great light* to those who live in this region. And he perceptibly supplied the image of this life-giving drink when, at the conclusion of the "wedding" "in Cana of *Galilee*"[4] he performed the *first* miracle, **[63]** the conversion of the water into wine. This is the reason why the Evangelist noted: "This, the first of his signs, Jesus did at Cana in Galilee."[5] Therefore the prophecy signifies these things when it says: *Drink this first, do it quickly.*

[9:2] For he wills that those who were deemed worthy of the great light of the saving theophany should produce fruit of the spiritual drink through works. Therefore it says: *O you people who sit in darkness, see a great light; O you who live in the country of the shadow of death, light will shine on you.* And who were those who were overpowered *in darkness and in the shadow of death* and who formerly were "without knowledge of God"[6] and who were enslaved in the *death* of the soul? Those who were without knowledge were *in darkness* before they received the illumination of Christ "the true light."[7] And those who were *in the darkness of death* were "those who committed mortal sins,"[8] according to the following verse: "The soul that sins, this one shall die."[9] In the present life it happens that "he who commits a mortal sin" is not in every way swallowed up by death (as he who cannot turn and be saved), but neither is he altogether delivered from it. Therefore he is said to be *in the shadow of death.* However, after shining on them first, the one who was prophesied

through the things discussed above gave the grace of the *great light.*

[9:3] This is the *country* in which he then acquired *most of the people*, and he chose from them the apostolic band. Therefore the text says next: *Most of the people, whom you have brought back in your joy.* But instead of *whom you brought back*, the other Greek versions translate this phrase *whom you magnified.* Therefore, at that time only those who lived in Galilee believed in the Christ of God (whom the present word mentioned), but now indeed *most* have believed. And although many remained in disbelief, it can be said that *most of the people* have received the *joy* of salvation.

In the verse at hand he speaks of the miraculous deed in the Gospel of our Savior, when indeed a multitude of about "five thousand" men was once fed from "five loaves"[10] in the indicated country. And once from "seven loaves four thousand men" were fed, "not including the children and women."[11] Therefore, according to Symmachus, the text reads: *They will rejoice before you as one rejoices in harvest.* And thus those who eat together *in harvest* were also accustomed to drinking together. And so interpreted according to the deeper meaning, we understand that the text is speaking about the apostles of our Savior **[64]** and their successors, who, presiding over his churches and laboring as harvesters even until now, share in ecstatic *joy* before their Savior. That they were "laborers" of the *harvest* of the Gentiles he revealed when he said: "The *harvest* is plentiful, but the laborers are few; pray therefore the Lord of the harvest to send out laborers into his harvest."[12] For truly the disciples and apostles of our Savior and those of his churches were "few," but they nevertheless carried out the great and abundant *harvest* of the Gentiles. And these same people divided the spoils of polytheism and the demonic error among themselves which the Savior

---

[4]Jn 2:1. [5]Jn 2:11 RSV. [6]1 Cor 15:34. [7]Jn 1:9. [8]1 Jn 5:16. [9]Ezek 18:4, 20. [10]Mt 14:17. [11]Mt 15:34. [12]Mt 9:37-38 RSV.

imself gave to them for plunder. Therefore also he verse above called out: "Quickly seize the poils, plunder in haste."[13] For after demolishing he error of idolatry, during which time the free souls of people had been "plundered" by him, he appointed his disciples and apostles and assigned their successors to the superintending of he harvest. And those who reaped rejoiced as *hose who rejoice at the harvest and in the same way as those who rejoice dividing the plunder*, illed up with joy at the abundance of the fields of each church.

9:4] . . . *the yoke that was* formerly *placed on* heir spoils *and the rod that is on the neck* of heir spoils *had been taken away.* For the *yoke that was placed on them* was heavy to those souls who had been enslaved by the devil, *and he fatal rod that was on their neck* pressed against it and forced it to bend down. Once these *had been taken away,* it was quite right that *those who divide* these *spoils* should rejoice. And how *the yoke and the rod that had been placed on their neck was taken away from them* he makes quite clear when he says next: *For he was scattered the rod of the exactors.* But instead of *the exactors,* Aquila translates this phrase: *the yoke of his burden and the rod on his shoulder, the stick of the punisher;* and Symmachus says: *the yoke of his burden and the rod on his shoulder, and the rod of the exactor was broken;* and Theodotion likewise translated this word as the *exactor. The exactor* is singular and signifies *the punisher* (revealing the devil), who punishes and brings the souls of people to their end, and *he exacts* payment from those who are well supplied with sin by him. And he who stripped off the heavy *yoke* has broken even this *rod of the exactor,* but afterward it is probable that there were many others who worked together with the devil, and of these there were some who were *exactors* to him. For there were many who were *punishers* of the human race.

He took away the yoke and the rod, and he did [65] these things against them *on the day that was on Midian*. In the story of Gideon in the book of Judges we read that the enemies were conquered not by arms but by an invisible and divine power. And so the enemies were thus conquered as *on Midian* with a hidden hand. And now the text says that *the rod of the exactor* (i.e., of the devil and of those who *punish* the souls of people with him) *will be scattered*.

[9:5] And those who were defeated *shall compensate for every garment and cloak acquired by deceit.* For since the devil stripped off the adornment and *garment* of the soul and cloaked himself in the tunic of excellence, when he had the stripped garment itself well in hand, he arranged it in a shameful fashion, and by deceit the opposing powers which are consulted as oracles were demanding this garment from him. It is rightly said by the prophetic spirit that they *will repay* all: *They shall compensate for every garment and cloak acquired by deceit.* And they themselves who used to *punish* the souls of people will *repay* everything at the revealed time, for *they would rather be burned by fire* than look on the Savior of the universe who lived among humanity.

[9:6] What this is about he states next when he says: *Because a child was born for us, and a son also given to us, whose sovereignty is on his shoulder: and he is named messenger of great counsel.* And he was the one who was called *son* and *child* and *Emmanuel.* This is the third time in the same prophecy where the *son* is also called *child.* Indeed the first time: "Look, the virgin shall be with child and bear a son, and you shall name him Emmanuel."[14] Then he added: "For before the child knows good or bad."[15] And the second time: "And I went to the prophetess, and she conceived and bore a son."[16] Then he added: "For before the child

---

[13]Is 8:3. [14]Is 7:14. [15]Is 7:16. [16]Is 8:3.

knows how to call 'father' or 'mother.'"[17] And the third time is in the text at hand through the word which said: *Because a child was born for us.* For this very reason the *child* is this *son*, who was given as a gift from God to those who have believed in him and who has many more names than those stated above. *And he has been named messenger of great counsel.* And although this name may seem rather ordinary, it points to something beyond mortal nature, even angelic.[18] For he addressed him not simply as *messenger*,[19] but as *messenger of great counsel.* And what else could *the great counsel* be except the *counsel* of the great God [66] concerning the calling and salvation of all nations, which the *messenger* himself, our Savior, would minister in the benevolent *counsel* of the Father? According to the Hebrew Scriptures he has been honored with greater forms of address than *messenger*, for it is said that he bears *the government on his shoulder.* For the *government* of the prophesied *child* (that is, the glory and the honor and the kingdom) is the *government* that is *on his shoulder* and over all (clearly, the government should be understood as the arm of the divinity in him). He has been called *messenger of great counsel* because of his divinity, for he alone understands the secret things of the fatherly *counsel*, and he is the *messenger* to the worthy. We said that he has been deemed worthy of an even greater title than *messenger*, for the Hebrew text reads, as translated by Symmachus: *And his name will be called marvelous, able to advise, strong and powerful, eternal father, ruler of peace*; and Aquila says: *His name is called wonderful, counselor, strong, powerful, father still, ruler of peace*; and according to Theodotion's translation: *And she called his name wonderful, counselor, strong, master, eternal father, ruler of peace.*

But instead of *strong*, the Hebrew text has *El*, which means God. For there are many passages in Scripture where *El* stands for God, and the text at hand should likewise be counted among them, for through the wording of the Hebrew God is proclaimed to be the *child born for us.* Accordingly, in the above prophecy concerning the *child born for us* and the *son given to us*, along with the other names and *El*, according to the Hebrew text, it is clear that the prophecy makes him known to be God. And so he is called *El Gibbor*[20] in the Hebrew tongue. But Aquila translates this phrase as *strong, powerful*, and Symmachus does as well. Theodotion translated this phrase as *strong, master, protector*—among which titles it is probable that he included the name of God as the *child born* for us. And we would not miss the mark to translate the phrase *powerful God*,[21] since it has been pointed out to us that the word *El* translates to "God." And so we have boldness to call him so. The phrase *El Gibbor* in the Hebrew tongue is translated *strong, powerful* in the Greek, and the name *Emmanuel* includes *El* in it and additionally takes on the phrase *God with us.* And such names of the revealed *child* present his nature as superior to that of a mere man. Now I suppose that there are those who distrust the Septuagint because it is silent concerning the true recipient of the portentous and surpassing greatness of these names,[22] but in another way this is stated summarily in the literal meaning: *And he is named messenger of great counsel.* [67] And how has he said *father of the coming age*, for we will understand that it is our father Adam who is being handed down who is of "the present age"[23] and of the mortal race of people. But "just as in Adam we will all die," according to the apostle, "so we will all be made alive in Christ."[24] If therefore he was speaking about the new age when he said, "Christ the firstfruits, then at his coming those

---

[17]Is 8:4. [18]In Greek, the word for "messenger" is the same as that for "angel." [19]Or, "angel." [20]The RSV translates these two Hebrew words "Mighty God." [21]θεὸν δυνατὸν. [22]There is an extensive lacuna in the text at this point. [23]See Gal 1:4. [24]1 Cor 15:22.

who belong to Christ, then comes the end,"[25] he would have said *Father of the coming age* of grace and again *peace of the rulers*. "For he is our peace,"[26] "making peace for all things whether on earth or in heaven"[27] "and reconciling the world"[28] in himself to the Father. He said next after these things: *For I will bring peace on the rulers and health to them*. And what sort of *rulers*? Or are these the ones who were appointed to rule his church with him? I speak of his disciples and apostles and those who received the succession from them throughout the whole empire. To them it was given to have a *healthy* and *peaceful* soul within themselves; to them he said: "My peace I give to you; my peace I leave with you."[29]

[9:7] And in addition he says: *his sovereignty is great*, instead of how Symmachus translated it: *For his instruction was fulfilled, and his peace has no boundary*, or according to Aquila, *there is no end*, or according to Theodotian, *there is no limit*. And *his sovereignty is great* you will understand as his church which can be seen throughout the entire empire. One could also conceive of it rather as the testimonies of the apostle concerning him, through whom he says: "According to the working of his great might which he accomplished in Christ when he raised him from the dead and made him sit at his right hand in the heavenly places, far above all rule and authority and power and dominion, and above every name that is named."[30] Therefore, the *sovereignty* of our Savior is *great*. And again, *and there is no end to his peace*. For it is unending, undecaying and unlimited; therefore it has been said: "Righteousness will rise in his days, and peace will abound."[31] After saying this concerning the *child* who was born, he adds yet also these things concerning him: *on the throne of David and his kingdom, to make it prosper*. And he

accurately preserves how it was said that he would take his seat not just *on the throne of David*, but more generally *on the throne of David and his kingdom, to make it prosper*, which we understand to imply that he will come in order to *prosper the* [68] *throne of David* and "the booth of David that is fallen."[32] For after the kingdom of David had been subjected and overthrown from the time of the captivity of the people in Babylon, there were also prophecies foretelling that the *throne of David* would shine forth in righteousness as the light of the sun throughout all civilization. This same promise has come to be fulfilled in him who was descended "from David according to the flesh"[33] and who shines over the souls of people and consolidates his kingdom through all the nations of the entire empire. For in this way *he restored the throne of David*, not in arms and staves but *with judgment and with righteousness*. And he did so *from this time onward and forevermore*, on the one hand *from now*, signifying the time when the rule had been ordained, through to the time of the advent of his sojourn among humanity, and *forevermore*, indicating his boundless and lasting kingdom.

One should note first that it was foreknown and announced that he "would be born of a virgin,"[34] second that, concerning the question before us, as it were, the Lord introduced how this will happen when he said: "And I went to the prophetess, and she conceived and bore a son," and third that he does not mention the virgin conception or the manner of the incredible pregnancy according to God. We learned these things concerning this child in advance, and he instructs us in detail in the secrets of his theology, and all these things are said concerning the advent of the little child. I do not know how those of the circumcision who do not wish to receive our Savior would

---

[25]1 Cor 15:23. [26]Eph 2:14 rsv. [27]Col 1:20. [28]Cf. 2 Cor 5:19. [29]Jn 14:27. [30]Eph 1:19b-21a rsv. [31]Ps 72:7. [32]Amos 9:11 rsv. [33]Rom 1:3 rsv. [34]Cf. Is 7:14.

understand these words, for the works testify concerning him and the accomplishment of the deeds is confirmed. *The zeal of the Lord of hosts will do these things.* What could the *zeal* be if not the good after which he strove, since it was fitting for him to save all those who were oppressed by the devil and who had been drawn down into godlessness?

[9:8] After outlining the story of the origin of Emmanuel, the word returns to the prophecy about Israel, for whose sake the Word made mention of Emmanuel. For since the people who were called Israel are ruled in Samaria and were in an alliance with the king of Syria, he prepared to besiege Jerusalem. Ahaz was anxious about the attack of "the two kings,"[35] and the prophet was ordered to predict the things that have been recorded, among which were also the predictions concerning Emmanuel, and he again vigorously resumes the extended discourse concerning Israel. I am speaking about the prophecy from the people who are ruled in Samaria, through whom he says these things. For this reason *the Lord* did not *send death* or a terminal *word* of wrath *on Israel but on Jacob*, since Israel is his people eternally. For *he sent* this not primarily *on Israel* but *on Jacob* since they were backslidden and more fleshly. And *death* or a terminal *word* of wrath was sent on Jacob [69], on those who thought they were good enough not to deserve wrath or to be overtaken by *death*; but I say it *came* on those who are called Israel. And the difference between Jacob and Israel was evident even during the lifetime of the patriarch himself. For he was called *Jacob* according to his birth in the flesh, but after he had advanced in maturity according to God, he was deemed worthy of communion with God. And he was pronounced *Israel* by the one who wrestled with him and said: "Your name shall no more be called Jacob, but Israel will be your

name, for you have striven with God."[36] In the same way, therefore, those who are void of reason and fleshly from among the Jewish nation he calls *Jacob*, but those who are thought to be rational among them he dubs *Israel*. Accordingly, the Word accuses also those who are supposed to be superior as also worthy of *death*, therefore he said: *The Lord sent death against Jacob, and it came on Israel.*

[9:9-10] And who *Israel* was he states next: *And all the people of Ephraim will know it, and those who sit in Samaria with pride and uplifted heart, saying: "The bricks have fallen, but come, let us hew stones and cut down sycamores and cedars and build ourselves a tower."* For these are those who dwell in Samaria, those who are known as *Israel* and who are called *the people of Ephraim* because they are ruled by the tribe of Ephraim, those who scorn and disparage Jerusalem. They said that they would build it *with bricks* and that they would have roofs of *sycamores* or, according to the other Greek translations, of mulberry trees.[37] Then they prepared to improve the city and promised that they would *build* it with hewn *stones* and *cedars*. Instead of the temple in Jerusalem, they said that they would erect *a tower for themselves* in Samaria.

[9:11-13] Therefore, since they dared to speak such things, the Word threatens them, saying next: *And God will strike those who rise up against him on Mount Zion, and he will scatter his enemies.* For after such things, they were emboldened *against Mount Zion* and against the God who is revered in it, and the Word threatens that he will humble them and *dash* them *down* from the great height of their arrogance. For he was about to deal with *those who rise up against Mount Zion* and who act profanely against God *himself*; he says he will humble and *strike* them. He will *scatter* not

[35]Cf. Is 7:16. [36]Gen 32:28. [37]The two words Eusebius uses are closely related and would probably both be best translated "sycamore."

52

only them but also all *his enemies*, meaning those in Damascus who were allied with Israel, as explained above. And he announces that he will *dash down* from the other nations all *those who rise up against Mount Zion* and against God in that revered place, those who were *from the rising of the sun* and those who were *from the setting of the sun*, and *the Greeks* in between these peoples. [70] For all of these *devour* the aforementioned *Israel with open mouths*, and, reinforcing[38] the error of their idolatry, they promised to come to their aid and to be allied with *those who rise up against Mount Zion*. May you never sin by *devouring with the open mouth* of the Greeks and of the other tribes, that is to say, those who advance into apostasy through the deception of "the wisdom of this age"[39] of the Greeks. For Israel, who is at present accused by the prophet, was of this sort. Therefore the *anger* of God was *raised* against them and *his hand uplifted* and poised in wrath against them. And thus neither *did they turn back* nor *did they seek the Lord of powers*. "But by their hard and impenitent heart they were storing up wrath for themselves on the day of wrath."[40] This phrase does not mean that God is angry in an emotional sense, but according to the customary language found in those books called Scripture, the phrase refers to the punishment that will come against them.[41]

[9:14-16] Instead of *so the Lord took away from Israel*, Aquila has *so the Lord will destroy*, and Symmachus has *so the Lord will utterly destroy* and Theodotian *so he took away*. They translate the phrase as though God were about to do these things, "things not yet done"[42] which he predicted, turning those who would listen to repentance, so that they would not suffer what had been threatened. And he says that he will do all these aforementioned things *in one day*—and these events have clearly occurred. That is, they have occurred at one and the same time. For when he said the *head and tail* he was appealing to the imagery of an irrational animal. For humans do not have *tails* but irrational animals do, with which he compares the people. The *head and tail* may refer to the rational and the irrational or the rulers and the least of the subjects, as he then indicated quite plainly when he said, *the great and the small*. But instead of *and those who admire persons*, Symmachus translated it *and the venerable*. And therefore we may say that this *venerable one* and *the elder* would be the head. But *the tail is the prophet who teaches lawless things*, which, as it were, is the least part of an irrational animal. The Word threatens that these *will be taken away* and utterly destroyed in one day, and those whom the Word says are deceiving false prophets speak wrongly about these things and while *congratulating the people, lead them astray in order to devour them*, taking from them a profit for themselves.

[9:17-21] This is why he thus lays out these threats before them: *Therefore God will not rejoice over their youths, nor will he have compassion on their orphans and widows*, and the rest. He threatens that, as the good farmer of souls, God will do these things, in order that the *lawless* might be made to vanish from among them, just as tender herbs are consumed *by fire*. This is what he means when he says: *And the transgression will burn like a fire, and like dry grass will it be consumed* [71] *by fire, and it will burn in the thickets of the forests and devour everything around the hills*. For he says that the aforementioned wrath of God

---

[38]Eusebius is again punning here. He uses a word which can mean either "to lay down as a foundation" or "to cast down." Eusebius is saying that the political allies of Israel are both laying down a basis for the continued idolatry of Israel and that these supposed allies are causing the downfall of Israel. [39]1 Cor 2:6. [40]Rom 2:5. [41]The precise meaning of this theologically significant sentence is unfortunately marred by lacunae. [42]Is 46:10 RSV.

that comes according to these metaphors will wreak havoc among them, so that *brother* will rise up against *brother*, and nearly no one will be spared. All will be declared enemies and foes of one another. Conditions among them will escalate to such an extent that internecine war will erupt, as between the two tribes *Ephraim* and *Manasseh*, who were from one father, Joseph, who were united in one kingdom and who built one and the same city Samaria. They will rise up against each other, and they will devour the *arms* of one another. No longer devoting themselves to the war against Judah or the siege of Jerusalem, they will sharpen their own swords to their own hurt and slay themselves. And the wrath of God will not come on them until these things happen. And still further things will come on them. Just as God threatened that "he would put enmity between her and it,"[43] "between the serpent and the woman,"[44] so there will be enmity even between those who are good and amiable. Thus also now God proclaims that he will turn the harmony of those charged by the prophet to cacophony.[45] All this parallels the saying of the Savior recorded in the Gospels: "Do not think that I have come to bring peace on earth; I have not come to bring peace on the earth, but a sword. For I have come to set a man against his father, and a daughter against her mother, and a daughter-in-law against her mother-in-law."[46]

[10:1-3] I speak of the people called Israel, of the Jewish people who are ruled in Samaria. The present word accuses them of these things as before, saying that they compile false prophecies for quarreling and contentiousness from those who write the true prophecies of God. Therefore they were the greatest false prophets, those in Israel who whether opening their mouths or writing acted contrary to the true prophets of God. And they drafted lawless documents, full of every kind of sexual perversion, rather than holding to the divine Scripture of the law and judging in accordance with it.[1] And those who acted contrary to the law oppressed the *poor* who ought to be pitied, and resorting to violence they seized everything from the inexperienced, the *orphans* and the *widows*. And you might say that such are they who even now pervert the souls of the innocent through their wretched writings, whom the prophetic word threatens saying: *What will they do on the day of visitation*, when *affliction* and wrath *will come* against them *from far away?* For the wrath is from afar **[72]** because it is driven away from my God. It is to you, among whom these exist, that these things are said. Because you resort to violence, you bring God's wrath on yourselves, and when it comes, *to whom will you flee for help?*

[10:4] Then as usual he adds: *For all this his anger has not turned away, but his hand is still uplifted.* For they continue on in these same absurdities as those accused by the Word, and so it follows that the wrath would continue to be against them. He then asserted the charges against the people even as far as to tell those who were threatened by the prophecy that the Assyrians would come on them and besiege Samaria and ravage all their land and carry off nine entire tribes of the Jewish nation as captives into Assyria. And they did this during the reign of King Hezekiah in Jerusalem, when the kingdom of Israel had arranged itself for battle in Samaria and was completely destroyed. And when the battle came to an end, of the entire nation, only the two half tribes were left remaining as ruled by the successors of David in Jerusalem. For this reason, after

---

[43]Gen 3:15. [44]Gen 3:14. [45]Eusebius's allusion to Is 9:11 is not possible to catch in the present translation. Eusebius says literally that God will "disperse their harmony," thus echoing the line that God "stirs up their enemies" (RSV). [46]Mt 10:34-35. **Chapter Ten** [1]The manuscript is damaged at this point, rendering this translation provisional.

sserting the prophecy concerning Israel, the Word then turns from them to what would appen to the Assyrians themselves and in the ollowing foretells what was about to happen o them because of their attacks.

10:5-6] Subsequent to the captivity of the eople called Israel, the Word turns to the aptors—the Assyrians whom he threatens vith the aforementioned. And because the eople had already been carried away by the Assyrians and Samaria had already been esieged when the prophecies at hand were leclared, it is clear that what is said is from the mouth of the king of the Assyrians: *And I took Arabia and Damascus and Samaria. As I took these, I will also take all the countries.*[2] And gain: *For as I did to Samaria and to the works f her hands, thus will I do also to Jerusalem.*[3] And history informs us that "in the days of Ahaz, the king of the Assyrians invaded Samaria and besieged it."[4] At first he took captive only a certain portion of the people, but then, after Hezekiah had been succeeded by Ahaz, he "relocated" all the people to Assyria. And after the Assyrians had done this, the present word expounds in detail the aforementioned things pertaining to them, saying: you are a *rod* of instruction and one that will return on itself, for it was necessary for the people who refused to be chastened by the prophetic words to receive a trial. For this reason I raised up the Assyrians against this people as my *rod*, and I delivered the people into the *hands* of the Assyrians, so that through them the *anger* and the *wrath* (which the people brought on themselves) might come on them. It was therefore through the Assyrians that *I sent my anger against the lawless nation* who was then supposed to be my people. And I allowed the Assyrians to wage war and to spoil and to plunder and to raze all *their cities* to the ground and turn them *into dust.*

[10:7-11] [73]And although Assyria had received authority from me, *he did not plan thus,* but he was puffed up in his prideful thinking, and in his imperial power he conquered my people. But, not being content to besiege only them, he threatens to attack countless nations and plunder the valuable articles dedicated to God. For this reason then, those who were subject to him marveled at him and said: *You alone are ruler.* And he answered them and said: No longer call me *ruler* or lord, because *I have* not yet *taken all countries* everywhere, neither have I brought into subjection the *country above Babylon* nor *Calno, where the tower was built* during the time of the dispersion of tongues. But so far what I have conquered have been exceedingly small and insignificant, *for* up to this point I rule over *Arabia and Damascus and Samaria.* But he adds, *as I took these, I will also take all the countries.* And while the Assyrians were making such boasts, the prophetic word rightly arose and inveighs against their ruler and says the following: "Woe to the Assyrians,"[5] because they did not understand that my *anger* is against all who sin and that God has given them the authority of such a rule. And those who failed to reckon with this assumed that they had ruled over the nations by their own power. The above statements are addressed to the Assyrians, but in what is adduced next, God himself threatens Jerusalem and says: *Wail, you graven images in Jerusalem! For as I did to Samaria and to the works of her hands, thus will I do also to Jerusalem and to her idols.* And the book of Kings informs us that during the reign of Ahaz and in the period after this, those who were called the people of Judah used to commit idolatry right in Jerusalem. Accordingly, the Word threatens that precisely the same things would be suffered in Samaria as in Jerusalem, and he predicts these things admonishing those who hear to conversion and

---

[2]Is 10:9-10. [3]Is 10:11. [4]Cf. 2 Kings 17:5. [5]Is 10:5.

repentance, and recalling them to their senses in fear to the pattern of godliness. For it was not Assyria that said it had something against Samaria, but God, because of the ungodliness of the inhabitants. Therefore, according to the word of the righteous one, it was reasonable that those in Jerusalem would be delivered over to precisely the same siege as those who administer the affairs of their relatives who suffered the aforementioned. One should know that the eleventh volume of Origen's interpretation of the prophet came up to this point.

[10:12] The Word informed the reader beforehand about the Assyrian capture of Samaria and about the threats against the Assyrians and foretells that Jerusalem would suffer precisely the same things because of the same idolatries. Following the verses above, he teaches that, up to this point, the Assyrians and their ruler—although such things had been prophesied—acted boldly and conquered Samaria and Damascus. Nevertheless, they will have authority for a time as a sort of prelude to the final act, [74] after which their long rule of many years will no longer be established, and their kingdom will be entirely destroyed. And when this time might be he makes clear when he says: *And it shall be that when the Lord has finished doing all the things in Mount Zion and in Jerusalem.* For *when* the Lord *has finished doing* he shall bring to completion *all the things* that he ordained. And he ordained the things that were conveyed in the prophecies and the things that have been written in the Holy Scriptures concerning what happened in those places. Then at that point the Word says that *he will bring his wrath against the great mind,* or according to Symmachus, he says: *I will examine the fruit of the festivities of the heart of the king of Assyria and the boast of the loftiness of his eyes.*

[10:13-14] For this one did not give glory to God either, nor did he pay attention to him. The God of the universe was the one who handed over to him Israel and Judah and all those worthy of punishment. But he became proud and thought to himself, according to Symmachus: *By the strength of my hand I did it for I am wise, and I relocated the boundary of peoples, and I confounded their kings, and as a conqueror, I led down their inhabitants. And my hand found all the power of the peoples as a nest, and I gathered all the earth as one gathers abandoned eggs.* For this very reason, because of their overbearing arrogance, certain opposing forces came: "the ruler of the kingdom of the Persians and the ruler of the kingdom of the Medes and the ruler of the kingdom of the Greeks."[6] And so, one could say that it was the ruler of the kingdom of the Assyrians who had made the false pretensions and uttered the statements discussed above.

[10:15] Therefore this concerns the kingdom of the Babylonians. They besieged Jerusalem and burned down the temple and seized all the sacred vessels and the ornaments in it and dedicated them to their idols back in Babylon. And concerning him who dared to say such terrible and desperate things, the prophetic word answers saying: Then, O most foolish of all, do you not see that an *axe does not swing* itself to chop down a *tree* except someone uses it? Neither does a *saw* saw anything in half unless someone *pulls* it, nor does a *rod* smite anything nor does a *log* spontaneously strike anything unless set in motion. Therefore, it is necessary to understand that such power was yours only for as long as you were in the service of the anger of God—the power to prevail over countless nations, not only to stop them from advancing but even to slaughter them and dash others down, the power to reduce entire cities to slavery and to overthrow

---

6Cf. Dan 10:13, 20; 8:20-21.

umberless multitudes. But as with every *saw* nd *axe* and *rod* wielded with a hand, you vould be able to do nothing unless the Lord lelivered those worthy of punishment into our hand. And now, since you did not understand any of this [75], you raised yourself up nd presumed yourself to be *the great mind.* ?or you did not place before your eyes "the peace of God which passes all understanding."[7] And you thought that you were the highest *mind* and the greatest of all. You were arrogant before God with your haughty eyes. You ntended to confound the territorial boundaries of the nations, which God had drawn and vell ordained. "When the Most High separated the nations, when he scattered the sons of Adam, he fixed the bounds of the nations according to the number of the angels of God."[8] And you thought you were *wise*, and in your fallacious understanding you imagined that you were able to meddle with the boundaries that had been well appointed by God and to bring the *empire* into subjection to yourself. For you thought that no one was overseeing your actions nor that God would assist the people on the earth, and for this reason, you assumed that you would prevail over the nations of the empire who would be like deserted chicks or like *abandoned eggs.*

[10:16-19] Therefore it is necessary to be smart enough to understand that you would not have prevailed even against those nations had God not consented. For where did you receive such authority if God had not allowed it? And did not God use you as an instrument for the vengeance, and punishment of those who are in need of correction? But since "you did not reason thus"[9] and neither did you acknowledge the source of such authority as was yours, know that *the Lord of hosts himself,* the master of all power, and his angelic army *will send dishonor on your honor, and a burning*

fire will burn on your glory. The God who of old enlightened his own people, he himself *will be the light of Israel,* and he will be a fire *sanctifying them* and the arrogant among you. But instead of: *and he will sanctify them with a burning fire,* Symmachus has *and his holy one will be for a flame.* For "the Holy One of Israel,"[10] he who has been a light to his people and he who was *a flame* and *a fire,* he says this to you, Assyria—you who dared to imagine ungodly and inflated things. And to *hills* and *mountains* and *woods* he fittingly compares the multitude of Assyrians and those governing her and in positions of authority over others just as though they were *hills* and *mountains.* But these indeed *will vanish,* that is, those who were of old dreadful and hot with fury will involuntarily cool in death. For death will devour them; in a single night their souls and bodies will be spent. For their souls have been destroyed at once with their bodies; this is clear for every one of them. And through these phrases he indicates the strength of one's life. But instead of *and it will devour the wood like grass,* Symmachus says: *and in one day it will devour all that had been stored up and reserved, and the* [76] *glory of his wood and of Mount Carmel will be wasted from soul until flesh. And he who flees will faint, and the trees that are left over from its woods will be for a cipher, and a child will write them down.* It should be clear that he calls the multitude around him *woods,* and the rich and upper class he calls *Mount Carmel.* He definitely says that everything *will be consumed* by the punishing power of the aforementioned *fire.* And whenever these things might occur for him, he will flee, running away, and all those with him will do the same. And if there might be a few small trees remaining, they will be so few that even a *child* will be able to count their *number* and to record in writing those that remain from the vast number of those that were destroyed.

---

[7]Phil 4:17. "Understanding" here is the same word as "mind," as in "the great mind" in the line above. [8]Deut 32:8. [9]Cf. Is 10:7. [10]Is 1:4.

These statements have both a literal and a deeper sense. Interpreted literally, they are about Nebuchadnezzar when he burned down the temple and the city. But, interpreted in a deeper sense, they are about the power that opposed the nation of the Assyrians. Before these things happened, the government caused the kingdom to flourish and brought it to its best days, but then what had been prophesied befell the kingdom. The dominion of the Assyrians was indeed demolished in a moment. The Medes and the Persians then took power.

[10:20-21] He says that in that time all the aforesaid prophecies will happen, prophecies which were clearly against the ruler of the Assyrians. Those who remain from the captives of the Jewish people, who escape enemy territory and return to their homeland, will no longer devote their attention to evil demons, who of old plagued their souls (although they themselves were worthy of the evil they inflicted), but at last they will devote themselves solely to their Redeemer and Savior. And these things were fulfilled literally during the reign of Cyrus, the king of the Persians, who released all the Jews from captivity. This was the time of Zerubbabel and Joshua the great priest of Jehozadak, when the captives returned with Ezra and Nehemiah. They erected the temple and they reinstated the city.[11] Other historical events are clearly indicated through a literal reading of the passage at hand. Let us consider, for example, the phrase *what remains of Israel and those of Jacob who have been saved*. For they,[12] he says, no longer trust in those who have wronged them, although they did so during the time of Ahaz the king. For it is written in Kings: "Ahaz sent messengers to the king of Assyria, saying, 'I am your servant and your son. Come up, and rescue me from the hand of the king of Syria and from the hand of the king of Israel,

who are attacking me.' Ahaz also took the silver and gold that was found in the house of the Lord and in the treasures of the king's house, and sent a present to the king of Assyria. And the king of Assyria hearkened to him; the king of Assyria marched up against Damascus, and took it, carrying its people captive, and he killed Rezin."[13] **[77]** But he says, *no longer*, for those who return *will trust in God, the Holy One of Israel, in truth. And what remains of Jacob will hope in the mighty God*. But here, instead of *in the mighty God*, the Hebrew version preserves *El Gibbor*, which very name was one of the titles bestowed on the "child born to us," concerning whom it said: "and his name will be called Messenger of Great Counsel."[14] For there the Hebrew has *El Gibbor* among his names, and again the Hebrew mentions this name also in the text at hand about *what remains* of the people.

[10:22-23] And he continues on: *And if the people of Israel become like the sand of the sea, the remnant will be saved, for he is completing and cutting short a reckoning with righteousness, because the Lord will perform a shortened reckoning in the whole world*. Therefore, in the first place, this verse is speaking about those who were left behind, and who returned from the captivity. Then, second, the Word tentatively continues and says: *And if the people of Israel become like the sand of the sea, the remainder will be saved*. But after a pause he presents another sense. For the *sand of the sea* is innumerable, but it is useless for farming. Therefore, when he says that *the people of Israel* should disperse as a countless multitude and that it was useless for the production of fruit according to God, the Word is thus signifying that their multitude perished and that only *the remnant will be saved*, but *the remnant* is the unprofitable part of the nation that inhabited the land after the return

---

[11]There is a lacuna at this point in the text. [12]There is another lacuna at this point in the text. [13]2 Kings 16:7-9. [14]Is 9:6.

journey from Babylon until Roman times. For they were *the sand of the sea*, from which only *the remnant was preserved*, from whom his disciples, apostles and evangelists believed on the Christ of God.

And where he says *the Lord will perform a shortened reckoning in the whole world*, "the gospel" of the new covenant which was "preached" "in the whole world"[15] is clearly implied. And *the evangelical word was shortened* in that it was not contained in the precepts of Moses. And the apostle cited the words discussed above as follows: "And Isaiah cries out concerning Israel: 'Though the number of the sons of Israel be as the sand of the sea, only a remnant of them will be saved; for the Lord will execute his sentence on the earth with rigor and dispatch. And as Isaiah predicted, 'If the Lord of hosts had not left us children, we would have fared like Sodom and been made like Gomorrah.'"[16] One should know that the twelfth volume of Origen's exegesis of the prophet came up to this point.

[10:24-27] [78] The Word finished the prophecy concerning Judah and Jerusalem, and it was clearly indicated that those who were in Samaria and Israel would suffer a fate similar to those who were delivered over to the ruler of the Assyrians in the Assyrian siege.[17] And these things were to come afterwards in far distant times, when, as we said above, they would live holy lives. But for the present, Isaiah the prophet made the attack known to Hezekiah the king and the inhabitants of Jerusalem. And they grew desperate when they heard the prophet's words because they did not want to suffer the same things as those who dwelled in Samaria. He exhorts them not to fear the Assyrians. For, although he says that the king of the Assyrians will come and wage war against Jerusalem and that for a short time those dwelling in it will be stricken with a test

as though they were hit with a *rod*, the king's attack will be ineffectual and he will turn in flight. And these things were fulfilled while Hezekiah the son of Ahaz reigned in Jerusalem. Hezekiah was a man very different from his father, for he was righteous in all his ways and God-loving. For this reason the Lord says concerning those things which were revealed: *O my people, who live in Zion, do not be afraid of the Assyrians*. For even if the king of the Assyrians should turn on me and attack me, nevertheless he will visit you with a *rod and strike you*, but neither with swords nor with battle spears, but after arresting you with the law, he will attack you. And this *stroke* of a rod that will come against you will be contrary to the law. *For yet a little while and the anger will cease.* And no one knows the reason why the Assyrians having been spared, were allowed to be *a stroke* against you. For you were *on the way toward Egypt* because you again surrendered yourself and devoted yourself to idolatry during the time of Ahaz. And because of this I have delivered you to the *rod* of the Assyrians, in order to teach you discipline and correction. But *my anger will not cease* as such until you, together with your king Hezekiah, change and acknowledge God and the superiority of his way. This is when my vexation against you *will cease*, and when I shield you and am your salvation, Assyria will flee in shame through your land and through your cities, running away from place to place. But instead of *for I bring a stroke on you so that you may see the way of Egypt*, Symmachus says: *I will strike you with a rod, and I will raise his staff against you on account of the way of Egypt*.

For Assyria will do these things to you *on account of the way of Egypt*, and he says, after traveling this way, *God will stir up for him a scourge like the stroke of Madiam* at the place of affliction. But instead of this, Symmachus translates the verse in this manner: *And the*

---

[15]Mt 24:14. [16]Rom 9:27-29 RSV. [17]A series of lacunae obscure the meaning of this sentence and the next three following.

Lord will arouse on him the scourge of powers like the stroke of Madiam in Shur-Oreb. And the story about Moses is found in the book of Numbers, at which point in time "The Lord called to Moses, saying, 'Avenge the **[79]** people of Israel on the Midianites,'" and next Moses spoke to the people: "Arm your men for war, and draw up in battle before the Lord to execute the Lord's vengeance on Midian, a thousand from each tribe."[18] Then "he slew every male and the kings of Midian,"[19] among whom was "Balaam the son of Beor."[20] And this happened in *Shur-Oreb*. For the desert was called *Shur*, as the Scripture informs us when it says: "Then Moses led the children of Israel onward from the Red Sea, and he led them into the wilderness of Shur,"[21] and the mountain was called Horeb. For it has been written: "And the Lord said to Moses, 'Pass on before the people. Take in your hand the rod with which you struck the Nile, and go. Behold, I will stand before you there on the rock at Horeb.'"[22] Therefore, then, they brought the *plague* on themselves in *Madiam*, and he says: thus I will do to the Assyrians, and those who strike with my *scourge* will turn into *the way of the sea. And the yoke of Assyria will be taken away from your shoulder, and the fear of him from you.*

[10:28-31] And you will be free, having been delivered from all *fear*. And he who formerly fled *will come to the city of Aggai*; then from there *he will pass on* to another place, and after becoming quite weary, *he will put away his baggage*. He will then cross over from there to somewhere else, and from that somewhere else into the *city* called *Saoul*, then into yet another place, and thus he will disappear in shame.

[10:32] And you will be encouraged and will finally find relief, no longer being under the yoke of Assyria. Therefore, those who are able are commanded to *encourage* you and to *summon* you from there to do this now. For, he says, *Encourage her today to remain in the way; O mount, as well as you hills that are in Jerusalem, with your hand encourage the daughter of Zion*. For because she was not to flee but *remain* and stand firm in the face of the chastisement that was soon to come, he says *encourage the daughter of Zion*, clearly referring to the inhabitants of Jerusalem. And he is careful to include the word *today*. For the things previously discussed concerning the ruler of the Assyrians, he was referring to the far distant time of Nebuchadnezzar, but the present things were spoken about *today*, about the things during the lifetime of the prophet Isaiah. Therefore he says: *encourage her today to remain in the way*. *Encourage* the people not to flee now, *today*, during the Assyrian attack on King Hezekiah so that he *remains* and learns not to flee. And now Assyria too, once it has stopped its assault, will suffer such things. And he commands certain people to *encourage* Jerusalem, adding next: *as well as you hills that are in Jerusalem*. For he enjoins those who have risen above and who have been raised in soul and mind according to God to *encourage* the people. For probably the stroke from God that inflicted the Assyrians was the plague that caused "one hundred and **[80]** eighty-five thousand"[23] to fall in one night. And those who survived with the king himself ran in flight through the cities, villages and places previously mentioned in the prophecy. And so while fleeing, Assyria went about *by the way of the sea, on the way toward Egypt*,[24] and history informs us that the Ethiopians rose up against him. At this point the prophecy spoken concerning Assyria comes to an end, and the next statements concern God and represent a new section.

[10:33-34] The Word repeatedly mentioned the Assyrians, those who had ruled them, and

---

[18]Num 31:3-4. [19]Num 31:7-8. [20]Num 31:8. [21]Ex 15:22. [22]Ex 17:5-6. [23]Cf. Is 37:36. [24]Is 10:26.

he high-minded among them. Now he describes in detail the downfall of the ruler, a downfall which had been revealed through what was discussed above concerning the government of the nation. And there were at that time governors of districts and governors of peoples and kings of nations, such as Egypt, Arabia, Tyre, Sidon, and the other nations. They were idolaters and insulted God, thinking inflated thoughts of themselves as exalted and high. For this very reason, then, after the aforementioned pronouncements concerning the downfall of the Assyrians, he prophesies also concerning these very governors, foretelling their absolute destruction when he said: *For behold, the Sovereign, the Lord, will mightily confound the glorious ones, and the lofty will be crushed in their insolence, and the lofty will be brought low in their insolence*, and so on and so forth. Then, after the time had arrived when these things were to happen, the appearance of Christ among people came at precisely the right time. Through the things discussed above, he informed us in advance about his virgin birth and the way it would come about. And his worthy names were announced beforehand to those who then reflected on his wonders, as to those who now do so, from what race and what tribe he would arrive, and how he would appear. And in the same way he also indicates the downfall of the restored government, as well as the downfall of other governments that had once reigned over every nation, ruling through both provincial and imperial governments. Their leaders had ruled among the Jews and the nation in general and the invisible powers and evil spirits and demons, and they prevailed over the error of polytheism which has existed in all nations since ancient times. Then the Word threatens that the destruction of all these governments will come with the theophany of the Savior: *For behold, the Sovereign, the Lord of hosts, will mightily confound the glorious ones, and the lofty will be brought low in their insolence, and the lofty will fall by dagger, and Lebanon will fall with its lofty ones.* You see that he speaks of the *lofty ones* very frequently and with various expressions. Their community was in *Lebanon*, and thus he compares the most lofty among them to cedar trees. Therefore, it has been said elsewhere: "I have seen a wicked man towering like the cedars of Lebanon,"[25] and again, in another place: "The voice of the Lord breaks the cedars, and the Lord will break **[81]** the cedars of Lebanon. He will make them small, *even Lebanon*, as a calf."[26] Accordingly, the Word first announces that *the Lord of hosts* will do this, and I say that he will break all human forms of government, whether national or imperial. And since in many places in the Holy Scriptures Jerusalem is referred to as *Lebanon*, as we often pointed out, it would be reasonable to suppose that he indicates the fall of Jerusalem and the fall of the rulers of the Jewish nation, who once possessed such power, when he says: *And Lebanon will fall with its lofty ones.*

[11:1] And how the ruin and fall of all of these will occur he presents next when he prophesies: *From the root of Jesse a rod shall appear*, which *will bring low* and break all those who were shown to be *lofty*. Thus the following is appended: *And a rod will come out of the root of Jesse.* But instead of *from the root*, the other Greek versions unanimously translate the phrase *from the stump.* For there was the tribe and there was also the fatherland from which the Savior came. The fatherland was as a *stump* which no longer had branches since the abandonment of the kings of the Davidic succession after the Babylonian captivity. For this reason, it seems to me that the race of David according to the flesh is called the *stump*, and David's father was Jesse. But lest

---

[25]Ps 37:35. [26]Ps 29:5-6.

someone assume that the prophesied king would be like David, he did not say *from the root* of David but of Jesse, because he would resemble Jesse in his respectable way of life. For *Jesse* was poor and in a position of no authority according to the world. Therefore, the text aptly says *from his root*, or, as Aquila says, *a little rod will come out from* an old *stump*. He rendered it as *little rod*, thus presenting the humble estate of our Savior according to the flesh. And likewise he uses the terms *branch* and *shoot* for the same reason. But instead of *and a blossom shall come up out of his root*, Aquila writes: *and a branch will grow from his root*; and Symmachus: *and a shoot will grow from his root*.

[11:2-3a] Therefore the *little rod* or the *branch* or the *shoot*, perceived according to the flesh, was our Savior the man. But it is clear from the statements adduced next that God the Word indwelled him, for the text says: *And the Spirit of God shall rest on him, the spirit of wisdom and understanding, the spirit of counsel and might, the spirit of knowledge and godliness, and the spirit of the fear of God will fill him.* For in these things "the whole fullness of deity"[1] of the only-begotten God is signified, concerning whom the Evangelists say: "from his fullness have we all received,"[2] and the apostle: "For in him all the fullness of deity was pleased to dwell bodily."[3] For from among the remaining prophets "each has received his own special gift from God,"[4] and likewise each one of the apostles has been allotted a share "from the fullness."[5] But he was where "the whole fullness of the deity"[6] dwelled, from which no human has ever been able to [82] *come out* except the prophesied *rod from the root of Jesse.* In him the *Spirit* of God dwelled, and it is concerning him that the apostle said: "Now the Lord is the Spirit,"[7] *the spirit of wisdom and*

understanding. And "wisdom" is what proceeds from the *Word* of God, "through whom all things were made."[8] "For he made all things in wisdom,"[9] and "God *by wisdom* founded the earth,"[10] and according to the apostle: "Christ, the power of God and the wisdom of God."[11] And so *the spirit of wisdom* was on him whose advent had been prophesied neither for an hour nor for a day nor for any brief period, but *the spirit of wisdom rested on him* as on the literal temple. This was the *spirit of counsel and might.* Therefore, as discussed above, he was called the "Messenger of Great Counsel"[12] and "Christ, the power of God and the wisdom of God."[13] But the same spirit is also referred to as *the spirit of knowledge and godliness; the spirit of the fear of God.* One is not to understand these many spirits as entities separate from one another. Rather, just as we understand the same word of God to be "light"[14] and "life and resurrection"[15] and a myriad of other things according to one's reflections on him, so also should we understand *the spirit of wisdom and understanding and counsel and might and knowledge and godliness and of the fear of God.* One should understand all these titles as referring to the one and the same Word who proceeds from God and who *rested* on him who descended *from the root of Jesse* and "from David according to the flesh."[16]

[11:3b-4] Therefore, he then addresses the interwoven existence of the unique Son of God, who assumed the existence of a son of man, demonstrated here in this text, and who experienced the realities of human existence and lived his life as a member of the human race. He then writes: *He shall not judge on the basis of reputation or convict on the basis of report, but he shall administer justice to a humble one and convict the humble ones of the earth.* Symmachus translates this verse some-

---

Chapter Eleven [1]Col 2:9. [2]Jn 1:16. [3]Col 1:19; 2:9. [4]1 Cor 7:7. [5]Jn 1:16. [6]Col 2:9. [7]2 Cor 3:17 RSV. [8]Jn 1:3. [9]Ps 104:24. [10]Prov 3:19. [11]1 Cor 1:24. [12]Is 9:6. [13]1 Cor 1:24. [14]Cf. Jn 1:4. [15]Jn 11:25. [16]Rom 1:3 RSV.

what more clearly: *He shall neither judge by what he sees nor shall he convict by what he hears, but he shall judge the laborers in righteousness and convict the poor of the earth in uprightness.* And one finds in the Gospels that our Savior and Lord *did not judge on the basis of reputation.* "Showing no partiality to anyone,"[17] he once fearlessly convicted the scribes and Pharisees and the rulers within the temple precincts, and he said to them: "The kingdom of God will be taken away from you and given to a nation producing the fruits of it."[18] And he did not convict on the basis of report. For indeed they approached him and said: "Teacher, we know that you are true, and teach the way of God truthfully, and care for no man; for you do not regard the position of men."[19] But he *did not convict on the basis of their report.* For this reason "Jesus, aware of their malice, answered, 'Why put me to the test, you hypocrites?'"[20] And **[83]** *he administered the justice of the humble,* and *he convicted the humble of the earth* or, in Symmachus's version, *he convicted the poor* in uprightness. The poor, we presume, are those whom he congratulated when he said: "Blessed are the poor in spirit, for theirs is the kingdom of God."[21] Such were his apostles and disciples, whom he refuted and once said even to them: "Are you also still without understanding?"[22] and again: "Do you not yet perceive or understand?"[23] and once he said to Peter: "O man of little faith, why did you doubt?"[24] And we see that he rebuked and refuted them in an abundance of other passages, and knowing this in advance, the prophecy foretells the above.

Then he adds next: *He shall strike the earth with the word of his mouth, and with breath—through his lips he shall do away with the impious.* And you will understand this after you hear what he said next: "Do not think that I have come to bring peace on earth; I have not come to bring peace, but a sword."[25] And the "sword" was *the word of his mouth, by which* he was doing away with *the earth* and the earthly mindedness of those who have believed in him. *And by his spirit*[26] *he shall do away with the impious,* "rebuking"[27] the godless and impious demons and driving them far away by the word borne through his lips, so that they cried and said: "What have you to do with us, Jesus, Son of God? Have you come to torment us before the time? We know who you are—the holy One of God!"[28]

[11:5] *But he shall be girded with righteousness around the waist and bound with truth around his sides.* Symmachus translates this rather: *and righteousness will be the girdle around his waist, and faith the girdle around his flanks.* And just as a king is girded with a golden belt and precious stones, so in the same manner as a belt, as prophesied, he divides *righteousness* and *truth.* From here we may understand that the text is speaking of the divinity of the Word. For he was righteousness, as the apostle informs us when he says: "Whom God made our wisdom, our righteousness and sanctification and redemption."[29] And it is recorded that in the Gospels the Savior himself said: "I am the light, and the *truth* and the life."[30] Therefore, *truth* and *righteousness* were bound around the *sides* and *waist* of him who was "from the root of Jesse"[31] in a royal and military fashion, displaying the inspired power of his word against unseen and invisible enemies. Through such metaphors as these, he portrays the prophesied one.

[11:6] He then delineates his achievements, informing us that through his grace and divine excellence, even the rapacious and greedy

[17]Gal 2:6. [18]Mt 21:43 RSV. [19]Mt 22:16 RSV. [20]Mt 22:18. [21]Mt 5:3. [22]Mt 15:16 RSV. [23]Mk 8:17 RSV. [24]Mt 14:31 RSV. [25]Mt 10:31 RSV. [26]The word for "breath" in Greek, as in Hebrew, is also the word for "spirit." Although this word is translated "breath" in the citation above, the context clearly demands that the term be translated "spirit" here. [27]Mt 17:18. [28]Mt 8:29. [29]1 Cor 1:30 RSV. [30]Jn 14:6. [31]Is 11:1.

wolves among people [84] will turn from their depravity, and their souls will flock together as tame and meek lambs in one church. But other people, savage and completely wild, who are no different at all from *leopards*, putting away their beastly dread, *they shall rest with the kids and together with* the simple and pure. And others, whose dispositions could have been likened to *lions*, abandoned their savage-hearted and flesh-eating ways, and *they shall graze* together with the newborn in the church as *calves and bulls*, and they shall partake of the same nourishment of the divine Scriptures. And if one should look inside the church of God, where noble people who have been decorated with worldly honors and awards are gathered together with the poor and the commoners, he would not hesitate to say that the Scripture has been fulfilled which said *the lions will graze with the calves*. And along with all those who were referred to as *wolves* and *lambs* and *leopards*, he says that *a little child will lead* the *kids* and the *lions* and the *calves* and *bulls*. The text reads *he will lead* instead of *he will gather together*.[32] And we are to understand that those in the church of Christ who possess deeper insight than politicians because of their simplicity of soul and guilelessness in reality are not all that different from infants.[33] Nevertheless, these infants govern those gathered together from every race.

[11:7] And he says: *and the ox and the bear shall graze together, and their young shall be together*. Here the text is speaking about the offspring of reserved and amiable people who are suited for the cultivation of the soul and of people of a different sort who are wild in their dispositions. He describes their fellowship in the same way, and when you see the well-behaved children of the rich and poor, of the bad

and good, you will testify to the truth of the prophecy which says: *and their young shall be together*. And though the *lion* is carnivorous by nature, he shall be nourished with *husks* as a herbivorous animal. So too there are savage and coarse people who understand only the literal interpretation of the graces of the divine Scripture. The divine Scripture is the nourishing word of souls, but its secrets escape the notice of our minds, for the meaning is surrounded by a *husk*.

[11:8-9] Now concerning the *young child*, who was mentioned a little earlier, the text says: *he shall put his hand over the hole of asps*, and it says that he will not be hurt. *Holes* and also *nests of asps* and their offspring are perhaps the bodies of those who are vexed by demons, whom the lurking, slithering and venomous spirits infest. The demons inhabit the faculties of their bodies as *holes*. These are the *young children* of Christ, who although he was absolutely human still was "an infant in regard to evil."[34] They drive away demons in the power of the Savior, for he laid [85] his *hand* on them and now nothing is able *to hurt* them, since the one proceeding "from the root of Jesse"[35] "gave authority"[36] to his children "to tread upon serpents and scorpions, and over all the power of the enemy."[37] He proclaims that all these will be *on his holy mountain*. And what has been revealed above is none other than the heavenly and evangelical word, on which "the house of God"[38] and "his church is built."[39] And, therefore, lest anyone assume that the *holy mountain* spoken of here is that which is among the Jews in a corner of Palestine, he makes his meaning perfectly clear when he adds next: *because the whole earth has been filled to know the Lord like much water to cover the seas*. He thus signifies the church of

---

[32]Eusebius here notes that the text reads ἄξει rather than the related compound verb συνάξει. [33]Perhaps Eusebius recalls the ancient tradition, transmitted by Papias, that in the earliest church, "child" was a complimentary term, reflecting the guilelessness of the person so named. [34]1 Cor 14:20. [35]Is 11:1. [36]Lk 10:19. [37]Lk 10:19 RSV. [38]Cf. Is 2:2. [39]Mt 16:18.

God, which has been established throughout the whole world, and the righteous knowledge which is preached in it, which exposes the bitterness of evil living, flooding the soul with many rivers and cleansing it of all sordidness.

11:10] And *there shall be on that day* clearly indicates that it will be during the prophesied time that this one who *shall be raised* "from the root of Jesse"[40] himself *shall arise*, clearly indicating the resurrection from the dead, after which the "rulers and leaders of the nations"[41] *and nations shall hope in him*. For the king will not be from the Jews, as David and his successors were. But he will conquer Israel's narrow quarters, and he will rule everywhere on the earth. And nations shall hope in him, thus fulfilling the prophecy which was spoken by Moses: "A ruler shall not be wanting from Judah and a leader from his thighs, until the things stored up for him come, and he is the expectation of nations."[42] And he brings the verse to a conclusion by saying: *and his rest shall be honor*, or, in the very apt phrase of Aquila and Symmachus: *and his rest shall be glory*. For after informing us about his first advent and birth among people and about everything in between until such an end as will be, he states: *and his rest shall be glory*. Not even mentioning his death, he speaks of his *rest* as *glory* and *honor*. For that was the end of our Savior's dispensation among people. Our Savior himself proved this when he said in the prayer to his Father: "Father, glorify me with the *glory* which I had with you before the world was made."[43]

The one who would proceed "from the root of Jesse"[44] was none other than Christ, and the children of the Jews themselves confess that this is so when they say that the prophecy discussed above is clearly about the expected and anointed one who would come among them. But now, even after a thousand [86]

years have passed from the time of the prophet Isaiah and the time of Christ to us, they maintain that the prophecy still has not happened. They are forever reflecting, but their theories have run aground, and they so extend the timeframe of the prophecy in order to discredit it as untrue. They rob themselves of the hope of the prophecies. Futhermore, they try to interpret the sense of the prophetic sayings, as the apostle says, "without understanding either what they are saying or the things about which they make assertions."[45] But in order that we might attain what was discussed above, he then prophesied that *the one who is raised from the root of Jesse shall rule the nations*. And he adds: *nations shall hope in him*. He is certainly remembering the Jewish faction in what was discussed above, and he does not assume that anything prophesied would benefit the people of the circumcision.

[11:11] Therefore he teaches that *on that day*, that is, in the time of the epiphany of the prophesied one, *the Lord will further display his hand to show zeal for the remnant that is left of the people*. But Aquila writes instead: *the Lord will apply his hand a second time to acquire the remainder of his people*; and Symmachus: *the Lord will apply his hand for the second time to show zeal for the remainder of his people*. For just as he once freed the Jewish people when they were "subdued in affliction"[46] in Egypt, displaying *his* wonder-working *hand* through Moses and doing incredible miracles in the land of the Egyptians, so in the same manner *he will again apply his hand for the second time* and perform incredible works in order to *acquire the remnant of the people* and to *bless them*. And again here also, when he says *the remainder* and the *survivors of the people*, he is speaking about what he addressed above when he said: "And if the Lord of hosts had not left us offspring, we would have become like

---

[40]Is 11:1. [41]Cf. Is 55:4. [42]Gen 49:10. [43]Jn 17:5. [44]Is 11:1. [45]1 Tim 1:7. [46]Ex 3:7.

Sodom and been made similar to Gomorrah."[47] And this "offspring" of the prophesied one is the apostles and disciples and evangelists, the "remnant chosen by grace"[48] from the entire diaspora of the Jewish people among all nations. For whether in the territory of the *Assyrians* or whether in *Egypt, Babylon, Ethiopia* or whether in the land of the Elamites, or whether in the rest of the world, there were certain of the Jewish nation who had been dispersed. He says that he will glorify and *bless*[49] those who have believed on the Christ of God and who are the "remnant chosen by grace."[50] And this has in fact been fulfilled through his disciples and apostles. And the church of God was composed of the rest of the Jews who had received [87] the word of Christ, and the calling of all nations was accomplished through them. For "the twelve apostles"[51] of our Savior were the first, and the "seventy disciples"[52] followed. Paul mentioned "brothers" to whom the Savior "appeared at one time"[53] after the resurrection and many other apostles.

Paul and Barnabas and Timothy and all the others were also of this band whom Paul called "his fellow workers and fellow soldiers."[54] The Acts of the Apostles also sets out their record and preserves the account that it was they "who were gathered together in one accord on the day of Pentecost"[55] "and after being filled with the Holy Spirit, they spoke" "in other tongues, as the Spirit gave them utterance."[56] It is also concerning them that the Scripture testifies when it says: "Now there were dwelling in Jerusalem Jews, devout men from every nation under heaven. And at this sound the multitude was gathered together, and they were bewildered, because each one heard them speaking in his own language. And they were amazed and wondered, saying, 'Are not all these Galileans? And how is it that we hear, each of us in his own native language? Parthians and Medes and Elamites and residents of Mesopotamia, Syria and Cappadocia, Pontus and Asia, Phrygia and Pamphylia, Egypt and the parts of Libya belonging to Cyrene, and visitors from Rome, both Jews and proselytes, Cretans and Arabians, we hear them telling the mighty works of God in our own tongues.'"[57] Then, those mentioned above "received the word" from Peter, elect among them, concerning the grace of the Savior and "were baptized, and there were added that day about three thousand souls."[58] And again, at another time, many of the Jews "believed, and the number of the men came to about five thousand."[59] And yet again the Scripture records what James said to Paul: "You see, brother, how many thousands of Jews have believed, and all of them are zealous for the law."[60] And the apostles and the first evangelists of the word preached among the rest of the Jewish people, and there were countless Jews from every nation who preached the Christ of God. And it was through them that the gospel was spread abroad to every nation "while God also bore witness among them by signs and wonders and various miracles and by distributions of the Holy Spirit."[61] God blessed them[62] and honored them in the presence of all those who received the word they proclaimed.

[11:12] And he says also that "the remnant chosen by grace"[63] *will raise a signal among the nations and* before all *he will gather the lost of Israel and the dispersed of Judah, those in the four corners of the earth.* For they received a command "to go" "to the *lost* [88] sheep of the house of *Israel.*"[64] This they did, preaching the

---

[47]Is 1:9. [48]Rom 11:5. [49]Eusebius's phrase here, ζηλωτοὺς ποιήσειν, is very close to the LXX, ζηλῶσαι ("to show zeal"). [50]Rom 11:5. [51]Mt 10:1. [52]Lk 10:1. [53]1 Cor 15:6. [54]Phil 2:25. [55]Acts 2:1. [56]Acts 2:4. [57]Acts 2:5-11. [58]Acts 2:41 RSV. [59]Acts 4:4. [60]Acts 21:20 RSV. [61]Heb 2:4. [62]Again Eusebius's language is a variation of the LXX, changing the meaning from "to show zeal" to "to bless." [63]Rom 11:5. [64]Mt 10:6.

gospel "freely" at first among "the sick whom they healed, the lepers they cleansed, and among those from whom they cast out demons."[65] They thus did what was commanded them to do: to preach "first"[66] to those from the circumcision, gathering those who believed from among them into the church of Christ, those who were formerly lost. This is precisely what the Savior taught his disciples to do when he said: "Go to the *lost* sheep of the house of Israel."[67] These things they did *in the four corners of the earth*, penetrating the east and west and north and south. "They communicated the evangelical word first" to them, and then they preached "to all the other nations."[68] For this reason the text says: *and he will gather the lost of Israel and the dispersed of Judah.* And who *will gather the lost of Israel* except the apostolic band and him whom they preach, he who is "from the root of Jesse"[69] and in whom God the Word dwells? Then they were *gathered* into one church, no longer divided or separated from one another as before.

11:13] For the tribe of *Ephraim* and the peoples they ruled in Samaria lived separately from the tribe of *Judah* and those who dwelled in Jerusalem. Therefore he says that *the jealousy of Ephraim shall be taken away* from their midst, so that no longer *shall Ephraim be jealous of Judah or Judah of Ephraim.* This in fact transpired during the time of the prophecy, as has been made clear through what was discussed above.

11:14] He next says about them: *But they shall fly away in ships of foreigners; together they shall plunder the sea.* For it was entirely appropriate to state that they who travel through the nations should journey through *sea*, since they *rushed* with speed and finishing the course through the *sea*, so that in a short time they had preached the gospel to many nations. Some-

times they traveled over land by foot; sometimes through the *sea*, not proclaiming the gospel to the Jewish helmsmen but to those who received the word of Christ. And in the same way *they were plundering the sea*; this means the islands which received the word. Landing on these islands, they committed themselves to the saving teaching. And you can know the full completion of the word from a single example: Paul the apostle was one of those who were prophesied. He journeyed around the Roman Empire by sea and came down "to the island of Malta,"[70] where he performed an awesome miracle before the natives. He healed the bodies of the sick and astounded those who looked on, and so he *plundered* and carried away many by the saving teaching. Therefore the text says: *But they shall fly away* **[89]** *in ships of allophyles;*[71] *together they shall plunder the sea and those from the rising of the sun.* Therefore it says that the disciples of Christ *shall also plunder those from the rising of the sun.* And so it is reported that certain of them traveled as far as the countries of Persia and India.

And later, during the time of the prophet, it seemed that the *Edomites* and Ammonites and *Moabites* and these Arabic nations around Judea would take up weapons of war against the Jews because of their absurd idolatry, although these same Jews were still precious to God. The Word was justified in mentioning these nations by name, since they too would receive the fear of God that was about to be preached by the apostles. Therefore he says that *they shall lay their hands on Edom and on Moab*, and he prophesies that *the sons of Ammon shall obey* the preaching. These nations are composed of those who live in Arabia, and they used to be extremely superstitious, but now they have received the word of Christ. And so, although it seemed incredible, he prophesied that those who were hostile and

---

[65]Mt 10:8. [66]Acts 13:46. [67]Mt 10:6. [68]Acts 13:46. [69]Cf. Is 11:1. [70]Acts 28:1. [71]"Foreigners," a common translation of the Hebrew word for Philistines.

opposed to the Jewish service of God would one day submit to the preaching of the gospel. And he says in Symmachus's version: *Edom and Moab will extend their hand.* This was in fact fulfilled when the disciples of our Savior stretched out their *hands* to those who dwelled in Arabia and accomplished the deeds that they did. It was prophesied that God would fill these cities with churches when it was said: *And they shall first lay their hands on Moab,* and again: *But the sons of Ammon shall obey first.* It is necessary to note that only the Septuagint and neither the Hebrew version nor the other Greek translations provides the additional word that they *will obey first.* The grace of Christ that was proclaimed by the apostles will be extended also to them.

[11:15] The three Greek versions unanimously translate the next verse as follows: *And the Lord will curse the tongue of the sea of the Egyptians.* The Word is accustomed to calling the multitude of ungodly people "the sea," for the sea is full of evil salt water. He says that the Lord *will curse,* so that that they might no longer confess with the *tongue* the superstitious error in Egypt and instead learn "to speak" the sayings of God and "to swear by the name of the Lord."[72] It is important to understand that when in the above discussions the word mentions our Savior, it is Jesus who is being identified. In the Hebrew version the text reads: "Behold, God is my Savior; I will trust in him."[73] The Hebrew word underlying the translation "my Savior" is Jeshuathi;[74] and again, in the phrase "out of the springs of salvation,"[75] where the Greek reads "of salvation," the Hebrew is Jeshua. Thus the word did not delay in mentioning the *Edomites* and the *Moabites* and the *sons of Ammon* among the above names, [90] for they were the most superstitious nations, and they were hostile

and opposed to the God of the prophets. And yet, incredible though it may be, he prophesies that these very nations will receive the doctrine of Christ. In the same manner, he also speaks propitiously of the idolatry of the Egyptians, for it will indeed be abolished at the revealed time. But the present word does not concern the Egyptians. For the prophecy concerning the Egyptians is spelled out in the familiar oracle which commences: "A vision concerning Egypt," from which "there is a remnant, chosen by grace."[76] He prophesies these things when he teaches that after the entrance into humanity of the one who proceeded "from the root of Jesse,"[77] those who received this one would be a "remnant, chosen by grace."[78] It is they who will fill Israel as well as the other nations and the land of the Egyptians with the doctrine of Christ, and no one will stand in their way.

And we already observed in the preface to this commentary that sometimes the prophetic message is to be rendered literally and not allegorically, and sometimes, when the people are unwilling to listen, the spirit is forced to express the prophecy as an allegory. Therefore, the Word was forced to speak figuratively about "the rod from the root of Jesse"[79] and "the blossom" and "the stump," but now the Word is no longer obliged to speak allegorically about the righteous Jesse. So too, the statements about the beasts were really figurative statements about people who behaved like beasts, but now the nations whom they were said to rule are no longer depicted allegorically. Thus, one should affirm that among these the land of *Egypt* means the literal country of the Egyptians, but at the same time, the *sea* and *river* are allegorical expressions, in as far as he says that they will be *laid waste* at the prophesied time, when it is said that "the Lord will further display his hand."[80] In the

---

[72]Cf. Is 19:18. [73]Is 12:2. [74]This is the Hebrew word from which the Greek name Jesus is derived. [75]Is 12:3. [76]Rom 11:5 RSV. [77]Is 11:1. [78]Rom 11:5. [79]Is 11:1. [80]Cf. Is 11:11.

ddition, it is clear that others who are very imilar to them in the deeds practiced among hem will be born afterwards, from among vhom the *hand* of the Lord led out through Moses the children of Israel from the land of Egypt and led them through the Red *Sea*. He ed them "into the land of promise"[81] which formerly had been occupied by other peoples. Now, in the one "from the root of Jesse,"[82] the same *hand* of the Lord supplements the good hings provided in the apostles of the Savior and in the Jews who were preachers of the saving gospel. And from people who were expected to be agitators he created zealots who stood unhindered against the whole world, even against Egypt itself, and no one stood in heir way. They went down to destroy the idols of the Egyptians. Those who fled from Pharaoh and the Egyptians came out with Moses, but the disciples of Christ entered into Egypt voluntarily, preaching the saving word. And the sea was literally divided before those who were with Moses, and the water of the Nile changed into blood. But there were additional good hings that were revealed as having occurred at that time: the Egyptian sea was made into a desert, **[91]** and their river was utterly abandoned, both of which were impediments to the preachers of the saving gospel, who could now traverse the lands of the Egyptians and indeed effect the overthrow of their superstitious polytheism. And the one preceding "from the root of Jesse"[83] gave the knowledge of God and of his Christ to all. One should note that the text says that *the Lord will make* not the land of Egypt *desolate* but its *sea*, and this clearly refers to its many idolatries.

As the undesirable catches are cast back into the sea, is it not, therefore, appropriate to say that the tongue of godless and profane people who once did not know God is revealed to be that of Pharaoh, who said: "I do not know the Lord, and I will not let Israel go"?[84]

The word prophesied what happened next. And thus *the tongue of the sea* of Egypt *was accursed*, so that those demons among it who once cried out oracles and divinations would be silent, and so that their fraudulent art of groaning through people would be undone. All these things were in fact fulfilled when the evangelical preaching was proclaimed to them in Egypt. And from among them and also among us ourselves, the all-powerful extinguished those who were supposed to be gods by the Egyptians and all the godless and irreligious people throughout the whole world who acted like the Egyptians in their idolatry. Then the sea, rising like a flood and covered with waves, enveloped the last desert. The text says that the Lord *will make the sea of Egypt desolate*, that is, their many idolatries. And not only *will he make the sea desolate*, but also *he will lay his hand on* its *River*, the Nile, which had always been associated with the kingdom of the Egyptians. It is thus clear that the *violent wind* should be understood to be the Roman ruler who earlier conquered the kingdom of the Egyptians. Therefore it has been undone, for the *river* was *struck*, sunk into deep gorges, transformed into *seven gullies*. One will understand this verse only when he perceives its deeper meaning. The *River* which was once a mighty current is the kingdom of Egypt, for it predominated over all nations in that area. But after it was *struck* and undone, certain regional rulers governed it for a time. For indeed the Libyans administered a part, and the Thebans a territory belonging to Egypt and Alexandria itself. And on the one hand, there were regions that were honored with political independence, where the governance was entrusted to the common people and citizens. But on the other hand, there were regions that were governed by soldiers and military forces, and these regions were administered by the great authority of the revealed

---

[81]Cf. Heb 11:9. [82]Cf. Is 11:1. [83]Cf. Is 11:1. [84]Ex 5:2.

rulers. Thereupon, being of no consideration, the *gullies* were rightly disregarded, for in comparison with the *River* that once rose like a flood against them—I am speaking of the king—which all at once and with one current washed up on both sides [92] of the nation of Egypt, it washed up with one royal and predominant power over all. Thus the Egyptian *river* was *struck*, and the regional *gullies* were set in its place in order that the rest of Egypt might be covered over with those who preach the gospel of Christ, no one standing in their way and no one hindering them.[85]

[11:16] Therefore, the Egyptian kingdom was no longer associated with demonic activity, for it was extinguished at the season when the evangelical preaching was announced among them, as the word says: *And there shall be a passage for what is left of my people in Egypt*, but he says, *it shall be for Israel as the day when they came out of the land of Egypt*. The people of Moses crossed the Red Sea on foot "on dry ground,"[86] and then after the passage, "They sang this song, saying, 'I will sing to the Lord, for he has triumphed gloriously.'"[87] In the same manner, the Evangelists of our Savior who were prophesied to come, those who were the remnant from the entirety of the Jewish nation, they finished the course unhindered and ran through the whole land of the Egyptians, preaching the gospel to the Jews in their synagogues. They arranged the conversion of the nations through the church of Christ, just as Moses taught those who were rescued to "sing a new song."[88]

[12:1-2] And this is what was foretold by the prophetic word, saying: *And you will say in that day: I will bless you, O Lord, for you were angry with me, and you turned away your wrath from me, and you had compassion on me. Behold, my*

God is my savior; I will trust in him and will be saved, and I will not be afraid, because the Lord is my glory and my praise, and he has become my salvation. Those who proclaimed the Christ of God were taught to say these things in the land of the Egyptians, so now the Egyptians themselves have received the Christ of God. For the aforementioned "river"[1] is no longer present among them, nor "the sea" that was formerly covered with waves. Therefore, the text says, *Behold, my God is my savior; I will trust in him, and I will not be afraid*, because there are no longer any who frighten them away or any who forbid them from serving God according to the word of Christ. And so the text says: *because he is my glory and my praise, and he has become my salvation*. And in the phrase *you were angry with me*, they present a confession of their former sins, because of which the Egyptians were worthy of the wrath of God before they received the call of salvation. And the phrase *you turned away your wrath, and you had compassion on me* speaks of the forgiveness of sins that was granted to them after the call. "For grace and truth came through Jesus Christ."[2] The release from bonds and the remission of sins was granted even to the Egyptians and to all who received the Son of God.

[12:3] [93] After these things, the text adds: *And with joy you will draw water out of the springs of salvation*. And again here one should understand the *water* and the *springs of salvation* allegorically. And you will understand these things when you hear what the Savior himself said: "If any one thirst, let him come to me and drink. He who believes in me, as the Scripture has said, 'Out of his heart shall flow rivers of living water.'"[3] Accordingly, the *springs of salvation* are the evangelical words which gush out from the Holy Spirit, just as the

---

[85]Eusebius would seem to be reflecting on Acts 28:31. [86]Ex 14:29. [87]Ex 15:1. [88]Ps 33:3. **Chapter Twelve** [1]Cf. Is 11:15. [2]Jn 1:17. [3]Jn 7:37-38 RSV.

prophetic words of Israel were called springs in the Scripture which says: "Bless God in the great congregation,[4] the LORD, O you who are of Israel's fountain!"[5] For it is prophesied that the Egyptians will drink *from the springs of the word of salvation* and those who served the cup *of salvation* to them.

[12:4-6] After the above, he continues on to say: *And you will say in that day: Sing hymns to the Lord; call his name out loud.* The phrase *you will say* speaks of the band of the evangelists of our Savior. And he says, *in that day* (clearly referring to the prophesied time) *you will say* (that is, the preacher of the saving gospel) to those among the Egyptians who received the message. *Sing hymns to the Lord; call his name out loud; declare his glorious deeds among the nations; remember them, because his name has been exalted.* For you (the apostolic band) *will say* these things, instructing those who become your "disciples,"[6] charging them not to keep silent but to go forth as a shout audible to all of the saving work of grace. Then again he tells them to teach and say: *Sing hymns to the name of the Lord, for he has done exalted things; declare these things in all the earth.* After all these things, he says besides: *Be glad, and rejoice, O you who dwell in Zion, because the Holy One of Israel has been exalted in your midst.* But already the evangelical word had been delivered throughout the greater *Zion*, where the church of God was built. Therefore, since *the Holy One of Israel has been exalted in the midst* of his church, it is right that he says *be glad and rejoice, O you who dwell* in it and *you* who have *the Holy One of Israel* himself among you also. He dwells among his people according to the promise he made when he said: "For where two or three are gathered in my name, there am I in the midst of them."[7] And again it was declared in the name of the

prophetic spirit that *Zion* should *be glad* and *rejoice.* He charges those who dwelled in it with these words in order that he might lead them from the circumcision to tranquility. They think that these things are said concerning them, and they treat the book with respect, saying that it deserves glory because it always prophesies elegant things about them.

[13:1] [94] After the Word brings to a close the prophecy concerning the one who proceeded "from the root of Jesse"[1] and after prophesying about all the things that happen at the coming of Christ, he commences another theme: *against Babylon.* He then lays out a second theme: "concerning the Philistines,"[2] whom the Scripture is accustomed to calling Palestinians. Then comes a third one, "the word against Moab,"[3] and then "the word against Damascus."[4] After these comes "a vision concerning Egypt."[5] Then comes, sixth, "the vision of the wilderness,"[6] and then "the vision concerning Edom,"[7] and afterwards, "the oracle in Arabia,"[8] which is succeeded by "the vision concerning the ravine of Zion"[9] and at last "the vision of Tyre."[10] Thus, these ten prophecies should be read as a whole and all concern the nations of other tribes, among which "the ravine of Zion"[11] is also included, for the prophet catalogued the Jewish people with the other nations. And the knowledge of Christ and of the promise of good things was preached to them. He preaches the word concerning the judgment of God to all universally, persuading all to live in the fear of God, remembering the place where God judges. It was necessary that he deliver the prophecies concerning these ones as well to the Jews in order that, from the foretelling of events that were about to happen and from the outcome of the predictions, they might be persuaded that "it was truly God who spoke to them through

---

This Greek word could also be translated "churches." [5]Ps 68:26 RSV. [6]Mt 28:19. [7]Mt 18:20 RSV. **Chapter Thirteen** [1]Cf. Is 11:1. This section runs from Is 14:28-32. [3]Is 15:1. [4]Is 17:1. [5]Is 19:1. [6]Is 21:1. [7]Is 21:11. [8]Is 21:13. [9]Is 22:1. [10]Is 23:1. [11]Cf. Is 22:1.

the prophets"[12] and that it was he who provided them with their foreknowledge and that he advised what was advantageous.

First, therefore, he sets out the *vision against Babylon*. He said before at the beginning of the whole book that it was "a vision against Judea and against Jerusalem,"[13] for as we read later: "God shows no partiality."[14] He began with their houses, and he will direct the word again to them. He places Babylon with the nations of other tribes, and this royal city was the largest and most powerful city of the Assyrians.[15] The Assyrians first are said to have prevailed over the world for a period of one thousand three hundred years until those who besieged Jerusalem led the Jewish people into captivity in their own land. For in this act of the Assyrians, their strength was destroyed all at once and not over a period of time. And continuing the above discussion, it was indicated in advance that the Assyrians would take Israel and Samaria. And since Jerusalem was about to experience a siege that was similar to the one against Samaria, he prophesied the end of Jerusalem as well. He described in detail how the Assyrians themselves would prevail and become their rulers. He now teaches what concerns the royal city which had always been present among them, but not so that the Babylonians themselves might learn about the things that would happen among them. Rather, I expect that the prophecy is for those who were not present and yet [95] received it as of utmost importance, so that they might know the coming righteous judgment of God on all humanity, so that they might have consolation during all that would happen to them and so that the Word would be vindicated. The Word is about to make a threat specifically *against Babylon*, but we are to understand that the prophecy is published generally concerning the judgment of God, as

concerning God's place of judgment against all those who rule profanely and arrogantly over the whole world. And after this general teaching he passes on to the specific threat *concerning Babylon*.

[13:2-3] *On a mountain in the plain raise a signal; raise up your voice to them; encourage them with your hand; open, you rulers. It is I who instruct, and lead them. Mighty ones come to fulfill my wrath, at the same time rejoicing and reviling.* These things are cited in the prophecy by the divine Spirit from the Word from the mouth of God. It is he who commands the angels around him *to open* the closed doors; he who commands those who are within to advance, to hurry, to come to the aid of the godly. And I suppose that these statements make it clear that the land under discussion was divided by opposing political powers, just as conquerors place into prison those they have overpowered. And is it possible that this is what is called "the abyss," which the Word teaches is full of "dragons" when it says: "dragons and ocean depths"?[16] Wherefore also the demons "begged"[17] the Savior not to send them "into the abyss," saying: "Have you come to torment us before the time?"[18] For they were not ignorant that the time would come when they would be locked up "in the abyss."[19] Therefore, the *mighty ones* are either the personification of opposing political powers or the "angels" who came down from heaven, from whom "the giants were born."[20] The Scripture of Moses mentions them when it says: "the sons of God saw that the daughters of men were fair; and they took to wife such of them as they chose."[21] Then it says that "those born"[22] from them were "those who were named *giants* forever." Whether these are the souls of those beings, or whether they are the spirits of those who have begotten them or

---

[12]Heb 1:1. [13]Is 1:1. [14]Rom 2:11 RSV. [15]Herodotus also refers to Babylon as a city of Assyria in his *History of the Persian Wars* 1.178, as does Judith. [16]Ps 148:7. [17]Lk 8:31. [18]Mt 8:29. [19]Lk 8:31. [20]Bar 3:26; Gen 6:4. [21]Gen 6:2 RSV. [22]Gen 6:4; Bar 3:26.

whether they are other rebel powers, he has cast them forth from the heavenly realm into darkness and "chains,"[23] there to be held until delivered over during the time "of the judgment." When the universal judgment shall come to the place of God's judgment, the Christ of God will judge every race of humanity "after sitting down on his glorious throne,"[24] just as he taught: "He will send out his angels, and they will gather all nations with a loud trumpet call from one end of heaven to the other."[25] Indeed, he will bring about the resurrection of the dead and the judgment of all nations according to God's standards [96] through the angels who surround his throne. For it says: "He will send out his angels with a loud trumpet call, and they will gather his elect from the four winds, from one end of heaven to the other."[26] And he will lay out punishments for those who are to be punished, just as a judge at trial in a civil courtroom. Accordingly, in the above, he commands the angels at attention *to raise a signal on a mountain in the plain.* He calls this earth and every dwelling place for people a *mountain in a plain.* He commands them to produce and set up a *sign* of the coming judgment of God, but also *to raise up their voice,* calling to counsel those who are to be judged according to God's standards.

Then he says next: *Encourage them with your hand; open, you rulers.* But Symmachus says rather: *Move your hand and let the doors be opened.* For he had commanded the aforementioned powers to be cast into "outer darkness,"[27] where they had been shut out. Therefore he adds: *open the doors.* They could never *be opened* except by the one who stands as my judge and the ones served by your and my angels. They *opened* the *doors* at my signal; *raise up your voice to them.* They urge those who are called to hurry up. For it is *I who instruct, and I who lead them.* And who they

are, he clearly presents next when he says: *Mighty ones come to fulfill my wrath, at the same time rejoicing and reviling.* Theodotion translated this in alignment with the Septuagint when he said: *And I called my mighty ones.* Aquila and Symmachus have *powerful ones* instead of *mighty ones.* Thus, he will call the vengeful powers, through whom wrath will be administered against the ungodly. These are the ones who rejoice over another's misfortune, who are said to be *mighty* and who exact all that is vowed. They *rejoice* in *reviling* and punishing the ungodly; they have neither compassion nor kindness nor benevolence but are only cruel-hearted and inhuman. Therefore, although we grieve for those who are perishing, they *rejoice and revile.*

[13:4-5] Therefore, what he says next concerns the nations that will be judged: *A voice of many nations on the mountains like that of many nations! A voice of kings and of nations gathered together!* For nothing but the voices of those who are about to be delivered over to vengeance will escape, confessing their wickedness. And all nations and their *kings* will answer with one and the same voice, lamenting their miserable circumstances. He then reveals the cause of the cry from the *nations* and *kings* when he says: *The Lord of hosts, or the Lord of powers or the Lord of armies, has commanded a heavily armed nation to come from a distant land, from the utmost foundation of heaven—the Lord and his armed men—to destroy all the world.* [97] And those who were called *mighty ones* above are here described as *heavily armed,* who were long ago shut out *in the foundations of heaven,* whom the judge of all will summon when the time comes *to destroy all the world* of the wicked after the separation of the righteous. And so it is said in the Gospels: "when the Son of Man will sit on his glorious throne,"[28] he will first call those "on the

---

[23]2 Pet 2:4; Jude 6. [24]Mt 19:28. [25]Mt 24:31. [26]Mt 24:31 RSV. [27]Mt 8:12. [28]Mt 25:31.

right"[29] into "the kingdom prepared for them from the foundation of the world." After they are admitted and gathered into the promise, the threat "of fire"[30] will be carried out on the rest of the nations and those found on the left.

[13:6-8] The Word teaches that these things will happen in the day of judgment. He calls forth those who have not yet come to this day and those who are still present in this life, exhorting them that there is yet time to turn and bewail their wickedness and cry aloud. This is why he says: *Wail, graven images, for the day of the Lord is near and destruction will come from God!* For he does not say that what has been threatened has already been administered, but rather that such things have not yet occurred. Therefore, weep, lament and wail, and atone for your wickedness, for the aforementioned day of the wrath of God is about to arrive, in which *every hand will be weakened, and every human soul will be afraid, and the elders will be troubled, and pangs will seize them, as of a woman in labor. And they will bewail one to another and be amazed, and they will change their face like a flame.* Here he refers to those *elders* who stand up in public to speak for the cause of godlessness, those who supply leadership to the error of idolatry and those who teach atheistic and profane doctrines, on whom everything recounted earlier will descend. The color of each one's *face will change* as they are perplexed and overcome by an unexpected and dreadful fate.

[13:9-10] To this he adds: *For behold, the day of the Lord's fury comes, a day of wrath and anger, to make the whole world desolate and to destroy the sinners from it.* He says that during that time *the stars of heaven and Orion and all the ornament of heaven will not give light, and it will be dark when the sun rises.* For during the time of the consummation, neither *the sun* nor *the moon* nor *the stars will give* their *light* to the ungodly, to those who will be delivered over to retribution and vengeance. Those luminous bodies which turned from their own function to another will receive a better assignment. In the same way, those who attain regeneration will no longer be slaves to bodily futility but shall "be set free from the bondage to decay,"[31] according to the apostolic word.

[13:11] [98] In order that they might attain this glorious and highest rest over all of heaven and earth, the luminous bodies retired in darkness, and the ungodly were delivered over to suffer what had been prophesied. It was concerning them that it was said: *And I will command evils for the whole world, and for the impious, their own sins.* Therefore, all these things were spoken generally concerning the judgment which would come at the end of the world against the ungodly. It is therefore for all of these that the Word spoke of *the world* rather than Babylon. If our observation is correct, we may divide the meaning of the prophecy into the generic sense concerning the universal judgment and the specific sense concerning Babylon. Therefore, he made references to the prophecies concerning *the world* in a variety of ways. For he said: "The Lord and his armed men will come to destroy *all the world*,"[32] and "For behold, the incurable day of the Lord comes, a day of wrath and anger, to make the *world* desolate,"[33] and once more: *I will command evils for the whole world.* In these statements, the prophecy did not once mention Babylon but rather delivered a general lesson concerning the "righteous judgment of God."[34] It is concerning this which the text continues on to say: *And I will destroy the pride of the lawless and bring low the pride of the arrogant.* Now why did he speak only of the Babylonians so harshly and not of other nations as well, such as the Galatians and their

---

[29]Mt 25:34. [30]Mt 25:41. [31]Rom 8:21. [32]Is 13:5. [33]Is 13:9. [34]Cf. Rom 2:5.

demigods or the Spaniards? For we know of none other that vexed the Jewish nation at that time, nor do we read of any others who continually attacked them. And then they plundered Jerusalem and ravaged their land. Thus the Word informed those who were about to be besieged of what would certainly happen at the hand of their enemies.

[13:12] Passing on from the universal judgment of God discussed above, the word adds to these things and teaches what will happen to the ungodly throughout the whole world and what will overcome those who rule the nations as godless tyrants. It is concerning those arrogant and exalted ones, those who prevailed over the nations on the earth during various times and seasons, that he says: "I will destroy the pride of the lawless and bring low the pride of the arrogant."[35] But instead of this, Symmachus writes: "And those who have been forsaken will be honored; I will value men over gold and a person over the stone of Ophir."[36] For he says that what had been scarce will be found to be plentiful among them and that it will attract the notice of everyone.

[13:13] But he who redeems the rational nature of humanity will not be found among them. For there were certain wild individuals who had reverted to a bestial existence. Thus *heaven*—I am speaking of the heavenly powers, that which had been created by God—was moved against them and was vexed along with God at the loss of all sense and pretentiousness and godlessness of those whom we have identified. Therefore, it has been written: *For heaven* [99] *will be enraged, and the earth will be shaken out of its foundations, because of the fierce anger of the Lord.* I suppose that when the text says that *the earth will be shaken out of its foundations,* it is speaking of the consummation.

[13:14-15] He says that if any one among them should flee in an attempt to reach safety, these too will be easily caught. They are not like mature *gazelles* which bound with nimble and fleet-footed movements but rather like a *little gazelle.* It is for this reason that the other Greek translations render this word *little gazelle.* And they are likened to *a wandering sheep* that is neither being looked for nor *gathered.* Those who flee on the right hand will pray to find a place of refuge among their relatives, but they shall certainly not find it, for *there will be no one to gather them.* It is for this reason that the text says that *they will be overcome* by them, or, as the other Greek versions translate it, *they will be massacred.* And those *who are caught will be gathered* together and slain as one person by *the dagger of the wrath of God.*

[13:16] Not only those who were said to be arrogant, but the avenging angels who will overtake them will dispose of them as well: *And they will dash their children in front of them, and they will plunder their houses and take their wives.* As those men will be punished, so their godless and profane *wives* will be subject to an equal retribution, and even *their* ungodly *children.* Following the depravity of their own way of life, others will appropriate their houses, which we could suppose represent their souls. He therefore threatens that all the ungodly and the lawless and the arrogant would suffer these things in the time of the universal judgment of God. Here he predicts specifically what would happen in Babylon to the Babylonians and to the king of the Chaldeans, tailoring the prophecy especially for them. It is for this reason he addresses the word directly to the Babylonians. We should note that the fifteenth volume of Origen's commentary on the prophet came up to this point.

---

[35]Is 13:11. [36]Is 13:11.

[13:17-18] To confirm the factuality of the statement *see, I am stirring up the Medes against you*, we may investigate the histories of the Greeks, the Chaldeans and the Assyrians, as well as those of the Medes. Our own records in the book of Chronicles preserve an account of what we experienced. Accordingly, the Medes appeared and cleared away the administration of the Assyrians. But Cyrus, who was the first king of the Persians, subdued them. It was he who annulled the captivity of the Jews and gave authority to those who wanted to return to their homeland and to rebuild the temple of God. Therefore, with a view towards the literal fulfillment of these things, the prophecy now says: *See, I am stirring up the Medes against you*, and he later makes mention of "Cyrus"[37] by name.

[13:19-20] [100] He says concerning Babylon: *And Babylon, which is called glorious, will be as when God overthrew Sodom and Gomorrah. It will not be inhabited forever.* We should note that this in fact proved true, and Babylon is even now uninhabited and absolutely desolate, as the reports of these places that reach us testify. When he says *nor will Arabs pass through it*, I suppose he is speaking of those whom we call the Saracens. Those who advance these claims used to pitch their tents in Babylon itself. And thus it is shunned by its nomadic neighbors even as it is by those from faraway countries, so that no *shepherd* from *Arabia* pastures any of his animals there since it has been truly left utterly desolate. One should know that the nations of the Saracens extend all the way to the borders of Assyria, and he says that the innermost desert is occupied by the *Arabs*. For those who dwell in adjacent countries own the land of the *Arabs*. It is for this reason that Symmachus writes: *No Arab will pitch his tent there.* There is also another Arabia situated in the land of Persia,

which is called Arabia the blessed, and even those from this Arabia are able to verify the saying. But since *shepherds* often pasture their flocks in desolate places and there construct pen folds for their animals, he predicts that Babylon will be no good even for this when he says: *Nor will Shepherds rest in it.*

[13:21-22] Therefore he prophesies that Babylon will be absolutely empty and no longer inhabited by the domestic and useful animals that had dwelled among it. And when he says *wild animals*, we read this as a prediction that there will be certain obscure and unknown creatures, certain wild and savage demons and spirits in it. Therefore, instead of *wild animals*, the other Greek translations have rendered this word *sieim*.[38] Instead of *sirens*, they have *ostriches*, and instead of *Donkey-centaurs*, they simply transliterated the word *iim* from the Hebrew because of the obscurity of the meaning. And in the same way, instead of *hedgehogs*, the three translations render this word *sirens*, perhaps because of the deception of such demons, since the Greeks say that these *sirens* are sweet-voiced and deceptive spirits. After all these things he says: *it is coming quickly and will not delay.* For every period of time that is considered to be very long in human terms is reckoned as very short before God the judge, and therefore it has been said: "a thousand years are as but yesterday before him, as a watch in the night."[39] But what was foretold in the prophecy did not happen for a long time—the prediction of what the Babylonian empire would suffer at the hand of the Medes.

[14:1] Following the prophecy against Babylon, he speaks of the return of the Jewish captives from [101] Jerusalem which Cyrus authorized when he says that after going back *they will rest on their own land, and the gioras*

---

[37]Cf. Is 44:28; 45:1.   [38]A transliteration of the Hebrew word for "wild animals."   [39]Ps 90:4.

will be added to them. But instead of *the gioras*, the other Greek translations render this word *he sojourner*.[1] For thus he says that they will prosper *on their own land* so that other tribes will seek after their godliness, and their *sojourners* will be *added to the house of Jacob*. For although they were not from among them, they sojourned and dwelled among them, and thus there was no difference between the natives and those who were originally from other tribes.

[14:2] And when they return from Babylon to the land of Judah, he says that *nations will take them and bring them into their place*. These things were accomplished as we read in the record preserved in the Scripture of Ezra, for King Cyrus issued an edict giving authority to those of the Jews who wanted to return to their own land and to rebuild the temple in Jerusalem. The Scripture adds to this: "Then rose up the heads of the fathers' houses of Judah and Benjamin, and all who were about them aided them with vessels of silver, with gold, with goods, with beasts and with provisions."[2] Therefore, Zerubbabel the son of Shealtiel and Joshua the son of Jehozadak led them, and the prophets Haggai and Zechariah joined them. And after Cyrus, Xerxes, the king of the Persians, sent away Ezra "the scribe of the law"[3] with letters ordering all the rulers of the nations between the country of the Persians and that of the Jews to cooperate with Ezra. This then was the second group of those who returned with Ezra. After these things, when Nehemiah was again going up to Jerusalem, the king of the Persians issued letters "to the governors of the province beyond the river,"[4] and this same "king sent powerful rulers and leaders with him,"[5] as well as guards. The prophecy thus signifies these things when it says: *And nations will take them*

and bring them into their place. The prediction *and those who captured them will be captives, and those who dominated them will be dominated* was fulfilled when the Persians and the Medes overpowered the entire Assyrian empire with their own forces and brought the Babylonians under their control.

[14:4-7] Thence, the prophetic Spirit now presents a teaching in the prophetic Scripture concerning the events that would occur in the times after these things: how it is necessary to glorify and bless God for the kindnesses that he has bestowed on them and how it is necessary to lament over the kingdom of Babylon. Therefore he says: *And you will say on that day: How the exactor has ceased*. One should know that the sixteenth volume of Origen's commentary on the prophet came up to this point.

[102] Therefore, the text says, *you will say on that day: How the exactor has ceased and the taskmaster has ceased!* But instead, Symmachus adduces in his translation: *How the tribute was imprisoned! The Lord has crushed the staff of the ungodly, the staff of those in power*. And again, instead of *it rested confidently, all the earth*, Symmachus says: *It rested and enjoyed tranquility, all the earth*. And he says besides: *Be glad and exult! For even all the pines rejoiced over you, the cedar of Lebanon*. Again, the *pine* and the *cedar of Lebanon* speak allegorically of those absolute rulers who raised themselves up, of those who were besieged by the Babylonians and those who were cut off from their homeland. It was likely they who were to *rejoice over* the fall of the one who is here identified.

[14:8-21] He says that they were sated with your destruction when he writes: *Since you fell asleep, the one who is to cut us down has not come up*. Therefore, it is those on the earth who will say these things, and those who have

<hr />

Chapter Fourteen [1]The word for "sojourner" could also be translated "proselyte," and it may be in this sense that Eusebius uses the word in the next sentence. [2]Ezra 1:5-6. [3]Ezra 7:12. [4]Neh 2:7. [5]Ezra 8:1.

departed their earthly life, and after leaving behind their chains in the regions of Hades, they *rejoice*, and in his destruction, they will forget the coming events. Hades and the power which is set over the souls of those who have died overtook all there, and just as a prison guard, it will rise up against you from the innermost places of darkness below with anger and wrath. And just as this ruler and those in power there arose from their proper thrones, so it will be with *all the mighty ones*, or, as is found in the other Greek translations: *the Raphaeim*.[6] And these are they about whom he expounds when he says: *Those who ruled the earth, those who have roused from their thrones all the kings of the nations*. And they who do these things to the condemned king of Babylon, when they see the nakedness and desolation in body and soul of the one who once ruled Babylon, they will say: "Would it not be better for you to die; will you not choose such at our hand?" For your life on the earth and your riches and *glory* and extensive dominion is nothing, if you are to receive nothing more than "dust and ashes"[7] from all of these things, *worms* and the *decay* of the flesh. And we thought that you were not dead, but we were deceived by the splendor of your *glory*, which was the most brilliant light in the sky, which we compare with that called the *Day Star*. And you thought you were greater than these and pranced about, and in your mad arrogance you dared to consider yourself to be like the *most high* God and imagined that *you would set* your *throne* above the heavenly arches. And we who were cheated by your deadly conniving purposed for these things to happen to you, for you thought [103] such great things about yourself in your drunken excitement. Then came the time when you were refuted and you fell. A similar end did not come on the other people. For, indeed, they returned in tranquil-

ity and peace to their own homes, as it is recorded, but you had your life taken away by the sword of your enemies; as an unburied *corpse you will be cast out*, exposed as fodder for beasts and birds. And one should know that the seventeenth volume of Origen's commentary on the prophet came up to this point.

Symmachus renders the sense of the passage in this way: *You too were wounded even as we were, and you were exposed among us. But your arrogance was brought down, your mouth was silenced in death, dust[8] was spread beneath you, and a worm will be your shawl. How did you fall from heaven, O Day Star of the dawn? You are knocked to the ground, O you who wounds nations. You said in your heart: "I will ascend to heaven, I will raise up my throne above the stars of heaven, and I will sit on the appointed mountain in the regions of the north. I will ascend to the highest cloud, I will be likened to the most high. But you will be brought down into Hades, into the depths of the pit. Those who see you will look down, concerning you they will reflect: "Is this the man who disturbed the earth and made kings to tremble, the one who rearranged the whole world as a wasteland and overthrew its cities?" You did not send away its prisoners to their houses. All the kings of the nations have fallen asleep in honor, each in his own house. But you will be cast out from your grave as an abominable abortion, attempting to enter into the heights but, weighed down with a sword, descending to the foundations of the pit.* In the Septuagint, the text then says: *As a cloak stained with blood will not be clean, so neither will you be clean, because you have destroyed my land and killed my people*, and the things which follow next. But instead of this, Symmachus rendered the text: *As stinking corpses you will not take part with them in burial, because you utterly destroyed your land; you killed your people. You will not be called*

---

[6]A transliteration of the Hebrew word meaning "ghosts." [7]Cf. Gen 18:27. [8]This is a hapax legomenon in the Greek corpus, seemingly having to do with the word for creeping insects.

forever, you evil-doing seed. He prepared his sons for slaughter because of the lawlessness of their fathers, lest they arise and inherit the land and fill the face of the cities of the whole world. This is how it is worded in Symmachus's version, and Aquila and Theodotion chime in with him and sound the same deeper sense. For he says that the *king of Babylon* himself *destroyed his own land.* Therefore he says: *You utterly destroyed your land.* But he also teaches that *he had killed his own people* and *prepared his sons for slaughter.* And again, the text reads according to Symmachus as cited above: *"Is this the one who rearranged the whole world as a wasteland and overthrew its cities?" You did not send away its prisoners.* And the Babylonian empire *destroyed its own cities,* and as such **[104]** *did not send away its prisoners,* so that *it utterly destroyed its own land and killed its people, and prepared its sons for slaughter.* It is worth the effort to examine carefully this phrase. For if indeed it had been translated as in the Septuagint—*Because you have destroyed my land and killed my people*—then we would find nothing unusual. For, as everyone knows, the Babylonians attacked the land of Israel and besieged it and took prisoner those who once bore the title the people of God. According to the other Greek translations and the Hebrew text, however, it says that *it utterly destroyed its own land and it killed its own people,* and to grant *its own children as a sacrifice.* He speaks in riddles, lest you see the invisible and unseen power which was set in the nation of the Babylonians. And the prophet Daniel also teaches about such angels among the nations. And also Gabriel, the angel who interacted with him, introduced himself to him with these words: "And behold, the ruler of the kingdoms of the Persians and the ruler of the kingdoms of the Greeks and the ruler of the kingdom of the Medes came against me, and there was no one with me except Michael your

ruler."[9] Therefore, it is probable that there are certain rulers who are set over each nation, as also Moses affirms in the Scripture which says: "When the Most High was apportioning nations, as he scattered the sons of Adam, he assigned boundaries to nations, according to the number of the angels of God."[10]

Therefore, Babylon had a fine arrangement, and there was a palace and those in positions of power there had great dominion, and perhaps also the ordained spiritual powers joined in assisting them to accomplish these great things. But since the secular kingdom had lost its presence and the one ruling and establishing everything among them, when his time was up, one received a band of similar beings, and *all those who were called Raphaim* and *the mighty ones* stood with him. And they and these certain powers were probably other nations which were not governing properly at the time. Therefore, we should state that it was this ruler of Babylon himself who *utterly destroyed his own land,* lest one suppose that it was God who *killed his own people* and delivered over *his own sons to sacrifice.* Is God to be held responsible for the destruction of his subjects, just because it is supposed that God was among them? And if anyone might assume this to be the case, he should observe the whole word of the prophecy, which had been predicted concerning the king of Babylon, which refers to that power. For because in his pride he attempted to secure for himself the glory of God among the subjects, it is right that he is rebuked with the word: *You said in your mind, "I will ascend to heaven; I will set my throne above the stars of God; I will be like the Most High."* And you will be able to apply the other statements from the passage and align the other revelations delivered in the prophecy to the historical reality of the kingdom of Babylon.

[14:24-25] [105] These are added to what was said concerning the Babylonian ruler and

---

[9]Dan 10:13, 20-21. [10]Deut 32:8.

concerning the city itself and the nation of the Assyrians. The prophet thus declares: *This is what the Lord of hosts says: As I have said, so shall it be, to destroy the Assyrians on my land and on my mountains*, thus teaching that even the land of the Babylonians and the mountains on it did not belong to them. "The earth is the LORD's and the fulness thereof."[11] Therefore, he says the Assyrians *shall be trampled*, being subdued by those who later prevail over them. *And their yoke shall be removed from them*. For when they conquered their subjects, they hung a heavy and burdensome *yoke* on them. *And their renown shall be removed*, although this glory once rested on their *shoulders*. For thus it has been said about the Savior: "The government will be upon his shoulders."[12] Thus it is here said that *renown* of the Assyrians is *on their shoulders*, although the Word threatens that *it shall be removed* from them.

[14:26-27] Up to this point the prophet has sketched out a word concerning Babylon, but now the prophecy returns again to the first theme, which we discussed above, and says: *This is the plan that the Lord has planned against the whole earth*. For judgment has been carried out against Babylon and its inhabitants, and it was such as befitted all the godless and vile people who held power over the whole world. For according to the word of the righteous one, those who are ungodly in the same way will suffer the same punishments. For this reason he says besides: *And this is the hand that is raised up against all the nations of the world*, and so we are to think of the nations of those godless and vile people. For he has not come to carry out these things rashly against the godly and those who are dedicated to God. Therefore, he finished in the same way that he began, remembering the impending universal judgment of God with a view toward conversion. But all those who appeal to

the Scripture should not suppose that anything that was said concerning Babylon was addressed to them. And none of it was addressed to us either, but these things were said about them alone. And now the Word turns of necessity even to anguish and fear, leading us to the universal judgment of God which awaits all. He of necessity calls these things to mind, just as at the beginning of the prophecy, so also at the end.

[14:28-29] Making another start at sketching out the theme of the "vision against Babylon,"[13] the Word addresses the houses of *those of other tribes*, whom the Hebrew text and the other Greek translations call *Philistines*. The Greeks, however, changing their name, called them Palestinians. Indeed, when Ahaz was living in Jerusalem and those in the other Jewish cities were committing idolatry, whom history makes clear were from other tribes but were living on the same land, then those who were called gods by them but were evil demons rejoiced [106]. They probably rejoiced at the error and destruction of Ahaz and the people under him called Judah. For the people called Israel and the kings in Samaria had already been taken captive by the Assyrians. And therefore the book of Kings records: "The Lord humbled Judah because of Ahaz king of Judah[14] since he led the people into apostasy from the Lord."[15] And it is written concerning the other tribes: "And the Edomites had again invaded and humbled Judah, and carried away captives. And the *other tribes* invaded the cities of Palestine and destroyed Bethshemesh."[16] But here, instead of "and the *other tribes* invaded the cities," other texts state that it was *the Philistines* or the Palestinians who attacked Ahaz. For no longer is he sent to you *to make the dying rejoice*—that is to say, the ungodly *king* whom you formerly caused to rejoice—but rather Hezekiah, the God-fearing man, who succeeded Ahaz as is recorded in the

---

[11]Ps 24:1 RSV. [12]Is 9:6 RSV. [13]Cf. Is 13:1. [14]"Judah" is recorded in the LXX, "Israel" in the MT. [15]2 Chron 28:19. [16]2 Chron 28:17-18.

second book of Chronicles and in the fourth book of Kings.[17] Therefore, just as it was possible for *the other tribes to make the dying rejoice* and cheer the ungodly Ahaz, so also the righteous man Hezekiah, and at the right moment the prophecy declares to them: *May all of you of the other tribes not rejoice.* For while Ahaz was yet living, he caused all the enemies of God *to rejoice* through what he did among you. But it was because the *yoke* of Ahaz *had been broken* and he was neither able to subjugate you nor to place on you the *yoke* of his rule that evils were multiplied.

The slithering and venomous power of evil spirits multiplied from the one who *struck you*, and now you are no longer to rejoice as before over the kingdom of the one who succeeded the God-loving man. For he has placed over you the one *striking* and beating and chastening you. And thus these things were fulfilled literally in Hezekiah, concerning whom it has been said in the fourth book of Kings: "He smote the other tribes as far as Gaza and its territory, from watchtower to fortified city."[18]

This may be the meaning of the verse: *May you not rejoice, all you of other tribes.* They were proud of those things which were supposed to be gods among you, although they were nothing, and you *broke* the wickedness of the present time, as if *the yoke of him who struck you* had been utterly *broken.* But these things did not happen to you because of your evil. For when no one *struck you*, humbled you or was severe with you, there was much provocation of evil among you. For those *snakes* once lurked in your souls, in your priests and temples, and in your gods as well, evil demons producing fearful offspring and birthing *evil seed*, so that the *snakes* born from them will be the worst of all venomous creatures. And from these came other *snakes* which could fly through the air. Therefore, these things were not only among you at the present time but also among the

other tribes, and even now they multiply even among those who bear the title the people of God. Thus, **[107]** the verse about the *snakes* and the *offspring of serpents* that fly through the air has in every way been fulfilled in the injurious spirits. And so the *snakes* and *serpents* of the one who murdered all these and who was exalted during this time will be gone, as will their evil *offspring*, so that they will no longer effect these things among humanity.

[14:30-32] Therefore, *I will wipe out* this slithering and venomous race *with famine*, and the predicted *famine* will bring to an end the usual supply of food, clearly what was offered through sacrifices in the demonic cult. He will nourish the *poor* and *he will rest in peace*, no longer vexed by the deceitful snakes. It is certainly possible that these things were fulfilled during the time of Hezekiah. For those who were once poor according to God among the entire Jewish nation he restored with spiritual food and teaching. On the good principle of religious law, he also appointed that they be nourished by the divine lessons and reared in the sacred doctrines. All these things happened, as the records about this matter inform us, during the time of Hezekiah.

And he speaks of the king of the Assyrians, who came up from the northernmost regions during the time of Hezekiah and subjugated those of the other tribes who lived in Palestine. He besieged their cities and took large numbers of captives from among them and burned up the gates of their cities. For the greatest evidence for them will be that God is the guardian of his city so that it suffered nothing as the other cities.

For neither through marshaled and armed men nor through the ruling king of the nation but through God himself will salvation come to the people. These things were fulfilled literally "in the fourteenth year of the reign of

---

[17]2 Chron 29:2; 2 Kings 18:3. [18]2 Kings 18:8.

King Hezekiah"[19] when the king of the Assyrians attacked and conquered the other cities in Judea but after attempting to conquer Jerusalem returned without success.

[15:1–16:4] Those who lived in Moab were arrogant about their gods. They laughed and jeered at the God of Israel, and because of this, the prophetic word delivered this prophecy concerning them. And so, starting with their exceeding ignorance of God, he called on *night* and *darkness* and threatened that destruction will come on them in the same *night* when he says: *By night Moabitis will perish; for by night the wall of Moabitis will perish.* Then, next, concerning the place in which their idolatry had been established, he adds: *For Lebanon will perish! Where your altar is, there you will go up to weep.* And he mentions their altars again at the end of the prophecy when he says: "Moab has become weary at the altars, and it will enter the works of its hands in order to pray but will not be able to deliver him."[1] I suppose that it is clear from this that [108] this is the cause of the present theme of the destruction of the idolatry that surrounds the Moabites. It is also predicted that other things are about to happen in it and in the city and in the lands around it, even in the surrounding villages and cities. These things were fulfilled in history in the attacks of the Assyrians and Babylonians. During the time after these things happened they conquered the land of the Arabs, and this is what God threatened when he said that *he would bring Arabs.* It is possible that he was speaking of those who live adjacent to the Arabs or the Saracens discussed further on, to whom the Word says that he will deliver Moab. Therefore, it is not necessary to document exactly all that hap-

pened among the other cities on either side of Moabitis, nor need we elaborate on what happened to the villages and lands that were mentioned in the prophecy. I am speaking of *Nabau, Hesebon, Eleale, Iassa, Debon,*[2] *Louith, the way of the Arabs, in which the water of Nemrim is found, Agallim, the well in Ailim, the water of Debon, Ariel, Adama, and the place called Arnon.* For even now these places and villages on both sides of the land which is now called Areopolis are still well known, and it would be needless to elaborate now on how all that was threatened concerning these cities was fulfilled literally and once for all during the times of their besieging.

I suppose that the figurative interpretation[3] of these things must be that the Word was prophesying that the "Medes" from among the Babylonians would rise up against Babylon. Thus, God says even now to the Moabites that *he would bring Arabs. For I will bring Arabs to the ravine,* and again: *And the water of Debon*[4] *will be filled with blood, for I will bring Arabs on Debon.* And they say that the great village *Ariel* can still be seen in the land of the Areopolitans, and so too *Sior* and *Esebor* and the others, although someday they may be completely covered over.

Why then would it be appropriate and profitable to document the prophesied events so exactly, since it is clear that God had always had foreknowledge of all predicted destruction and desolation, and since the church had been established among the people from whom the idols—which had formerly been thought to be gods—were driven away. Nothing could be more amazing. The Word prophesies these things through the following: *For Debon*[5] *will perish, where your altar is,* and again: *Because your alliance has been taken away, and the ruler*

---

[19]2 Kings 18:13. **Chapter Fifteen** [1]Is 16:12. [2]In the LXX, at this location in the text, one finds "Segor" instead of "Debon," and at the next instance of "Debon," one finds "Remmon." [3]Here Eusebius uses the term θεωρία, a term that more generally means "speculation" or "theory." [4]Again, in the LXX, one reads "Remmon" in this verse. [5]Here, it is seen that probably "Debon" is an erroneous reading of "Lebanon," for the l (Λ) and d (Δ) in Greek are very similar in the capital form.

who trampled on the land has perished. In saying these things, he is speaking of either the evil demon that rested over the nation or the ruler of an individual nation, such as the ruler of the kingdom of the Persians or the ruler of the kingdom of the Greeks or the ruler of the Babylonians. Therefore, this demon lay in wait in the city of the Moabites, and they supposed that they would receive aid from it. Thus, he says in symbols that the cities would be destroyed, seeing that he tramples down their souls. He beckons [109] them to trample down the earth, so that they are able neither to lift up their heads nor look up. Therefore, he says: *Because your alliance has been taken away and the ruler who tramped on the land has perished.*

[16:5] After the destruction of this one, he says next: *Then a throne shall be restored with mercy, and he shall sit on it with truth in the tent of David, judging and seeking judgment and diligently procuring righteousness.* One sees the miracle of the Word presented in the conclusion of the prophecy. For there he predicted the disappearance of idolatry from among the aforementioned peoples, and he announces the hope of good things to come among them. He said that the *tent of David* and the *throne* of God would be established among them. Further, this would not come about by human effort but by the *mercy* and benevolence of God. Therefore, it has been said according to Aquila: *And a throne will be prepared in mercy;* and according to Symmachus: *And a throne will be prepared in pity;* and according to Theodotion: *And a throne will be prepared with mercy.* And certainly the one by whom *it will be prepared* is Christ, he who would be born "*from the seed of David.*"[1] Accordingly, he says that *throne* of Christ will be among the Moabites, on which *he shall sit with truth in the tent of David.* Thus, the prophetic Spirit is

accustomed to calling the church of Christ *the tent of David,* since it is also its custom to name the Christ himself David, because he had been born "from the seed of David according to the flesh."[2] For this reason, he refers to the church as the *tent of David* and to the seat in front as a *throne,* which the church warden maintains as the bodily *throne* of Christ.

And that these things are said concerning the church of the Gentiles, the Scripture of the Acts of the Apostles confirms. For there it has been recorded what James, who served as the first bishop of Jerusalem, said: "Brethren, listen to me. Simeon has related how God first visited the Gentiles, to take out of them a people for his name. And the words of the prophets agree with this, as it is written, 'After this I will return, and I will rebuild the tent of David, which has fallen; I will rebuild that of it which has been trampled down,[3] and I will set it up, that the rest of people may seek the Lord, and all the Gentiles who are called by my name, says the Lord, who has made these things known from of old.'"[4] It is clear then that by addressing the prophecy concerning the *tent of David,* [110] he also raises the subject of the call of the Gentiles. He says, therefore, that these things will happen, not in types and symbols but in truth. For the *tent of David* will be established among the most superstitious Moabites, and the one who rules *shall* take his place on his *throne, judging and seeking judgment and diligently procuring righteousness.* But according to Symmachus, the text reads: *he shall sit down on it in truth in the tent of David, judging and seeking judgment and quickly for righteousness.* And could anyone who had witnessed these things with their own eyes deny that it was the result of the word that the *throne* of Christ was established among the churches of God, even in the Areopolis and in the lands all around it and in the other cities

---

Chapter Sixteen [1]Cf. Rom 1:3. [2]Rom 1:3. [3]Eusebius changes the Greek word here ever so slightly so as to change "its ruins" to "that of it which has been trampled down." Whether the change is purposeful or not is debatable. [4]Acts 15:13-18.

of Arabia. And those demons who formerly worked dreadful deeds among them will no longer be remembered even in name.

[16:6-14] Symmachus makes the meaning of these things very clear and renders it in this way: *We heard of the arrogance of Moab, in his vanity and arrogance he is exceedingly arrogant. And his wrath and his arms are not thus. Because of this Moab shall wail, and concerning Moab all shall wail; wounds were found among those who rejoiced in the earthen wall. The branches of Hesebon were stripped bare, the vine of Sebama. The lords of the Gentiles cut off her offshoots. She was touched as far as Iazer; they were led into the desert. Her emissaries failed to cross the sea. Because of this I will weep with the weeping of Iazer for the vine of Sebama. I will make you drunk with my tears, O Hesebon and Eleale, because he fell on your fruit and on your trampled harvest. And joy and cheer were taken away from your Mount Carmel, and they will not be glad in the vineyards, neither will they drink wine. The one treading will not tread for the vats, for I stopped the movements of the treaders. Therefore my belly will resound like a harp to Moab, and my inward parts will be like an earthen wall. And it will be that when he appears Moab will toil and enter into the high places and pray for her sanctification, but she will not be able to do it. This is the word which the Lord spoke concerning Moab. And now he said: "In three years, as a hired worker counts them, the glory of Moab will be dishonored with all its great population. It will be a very short while from now and not much longer."*

[16:6] The power of the Moabites was great at the time when these things were prophesied, as had already been established in witness of the voice of the prophet Jeremiah. When he spoke

out in opposition to Jerusalem, the Moabites disparaged Israel and laughed as not deserving any thought at all, for they were very proud of their idols. And the prophecy presents this when it says: *We have heard of the pride of Moab: exceedingly proud he is; you have removed his arrogance.* But according to Symmachus, the text reads: *We heard of the arrogance of Moab, in his vanity* [111] *and in his arrogance he is exceedingly arrogant.* But he also says: *And his wrath and his arms are not thus.* But in the Septuagint, the words describing his arrogant deeds are different: *Your divination is not thus, no not thus.* For since they were proud of their own God and their divinations, he says that it will be *not thus.* The demon among them divined such things, and even though nothing in the oracles that it proclaimed to those who attended came true, they still thought that the demon was God. And thus their lying spirit will be disgraced at the present time. It is for this reason that he adds at the conclusion of the prophecy: "And it will be for your shame, because Moab has become weary at the altars, and it will enter the works of its hands in order to pray but will not be able to deliver him."[5]

[16:7-8] And what has been said in the meantime signifies that there will be a change in the former daintiness of the Moabites. Thus, he predicts that those in it who rejoiced will *mourn* and *wail: Moab shall wail, for in Moabitis all shall wail,* and again: *The plains of Hesebon will mourn.* And we should note that the nineteenth[6] volume of Origen's commentary on the prophet came up to this point. Then he states next: *The vine of Sebama. As you swallow up the nations, trample down its vines as far as Iazer,* and the rest. Through this he adumbrated the change in their land to

---

[5]Is 16:12. [6]The last volume Eusebius mentioned was number 17. Perhaps a lost volume accounts for Eusebius's brevity in commenting on the last several chapters. Or, perhaps finding the material uninteresting, Eusebius skimmed by it, not thinking it worth while to mention that he also had combined volumes 17 and 18.

aridness and utter desolation, and it was over this change that he predicted that they would weep aloud.

[16:9-10] Then the prophet laments, deeply pained and grieving over the destruction of the souls of those who had been deceived among them. He had exhorted them earlier to wail and had already admonished them to weep aloud in repentance for their sins. But since they had not done this, he takes up "weeping" for them and says: *Therefore, I will weep with a weeping, and I will make you drunk with my tears.* And he teaches us what the reason for the *weeping* is when he says: *Because he fell on your fruit and on your trampled harvest.* And in the *fruit* and *harvest* and in the *vine*, to which he frequently alludes, he is speaking of the flourishing and bloom and the youthful tenderness of their lives, for they spent their lives getting drunk and partying and reveling in their godless impieties.

[16:11-12] For this reason, he wept aloud for their destruction and said: *Therefore my belly will resound like a lyre on Moab, and my inward parts will be like a wall that you have restored. And it will be for your shame.* For, he says, my *tears* and my *weeping* is for no other purpose than *for your shame*. Then he predicts the disappearance of the idols they had thought were gods: *Because Moab has become weary at the altars, and it will enter the works of its hands* —or, according to the other Greek translations: *Into its sanctuary*—*in order to pray but will not be able to deliver him.*

[16:13-14] And *this* is the conclusion of the word of God *which he spoke against Moab*, to which you will add what has been said above. For in the place of the desolation of their altars and [112] the destruction of their gods, "A throne shall be restored with mercy, and he

shall sit on it with truth in the tent of David."[7] This verse has been inserted in the middle of the prophecy and is rather mysterious precisely because the Holy Spirit dealt out the knowledge of these things only to those who would understand and who were deemed worthy of contemplation. But instead of *the Lord spoke against Moab at the time he also spoke*, the other Greek translations say: *What the Lord spoke against Moab, he spoke from then even until now.* It is extremely important to note the precise wording of the Scripture, for it says *from then he spoke* and so too the Lord *speaks even until now* through the prophetic revelation. Thus, what was formerly prophesied in words is now accomplished in deeds.

In place of the Septuagint's translation *in three years of a hired worker, the glory of Moab will be dishonored*, the Hebrew text and the other Greek translations insert a conjunction in between the clauses, thus presenting the meaning more accurately. For in Aquila's version, this verse reads: *In three years of a hired worker*; and in Symmachus's version: *From then even until now, the Lord spoke, saying: "In three years as counted by a hired worker"*; and in Theodotion's version: *From then even until now, the Lord spoke, saying, "In three years as the years of a hired worker."* Then, as a new clause, the other Greek translations and the Hebrew text say: *The glory of Moab will be dishonored with all its great population.* For when the conjunction is inserted, it presents another meaning than when *and the glory of Moab will be dishonored* immediately follows. And, as discussed above, it was revealed that *in three years* all the aforementioned that *the Lord spoke to Moab* through the prophet would happen. The Lord hired the prophet and kept him busy with the prophecy concerning these things. For the prophet did not put forth the entire and extended word of the prophecy as a single piece as we read it

---

[7] Is 16:5.

when we gather together in a crowd for the public reading, but all that was said to him was delivered separately and in parts at different periods of time over the course of *three years*. And so, *the Lord spoke* these things *in three years* through the prophet, and this was the conclusion of the words of God: *And the glory of Moab will be dishonored with all its great population, and only the smallest and least respected will be left behind.* This too was literally fulfilled, as is obvious to those who travel to these places.

[17:1-3] Just as the Word delivered a prophecy that was precisely appropriate for Babylon and the other tribes that lived in Palestine, and just as the Word prophesied things specifically directed towards Moab, [113] so in the same manner *the* prophetic *word* also threatens that an end will come *against Damascus*. For he says that it *will be removed from among cities*; or, according to Theodotion, he says that it *will be discharged from among cities*. And this happened during the times of the Assyrians, as was explained above. The Scripture at hand refers to the king of the Assyrians when it says: "And I took Arabia and Damascus and Samaria. As I took these, I will also take all the countries."[1] And history confirms the accuracy of this word, for it has been written in the fourth book of Kings: "The king of Assyria marched up against Damascus, and took it, carrying its people captive to Kurenen,"[2] or, according to Symmachus: "To Kirran, and he killed Rezin." But these things came to pass before the prophecy at hand. It seems that the present word was fulfilled literally during the time of Jeremiah the prophet, at which point the king of Babylon attacked Jerusalem and again seized Damascus, all at once ripping it from its foundations. This is what Jeremiah is speaking about when he says: "Damascus has become feeble, she

turned to flee, and panic seized her; anguish and sorrows have taken hold of her, as of a woman in travail. Why did he not forsake my city? He loved the village,"[3] or, according to Symmachus: "the laudable city, the mother city of merriment."[4] "Therefore her young men shall fall in your squares, and all the military men will fall in that day, says the Lord of powers. And I will kindle a fire in the wall of Damascus, and it shall devour the thoroughfares of the son of Ader."[5]

Accordingly, the prophecy at hand foretells the same things as those above when it says: *See, Damascus will be removed from among cities and will become an abandoned ruin.* And the word *forever* at the end is found only in the Septuagint; it appears neither in the Hebrew nor in the other Greek translations. For this reason, one may not conclude that the text certainly posits that the ruin of *Damascus* will be forever, especially as it fell during the siege of the Assyrians, when they also conquered Jerusalem. But just as the Jews rebuilt Jerusalem after they had returned and repopulated the land, so also it was with *Damascus*. After the city had experienced all that had been foretold by the prophecy, the city was then also reconstructed, and it was again established as the capital. And so it remained as such until the times of the apostles. For example, Paul mentions the king of Damascus in the Scriptures thus: "At Damascus, the governor under King Aretas of Damascus guarded the city in order to seize me, but I was let down in a basket through a window in the wall and escaped his hands."[6] Therefore, we submit that the first events of the prophecies occurred during the times of the Assyrians, [114] when *Damascus* was besieged for a first and second time. And it is probable that similar things transpired during the time of the Persians and the Macedonians. During this time, as the city was rebuilt and besieged, the saying was

---

Chapter Seventeen [1]Is 10:9-10. [2]2 Kings 16:9. [3]Jer 49:24-25. [4]Jer 49:25. [5]Jer 49:26-27. [6]2 Cor 11:32-33.

fulfilled: *See, Damascus will be removed from among cities and will become an abandoned ruin, to be a fold and resting place for flocks, and there will be no one to drive them away.*

Then comes the following verse: *And no longer will it be strong enough for Ephraim to flee to it for refuge, and no longer will there be a kingdom in Damascus.* This perhaps came about during the Roman times, when, after the coming of our Savior, the whole district was laid waste and the *kingdom of Damascus* was destroyed. The first part of the prophecy makes it clear that the absolute disappearance of Damascus is not predicted, but rather a partial fall. This is made clear through the phrases *no longer will it be strong* and *no longer will there be a kingdom in Damascus.* For the prophet says how it will be: it will certainly not be as strong as it used to be, nor will it again possess such an extensive rule. And in another way, it befell these places, when the prophecy announced beforehand humiliation for the private lives of those who dwelled in Damascus. And thus we are accustomed to saying that the rich and those of rank fell and were driven to extreme penury when they were deprived the privilege that they had possessed. This is what the following verse is about: "The house of Israel has fallen, no more to rise."[7] Therefore, in saying *see, Damascus will be removed from among cities and will become a ruin, abandoned forever,* he adumbrates the downfall of the imperial power that the shining city had once possessed. For it alone of all Syria was dominant, for the cities which exist in Syria today had not yet been built. For Antioch and Apameia and Laodicea and other such cities appeared after these things, after the death of Alexander the Great,[8] but before *Damascus* came to dominate all the cities of Syria as the imperial city of the Syrians. Therefore, it was about to fall from the imperial honor and to be abandoned as mediocre and abased and insignificant, so that in the *city* as well as in the country, its empty terrain would be inhabited by common people as herds and *flocks,* and no enemy would trouble them any longer. For this reason it has been said: *See, Damascus will be removed from among cities,* which very clearly means *from among imperial cities.* This is what we are to understand as contained in the verse: *She will become a ruin, abandoned forever, and to be a fold and resting place for flocks, and there will no longer be anyone to drive them away.*

These things found fulfillment during the Roman rule when *Damascus* was in part reestablished. For he says that the former imperial city would completely disappear. And thus the prophecy foretells that the city which would be re-established and which we know today would no longer be awarded the imperial honor or rule the nation of the Syrians. But that which [115] formerly possessed great power has fallen, and in a single night it has been *abandoned to be a fold for flocks and a resting place for cattle.* The Word is accustomed to calling worthless land a place to graze herds. No one besieged the city of Damascus while it was under Roman administration, and it should be clear to everyone that it was not able to act as an ally to the Jewish nation while it was in such a situation. Therefore, the text says: *And no longer will it be strong enough for Ephraim to flee to it for refuge, and no longer will there be a kingdom in Damascus and the rest of Syria.* Do not suppose that he says *Damascus* will be deprived of the imperial honor and that another city of *Syria* will be awarded it, for he says *a capital*[9] will no longer be in Damascus or anywhere else in the nation of Syria. He next teaches the reason for this when he says to the city's face: *For you are not better than the sons of Israel and their glory.*

---

[7]Amos 5:2. [8]Eusebius knows this figure as Alexander of Macedon. [9]Eusebius has altered the text very slightly here, effecting a not insignificant change in meaning.

For if those who were once called the people of God fell from their place of honor and lost the independence and kingdom that had once been administered among them, then it is not for you, *O Damascus*, who suffered similar things to be terribly upset. *For you are not better than the sons of Israel and their glory*, which has been taken away.

[17:4] Because *the glory* had been taken away from them, he continues on to say: *This is what the Lord of hosts says: On that day there will be a failing of the glory of Jacob, and the riches of his glory will be shaken.* These things were also fulfilled after the advent of our Savior. For I say that in one day, as one always counts a day, at one and the same time, the dignity of the people of the circumcision and the *kingdom of Damascus* was destroyed. Therefore the text says: *On that day there will be a failing of the glory of Jacob.* And thus describes the sight not of the absolute destruction of the nation but only *of their glory* which they possessed before the demolition. For, indeed, the former *glory* of this people, the holiness and the kingdom, the sanctity and their lawful worship existed very long ago, when there was also a gracious prophet and national freedom and other such things among the Jewish nation. But the Word declares that *they will be shaken* all together and will fall and be completely abandoned.

[17:5-6] He says how these things will occur: *It shall be as if someone were to gather the standing crop.* Indeed, as *ears of corn are gathered in harvest* or as a bare stalk in the field is *left*, so also he says it will be with the Jewish people, for the *ears of corn* among them have been cut off and only the *stalk* has been *left* among them. And if a certain holiness of speech may be found among them, this too will be cast aside as an *ear of corn*, and not as one growing in a plain but rather in a deep,

parched and *sterile ravine*. I would suppose that the *ear of corn* represents the band of the disciples and evangelists of our Savior, concerning whom it was said [116] as discussed above: "And if the Lord of hosts had not left us offspring, we would have become like Sodom and been made similar to Gomorrah."[10]

Because he was attempting to impress this on their memory, he declared these things in another metaphor when he said: *or like berries of an olive tree—two or three on the topmost height, or four or five left on its branches.* For he says that there will be such a dearth of those who are saved from Israel during the time of which the prophecy speaks that all will be cast aside as one *ear of corn*. And those who are chosen from among them will be *just like berries of an olive tree—two* or perhaps *three on the topmost height.* Here the Word foreshadows the heights to which the apostles would ascend, which the Savior sometimes called a pair and sometimes three, and the Gospels introduce these three as the chosen of the chosen. What I mean is that we read that it was "Peter, James and John alone whom Jesus led up the mountain"[11] to witness his transfiguration, and again Jesus received them alone to witness the resuscitation "of the daughter of the synagogue ruler."[12] And the other numbers mentioned besides the *three* were *four* and *five.* They add up to the number nine *on the topmost height on the olive tree.* And if anyone should count up the *two* and the *three* and the *four* and the *five*, it would make fourteen in all. One could perhaps say that the twelve would be the first apostles, but not least were also the excellent Paul who was "called an apostle"[13] and "James the Lord's brother,"[14] who is remembered as the first bishop of the church that was established by the Savior himself in Jerusalem. These all were *on the height of the olive tree.* I would say that the passage at hand is speaking of the succession of the Jews. And

---

[10]Is 1:9. [11]Mt 17:1; Mk 9:2. [12]Mk 5:35. [13]Rom 1:1. [14]Gal 1:19.

the divine apostle knows to compare the succession of the Jews' lineage with an *olive tree* and to call them the "holy root"[15] and "first-fruits" and "cultivated olive tree."[16]

These then are the rare *berries of the olive tree* that have been scavenged from it, and what has been rendered an *ear of corn* is also scarce. It is for this reason that the prophetic word says: *And it shall be as if someone were to gather an ear of grain in a sterile ravine or like berries of an olive tree—two or three on the topmost height.*

[17:7-8] After the reference to the apostles, and moving on from the former polytheism of the Gentiles, he then prophesies the conversion of the whole world to God. Thus the text says next: *This is what the Lord God of Israel says: On that day a man will trust in the One who made him, and his eyes will look to the Holy One of Israel, and no longer will they trust in the altars nor in the works of their hands, which their own fingers have made, and they will not look at the trees or at their abominations.* For they will no longer offer sacrifices in groves and in the high places among the *trees* [117] as they did formerly. But *in that day*—clearly, at the time to which is referred—those who were once "aliens"[17] from the knowledge of God and "strangers to the covenants of promise" will acknowledge *the Holy One of Israel* alone.

[17:9-11] He then writes of the call of the Gentiles: *On that day*—that is, at the same time mentioned above—*your cities will be abandoned, just as the Amorites and the Hivites abandoned them before the sons of Israel, and they will be desolate, because you have abandoned God your Savior and have not remembered the Lord your God.* Thus, very surprisingly, he candidly prophesied that their cities would be not only abandoned but abandoned as the cities of the *Amorites and the Hivites*

had been. For he says that just as those who passed by the cities and lands that had been destroyed and occupied them, so too your *cities* will have other inhabitants, and you will be cast away and banished. And that this happened is plain to see. And indeed Greeks dwell in Jerusalem itself and many other *cities* in Israel, although no one dares to set foot in the place in the temple which is for Jews only. And a great many of them were besieged by the Romans and ripped from their foundations and turned over to their final desolation in accordance with the prophecy. And he says that these things would overtake them, since *they have abandoned* their own *Savior.* Here, the Hebrew text mentions our Savior Jesus himself, for as we have noted, the name Jesus is translated as *Savior* in the Greek language. And this was the reason why the text says that all the aforementioned things will befall them: *Because they have abandoned God their Savior and have not remembered the Lord their helper at all times.*

The Gospel teaches us how he was their *helper* at all times when it says: "How often would I have gathered your children together as a hen gathers her brood under her wings, and you would not!"[18] And it also teaches that there was another reason for which the aforementioned things would befall them: because *they planted an unfaithful plant and an unfaithful seed.* This is established in as far as they were not faithful to the Christ of God who shone forth from among them first. He says that if you plant this *unfaithful seed* and *unfaithful plant* in your soul, then you will be led astray. But if one should change and plant seed that will grow in the *morning* light of the gospel in the world, then one is sowing another *seed* in his understanding. It was concerning this seed that the Gospels say: "A sower went out to sow,"[19] and: "The kingdom of heaven may be compared with a man who sowed good

---

[15]Rom 11:16. [16]Rom 11:24. [17]Cf. Eph 2:12. [18]Mt 23:37 RSV. [19]Mt 13:3 RSV.

seed in his own field.["20] And when the light of the "sun of righteousness"[21] rises in the *morning, it will blossom for harvest among you*, so as to distribute a good portion to all of those among you [118] "who were born of God"[22] through the saving teaching. Returning again for a minute to the oracle given to Damascus, the prophecy included similar things in its word concerning that city, since the prophet had finished the oracle concerning Israel.

[17:12-13] After foretelling the conversion of the Gentiles to God and the unfaithfulness of the Jewish nation to Christ, the Word turns to address the multitude of nations who remain in unfaithfulness like Damascus itself and the other lands and who are about to persecute and besiege the church. Accordingly, he appeals to the imagery of a *swelling sea* and says that they will be driven into confusion and that *they will be troubled*, nonplussed by the evangelical preaching that reduces the error of idolatry to nothing. Therefore, the text says: *Ah, the multitude of many nations! It will roar like water*. For just as the *backsides of the sea* hunch and are raised up when driven by a storm and *troubled* by the winds, creating a great noise that terrifies those on the open seas, so also the multitudes of those Gentiles who remain in unfaithfulness and idolatry in Damascus itself and in the other countries are easily perturbed by the spirits of the air, and they rise up and *roar* as the *sea* against the church of God. For this reason, the text says: *They will roar like water, many nations like much water, as when much water is carried*.

See how many metaphors he uses to speak of the godless and profane judgment of the aforesaid individuals, comparing their wrath first with a *swelling sea*, then their decrees against the church with *roaring water* and third with *much water being violently carried*. He

thus indicates the fluctuating and transient character of their lives. And when he says *much water being violently carried*, he is speaking of those who go with the flow and are driven by others to attack the church. But he provides an outline of their end when he says next: *And he will drive him away and pursue him*, or, according to Aquila: *And he will rebuke him and chase him far away*; or, according to Symmachus: *And he will admonish him and chase him far away*. And whom *will he admonish* or *rebuke* but the aforementioned *multitude* of the unbelieving *nations*, or the devil who is at work among them? And who *will rebuke* them but he concerning whom it has been said: "The Lᴏʀᴅ who has chosen Jerusalem *rebuke you*"?[23] He then says what will happen when the Lord *rebukes* him: *He will pursue him far away, like the dust of chaff when they winnow before the wind and like a squall that drives a circling dust cloud*, or, according to Symmachus: *And like a sudden whirlwind*.

[17:14] Then he states next: *Toward evening there will be lamentation; before morning, and it will not be*. For those who were arrogant toward [119] the church as a *swelling sea, there will be lamentation* at the sunset of their life and at their very end, when they will be banished from the dawning age of the morning light of the sunrise which now shines on the righteous. The text says: *And this is the portion and the state of those who despoiled you*. And it is quite clear that the *you* represents those who seek refuge in the church of God.

[18:1-2] In the Acts of the Apostles, it is recorded what the rulers of the Jews said to Paul, who resided in Rome at the time, when he was discussing faith in Christ with them: "We have received no letters from Judea about you, and none of the brethren coming here has

---

[20]Mt 13:24. [21]Cf. Mal 4:2. [22]Jn 1:13. [23]Zech 3:2 ʀsv.

eported or spoken evil about you. But we desire to hear from you what your views are; for with regard to this sect we know that everywhere it is spoken against."[1] And in saying this, they made it clear that before Paul came to reside in Rome, they had been directed not to welcome the preaching of Christ. Not only had they been instructed to do so, but also the Jews of every land. It is for this reason that the text says: "For with regard to this sect we know that everywhere it is spoken against."[2] And so the Jews "everywhere" were all in agreement to "speak against" the word of Christ. We found among the old ordinances that, when the priests of the nation and the scribes and elders who divide the Scriptures dwelled in Jerusalem, they sent off emissaries to the Jews everywhere in all nations, attempting to discredit the teaching of Christ as a strange sect and not properly of God. They thus commanded them through letters not to welcome the Christian message.

Therefore, it would seem that this is what the prophecy at hand means when it says: *Ah, wings of a land of ships beyond the rivers of Ethiopia—he who sends hostages by sea.* But Symmachus said *apostles: He who sends apostles by sea.* Aquila rendered the word *elders: He who sends elders by sea.* You see how the Word deems as miserable the aforementioned rulers of the Jews and their land which evil overtook as far as Ethiopia. Therefore, the text says in Symmachus's translation: *Woe to the land, in which there is the sound of a wing, beyond the rivers of Ethiopia.* By this he means that the sound of the evil went on *beyond* the lands of the Ethiopians even to the ends of the earth, and it came to the inhabitants of the land of the Jews as though in flying ships. And these apostles[3] brought their *papyrus letters* with them and, navigating the waters, sailing the *sea* and traversing everywhere on land, they

stood in the way of the word of our Savior. And it is convention even now to call those who bear circular letters from the Jewish rulers *apostles.* He thus foreshadows these things when he says this. But, next, instead of *for* [120] *swift messengers will go,* all the other Greek translations write: *Come, swift messengers,* as though it were the beginning of an imperative sentence. And it seems to me that this is an imperative spoken to the disciples of our Savior. And because the disciples proclaimed the good news to all people, he called them *swift messengers,* thus distinguishing them from the Jewish apostles. Therefore, he says to them, the *messengers* of the good news, you, the disciples of Christ: *come.* This is what the Savior himself commanded you when he said to you: "But *go* rather to the lost sheep of the house of Israel,"[4] and: "Go and make disciples of all nations in my name."[5] And he says that when you *come,* you are to be *swift* and light so that you will be ready for the journey. This is what he exhorted them to do when he said: "Take nothing for your journey,"[6] and: "Take no gold, or silver or copper in your belts, no bag for your journey, do not have tunics, or sandals or a staff."[7]

And so, he said quite accurately that they were *swift messengers,* and he orders them *to come to a high nation and to a foreign and fierce people.* For *they were sent* not to their brothers or relatives with whom they were already acquainted but to those people in every nation who are estranged and of another race. This nation was truly *high,* for it stood firmly on nothing but was deceived "and carried about with every wind"[8] of the error of polytheism. And they were a *fierce nation,* for they were hostile and belligerent toward the word of godliness. Therefore, he likewise encouraged those *swift messengers* to go and preach to them, and to traverse the ends of the earth. For

Chapter Eighteen [1]Acts 28:21-22. [2]Acts 28:22 RSV. [3]Eusebius here is using the term as "emissary," not in the Christian sense of "apostle." [4]Mt 10:6 RSV. [5]Mt 28:19. [6]Lk 9:3 RSV. [7]Mt 10:9-10. [8]Cf. Eph 4:14.

this reason, the text says: *Who is beyond it?* Or, according to Symmachus: *Beyond which there is nothing?* And this is the *estranged* and *high nation without hope*, as the apostle says: "We once had no hope and were without God in the world."[9] And the prophet himself whose words we are considering prophesies then about those *without hope* when he says next: "And those *without hope* among people shall be filled with joy."[10] And therefore *they were sent to a nation without hope* and *to a nation trampled down* by the devil and all demonic activity.

[18:3] Then he puts courage into them when he says: *Now the rivers will be all like an inhabited country; their country will be inhabited; for now* in your journey *the rivers of the land will be inhabited and all their lands.* It seems to me that when he speaks of *rivers*, he is foreshadowing the multitudes of people who will come to acknowledge God, and their *lands* then would stand for the churches. For as **[121]** he above compared the "multitude of unbelieving nations" with "a swelling sea and troubled water,"[11] so now he portrays the people of Christ as sweet and gently flowing *rivers.* Thus, it is clear that their *land* is the church. Therefore, they were once uninhabited *rivers* and "aliens to God,"[12] and their *land* was desolate of piety. But now, he says, through your preaching, the *rivers* and their *land* will become part of the inhabited world. And he will grant this *signal* of Christ to them—although it will not be recognized, even though it will be manifest to all—*as if a signal were raised from a* high *mountain* or *as the sound of a trumpet* sounding loudly. In the same way, your preaching will be clear, audible and renowned among all people.

[18:4] And he teaches how the *rivers* and their aforementioned *land* will be peacefully

inhabited when he says: *Because thus the Lord said to me: There will be safety in my city.* And the aforementioned *land* is the city of the Lord. For this reason, *there will be safety in it,* because I will guard it and keep watch in all quarters. Thus it has been rightly said: "Glorious things are spoken of you, O city of God,"[13] and: "There is a river whose streams make glad the city of God."[14] And thus the Word is accustomed to calling the city in which *there will be safety* the "city of God." And he adds that there will be *light in the same city,* not the natural light we know but light which he compares with the rays of the midday sun. And this *light* will be *like the midday heat,* and he says that *in my city* there will be neither injury nor pain for those on whom this light shines, because there will be a cloud overshadowing them *as in the days of harvest.*[15]

Therefore, the Word of God himself is the *light* and the one who "enlightens"[16] his church through everything. The Holy Spirit is the *cloud of dew* that overshadows the height of the knowledge of the only-begotten Son of God, so as to conceal it from those who are not believers. The Holy Spirit, whose movements are like that of a cloud, brings about the greatest and highest expressions of the theology of Christ.

[18:5-6] And he says that these things will occur *before the harvest.* He is thus clearly speaking of those in the churches of God who bear fruit and are stocks of corn, budding and reproducing ears of corn. It was concerning them that it was said above: "They will also rejoice before you like those who rejoice at the harvest."[17] The Savior also said: "Lift up your eyes, and see how the fields are already white for harvest,"[18] **[122]** and again: "The harvest is plentiful, but the laborers are few; pray therefore the Lord of the harvest to send out

---

[9]Eph 2:12.　[10]Is 29:19.　[11]Cf. Is 17:12-13.　[12]Cf. *1 Clem.* 7:7.　[13]Ps 87:3 RSV.　[14]Ps 46:4 RSV.　[15]Much is lost from the last clause of this sentence due to the poor condition of the manuscript at this point. However, the sense is clear.　[16]Jn 1:9.　[17]Is 9:3.　[18]Jn 4:35 RSV.

laborers into his harvest."[19] And therefore the *light* of the divine Word will be like the *midday sun* at its height *in his city*. And because the *cloud of dew* of the Holy Spirit passed over and kept people from part of the knowledge, he overshadows the *city* itself, in order that as *in the days of harvest* and in the days *before the harvest*, so also the *light* might shine forth but *the cloud* would still overshadow the city. And these things will occur around the *city* of God before the end and *before the harvest*; and after the *harvest*, at the end of the present life, those who are deemed worthy of the height of the divine Word will take part in that end. Then, to apply another image for the end—that of the fruitfulness of the church—the fruit borne by everyone who has been gathered into the church of God will be separated out. For with the grapevines, whenever the farmer finds that the *clusters of grapes* are *unripe*, he not only *cuts off* what is extraneous and unprofitable from the *branches* but also what is imperfectly formed and dead from off the *clusters of grapes*. For as the extraneous and unprofitable grapes are not necessary and he is not very hopeful that this fruit will come to term, he removes all this with the skill of a husbandman, in order that he might not allow the healthy *clusters of grapes* to spoil.

For this reason, *he will take away* these grapes and hand them over for food *to the birds of heaven and to the beasts of the earth*. And he will keep the fruit that comes to term through all his care. He says that this will not occur during the time of the *harvest*. For the extraneous *branches* of the grapevine and the unprofitable *clusters of grapes* which he *took away* and *cut off* will be used as fodder for the forces of retribution. And the good *clusters of grapes* that bear fruit—that is, the souls of good hope—they will come into the presence of God. The Savior said that he himself was "the grapevine,"[20] and he called the disciples

"the branches." And it would be reasonable to understand the *clusters of grapes of the branches* as those who were taught by the apostles. He informs us that the dead and unprofitable *clusters of grapes* in which no sap runs will all be cast away at the time of the judgment, as the *branches* that bear no *clusters of grapes*. The traitor Judas was one of those unprofitable *clusters of grapes that was to be cut off*.

But instead of *then he will take away the little clusters with pruning hooks*, and the rest, Symmachus says: *And he will cut off what is shabby from it*; and Aquila: *And he will cut off the unnatural growths from it, and he will leave them with the pruning hooks for the birds of heaven and for the beasts of the earth. And the birds of heaven will gather on them, and all the beasts of the earth will come on them*, which are clearly enemies and the forces of retribution.

[18:7] [123] Such is their end, and making mention of the fruit-bearing *branches* and the healthy *clusters of grapes*, he next pronounces: *And gifts will be brought to the Lord of hosts from a people afflicted and plucked*. And this is perhaps about the one who travels "the narrow and hard way that leads to life."[21] And he has been *plucked out* or withdrawn from the common worldly life, but he is great and important before God. For this reason the text says: *And from a great people*. And he says that these *gifts will be brought to the Lord of hosts henceforth and forever*. For in the present life and in the age to come, the identified *people* did not hesitate to offer up reasonable *gifts* and bloodless sacrifices to God. And it was in reference to this people that it was said above: *A nation trodden down and having hope*. Because of the endurance of their *hope*, the text says: "And endurance produces character, and character produces hope, and hope does not disappoint us."[22] The text says this because

---

[19]Mt 9:37-38 RSV. [20]Jn 15:1. [21]Cf. Mt 7:14. [22]Rom 5:4-5 RSV.

those who persecuted the people and trampled them down have also been *trodden down*. Therefore, according to Aquila, it has been said: *An enduring nation that has been treaded on*. You see why he called the *people plucked but enduring*. And he says besides: *Which is in a part of a river of his land*. And whom does this *his* refer to but God?

For it seems that this *nation in a part of a river* of God's *land* should be understood as that which was given citizenship in the church of God, as it is said: "For we know in *part* and we prophesy in *part*."[23] For the land did not contain the whole *river*, that is, the word of God. For this reason, it is said that the *nation* is *in a part of a river* of God's *land*. And the other Greek translations say: *Whose rivers divided the land*. For the enemies of this *nation* of God were persecutors when they *divided the land*, when those who are treacherous plague them, *pressing and treading down* those of the city of God. It has been said about them: "The *rivers* came, and the winds blew,"[24] and again: "The torrent would have gone over us; then over us would have gone the raging waters."[25] And from among all of these—the *people* once *afflicted and plucked* but now set free and the *nation trodden down* but still *hoping in God*— they *will offer gifts to the Lord of hosts*. And the text says that they *will make an offering in the place where the name of the Lord of hosts* is, *in Mount Zion*. For the people who have suffered such things are deemed worthy "of the heavenly city,"[26] and they will offer spiritual sacrifices by the high priest, by the Son of God, *in the place where the name of the Lord of hosts is, in Mount Zion*. The apostle says concerning this: "But we have come to *Mount Zion* and to the city of the living God, the heavenly Jerusalem."[27]

[124] This is the end of the prophecy

against Damascus, which began with the times discussed above and ended with the "close of the age,"[28] the thrice-blessed finish line for the champions of godliness.

[19:1] When one understands the sense correctly, one perceives why the expression *vision of Egypt* is appropriate. The prophet did not say "a vision of Babylon," but "a vision against Babylon,"[1] or "a vision of Judea and Jerusalem" but "a vision, which Isaiah son of Amos saw—which he saw against Judea and against Jerusalem."[2] Neither did he say "of Damascus"[3] or "of Moab,"[4] but he now speaks of a vision of *Egypt*. The text does not say "a vision against Egypt" but *a vision of Egypt*. This could mean that Egypt is about to see and witness with its own eyes what has been unambiguously prophesied concerning it or that the prophet has seen a vision which announced beforehand something beautiful for the Egyptians.[5] For what news that would be brought to the Egyptians could be better and more blessed than that the Lord would deem them worthy of his advent and that he would grant them his knowledge?

One could say that this has been fulfilled in history when the Lord himself, "the one who was in the beginning with God,"[6] God the "Word," lived in the land of the Egyptians. He was neither bodiless nor invisible but indwelled the *swift cloud* of the body, which had been raised up "from the Holy Spirit"[7] and the holy and prepared virgin. For if the line *sitting on a swift cloud* had not been added, we could still have arrived at the idea anyway, for as we know, God the Word was everywhere in bodiless and divine power, since he "fills all things."[8] "He was in the world, and the world was made through him."[9] And he states that his coming will be in Egypt, foreseeing that his

---

[23]1 Cor 13:9. [24]Mt 7:25. [25]Ps 124:4-5 RSV. [26]Heb 12:22. [27]Heb 12:22 RSV. [28]Mt 13:39. **Chapter Nineteen** [1]Is 13:1. [2]Is 1:1. [3]Is 17:1. [4]Is 15:1. [5]To reflect this second sense of the phrase that Eusebius identifies as possible, one might translate it into English: "A vision *for* Egypt." [6]Jn 1:1. [7]Mt 1:18. [8]Eph 4:10. [9]Jn 1:10 RSV.

sojourn would extend even as far as them. But according to this manner of speaking, someone should not say that he was in another part of Egypt entirely. But now, speaking definitely *for Egypt*, he says that the Word *will come* riding *on a swift cloud*, thus it is clear that his coming will be bodily and unique. And one might say that he who was constituted in this succession was deemed worthy of the passage into humanity, the God who was born from the holy virgin, whom the prophecy calls "Emmanuel."[10] For just as a *cloud* is not constituted from anything but air and vapors from the earth, so also the body which he took up "from the Holy Spirit"[11] was also from earthly substances, as was the *swift cloud* on which the Christ of God, who dwelt "in Egypt"[12] during the period of his infancy, [125] sits. And this was sufficient for the Egyptians to be greatly benefited in unspeakable power before the Savior left.

And according to the deeper sense, it was especially needful that the Lord would come to the Egyptians, since they were of all people most superstitious. They not only believed that the reasons for everything were decreed by the stars of heaven, but they even fashioned idols after the image of irrational animals and untamable beasts, birds and reptiles. And so they conducted everything without proper authority and in an unpremeditated way, so that also their king could say with a bold face: "I do not know the LORD,"[13] and: "Who is the LORD that I should heed his voice?"[14] *And the handiworks of Egypt will be shaken at his presence, and their heart will be dismayed within them.* Therefore, the *handiworks* are perhaps the sculptures and the lifeless statues of wood. But he says that the lifeless statues of wood *will be shaken*, and *their heart* (clearly, the demons) *will be dismayed*—or, according to the other Greek translations—*will melt* by an unseen and invisible power. And all these

things were fulfilled when the churches of God adorned all Egypt, gently quelling the demonic activity for a little while.

These things happened in fact among them when the churches of God were settled throughout the whole of Egypt, and the Lord himself dwelled among the Egyptians, visiting his churches, according to the verse: "Where two or three are gathered in my name, there am I in the midst of them."[15] And therefore the churches were shining in his grace and there demolished the error of the demons.

[19:2-3] *And Egyptians will rise up against Egyptians, and a man will war against his brother, and a man against his neighbor, city against city and province against province, and the spirit of the Egyptians will be troubled within them, and I will scatter their counsel.* And instead of *and they will rise up*, Aquila says: *And I will make the Egyptians to be at variance with the Egyptians*, and, Symmachus says: *I will trouble the Egyptians with the Egyptians.* And Theodotion says: *I will stir up trouble for the Egyptians with Egyptians.* These things were fulfilled when the evangelical preaching was spread abroad in Egypt, where the lifeless statues of wood were rocked from their eternal and unmoved position, so that they no longer were situated in a firm position because of the quaking that sprang up among them. And the evil demons that lurk among them were discovered to be nothing at all. For families throughout the whole of Egypt were upset, and the houses and cities of the inhabitants were divided and severed and estranged from one another, and this happened when the people ran to the evangelical preaching and withdrew from the demonic and Egyptian error, and those who [126] remained in this error became hostile and implacable toward the others. And thus *Egyptians were raised up against Egyptians, and a man warred against his neighbor,*

---

[10]Is 7:14. [11]Mt 1:18. [12]Mt 2:13. [13]Ex 5:2 RSV. [14]Ex 5:2 RSV. [15]Mt 18:20 RSV.

and a man against his brother and even city was at variance *against city and province against province*. And districts are still called *provinces* among the Egyptians, and these districts shall be at variance against one another because of their proposed actions. The life of the godless was separated from the government in relation to God, *and province* assembled against *province*. The evangelical law overturned the customs of the Egyptians, and then the law of idolatry warred once more against the saving word. And all these things were so, and the Egyptians were in agreement about their evil and in harmony concerning the error of polytheism, but the Lord confounded those who dwelled among them. Therefore, the text says according to Aquila: *And I will set Egyptians at variance with Egyptians*, and according to Symmachus: *And I will dash the Egyptians together with the Egyptians*. And relatives and sisters will be against each other too. The Lord taught the same thing in the Gospels but with other words when he said: "Do not think that I have come to bring peace on earth; I have not come to bring peace, but a sword,"[16] and the rest.

And these things being so, the Word says that *the spirit of the Egyptians will be troubled*, or, according to Symmachus: *And he will break the spirit of Egypt within it*, or, according to Theodotion: *And the spirit of Egypt will be shattered within it*, or according to Aquila: *And the spirit of Egypt will dissolve inside of it*. And those who were *broken* and *troubled* were Egyptians who contrived evil *counsels* against the advancement of the church, but the Lord says: *I will scatter their counsel*. And some will be at a loss because they will act according to their old custom and turn to those who are supposed to be *gods* among them, and they will receive oracles and divinations concerning the actions of those who raise an uproar against them. Therefore, the text says: *And they will consult their gods and their images and those who speak out of the earth and the ventriloquists.* But no longer will any of these frequently be found among them, and they will fall into a final distress.

[19:4] Therefore, those who live anywhere in these lands will suffer these things, and the Word says that all *Egypt will be delivered into the hands of cruel lords, and cruel kings will lord it over them*. I consider that this indicates the time of the prophesied event. For it signals that this transition in the kingdom of the Egyptians will occur during the period when the Lord arrives in Egypt. And who would not be amazed when considering the period of the preaching of the saving word and how it disbanded the kingdom of the Egyptians, so that from that time until now they have no longer had their former [127] autonomy. But I say that the Ptolemies were in power, and then their Roman lords appeared. And instead of *and cruel lords*, Aquila writes: *And the king who has prevailed will exercise authority over them*; and according to Symmachus: *And a strong king will exercise authority over them*, and Theodotion: *And a strong king will lord it over them*. And you could say that this occurred during the time of the birth of our Savior when one from the kingdom of the Romans was sovereign. And therefore Augustus truly *prevailed* and was the first *strong king*, and he subjected Egypt to the Romans. He descended from the succession of the Ptolemies, who had ruled among them long ago. And those who *prevailed* during the Roman era were absolute and *strong* (or, according to the Septuagint, *cruel*) *kings*, and they reduced the nation of the Egyptians to slavery. They have declared that the military leaders over Egypt were very *cruel* to them during these times. Therefore, the text says concerning them: *And I will deliver Egypt into the hands of*

---

[16]Mt 10:34 RSV.

men, cruel lords,[17] but according to the other
Greek translations they are called cruel lords.[18]
But I say that these rulers were only called
rulers of parts of the land.

19:5-7] The text says next: And the Egyptians
will drink the water that is by the sea. But
instead, Aquila says: And they will drink up the
waters from the sea; and Symmachus: And they
will drain the waters from the sea. The Word
speaks of the sea as a figure for the multitude
of rebellious Egyptians. It will be a strange
sight among them when you offer someone a
cup of water. For they will no longer endure
the water of the river or from another Egyptian source, and as it is not fit for drinking
since it is seawater, he says that they will drink
fresh and strange water. And this was what was
abundantly supplied to them from "the springs
of salvation"[19] from the Lord. Therefore, when
he added to these things the little statement:
"Ah, the multitude of many nations! Like a
swelling sea and the backside of many nations
will roar like water. Many nations are like
much water,"[20] it was clear that he would cast
those who are rebellious from the nations into
the waters and the "swelling sea." And the
phrase and the river will fail could perhaps
mean that their kingdom would no longer be
established. And that the Word is clearly
speaking of the kingdom of the Egyptians
when he said the river will fail, we already
presented earlier in the prophecy concerning
the one who would proceed "from the root of
Jesse."[21] For it was said: "And the Lord will lay
his hand on the river with a violent wind and
will strike seven gullies so that he may cross in
sandals."[22] For such things are also prophesied
in the text at hand, which says: But the river
will fail and every gathering of water will be
dried up, and the passage discussed above said:
"It is a nation without hope and trampled

down, where the rivers plundered the land."[23]
The word is not about the physical rivers
which **[128]** we have described in the Onomasticon.[24] It seems to me that when the prophecy
says that the river will fail and be dried up and
again, after the first one, other rivers and
canals and every gathering of water will fail, the
prophecy foreshadows the dissolution of the
kingdom of the Egyptians and of the former
system of district administration. But since
there were certain enemy powers among them,
he prophesies that the synagogues among them
and their kingdoms would cease at the indicated time.

And he prophesies that the rivers would be
calmed and stilled, thus that the kingdom of
the Egyptians would be demolished, when he
adds next: "And then I will settle their waters
and cause their rivers to run like oil."[25] Next
he says that all that used to grow there would
disappear, the reed around the river, and
certainly also the papyrus and the green marsh
grass, and even what sprouts in the river itself.
All such things are found around the river of
the Egyptians. And I would say that these
things signify the absolute drying up of the
waters, so that there will not be even a trace of
any water either in the river or in the marsh,
neither on the banks of the river nor in the
middle, neither will there even be any stagnant
water in the canals. Therefore, in these
statements the prophecy leads us to believe
that even the people too will disappear and
that there will be nothing left for anyone to
seek. And so it follows that all the water from
so great a river will fail, and every animal will
die, since they will be deprived of the river.

But now, after the failure of so many water
sources, he mentions the people who will be in
Egypt then. And he says that there will be an
altar in Egypt, and the Egyptians will sacrifice
to the Lord, and he will send a man to them who

---

[17]κυρίων σκληρῶν.   [18]σκληροὶ κύριοι.   [19]Is 12:3.   [20]Is 17:12-13.   [21]Is 11:1.   [22]Is 11:15.   [23]Is 18:2, 7.   [24]In Eusebius's words, "The Places."   [25]Ezek 32:14.

*will save them, and the Lord will be known to
the Egyptians.* Who would not be wise to investigate how they could live through the failing
of all the water, since the land will not even
have any *green marsh grass?* But the Word
forces us to adopt a figurative interpretation,
so that even if we do not want to we have no
other choice but to understand the *rivers* and
Egyptian *waters* either as the plenitude of
Egyptian power or as their kingdom which
once was flooded with water. From the
perspective of another interpretation, we could
also conclude that it is philosophy, which once
had a golden age among the Egyptians,
concerning which it has been said: "And Moses
was instructed in all the wisdom of the
Egyptians."[26] For as their philosophy was
great, so their rushing river was great, the
word of venerable wisdom among them. But
this mighty river eventually was reduced to
many *canals* and to many *rivers*, each school of
philosophy having its own disciples. And from
it grew up neither grapevines nor olive trees
nor any necessary and fruit-bearing trees, but
papyrus and a reed and green marsh grass.

[19:8] [129] The text says that those who fish
(clearly, those who hunt the souls of people) in
the *failed* Egyptian *waters* will *mourn.* And you
should know that those whom the prophecy
calls *fishers* and *anglers* are not ordinary fishers
and netters but rather are the apostles and
disciples of our Savior, to whom it was said:
"Come, and I will make you fishers of men."[27]
For through their teaching they hunted for the
souls of people for salvation and thus are to be
differentiated from those called *fishers* and
anglers of the Egyptians, those who of old were
teachers of philosophy among them. For
through their Egyptian magic, they ensnared
those whom they caught, enticing them as with
hooks. And you should understand what their
seines are from the parable of our Savior, when

he said: "The kingdom of heaven is like a net
which was thrown into the sea and caught fish
of every kind."[28] Therefore, just as in the
parable the people are said to be *fish* and the
seine is said to be the evangelical word concerning the kingdom of heaven, so also here the
seine and the *casting nets* are perhaps the
intricate rhetoric of the Egyptians. And those
netted and caught by them then would be the
fish, for they are dragged down by the beguiling
sophistry of their every godless superstition.
And the text says that the *anglers* of Egypt *will
groan* and then *mourn*, because they no longer
have work since the Lord who lived among
them destroyed their every wisdom, as the verse
says: "I will destroy the wisdom of the wise, and
the cleverness of the clever I will thwart."[29]

[19:9-10] Thus you should understand that
the split flax that *they work* is not stiff or
unbroken *flax* but *split* (clearly, their philosophy has been split apart and severed), and
likewise with their *linen* which grew in the
river of the Egyptians and was watered by it.
For this reason the Word says that the *workers*
of these materials *will groan.* Then there was
no longer an abundance of their philosophical
fabrications, nothing more to spin according to
the circuit and system of their wisdom. For
just as one spins with *split flax* and *linen*, so
they contrived systems and circuits that were
plausible to them at least, contrived with
deceptive words that conceal falsehoods. The
text says that not only these *will groan*, but
also all those who *make beer*—not wine from
the grape, but Egyptian *beer.* It was counterfeit
and muddy, but they enjoyed it as the drink of
choice when the Lord lived among them. And
it is rightly said that the Egyptians *will mourn*
because of the lack of water, and the souls of
the workers will be pained. Therefore, he
threatens that the sophists[30] of Egypt will
suffer these things, those beer brewers and

---

[26]Acts 7:22 rsv. [27]Mt 4:19. [28]Mt 13:47. [29]1 Cor 1:19 rsv; cf. Is 29:14. [30]This word could either mean "sophist" or "expert craftsman."

workers of *split flax* [130] and *linen*, and fishers, and those who revere the Egyptian river and Egyptian philosophy. Another prophet attempted to avert the people from Egyptian philosophy when he cried: "What do you gain by going to Egypt, to drink the waters of the Nile?"[31]

19:11-15] And those things stated next are about the unseen rulers, who at that time especially watched over the greatest and most prominent cities of Egypt. What I mean is that the prophet addresses *Tanis* and *Memphis* in this way: *And the rulers of Tanis will be fools; as for the wise counselors of the king, their counsel will become foolish*; and again: *The rulers of Tanis have failed, and the rulers of Memphis have been exalted, and they led Egypt astray*. But according to Symmachus: *The rulers of Tanis struggled, the rulers of Memphis stiffened up; they deceived Egypt*. In saying these things, he presents all the meretricious arts as demonic idolatry, and he says that the rulers of Egypt had a palace here in the days of Moses. Therefore, the text says that there were "signs in Tanis's plain,"[32] wonders during the times of Moses and wonders there now as well. And, therefore, he says that those ruling demons *became fools* when the Lord lived in Egypt by the Egyptian river, and although they professed wisdom, the Lord was not present among them. But he rebuked them and charged them of possessing no wisdom at all. And they were truly *fools* during the coming of the Lord. And the kings of Egypt relied on the oracles delivered by the ruling demons just as they would the pronouncements of their advisors, and thus they were seduced by these divinations and oracles and the other demonic frauds. Therefore, the text says: *And they led Egypt astray*. Then the Word declares as though speaking to the Egyptian demons themselves: *How will you say to the king, "We are sons of sages, sons of kings who were from the beginning?"* How can you seriously say that, since you are perfectly aware that there is no longer a king among you? And how can you say that you yourselves are *sons* of those who were once *kings* and to whom sacrifices were presented—Horus and Isis and Osirus and Tufona—or of the family of the gods, heroes and spirits of the dead who once dominated Egypt? How can you say that you yourselves are the *sons* and descendents of gods and *kings*, those whom the prophecy speaks of as the *rulers of Tanis and Memphis*? And how could you be gods, or what sort of wisdom could you possess, since you were neither able to know nor declare in advance your sentence and the destruction of the kingdom? You were their advisors, but you murdered them with your manifold delusions.

[131] He addresses these advisors and Egypt itself when he says next: *Where now are your wise men? And let them also declare to you and say what the Lord of hosts has planned against Egypt*. And where are your wise gods, who through divinations and oracles promise to announce the things that are about to happen? Let them stand before all and say *what the Lord of hosts has planned against Egypt*. But there is none who can tell it. For none of the evil demons knew the counsel of God, but neither did anyone else. *The rulers of Tanis and Memphis have failed*—those who were once *exalted* and *led Egypt astray* by the consent of the Lord. For since those mentioned above could neither observe all foreknowledge nor oversee it either entirely or partially, they would have been powerless to *lead Egypt astray* if the Lord himself had not allowed this to happen to them. He *prepared for them a spirit of error*, and for this reason the Egyptians *went astray* just like *drunkards*. And so strong was the Egyptian *drink* that their men were like *a drunkard and one who vomits . . . together* from

---

[31]Jer 2:18 RSV. [32]Ps 78:12.

the great excess of *drink*.

And one may gauge the potency of this drink in as far their idolatrous practices are not like those of other people; they make idols in the form of irrational animals. Therefore, the text says: *As the drunkard and the one who vomits are led astray together*, or, according to the other Greek translations: *As the drunkard is led astray when he vomits*. Above all, the question is whether we should understand the *drunkard and the one vomiting* as the same person or not. For *together* refers to them both, so that we understand that the one *vomiting* is also drinking and drinking to get drunk, and again the one *vomiting* is also the one *vomiting* from his drinking. And by such drink the aforementioned *rulers of Tanis and Memphis led astray* the souls of the Egyptians, for whom the Lord himself *prepared a spirit of error*. For the demons were evil and were enemy powers with a mind contrary to God, and they attempted to do battle with God. For this reason they were delivered over to error, since God judged them to be evil and worthy to be delivered over to error. And these emit their own evil on the Egyptians just as a deadly poison, and *they led Egypt astray, as the drunkard and the one who vomits are led astray together*.

The Lord lived in Egypt because of them, in order that, once he had brought them to their senses from their error, he might completely dispel their errors. Therefore, the text says: *And there will no longer be a work for the Egyptians that will make head or tail, beginning or end*. For tasks that previously had been accomplished among them will now be unprofitable and ineffective, so that no work among them will have either *beginning* or *end*, and the good Lord worked it this way. For long ago there were works of the error of polytheism among the Egyptians that had a *beginning* and an *end* and what was thought to be an outcome. And he says that during the aforementioned time when the Lord comes to them *there will no longer be a work* among them that is fulfilled and completed and finished. But even if a work ever be found, it will be one without beginning or commencement and without end or [132] conclusion. This then will in fact be the case[33] because they have not completely forsaken their idolatry. And so it is that the matter will have neither *head* nor adequate *end*.

[19:16-17] During the time of the arrival of the Lord into Egypt, to which we already referred, he prophesies that there will no longer be a manly spirit among the *Egyptians* but, as *women in trembling and fear*, their constitution will dissolve because of the *hand* of God that will rest on them. And what else should we understand the *hand* of the *Lord* to be but his said right hand, the Roman power that subjected the Egyptians and brought them under their hand because of the coming of the Lord? For it has been recorded that the devil also once said to God concerning Job: "But put forth your hand now, and touch all that he has, and surely he will curse you to your face."[34] Accordingly, the power that was served by the will of God and that conquered the ruler of Egypt was the Roman army, which is also called the *hand* of Rome. And that the *Egyptians* serve the Romans like *women* with *fear* and anguish, it is not necessary to say anything.

But the *land of the Judeans* became a *terror* among the *Egyptians* to whom the Lord came. And you would not be wrong in saying that the *land of the Judeans* represents the divine Scriptures, since the land is said to possess an extreme reverence and faith and acknowledges the Lord "with fear and trembling."[35] It believes in reverence, no longer blasphemes as before but honors and respects the Lord, because he was preached in it. For this reason, every person who reads the Scripture among them

---

[33]Eusebius puns here: in Greek, "in fact" is said "in work."   [34]Job 1:11.   [35]Cf. 2 Cor 7:15.

produces the *fear* of God among them. "The fear of the Lord is the beginning of wisdom."[36]

[19:18] And during the same time, when it is prophesied that these things will occur, the Word says that *five cities* will be established *in Egypt*, speaking and *swearing* not in the *language* of the Egyptians but in *Chananite*. They once believed in the gods of their ancestors, but now they adhere to the God who is known among the Jews; they believe *in the name of the Lord of hosts*. And this was the one "on a swift cloud"[37] who lived among them. And what is remarkable is that the Hebrew text uses the word current among the Egyptians, for the Egyptians call Hebrew the *Chananite language*. Whenever they use Hebrew words in the church of God, they are "alleluia" and "amen" and "Sabbath" and such others as are found in the divine Scripture. And when it says that when they swear to the Lord and make an oath in his name as well as in the name of the gods of their ancestors, they honor the *Lord of hosts*, who is known only among the Jews, **[133]** it is not necessary to say anything concerning the truth of the same prophetic and sanctioned voice. And it is important not to misunderstand that, although the *cities* in the prophecy are said to be *five*, they count as *one*. And for this reason they all are called by one name, *Asedek*, although Symmachus translates the name *Sun*. Therefore one might conclude that this city is the holy church of God, especially since in the Septuagint it is called *Asedek*, which means *righteousness*. In Symmachus it is called *sun*, about which it has been said: "For those who fear my name the sun of *righteousness* shall rise, with healing in its wings."[38] To be accurate, the city is called *Areopolis* in the Hebrew, according to which the final phrase would be translated: *The one city will be called the city of the earth*. For of

all the cities in the world, God is seated only in this one, and so it has been said: "Glorious things are spoken of you, O city of God."[39]

And one could say that there are *five cities* of God within the church, for the various offices could be distributed into five divisions. Thus, one would count the first division as that of the bishops,[40] the second as that of the presbyters, the third as that of the deacons, the fourth as that of the enlightened in Christ, and to these one might add those who happen to be present. And so these offices would come to *five* divisions in the church of God. For this reason it has been said that *five cities will speak* in *one language*, which the Egyptians supposed was *Chananite* and in which they will *swear by the name of the Lord of hosts*. One begins to see the wonder of the word when he understands that the Egyptians used to be the most superstitious, and of all people enemies of the Jews and accustomed to blaspheming their God. It is said in the Jewish Scriptures that they will adopt the fear of him who bears the title among the Jews the *Lord of hosts*, so that they will swear oaths by his name. And he rightly said that the church was the *city* of the light of the *sun* because Christ is the light of God enlightening every man, coming into the world."[41] Therefore, the text reads in Symmachus's version: *The one city will be called the city of the sun*.

[19:19] And after the Word prophesied about the city of God that will be established in Egypt and about the various offices in the city, he mentions that there will be an *altar* in the city of God, and this will be miraculous. For he says that when the idols that the Egyptians formerly supposed to be gods have been destroyed, and "their river has failed,"[42] and "the rulers of Tanis and Memphis have been made fools"[43] and when all that has been announced beforehand has happened, then an

[36]Ps 111:10. [37]Is 19:1. [38]Mal 4:2. [39]Ps 87:3. [40]The word Eusebius uses is "presidents; those who sit in the front." [41]Jn 1:9. [42]Cf. Is 19:6. [43]Is 19:11.

altar will be established to him whom the Jews revere as the Lord. And now we have seen the fulfillment of these deeds with our own eyes, and so the final accomplishment [134] of the word no longer awaits a time in the future. And as it has been said that there is "one faith"[44] and "one baptism" and one church, so also there will be one *altar*, and the altar of which we speak is the one found in all of the churches across Egypt. And the one *stele* that will be erected with the altar in the city is the evangelical Scripture, and it will differentiate the faithless from the faithful among the Egyptians. For this reason, the text says: *And there will be a stele to the Lord at its border.* Therefore, when he speaks above of the "terror" that will happen "to the Egyptians"[45] and the "land of the Judeans," he is speaking about the Jewish Scriptures, the word of the old covenant.[46] And the *stele* which we have paired with the *altar* of Christ would be the gospel of the New Testament, which distinguishes those who believe in Christ from the unbelieving of the Egyptians.

[19:20] He says concerning these things: *The Lord will be a sign forever in the country of Egypt.* For this reason, having learned that they have been sealed with this *sign*, those Egyptians who have received the Lord made use of this symbol, and those who were in oppression appealed to this aiding *sign* and shouted aloud and called on *the Lord on account of those who oppress them.* And these were faithful Egyptians, but there were also Egyptians who remained in disbelief, concerning whom it was said at the beginning of the prophecy: "And Egyptians will rise up in revolt against Egyptians, and a man will war against his brother, city against city and province against province."[47] And they who are op-

pressed by those who *oppress* and persecute those who flee to God for refuge, they will indeed cry out *to the Lord*, and he will immediately present a *savior* for them, his Christ. Therefore, according to the other Greek translations, the text says: *And he will send a savior to them, and he will fight on their behalf.* It is perfectly obvious that this is about Jesus our *Savior*, for *Jesus* is how one translates the name from the Hebrew of the prophetic word. And instead of *he will save them—judging he will save them,* Symmachus writes: *And he will fight on their behalf, and he will deliver them.* And who will *deliver* them, and who is the *savior* who will be sent to help those who are oppressed because of him? *And judging he will save them,* if he finds them worthy of salvation by his invisible hand; he will pursue and judge those who *oppress* them.

[19:21] And, therefore, especially in this way *the Lord will be known to the Egyptians, and the Egyptians will know the Lord on that day,* that is, clearly in the time of their oppression. And having learned to be grateful, they will render *sacrifices* to him, since they will then have an *altar* among themselves and will then be deemed worthy by God to be priests. Therefore, according to Symmachus, the text reads: *And they will offer a sacrifice and an offering.* Then, it is necessary to understand the sense here, for the Word presents an introduction to the new law and [135] new covenant. For the law of Moses commanded that no *altar* be erected outside Jerusalem and that only those of the tribe of Levi and none other be priests to God.[48] But the prophecy foretells that an *altar* to God will be erected in Egypt and that there will be priests of the Egyptian race and that *sacrifices and offerings* will be offered up to the Lord of the prophets. The divine apostle says

---

[44]Eph 4:5. [45]Is 19:17. [46]παλαιᾶς διαθήκης. This phrase could also be translated "old testament," so long as one understands that Eusebius is not talking about the corpus of literature per se but the former covenant God had with his people. [47]Is 19:2. [48]Cf. Deut 12:5; Ex 32:26-29.

omewhere: "And when there is a change in the priesthood, there is necessarily a change in the law as well."[49] And concerning these things, he states next: *And they*—clearly, the Egyptians—*will make a vow to the Lord and repay it.* For, promising with *vows*, they will not fail to fulfill those promises that are fitting for God, and therefore they will endure until death in their godly struggle.

19:22] Then he adds: *And the Lord will strike the Egyptians with a blow and heal them with healing, and they will return to the Lord.* "For the Lord disciplines him whom he loves and scourges every son whom he receives."[50] Therefore, because he loves them, it is right that *he will strike the Egyptians*, but only when there is a need for discipline and correction and not for long. But, withholding nothing, *he heals them with healing.*

[19:23-25] And he says that during the same *day*—that is, during the identified time—*there will be a way among the Egyptians to the Assyrians, and the Assyrians will enter Egypt, and the Egyptians will go to the Assyrians, and the Egyptians will be subject to the Assyrians.* And here I suppose that the Scripture is calling them *Assyrians* who are now called *Syrians*, for those who live in Syria and Mesopotamia were once called *Assyrians*. And the Egyptians and Assyrians were enemies, and they of all peoples continued to be adversaries. But now, the present word prophesies that there will be fellowship and interrelations among them, although this has never been the case yet. For, before the Roman rule, the Egyptians and the Assyrians had completely separate kingdoms. The Egyptians had the Ptolemaic empire, and the Syrians from Antioch and Demetrius. And Judea lay exactly in the middle and was governed by its own rulers. And the nation of the Jews was caught

in the middle when Syria waged war against it and when the Ptolemies waged war against it. But the Syrians were always enemies with the Egyptians, and the Egyptians fought with the Syrians, and thus they were segregated and defensive in their stance toward one another. Indeed, such things happened in the old days, but the present word preaches that there will be the deepest peace in Egypt and fellowship and interrelations after the arrival of the Lord, saying: *There will be a way among the Egyptians to the Assyrians, and the Assyrians will enter Egypt, and the Egyptians will go to the Assyrians, and the Egyptians will be subject to the Assyrians.* **[136]** *And Israel will be third blessed among the Assyrians and among the Egyptians.* Therefore, he gathers together the old enemies and adversaries—I am speaking about the Syrians and Egyptians and Israel—and says that they will all enjoy one blessing from God. Israel will then no longer be proud or arrogant toward the others, as though they were the only ones who were *blessed* and as though they were the only people of God. But the prophecy also teaches that even though they will enjoy this blessing, the Egyptians will be subject to the Assyrians (I am speaking about the Syrians).

Would one, therefore, who has seen with his own eyes the Roman encampments of Syrian troops lying in wait against the commander of the Egyptians, and the Egyptians subject to them—would he not be astounded at the fulfillment of this prophecy? And who would not be amazed to see Egyptians traveling without fear through the land of the Syrians or Syrians going freely about their business among the Egyptians, instead of reducing the other to slavery by the power of the ruling authorities in their own lands? But the most incredible thing of all is that during that same time there will be people among the Syrians and Egyptians and in the land of Israel

---

[49]Heb 7:12. [50]Prov 3:12.

who will be *blessed* by God, so that Israel will no longer differ at all from Egypt and Syria, neither will Syria be superior to Israel or Egypt in the sight of God, nor again will Egypt be inferior to Israel and Syria in the sight of God.[51]

The good will that those who were once enemies and adversaries with one another will share at the coming of the Lord will be tremendous, the prophet says. Therefore, on the one hand, the people of the Lord were allied with Egypt itself, just as the people of Syria can be immediately recognized through the great quantity of the churches. And, on the other hand, the people from the Israelite race were most numerous at the time the gospel was first preached, when the disciples of our Savior and the apostles and all the evangelists and those from the circumcision feared God and acknowledged the Christ of God, as did the Egyptians and Syrians. For this reason they were all in common deemed worthy of one and the same blessing from God. Therefore, the text says: *Blessed be my people that are in Egypt and among the Assyrians, even Israel my heritage.* But according to the other Greek translations, the text reads: *Blessed be my people Egypt and Assyria,* not as though speaking of the Jews in Egypt but the Egyptians and the Syrians themselves. And when it is said that *Israel will be third among the Egyptians and among the Assyrians, blessed in the land that the Lord of hosts has blessed,* we should not suppose the land to be anything else than the land of the church of God. And it is possible to understand *Israel* and the whole band of saints and God-loving people from the Jewish nation who have passed on from this life. For this reason, the text says: *Even Israel my heritage.* "For when the Most High gave to the nations their inheritance, the Lord's portion is his [137] people Jacob, his allotted

heritage Israel."[52] Then only Israel was mentioned, but now the Egyptians are also said to be his *people*, and likewise the Assyrians his *blessed people*. And in the phrase *in the land that the Lord of hosts has blessed*, one might find a reference to the heavenly land, concerning which the Savior said: "Blessed are the meek, for they shall inherit the earth,"[53] and again: "It is the heavenly Jerusalem and the heavenly Mount Zion of God."[54]

[20:1-3] It would seem that the things discussed above are contrary to those which have just been said. For before the Word indicated that there would be peaceful relations between the Egyptians and Assyrians, but now he says that the *king of the Assyrians* will take captives from the Egyptians, *young and old, naked and barefoot.* And a solution to the difficulty might be found if we understand it in the manner of the prophetic Spirit. For as he turned toward Egypt, he was able to see what was momentarily about to happen to the Egyptians during the time of the prophet, but then he looked away toward the pleasant things that would result concerning the land of the Egyptians later in times far distant. Then, after prophesying about the pleasant things first through the above, he turns toward what would happen in the immediate future. And these were painful for the Egyptians and were not fulfilled in far distant times but during those which the prophet announced. And of necessity, after prophesying about what would happen in the immediate future, the divine Spirit concluded what would happen concerning the arrival of the Lord into Egypt and concerning the good things that would occur among the Egyptians. He did this in order that, from the fulfillment of the present prophecy, the people would believe that what was prophesied to happen later in times far distant would indeed happen

---

[51]Eusebius's clear intention is to place these three countries on a level footing, and therefore he has created three statements, each one headed by one of the three countries. [52]Deut 32:8-9. [53]Mt 5:5 RSV. [54]Heb 12:22.

or those who listened then, at that time, to the prophetic words.

Therefore, the things discussed beforehand are not contrary to those prophesied above. For on the one hand, he referred to the times that would come in the distant future, and on the other hand, he proclaims about what will happen in the near future. For during the time of the prophet Isaiah, when the king of the Assyrians was in power, after approaching the nation of the Palestinians, he took Azotus, which was then the greatest and most prominent of the cities in the area. And when the cities had been conquered, the prophet was commanded to go about in public without even one garment because of the heights to which philosophy had reached in them. And he was commanded to lay aside his garment, which had not been woven from wool but from goats' hair, and thus to present himself as absolutely *naked*, since he did not have a second covering of animal skin. He was also commanded to remove his *sandals*, or, according to the other Greek translations, *shoes*. And after passing over these things, God says that when the Egyptians are attacked by the Assyrians, they will share the same appearance as the prophet. Not only *will they be led away naked and barefoot*, but the feared *Ethiopians* will also act as an ally and enter into an alliance with them. For [138] because the Ethiopians were numerous and very powerful by the standards of the time, the Egyptians felt confident and disdained the Assyrians. But God demonstrates what is about to happen when he says: *Just as my servant Isaiah has walked naked and barefoot for three years, there will be signs and portents to the Egyptians.*

[20:4-6] See those who were conquered by the Assyrians being *carried away naked and barefoot*, in keeping with the example that the prophet had left for them. Therefore, the text

states next: *Naked and barefoot and with uncovered shame, thus the king of the Assyrians will carry off the Egyptians and the Ethiopians.* And after capturing the Ethiopians, *the Egyptians will be ashamed* and blush before those in whom they had confidence and *trusted,* so that *those who dwell in this island*—clearly, in the land of the Egyptians—will condemn and blame themselves. And he called it an *island* because they streamed around from every side and encircled them by the river. And he says that they will condemn themselves and regret that they hung their hopes on people rather than the God of the whole world. *And how* will they be able *to be saved,* when those who expected to find help suffered such things? And what is astounding is the prophetic life, which the apostle also presents when he says: "They went about in skins of sheep and goats, destitute, afflicted, ill-treated."[1] And the Scripture at hand presents Isaiah as without even a sackcloth garment, clearly mourning and bewailing those who had fallen far away from God because of their own impieties. And the fact that he was willing to go about *naked* when ordered to do so, and not to delay but to perform this immediately and before the eyes of everyone around him—this is perhaps the greatest evidence of his obedience and devotion to God. Led on to desperate courage and unyielding resolution, he threw his reputation among people to the wind.

[21:1-2] I suppose that, seeking to maintain a literal reading of what as discussed above, he resumed the subject of the words contained therein: "Babylon has fallen, it has fallen, and all its images and the works of its hands have been crushed."[1] For these things have been said outright concerning Babylon. And the Word that advances anew says: *The Elamites are on me, and the envoys of the Persians are coming on me.* But instead of this, Symmachus translates

---

Chapter Twenty [1]Heb 11:37 RSV. **Chapter Twenty-One** [1]Is 21:9.

it: *Arise, Elam, go to war, Medes.* And the Hebrew text and the other Greek translations have *those from among the Medes* here. And these are the ones who *descended* on the ruler of the Babylonians, as the prophecy concerning Babylon indicated through what was discussed above when it said: "See, I am stirring up the Medes against you."[2] And, therefore, it was not long afterwards that the Persians who succeeded the Medes cleared away the remnants of Babylon. And, therefore, I think that **[139]** what was said beforehand has been said rightly. And what does the Word mean when he says: *The vision of the wilderness?* Here, he already calls Babylon a *wilderness* because of the things that have been prophesied concerning its desolation.[3] Accordingly, the *vision of the wilderness of the sea* signifies the desolate *sea* of Babylon. And if anyone were to ask what this inauspicious word (which was once fulfilled through what was discussed above in the prophecy that we have explained concerning Babylon) concerning Babylon means, we would say that, because "The king of the Assyrians would lead away the captives of Egypt and of the Ethiopians, young and old, naked and barefoot,"[4] as we recently said, the Word signifies of necessity what sort of terrible things will soon happen to the Assyrians. For just as God fairly punished the Egyptians through the invasion of the Assyrians, so he also purged their arrogance when he delivered the Assyrians over to the Medes, and then he subjected the Medes to the Persians, and finally he chastened them with others. And so the above sequence will no doubt go on and on.

Once the heading "the *vision* of the desolated *sea*" has been stated, the Word leads on: *As a whirlwind might pass through a wilderness—coming from a wilderness, from land—dreadful and harsh is the vision declared to me.* I suppose that these things are said directly to Babylon itself. It is as if, after receiving the report of the evil that was about to befall it, it wishes that the report would pass and that the anticipated things would not happen. Therefore, the text says: *Dreadful and harsh is the vision declared to me, just like a whirlwind might pass through a wilderness.* For it may be that he says that it passed through and passed by on the other side like a *whirlwind coming from a wilderness.* For if the very report of the *vision* that had been made known to me was harsh and caused terrible fright, how then will it be when it actually comes up like a *whirlwind coming from a wilderness* and when it *passes through* and overtakes and comes on me so that I have no firm footing. For I learned who the *betrayer betraying and the lawless one acting lawlessly* would be, for I heard their name from those who declared the vision to me: it is the *Elamites* and the *Medes* who *will come on me,* and they are the forerunners of the Persians. It is for this reason that one would not be wrong to say that they are the *envoys of the Persians.*[5] Therefore, what should I do about the *whirlwind* of those who are about to attack me? *Now I will groan,* although I did not used to do so, but since it was proud and arrogant toward the other nations, it will now heave a sigh to those around. But *now* the speaker is Babylon, and the people in it are those who say *I will groan and comfort myself* with a sigh.

[21:3-4] The message concerning what was spoken about above had been fastened around me, and thus *my loins,* which had once been robed neatly and stylishly, were *filled with weakness.* Pain and distress gripped me—Babylon, which once towered above all others—and I became fearful as a *woman in labor.* I acknowledge that *I did wrong,* and these things happened to me when *I did* not *listen* to those who were exhorting me and when I did not

---

[2]Is 13:17. [3] In Greek, the word for "wilderness" (ἔρημος) and the word for "desolation" (ἐρημία) are cognate. [4]Is 20:4. [5]The word for "envoy" here is πρέσβεις, a word that also means "elder" and hence also includes overtones of "forerunner" or "antecedent."

hasten [140] *to see* anything correctly. There-fore, the text says: I have confessed that *I did wrong not hearing; I hastened not seeing. My heart wanders, and lawlessness overwhelms me; my heart has turned to fear.* But instead of this, Symmachus has: *My soul wandered; my heart was troubled; my once calm state of being drew me into an uproar, it drove me into confusion.*

[21:5-6] I suppose that these words are the prophet's dramatization of what Babylon would say, or perhaps what the people who live in it would convey. The prophetic Spirit addresses the Medes and the Elamites and the envoys of the Persians, stirring them up and inciting them to war against the Babylonians. Therefore, he says as though to them: *Prepare the table; eat; drink! Rise up, rulers; prepare the shields!* And the subject who speaks these things is the prophet being moved by the prophetic Spirit, when *because thus the Lord said to me: "Go, post a lookout for yourself, and report whatever you see,"* or, according to the other Greek translations: *Let him report whatever he,* clearly, *the lookout, sees.*

[21:7-9] Then he says that the *lookout* was posted according to the command of the Lord, *and he saw two riding horsemen,* or, according to Symmachus: *And he saw a chariot and a yoke of horses.* Therefore, this is what he saw first, and after this *pair of horses* he saw another *two horses,* one riding a *donkey* and another riding a *camel.* And these things were signs and sym-bols of the marshaling of the enemies who approached riding in *chariots* and on beasts of burden and animals drawn by reins. Therefore, *the lookout* whom God charged by the prophet saw these things. The text says: *Listen with much listening, and call Ourias to the watch-tower.* Then he commands his own ears to attend and to *listen* to the word that was about to be delivered and to *call Ourias to the watch-*

tower. But instead of *Ourias,* Aquila renders the word as *a lion,* and Symmachus as *a lioness,* and Theodotion as *Ariel.* And none of these translations render it *Ourias,* since the Hebrew text does not mention *Ourias.* For when he made mention of "*Ourias the priest*"[6] above, he was speaking of the man in other letters, but now in another text and in other letters, the Hebrew word means *lion,* or, perhaps, as Symmachus says, *a lioness.*

Therefore, the Lord commands the prophet *to listen with much listening* to what is about to be spoken and then *to call* either the *lion* or *Ariel,* so that after he comes with the *lookout* he might see what the prophet together with the *lookout* saw. This is what the word indi-cates when it says next: *I stood continually by day, and* [141] *over the camp I stood the whole night.* Accordingly, the prophet stood together with the *lookout* waiting to see the visage of the *lion* or the *lioness* or *Ariel.*

And after waiting patiently for the space of *the whole day and night,* he states: *And look, he himself comes.* But who is this? Is it *Ariel* mounted on *a pair of horses?* For this reason, the text says: *And look, he himself comes, one mounted on a pair of horses.* And who was this then? An avenging angel who was about to fulfill what had been prophesied concerning the besieging of Babylon? Or perhaps it is he who was called *Ariel,* the one who "prowls around like a roaring lion, seeking someone whom he might devour."[7] And then the prophet saw him, and he watched as an avenging angel worked the destruction of Babylon. Therefore, he cried out: *Babylon has fallen, it has fallen, and all its images and the works of its hands have been crushed to the ground.* For, since *Ariel* has been ordered to do these things, the prophet lets out this cry. Therefore, two *lookouts* are presented in this passage and two visages are seen. Indeed, the first *lookout* saw a *rider of two horses and a*

6Cf. Is 8:2. 71 Pet 5:8.

rider of a donkey and a rider of a camel, and the second, who was the prophet himself, saw not riders of camels or donkeys but one mounted on a pair of horses, that is, on the lion or Ariel, who brought about the aforesaid fall of Babylon and the crushing of its supposed gods. Therefore, according to Symmachus, the text says: Babylon has fallen, it has fallen, and all the images of its gods have been crushed. Therefore, the report of the first lookout is inferior to the prophet's, for although he saw a multitude of military men about to come on Babylon, the second, who was the prophet himself, saw the ineffable visage of the angel (at least, I suppose it was an angel) who brought about the fall of Babylon. Then, indeed, the prophetic Spirit rightly cried aloud and said: Babylon has fallen, it has fallen, and all its images and the works of its hands. Anticipating this, the Lord said to the prophet: Listen with much listening (this listening is clearly the report concerning Babylon and its images). I suppose that this signifies the utter destruction of the kingdom of the Assyrians which would come by the judgment of God. And the messenger would have appeared foolish, except that he had been cast away by the prophet according to the command of God.

[21:10] And thus, for the rest, the prophet brings to light these things from those which have been done. And although he heard, he also saw those who have been left and those who are in pain among the people. And these who lamented bitterly against the people and barely survived from the error of the many were very few indeed. It is they whom the prophet addresses when he says: Hear the things I have heard from the Lord of hosts; the God of Israel has announced them [142] to us. For what he revealed to me he also brought to light for you through my interpreter. This is the end of the prophecy concerning Egypt, after which the Word turns to another theme.

[21:11] The Word has not idly made the prophecy concerning these things, but because the enemies of Israel were constantly attacking them, the narrative testifies to these things. As the psalm says: "They conspire with one accord; against you they make a covenant; the tents of Edom and the Ishmaelites, Moab and the Hagrites, Gebal and Ammon and Amalek."[8] You see how he places Edom before all of the enemies of the people of Israel. And this nation was great all around Petra in Arabia, and they were descendants of Esau. And Esau was the brother of Jacob, who is also called Israel, and all the Idumeans are from him. Thus, the Idumeans and the Jews are the children of brothers. For Edom was called Esau, and, for this reason, the Idumeans are from him. And so, the Idumeans were constantly rising up against Israel, and the prophet rightly sees a vision concerning them and foretells what would happen to them. It would appear that God addresses those who are known to himself when he says: He calls to me from Seir. The other Greek translations say he calls to me those who flee from Seir. And the mountain of Esau in Arabia was called Seir, in which he established the seat of his empire. And it is still called Seir by people in this region up to the present. Therefore, to those anguishing in fear of the Idumeans, he says: come quickly to me, and once you are by me, guard your battlements.

[21:12] And I will guard you during the day and during the night, and you will be by me. Therefore, if anyone among you needs help, let him inquire from me. Therefore, it seems to me that these things were said to those who were terrified and in fear of the Idumeans. God calls them to himself and promises to give them help, if they stay beside him.

---

[8]Ps 83:5-7.

21:13-15] The prophet says these things next, taking up another theme from the Holy Spirit. For this reason, he called the word a *statement*,⁹ although the *statement* is no longer addressed only to the Idumeans but is now also for the rest of those who live in Arabia and for those who were the enemies and adversaries of Israel. Concerning them, he says: You were always brimming with confidence and thus gradually became arrogant against my people, and thus now, after learning what would befall you, you came back to your senses.

For already your adversaries have set about cutting you down, and it may happen that most of you perish; but perhaps only one or two, or maybe at least a few, **[143]** if they should flee would thus escape with their lives and obtain salvation. I exhort them to prepare *bread* and *water* for those who are already weak and for those who have fainted. And, therefore, no longer having a city to dwell in, they will *lie down in the evening in the thicket* and in the desert places as they come on them. But, in order that they not perish in the famine, I exhort that they present *bread* and drink to those who are fatigued and dehydrated from exertion. And thus I say these things to you who live in the land called *Theman*, for whom it would be fitting to receive the refugees with kindness and to extend humanitarian aid, since they are not able to dwell in the city and thus must pass the nights in the *ways* and *thickets*. Therefore, you must not pitilessly disregard those perishing in the famine or those saved from the *dagger* of the enemy. From the *multitudes* of those who have perished or been carried away and settled in other places, there are so few who have just barely been able to escape.

[21:16-17] After bringing these things to light, God commanded that they would soon happen. For a whole *year* will not pass before the city will vanish, the city that was once exalted among all and splendid and prominent among the *sons of Kedar*, the city that was founded by the military youths and that was full of *strong* archers. The city *will fail*, so that there will be a very small number of men around. These things have been determined and judged by the *God of Israel* so that those things which have been revealed might teach them not to attack his people contemptuously. Thus, we conclude our discussion of this prophecy after only a few words.

[22:1] "For God shows no partiality."¹ Because of this, in the middle of the refutations against the other tribes, the Word also throws in a refutation concerning Zion, in which God places the inhabitants of Jerusalem along with the other tribes. And God votes against them.² It has been said also in Amos, from the mouth of God to the Jewish people: " 'Are you not like the Ethiopians to me?' says the Lord. 'Did I not bring up Israel from the land of Egypt, and the Philistines from Cappadocia and the Syrians from the pit? Behold, the eyes of the Lord God are on all the kingdoms of the earth.'"³ And it is also certain that *the words of the ravine of Zion* discussed above have not been said concerning *Zion* itself but concerning the *ravine* that is adjacent to it. For this reason, the present word says: "And your choicest ravines will be filled with chariots, and the cavalry will block your gates."⁴ I suppose that through these things, when he commands those who were accepted among the other tribes to explain this from the writings of the other tribes, God is speaking of the casting aside and the final disposition of Israel. And I suppose also that the fall of Jerusalem is

---

⁹It would seem that Eusebius imports this word *statement* from one of the other Greek translations, for it is not present in the LXX. **Chapter Twenty-Two** ¹Rom 2:11 RSV. ²Literally, "And God places a pebble against them." In ancient Greek culture, one would vote by dropping a pebble in a jar, and then the votes would be tallied when the stones were counted. ³Amos 9:7-8. ⁴Is 22:7.

clearly indicated when he speaks of the *ravine of Zion*.

[144] In any event, God finds fault with those who have fallen from the height of the godly government of the Jewish nation; it is just as though they have fallen down into the ravine of the depths of evil. For indeed "Mount" Zion is "high," on which the temple of God was built. Therefore, the text says: "Go up on a high mountain, you who bring good tidings to Zion,"[5] and: "You have come to Mount Zion and to the city of the living God, the heavenly Jerusalem."[6] And in the above verse, it is seen that Mount Zion signifies the evangelical word. And those who have fallen away from this hope into the adjacent *ravine* have fallen into Zion. For evil is next to every virtue, and whoever slips from virtue falls into evil. And thus also everyone who fails to attain faith is diverted into faithlessness. And therefore the people of the circumcision have fallen from the height of the gospel and from "the heavenly Zion,"[7] and being alienated, they have been diverted into the cliff of faithlessness. For this reason, God counted them as among the other nations. And so the prophecy adumbrates their final casting aside when he inscribed *the word of the ravine of Zion*. Because they were "puffed up without reason"[8] and were in the depths of evil, he says to them: *What has happened to you that you have all gone up to useless housetops?*

[22:2-3] Foreseeing in the Spirit their cries against the Savior and their godless slander against him, because of which they were cast away, the prophet states: *The city was filled with people shouting.* Since then "there is a sin which is mortal"[9] and "the soul that sins shall die,"[10] he adds the following, signifying the death of their soul: *Your wounded were not wounded by broadsword, nor were your dead men dead in battle.*

And he states: *Your rulers have fled*, or, according to Symmachus, *have been driven out* and according to Theodotion, *have been removed*. Therefore, there will no longer be a king among them to revere as there used to be neither governors nor high priests nor prophets, but neither will there be Pharisees nor Sadducees nor any such rulers as used to be among them. For they *have all been removed*, and those who were *caught* are still *painfully bound* by him who besieged these souls, since "each one is bound in the chains of his own sins."[11] Therefore, the text says: *And those who were caught have been painfully bound.*

[22:4-6] After being enabled to see these things by the Spirit, the prophet loudly bewails the Jewish people's final fall as if into a ravine from so great a height, saying: *Therefore I said, Leave me alone; I will weep bitterly; do not prevail in comforting me for the ruin of the daughter of my race*, or, according to Symmachus: *Do not attempt to reassure me about the suffering* [145] *of the daughter of my people.* For I know that the text says this accurately and that the prophet foresees this in the Spirit, all because of the aforesaid. The city that is dedicated to God *will be caught*, and everyone in it will be delivered over to the hands of the enemy. Therefore, I now lament bitterly and weep aloud for myself with genuine pity, and for the aforementioned ones. *A day of trouble and destruction and trampling and wandering from the Lord of hosts* has come over the *ravine of Zion*. And I suppose that this is said concerning those who were united as one in the plot against our Savior. He adds concerning them: *They wander on the mountains, from their small to their great*, thus signifying the people together with their rulers.

Then he advances the threat against them when he says: *Now the Elamites took quivers—riders of horses and a gathering for battle.* He

---

[5]Is 40:9. [6]Heb 12:22 RSV. [7]Heb 12:22. [8]Col 2:18 RSV. [9]1 Jn 5:16 RSV. [10]Ezek 18:4 RSV. [11]Prov 5:22.

hus indicates the opposing and invisible forces, the enemies and adversaries to whom God handed them over. And we could interpret the *Elamites* as those who overlook, since they disregarded the salvation of those perishing and spared no one. Probably we could call the soldiers who besieged them the *Elamites*, who stood in battle array with *horses* and great numbers of troops in the aforementioned *ravine of Zion*. They then led them for the last time into the wilderness.

[**22:7-11**] Therefore, the text states next: *And your choicest ravines will be filled with chariots, and the cavalry will block the gates of Judah.* They will enter *into the houses of the city*, not now and not at the present time, but *in that day*, I mean, at the prophesied time. And, in the process of subduing every place and every corner of the city, they will spare no effort to *uncover the secrets of the houses of the citadel of David*. And these things were the secret tokens of the kingdom or perhaps the things laid up in store for use in holy ceremonies, which no one was allowed to observe except "the high priest only."[12] And he then says that these things will be delivered over to the adversaries. But instead of *and they saw that they were many*, Symmachus says: *And you will see that the fractures in the house of David were multiplied.* He blames those who were *in the ravine of Zion*, first because *they turned the waters* which were *in the old pool into the city*, and second because they were contrived to secure *water for themselves between the two walls.* And the word of the inspired Scripture was the *water of the old pool* in the city. Although it did not belong to them, in turning the *water for themselves*, they contrived "traditions of the elders,"[13] "teaching as doctrines the precepts of men."[14] The Savior also finds fault with them

and refutes their transgression of the law[15] when he says: "For the sake of your tradition, you have made void the word of God, hypocrites!"[16] And Jeremiah also foreshadows this very same thing [146] when he says: "They have forsaken me, the fountain of living waters, and hewed out cisterns for themselves, broken cisterns, that can hold no water."[17] Therefore, thus *they turned the water of the old pool* in the city and contrived to secure foreign *water for themselves from between the two walls.* I am speaking of the *old* and new covenants. For it is from between these *two walls* of the city of God (clearly, the community of God) that those who are accused contrived foreign *water for themselves* that was not their own—"the traditions of the elders."[18] Those who are called deuteronomists[19] among them are very proud of these traditions.

And they dared to do something yet worse: *those who demolished the houses* of the city made use of their stones for the construction of their own *wall.* And they are still doing this even to the present whenever they remove the words of the divine Scripture and surround the houses with walls of myths, erecting a certain hedge or fence or wall around them with their own myths. For just as they contrived to secure foreign water for themselves, so they also erected their own *wall*, using the stones, that is, the sayings, of the divine Scriptures. And he says that you did these things *not looking up* to God *who made it from the beginning and who fashioned it* (I am speaking of the *old pool* of the inspired Scriptures which poured forth from the spring of the divine Spirit).

And Symmachus translated this verse in the following manner: *And you drew water for yourselves from the lower pool, and you numbered the houses of Jerusalem, and you demolished the houses to fortify the wall. And you*

12Heb 9:7. 13Mt 15:2. 14Mt 15:9 RSV. 15The word Eusebius uses here carries with it the idea of side-stepping the law. 16Mt 15:6 RSV. 17Jer 2:13 RSV. 18Mt 15:2. 19δευτερωτής. This is a word found for the first time in Eusebius (and subsequently used by Epiphanius, but very rarely indeed). It refers to those who are the keepers of the Jewish traditions, δευτερωσις.

constructed a water system between the walls and the old pool, but you did not pay attention to him who made it, and you did not see him who fashioned it from afar. And Theodotion translated this verse thus: *And you were gathering water from the pool below, and you numbered the houses of Jerusalem, and you pulled down the houses for the fortification of the wall. And you constructed an irrigation system between the two walls with the water of the old pool, and you did not look to him who made it, and you did not look to him who fashioned it from a distance.*

[22:12-13] Next the text says: *And in that day the Lord of hosts called for weeping and lamentation and shaving and girding with sackcloth, but they engaged in joy and gladness, killing calves and slaughtering sheep in order to eat meat and drink wine, saying: "Let us eat and drink, for tomorrow we die."* Therefore, even for such impudent deeds, God "does not will the death of the sinner but his repentance,"[20] and he ordered them to lament and to mourn deeply for their [147] destruction. But, finding themselves in such a sorry situation and giving up all hope of their own salvation, they drove headlong into desperation. They surrendered themselves to drunkenness and luxury, as if the judgment of God would not catch up with them after the conclusion of this mortal life. And so, making use of this same Scripture text, the divine apostle says: "If the dead are not raised, 'Let us eat and drink, for tomorrow we die.'"[21]

[22:14] But he says that all these things did not escape the notice of *the ears of the Lord of hosts.* For this reason, as if imprisoned in the chains of God, the verdict of their sin has been declared against them, saying: *and this sin will not be forgiven you until you die.* See then the magnitude of the impending verdict, and understand that the report of the idolatry of

the people is not at all slanderous. The report is true, "because they went up to useless house-tops,"[22] and because they filled the *city* with their crying and because, "turning the old pool," they contrived to secure foreign *water for themselves,* and because they constructed a "wall" for themselves "by demolishing the houses of the city."[23] In doing these things, they senselessly contributed to their own destruction. But the prophet was not thus affected by the destruction, but lamenting deeply for them, he said: "Leave me alone; I will weep bitterly."[24] And the cause of the bitter weeping then was that their end had been appointed, and the verdict was declared by God, saying: *This sin will not be forgiven you until you die.*

[22:15-25] *Somnas and Eliakim,* those who are identified in the passage at hand, were contemporaries with Hezekiah the king, as the narrative in Scripture records. But the prophet himself, who is also present in the passage at hand, teaches in what is stated next that when the king of Assyria set on the city and "stood before the conduit of the upper pool in the way of the fuller's field, there went out to him Eliakim the son of Chelkias, the steward, and Somnas, the secretary." This, however, fits in at a later part of the story. Therefore, the Hebrew text says that *Somnas* was a high priest but a voluptuary and a man of an indecent lifestyle. The result was that he abandoned and deserted the people to Sennacherib, the king of the Assyrians. The prophet is ordered to march *to the priestly chamber,* or, according to Symmachus, *to the tentmaker,* or, according to Aquila, *to the one dwelling in a tent.* They translated it *the priestly chamber,* since he said about it: "O, how vain! How excessive that *you carved out* for yourself *a tomb in the rock on the height* and that you chiseled out in it letters as signs for your own remembrance! Did you not

---

[20]Ezek 33:11. [21]1 Cor 15:32 RSV. [22]Is 22:1. [23]Cf. Is 22:10. [24]Is 22:4.

now that the *Lord of hosts* has carried away
the mountain against you? Did you not know
that he ordered **[148]** that the honors that you
possessed be taken away from you and that you
be stripped of the *robe* around you and of the
crown and of the other glories? You will *die in
the land that is furthest away from here, a
foreign and distant and colonized country.* You
had cultivated an excessive taste for beautiful
things and amassed riches and *chariots* and
everything else that is vain, and you are still
even now surrounded by them."

For all these things will be *something
trampled down,* for they will be demolished and
thrown away from the high priesthood, and
shown to be worthless. And God, being a
righteous judge, will distribute to each as
appropriate according to true values. And he
will do these things to you, but to your *servant
Eliakim* who has proven himself to be a good
*bondman, I will clothe him with your robe and
crown* of the high priesthood, and I will honor
him by putting into his hands the administration with which you had been entrusted up to
the present time. For this man is worthy of
these things. And since he was led forward by
God, he will not be arrogant and a braggart as
you were. But, as a father, he will offer the land
to all those who will be under his administration. For this reason, *I will give* to this gentle
and meek one *the glory of David,* the most meek
and most righteous king. And thus he will *rule*
the people with great authority, in such a way
that *no one* among his subjects *will contradict
him.* And he will be firmly rooted and established and securely positioned in his office, so
that *everyone who is glorious* among the people
will neither contend with him nor look on him
with envy, and neither will there ever be any
slander about him, but *they will trust in him* as
in a father. And therefore everyone, *from small
to great,* will depend on him, everyone being
confident in him for their care.

These things will happen to Eliakim, but
the aforementioned things will happen to
Somnas. For he, even he who is now *fastened in
a secure place,* he *will be removed* and replaced,
since he ran the administration with which he
was *entrusted* neither correctly nor faithfully.
For this reason, he will be transferred, and his
honors *will be taken away, and his glory will fall*
from him. And these things will happen to
him, since God has sentenced him to suffer
these things. And the Word chastens us and
calls us to our senses through these things,
exhorting us not to be conceited or elated by
past successes and so unmindful of the judgment of God. Accordingly, someone could
conclude that the things discussed above in the
prophecy before this one about the "ravine of
Zion"[25] could be linked to the suffering of our
Savior and that the prophecy refers to these
things. One could say that the fall of *Somnas*
from the priesthood is a concrete picture of the
Jewish priesthood according to the law of
Moses. And he foretells **[149]** that after the
suffering of the Savior, the Jews will experience what was prophesied and be kept from
the priesthood. And *Eliakim* could be interpreted as a symbol of the resurrection of God
to a new and fresh priesthood, which the
resurrection of our Savior established in his
church throughout the whole world.

[23:1] On the one hand, the prophecies
concerning the other tribes distinguish
between events that had already occurred and
others that would be accomplished only in the
distant future, and they furthermore state that
nothing will interfere with you. But now, on
the other hand, the individual word comes
along and arrives in godliness in order to say
that these events will happen among the
aforementioned Gentiles according to each
prophecy. And what is remarkable is that each
individual prophecy is addressed to each

---

[25]Is 22:1.

nation separately, and among these very prophecies these serious matters are again delivered especially by the godly word. At once, therefore, the vision concerning Babylon—in which we see that it will come to final desolation and will be destroyed by the Medes and by the ruler of the Assyrians—awakens us to the catholic doctrine of the awaited "righteous judgment of God."[1] There will certainly not be an altar in Babylon, and it was said that there will not be any godly people in it. And the "vision of Egypt"[2] is not about the actual wilderness but speaks of the idolatry which is among them, and he says that there will be an abundance of the fear and knowledge of God among the Egyptians. And thus he added something specifically about "Moab"[3] when prophesying the disappearance of the altars from among them. And he foretells that the throne of Christ and the church of God will be established among them. And just as in the prophecy "concerning Damascus"[4] he said that a great conversion would come to those who formerly did not know God, so also, searching carefully through Isaiah up to the present prophecy, we have interpreted each prophecy concerning a specific place separately. And therefore, what was said "concerning Tyre"[5] indeed has a certain individual significance and speaks of what was about to happen to it, and these things were fulfilled in the past during the times of the Assyrians under whom Tyre was besieged and suffered what was spoken of in the prophecy. But the Word draws a conclusion to this theme when he says: "And its merchandise and its wages will be holy to the Lord; it will not be gathered for them, it will not be gathered for them, but for those who live in the presence of the Lord."[6] Thus bringing up the subject of godliness, he presents the main point of the prophecy.

Therefore, *the word* concerning *Tyre*

foretells the coming siege of the city. For after Assyria had conquered the other nations, it also took Sidon itself, as is recounted in the secular[7] histories as well. And, therefore, we discovered among the records in Scripture that after the king of the Babylonians came on the Assyrians, he then plundered not only Jerusalem and Palestine but Arabia and Damascus as well, and he conquered the entire Phoenician race. For God judged the people who called themselves his own—I am speaking about Israel—when the Assyrians came on them with terrible severity. But neither did God pass by the other nations, nor did he leave them unpunished who had risen up against Israel and [150] captured it. Were these not "the tents of the Idumeans and the Ishmaelites, Moab and the Hagrites, Gebal and Ammon and Amalek, the other tribes with the inhabitants of *Tyre*"?[8] You see then that *Tyre* is also mentioned as one of those who were attacked during the time when the people were besieged. Therefore, the prophecy rightly indicates the events that were to befall Tyre at the time of its desolation, which was predicted to be great, as the desolation of Jerusalem was great. And therefore he says: "And Tyre will be abandoned for seventy years, like the time of a king, like the time of a man."[9]

Therefore, during the period in which the city of Tyre endured such great desolation, there were probably no longer any sailors importing merchandise as used to be their practice, but rather they ceased from all their sea trade. Therefore, the text says: *Wail, O ships of Carthage, for it has perished, and people no longer come.* And why else would the prophecy then mention *Carthage* except that there was at that time some sort of alliance between the people of Tyre and Carthage? For at that time, those who dwelled in Africa welcomed those from Tyre, and they were the

---

Chapter Twenty-Three [1]Rom 2:5. [2]Is 19:1. [3]Is 15:1. [4]Is 17:1. [5]Is 23:1. [6]Is 23:18. [7]Literally, "outside." It is not clear from what Eusebius considers these histories to be "outside." For example, does he mean "noncanonical" or "non-Jewish"? [8]Ps 83:6-7. [9]Is 23:15.

first ones to settle *Carthage*. Therefore, after Tyre disappeared, the merchants who used to convey wares from it to *Carthage* lost their business, as did those who used to sail from *Carthage* to Tyre. Therefore, the text says: *Wail, O ships of Carthage, for it has perished, and people no longer come from the land of the Kitieans* or *from the land of the Chetteim*, according to the other Greek translations. And although the text does not explicitly mention Cyprus, Kition is a city in it, through which those who set sail from Tyre passed. He next states the reason why there was no longer a trade alliance with Tyre when he said: *It has been led captive*, clearly speaking of Tyre.

[23:2-7] But instead of *to whom have they become similar?* Aquila says: *Keep silent!* And Symmachus says: *Be silent, you who dwell on the island.* For at this time when they were conceited and exalted and spoke in arrogant words, the Word urges them to be humble and *keep silent*. And these individuals were precisely the *merchants of Phoenicia*, and one could say that they heap up great wealth *as in harvest*, since their activities are unceasing. But now, since all whom they considered to be good were taken away and since they were deprived of them, they were overcome by shame, and it came not only on them but also on those who dwelled in Sidon and those who were from the same land. In a single night, a voice arose precisely *from the sea*, lamenting deeply because they no longer had anyone who had *reared young men and virgins*. As they were once children of the sea and looked after by it when business at Tyre was booming, so now when business failed, it was fitting for them to bewail the *sea* and their *strength* and to lament as one grieves for deceased children. But he also says that Egypt, although lying in the same region, will grieve and reflect [151] and anguish over its condition, and thus it will not

suffer at all like Tyre did. And to those who did not perish in Tyre but survived he says that, if they are able, they should cross over and flee to their settlements established in *Carthage*. And staying there, weep aloud for your own land, not blaming anyone else for the things you have suffered but blaming your own arrogance and *your pride*, in which you attempted to clothe the world.

[23:8-9] And the things that have happened to you and that you recorded, O Tyre, they were not decreed by fate. But inquire among yourselves *who has planned these things*, who decided that your land would experience these things? For when you inquire you will discover that these things happened to it by the righteous judgment of God. For *the Lord of hosts*, who is the subject of learned discourses only among the Hebrews, has removed this mountain, thus bringing low *the pride* and arrogance not only of Tyre but also of the rest of the godless and irreligious nations. For this reason, he warned in the things discussed above that similar things would happen "to Babylon"[10] and "to Moab"[11] and "to Damascus"[12] and to the other cities listed above. For "God resists the arrogant but gives grace to the humble."[13]

[23:10-11] Therefore, do not be haughty any longer, O you who boasted about the riches supplied by the sea. And now that you have been humbled, occupy your *land* and till the ground and be nourished from the fruit of the earth, for the profits from the sea have ceased. For while you enjoyed these things, you did not foster your own prosperity, but you were insolent and *irritated kings* and all those who lived in neighboring countries. But it was no longer allowed for you to do these things, neither against others nor against your neighbor Sidon, whom you used to endeavor to wrong.

---

[10]Is 13:1. [11]Is 15:1. [12]Is 17:1. [13]Prov 3:34.

[23:12-13] But *even if you go away to Kition,* which as we mentioned above is a city in Cyprus, as to an acquaintance or an old and familiar friend, *not even there will you have rest* from the one who pursues you from every side and will shut you up in prison. But if you wish to run away *to the land of the Chaldeans,* know that Babylon, their royal city, will be desolate because those who dwelled in it were ungodly and haughty people. And thus *its wall has fallen*—I am speaking of the royal power with which it was once fortified.

[23:14-15] Therefore, what other sort of refuge will you have, or from where will you procure hope of salvation for yourself? For this reason, it is appropriate for you expatriates to wail—I am speaking of the Carthaginians— you who were once the *fortress of Tyre.* And all that was prophesied against Tyre will be accomplished in only a few years, in which time also [152] the city of Jerusalem, which is dedicated to God, will become a wilderness. For God passed judgment for the *period of a man's* life—that is, *seventy years*—so as to place a boundary around the desolation that would come on Tyre and to delimit the many years' *reign* of the *one king.*

[23:16-17] During these *seventy years,* all people will sing a song, an ode about your desolation, since they will have seen that you were deprived of your honor as a woman who has fallen from decency. And now, return from the time of your desolation, *wandering* and transferring from place to place and among the other nations giving yourself over to prostitution, thus having been *forgotten* by God. And if you are able to *take up the lyre* and to employ your instrument no longer as a prostitute but in prudence, then *play the lyre much and sing much* in prayers and supplications to God. For in this way you will be ever *remembered* before

God, if you should employ your mouth and sense faculties, which have been intricately joined together as a *lyre,* in order to live discreetly, *singing* pleasingly to God. For thus *you will be remembered,* and you will be deemed worthy of remembrance by God himself. And, therefore, since the aforementioned time of his *visitation* is now quite finished, you will once more be present, and *you will be restored to your ancient condition,* so that a *market center* will again be established in you. People from every quarter will eagerly stream together to you, and they will bring their business to you.

[23:18] And after sorting through what pertained to the desolation that would sweep over Tyre, and concerning its renewal, which still even now is established, the Word passes on and avers: *And its merchandise and its wages will be holy to the Lord.* And when we carefully examine the reading in Aquila's translation, we find that it says: *And its merchandise and hire*[14] *will be sanctified to the Lord.* And, therefore, to be accurate, the Hebrew text states the words *merchandise* and *hire* separately, in contradistinction to the Septuagint, which says: *The merchandise and the wages.* But according to Aquila, the text reads: *Its merchandise and its hire will be sanctified to the Lord.* The text does not say *all its merchandise* or *all its hire,* but a certain part of the merchandise and a certain part of the *wages will be sanctified to the Lord.* And this also has been fulfilled among you, for the church of God has been established in the city of Tyre. Therefore, as much of its hiring occurred among the other nations, so also the things being supplied from its business will be sanctified to the Lord as prophesied in the church. Those who carry these goods offer them in reverence, not for themselves, however, or in order to profit from the gifts which are presented to God, *but for those who live in the presence of the Lord,* clearly for those who

---

[14]Having the connotation of a prostitute's hire.

ttend the altar. "For in the same way, the Lord [**153**] commanded that those who proclaim the gospel should get their living by the gospel,"[15] and: "Those who serve at the altar are to share in the sacrificial offerings."[16] Therefore, for these ones themselves as for the priests of God *who live in the presence of the Lord*, those being identified above offer firstfruits and thus fulfill in fact what the prophecy said. *And its merchandise and its hire will be sanctified to the Lord, and it will not be gathered for them but for those who live in the presence of the Lord*. And the Word shares in the amazement that the people of Tyre, who were always idolaters and the enemies of Israel, should offer gifts and firstfruits from their *merchandise* to the God of Israel. And the greater part of this word has in fact already been fulfilled among you.

After these things the text says next: *All its merchandise will be used to eat and drink and be filled, as a satisfaction, a memorial in the presence of the Lord*. Symmachus translated this most lucidly as follows: *Its merchandise will be used for those who live before the Lord to eat to satisfaction and to be clothed in respectability*. And this rendering is in alignment with the sense of the Septuagint: *For part of its merchandise will be for those who live in the presence of the Lord, so that they may eat and drink and be filled for a covenant and for a memorial in the presence of the Lord*. If we reproduce the above verse precisely as it appears in the Septuagint, then it reads: *All its merchandise will be used to eat and drink*. But neither the Hebrew text nor the other Greek translations say that *all its merchandise* but rather only a part of its *merchandise* and of the *wages will be for those who live in the presence of the Lord*, and this clearly indicates that it will be offered to the faithful among those who dwell in Tyre. The conclusion of the prophecy is demonstrated to have been fulfilled in the word which is delivered now. For anyone who is conversant with these things

will find the prediction astonishing, since it was delivered so long in advance of the times. The Word says that those idol worshipers who were absurdly impassioned about the error of polytheism and who had always been enemies and adversaries of the Jews will experience a transformation, so that they will come to know the God who is revered among the Jews, and they will bring gifts to him. And, by the grace of our Savior Jesus Christ, these things have in fact been accomplished. This provides an outline for the coming prophecies concerning the other Gentile nations, and the prophet next commences a new theme.

[24:1-2] The prophet now begins the section "against Judea and against Jerusalem."[1] In between the time when he introduced the subject and now when he finally advances, he has said many things "concerning the allophyles." After partially developing his discourse about the Gentiles, following through the things discussed before, he sets forth a universal prophecy which is delivered concerning the entire world, since "the earth is the Lord's and everything in it."[2] And so it is right that the one who cares for all people should command that the world [**154**] comprehend that God's judgment will be for everyone, for "on that day, God will judge the secrets of people."[3] And in the things discussed above, he delivers a universal instruction, ever watching out that he not give the wrong impression, thus addressing the prophecy specifically neither to Judea nor Samaria, and neither to Tyre nor to Damascus or Babylonia or any other nation. But clearly the Word states this concerning the consummation of life and the judgment that will take place after all these things. And thus all people might be taught the things that will happen to the ungodly after the present life and the good things that have been stored up for those who fear God.

---

[15]1 Cor 9:14. [16]1 Cor 9:13. **Chapter Twenty-Four** [1]Is 1:1. [2]Ps 24:1. [3]Rom 2:16.

And he started with the more gloomy in order that he could stop with the more pleasant. For this reason, he says: *Look, the Lord is ruining the world and will make it desolate.* As those on the earth will be judged, they will be transferred to certain other lands all throughout the entire world, thus leaving the former habitation of humankind desolate, since there will no longer be anyone to dwell in it. And he says about the *surface* of the earth—about its appearance—that *he will uncover* it and bring those who have been buried in it to the light. This Word is signifying the manner of the resurrection of the dead. *And he will scatter those who dwell in it,* or, according to Aquila and Theodotion, *he will scatter abroad,* as in all directions according to the analogy of the deeds of each one. For "where my Father is there are many rooms,"[4] and God's world is great and expansive and is able to welcome all and every soul that has been made a citizen of the age on earth. But, indeed, Hades and the regions under the earth await the ungodly, who will be consigned to the dark, enclosed chamber without any light, as the verse affirms: "They shall go down into the depths of the earth; they shall be given over to the power of the sword; prey for foxes they shall be."[5] But the godly "shall be caught up together in the clouds to meet the Lord in the air; and so we shall always be with the Lord."[6]

And when the bodies that are concealed in the earth shall be *uncovered,* those who are to be judged "will stand before the judgment seat"[7] of the great judge. Then they shall all stand as equals, and those who once gloried in this mortal life will not at all be privileged by what they possessed, whether it was a superior rank or race or riches. "For they shall all stand" then as equals "before the judgment seat of God."[8] And thus it will also be with the *priest,* so that the *people* will be as the *priest,* and all will be as one another, "since God shows no partiality."[9] For this reason, we read in Job: "The small and the great are there, and the attendant no longer lived in fear of his master."[10] And it will be this way also for the *servant* and the *master* and she who was once a *maid* and her supposed *mistress;* they will all stand as equals. But it will be so for those who *sell* and *buy* in great abundance, and so those who *lend* will be as those who plead for a loan and those who *borrow* in penury and need in order to purchase necessities.

[24:3-4] Next, he inserts this statement after what has already been said: *The earth shall be ruined with ruin, and the earth shall be plundered with plundering, for the mouth of the Lord* **[155]** *has spoken these things.* For the declaratory voice of God that was borne through the prophet says that there will be a worse word for those who have been appointed, whom he calls the *earth* because of their earthy thoughts. For just as it was said to Adam, "earth you are and to earth you shall return,"[11] so also vengeance has been threatened at the time of the judgment of God for all the lovers of pleasure and lovers of the body and those who thus will be found to be earthly and fleshly. And as public officials who exact debts, so certain others will arrest those who dared to deliver themselves over to *ruin* and to treat with contempt the image of God in them.

And these particular ones are doubtless avenging and punishing demons who will *plunder* and seize their souls when those who acted in ways worthy of mourning *will mourn* for themselves. For this reason, the text says: *The earth mourned, and the world was ruined.* And he makes it clear who the *mourning earth* and the *ruined world* are when he adds: *The exalted ones of the earth mourned.* For the wrath of God will pursue especially after them, since "he resists the arrogant but gives grace to the humble."[12]

---

[4]Jn 14:2. [5]Ps 63:9-10. [6]1 Thess 4:17. [7]Rom 14:10. [8]Rom 14:10. [9]Rom 2:11. [10]Job 3:19. [11]Gen 3:19. [12]Prov 3:34.

[24:5] But instead of *and the earth behaved lawlessly because of those who inhabit it,* Symmachus says: *And the earth was defiled by blood by those who inhabit it.* For the aforementioned *exalted ones of the earth defiled the earth with blood,* murdering and thus filling it with blood. And the *earth* suffered these things *because of those who inhabit it, because they transgressed the law and changed the ordinance—they disbanded an everlasting covenant.* For all people who have inhabited the world from the very beginning, "Greeks together with barbarians,"[13] all have inherited the natural *law* and the *ordinances* of God. They have this law "written"[14] in their souls. And because they have been given a glimpse of the *eternal covenant* through general revelation,[15] they have become "transgressors"[16] of the natural *law.* Therefore, it is with good reason that those who are to be judged will stand in the divine court of justice and render an account for their transgression.

[24:6] And *therefore a curse will devour the earth, because those who inhabit it have sinned.* And just as in the beginning of the creation of the world, while there was not yet any foundation of sin, "God blessed man,"[17] so also at the "consummation of the age"[18] he says that *a curse will then devour the earth,* or, according to Symmachus: *Because of this curse the earth mourned.* For *because of the curse* that came on all people, the *earth,* as the mother who had given birth to them and nursed them, will take up mourning for them. And again, instead of *therefore those who dwell in the earth will be poor,* Symmachus said: *therefore they will be* [156] *exhausted.* And of all those who will suffer these things on the *earth,* a certain *few will be left,* and they will be those who preserve "the likeness of the man of heaven"[19] in their souls.

[24:7-11] But instead of *the wine will mourn,* Aquila renders this as *the vintage mourned,* expressing the transient nature of human pleasures and the adornment of the body through the example of spoiling fruit. And then he says that *all will groan,* speaking of those who traveled the "wide and broad"[20] way in this present life and those who squandered their own lives "in drunkenness and profligacy."[21] They no longer get any pleasure from their lusts but are put to shame by the disgraceful things that they did and by their "abominable"[22] deeds, pouring down disgrace on themselves. Therefore, it is said somewhere: "Those who sleep in mounds in the ground will arise, some to everlasting life and others to contempt and everlasting shame."[23] Now the *wine* and what is called *sikera*[24]—although in the other translations it was called an *intoxicating drink*—is sweet, but during that time it will be *bitter* to them. And then *every city will shut up the house so that no one can enter.* For now there will no longer be governments such as there are now, in which the ungodly act out the evil in their minds. And the word frequently speaks of human wantonness as *wine* and, in the image of an evil, *intoxicating drink,* sketches how the torpor of the soul is encouraged alongside the natural understanding of sound conclusions. And when they are sobered up from their *intoxicating drink* and chastised, they will let out mournful sounds and cries. For this reason, the text adds: *Wail everywhere for the wine; all the joy has ceased.*

[24:13-14] But after the aforesaid things, the prophecy adds: *All these things shall be on the earth, in the midst of the nations.* This statement is clearly teaching about the universal judgment. Then he adds: *Just as when someone*

---

[13]Rom 1:14. [14]Rom 2:15. [15]ἐν ταῖς κοιναῖς ἐννοίαις. This could also be translated "through common thoughts." [16]Rom 2:25. [17]Gen 1:28. [18]Mt 13:39. [19]1 Cor 15:49. [20]Mt 7:13. [21]1 Pet 4:3-4. [22]1 Pet 4:3. [23]Dan 12:2. [24]This is a transliteration of the Greek word meaning "strong drink."

gleans an olive tree, so shall people glean them. Thus, nothing will be left of the ungodly, but the judgment of God will come on each person. But instead of *even when the harvest has ceased, these will cry aloud with their voice,* Symmachus renders it quite differently, presenting his interpretation: *As mere gleanings gathered at the end of the harvest.* Then, up until this point, he set forth the meaning from another beginning when he stated: *These will lift up their voice.* First, therefore, it has been rendered with the meaning of those who are first. For as those who gather up the fruit of the *olive tree* are accustomed to knock the branches and thrash about with reeds until there is scarcely even one olive remaining, and so after the *harvest* certain individuals go back and gather up the torn olives and the small clusters that still remain, so in the same manner they will also gather up the ungodly until every single one has been brought to the judgment of God. They will indeed suffer these things, *and these will lift up their voice.* And about whom is this verse speaking if not those of a superior class? And *these* are perhaps [157] those who have been deemed worthy of blessedness in the presence of God. For this reason, Symmachus states next: *And these will lift up their voice, they will rejoice exceedingly when the Lord is glorified.* But according to the Septuagint translation, they will indeed be delivered over to punishment and suffer the last *harvest.* And every one of them will be gathered up, and they will let out *sounds* and *cry* when they are punished. But those whose destiny is in God *will rejoice together in the glory of the Lord.* For then the Lord himself shall come "in the glory of his Father,"[25] "with power and great glory."[26] Therefore, it is in this *glory* of their *Lord* that those who have placed their hope in him *will rejoice.* But instead of *the water of the sea will be troubled,* Theodotion translates this as *the*

waters roared, thus signifying the magnitude of the shout that those *glorifying* their Lord will raise. For their *voice* will be comparable to a blast of the *sea.*

[24:15-16] And *the glory of the Lord will be in the islands.* This clearly refers to the churches in the middle of the nations which were once unbelieving, for it is as though they were set apart in the midst of the sea, but the *glory of the Lord* will then shine on them. Thus, the Word praises and acclaims the God who is given *glory* in the *islands.* Therefore, he says: *O Lord God of Israel, from the wings of the earth we have heard wonders: hope for the godly one,* or, according to Symmachus and Theodotion: *From the wings of the earth we have heard psalms,* or, *singing,* according to Aquila. For, marveling at his just judgment, those whose destiny is God *rejoice together in the glory of the Lord,* and those who *rejoice* send up hymns and most thankful singing to him. Then also the prophet marvels at this, for *the islands from the wings of the earth* have been deemed worthy of the glory of the Lord, and they sing hymns and *psalms* to him. And when the text mentions the *islands* in the passage in which it says *we heard psalms,* I read this as speaking about the churches and the parishioners in them. But if one prefers the alternate reading *we heard wonders,* the text would then be speaking about the incredible miracles of God. For the allophylites and those of another race and the barbarian nations passing through to the *opposite side of the earth* to sing *psalms* praised the God of the prophets who turned them away from the gods of their parents, which was a great and tremendous wonder. Then the text adds: *Hope for the godly one.* For since he has passed through those things that have been threatened for the ungodly, he then next leads on concerning those whose destiny is in God and says that *they will rejoice together in the glory of the Lord*

---

[25]Mt 16:27 rsv. [26]Mt 24:30 rsv.

and *the glory of the Lord will be in the islands.* So then, after speaking about "the righteous judgment of God"[27] he subsequently went on to the phrase about the *hope for the godly one,* for a good *hope* of salvation is held out for every just and *godly* person, whether he is an allophylite or whether he belong to the seed of Abraham.

[158] In Symmachus's version, this verse reads: *And he said: My mystery is for me, my mystery is for me.* For the prophets who glorified God in the aforementioned incredible wonder and those who mentioned the *hope* of the *godly* (but not saying what precisely what was being hoped for) and those who long to learn and know "what God has prepared for those who love him"[28]—God counsels them all to keep silence when he says: *My mystery is for me, my mystery is for me.* For he says that it is not yet time to reveal "what no eye has seen, nor ear heard, nor the heart of man conceived, what I prepared for those who love me."[29] And because the prophet was able to see these things at a glance by the Holy Spirit, he mourned deeply for the ungodly, foreseeing their destruction. And as he had glorified God for the *hope* of the *godly,* so also he next laments those who are perishing because they have cast away the benevolence of God: *Woe to those who reject, those who reject and the faithlessness of those who reject the law.*[30] But instead of *woe to those who reject,* the text reads in Aquila's version: *Woe is me, those who reject rejected,* and according to Symmachus: *O my, those who reject rejected.* You see how they felt sympathy for those who were perishing. The people of God were deeply pained for them because of their love of humanity, and so they were restless in mind and upset and said *woe is me* for those transgressors who *rejected.*

[24:17-20] Then, he next continues on to the threat against them and says: *Fear and pit and snare are on you who inhabit the earth! And it shall be that the one who flees from the fear shall fall into the pit, and the one who gets out of the pit shall be caught by the snare.* And he adds: *Because windows have been opened out of heaven.* He thus adumbrates the visitation of God in his mysterious and contemplative power over the universe, with which he observes all things as through *windows of heaven.* These windows indeed appear to be shut every time God overlooks the sins of those on the earth and does not prosecute those who offend. For it seems as though he is turned away and does not see those who sin. And when he proceeds against those who have sinned, it is as though *the windows of heaven* are thrown open. And the *windows of heaven* are probably what are also called the heavenly gates, concerning which it has been said: "Raise up the gates, O you rulers, and be raised up, eternal gates, and the king of glory shall enter."[31] Therefore, all the gates *will then be opened* for the Lord of the kingdom, and so that those who are under his rule may enter through them. But now, what could it mean that *the windows of heaven will be opened?* He says: *The foundations of the earth will be shaken, and the earth will be troubled with trouble, and the earth will be perplexed with perplexity.* And the earth (clearly indicating those who once inhabited it) will suffer all these things. And he says that they will suffer such things so that they will act as though they were drunk and had a hangover from the excess of their evil deeds. [159] The earth, which has been clearly identified in the above statements as the soul of the ungodly, will be like a *garden-watcher's hut.* As we have seen above, this indicates that it will be like a wilderness, concerning which it has been said: "Zion shall be plowed as a field; Jerusalem shall become as a *garden-watcher's hut.*"[32]

---

[27]Rom 2:5. [28]1 Cor 2:9 RSV. [29]1 Cor 2:9. [30]In Greek, the word for faithlessness [ἀθεςία] is very similar to the word "to reject" (ἀθετέω), and thus it is clear that Eusebius is drawn to this sentence not for its logical sense but for its rhythmic sound. [31]Ps 24:7, 9. [32]Mic 3:12.

And these things will happen on the earth—I am speaking about those who once inhabited the earth—because *lawlessness has prevailed on it*. For this reason, he says at the conclusion of the word: *And it will fall and will not be able to rise*. For, indeed, the earth and earthy flesh and the body-loving soul and those who once inhabited the earth all once *fell*, in that they underwent death in this mortal life. But they will also experience the universal resurrection and "stand before the judgment seat of God"[33] "so that each one may be repaid for what he has done in the body, whether good or evil."[34] This will take place when they are judged and fall from all good hope, and then they will be delivered over to the punishments that have been threatened. It is at that time that those who have fallen away from God *will no longer be able to rise*.

[24:21-23] But after completing the word concerning the habitations of the earth, the prophecy next turns to address the *heaven* and the heavenly regions: *In that day*—I am speaking about the identified time of the judgment of God—*God will bring his hand against the ornament of heaven*. In this statement, he adumbrates the consummation of the universe, when "heaven and earth will pass away."[35] For then, according to the saving teaching, "the sun will be darkened, and the moon will not give its light, and the stars of heaven will fall, and the powers of the heavens will be shaken; at this time the sign of the Son of Man in heaven will appear, and all the tribes of the earth will mourn, and they will see the Son of Man coming on the clouds of heaven with power and great glory."[36] The prophetic word adumbrates and teaches all these things when it says: *And it will be in that day that God will bring his hand against the ornament of heaven*. It was Moses' custom to call the sun and the moon and the

stars *the ornament of heaven*,[37] as when he said: "Pay attention lest you lift up your eyes to *heaven* and, seeing the sun and the moon and the stars all *the ornament of heaven*, you be drawn away and worship them."[38]

And thus, in the course of the present prophecy, he states what *the ornament of heaven* is when he says: *And the brick will be dissolved, and the wall will fall*. But instead of this, Symmachus renders it in this way: *And the moon will shy away and the sun will be ashamed*, and Aquila: *And the moon will be disgraced, and the sun will be ashamed*, as Theodotion also says: *The moon will turn away in shame, and the sun will be ashamed*. You see that in *bringing his hand against the ornament of heaven* he brings about the end [160] of all that is visible. And when he says *God will bring his hand against the ornament of heaven* and then adds *and against the kings of the earth; and he will gather them together in her synagogue and they will shut them up in a prison and in a fortress*, it seems to me that he is speaking of the "rulers of this age"[39] when he says *kings of the earth*. And thus also in Daniel, it is the one who calls himself Gabriel who is identified when the text says: "And the ruler of the kingdom of the Persians and the ruler of the kingdom of the Greeks and the ruler of the kingdom of the Medes came out to meet me."[40] And the Word answers and says that these *kings* and all such visible rulers of the nations will be gathered together by the hand of God and will be cast *into prison and will be shut up in a fortress*. For this reason, Symmachus's version reads: *Against the kings of the earth; and they will be gathered together as a group in bonds, and they will be shut up together in a pit and in an enclosure*. For it was on the coming of the kingdom of Christ and the new age that he was to rule over "the principalities and the powers and the world rulers of this present

---

[33]Rom 14:10. [34]2 Cor 5:10. [35]Mt 24:35. [36]Mt 24:29. [37]The phrase does read strangely in Greek: τὸν κόσμον τοῦ οὐρανοῦ. This is the Greek translation of the Hebrew phrase often translated into English "hosts of heaven." [38]Deut 4:19. [39]1 Cor 2:6. [40]Dan 8:20-21.

darkness and the spiritual hosts of wicked- ness."[41] Then they were to be cast into the nearby "pit"[42] which "they dug for themselves." For every ungodly one who "digs a pit and cleans it out shall fall into the hole he made."[43]

But those identified *will be shut up together in a prison* appropriate for them in order that there might not be a disturbance among those who are ruled by God. And they will be there because they have done such evil deeds, and the judge of the universe will judge them there in their bonds and will be resentful toward them. For this reason, the text says according to the Septuagint: *Through many generations will be their visitation*; and according to Symmachus: *After many days they will be visited*; and according to Aquila: *And from a multitude of days they will be visited*; and according to Theodotion: *Through many days they will be visited*. But by whom they will be visited, the text does not say. It does not necessarily follow that they will be visited by God, since the ineffable Word has kept silent on this point. Then also the *sun* itself *will be ashamed*, seeing those on whom it once shone cast into the dishonor of judgment and punishment. And so too, the *moon will be ashamed*, shutting its eyes to the victories of those who work godlessness on the earth. And in a short time they will be made by them just like those certain stewards who were charged to oversee and manage the house of the master. The master stands over them in order to see those who are subjected to chastising by various punishments. In the same way, those who have excelled in ungodliness, assisted by the light of the sun and the moon, will shortly be judged by the will of God; the other Greek translations say that they would *turn away and be ashamed*. According to the Septuagint, there is absolutely no mention [161] of either the *sun* or of the *moon* in this verse, for this is all

rather shrouded in the text: *Then the brick will be dissolved, and the wall will fall*, concealing that those who interpret the word based on the Greek text render the Scripture so as to reflect the different meanings in the verse.

To all these things he adds: *Because the Lord will reign in Zion and in Jerusalem, and before the elders he will be glorified*. For it was necessary that our Savior teach us about his hidden heavenly kingdom in the word concerning the consummation, which is to come after the destruction of the rulers and of the authorities. As we noted, Zion and Jerusalem are frequently referred to as "heavenly"[44] according to the apostolic diction. The king- dom of Christ will then be established, when *before his elders he will be glorified*. For those whom he honored with an ecclesiastical rank in this present life he consecrated as *elders*, and he will deem these very ones worthy of his divinity. For this reason, Symmachus's version reads: *And his glory will be openly displayed before the elders*.

[25:1-5] After finishing the prophecy about the universal judgment of God, which also encompassed the completion of the kingdom of Christ and "the glory of his elders,"[1] the word exclaims in absolute wonder and says: *O Lord, my God, I will glorify you; I will sing hymns to your name, because you have done wonderful things—an ancient, true plan*. And we will understand how this was an *ancient plan* if we pay attention to the voice of the Savior, which addressed those who would be established by his right hand: "Come, O blessed of my Father, inherit the kingdom prepared for you from the foundation of the world."[2] And rushing on, the apostle writes: "Even as he chose us in him before the foundation of the world, that we should be holy and blameless before him. He destined us in him to be his sons."[3] Therefore,

---

[41]Eph 6:12. [42]This word is the same word translated as "cistern" in Jer 2:13. Eusebius here appeals to the more sinister connotations of the word. [43]Ps 7:16. [44]Heb 12:22. **Chapter Twenty-Five** [1]Is 24:23. [2]Mt 25:34 RSV. [3]Eph 1:4-5.

this *plan* was *ancient*, and these deeds were truly *wonderful things* which had been destined "before the foundation of the world" which would be fulfilled "at the end of the age,"[4] when "he will put all his enemies under his feet"[5] and "when he will destroy every rule and every authority and power."[6]

At that point in time, when all evil has been brought under his feet and "after the last enemy death is destroyed,"[7] then "God will truly be all in all."[8] And our Savior and Lord will rule during the new age, and "before the elders he will be glorified,"[9] when also "all his saints"[10] "will reign in life,"[11] "reigning together"[12] with their own Savior. This was the *ancient plan*, and these deeds were the *wonderful things*, at which the prophet marvels and glorifies God. Then, praying [162] that these things would happen, he adds: *May it be so*, thus striving and longing that the accomplishment of these good things may soon be established. Indeed, this was an *ancient plan*, because of the foreknowledge and predetermination of God and because of the *true* completion of the end.

But, indeed, on behalf of those who were to be deemed worthy of the blessedness, he prayed and said: *May it be so*. And concerning the things that have transpired in this mortal life, he adds: *Because you have made cities a heap, fortified cities, so their foundations might fall; the city of the impious will not be built forever*. And concerning these things, he says therefore: *I will glorify you*, because you removed the *cities of the ungodly* and obliterated their godless governments and unholy buildings. And surely those from among them whom you preserve *will bless you* or *will glorify you*, according to the other Greek translations. And these are the *people* who went along begging during the first age because of you, and the *cities* of those who were once *ill-treated*

persons, who were *wronged* by those who persecute those who fear God. They *will bless you* in your church, and it is right that they who were examined strictly by various governments *will bless you*, since now *you have become a helper to every humble city and a shelter to those who are dispirited because of poverty*. For also when they were *humble* and fainthearted and in *poverty* and denied of even the most simple luxury, you were their *helper* and *shelter*. And you were a *shelter* for the *thirsty* at that time, as we read: "My soul thirsted for you,"[13] and "my soul thirsted for the strong and living God."[14] You again were a fountain sprinkling them and watering them through the channel of the Holy Spirit. And you strengthened those who were discouraged with endurance by the power of your only-begotten Word.

[25:6-8] And in order that the children of the Jews not suppose that these things were said concerning them, he adds that the grace of Christ necessarily pours forth on all the nations: *On this mountain the Lord of hosts will do it*[15] *for all nations*. And what is it that he *will do*? The other Greek translations next tell us that it is a *drink*. But the Septuagint says: *They will drink joy; they will drink wine*. Accordingly, in this verse, he prophesies that the Lord will prepare this celebration[16] neither for Israel nor the Jewish people exclusively but for all nations. It will not take place in the holes of the earth or in the ravines or in the plains, or on many mountains, but on a certain *mountain*. He shows us precisely where it will take place when he says: *On this mountain*. And he said how all *this* would take place when he said a little earlier: "Because the Lord will reign in Mount Zion and in Jerusalem, and before his elders he will be glorified."[17] For in the *mount* of his kingdom, where he will display his *glory* in the elders, there he pre-

---

[4]Heb 9:26. [5]1 Cor 15:25. [6]1 Cor 15:24. [7]1 Cor 15:26. [8]1 Cor 15:28. [9]Is 24:23. [10]Cf. Dan 7:18. [11]Rom 5:17. [12]2 Tim 2:12. [13]Ps 63:1. [14]Ps 42:2. [15]This is a literal translation of Eusebius's words. The word *feast* does not appear in the LXX text. [16]συμπόσιον. [17]Is 24:23.

pared the party, and the *drink* of immortality
will be given to those among the nations. For
this reason, the text says: *On this mountain*
[163] *they will drink joy; they will drink wine;
they will anoint themselves with perfume.* And
the apostle spoke about this mountain when he
said: "You have come to Mount Zion and to
the city of the living God, the heavenly
Jerusalem, and to innumerable angels in festal
gathering, and to the assembly of the first-born
who are enrolled in heaven."[18]

Therefore, it is not those who are of Israel
but those who are deemed worthy of the
promises from every nation who *will drink joy
and will drink the wine* from "the true vine,"[19]
concerning which the Savior said: "I shall not
drink it until I drink it anew with you in the
kingdom of heaven."[20]

And they will anoint themselves with perfume. No longer will they receive "the guarantee of the Holy Spirit,"[21] for they will then
participate in "the fullness of the divinity"[22] of
the Son of God. And no longer "will they know
in part and prophesy in part,"[23] but in perfection "they will be partakers of Christ,"[24] so
that they will be shown to be "kind"[25] and
"children of God and heirs of God and fellow
heirs with Christ."[26] And in these statements,
the evangelical word delivers for us images and
symbols in the mysteries of the new covenant
through the mysterious anointing and through
the saving blood, in order that once we have
been proven in these, we may partake of what
is better. He says: *Deliver these things* which
were spoken *to the nations,* for Israel was not
worthy of them.

And as someone might deliver a deposit of
truth in a mystery, so he says that the word
concerning the aforementioned is a mysterious
word. *Deliver this to all the nations, for this
counsel is against all the nations.* For this very
reason, the prophet rightly glorified God and

was amazed at the grace of God, and so he
said: "Because you have done wonderful
things—an ancient, true plan."[27]

After these things, he next makes it quite
clear what will happen to the nations that are
godless and hopeless because of the fact that
they wait expectantly on idols and demons:
Death, having prevailed, swallowed them up.
But, nevertheless, after the beneficent Savior
of the universe rescued the souls of humanity
from *death* and set them free from the diabolical error of polytheism, *he then took away every
tear from every face; and the disgrace of his
people he took away from all the earth.* And the
disgrace of the people from the nations was the
idolatry that mastered them. Although *God
took away the disgrace* and the *tear* from this
people, there are yet so many souls who weep
aloud because of the philanthropic[28] destruction. Therefore, this is how the text reads
according to the Septuagint translation, but
according to the other Greek versions, the
word presents another interpretation. Symmachus renders the text very clearly as follows:
*And, in this mountain, he will devour the face of
the person in power who has authority over all
the nations, and when the anointing has been
anointed against all the nations, he will make
death to be swallowed up in the end. And* [163]
*the Lord God will wash away every tear from
their faces, and he will take away the disgrace of
his people from all the earth, because the Lord
has spoken it.*

And the translations of this passage in the
other Greek versions are equally forceful, and
it seems to me that their meaning is essentially
identical. When, during the aforesaid time,
after the Lord has hosted the celebration[29] on
the mountain among all the nations, when he
will deem them worthy to partake in the *wine*
and the *perfume* and of his secret mysteries,
then at that time *he will make them to be*

---

[18]Heb 12:22-23 RSV. [19]Jn 15:1. [20]Mt 26:29. [21]2 Cor 1:22. [22]Col 2:9. [23]1 Cor 13:9. [24]Heb 3:14. [25]Eph 4:32. [26]Rom 8:17. [27]Is 25:1. [28]Eusebius's point may be that this destruction resulted in something that was ultimately good for humanity. [29]συμπόσιον.

swallowed up and *the face of the person in power who had authority over all the nations* to disappear (the text is here speaking *of death*). And thus the Lord who rules over the afore-mentioned *mountain* will *swallow* him *up*, so that he will no longer be seen anywhere (I am speaking of *death*), him whom the prophecy called *the person in power*. And the apostle did not shrink back even from calling death a king[30] when he said: "Death reigned from Adam to Moses,"[31] and so also: "The last enemy to be destroyed is death."[32] Here the word rightly says that *the face of the person in authority* will be destroyed. But instead of *the face of the person in authority*, Aquila and Theodotion render this phrase: *The face of darkness*. And to what does the *darkness* refer if not the land that is full of the *darkness* of death? Therefore, then, when the "saints will reign together"[33] with the Son of God, *death*, although formerly *swallowing up* everyone, will itself be *swallowed up*.

And this is the reason why: *The anointing has been anointed in all the nations*. For since they have been *anointed* with an anointing, they will no longer be subject to death, but, as partakers of immortality and eternal life, they will bring death to a state of inactivity, so that it is itself dead. Therefore, the text says: *Now that the anointing has been anointed against all the nations, he will make an end of death so that it will be swallowed up*. And then, when *death* is out of the way, *the Lord God will take away every tear from every face, and he will take away the disgrace of his people*. For it was not an insignificant *disgrace* for "those people who were made in the image of God"[34] to fall from eternal life and to be subjected to *death*. But the *disgrace* will be taken away when "death will be destroyed"[35] and when darkness will vanish. And when the kingdom of Christ will shine forth in eternal life, then those who have

been set free from all the nations that were formerly evil will experience the full benefit of this eternal life. And they will be deemed worthy of the promises of God.

[25:9-12] And, *in that day*, when *death has been swallowed up* at the time of the resurrection, the children of the new age will sing a song of thanksgiving, seeing their own Savior in glory. *And they will say: Lo,* **[165]** *our God, in whom we were hoping*. For we used to have hope in him, believing in the divine teachings concerning him, and in this way we were able to endure the painful trials that came on us, but now we see him with our eyes. And, indeed, they *will say* these things, and he will *give rest* to them in the aforementioned *mountain* of his kingdom. And they will indeed enjoy the benefits of those good things which have been promised. And *Moabitis*—or Moab, according to the Hebrew text—will undergo the punishment of its own godlessness. It will be *trodden down* in the manner of a *threshing floor with wagons*, so that *its hands* will be weak and worn out from faintness. Therefore, Aquila says: *And Moab will be threshed out under him as chaff is threshed out*; and according to Symmachus: *And we will thresh Moab as a threshing of chaff in mud*. He next states who they are who are *treading* it *down* and *threshing* it when he adds: "And the feet of the gentle and humble and the steps of the poor *will trample* it."[36] And I suppose that the evil demon and the opposing power which was once revered as a god among the Moabites is here referred to as *Moab*, which then was proud and arrogant against the God of Israel. And the nation was afflicted by it, and thus Moses dared to do such things because the people had given themselves over to fornication and "joined in worshiping the Baal of Peor."[37] This was the idol of the Moabites. Because of

---

[30]In Greek, the noun "king" is cognate with the verb "to reign." [31]Rom 5:14 RSV. [32]1 Cor 15:26 RSV. [33]Cf. 2 Tim 2:12; Dan 7:22. [34]Gen 1:26-27. [35]1 Cor 15:26. [36]Is 26:6. [37]Num 25:3.

this, the things discussed above are prophesied against it as against the certain dreadful power which wars against God.

In the vision concerning Moab and concerning its demon, Moab itself is addressed: "Because your alliance has been taken away, and the ruler who trampled on the land has perished."[38] Therefore, since this fearful and evil demon was among the people of the Jews, as it was supposed, the present prophecy teaches the end that will follow at the time of the universal judgment of God when it says: *And Moab shall be trodden down, and he will send forth his hands, as he himself brought others low to destroy them,* so also *he will suffer similar things.* But Symmachus says: *And we will thresh Moab down as a threshing of chaff in mud; and,* while it is being threshed and trodden down, *he will spread out his hands as one who is bathing holds them out in order to swim, and his arrogance will be brought low with the downward strokes of his hands. And your fortress with its high walls will bend down and cleave to the earth.* And the *walls* of its *fortress* are the powers which, although they were fortified, the Word says will be demolished. He teaches that these things will happen to the evil demon that once prevailed over the Moabites as well as those others that are supposed to be gods, thus leaving us with an example of what will come on the other opposing powers.

[26:1] [166] For it was necessary for us to learn in advance how the end of death and of the other opposing powers will occur during the time of judgment, and not to be ignorant of their destruction. After our Savior has received back his kingdom in the heavenly mountain, those who are worthy of the promises *will sing in that day* the heavenly *song* "while living in the heavenly Jerusalem,"[1] which the word above calls the present *Judea,* which

is to be found in the land of the earthly Jerusalem. Therefore, for the children who listen together with the people of the Jews, there is rejoicing and an exhortation to hold on to the hope of the things discussed above. And at the same time he presented Judea as somehow signifying the true land and expanse of the "heavenly Jerusalem," but we may indeed understand the text to be referring to Judea and to the God-fearing government of the divine and evangelical spirits. This is "the city of God." Then, *in that day,* they will sing the aforementioned *song.* And the prophecy informs us what sort of *song they will sing,* for the Holy Spirit then delivers the song through the prophet, prophesying and saying to the face of those ones themselves: *Look, a strong city, our salvation.* For this refers not to the *strong city* on the earth that was frequently captured by adversaries, but this refers to the true *strong city of God;* this refers to *our salvation.* According to Symmachus, those who *sing the song* will say: *We have a mighty city,* and according to Aquila: *The city of dominion is our salvation.* But instead of either *salvation* or *deliverance,* the Hebrew text unambiguously is speaking of *Jesus,* for we find the very same letters with which the name of our Savior is written in Hebrew. The city of the blessed will be our Savior himself, and he will be their *wall* and *outer wall.*

[26:2-8a] And he will be all things among them. If we may understand the "heavenly Jerusalem" as interpreted above, then it follows that we may also understand Jerusalem's *gates* as signifying the entrance of those who are in a certain position but the exclusion of all others. For he does not wish to *open* the gates for the Jews, neither for Israel nor for those who simply happen to be there, but only for those who *keep righteousness* and *truth* and *peace.* Therefore, he continues: *Open the gates; let a*

---

[38]Is 16:4. **Chapter Twenty-Six** [1]Heb 12:22.

people enter that keeps truth, that lays hold of truth and keeps peace. And concerning these gates, a certain God-loving man continues on and says: "*Open to me the gates of righteousness, that I may enter through them and give thanks to the* Lord."[2] And it is proper that he says to *open* the *gates* for those specified above, since *in you have they hoped, O Lord God, who humbled and brought down those who dwell in lofty places; you will cast down strong cities and bring them down to the ground.* This is quite similar to what was said before in the verse: "Because you have made *cities* a heap, *fortified* [167] *cities* so their foundations might fall."[3] And now, therefore, presenting the same theme of "the righteous judgment of God,"[4] he resumes glorifying God and saying: *O great, everlasting God, you have humbled and brought down those who dwell in lofty places.* But, indeed, those whom you brought down from the height and *humbled,* and whose *cities* you demolished and whose mortal life you brought to an end, making their godless and wicked cities vanish, those were your meek kinsfolk, whom you blessed when you said: "Blessed are the meek, for they shall inherit the earth."[5] You exalted them who were at first *humble,* but now, during the time of your righteous judgment, you made the rulers of those who were once arrogant to be *trampled. Then the way of the godly was made straight.* For there is no longer anyone who is in the way, and *the way was* without obstacle and free from interference. And the reason for this was "the righteous judgment of God."[6] For this reason he says besides: *For the way of the Lord is judgment.*

[26:8b-9] After discussing in detail what sort of end that will seize the ungodly and what sort of hope awaits the righteous, and how the kingdom of Christ will be, and how the "gates"[7] of the city of God in heaven "will be opened" only for the worthy, and how those who enjoy

the full benefits of the promises will "sing a song"[8]—following the discussion of all this, the prophet sends up cries to God from his own mouth and from those all around him, saying: *We have hoped in your name and in the remembrance that our soul desires.* For as he had been present when the prophetic words had been accomplished and as he had seen in his soul the deeds themselves with eyes that had been enlightened, he looks away from all else toward God above, and he praises in song the benefactor of so many good things, sending up praise and saying the things stated above. For the things which have been stored up for you are worth hoping for, and I say to you that these things are the desire of my *soul.* For you, O Lord, are my desire and the divine passion of my soul. Therefore, my *soul desired* you, for the very remembrance of your *name* overwhelms our soul and awakens longing for you. Therefore, we do not sleep during the *night* time, but rather, having been aroused *in spirit,* we keep you in mind as our desire. And thus it shall happen that "the nights are as bright as the days for us."[9] For this very reason, *your ordinances* and your words were given to us who yet sojourn *on the earth* that they may serve as our *light* all through the *night* and through the day. After crying these things aloud in his excellent composition to God, the prophet turns to us and encourages us to walk down the same road with him. Therefore, he says: *Learn righteousness, you who dwell on the earth.*

[26:10] But instead of *for the impious one has come to an end,* Aquila and Theodotion translate this phrase: *The impious was shown mercy,* and Symmachus: *The impious was presented with a gift.* [168] And the Word encourages those who were once found among the number of the impious to be quick to repent, because the judgment of God awaits all people. Because of this, everyone is encouraged to *learn right-*

---

[2]Ps 118:19 rsv. [3]Is 25:2. [4]Rom 2:5. [5]Mt 5:5 rsv. [6]Rom 2:5. [7]Is 26:2. [8]Is 26:1. [9]Ps 139:12.

ousness, because our beneficent God had mercy even on those who were overtaken among the impious because they repented. But if anyone should not be persuaded by the preaching and fail to *learn righteousness* and to practice the *truth*, he will be *taken away* from the living and will not see *the glory of the Lord*.

[26:11] After he said these words of encouragement to us, he again looks up and, on seeing the divinity of the Savior taken up into heaven, he cries aloud: *O Lord, your arm is lifted up, and they have not known it*. For since they were depressed and had fallen far away from the knowledge of his divinity, the impious groped about in the darkness of their own ignorance. But on seeing the *uplifted arm* of the universal judgment that will befall them, those who once blasphemed him as though he did not exist will restrain themselves and cease from their desperate and shameful deeds. And when they see the blessed enjoying life to the full in the heavens, they will be jealous. And *jealousy* will especially lay hold of those *people* who did not wish to receive the chastening of God during this present life. Therefore, when he says *jealousy will take hold of an uninstructed people*, he adumbrates those of the circumcision who have not received the grace of God through Christ. Then he says next: *And fire will now consume the adversaries*, which is the same sentence as is laid down in the pronouncement: "Depart into the eternal fire prepared for the devil and his angels."[10]

[26:12-13] After saying these things, he again turned his attention to God and sent up a petition, saying: *O Lord, our God, give us peace, for you have granted us all things*. For, indeed, all things are from you, what delights us as well as what does not. But the greatest gift from you is *peace* in relation to you, in order that we might be free from any divisions toward you. And living at peace with you, our souls will be preserved through all. And so it will be, if you deem us worthy to be made your own possession. And, because *we know no other* except you, we have placed our trust *in your name* alone. Therefore, as we have gained nothing in this life except you, we justly entreat you to make us worthy to become your share and portion.

[26:14] He says, therefore, that we are yours, O Lord, and you are our possession. But there are those who give themselves over to "mortal sins,"[11] and because of this their souls are *dead*. "The soul that sins shall die,"[12] and thus it will not see the eternal *life* promised to the saints. Nor will the attending *physicians* be able to assist them and bring about salvation during the time of the [169] judgment, nor will they be able to *raise* them *up* from their fall. For if you—the great and fearful and righteous judge—delivered them over to destruction, who among *physicians* will be able to save them? But instead of *and you have taken away all their males*, Symmachus translates this: *Their every remembrance*; and Aquila and Theodotion: *Their every memorial*. For it was necessary that *their every* evil *remembrance be taken away* during the indicated time of the judgment. And if one prefers the reading *all their males*, then the Word introduces a great kindness. And so, indeed, those who have sinned will not themselves be completely obliterated, nor will they be utterly *destroyed*, but only the indicated offspring, for their soul had given birth to evil thoughts. For he says that these evil thoughts will be done away.

[26:15] And again, concerning the verse: *Increase evils on the glorious ones of the earth*, we do not find the word *evils* in either the other Greek translations or in the Hebrew reading. But rather, all of the other translations say: *You increased in the nation in which*

---

[10]Mt 25:41. [11]1 Jn 5:16. [12]Ezek 18:4.

you were glorified. In alignment with all these translations, we follow and understand this verse in this manner: that he *increased* something in the nation. This is precisely what we will understand from the saving word which says: "To every one who has will more be given, and he will have abundance."[13] Therefore, indeed, for those who have acquired good things for themselves, *he increased* what he dealt out, "what no eye has seen, nor ear heard, nor the heart of man conceived."[14] But to those who stored up *evil things* for themselves, he will again *increase* things that correspond to their works. Then, he next adds: *You removed to a distance all the boundaries of the earth.* For they positioned themselves far away from God, and he likewise distanced himself from them. For this very reason, so that the household of God might not suffer this judgment because of the ungodly, they ask urgently in prayer: *O Lord, our God, take possession of us.*

[26:16] The prophet foresaw the universal judgment just as though he had been present in the judgment and as though "standing before the judgment seat of God."[15] He saw these things while praising God and while beseeching him and while giving thanks to him, while relating in detail the repayment that God will award to the worthy and while setting down the punishments against those who were unworthy. And he delivers to us all these things through his writings so that we might be disciplined and instructed in all that he himself knew by the divine and illuminating Spirit. And, therefore, he says that the time was now when, O Lord, traveling the "straight and narrow,"[16] we strove earnestly for godliness. But even in that *affliction* we were not unmindful of you, and it was in fact by remem-bering you that we were able to stay strong and say: "We are *afflicted* but not crushed, persecuted but not forsaken; struck down [170] but not destroyed."[17] And, therefore, we were disciplined in the affliction, knowing that "the Lord disciplines those he loves."[18] And we consider every *affliction small* because of our longing for you, and so we say: "The sufferings of this present time are not worth comparing with the glory that is to be revealed to us."[19]

[26:17-18] Therefore, in enduring every hardship, we resembled a woman in *travail*, who lets out cries as she is about to bring to the light that with which she is pregnant. For *so were we to your beloved.* For they have your only-begotten Word within their soul, and the *fear* with which we reverence you is dispersed from you into us. And in accord with our noble birth, we bear the afflictions that have been laid on us, struggling lest we miscarry and lose *your beloved*, with whom we are now pregnant, and lose our God-inspired *fear.* And then, after enduring, we are not disappointed by hope, but *we produced the spirit of your salvation.*[20] For the *salvation* of your *spirit* was the end of the pregnancy *of your beloved* and of his *fear.* After publicly giving birth, we appointed people *among all the inhabitants of the earth*, so that they might learn of this and themselves profit by being eager to conceive *from your fear* and thus to *bring to birth* the same *spirit.* For those who neither receive this *fear* nor *produce the spirit of salvation* but rather are barren and without fruit will fall from the hope found in you. But those who are your share and those who endured every *affliction* because of you, even if they had to "fight to the death"[21] against sin, they will certainly not fall from the life that is found in you.

---

[13]Mt 25:29 RSV. [14]1 Cor 2:9 RSV. [15]Rom 14:10. [16]Mt 7:14. [17]2 Cor 4:8. [18]Prov 3:12; Heb 12:6. [19]Rom 8:18 RSV. [20]The Greek word here may be translated either "wind" or "Spirit." The NETS translators have chosen "wind," and the verse in this case holds a meaning of disappointment and futility. However, Eusebius clearly sees this statement as one reflecting hope and fulfillment, and thus the word must be rendered "spirit" in this context. [21]2 Macc 13:14.

[26:19] *For the dead shall rise*, or, according to Symmachus and Theodotion: *Your dead shall live*, or, according to Aquila: *Your deceased shall live*. And his *dead* could either be specific individuals or perhaps his holy martyrs. But there are others in addition to the above *dead*, concerning whom it has been said: "But the dead will not see life, nor will physicians raise them up."[22] They were the *dead* who "committed a sin which is mortal,"[23] but the *dead* of the Lord who endured every tribulation until death because of him, *they shall rise* even after their burial *in the tombs*. But instead of *they shall be raised*, the other Greek versions translate this phrase *they shall be awakened*, as though they were asleep rather than dead. For this reason, the death of the saints is called sleep, and, in accordance with sleep, the resurrection is referred to as waking up. Therefore, according to the other translations, the text says in the first line: *Those in the tombs shall awaken*; and in the second line, according to Symmachus [171]: *They will rejoice exceedingly*, or, according to Aquila: *They will sing praises*, or, according to Theodotion: *They will shout in joy*. And the reason for the resurrection is that the *dew from you* will be *for them*. For just as *dew* comes down on the earth silently and gently and causes the seeds which have been stored up in it to sprout and grow, so in the same manner *the dew from you* supplies *healing* and life and salvation to your *dead*, whose bodies were sown during their time on the earth. And you would not be wrong to say that the only-begotten Word of God is himself the *dew*. He besprinkles his dead with the life-giving drops of himself, which is at the same time healing for maladies,[24] if anything has gone wrong for them from a human perspective, as well as affording the resurrection and salvation and eternal life which will be given to them. But such things will not be for *the impious*, for their *land shall fall*. For this reason, since they are ever falling away in their bodies and their souls, God will deliver them over to the one who will administer their punishment.

[26:20] After the teaching about the resurrection of the dead and the vision of the prophetic Spirit of the saints of God gathered together and all standing before the divine presence, then in turn he addresses the coming wrath for the ungodly. But those among the ranks of the saints carefully consider this and depart far away for a little while and *conceal themselves*, lest they become spectators of the destruction of the ungodly. Therefore, the text says: *Go, my people, enter your chambers*. And the *chambers* of the people of God are the "many rooms in my Father's house,"[25] which are appointed to each rank of the saints according to the righteous judgment of God. He says, therefore, about these *chambers* which *you* have prepared: *O my people, enter* and *shut your door*. Do not be preoccupied with the things that are happening far away from your *chambers*, but *hide yourselves for a little while, until the wrath of the Lord has passed*. And, hereafter, when it has passed, throw the gates of your *chambers* open wide with great authority and boldness, and go forth to be admitted to the eternal temple and the kingdom of God that has been promised to you.

[26:21] After these things, he then next teaches what the *wrath* that will come on the ungodly will do when he says: *And the earth will disclose its blood*. And so the souls of those who have been *slain* in it could not be hidden because they committed a "mortal sin."[26] For in this God said that his *wrath would come on them*. Here, what is called *wrath* are those "angels" who administer punishments. For as it was said to the Egyptians: "He sent among them his wrath and anger and affliction, a dispatch through wicked angels,"[27] so also now

---

[22]Is 26:14. [23]1 Jn 5:16. [24]This word means "physical malady" as well as "sin." [25]Jn 14:2. [26]1 Jn 5:16. [27]Ps 78:49.

the *wrath* of God has rushed against those who once *dwelled on the earth. He will disclose the blood* that was poured out on it, *and it will not cover the slain.* It perhaps indicates through these things the murder of the saints of God and the *blood* of the martyrs, concerning which also Moses said in his great [172] song in the Scriptures: "For he avenges the blood of his children, and he will avenge, and he will repay the enemies with a sentence, and he will repay the haters."[28] And each earthy soul and body-loving *blood*—I am speaking about those who have committed "mortal sins"[29]—will be acknowledged and *disclosed.*

[27:1] After these things have been accomplished, then one will be able to say: "The last enemy to be destroyed is death."[1] For this reason, at the conclusion of everything and after all else, the Word affirms: *On that day,* that is, during that time, *God will bring his holy and great and strong dagger.* But instead of *holy,* all the other Greek translations say *hard.* Therefore, he will deal out this judgment from afar and let loose against no one else, but he will *bring* it on this one only, for whom also it was reserved in proportion to his evil. And who else could this be but the one who in the beginning supplanted the first man in the paradise of God and caused him to fall from his position before God? This was the one who was aptly called the *crooked snake* and the *dragon,* since he was dragged down to the earth and slithers about and lurks at people's feet, hoping to bite someone and drive his toxic venom into him and thus to cause him to fall from his upright journey that leads to God. Therefore, indeed, the rod of God is straight and is used for instruction, as we read: "Your royal scepter is a scepter of equity."[2] It has been reserved for those who have committed curable sins, and it was brought on them for

their instruction and betterment and for the profit of their soul. But the one who never did anything upright or straight but was always completely and continually bent and crooked lies on his abdomen on the earth and crawls on his belly, lurking around the feet of all in order to supplant them and cause them to fall after the ungodly. He will be delivered over to a *hard* and *great* and *strong dagger,* for the great judge has dealt out a sentence only for him. And what could this *dagger* be—which the Septuagint said was *holy* and *great* and *strong*—except "the word of God, which is living and active, sharper than any two-edged sword."[3]

Here he calls the action of judgment a *dagger,* but he also says that it is *holy.* He consoles them in their fear of the threatened judgment, and at the same time he points out that those who are punished will not be subjected to destruction and that the reason for their holiness is that they repented. For God does not wish to destroy those he chastises, but to cleanse and to sanctify those whom he reforms. But then, when he attacks his rival and opponent, the *dragon* that has had so many victories against him, *he will kill* him. And he will remove his very being from the realm of what exists, so that he will no longer be, nor will he be counted among what exists. It is for this reason that he was not even deemed worthy of the wrath of God. For this wrath was instructive and reformatory, as he teaches when he avers: "O Lord, rebuke me not in your anger, nor chasten me in your wrath."[4] This is spoken on the one hand about an anger that possesses a reproving power and, on the other hand, about a wrath that has an instructive power. Therefore, he pursued those who have committed sins that are lesser in degree and brought reproaches on them and chastened them, but the *dragon* was worthy of neither reproaches nor training but only of absolute annihilation.[5]

---

[28]Deut 32:43. [29]1 Jn 5:16. **Chapter Twenty-Seven** [1]1 Cor 15:26. [2]Ps 44:7. [3]Heb 4:12. [4]Ps 6:1. [5]The word indicates "disappearance" or "vanishing," but in this context, "annihilation" would seem to be a fair translation.

Because of this, God will first bring his *holy* [173] and *great* and *strong dagger* against him. And the one who sees the dagger will surrender himself *in flight*, but he will do this thoughtlessly and frantically, since it is rightly said: "Where can I go from your Spirit, and where can I flee from your presence?"[6] But, except he endeavor to *flee*, the *holy* and *great* and *strong dagger* of God will apprehend him and *kill this crooked* one and will take away all his essence from existence. And just as one *flees away* into the innermost room of the house in order to hide himself, so he attempted to do so in that which was called the *sea*. Concerning this sea it has been said: "This great and wide *sea*; there are creeping things without number, living things small and great,"[7] and "this is the dragon that you formed to play in it."[8] And in Job, the one who identifies himself as the Lord taught about this when he said: "And will you draw out a dragon with a fish hook, and put a halter around its nose? Or will you fasten a ring in its nostril?"[9]

Concerning these things, he adds: "He is the first of the Lord's creation, made to be mocked by his angels,"[10] and again he says: "He is king over everything that lives in the water."[11] And in these things, the Word teaches that he is released on all sides because he has given up his life "to be mocked by the saints of God,"[12] who are exercised in battling with him, at one time casting "fishhooks"[13] around him, and at another time fettering him by "putting a halter around his nose"[14] and at another time piercing him with a "ring."[15] This is why it has been said: "Made to be mocked by his angels."[16] But after this hunt and contest, he confronted the athletes of God, and those who train exhibited a proof of their own prowess against him and through their contest with him. And the "dragon"[17] himself continued to be "mocked"[18]

when the contest had come to an end, and "the righteous judgment of God"[19] then presented rewards to those who contended until the consummation of the universe.

After the judgment against the ungodly, *God will bring his holy and great and strong dagger against the dragon, a fleeing snake, against the dragon, a crooked snake.* But according to Symmachus, the text reads: *Against Leviathan, the crooked snake, and in that day he will slay the dragon in the sea;* and Aquila says: *On Leviathan, a snake who has become dried out and dispersed, and in that day he will slay him with the sea monster in the sea;* and Theodotion says: *On the dragon, the strong snake, and on the dragon, the crooked snake, and he will slay the dragon in that day in the sea.* And the *snake* and *dragon* is also called *Leviathan*, and this name was given to him from the Lord. And this was indeed the "great sea monster,"[20] although we read that the Lord "subdued" him: "He who is about to subdue the great sea monster."[21] And in this context he is called *Leviathan*, as well as in the psalm which says: "This is the dragon that you formed to play with it,"[22] [174] for according to the Hebrew text he is called *Leviathan*. And likewise in the verse in Job which says: "And will you draw out a dragon with a fish hook?"[23] again he is called *Leviathan* in the Hebrew. In the same way, this many-headed and many-named *dragon* is at once called a *snake* and the devil and Satan and a "great sea monster"[24] and *Leviathan*, and in other contexts also a "lion"[25] and a "serpent."

In that day—that is, in the time of the consummation of the age—God, the judge of the universe, *will kill the dragon* with his *dagger*, and *in that day* he will deeply wound this one. And in his first coming to humanity, the Christ of God did not assail him as with a

---

[6]Ps 139:7. [7]Ps 104:25. [8]Ps 104:26. [9]Job 41:1-2. [10]Job 40:19 LXX. [11]Job 41:34. [12]Cf. Job 40:19 LXX. [13]Job 40:25 MT. [14]Job 40:25 MT. [15]Cf. Job 41:2 LXX. [16]Job 40:19 LXX. [17]Cf. Ps 104:26. [18]Cf. Job 40:19 LXX. [19]Rom 2:5. [20]Cf. Job 3:8 LXX. [21]Job 3:8 LXX. [22]Ps 104:26. [23]Job 41:1. [24]Cf. Job 3:8 LXX. [25]Cf. Ps 91:13.

dagger, and he did not *kill* him but rather only stepped on him and trampled his powers. For this reason it has been said to his face: "You will tread on the asp and the serpent, and you will trample the lion and the *dragon*."[26] And now, indeed, "he has trampled down" and still even now "he treads down," for he has given "authority to tread on *snakes* and scorpions, and over all the power of the enemy"[27] to his disciples. And at the indicated time of the consummation after everything, the *dagger* of God will apprehend the ungodly and seize him who *flees*, and he will *take him away* from existence so that he will no longer exist. Here also the Word of God continues to delineate the universal judgment, as he had been doing beginning with the verse: "Look, the Lord is ruining the world and will make it desolate."[28] Now that the prophecy has brought a conclusion to this theme, it commences a new and different one.

[27:2] Then the prophet commences another theme about *a beautiful vineyard—a desire*, imagery that had been used in the prophecy above when discussing the universal judgment of God. He first stated the threats against Jerusalem and against its inhabitants because of their unbelief in the Lord. Then he discussed how the apostolic preaching was spread abroad throughout the whole world. Then he remembered the women with Mary Magdalene who saw the saving resurrection, and he expounded the conversion to God of those nations who were formerly idolatrous. Then he prophesies concerning the council of the Sadducees and the Pharisees and high priests who assembled against the Savior, and he prolonged the word a little concerning this point. But he makes Jerusalem the starting point when he says: *A beautiful vineyard—a desire*. And this *vineyard* was the very one concerning which it was said above: "The beloved had a vineyard on a hill, on a fertile place."[29] And he makes it perfectly clear when he says a little later: "For the vineyard of the Lord of hosts is the house of Israel."[30] Therefore, this *vineyard* was *good* and *a desire* when "Jacob became the Lord's portion and Israel a measured part of his inheritance."[31] Therefore, to make sense of this, one should think back to the time when David reigned and all he accomplished, or when another righteous king is attested to have existed. He will thus see how the *vineyard* was *good* and how it could have been said to have been *a desire*. And, therefore, this *vineyard* has been adorned with prophets and spiritual people and with the honor of the priesthood and the eminence of the high priesthood and with the appearances of angels and even with the visitation of the Lord.

[27:3] [175] And now the Word *begins singing* about it, informing the reader that it says that it is a *city* in the vineyard: *I am a strong city, a besieged city*. For it truly was a *fortified city* when a "hedge"[32] had been set up around it and it had been "fenced in" and secured from all directions. Thus it was *fortified*, so that nothing damaged it although it was *besieged*; but even though indeed it had been such a *vineyard*, now it has been abandoned and become unfruitful, so that it has been said concerning it: "I will take down its hedge, and it shall be plundered, and I will demolish its wall, and it will be trampled down, and I will abandon my vineyard, and it shall certainly neither be dug nor pruned."[33] And he teaches what the reason for this will be when he says: "Because I waited for it to produce a cluster of grapes, but it produced thorns."[34] In the passage at hand, he gives this reason: *In vain have I watered it*. For all such expense on the aforementioned *city* was wasted and, therefore, it *will be taken by night* by those who *besiege* it. For it was overtaken in the darkness even though the prolonged light had made it easy

---

[26]Ps 90:13. [27]Lk 10:19. [28]Is 24:1. [29]Is 5:1. [30]Is 5:7. [31]Deut 32:9. [32]Is 5:2. [33]Is 5:5-6. [34]Is 5:4.

for the adversaries to take it. And so, when the final fall came, it did not have a wall fenced around it or guarding it. For it had been taken down by him who said: "I will take down its hedge, and it will be plundered, and I will take down its wall, and it will be trampled down."[35]

[27:4] Nevertheless, although these things happened, the prophet continues on and says in his composition to them: *Who will set me to watch a stalk in a field?* For even though that "wasteland"[36] "produced thorns instead of a cluster of grapes"[37] and had nothing more than a *stalk* in it, he nevertheless loved it and took care to *watch* over it. But according to Symmachus, the text reads: *Who will give me over to a land that is dry and that has been abandoned in battle?* This would appear to us to be an equally valid translation. And so the text says that I wished to be a guard for the aforementioned *field* or the *vineyard* or the once *fortified city.* And he made me *set aside* what became *enemy territory* for me, and so much so that I delivered it over to fire after it had been besieged.

[27:5-6] Therefore, the prophecy rightly adds: *I have been burned up. Those who dwell in it will cry out.* For the fire of the judgment of God will force even those who do not want to confess back into their place. And the adversaries of God indeed will come to such an end, but we who are of another division and who have been chastened—our suffering having been caused by those same adversaries—*we will make peace with him.* And the prophetic word addresses these things to those who happen to be of his own household and class, advising them and encouraging them. For this very reason, it says: *Let us make peace with him,* all you who are *coming.* And they are those whom he presents when he says next: *The children of Jacob, Israel, shall bud and blossom, and the world will be filled with his fruit,* clearly fore-

shadowing the apostolic band. And therefore, the apostles were the *children of Jacob.* For they were those who went out from the nation of the Jews and who *budded* from the "Israel according to the flesh,"[38] and they produced a *blossoming* shoot [176] and a sweet-smelling flower that has filled up the whole *world* with its fragrance.

[27:7-9] After these things the text says: *Will he be smitten even as he himself was struck? And will he be killed even as he himself has killed?* The sense of the word is as follows: those who preached evil for the Gentiles were themselves not given peace in return, were they? For there were those who struck and persecuted them and who inflicted blows on them, but there were also those who most beautifully preached peace to them. And, therefore, those who did wrong from among the Gentiles did not suffer the same things as the heralds of peace, did they? For, indeed, they struck others but were not struck in return, and they killed but were not killed in return. *Fighting and rivaling* they were persecuting them, and *they sent them away.* And they neither withdraw from peace nor from preaching good news to them. Therefore, as though to the unfaithful from among the Gentiles, the Word says next: *Were you not the one who conspired with your harsh spirit to kill them with a spirit of wrath?* For the unfaithful from among the Gentiles *conspired* these things against the apostles of our Savior, possessed of a *harsh spirit,* and, with this *spirit of wrath* inside them, they think about nothing else except how *they might kill them.* But those who *budded* and *blossomed* from *Jacob* and who suffered these things, they bore all things nobly because of Christ. This is why the text then adds: *The lawlessness of Jacob will be removed. And this is his blessing when they might remove his sin.* And he says that these things will be the reasons for the removal *of the*

---

[35]Is 5:5. [36]Cf. Is 5:6. [37]Cf. Is 5:4. [38]1 Cor 10:18.

sins of Jacob, and because of these things he will grant him *the blessing of removing his sin*. And if, as the apostle says, "she will be saved through bearing children, if she continues in faith and love and holiness, with modesty,"[39] it follows that since *Jacob budded children* and *blossomed* such fruit, he will share in their *blessing* through their virtue. And the Word signifies that many will be saved through the apostolic grace and those who follow after the apostles in this life.

He says specifically that these things will happen when the aforementioned *children of Jacob* and the bloom from *Israel* will have traversed the *world* and filled it with their God-fearing teaching. Then, through his power, they will refute the error of polytheism which had forever prevailed over the Gentiles so as indeed *to make all the stones of the* idolatrous *altars broken pieces like fine dust*. They will make the *trees* and *groves* around their temples disappear, and they will bring about their desolation, although they were once so great as to be compared with *oak trees*.

[27:10-11a] Therefore, the ones indicated above will indeed accomplish these things, but the once *inhabited fold*—the people of Israel—*will be left deserted, like a forsaken fold*. They did not wish to follow after "the good shepherd who lays down his own life for the sheep,"[40] and for this very reason, the land of their [177] soul *will be turned into a feeding place for a long time*. Thus will the verse be fulfilled among them: "A boar from the wood ravaged it, and a lone wild beast fed on it."[41] *And there*, he says, *they will rest*, clearly "those who devour and ravage it."[42] And it will turn into a wilderness, so that *nothing green* will be found *in it*. For this reason, the text says: *There will be nothing green in it*.

[27:11b] He calls on *women* because there were no men to be found among them who were

worthy of salvation. Therefore, he encourages the *women* to come quickly to witness the *spectacle* of the incredible and marvelous works so that they might come and *enlighten* "the people sitting in darkness"[43] and their *abandoned city*. Therefore, according to Aquila, the text reads: *The women are coming and enlightening it*; but according to Symmachus: *The women are coming and making it visible*. And the *it* is the *city* mentioned above, concerning which it has been said: *For the fortified city which alone was beautiful has been abandoned and left behind as a desert*. And these things have been fulfilled literally and in history at the resurrection of our Savior, for we read in the Gospel of Matthew: "There were many women there, looking on from afar, who had followed him from Galilee, ministering to him; among whom were Mary Magdalene, and Mary the mother of James and Joses, and the mother of the sons of Zebedee";[44] and in the Gospel of Luke: "And those women who had come with him from Galilee followed,"[45] and the rest. Therefore, *the people did not have understanding* in as far as they were not persuaded by the preaching of the apostles, and yet the word was received by the Gentiles. Because of this, the divine Spirit calls the women to bear witness to the preached word, but later he saw that the people were blind. *Therefore*, he says, *he that made them will not have compassion, nor will he that formed them have mercy*.

[27:12-13] *And it shall be on that day*—that is, during the indicated time—*that the Lord will fence them in from the channel of the river*. But instead of *to fence in*, all the other Greek translations read *he will strike*, clearly signifying that the Lord *will strike* those faithless ones and the people without understanding. Then he specifies where this will take place when he says, according to Symmachus, but the other Greek translations present the basic meaning: *from the*

---

[39]1 Tim 2:15. [40]Jn 10:11. [41]Ps 80:13. [42]Cf. Ps 80:13. [43]Cf. Is 9:2. [44]Mt 27:55-56. [45]Lk 23:55.

channel of the river to the torrent of Egypt. And I suppose that this verse points toward the war against the nation of the Palestinians that befell the Jews after they committed the daring deed against Christ. And, therefore, it would appear that the Word is speaking of their boundary with Palestine when he says *from the river,* and perhaps he is speaking of the Jordan when he says *as far as Rhinocorura.* And this is the city which lies on both sides of the boundary between Egypt and Palestine. And, therefore, according to the other Greek translations, the text reads *as far as the torrent of Egypt,* and thus the Word adumbrates, as I said, that there would be a war between the Jews and the nation of the Palestinians.

[178] Next he orders the messengers of the Word when he says: *But as for you, gather one by one the children of Israel.* For the people did not all wish to be present for the saving preaching. *For the people are without understanding,* and even if there are scarcely any among them, *gather one by one the children of Israel.* For the beloved ones will be saved, even if it is only *one by one,* or two, or only a few of them from each city or from each nation. Therefore, *gather* these *one by one,* and *a great trumpet will sound* among the other nations, and the Word will cry to those who listen from among all the people. For this reason, the text reads: *And it shall be on that day that he will trumpet with the great trumpet, and those who were lost among the people of the Assyrians and those who were lost in Egypt will come and bow down to the Lord on the holy mountain at Jerusalem.* In saying Egyptians he signifies the idolaters, and in saying *Assyrians* he signifies the adversaries of Israel who besieged the land of Judah. It is concerning them that he says that through the word of the *great* evangelical *trumpet*[46] of him who preached truly, those

who were once idolaters among the Gentiles and hostile and opposed to the worship of the God of Israel, they are the ones who will change and convert and come to God. And so, those who were once lost in the error of idolatry, after being changed and striving to come to the knowledge of the word of God, will receive salvation through Christ.

[28:1] In the Spirit, he sees the assembly of the godless who are ashamed of our Savior. And he calls their complicity in evil and their unanimity in evil a *crown of pride* when he cries aloud and says: *Ah, the crown of pride.*[1] And thus he adumbrates the council of the Pharisees and chief priests and the other rulers of the Jewish people. They came together from various ranks, and so he compares them with a *crown,* and not a crown of honor or glory either, but *of pride* and of dishonor. For this reason he says: *Ah, the crown of pride,* or, according to the other translations: *the crown of arrogance.* They were arrogant and desperate braggarts, among whom also were the *workers of Ephraim.* And it is said that Judas the betrayer was from the tribe of Ephraim. And he calls him a *worker* because he was bought off to deliver over the teacher. But he was also *the flower that has fallen from glory.* For he shared in the *glory* of the apostolic band, but because of his turn for the worse, he became *the flower that has fallen from glory.* And the apostles of our Savior were called a *flower* and bud only a little earlier, when it was said concerning them: "Children of Jacob, Israel shall bud and blossom and the world will be filled with his fruit."[2] But the text says that the betrayer *fell* from them, for *the flower has fallen from its glory.*

[179] And all those mentioned above were gathered together *on the top of the stout mountain.* The Word thus indicates the seed of

---

[46]Eusebius's word choice here can be linked to Origen's homilies on Josh 7:1. **Chapter Twenty-Eight** [1]The two words translated "complicity" and "unanimity" in this sentence are probably meant to bring to mind the interweaving and interlacing of the crown of thorns that was set on Jesus' head. [2]Is 27:6.

those who have been fattened in soul, concerning whom it was said: "The heart of this people was made fat."[3] Accordingly, the *top of the stout mountain* would be the rulers of the people that have been fattened, since those rulers were their head. We also interpreted the line about *the flower that has fallen from glory* in reference to them, and therefore he deems them unhappy. But instead of *on the top of the stout mountain*, Aquila translates this phrase: *ravine of filth*; and Symmachus: *ravine of fattiness*; and Theodotion: *ravine of fat*. But the Hebrew text says *Gethsemani*. Although, I once heard someone from among our beloved explain that the place that is called "Gethsemani"[4] in the Gospel is where the betrayer with *the crown of pride* approached the Savior and betrayed him.

[28:2] And these were the ones who were *drunk without wine*, whom he next threatens and says: *See, the wrath of the Lord is a strong and hard thing, like hail. Violently rushing down like a great flood that sweeps a country, it will give rest to the land with hands and feet.* For thus he says that the *wrath of the Lord* will come down against those who are *drunk without wine*, and he compares it with *hail* falling down on the heads of people who *have no shelter* and with *water* that *rushes down* and creates its own channel through the earth. This is how he says that the wrath of God will be vented against those indicated.

[28:3] Then he adds next: *The garland of pride will be trampled—the worker of Ephraim.* Indeed, they were once a *garland of pride* for those who stand prepared to affront, and for this reason they were called a *crown of arrogance*. And he will distribute such an end to them that they will be *trampled*. Therefore, they were *trampled* by the wrath of God that overtook them and by the adversaries who

enslaved them, adversaries who profaned[5] their city and appropriated it for themselves and banished those who had once lived there.

[28:4] Therefore, while discussing *the garland of pride*, and particularly concerning *the flower that has fallen from its glory*, he adds next: *And the flower that has fallen*[6] *from its glorious hope on the topmost of the lofty mountain will be like an early fig; the one who sees it will want to eat it up before he takes it into his hand.* And such a one was Judas, who indeed was a flower, but one that *fell from hope* in God and *from glory*. And, indeed, they were once *on the lofty mountain*, but that is not to say that they were *on the top of the stout mountain*. For the present prophet informs the reader that he was also one of those who were on *the lofty mountain* [180] when he says: "Go up on a high mountain, you who bring good tidings to Zion."[7] But he was the kind of person who could be compared with an *early fig*, an unripe fruit, on the one hand considered good when in season, but on the other hand unprofitable because its fruit was not mature and suitable for eating. This is why he who slanders what is good was perceived to be *early*, for he was quick and snatched away beforehand because *he wanted to eat it up before he takes it into his hand*. And, therefore, he was in fact able *to eat it up*.

[28:5-6] But, indeed, he says that the things concerning the *crown of pride* and *the flower that has fallen* will happen *in that day*, clearly during the same time that *the Lord of hosts will be the garland of hope, which is woven of glory, to what is left of the people*, that is to say, *for those who survive* from the destruction of all the people. And they were the apostles and disciples of the Savior, for whom he promises that the Lord himself will be a *garland of hope*. Because it is said that "they will sit on thrones,

---

[3]Is 6:10. [4]Mt 26:36. [5]The Greek word can have either the sense of "profanation" or "trampling." [6]Eusebius has here inadvertently omitted the Greek word translated "that has fallen." [7]Is 40:9.

udging the twelve tribes of Israel,"[8] the text then says that the Lord himself will be *also a spirit of judgment* for them. He will also be their *power*, so that they will be able *to turn the* people *from the city* to the *gate* of the church.

[28:7-8] These things indeed happened concerning the apostles; then the Word once again turns to address those of elevated ranks when he says: *For these have gone astray with wine.* And he explains who *these* are when he says *the priest and the prophet.* You may see that they were *the crown of pride,* and it is clear that *the priests* and those who are called their *prophets* in the verse above are those who indeed claim prophetic honors for themselves. He says that all *these went astray from wine* and *because of sikera* from "the poison and bitterness and rage of serpents."[9] *They went astray because of sikera,* although the other Greek translations call it an *intoxicating drink.* And he ensures that the *wine* and an *intoxicating drink* at hand are understood to be different, lest anyone should assume that they are the same, when he says above: "those who are drunk without wine."[10] So then, this *wine* was not the same as what was called *sikera* or an *intoxicating drink,* by which the leaders were led astray. Then he adds: *This is an omen.* For truly it was an omen and an apparition for them all together to suffer such things and to intend such terrible and godless counsel which will be foiled by a *curse* from God. Because of these things, Judas, who betrayed the Savior, earned a reputation as one driven by *greed,* but the leaders pretended to act on behalf of the *greed* of the people. And, for whatever reason, the word of Christ did not immediately destroy them, although from the very beginning they contrived a plot against him. For this reason, the text says that they planned *this counsel for the sake of greed.* And he calls the *counsel* a *plot.*

[28:9] [181] After describing the prophecy concerning "the crown of pride"[11] and that which followed next, the Word turns again to speak of the apostolic rank, for whom it was said that "the Lord of hosts" himself would be "a garland of hope"[12] and "a tiara of glory." And he teaches precisely this, I mean, that the apostolic band was to be prepared and ready for the afflictions that were to come on them because of the Word of Christ. And, therefore, he mentions them when he says: *To whom did we declare evil things, and to whom did we declare a message?* But who would have been eager to receive the *evil* things that have been announced if he had spoken more clearly about this evil? And so he speaks more generally of difficult circumstances and painful experiences, but he clearly means sufferings and tribulations for the sake of godliness. To whom do we announce these things? Let him listen, because we do not only declare *evil,* tribulation, suffering and painful experiences for him, but we also declare the good *report* that those who have contended well will be repaid with rewards. You listened, you who have been *weaned from the breast.* For this word is for you apostles, and the things that we announce concern you. Indeed, "when you were children"[13] and nourished with milk at the breast, no such demands were laid on you because of the immaturity of your youthful understanding. And then you were nursed "by the custodian"[14] of the "law" and by the elementary teachings of the word of the fear of God. But now, "after increasing in stature,"[15] you were released from your custodian, and you entered into the mature teaching, now *weaned from* the *milk* of the law and *pulled away* from your Jewish mother and her bodily forms of worship.

[28:10-11] So then, by ever more sharing in the mature and saving nourishment of the gospel,

---

[8]Mt 19:28. [9]Deut 32:32. [10]Is 28:1. The phrase translated "those who are drunk" (οἱ μεθύοντες) is cognate with the word translated "an intoxicating drink" (μέθυσμα). [11]Cf. Is 28:1. [12]Cf. Is 28:5. [13]Gal 4:3. [14]Gal 3:24. [15]Lk 2:52.

you will be prepared for *tribulations*. For those who strive after godliness must expect *tribulation*, and not just once but also a second time after the first. These things are addressed to the apostolic band and to all who are discipled in the saving gospel. And we do not have to say any more about the tribulations or mention that they had despaired of their salvation, as those who were ever born in *tribulation*. For in a little while the *tribulation* will be over, and he will award you your trophies. And you shall be presented as champions, crowned with the "garland of hope which is woven of glory."[16] For this reason, he continues on to say *hope on hope*, and not after a little interval from the *tribulation*. For the interval between them is brief. Therefore, he says *yet a little, yet a little*. "For *tribulation* produces endurance, and endurance produces character, and character produces hope, and hope does not disappoint us."[17]

[182] You will acquire these things from the *tribulation because of contempt from lips and through a different tongue*. For those who disparage, afflict, mock, slander and blaspheme you will do so with a very different[18] *tongue*, which you will be able to despise because of the *little hope* that you received. Therefore, although these statements usually refer specifically to the apostles and disciples and evangelists of our Savior, in this context the Word teaches prophetically about the Jewish people. For those who learn to be disciples of Christ *will speak* and persuade them of these things concerning the *tribulation* and the *hope in tribulation* so that they will come to the resurrection that is reserved in the presence of God—what I am speaking about is that although they are oppressed, they will endure all things for the sake of godliness.

[28:12-13] And *this* is the supposed *rest, and this destruction by thirst and hunger* is "the

godliness which is of value."[19] And, indeed, *they will speak* these things *to this people*, and the Word explains these things to the unfaithful from among the circumcision, but *they will not want to hear*. For this reason he says that *the oracle of the Lord God will be to them*, and in another place, *affliction on affliction*. For, because they were unwilling to suffer because of Christ and to walk "the narrow and hard way"[20] and instead went off on the "broad"[21] and "easy" way, *they will fall backwards and will be in danger and crushed and taken*. Those who are unwilling to take up the aforementioned *oracle of the Lord* will receive all these things, and they will in fact deserve their *falling* and *crushing*.

[28:14] And, seeing that they piled up such things as these for themselves because they did not believe the aforementioned word, he declared to them next: *Therefore hear the word of the Lord, you afflicted men and rulers of this people that is in Jerusalem*, or, according to Symmachus: *You scoffing men, those in authority over this people in Jerusalem*. For there are *scoffing men* and others among the Greeks who ridicule the word of Christ, and, lest anyone should assume that the things discussed above are said concerning others, he then specifically and of necessity added: *Those in authority over this people*. And seeing that they did not preside over the people in Jerusalem but rather those in all Judea and Galilee, one could say that he distinguishes accurately between the *rulers* and *those in authority over the people*.

[28:15] They are the "crown of pride"[22] which was mentioned above, and this verse is therefore addressed to them, since *you have said* to them: "*We have made a covenant with Hades and agreements with death*." For you have said: "*We have made falsehood our hope, and in falsehood we will be sheltered*." Accordingly,

---

[16]Cf. Is 28:5. [17]Rom 5:3-5. [18]This Greek word for "different" can also mean "less than good" or "mediocre." [19]1 Tim 4:8. [20]Mt 7:14. [21]Mt 7:13. [22]Cf. Is 28:1.

these things were intended for others [183] and are addressed to the aforementioned scoffers[23] who scoff and ridicule the word of Christ. Through these things, it is taught that it would be fitting for them to anticipate *affliction on affliction* but also *hope on hope*, because they had forged a friendship and made peace with *death* and secured a *refuge in Hades*. And, after doing so, they anticipated that they would not be tested by *affliction* and that nothing distressing and unpleasant should befall them. And if the *storm* should come on you, it will overwhelm and assail the opposing power, but it will not come on you. Because of your friends, you understood the opposing power to be *death* itself.

[28:16] Therefore, *you have said* these things to them because you listened, for the Lord of the universe commanded even you to speak. You did not receive the grace that was proclaimed to you first of all, but I placed myself as a *precious and honored stone* at the topmost corner, and I will make myself high and distinguished and prominent among all, so that *everyone who believes in him* will not fall from hope. But according to the other translations: *the one who believes will not be anxious.* For *the one who believes* will be patient and wait for the gospel of the word. This gospel is probably what the *stone* refers to and so would be the same rock concerning which the Savior said: "On the rock I will build my church."[24]

He announces: *I will lay this stone for the foundation of Zion*, and in fact he has done what he said he would do: "On the rock I will build my church."[25] For we frequently interpret Mount *Zion* to be the evangelical preaching and the church that has been *founded* on it. And he promises that he will *lay this precious* and *chosen* and *honored stone for the foundation* of the church. And so it has been called *corner stone* or the *corner foundation stone*. The *stone*

may also refer to the human body of our Savior, since we read in Daniel that he saw "a stone cut out from a mountain without hands."[26] Indeed, the *stone* is to be understood as the human body of the Savior and the mountain as his divinity.

[28:17-18] And he says that he will *turn judgment into hope* by this *stone*. For although this *stone* judges, it will also protect the good hopes of those who are judged, because by it *mercy* has been united with the most just *weight balances* and scales. For this reason the text says: *My mercy will become weight balances.* And so these things have been said concerning the *stone* and those things spoken of above. And after saying: "We have made falsehood our hope, and in falsehood we will be sheltered,"[27] he next adds: *And as for you who trust vainly in falsehood, I tell you that the tempest will not pass you by, lest it also take away your covenant of death.* He tells them not to be deceived when he says: because we were treated kindly *in death, the tempest* [184] *will not come on us*, neither will we be tried by a certain distress. O you who *trusted in a lie* and said "we have made falsehood our hope, and in falsehood we will be sheltered"[28] and *even if a storm passes by, it will not pass by us.* Therefore now hear and learn that *he will take away your covenant with death, and your hope in Hades will not abide.* For you entrusted yourselves to *death* and to an unsound course of action, and in *Hades* you placed your hope. For this very reason, *if a rushing storm comes, you will be washed under it.*

[28:19] If also it is about *to pass by* and *depart*, it will yet draw you far away and *take you along.* And this will not happen to you in the distant future but *early, early*, that is, soon, the visitation of God will come on you and will begin to approach. *In the day* but also *in the night it will*

---

[23]Is 28:14. [24]Mt 16:18. [25]Mt 16:18. [26]Dan 2:34, 45. [27]Is 28:15. [28]Is 28:15.

come on you, and this will be the end of your *hope*. For *you pledged yourselves to death*, and you surrendered yourselves *to Hades*.

[28:20] If you find such words as these unpleasant to your ears, then while *you are in straits* pay attention to what awaits you and do not say: *We are unable to fight* "on behalf of the truth,"[29] *and we ourselves are too weak to be mobilized.* For if you will be willing, you will be gathered into the portion of God, and you will not be weak but will struggle on behalf of godliness. But if you voluntarily assign yourselves to *death* and *Hades*, know that the Lord will now come to you and bring wrath on you for all the aforementioned reasons.

[28:21] And the wrath of God will hang over you *as a very high and majestic mountain* against the *impious ones.* Symmachus says, *thus the Lord will stand as in the clefts of the mountain*, and instead of *and he will be in the ravine of Gabaon*, again he says *in the deep valley in Gabaon.* The story is recorded in the book of Joshua, the son of Nun, the successor of Moses, that when battling the Philistines, he prayed and said: "Let the sun stand at Gabaon and the moon at the ravine of Elom."[30] And then "the sun stood at Gabaon and the moon at the ravine of Elom," when "the sun stood still" for the entire period of a day until all the Philistines had been vanquished. Therefore, as this was done against the *ungodly in the clefts of the mountain, in the deep valley in Gibaon*, so also now the *Lord will rise up against* those who are here accused and *with wrath he will do the deeds*—deeds of bitterness—to those who have been asking for it. And so it will be given as a bitter antidote for the evil that lies under their soul. And the *wrath* of the Lord *will deal strangely*, and he will act according to *bitterness* and not according to his sweetness and kindness and goodness, but according to the punish-

ment deserved by them. And it would seem that the *bitterness* and *wrath* and *anger* and such things as were said to come from God indicate nothing other than the chastisements against the ungodly and the punishments that shall come on them from the divine court of justice.

[28:22] [185] Therefore, he says that such things await those of you who refuse to receive "the honored and precious stone,"[31] and for this reason he says *may you not rejoice* with an evil glee *or let your bands become strong.* With these *bands* you bound yourselves to the "covenant which you made with death and the agreement with Hades."[32] But there is hope of salvation for you, if you burst the *bonds* chaining you to death and withdraw from worldly merriment and cease from temporary pleasures. For you have already learned to what sort of end this leads. And do not suppose that I am a prophet because I announce these things to you. Rather, I have shared with you only the things that *I have heard* with the hearing of the soul that the *Lord of hosts* has spoken. For it was willed that you should not be ignorant of the *deeds* which have been adjudicated and ordained and settled. For judgment has not yet come on these people and still awaits them, but it has been already determined and decided in his presence. *You have heard* these very things, and I call you to be a witness.

[28:23] The Word continues to address these things to "the crown of pride"[33] that has been given away, and he exhorts those who rejected[34] "the chosen and honored cornerstone"[35] first to *give ear* and then to *hear* and to obey what was said. And he teaches them that those punishments that they deserve will pursue them. "For mighty men will be mightily tested."[36] And, indeed, he who is small and weak will suffer a lenient punishment that is

---

[29]Sir 4:28. [30]Josh 10:12. [31]Cf. Is 28:16. [32]Cf. Is 28:15. [33]Cf. Is 28:1. [34]Ps 118:22. [35]Cf. Is 28:16. [36]Wis 6:6.

appropriate to the smallness of his ability. But he who had great ability "will be mightily tested,"[37] as the Word justly says. And, therefore, the rulers and the priests and the leaders of the people will suffer a punishment worthy of the magnitude of the authority that had been entrusted to them.

[28:24-29] Then he introduces an illustration from nature. For, after all, there is "a time"[38] for farming the land and another time for plowing the land and another to sow seeds suitable for the soil that lies below. For he will plant *small dill* in one field and *cumin* in another, and *wheat* in one and *barley and various seeds*[39] in another, and *spelt* in yet another. Then, when the crops from all of these ripen in the harvest season, when he gathers each one individually and will *purify* as is appropriate to each one, then he will bring about the purification of all in this very place. He will neither use a *cart* nor those iron "wheels like saws"[40] which he has fashioned on the *cumin* and the *small dill*, the grain, *barley* and *spelt*. And, once again, he will not *purify* the grain by striking it with a *rod*. For the plants that have not produced will be *purified* like the *small dill* and the *cumin*, for he takes the *rod* on the weakest of seeds. When he strikes with a *rod, he will purify the cumin and the* [186] *small dill*. And he will run the iron *cart wheels* over the grain and the *barley* and the other plants growing nearby, and these *cart wheels* are sharp and will be able to easily cut out and to chop down what is useless except for the *fire*. And, therefore, in the same way, the farmer of souls and of the Word of God wills that the souls of people be renewed at the proper time through the spiritual teaching that plows up and opens up the words hidden in the depths, words that are attained by the plow of the word. For this reason, he commands:

"Renew for yourselves the newly plowed field, and do not sow among thorns."[41]

And when the *surface* of every evil soul that once produced thorns shall be *leveled* and taken away, then in a fashion corresponding to the variance of those who receive the seed, the seeds are scattered. On the one hand, there are certain small and seemingly insignificant seeds such as *dill and cumin*, and on the other hand there are more important and necessary seeds such as *wheat and barley, seeds and spelt*, which are sown because of their ability to reproduce generously and in various conditions. "For there are varieties of gifts, and there are varieties of working, and it is given to each one through the Spirit,"[42] and these gifts are furnished to these over here and other gifts to others over there. And when "the Lord of the harvest" shall arrive, "then the consummation of the harvest of the word shall take place,"[43] as the Savior taught. Then, fruit will be demanded in return, in accordance with the value of the seeds which each one received. And those who received a moderate amount of seed but failed to produce a corresponding crop will receive a trial of moderate correction and chastisement, for example, beating with a *rod*. But those who have been deemed worthy of more seeds and more perfect gifts, if they fail to return fruit worthy of the privilege that has been supplied to them, they will be delivered over to great hurricanes of chastisement.

And so it is with you who have been appointed rulers, leaders, teachers of the people and priests who occupy yourselves in such a glorious and honorable service of God. The Word says that you are a "crown of pride"[44] and the "hired workers of Ephraim," for you have dared to turn the people aside so that they "rejected"[45] "the honored and chosen cornerstone."[46] For this very reason, those among you who were given moderate abilities

---

[37]Wis 6:6. [38]Eccl 3:2. [39]The Greek word κέγκρος means "a small, seed-sized object." [40]Cf. Is 41:15. [41]Jer 4:3. [42]1 Cor 12:4, 6, 8. [43]Mt 13:30. [44]Cf. Is 28:1. [45]Ps 118:22. [46]Cf. Is 28:16.

will also be given a moderate judgment, but to those who have been granted greater and more extensive capabilities, more severe punishments will be applied. The text says according to Symmachus: *and God will discipline him with his judgment,* or, according to the Septuagint: *and he will be instructed by the judgment of God.* This verse teaches through an illustration from nature that just as a farmer applies fitting measures according to the principles of agriculture, so God does according to what he has supplied to every person. When it comes to the purification of seeds not all will be purified in the same way. Indeed, he will *purify* some through the *rod* but others through **[187]** harsh treatment, on whom the *wheel* of the *cart* will come. For these things did not come from human learning but from the instruction of God. The one who has been occupied in the field has been *instructed by God* and has been taught to receive this *judgment.*

According to Aquila, the text reads: *and the bread will be cut small* instead of *it will be eaten with bread.* For instead of *it will be eaten,* Aquila writes, *it will be cut small,* and Symmachus and Theodotion also write, *it will be cut small. But, not forever,* he says, *will he thresh him with a threshing instrument, neither will the wheel of his cart disturb him, nor will he winnow him with his hooves.* For he says that then the *wheel of the cart* will pass over the grain and that it will *winnow* the stubble all around, and the stubble will be *threshed* into fine chaff by the *wheels* and by the *hooves* of the oxen. But he will not ruin the grain, and by this he means that the essence of the soul will not be utterly destroyed, nor will it perish altogether in the chastisement which is borne on it. We understand this from when he said: *For I will not be angry with you forever, nor will the voice of my bitterness trample you.* He does not say that he will punish the ungodly so as to ruin their essence and to utterly destroy their souls, since

the image of the iron *wheels of the cart* which were prepared to ruin the grain was a negative example. Rather, he will clear away all the stubble in order to preserve the grain and to accomplish its purification.

And he says that all *these wonders* were for those who do not understand, and do not suppose that a man has said this. For the negative statement has been accomplished *by the Lord of hosts,* against which you ungodly *took counsel,* and it is to you whom these things are said. And if you should be such a one, then the *vain appeal* and consolation in which *you exalted* yourselves is addressed to you.

[29:1] The children of the Jews themselves acknowledge that what is deemed unhappy in the passage at hand, *Ariel,* is Jerusalem. And he says in particular that the altar that stood before the temple was called *Ariel.* This is clearly indicated in Ezekiel, where he says at the very end of the description of the city: "And these are the measurements of the altar by cubit of cubits (by cubits and a handbreadth); extent, depth, up to a cubit."[1] And then he adds: "And the Ariel[2] is four cubits, and from the Ariel and above the horns was a cubit. And the Ariel was twelve cubits in length by twelve cubits in breadth, square in its four parts."[3] The word *Ariel* means "lion of God," and this was because the altar was of God, and it devoured all the animal sacrifices that were offered on it. This is the reason why this name was given to it.

[188] And the phrase *the city, against which David waged war,* is not how the text reads in the Hebrew, but according to Aquila: *the village, the encampment of David,* and according to Symmachus: *the city, the encampment of David.* For it was Philistine before David subjected the Philistines and drove them away, and we are able to accommodate this meaning to the reading in the Septuagint. For one could

---

Chapter Twenty-Nine [1]Ezek 43:13. [2]The Hebrew word for altar is transliterated into the Greek of the LXX as Ἀριήλ. [3]Ezek 43:15-16.

thus say that it was *the city, against which David waged war* when it was occupied by the Philistines, and thus one could also say that it was *the city on account of which David waged war* or *on behalf of which David waged war*. Therefore, it follows that the present word is speaking about Jerusalem. For after the aforesaid things concerning the city's rulers, who were clearly identified as "the crown of pride,"[4] then the rest of the things that were about to be suffered because of their aforementioned transgressions were prophesied against the city. Thus the Word says to those who dwell in it that the time for them to *gather crops*[5] for themselves is now; by consent you were allowed one *year*, perhaps also a second year will be granted. For this is how long you will be deprived of spiritual food. Therefore, now is the time for you to make use of these years for the profit of your souls. And it seems to me that the time of the saving preaching is thereby foreshadowed, during which the Christ of God resided among them and announced "the acceptable year of the Lord and the day of retribution."[6] Perhaps also a second *year* is ordained for them, and accompanying that possibly even a third. Therefore, it was during this very time that he presented and showed them the doctrines of the kingdom of heaven. *Gather crops year by year, you will eat.* Now, the phrase *for you will eat with Moab* is altogether absent from the Hebrew text. Therefore, it is not found among the other Greek translations, and furthermore it would appear to be an aberration from the flow of the passage. In any case, however, he still says that the time is now: *Gather crops year by year, you will eat.*

[29:2] After these things happen, he will no longer permit you to *gather crops* so that you will be nourished in safety and peace. *For I will greatly distress Ariel*—clearly speaking of Jerusalem. But instead of *and its strength and wealth shall be mine*; Symmachus says: *And affliction and pain shall be mine, as for Ariel*; and Aquila says likewise: *And Ariel shall be pained and distressed*. For this very reason, a certain city of the Moabites was referred to as *Ariel* in the prophecy concerning Moab, concerning which it was said: "And I will remove the offspring of Moab and Ariel."[7] He says this aptly concerning Jerusalem, because such things will be mine in that *Ariel* of the Philistines.

[29:3-4] Then, he says next: *And like David I will surround you*. For just as David once surrounded the encampment at Jerusalem, when the city was occupied [189] by the Philistines, so also I the Lord now say that *I will surround you. And then, just like David, I will lay ramparts around you*.[8] For now, you who were the dwelling place of the Philistines have been filled with evil rulers and with "the crown of pride."[9] It was so filled following the daring deeds committed by those who live in Jerusalem against our Savior. And it has been recorded that, when broken in spirit,[10] the Savior himself said to Jerusalem: "If you, even you, had known what would bring you peace. For the days shall come on you when your enemies will cast up a bank about you and surround you,"[11] "and you shall be dashed to the ground."[12]

[29:5-6] Then, he continues: *But the wealth of the impious in it shall be like dust from a wheel and like flying chaff*. And all these things will be "in a moment of time,"[13] *and it shall be like an instant, suddenly, from the Lord of hosts*. For he says that *the visitation* that will be against them *with thunder and earthquake and a great voice, a rushing storm and a devouring flame of fire* will not come from people but from God himself. These things foreshadowed then that "the city would be burned with fire"[14] and the

---

[4]Cf. Is 28:1. [5]The Greek word γένημα could also mean "offspring." [6]Is 61:2. [7]Is 15:9. [8]Cf. 2 Sam 5:6-12. [9]Cf. Is 28:1. [10]The Greek word ἀποκλάω. [11]Lk 19:42-43. [12]Is 3:26. [13]Lk 4:5. [14]Cf. Is 1:7.

thunder and earthquake and *rushing storm* that God brought against it. These things are said concerning Jerusalem.

[29:7-8] The Word next prophesies in detail about those who would besiege Jerusalem: *And the wealth of those who marched against Mount Zion will be as one who dreams in sleep.* In this verse, the pleasure in this life of the luxuriousness of the Roman rulers is adumbrated. For these were they who brought the last siege on Jerusalem. It was necessary for us to learn something about them and to be taught what sort of end they will experience. Therefore, he says that their *wealth* and luxuriousness, which last only during this present life, are like those who dream in their *sleep* and think that they possess the very things they are dreaming about. For such is the appearance of present *wealth*. After the present *vain* existence, they will find that it was a *dream* and that the luxuriousness they thought they would enjoy will come to an end.

[29:9-12] Instead of *be faint and amazed* and the rest, Symmachus translates this passage thus: *Wonder greatly and marvel, be deluded and be drunk without wine, be disturbed apart from an intoxicating drink. For the Lord mixed a spirit of torpor against you and made your eyes dull and placed a covering over your prophets and rulers and those who see for you.* The Word finished the above discussed prophecy concerning "the crown of pride"[15] and concerning the siege of Jerusalem. And after presenting these things concerning those who are supposed to be of the people of the circumcision, he relates in detail and prophesies that they will indeed announce the prophetic Scriptures, but they will certainly not understand them. For **[190]** there is no advantage for those who authenticate a document with a seal if, as the Jewish people, they are unable to discern what is

inscribed therein. And so the prophetic words will be unknown to them, whether they should announce them from their mouths or whether they should be unacquainted with them. And, as he was about to prophesy these things, the Word cried out to them. And, if after all there will be release for you and he offers you what will be said along with astonishment of soul, it will be said for this reason: *Be faint and amazed.* But if you want it and if you otherwise *deceive* yourselves, and if he distorts the meaning of what has been said, in so being *deceived, you deceive yourselves*, and this one is no friend to you. But instead of *get a drunken headache*, all the other Greek translations say *be drunk without wine and be disturbed apart from strong drink.* For the drunkenness that comes from deceit is worse than that of *wine*, so that if you rejoice in *deceiving* yourselves and being *drunk* as some do against others, they see and misinterpret these divine oracles, as you should know. For *the Lord* himself *delivered* you *over to a spirit of deep sleep*, or, according to Symmachus, *of drowsiness.*

Then he adds: *He will close their eyes and those of their prophets and of their rulers.* For this very reason, when the Lord was incarnate and present with them, "they listened by listening but did not understand, and they looked on him with their eyes,"[16] as in a vision of the soul, but "they did not see, and *they closed their eyes* so that they would not see, and they stopped their ears so that they would not hear." Therefore, they first *closed their own eyes*, and because of this the *Lord* himself did these things to them and *to their prophets*—instead of to their teachers—and *to their rulers*, who promised to see *the hidden things* and to distinguish and to interpret the secret meaning that has been concealed exclusively in the sacred writings.

And so he will shut "their eyes so that they cannot see,"[17] since it was fitting that the

---

[15]Cf. Is 28:1. [16]Cf. Is 6:9; Mt 13:14. [17]Cf. Rom 11:8.

words not only from the other divine Scripture but also from the *book* of the prophecy of Isaiah at hand should be as a *sealed book*, for they were not permitted to know what was inscribed therein, even if they knew how to read or were altogether illiterate. For, indeed, even the one who knows how to read skillfully will not be able to discern what is in it because the *book was sealed*. But the one who is without experience in reading would not have been able to read it even if the *book* had not been *sealed*. And in such a way, the meaning of the prophetic text will not be understood by all people, but only by them about whom these things were prophesied.

But you paid attention, and therefore he says: *And these words will be to you.* For he says *to you*, indicating those who are present and who see and listen. For the word was directed toward the Jews, to whom he says the unknown meaning of the prophecy will be, and to whom it will be known because he will teach them in increasingly deeper lessons. He then says later about them: "On that day the deaf shall hear the *words of a scroll*, and the eyes of the blind will see, and they shall be glad."[18] **[191]** Therefore, the Word taught the law accurately through what was discussed above about the Jewish people and the remembrance by word of mouth, and he prophesies that those who lead the divine readings and such things will be in ignorance of the deeper meaning of the prophetic words.[19]

[29:13-14] And God says that these things will be on them, and he states the reason: because they pretend to *honor* God with their *mouth* and *lips*, but their intention was to circumvent the commandment. They pretended to *worship* him, but in fact they heeded certain "traditions *of men*"[20] rather than the *teaching* of his words, and they preserve these

traditions[21] "of the elders"[22] and hold them in utmost respect. Because of this he says that "the mind of the divine Scriptures"[23] certainly will be shut out from them. And he says that all their *people will be removed* from the place of honor in my presence, so that they will no longer be the "Lord's portion" or "Israel a measured part of his inheritance."[24] For this very reason, they were putting forward for themselves the wisdom of man and turning away from my wisdom and my word, and they were following certain other "traditions of the elders among them,"[25] holding to the wisdom of those considered *wise*. Because of this, they will not understand my Scriptures. And *I* myself *will destroy the wisdom of their wise, and I will bring the understanding of the understanding* among them *to nothing.*

[29:15] Then, for this very reason, they profess with their lips that they serve God, but in secret they perform base actions, being defiled with sorceries and uncleanness and a myriad of other unlawful deeds. Being occupied with all these things, they did not have God in view, and thus he justly deems them unhappy when he says next: *Ah, those who make plans deeply and not through the Lord,* although Symmachus translated this verse: *Ah, the depths that conceal the plan of the Lord, for their works were in darkness, and they said:* "*Who sees us, and who knows what we are doing here well out of the way?*"

[29:16] Then he adds: *Shall you not be regarded as the potter's clay?* For, as people, we are all as *potter's clay*, because our bodies are of clay. Does it not therefore logically follow that it is not possible to escape the notice of the maker? Is it possible for the one who has been made by him to do such works? And who is able or who will dare to say that God did not

---

[18]Is 29:18. [19]This sentence represents one possible reconstruction, as there are several lacunae in the text in the space of this sentence. [20]Mk 7:8. [21]δευτερώσεις. [22]Mk 7:3. [23]Lk 24:45. [24]Deut 32:9. [25]Mk 7:3.

create him? For if the *clay* that lies before the *potter* could never say these things concerning him, it is clear that all those who think out a *deep plan* within their soul and those who imagine that God does not know the *works* that they did *in darkness* are vain.

[29:17] But, as far as concerns these things, he says, *yet a little while and Lebanon* and another tribe from the Gentiles that is present in the land *shall be changed* into the land of the Jews, specifically Mount Karmelion,[26] or, as it is called in the Hebrew, *Carmel*.[27] [192] And there will indeed be a change for the better for *Lebanon*, and there will be a certain alteration of *Carmel* afterwards. For *shall* the fullness of our plants and good fruit *be regarded as a forest*? For this *Carmelos*, which is also called *Carmel*, is like a *forest* of unfruitful and uncultivated trees. And the *Lebanon* of the foreigners will be changed, as also the ancient *Carmel* was changed. And through these things the Word indeed speaks of *Lebanon* as the people of the Gentiles and *Carmel* as the Jewish nation, that certain *forest* of uncultivated and unfruitful trees which was once a forest like *Lebanon*. And the people of the Gentiles are now as the people of the Jews once were, filled with good trees and all kinds of plants and fruits.

[29:18-19] And then, when this change shall occur, *on that day*, clearly during the same time, those who were once *deaf shall hear the words of a scroll*, and what *scroll* would it be if not the very one at hand, concerning which it was said above: "And these words shall become for you like the *words* of this sealed *book*."[28] But on the one hand in *Carmel* which is being changed and on the other hand *in the thicket* "will be the *words* of the *book*" of the prophecy "which have been sealed." But again, for those who were considered as once *blind* and in the

thicket of Lebanon, the audible words of the divine Scriptures will be for those who were converted into cultivated and fruitful vines. And those who were formerly *in the darkness and in the fog*, so that they could neither see nor understand nor perceive because of the fact that their eyes were blind, after being deemed worthy to be spectators of an incredible conversion, they will also witness those mysteries that are stored up in the divine letters. Therefore it says: *The eyes of the blind shall see*, and those who used to be poor and lack every *good* thing *shall be glad*; for *they shall be full of joy* before the Lord, they for whom there was formerly no hope of salvation. For why should it be supposed that those who practiced the godless idolatries of their ancestors and those who were ungodly and estranged from the knowledge of God would come to such a hope? He therefore says: *And those despairing among people shall be filled with joy*.

[29:20-21] And all these shall enjoy the benefit of these things, since the one who formerly ruled over them and acted as their monarch was a *lawless* and ungodly governor. I am speaking about the devil, who was pursued for a long distance and *failed and perished*, who was *arrogant* and had formerly enslaved them. But those too who were under him were impious and unrighteous, and they were *utterly destroyed*, clearly evil demons, *those causing people to sin in word*. Therefore, it has been said somewhere: "They hated the one who *reproves in the gates* and have despised holy speech."[29] And it was they who *in vain turn away the just*. For, since [193] they have nothing onto which to deflect the blame, they shake off and *turn away* the *just word* and the *just* Christ of God, and they do this *in vain* and unjustly. For they *reproved* the prophets to their face, and they returned to their sinful actions. Those who pursue them laid a snare

---

[26]Καρμήλιον. [27]Χερμὲλ. [28]Is 29:11. [29]Amos 5:10.

or them, after taking counsel against them in order that they might destroy them.

It is the custom of Scripture to state things in the future tense rather than the past, as one finds in the sixty-sixth psalm,[30] for example: "a river they will pass through on foot,"[31] instead of "they passed through." And so too here, when the text says: *The lawless has failed* and continues on: *All those who reprove in the gates a cause of stumbling, they abandoned* the public places. But according to the conventions of the Scriptures, it states that it will come in a future time.

[29:22-24] The prophetic word even inveighs against them, and since you have been such a sort as these, he says: *Therefore this is what the Lord* of the universe *says to you. I am speaking about you who are called the house of Jacob,* who were not worthy of being called those loved by God and blessed. God himself *set them apart* and removed them, since in their works they proved themselves not to be worthy of Abraham. For "the children of Abraham" are recognized by their "works," as the Savior taught when he said: "If you were Abraham's children, you would do what Abraham did."[32] And according to Symmachus: *Thus says the Lord to the house of Jacob, the redeemer of Abraham,* but not the *redeemer* of these, against whom he inveighs. Therefore, he speaks thus to them. Indeed, it has been said concerning you that you will not understand "the words of this scroll."[33] And it has also been said concerning those who were once "blind" and concerning the unbelieving Gentiles that they will understand the words of the holy and inspired Scriptures. And they will see with the eyes of the soul the meaning of the divine words. And they will take up the knowledge of God, and those who were once lame will also share in the joy before him. But now indeed, when these things were being

prophesied you had no insight into the things being said. Therefore, *you are not ashamed now,* neither are you pretending that the things threatened against you will not happen, *nor* is he turning away the *face* of you who hear these things from the one who is present. And the time will come when *you will be ashamed* and you will turn away, and *you will turn* your *face* from this shameless and impudent opposition.

And when will this time be, or when will the fulfillment of my words come when your *children* will see those of another race and those who are of another people than yours glorifying *and sanctifying my name?* For then your *children* will be put to shame and will turn away, seeing the wonder of the conversion of the Gentiles, even as other tribes and certain people *will sanctify the holy One of Jacob and the God of Israel.* And they shall do this as those who wandered for a long time will take up again the fear of the God who is over all, and as they themselves who once were counted in error [194] will understand, and as those who murmur and speak out against providence *will learn to obey* and to keep my instructions. And the *faltering tongues,* which by nature could *speak* neither anything clearly nor truthfully, will come to speak the most clearly, *learning to speak words of peace,* since they have been set free from all wars and have made peace with God.

But instead of *Jacob shall not be ashamed now, nor shall he now change his face,* and the rest, Symmachus translates this passage as follows: *Jacob shall not be ashamed now, nor shall he now turn his face away, but when his children see the works of my hand in their midst, then they will sanctify my name and sanctify the Holy One of Jacob and the God of Israel, and those who wandered in spirit will prevail, and they will know and understand, and the grumblers will learn instruction.* Here the prophecy against "the crown of pride,"[34] which followed what was

---

[30]The text reads "sixty-fifth," for the modern arrangement of the psalms is not quite identical to the Septuagintal order. [31]Ps 66:6. [32]Jn 8:39 RSV. [33]Cf. Is 28:18. [34]Cf. Is 28:1.

threatened against "the dragon and the crooked serpent,"[35] comes to a conclusion. And one should read each of these as separate sections.

[30:1-5] After the Word brought an end to what was being threatened against "the crown of pride"[1] and all the rest of the things being threatened, he turns to address another theme. He prophesies about what the children of the Hebrews did during the time of the prophet Jeremiah, when the Babylonians captured Jerusalem and led away the people who remained in the land of Judea. This was the time of the prophet Jeremiah and Baruch and certain others, when the people were forced to flee because of the fear of the Babylonians, preferring to entrust themselves to the Egyptians rather than to serve the Babylonians. These things have been recorded in the prophecy of Jeremiah.[2] And the prophet Isaiah mentions events approximately fifty years before the time of Jeremiah. And therefore he writes concerning those very people who did not obey the voice of God through Jeremiah, forbidding them to go to the Egyptians and saying: *Oh rebellious* (or *transgressing*, according to Symmachus) *children, says the Lord; you made a plan not through me and agreements not through my Spirit, to add a sin to sins—those who walk to go down to Egypt but did not ask me, to be helped by Pharaoh*, and what was being said besides these things. And in these words he teaches that *there were leaders in Tanis, evil messengers*, clearly indicating that there were then demons among the Egyptians—calling them *evil messengers*—who were especially working many things in the city of Egypt called *Tanis*. And it was there that Pharaoh had his capital at that time. And all those who ruled the lands of the Egyptians were called [195] *Pharaoh* and had this title placed after their personal name. And a

certain one of them was called *Pharaoh Necho*.

And *Tanis* is mentioned in the psalm about the incredible wonders that were done through Moses, "in the land of Egypt, in Tanis's plain,"[3] as well as in the prophecy concerning Egypt, which this prophet himself teaches when he says: "Where now are your wise men? And let them also declare to you and say to you what the Lord of hosts has planned against Egypt. The rulers of Tanis have failed."[4] But here, indeed, he prophesied the coming of the Lord into Egypt, as is signified in "the failure[5] of the rulers of *Tanis*," and this was fulfilled at the time of our Savior's appearance among humanity. And through what was at hand during the time of Jeremiah, the Word did not say "the rulers have forsaken Tanis," but that there were then *leaders in Tanis, evil messengers*. It was they who said above that they were the "rulers of Tanis."[6] Nevertheless, he says these *leaders in Tanis, evil messengers, they will be of no profit at all*, and they will not come to the aid of those who flee to them for refuge or those who call to them for help. They will *profit* them nothing but rather will be a *shame* and a *reproach* for them. And these things were fulfilled in fact during the time when the king of the Babylonians conquered Egypt, and not only the Egyptians, but, in accordance with the principles of war, he also reduced to slavery the Jews who fled to them for refuge. For at that time the Jews' hope in Pharaoh turned into a *shame and a reproach* for them. One should know that the thirtieth volume of Origen's commentary on the prophet came up to this point.

[30:6-7] Next, he adds: *The vision of the quadrupeds in the wilderness. In affliction and distress, there are a lion and a lion's whelp, thence also asps and the offspring of flying asps.* And I suppose that through these things he is intimating a message about the gods of the

[35]Cf. Is 27:1. **Chapter Thirty** [1]Is 28:1. [2]Cf. Jer 50:7. [3]Ps 77:12. [4]Is 19:12-13. [5]This word (ἔκλειψις) could also be translated "defection" or "departure." [6]Cf. Is 19:13.

Egyptians. For it seems that every kind of *four-footed creature* is considered to be a god among them. But instead of *the vision of the quadrupeds in the wilderness*, Symmachus says *the burden of the beasts of the south*, and all the other Greek translations also render this phrase: *Beasts of the south*. Surely then the Septuagint is referring to the land of the Egyptians which lies in the southern regions when it says: *The vision of the quadrupeds in the wilderness*. For the whole *wilderness* was then God's and had been filled with *quadrupeds* which were deified among them and which the demons animated among them. It was for this reason that they were said to be in *affliction and in distress*. For due to much *distress* of soul and due to an excess of *affliction* they publicly proclaimed their gods among them. And it was precisely the evil demons who were afflicting and distressing their souls, among whom there were *lions*, *asps* and their *offspring*, snakes, and a myriad of other reptiles [196] as well as beasts. These were the perceived creatures that were the images of the evil demons that were being deified throughout the whole of Egypt. For truly they honored *lions* and *asps* and snakes and a myriad of other creatures as gods. And, therefore, they have named their cities after the animals they suppose to be gods. Thus, from the word for lion, they call the city "Leonto," and from the word for "dog," they call the city "Kuno,"[7] and they have named other cities after words for other animals too. Therefore, the prophet saw this *vision of the quadrupeds in the wilderness* of Egypt, and those of the Jews who fled for refuge carried off *their own wealth* to them. For they delivered the treasuries of their own soul over to the Egyptian error. And the text says that they carried away *their own wealth*, thereby clearly indicating their own irrationality and folly, on *donkeys and camels*. And they went *to a nation that shall not profit them*. For

neither the real *Egyptians* nor their supposed gods were about to *help* the Jewish people who fled to them for refuge.

[30:8-11] Those events that are announced next in the prophecy are absolutely clear, although I suppose one needs to interpret them in a broad context. The people had claimed that the prophet had lied when he warned them, using the authority of God, not to go down to Egypt. It is because of this that the present prophecy says: *Who were not willing to hear the law of God, saying to the prophets, "Do not declare to us," and to those who see visions, "Do not speak to us."* But according to Symmachus the text reads: *And saying to those who see, "Do not see for us correctly, tell us smooth things, see for us errors, stay far from the road, turn me away from the path, keep the Holy One of Israel from our face."* For this is what those who did not believe the voice of Isaiah said to him and to those who were like-minded with him.

[30:15-16] Therefore, after threatening them with what was said earlier, he then exhorts them saying: *When you turn back and groan, then you shall be saved.* And according to Symmachus, the text says: *You will be saved in repentance and repose, and your power will be in hope.* For, he says, if you fall down repentant in the place of Jerusalem and stop your attack against Egypt, *then you will be saved in tranquility* and experience *repose*. He also says that *your power will be in hope*, for in believing and hoping on God, you will be able *to be saved*. And he mentions those who *did not wish to hear* but said, "We will flee on horses." It is them whom he threatens with what is said in addition when he says that *you shall flee* indeed, but you will certainly not be able to escape the land of the Babylonians or the Egyptians, where you will soon find yourselves.

---

[7]The Greek word for dog is κύων.

[30:17] And he says that so many will flee, until they are left like a pole on a mountain and as a standard on a hill, or, according to Symmachus: as a pole on a high mountain and as an altar on a hill. For just as a ship which is falling apart and lost at sea raises a flag, and the pole on a high hill is put away **[197]** when there is no more need of it, so too the destruction of those who have been mentioned above will be like a flag.

[30:18] But he says that not quite all will be destroyed, but a certain few will *survive*, on whom *God will show mercy*. And he will be compassionate and keep them safe, and he will be glorified and *exalted when he shows mercy* to them. Therefore he is a righteous *judge*, for those who were indeed worthy of vengeance received it, and those who were deemed worthy of mercy received salvation in his presence. For this reason, *happy are all those who abide in him*, or, according to Symmachus, *who remain on him*. For it is good neither to abandon nor to give up on the help of God when misfortune overtakes you.

Following this then, after the Word announced what would happen during the time of Jeremiah the prophet in the oracles delivered above, he prophesies that the people would return from their captivity and that after going back, they would rebuild the temple in Jerusalem and again dwell in the city, and the entire country would be covered by Jews who would spend their time tilling the soil in the securest peace. And this was fulfilled in the days of Zerubbabel and Jeshua the son of Jozadak, when the temple worship was renewed through the ministry of Haggai and Zechariah. It was then that Ezra returned from Babylon and worked side by side with Nehemiah and achieved the restoration of the city, after which time the city remained impregnable and the temple remained safe

inside it for many years. Therefore, the Word predicts these things in the present oracle when it says: *And again God will wait to have compassion on you; therefore God will be exalted to show mercy to you*. And he goes on to say next: *Because the Lord God is a judge*. He is indeed a righteous *judge*, for he delivered those who in fact deserved it over to captivity, but because he is also righteous, he showed mercy to them and saved them. And, therefore, *the one who stays firm in him* is *happy*, or, according to Symmachus, *the one who abides in him*. And so, as a righteous and good *judge*, he will *again have compassion* on Zion, and Jerusalem will be inhabited a second time, and the people will once more dwell in it. And he calls God the glory of Israel, the Savior of the universe.

[30:19] And although it has been written *because a holy people shall dwell in Zion*, we should note that neither the Hebrew text nor the other Greek translations preserve the word *holy*. According to Symmachus, the text reads: *A people shall dwell in Zion*. For so it was that not all the *people* who inhabited Jerusalem after these things happened were *holy*. The Hebrew text in fact states: *She did not weep with weeping, "Have mercy on me."* For this reason, according to Symmachus, the text reads: *In Jerusalem you will not weep with weeping*, and likewise according to Theodotion: *In Jerusalem you will not be wept for* **[198]** *with weeping*. For those who, by the mercy of God, once again reached their fatherland and for those who rejoice and are glad, the time of weeping was no more, as the text says: "Coming they shall come with rejoicing, carrying their sheaves."[8] But this was only because they received the mercy of God. But instead of *the voice of your cry; when he saw, he listened to you*, Symmachus says: *To the voice of your shout, whenever it might be heard, he will hear you*. And this is similar to the verse: "According to your faith be

---

[8]Ps 126:6.

it done to you,"[9] as the Savior used to say. For he indeed says now *she did not weep*, but he is speaking of another time. But the Word always encourages her to shout out to God. For, he says, God will answer *your voice*. But according to the Septuagint, the text reads: *And Jerusalem wept with weeping, "Have mercy on me."* For when the land resounded loudly to God with the evil of its inhabitants, the powerful were broken off on behalf of the powerless and the better on behalf of the worse. Therefore, the text continues on to say: *The voice of your cry; when he saw, he listened to you.*

[30:20-24] And at the present moment in the passage, he then says: *The Lord will give you bread of affliction and scant water.* And after these things he next adds: *The bread of the produce of your land will be plenteous and fruitful*, and: *Then there will be rain for the seed of your land.* And he teaches through these things that at the beginning of the return to the land of Israel, the people experienced much *affliction.* Those who returned from the land of Babylon and from the surrounding areas were afflicted, and it was difficult for them to keep ritual worship at the holy site of the temple. This story is recorded in the book of Ezra. Therefore, the text says that *the Lord will give you bread of affliction and scant water; and those who lead you astray will not come near you anymore, because your eyes shall see those who lead you astray. Therefore they will no longer deceive you.* For even though there might be some who would attempt to deceive you, *your eyes shall see* them. And after seeing and observing them, *you shall not be deceived.* And again, although others might attempt to speak to you with deceptive and distorted words, *your ears shall not receive their words.* And if those deceivers might say: *"This is the way, let us walk in it, whether to the right or to the left,"* you will still not believe them, even if they say these things to them. But "you will travel by the royal road," walking in the middle and "neither turning aside to the right nor to the left."[10]

For this very reason, since you will no longer be deceived, *you will pollute the idols*, that is, you will drive out the polluted and unclean idols just as one who was apart would dispose of stinking dung and worthless filth. And when you might do these things, then *bread of affliction and scant water the Lord will give you. Then there will be rain for the seed* [199] *of your land, and the bread of your produce will be rich and abundant.* And all these things will be fulfilled among you, as you live to the end of your days in great prosperity and the securest peace, so that your animals and those farming the land will be provided with food from the surrounding environment.[11] These things were fulfilled in a subsequent period after Jerusalem had been restored, when those who were living in the fields in the country as well as those who busied themselves in the cities enjoyed rest and peace.

[30:25-26] Therefore, these events may refer to the times indicated above, and the text says next: *And on every lofty mountain and every high hill there will be running water*, and even the one who does not want to do so is pressed to strive after ethical conduct.[12] The sense of this passage is elucidated next: *On that day when many perish and when towers fall, the light of the moon will be like the light of the sun, and the light of the sun will be sevenfold, as the light of seven days, on the day when the Lord heals the destruction of his people, and he will heal the pain of your wound.* For he might save these things that he had previously mentioned and then indicates what follows from them. And, therefore, the text says that it might be necessary to consider the things that then followed what had been predicted, for after-

---

[9]Mt 9:29. [10]Num 20:17. [11]There is perhaps an echo of the tradition delivered by Papias (Irenaeus, *Adv. haer.*, 5.33.3) concerning the abundance that will characterize the millennium. [12]The Greek word here is τροπολογία.

wards the Word made bodily promises and said: *And the bread of your produce will be abundant and rich. And on that day your cattle will graze in a fertile and spacious place. Your bulls and oxen that work the land will eat chaff prepared with winnowed barley.* It is right that he should introduce divine promises to those of them who are bodily and worthy.

And he indicates what these are: *On every lofty mountain and every high hill there will be running water.* And he informs the reader when that time will be when he says in addition: *On that day when many perish and when towers fall,* or, according to Symmachus: *In a day of much slaughter when the great ones fall.* And when will this *day of much slaughter* take place, and when will *the great ones fall,* or when will the time of the universal judgment happen, after which will occur "the close of this age"?[13] Therefore, the text reads according to the Septuagint: *When towers fall and when many perish.* For *many will perish* during that time when what has been threatened will be rendered to the deserving. And what he teaches when he says that there will be *running water on every lofty mountain* and that the moonlight will be multiplied for them and that the sunlight likewise will be *sevenfold,* is that there will be much powerful light and *channels of water.* [200] Symmachus translates the passage: *And on every high hill there will be aqueducts of water.* And during that time, what has been promised will be rendered to the deserving. Those who are worthy of *slaughter* will be delivered over to *slaughter,* and those who were exalted and vainglorious in this present life *will fall* from their heights. For this reason, according to Aquila, the text reads: *In a day of much death, when those who possessed great power will fall.*

You see the outcome of the bodily promises that the Word has made to the bodily-minded among the multitude, but to those who rise above, the higher promises of him who has promised have been distributed in the mind and in the soul. And as you have often thought about "the heavenly Mount Zion,"[14] so also you should know that "the many rooms at my Father's place"[15] contain heavenly mountains, and those worthy of the kingdom of God will inhabit them. And, in any case, whether they are mountains or rooms, he says that there will be *running water* everywhere shooting forth from the "fountain," concerning which it has been said: "Because with you is life's fountain."[16] From this fountain, "the river of God" pours forth, concerning which it has been said: "The river's strong currents make glad the city of God,"[17] and: "The river of God was filled with water"[18] from the only-begotten Word of God, the giver of life, the Savior. Therefore, *on every lofty mountain and every high hill,* there will be the *running water* of immortality and eternal life, from which those who drink will be made immortal. When "the creation itself is set free from its bondage to decay,"[19] then it will receive repayment for all its sufferings. For this reason, too, the *moon* and the *sun* will enjoy a greater glory than they do at present as they perform the will of God. And he says that these things will occur *when the Lord heals the destruction of his people, and he heals the pain of your wound.*

Then he mentions neither Israel nor Jacob or even the Jews; instead he speaks of his people, as all those worthy to be called the people of God as the promise unfolded. And so, I suppose that the holy apostle Paul[20] was led to say: "For the creation waits with eager longing for the revealing of the sons of God,"[21] "because the creation itself will be set free from its bondage to decay and obtain the glorious liberty of the children of God."[22] You see, "the liberty of the children of God"

---

[13]Mt 13:39. [14]Heb 12:22. [15]Jn 14:2. [16]Ps 36:9. [17]Ps 46:4. [18]Ps 65:9. [19]Rom 8:21. [20]When the early church fathers spoke of the "apostle," they invariably meant Paul. [21]Rom 8:19 rsv. [22]Rom 8:21 rsv.

mentioned by the apostle Paul was the same thing that the prophet called the *healing of his people*. Therefore, "the creation will be set free"[23] along with his people at the same time, *in this day*, that is, at the time *when the Lord heals the destruction of his people*. Then the *sun* and the *moon* will be stronger than they are now, for their *light* will be magnified, and they will share in a superior glory. Therefore, it has been said: "Because the creation itself will be set free [201] from its bondage to decay and obtain the glorious liberty of the children of God."[24] And so "the children of God" and his people had much *ruin* and *pain* when they were living out their mortal lives. For they were in pain and suffering ruin, as has been said: "A broken and humbled heart God will not despise" and "sacrifice to God is a broken spirit."[25] It was they who were broken during their stay on the earth who mourned for those doing the things worthy of mourning, as the apostle Paul teaches when he says: "While we are still in this tent, we sigh with anxiety,"[26] "and I may have to mourn over many of those who sinned before and have not repented."[27] *God will heal the destruction and pain of these ones*, reassuring them that the promises will surely be fulfilled. The Savior also made this clear when he said: "Blessed are those who weep"[28] and "blessed are those who mourn, for they shall be comforted."[29]

[30:27] The Word warned those who fled for refuge to Egypt against the ordinance of God during the times of Jeremiah the prophet and informed them of what would befall them in Egypt. He next foretold in the prophecy to them that it was not necessary for them to give up hope on the rising again of Jerusalem. For those who fell away from it will come back again from the land of the enemy and will inhabit it again, and they will farm the entire land of Judea in peace and without fear. Then, after the promises that have been spoken in a bodily fashion, he adds on a discussion of the heavenly promises that will be repaid to the worthy after the consummation of the world, when the ungodly will be delivered over to destruction and calamity. After the Word prophesied these things, he adds on a discussion pertaining to the above-mentioned universal judgment of God. For this reason he says: *See, the name of the Lord comes after a long time*. Instead of *after a long time*, the other Greek translations said *from far away*. One should note that he does not say that the Lord himself will come, but *the name of the Lord*, thereby alluding to the Christ of God, concerning whom it has been said: "Blessed is the one who *comes in the name of the Lord*. The Lord is God, and he showed us light."[30] And the vengeful powers will follow closely after he comes and makes his glorious, second appearance, through which retribution will be brought to the ungodly and which the present Scripture passage calls *anger* and *wrath*. But instead of *his wrath is burning with glory* and the rest, Symmachus translates this as follows: *His wrath is inflamed and weighty and bears down his lips like a torrent, overflowing all in its path and coming up to the neck, sentencing the nations with a sentence of vanity*. But according to the Septuagint, the *burning wrath* or the opposing power will follow in the *glory* of the Lord. But it will do nothing without the order of the judge. Therefore it has been said: *The accomplishment of his lips, the accomplishment of his full* [202] *anger*. Following the delivery of the *oracle*, the *anger* will be brought on those who are to be punished.

[30:28] And when he sends *his breath*[31] on the ungodly, *it will come sweeping down* just as *water in a ravine* that *comes up to the neck* and

---

[23]Rom 8:21. [24]Rom 8:21 RSV. [25]Ps 51:17. [26]2 Cor 5:4 RSV. [27]2 Cor 12:21 RSV. [28]Lk 6:21. [29]Mt 5:4 RSV. [30]Ps 118:26-27. [31]The Greek word could be translated "breath" or "spirit."

sweeps away those who stand under vengeance. The text says that this corrective breath *will be divided* into many divisions, and the greatest distinction is for those who are to be chastised. Therefore, *he will confuse nations*, in as much as *they wandered vainly* and so *he pursued them* in the *error* of their former life.

[30:29] After saying these things, the Word next inveighs against those who pretended to reverence God but who consumed their lives in luxuries and comfortable living when he says: *Must you continually rejoice and continually enter my holy places as if you were keeping a feast? And as if you were rejoicing must you come in with a flute to the Lord's mountain, to the God of Israel?*

[30:30-31] After saying these things to those who pretended with hypocrisy to reverence God, he next adds: *And the Lord will make his voice to be heard, and he will show the wrath of his arm with wrath and anger and a flame of fire.* And he continues on: *The Assyrians will be defeated through the voice of the Lord, through the stroke with which he will smite them.* And the *Assyrians* by no means refers exclusively to the nation but would include all those who like the Assyrians ruled as tyrants and arrogantly proclaimed their conquests against people. And, anyway, even the children of the Hebrews transmitted the tradition that the statements about the *Assyrians* are to be interpreted as about those who flourish and enjoy prosperity, whom the present word teaches will be punished during the time of the judgment by the *stroke* that will be brought on them.

[30:32] Then the avenging demons who struck and smote them *from all sides* will surround them with toil and bring on punishments. Who they are he makes clear when he says: *From where the hope of help which he trusted came to them; they will wage war against him with drums and lyres.* And the hope of *help* for the ungodly was from their opposing gods, clearly then from powers and evil spirits. For they were attending to these as though they were gods, and they were hoping that *the hope of help* for them would be from them, not knowing that these themselves would be the ones who would be punishing them. "For the *anger* and wrath" which was sent "through wicked angels" will come against the ungodly, who also *will wage war against them with drums and lyres*, seeing that [203] they are those who rejoice in evil. And so it was said earlier on: "Mighty ones come to fulfill my wrath, at the same time rejoicing and reviling."[32] Therefore, those who were predicted to come *in turn will wage war* against the ungodly. Instead of friends, they will prove themselves to be enemies.

[30:33] And then even *they will be deceived*, since they will have to pay for all the sins that they committed. And he says these things because you are waiting for your former voluptuousness and arrogance. Therefore, you should realize that you have been *deceived*, because *it was made ready for you to reign*, as it is for all those who travel along the "narrow and hard" way[33] and for those who are "poor"[34] because of God and "persecuted for righteousness' sake."[35] For all those "the kingdom has been prepared,"[36] but not for you who walk along the "wide and easy way"[37] Therefore, the aforementioned *deep trench* of "sweeping waters"[38] has been prepared for you, full of *wood* and *aflame with fire*, so that every *valley* has been filled with nothing other than *wrath*, anger, *brimstone and flaming fire* for the punishment of those who will then be condemned. After finishing speaking about these things, he resumes the prophecy about those who fled to Egypt for refuge. And he goes on to speak of the following events.

---

[32]Is 13:3. [33]Mt 7:14. [34]Mt 5:3. [35]Mt 5:10. [36]Mt 25:34. [37]Mt 7:13. [38]Is 30:28.

31:1-3] In the prophecy concerning those who fled to Egypt for refuge, the Word vividly calls to mind the universal judgment of God and resumes speaking about the above-discussed threat. He deems miserable those who went down to Egypt in an attempt to secure aid. Because they thought that God would not be able to save them, although he had ordered them to remain in their place and to be rescued from the hand of the enemies, they sought their salvation from idolaters. It was they who are recorded as boasting before the God of Israel, they who placed their *trust in the Egyptians* and *chariots* and *horses*, failing to remember that their God at one time "threw the *chariots* of Pharaoh and his host into the sea."[1] Therefore, the Word censures them for acting as they did, because they did not place their *trust in the Holy One of Israel.* Thus, he threatens that the *evils* that they did not expect will overtake them in Egypt itself. Therefore, the text reads according to Symmachus: *The Egyptians are men and not God, and their horses are flesh and not spirit. And the Lord will stretch out his hand, and their aid will be weakened, and him who is aided will fall, and they will all be brought to an end together.* Indeed, the Word says *aid* in speaking of the Egyptians and *him who is aided* in speaking of them who flee to them for refuge.

Through the whole history which has been discussed above, the Word teaches that in times of persecutions, when it may happen that God judges his people or even delivers over his church to those who harass the service of God, it is necessary not to withdraw from the inspired faith, **[204]** or to abandon trust in God, or to give up hope of reconciliation with God or even to desert the Egyptian way of life but simply to desert the life of idolatry. For many in such times fall away from the word of true religion and attach their hopes onto the aid of idolaters.

[31:4-6] But, after what was said above, he then joins in a discussion of the return of those who will come back from the captivity whom God will then protect. And he says that just as a *lion,* the king of beasts and the strongest of all animals, rouses himself over his *prey* of food and, when charging at a shepherd of sheep does not turn around despite the *shouts of the shepherds* and the *multitude* of the herdsmen, thus the Lord himself will assault the enemies. And he will rescue his own people from them and reestablish them in their own place in Jerusalem. *So the Lord will shield* them, just as is commonly seen in the nature of birds when the mother of the chicks flies around the nest and fights on behalf of the chicks, *so also he will shield Jerusalem.* After God promised that he would *shield Jerusalem,* he next addresses those who entered into Egypt when he says: *Turn, you who plan a deep and lawless plan.* For it is still possible even now for them to repent and return to their land and for them to experience such blessings as God promised for their land.

[31:7] Then he promises that during that time when the people will return, there will no longer be any idolatry among them. Therefore, he says: *Because on that day people shall set aside their handiworks.* And history confirms this. After the people returned from Babylon and erected the second temple, there were no longer any idols to be found in Jerusalem.

[31:8] Then, inasmuch as they feared Assyria and abandoned their residences in Judea and fled for refuge to Egypt, he assures them of the fall of Assyria when he says: *Then Assyria shall fall; not a man's dagger.* He thus indicates the destruction of the kingdom of the Assyrians and their fall, so that the reputation of their kingdom, which was once very high, was brought down low. And he says that this will

---

Chapter Thirty-One   [1]Ex 15:4.

happen to them not due to any human attack but from the wrath of God himself against them. Although it seemed that it was human beings who engineered their destruction, it was in fact God himself who was the one who destroyed them through human beings. Therefore, it was said above in the prophecy concerning Babylon: "See, I am stirring up the Medes against you."[2]

[31:9] But instead of *for they shall be encompassed by a rock, as with a rampart, and they shall be defeated, and the one who flees will be caught. This is what the Lord says,* Symmachus renders the text thus: *This fearful rock* (and clearly he is speaking of the Assyrians) [205] *will pass away, and its rulers will be defeated, says the Lord.* He calls the Assyrians a *rock,* because their kingdom was once solid and firm and strong, although the Word also says that its destruction *will happen,* referring to the end of the dominion of the Assyrians. Then he says: *"Happy is the one who has a seed in Zion and kinsmen in Jerusalem."* And through this he urges those who were rushing to Egypt not to depart from the place where the temple of God was. But he also says that those who have *a seed in Zion and kinsmen in Jerusalem* will be happy because of the fact that the place would soon be renewed and receive again a glory that would be superior even to what it once possessed. Therefore, it was said elsewhere: "The last splendor of this house shall be great beyond the first."[3] And we are obliged to point out that none of the other Greek translations has the word *happy.* But instead of *who has a seed in Zion and kinsmen in Jerusalem,* Symmachus says: *The Lord has a fire in Zion and a furnace in Jerusalem,* and Aquila and Theodotion say: *There is a light for him in Zion and a furnace for him in Jerusalem.* And thus, the Word teaches that God, the Lord of the universe who threatened the above said things

against the Assyrians, *has a fire in Zion and a furnace in Jerusalem,* in order that when he wishes he may cast those who deserve to be burned up into this *fire* and into the blazing and roasting *furnace.* Therefore, it is not proper to look down on the city of God.

And these things also have been said about the church, inasmuch as it is the "glorified city of God," concerning which it has been said: "Glorious things were spoken of you, O city of God,"[4] and: "The river's strong currents make glad the city of God."[5] But there is also a *fire* and *furnace* in the city of God to burn up and consume the "wood and hay and straw"[6] in each soul. And perhaps it would be most adequately rendered: *A light for him in Zion and a furnace for him in Jerusalem,* for on the one hand we will choose to say that the *light* speaks of the light around which the worthy have been gathered, and on the other hand the *furnace in Jerusalem* speaks of the burning and destruction for those who deserve such.

[32:1-4] The rendering of the Septuagint joins these things to the verse discussed above. For this rendering predicts: *Then says the Lord: "Happy is the one who has a seed in Zion and a kinsmen in Jerusalem,"* and then says immediately following: *For see, a just king will reign, and rulers will rule with judgment.* For, since these things were about to happen in Jerusalem, he rightly deemed blessed those who were about to enjoy the benefit of these things there. But in the other Greek translations, the phrase *the Lord says* is joined to the above verse and the things then discussed form a new section. Therefore, according to Symmachus, the text reads: *See, the king will reign in righteousness,* [206] and according to Aquila: *See, the king will reign for the righteous one,* and the same according to Theodotion. Indeed, this refers to how Zerubbabel, who was from the tribe of Judah and from the lineage of

---

[2]Is 13:17. [3]Hag 2:9. [4]Ps 87:3, [5]Ps 46:4. [6]1 Cor 3:12.

David, led the children of the Jews in the return from Babylon, when they came back from their captivity during the times of Cyrus, the king of Persia. The fact that *rulers will rule with judgment* is in the plural may indicate that Jeshua was with Zerubbabel, who was of course the son of Jozadak the great priest, and there were also many others of whom we know because they are mentioned by them.

And I do not expect that they will be able to save themselves from the things that come on them next; I am speaking about the verse *and he will appear in Zion like a rushing river, glorious in a thirsty land*, and the things that follow this verse, certain of which did not find their fulfillment during the times of Zerubbabel. For this reason, as if the prophecy had been fulfilled in the events that transpired in Egypt during the times of Jeremiah, the Word starts a new theme and prophesies concerning the appearance of the Christ of God. For he alone among men appeared as the *righteous king*. And his apostles led with the *judgment* of him who was their own king as well as the king of the church. After commenting on Jeremiah's prophecy concerning those who went down to Egypt and after prophesying the return from Babylon to Jerusalem and the resettling of the people that would soon be in the land of Judea, immediately following he next delivers an oracle about Christ, saying that he would be the prophesied one who would bring about good for all people.

And, since he had prophesied the descent into Egypt many years before it happened, during the times of Jeremiah the prophet, and the return after the captivity, it was therefore nothing extraordinary for him to prophesy events that would happen even further on in the future at the coming of Christ, who is called a *righteous king, ruling in righteousness*, according to the other Greek translations. For inasmuch as the "righteousness of God has

been revealed" through his gospel not only "to the Jews" but also "to the Greeks,"[1] and the knowledge of God has been preached to people throughout the whole world, the Christ of God therefore *reigned in righteousness* over this new kingdom. For it was neither in looking for human esteem nor for honor and glory from among people that he ruled the kingdom but *in righteousness*. Therefore, his *rulers* also did not exercise their authority in order to be promoted to worldly honors but *ruled for judgment*. Therefore, according to the other Greek translations, the text reads: *And the rulers will rule for judgment*.

But instead of *the man will be hiding his words*, Symmachus says: *And there will be a man as a hiding place from the wind and* [207] *a shelter from the storm*. Therefore, what sort of man will he be if not the one who is called *righteous* above? For he is this man, who is not a man by nature but by nature superior to a man. But *there will be a man concealing* his divinity. Therefore, indeed according to Symmachus, the text reads: *As a hiding place from the wind and a shelter from the storm*, and according to Aquila: *As hiding from the wind and a hiding place from turbulence*. You see that the Word presents the hidden reality of his humanity, since, according to the Septuagint, he delivered "all that he said in parables."[2] Because of this it has been said: *He will be hiding his words and will be hidden as from rushing water*. For *rushing water* destroyed many of the people of the Jews. For this reason, on the one hand, *he hid* him from them and concealed *his words* from them, but on the other hand, he manifested them to his disciples. Therefore, he says that he will be manifest in his church when he continues on and says next: *And he will appear in Zion like a river*. And who *will appear* if not the *righteous king* himself? For he *will appear like a rushing, glorious river*. And what is this Zion if not the

Chapter Thirty-Two [1]Rom 1:16. [2]Mt 13:34.

place that receives those who had been *hidden* and are now again manifest? The text informs us about this great *river* when it says: *Like a rushing river, glorious in a thirsty land.* For this Zion that formerly was a desert and a *thirsty land* is the church of the Gentiles, concerning whom he says that *they will no longer trust in people.* But instead of this, Symmachus translated this verse: *And they will not be dimmed* (clearly referring to *the eyes of those who see*), so that they will see and be aware of the *river* that is evident to them in the church of God, clearly the only-begotten Word of God, concerning whom it has been said: "The river of God was filled with water,"[3] and: "The river's strong currents make glad the city of God."[4] And for this reason, the Savior himself taught: "But whoever drinks of the water that I shall give him,"[5] "out of his heart shall flow rivers of living water."[6]

He adds these things next: *But they will lend their ears to hear. The heart of the weak will apply itself to hear.* But instead of this, Symmachus says: *But the heart of the senseless will understand and know.* You see how he announces the understanding of the righteous king, who hid it from others, to those who used to be senseless. And he says that the stammering tongues will soon learn to speak peace, but according to Symmachus: *The tongue of the lisping will hasten to speak distinctly.* Accordingly, Zion and the thirsty land which was once a desert could be the church, as well as the heart of the weak and the lisping tongues, for the Gentiles formerly did not know God, and neither did they correctly speak of him. He promises them a change for the better.

[32:5-6] [208] To these things he adds: *And they will no longer tell the fool to rule.* Therefore, this is what they were formerly doing, when they were truly entrusting their own

souls to fools as their teachers, and they were the "wise men of this age, whose wisdom God made foolish."[7] Although they once foolishly entrusted their rule to this godless and polytheistic teacher, now the Word says *they will no longer tell the fool to rule.* But instead of *and no longer will your servants say, "Be quiet,"* Symmachus says: *Neither will the crafty be called savior.* For where the former rulers were *fools,* they never relied on those who wished to learn something and to inquire after the truth. Therefore, according to the Septuagint, the text reads: *And no longer will your servants say, "Be quiet," for the fool will speak folly.* And such a one as this was truly everyone who proclaimed "the wisdom of this age."[8] *And also his heart considered vain things in order to accomplish lawless things and to speak error against the Lord, in order to turn away hungry souls,* or according to the other Greek translations: *In order to strike* or *strike down hungry souls and to make empty the souls that thirst.*

[32:7-8] For those who were once the foolish rulers of humanity used to do all these things, and their *evil counsel which they planned was lawless, to ruin hungry souls* with their *words,* or according to Symmachus: *To ruin the meek with their lying speech and to scatter abroad the words of the humble.* For even if some humble person of modest means put forward a correct word of truth, this they did away with and scattered it abroad. And he says that the former things that used to be will no longer be in the new Zion. *For they will not tell the fool to rule, neither will the deceitful be called savior,* but he says that *the godly will plan intelligent things, and this counsel will remain.* And in Symmachus's version, after the narrative against the *ruling fools,* he continues on to say: *And the rulers will make imperial plans and the leaders will rise up.* And by this he means the apostles of our Savior, to whom the *righteous king* gave the rule of his church and

---

[3]Ps 64:10. [4]Ps 46:4. [5]Jn 4:14 RSV. [6]Jn 7:38 RSV. [7]1 Cor 1:20. [8]1 Cor 2:6.

adership over it. Therefore, it has been said from his lips: "But it is you, my leader and my familiar friend."9

One must take note that nowhere in these promises is it said that these leaders are from Israel, neither from the frequently mentioned Judah nor from Jacob, since the prophecy concerns Christ and those people who converted from error to his church. Therefore, it is right that at the beginning of the passage, as we read in the Septuagint, the Word should pronounce blessed "those who have seed in Zion and kinsmen in Jerusalem."10 And it is clear that this will occur in the new Zion and in the new Jerusalem of Christ, where the seed of those blessed men of old bloomed and bore fruit so that [209] the whole world has been filled with their blessing. Therefore, God's blessed prophets of old prophesied concerning them when they said: "If the Lord of hosts had not left us offspring, we would have become like Sodom and been made similar to Gomorah."11 But those who said these things have not become barren and sterile and childless like Sodom and Gomorrah." Therefore, those who procure for themselves such "seed" and such "kinsmen" as these are blessed in the church of God. Therefore it has been said: "Happy is the one who has seed in Zion and kinsmen in Jerusalem."12 And in many places in the prophecy discussed above you will find as you go along that the church of the Gentiles is often referred to in this way.

[32:9] The Word prophesied about the appearance of Christ and of his apostles and his dominion with right "judgment" when it said: "See, a just king will reign, and rulers will rule with judgment."13 Then, after continuing on to discuss the conversion of the Gentiles to God, he addresses the people of the circumcision and exhorts those who are broken off and cut off to lament as those who "who have fallen

away from the grace of God"14 because of their faithlessness toward God. And moving on, he says that their souls are unmanly and effeminate and calls them *women*. And it is clear that he is speaking about their synagogues in the prophecy. *Rise up, you wealthy women*, or according to the other Greek translations: *You flourishing women*. For there was a time when they were truly "rich according to God"15 and *flourishing*. If therefore he says that they are *rich* and *flourishing*, it is because it seems as though they are abounding and faring sumptuously in bodily riches. Therefore, the Word recommends to them that they not attend to the things that have been said in a sluggish or shoddy way but in an alert and orderly fashion. Therefore, he says: *Rise up and hear my voice*. But it is not as though he commands those who have fallen to stand up, is it? But instead of *daughters in hope*, the other Greek translations all say unanimously: *Obedient daughters*. For then they still assumed that they would always be *wealthy* and *flourishing*, and they were proud and *trusted* in their wealth. And one could say that the first *women* stand for the assemblies of the Jews in former days and the multitudes who were gathered in them, and then one would assume that the *daughters* would be their synagogues in the latter days.

[32:10] And then the Word enjoins that the people earnestly and attentively *listen* to both the commands that were delivered. Through this he teaches them to *mention* the days of a certain *year* and to do this with *pain* and in *hope* that it will continue well for them. In saying a *year*, the prophetic word teaches the time of the preaching of the gospel, during which our Savior and Lord lived among humankind and preached. And this is clear from what [210] is said next from the mouth of Christ: "The Spirit of the Lord is on me, because he has anointed me; he has sent me to

---

Ps 55:13. 10Is 31:9. 11Is 1:9. 12Is 31:9. 13Is 32:1. 14Gal 5:4. 15Lk 12:21.

bring good news to the poor, to proclaim release to the captives and recovery of sight to the blind, to summon the acceptable year of the Lord."[16] Therefore then, in *mentioning a year*, he intends to do the things *with pain* that have been declared, and the things having been kept silent by those who have had courage, but also *with* good *hope* to do this because of the *hope* that has been promised to those who regret what they have done. When therefore "the vineyard of the Lord was the house of Israel and the man of Judah was a beloved young plant,"[17] there was indeed a plentiful harvest among them. I am speaking about when the temple and the altar were established and when they offered presents and sacrifices according to the law, gathered from the entire nation just as from a vineyard. But now he says: *The vintage has been consumed and has ceased.* And even if at another time this *vintage* ceased during the captivity in Babylon, even then it was once again revisited and renewed in its place, but now indeed, as we learn, *it will no longer come.* The phrase reads, *it has been consumed and has ceased*, but according to Symmachus: *The vintage has been finished, it was announced that it will not come.*

[32:11-14] Therefore, he continues on and says what it is necessary for you to do in response to the things that have been predicted: *Be amazed; be grieved, you confident women.* He says that you should let "godly grief"[18] grip you and *be amazed* at your former disbelief, giving yourselves up "to repentance." "For godly grief produces a repentance that leads to salvation and brings no regret."[19] Therefore, demonstrate "fruits of repentance"[20] in your works, stripping away the covering of riches. Strip yourselves bare of luxury and prosperity and, in a masculine fashion, *gird up your loins and beat your breasts*, realizing that what was once your "desired vineyard"[21] has become a desert.

And what the *field* and the fruitful *grapevine* suffered he continues on to say next: *As for the land of my people, thorns and grass will come up.* He made this point earlier when he said: "And I waited for it to produce a cluster of grapes, but it produced thorns."[22] And he interprets these things when he goes on to say: "I waited for him to produce justice, but he produced lawlessness—nor did he produce righteousness, but a cry!"[23] For this very reason, he prescribed that they *beat their breasts* for these things, and especially because of the threat that was laid on them when it was said: *And the joy will be removed from every house.* And he says that although this *city* was once *wealthy*, its *houses will be forsaken* and deserted at the time when the *wealth of the city* and the revered and *desirable things* of the holy *house will be forsaken* by God. And he says that the one who once pranced about arrogantly and styled itself the city of God will become the dwelling of *wild donkeys and a feeding place of shepherds*, or, according to Aquila: *A feeding place of herds.* And who, after seeing the idolaters who settled in Jerusalem from all different nations, would not be entirely justified in saying that *wild donkeys* or *herds* will feed in it? For this reason, the text says: *The joy of wild donkeys, a feeding place of shepherds.*

[32:15] [211] For this very reason, because of these things, the Word ordered you to make a loud wailing and to continue with the lamentation *until* such a time as *a spirit from on high comes on you*, or, according to Symmachus: *A release from on high.* For although there are different kinds of spirits, nothing will be able to restore you and bring an end to the lamentation and the wailing until the *Spirit* that will be sent down *from on high comes on you.* And it was concerning this Spirit that the Savior said: "Behold, I am going away, but I will send to you the comforter, the *Spirit* of truth,"[24] and

---

[16]Is 61:1-2; see also Lk 4:18. [17]Is 5:7. [18]2 Cor 7:10. [19]2 Cor 7:10 RSV. [20]Lk 3:8. [21]Cf. Is 27:2. [22]Is 5:4. [23]Is 5:7. [24]Jn 14:16; 15:26.

gain: "until you receive power *from on high*."[25]
Therefore, since "Blessed are those who
mourn, for they shall be comforted,"[26] and
"Blessed are you that weep, for you shall
laugh,"[27] the things prophesied above are
appropriately added, for if they prove their
repentance through lamentation and weeping
and wailing, he gives a good promise that he
will restore them through the Holy Spirit.
And again, what has been said above is interpreted differently, for the text reads in the
Septuagint: *And Carmel will be a wilderness,
and Carmel will be regarded as a forest*, but
according to Symmachus: *And although
Carmel will be a wilderness, Carmel will be
regarded as a forest.* And it was said in the
passage discussed above: "It is not yet a little
while, and Lebanon shall be changed like
Mount Chermel, and Chermel shall be regarded as a forest. On that day the deaf shall
hear the words of a scroll, and as for those who
are in the darkness and those who are in the
fog, the eyes of the blind shall see. And the
poor shall be glad with joy through the Lord,
and those despairing among the people shall be
filled with joy."[28] But according to Symmachus, the text reads: *In yet a short time Lebanon will turn into Carmel, and Carmel shall be
regarded as a forest.*[29] When the text mentions
Lebanon as becoming the mountain in Phoenicia, it is clearly speaking about the Gentiles,
and, again, when the text mentions Mount
Carmel, which was formerly called by the Jews
and the people of the circumcision Chermel
(but clearly this is Carmel),[30] it is speaking
about the knowledge of circumcision. Accordingly, he says that Lebanon, that is, the people
from other tribes and other races, the Gentile
peoples, will be changed. And such a people as
those from the circumcision who were formerly
honored by God, he says that these very people
of the circumcision *shall be regarded as a forest*

called Chermel or Carmel. Therefore also the
Word indicates this when he states the things
in the passage at hand. According to Symma-
chus: *And there will be a wilderness in Carmel.*
For as it was said that Lebanon would be
changed into Carmel, here in this context it
says *the desert* in order that *the desert* and
Lebanon might be identified with one another,
thus clearly speaking about the church of the
Gentiles which will be changed into Carmel.
For just as "Jacob was the Lord's portion, and
Israel a measured part of his inheritance"[31] at
first, and Carmel also was aware of this, so too
Lebanon which was once a *desert* changed for
the better and became "God's portion." So
once again *Carmel was regarded as a forest*, and
a *forest* is a place where there are wild trees
[212] without any fruit. For this reason, we
frequently find in the divine Scripture that
"the nations that know not God" are called a
forest, as we have often noted.

[32:16-18] Then, next, already being deemed
worthy of great possessions, it is promised that
these things will be brought on the *desert*,
when it says: *Then judgment will rest in the
wilderness, and righteousness abide in Carmel.*
And this *Carmel* was in fact the *desert*, concerning which it was said: *And there will be a
desert in Carmel.* Accordingly, he promises that
judgment and righteousness will rest and abide
in the place that was once a *desert.* And for
this reason it was said above in the prophecy:
"Yet a little while and Lebanon shall be
changed like Mount Carmel."[32] And next, the
conversion of the unbelieving nations to God is
cited when the text says: "On that day the deaf
shall hear the words of a scroll, and as for
those who are in the fog, the eyes of the blind
shall see,"[33] and the rest. Therefore, he introduces similar things to those in this context
when he says that in the place that was once a

---

[25]Lk 24:49. [26]Mt 5:4 RSV. [27]Lk 6:21. [28]Is 29:17-19. [29]Is 29:17. [30]Eusebius here spells the word Κάρμηλος, although as quoted above, the word is usually spelled Χερμέλ in the Septuagint. [31]Deut 32:9. [32]Is 29:17. [33]Is 29:18.

desert, *judgment and righteousness will rest*, and there will be *works of righteousness* there. And he also says that in this very *desert, they will be confident forever; and his people will dwell in a city of peace.* For instead of that great and splendid city being demolished, God will establish another city, the church catholic,[34] and he foretells the godly administration that will exist in it. And according to Symmachus, the text says: *And my people will be settled in a house of peace.* In this context, neither Israel nor Jacob is any longer mentioned, but the one who remained in the new *city of peace*, the city of God, in which he says *his people will abide in confidence and rest with wealth.* And the apostle speaks of this *wealth* of the church when he says: "I give thanks to God through Jesus Christ, that in every way you were enriched in him with all speech and all knowledge."[35]

[32:19] Then, afterwards, we read above that the "anger" of God will come against the ungodly during the time of judgment, as he clearly states: "With wrath and anger and a devouring flame of fire he will thunder violently, even like *hailstones* falling down with violence."[36] And then he properly adds concerning those who are deemed blessed in the passage at hand: *And if hail descends, it will not come on you. And even those who dwell in the forests will be confident, like those in the plain.* You see how he gives good hope to the wild and fruitless plants of the *forest* that they will no longer be such souls in the *forest* but in the *plain* and level ground and in the cultivated land, so they may have good courage and be *confident* in their own fruitfulness.

[32:20] After the Word foretells these things, he subsequently congratulates those who cultivated this desert. For this reason he says:

Happy are those who sow beside every water, where ox and donkey tread. And through these things, he congratulates the apostles of our Savior and those first heralds of the gospel who preached to the Jews and Greeks, casting their seed to everyone, [213] "to the Jew first and also to the Greek."[37] For on the one hand, the *ox* would be the people who are called the circumcision and are in this verse represented by a clean animal because of the ancestors, and on the other hand, the *donkey*, which is unclean, would be the people of an idolatrous ancestry. Therefore, because the apostles of our Savior cast the gospel seed "to the Jews first and afterwards to the Greeks," the text rightly says: *Happy is the one who sows beside every water, where ox and donkey tread.* In this context, *water* alludes to the inspired Scriptures, which were *treaded* out by the Jews and the people of the nations.

[33:1] But, the prophet says, although I consider you to be *happy*, I see others who deem you to be unhappy and call you wretched, and I am speaking about your persecutors. Therefore, he says concerning them: *Woe to those who distress you*, and *woe to them* truly, because *no one makes you distressed, and the one rejecting you* thinks that he is *rejecting* people, but "he does not reject you" but "the one who sent" you.[1] And what the Savior said to his own disciples applies to a Christian sister as well: "he who rejects you rejects me, and he who rejects me rejects him who sent me."[2] One could say that there are two positions to be assumed during a time of persecution: that of the culprit and that of the one who suffers. The one suffering is happy,[3] but not the culprit. The culprit is the real wretch, not the one who suffers. But there will be *woe* for them in the extreme, since *the*

---

[34]καθολική ἐκκλησία; that is, the universal church. [35]1 Cor 1:4-5. [36]Is 30:30. [37]Rom 1:16. **Chapter Thirty-Three** [1]Lk 10:16. [2]Lk 10:16 RSV. [3]The Greek word here is μακάριος and could either be translated "blessed" or "happy." It is the word that Jesus uses to commence each of the beatitudes.

betrayers will be caught and delivered up to the one who seizes those who are thrown aside by God, and he will seize their souls and do away with them, as the text says next: and like a moth on a garment, so will they be defeated.

[33:2] The prophetic word deems happy those who were our Savior's apostles "to the Jews first as well as to the Greeks,"[4] who "sowed"[5] the heavenly and evangelical seeds, but he deems wretched those who "reject."[6] And when they rejected the apostles to their face, the speaker sends up a prayer: O Lord, have mercy on us, for we trust in you. For indeed, the seed of those who were disobedient to the evangelical preaching were delivered over to destruction, but you yourself, O Lord, are our salvation, and you are present with us in a time of affliction.

[33:3-4] Then, concerning those who were disobedient to the apostolic preaching, he adds: Because of the voice of the fear of you, peoples were astonished and nations scattered abroad. But according to Aquila, the text reads: From a voice of a crowd, and according to Theodotion: From a voice of a multitude, the people withdrew. He signifies the besieging of the Jewish nation, when a great number of their adversaries came on them, and they were astonished and scattered abroad from their own land into the nations. But instead of they were scattered from the fear of you, Symmachus says: Because they were raised up against you, as does Aquila. [214] And Theodotion says: They were scattered abroad because they were exalted against you. Then, as to them who were scattered abroad into the nations, he adds: But now your spoils—of small and of great—will be gathered; as someone might gather grasshoppers, so will they mock you. This verse presents those of the Jewish nation as easily conquered and led away and compares their number with grasshoppers. And when the text says that they will mock you,

it signifies that the adversaries not only will have them for sport and scatter their spoils, small and great, but also will mock them.

[33:5] After saying these things about them, he turns to address those in the church of God, and so he also glorifies God saying: God who dwells in lofty places is holy, Zion is filled with judgment and righteousness. And you will perceive from what is said that Zion has itself been filled with judgment and righteousness. Above the text said: "Then judgment and righteousness will rest in the wilderness."[7] Therefore, the desert which was mentioned above he now calls by name as Zion, signifying the church of Christ. For this was the place that once was a "desert,"[8] but then "in which judgment and righteousness came to rest." For this reason, God is now blessed, because this place was filled with judgment and righteousness.

[33:6] Then he says: By law they will be handed over. For it was by a new law that they were handed over, clearly by this new and evangelical law of Zion. And our salvation is in treasures. And what sort of treasures are these if not those that are "laid up in heaven"?[9] But instead of by law they will be handed over, Symmachus says: And the faith of your time will be the riches of salvation, wisdom and knowledge, the fear of the Lord, this is your treasure. But instead of this, the Septuagint renders the text: Wisdom and knowledge and piety have come to the Lord. For all these things are from people, just as a certain spiritual and acceptable sacrifice is offered up to God, and these things are found among people, wisdom and knowledge and piety are the treasures of righteousness. Therefore it has been said: Our salvation is in treasures.

[33:7] After these things, the text addresses the apostles and says: See now! They themselves will be afraid with fear of you; those who feared

---

[4]Rom 1:16. [5]Is 32:20. [6]Is 33:1. Again, this word could also be translated "the betrayers." [7]Is 32:16. [8]Is 32:16. [9]Col 1:5.

will cry aloud because of you. For the fear of you will fall on the faithless, and *they will cry aloud*, thus referring to those whom you once supposed to be terrifying. But according to Symmachus: *Behold, I will appear to them, they cried out earnestly.* And he continues on to say, who *cried out earnestly: messengers of peace wept bitterly*; and according to Aquila: *Behold, I will appear to them, I will cry out earnestly, angels of peace will weep bitterly*; and according to Theodotion: *behold, I will appear to them,* [215] *they cried out earnestly, messengers of peace will weep bitterly.* Therefore all the translations say: *I will appear to them*; clearly, the present word is saying that God *will appear to them.* And to whom does *them* refer if not they who treasure up for themselves the *treasures of righteousness and wisdom?* He says: *I will appear* to them. And these ones were the apostles of our Savior; to them indeed "I appeared."[10] And *the messengers of peace cried out earnestly*, and therefore *they wept bitterly*, *crying aloud earnestly* in prayers because of the destruction of his former people. For the apostles of our Savior were the *messengers who wept bitterly*, and they mourned because those whom they called to the *peace* of Christ did not listen and did not believe. And, therefore, when weeping over Jerusalem, the Savior himself said: "If you, even you, had only known what would bring you peace."[11] Therefore, even the *messengers of peace wept bitterly* as they deeply lament their destruction.

[33:8] Therefore, he continues on to say: *For the roads of these people will be made desolate; the fear of the nation has ceased, and their covenant with these is being put away, and you will not consider them to be men.* Symmachus translates this verse more clearly when he writes: *The roads were obscured; the one who travels along the path has ceased; he has scattered the covenant; he pushed away cities; he was*

not considered to be a man. And one does not read the phrase *the fear of the nation has ceased* in the Hebrew text, nor is it to be found in the Greek translations. Rather, one reads that *the roads* of the people of the circumcision *ceased*, that *their covenant* which was delivered to them through Moses *is being put away* and that *no one considers them to be men any longer.*

[33:9] Then, after these things, he adds: *The land mourned*, and then subsequently, because of what has been said about it, *Lebanon was ashamed; Saron became marshes; Galilee and Carmel will become visible.* But according to Symmachus: *The land wailed and was weak, Lebanon was put to shame, Sharon became unserviceable, and so too Bashan and Carmel became impassable.* All these things apply to the land of Judah, and I am speaking about Carmel and the places called Bashan and Galilee and Sharon and Lebanon. But in the things that have been mentioned earlier, between Sharon and Bashan and Carmel and Galilee, there the present passage is to be understood specifically about Jerusalem, because of the sacrifice that was made in it, where frankincense was also offered according to the law of Moses. And then he says that *Lebanon has been put to shame*, as if to clearly indicate that the sacrifice and altar have been put to shame, since the worship according to the law of Moses has been ended. And in others also Jerusalem is called *Lebanon*, as it has been said in Zechariah: "Open your doors, O Lebanon, and let fire devour your cedars."[12] And Ezekiel says: "The great eagle with great wings, who has the guidance to enter into Lebanon and snipped off the tender shoots of the cedar."[13]

[216] Then, translating the deeper sense[14] of the word, he continues on to say that Nebuchadnezzar will come into Jerusalem, and the eagle very clearly is the kingdom of the

---

[10]Lk 24:34. [11]Lk 19:42. [12]Zech 11:1. [13]Ezek 17:3-4. [14]διάνοια.

Babylonians and Lebanon is Jerusalem. But he
also says that the land that is called *Saron* or
Assyria became marshes or unserviceable, and
through these things he signifies that the most
fertile land of the Jewish nation will disappear;
clearly, this refers to the things which they
perceive in their souls. And the phrase *Galilee
will become visible* has been said because of
what was prophesied above concerning this
Galilee of the nations."15 "O you people who
sit in darkness, see a great light! A light has
dawned for those who sit in darkness and the
shadow of death."16 For because of these things
Galilee will become visible, and he says likewise
that *Carmel will become visible*. And what is
this or what is he speaking about above? Is he
perhaps referring to the verse: "And Carmel
will be as a wilderness"? Therefore, this
wilderness"17 which was "as Carmel" *will
become visible* along with *Galilee*.

[33:10-12] Therefore indeed the beneficent
God "sent messengers of peace"18 to the Jewish
people "weeping bitterly and entreating" them
to accept the peace that is being preached to
them. And since they did not receive them, he
continues on to say: *"Now I will arise,"* says the
Lord, *"now I will be glorified; now I will be
exalted. Now you will see; now you will perceive"*
his promised second coming in glory, when
they will see and receive a perception of his
divinity. And then *he will be glorified*, and *he
will appear*. And then they will know that *the
strength* of their *spirit was vain*. For *fire will
consume them*, and therefore it has been said to
their face: *The strength of your spirit is vain;
fire will consume you*. But instead of *and the
nations will be burned*, the Hebrew text and all
the other Greek translations say: *And the
people will have been set on fire*; clearly the
word is directed to those people to whom this
word also was addressed: *They will be as a
horn cast out and trampled in a field*.

[33:13] And these things were prophesied
concerning those of the Jewish people who did
not receive the grace that was preached to
them: "You will listen by listening" to these
prophetic words, "but you will not understand"19 and know because of these things that
have been spoken and written to you in the
Hebrew language. And I performed many
wonders for you *who are far away*, even as far
as the ends of the earth, and although I spoke
among you and what *I have done* was done in
your sight, those at the borders of the world
will know. And how *will they know* if not
because they "draw near to God"20 and
approach him and are trained in his *strength*.

[33:14-15] And they will be as stated above,
but *the lawless ones in my Zion . . . have gone
away*. Because of their departure, *trembling
will seize* them. Then, as **[217]** to those from
the people of the circumcision who did not
believe, he continues on to say: *Who will
declare to you that a fire is burning?* Concerning them he said a little earlier: "Fire will
consume you,"21 and again: *Who will declare to
you the everlasting place*, clearly referring to
the place "prepared for the devil and his
angels."22 Who therefore will be the one who
has seen these things and bears witness for
those who have not seen if not everyone
*walking in righteousness, speaking straight talk,
and everyone hating ungodliness and unrighteousness* and turning away from bribes, and
stopping *his ears so that he not hear a judgment
of blood and shutting his eyes so that he not see
an unrighteous deed*? And such a one as this
was each of the prophets of God and every
God-loving person, and such were the apostolic band and the disciples of our Savior.
Therefore, he says that everyone like this *will
announce to you that fire* "has been prepared"23
and *is burning* for the ungodly. But the one
who bears witness, he himself will make clear

15Is 9:1. 16Is 9:2. 17Is 32:15. 18Cf. Is 33:7. 19Cf. Is 6:9. 20Heb 7:19. 21Is 33:11. 22Mt 25:41. 23Mt 25:41.

to you the *place of everlasting* condemnation and keep watch lest you fall into it.

[33:16] And *this one* is far away from the *fire* and from the aforementioned *everlasting place*, and *he will live in the high cave and on the strong rock*, or according to Symmachus: *He will settle in the heights, and the enclosures of rocks will be his throne*. We are to understand through this verse that the discipline of the blessed and their life of philosophy is of the highest excellence. Therefore, he continues on to say: *Bread will be given to him, and his water will be assured*. But such a one as this who is disciplined in *bread* and *water* during the present life will have the glorious contemplation of the kingdom as a reward and fruit of his asceticism.[24]

[33:17] Therefore, the text continues on to say: *You will see a king with glory*. And who is this *king* if not him on whose account the present theme documents all these things, beginning from the verse: "See, a just king will reign, and rulers will rule with judgment"?[25] Therefore, people like these *will see* this one *in glory*, whom the Word describes above. They will attain these things, but to you it has been said: "Who will declare to you that a fire is burning?"[26] The soul *will see from far away* the heavenly "land of promise,"[27] and although you will not enter into it, you will see it from far away. For "the meek shall inherit" that "land,"[28] but those who have been cast aside far away from this land, they will fall into fear of their condemnation.

[33:18-19] Therefore, he continues on to say to them: *Your soul will muse on fear*. Then the Word again turns to the people of the circumcision and says: *Where are the scholars*, those who are custodians of the letter of the law and know nothing else and do not understand the promises of the text? Are they not those whom

the Savior deemed miserable in the Gospels [218] when he said: "Woe to you *scribes* and Pharisees, hypocrites!"[29] For this reason he says: *Where are the scholars? Where are the counselors?* For *where* will they appear in the day of judgment, those who gather together their disciples with flattery? For this reason h says: *The one who counts those gathering together, a small and a great people, with whom they took no counsel* but whom clearly they gathered together with flattery. But according to Symmachus, the text reads: *The one who counts those who have been gathered together, th shameful people. He will not look at a people difficult in speech, lest he hear the discourse of their tongue*. Therefore, indeed, he says you divert the *shameful people*, nurturing them in flattery and deceit, O you scribe of the law! And do you not know that he will see my *people difficult in speech*? But neither is there no understanding in the *hearing* of the *speech of the tongue*, concerning which it was said above: "And the stammering tongues will soon learn to speak peace."[30] But you *will not hear* these *tongues*, neither will you understand the *people of deep speech*. For whether it would be possible for they who are of no understanding to even understand these things, the text says concerning them: *So that a despised people could not hear, and there is no understanding fo the one who hears*.

[33:20] But instead of *Look, the city of Zion*, Aquila says: *Behold, the village of Zion*; and Theodotion says: *Behold, Zion, the city of our saints*. The Word addresses Zion and either exhorts it to look to the *city* which is called th *city of our salvation* or to look to *the city of our saints*. And again, he says next: *Your eyes will see Jerusalem*, so that you will know what is coming for Jerusalem and so that *your eyes will see* another *city* which is *the city of festivals*. And when the Word speaks of *deliverance*, he

---

[24]ἄσκησις. [25]Is 32:1. [26]Is 33:14. [27]Cf. Heb 11:9. [28]Mt 5:5. [29]Mt 23:13. [30]Is 32:4.

s speaking about the Christ of God, and the *city of festivals* is the church of God, which is also the *wealthy city* and the *tents that will not be shaken, nor will the stakes of its tent be moved forever, nor will its ropes be broken.* For, indeed, *the tents* of the Jerusalem of the Jewish people *were shaken* frequently, during the several times that it was besieged and even brought down to its foundation by those who warred against it. But he says that the *stakes of this new city* will be unmovable. And although one considers that it was harassed by persecutions and besieged, yet through endless ages it remains standing "on the rock."[31] For the one who said this "never lies":[32] "and on this rock I will build my church, and the gates of Hades shall not prevail against it,"[33] and again: "The rains fell, the rivers came, the winds blew and dashed against that house, but it did not fall, because it had been founded on the rock."[34] Because of this he says, *its ropes will not be broken.*

[33:21-22] He continues on to tell us the reason: *Because the name of the Lord is great to you, there will be a place for you—rivers and canals, broad and spacious.* He says that the name of the Lord will be this place in the new city, the unshakable and secure city. For this reason, because the city that has been built on this place has been built on the Lord, [219] it remains unshakable. According to Symmachus, the text says: *The Lord is mighty for you, a place of rivers, spacious canals, where a boat with oars shall not go, neither shall the commandment of the mighty one go across it;* and according to Aquila, the text says: *The Lord is exceedingly difficult to you, a place of rivers, wide channels at hand, an exceedingly difficult ship with oars and a galley shall not sail in it and shall not pass over it.* Theodotion renders the word of the prediction with approximately the same sentence: *The Lord will be the place of the city that has channels of rivers and wide canals,* so as to say: "The river's strong currents make glad the city of God,"[35] and again: "The river of God was filled with water."[36] And thus they are certain that these "rivers" "make glad the city of God"[37] so that neither the boat with oars nor the exceedingly difficult galley is unable to sail down them because the Lord is their place.

And the *rivers* come to the aforementioned *city* of God and serve in place of a wall encircling and surrounding the *city* and are just as uncrossable as any other barrier, making it inaccessible to the enemies and adversaries, because *the Lord is* the city's *great place.* For he was the rock on which it was built. And it says that he is *our judge,* and he is *our ruler,* and he is our *king* and Savior. The Lord is these things to us, and thus the *city* is impregnable, for the *rivers* which encircle it make it inaccessible to every enemy. And we will see that the word speaks of the *rivers* that enclose the *city* as equivalent to the great and full *river* whose "streams make glad the city of God."[38] And "his angels who always behold the face of the Father who is in heaven"[39] might also be the *rivers* that enclose his church. Such things as these the Word says concerning the *city* of God, but he will suddenly turn and inveigh against the ancient city.

[33:23-24] Thus he says: *Your ropes broke, because they were not strong. Your mast has bent so that it releases the sails;*[40] *it will not raise a signal until I give it up for plunder.* He signifies through these things the fall of the bodily Jerusalem, whose ropes and mast were broken, and just as the mast of a ship wrecked in the winter storms and waves, so it was bent. Jerusalem fell, and the ropes that held it fast were torn asunder. But according to Symmachus, the text says: *Your ropes were cast away*

---

[31]Mt 16:18. [32]Tit 1:2. [33]Mt 16:18. [34]Mt 7:25. [35]Ps 46:4. [36]Ps 65:9. [37]Ps 46:4. [38]Ps 46:4. [39]Mt 18:10. [40]The alteration in this translation is due to a slight and probably unintentional changing of the Greek text of the Septuagint's οὐ χαλάσει to Eusebius's τοῦ χαλάσαι.

and so they did not hold; and this happened to their mast so that it did not unfurl the sails. Then he distributed it as great spoils. When a ship breaks apart and suffers shipwreck in sea battle with its adversaries, the victors seize for themselves the spoils of those who have perished and they make plunder of everything. Thus, he says that when Jerusalem [220] fell and was delivered over to its adversaries, all the valuable and noble and priestly vessels in it were distributed for plunder, since God had given it up. For it was not on their own power that the adversaries had such strength so that they were able to conquer it. And, therefore, suddenly these lame people came and took plunder, limping along and, since they were maimed in the recesses of the soul, they could not walk in the way of godliness. And it was idolaters who tirelessly and without fatigue seized the wreckage of the fallen city. Therefore, the text says: Now, many lame will take plunder. And the people who dwell in them will not say, "I am weary." For their sin has been forgiven. For their sin has not been counted against those who besieged the city because this has happened as the judgment of God.

[34:1] And in the above passage we may conclude that the Word predicts the siege of Jerusalem, but next he speaks of the judgment against all nations, for as we read elsewhere: "Begin from my holy places."[1] And thus in the present passage he comments on the plunder of Jerusalem and its fall, prophesying the judgment against all the nations. For it is possible that the Word did not threaten that these things would happen only in Jerusalem but also in the other nations and among those who continue in their own unlawful and ungodly deeds. Therefore, the Word summoned the nations and the rulers and people, all the earth and all those in it. The world is what we are to understand when he says "earth," including

every element of the dry earth, but it also refers to those particular wild inhabitants and uncivilized people who live in the many deserted and forgotten places and make dwellings there in the world and in our nations, in cities and in buildings. Therefore he addresses the people of the world.

[34:2] Then the summons was directed to all together, witnessing to the awaited universal judgment of God, which he states in the present verse: Because the wrath of the Lord is against all the nations and his anger against the whole number of them, or according to Symmachus: Against their every power; and according to Aquila: Against their every army, to destroy them and to deliver them over to slaughter. But over to whom will he deliver them or to what punitive and vengeful powers?

[34:3-4] And there will be those who are wounded and dead from among those who were chastised, clearly speaking of those who "sinned a mortal sin,"[2] and during the time of the judgment when this mortal life is finished, their deeds will give off a foul smell. Therefore, the text reads according to Symmachus: And their foul smell will ascend. But instead of the mountains shall be drenched with their blood, the text reads according to Theodotion: The mountains will ooze over with their blood. And Aquila adds these things next: And all the hosts of the heavens will melt, and according to Symmachus: And every power of the heavens will melt, and [221] according to Theodotion: And all the powers of the heavens will melt. Therefore, these mountains refers to those concerning which it was said: And the mountains will ooze with their blood. For the powers of the heavens which we are considering are said to be the cause of the destruction described above. And they could be that concerning which the apostle says: "We are not contending

Chapter Thirty-Four   [1]Ezek 9:6.   [2]1 Jn 5:16.

against flesh and blood, but against the principalities, against the powers, against the world rulers of this present darkness, against the spiritual hosts of wickedness in the heavenly places."[3] For these *powers* which run across the airy regions are said to be *powers of heaven*, but the Scripture is accustomed to calling the things that fly through the air "birds of heaven":[4] "The birds of heaven and the fish of the sea."[5]

And the phrase *and all the powers of the heavens will melt* is not present in the Septuagint translation; it is marked with an asterisk in the other Greek translations.[6] And since it was necessary for us to know when these things will be, the present prophetic word teaches that after "the close of this age"[7] what has been foretold will happen. And therefore he adds: *Heaven shall roll up like a scroll, and all the stars shall fall like leaves from a vine and as leaves fall from a fig tree.* And the Savior said in the Gospels when he delivered his teaching about the end: "And the *stars will fall* out of heaven, and *the powers of the heavens* will be shaken; then will appear the sign of the Son of man in heaven."[8] But instead of *and all the stars shall fall like leaves*, Aquila writes: *And all their hosts will fall away as a leaf falls away from a vine and as a misshapen fruit from a fig tree*; and according to Symmachus: *And their every power will fall like a leaf falls from a vine and as a misshapen fruit from a fig tree*; and likewise Theodotion also: *And their every power will fall as leaves fall from a vine and as windfall fruit from a fig tree.* And you will have noted that the word that was translated *stars* in the Septuagint appears rather in the other Greek translations as *powers of heaven*. And what are the *powers* if not precisely what was just mentioned? According to Aquila: *And all the host of heaven will melt away*; and according to Sym-

machus: *And all the power of heaven will melt away*; and according to Theodotion: *And all the powers of the heavens will melt away.* Therefore, we understand these *powers* to be "the principalities and the powers, the world rulers of this present darkness and the spiritual [**222**] hosts of wickedness in the heavenly places."[9] The statement *they shall fall as leaves from a vine* has been said concerning the time of the judgment, when *heaven shall roll up like a scroll.*

And the Word indicates then that those who are worthy of the Word should note that heaven will neither be ruined nor destroyed nor obliterated, but "heaven shall roll up like a scroll."[10] The things that have been indicated are clear: "the scroll" will certainly not be destroyed but be "rolled up" as a writing in heaven which encompasses every deed that has transpired in the world. The opposing powers will drift away from the way of life into thin air, and they will fall away. Daniel teaches these things about the judgment when he says: "A court sat in judgment and books were opened."[11] And what sort of *scrolls* are these if not those in which all of the deeds of governments in every age have been written? You would not be incorrect to say they are the *heaven that shall be rolled up* as a *scroll*, on which the deeds of all have been inscribed as on a document. And then the opposing powers which once deceived many *shall fall* as *stars*, since "even Satan himself, disguised as an angel of light, has fallen like lightning from heaven."[12]

[34:5-6] And these *powers shall fall*, he says, when *my dagger has become drunk in heaven.* We should understand the *dagger* to be the chastising power, to which those who stand in need of such punishment will be delivered. But someone else might say concerning the consummation of all that is seen that the very

---

[3]Eph 6:12 RSV. [4]The Greek word primarily means "bird," but more generally it means any winged or flying creature. [5]Gen 1:26. [6]The asterisk appears in the Hexapla and in early Christian manuscripts as a text-critical marker. See Jerome's discussion in *Adv. Rufin.*, 2.25, 27. [7]Mt 13:39. [8]Mt 24:29-30. [9]Eph 6:12. [10]Rev 6:14. [11]Dan 7:10. [12]Cf. 2 Cor 11:14; Lk 10:18.

being of the elements will be undone as also *heaven* itself and the *stars* in it. And I say that the invisible *powers* in it and the bodies surrounding them will be stripped away in the transformation to a better life, and this is made clear from the statement of the apostle: "Because the creation itself will be set free from its bondage to decay and obtain the glorious liberty of the children of God."[13] And the abovementioned *dagger* of God first pursues after the evil and opposing *powers* that come along in the air and, second, those souls in the land of the ungodly. Therefore, he continues on to say: *It will descend on Edom and on the people of destruction.* And what will *descend* if not the *dagger*? And *Edom* is interpreted as earthly, and it is this soil that will be filled with *blood* after the *dagger* descends on it; it will be *gorged from the fat* of those who will be slaughtered.

And he says who these *lambs* and *goats* and *rams* were. Indeed, when he speaks of the *lambs*, or *young sheep* as it is translated according to the other Greek translations, he indicates those who pursue the common and everyday life. And the *bulls* and *rams* signify the many who were powerful among "rulers and authorities"[14] whom the *dagger* of God will pursue as [223] a *sacrifice*, working to slaughter and offer the aforementioned *lambs* and *bulls* and *rams*. And these things he will do in *Bosor*, which is to be interpreted as signifying, in the literal sense of the word, the resurrection of the flesh among them. Therefore he says that the *slaughter* in the flesh will be of those who are said to be teachers, *because the Lord has a sacrifice in Bosor and a great slaughter in Edom*, for every earthly soul will be pursued. For *Edom* is to be understood as those who are of the earth and *Edom* as those who are earthly, as these works are interpreted elsewhere.[15] Therefore the prophet himself

proceeds and next says concerning the Savior and the judgment which he will give: "Who is this that came from *Edom*, a redness of garments from *Bosor?*"[16] In this way he disclosed how his incarnate coming on the earth would be.

[**34:7**] But yet in the preceding verse he says that the *prominent shall fall* and the *rams* and the *bulls* when the *land will be drunk from the blood and from the fat* of those who are slaughtered by the *dagger* of God. But according to Symmachus, the text reads: *And the lofty wild oxen and the strong young bulls will be brought low, and the earth will be drunk with blood, and the scraps of their fat will be left behind.* And I suppose that the divine Spirit warned them with such threatening words in order to present the vengeance of God against the ungodly and to alarm those who attend to these words in the customary and coarse way, for they are neither able to understand all the penalties that will be brought on the ungodly nor are they able to comprehend the manner of the punishment. For this reason, he has spoken very coarse sayings using very common words of fear in order that, thus being afraid, those who hear these things might turn around.

[**34:8**] The Word alluded to the siege of Jerusalem when he says: "Your ropes broke, because they were not strong. Your mast has bent; it will not release the sails; it will not raise a signal until it is given up for plunder."[17] Then, next, after speaking about those nations who besieged it and about the judgment of God against the whole world that will come on all the ungodly, he resumes teaching the word concerning Zion and Jerusalem, teaching that a *year of recompense* and a *day of judgment* has come on it. And in the above verses he says: "Rise up, you wealthy women,"[18] "mention the

---

[13]Rom 8:21 RSV. [14]Eph 3:10. [15]Eusebius is drawing a play on words here. The word *Edom* in Hebrew comes from a root meaning "red" and came to mean "blood" or "humankind." The word therefore then also commonly meant "soil" or "earth." [16]Is 63:1. [17]Is 33:23. [18]Is 32:9.

days of a year in pain with hope."[19] Therefore, the present prophecy states when this *year* in the verse at hand came to be, the year when he determines that they will be stricken "with pain."[20] And it was necessary for the word from the mouth of Christ to be presented in the words which the prophet himself says next: "The spirit of the Lord is on me, because he has anointed me; he has sent me to bring good news to the poor, to proclaim release to the captives and recovery of sight to the blind, to summon the acceptable *year of the Lord* and the *day of retribution* for our [224] God, to comfort all who mourn so that to those who mourn for Zion glory is given."[21] You see how the phrases *year of the Lord* and *day of recompense* have been said in these verses, and it signifies the same in this context: *For it is a day of the Lord's judgment and a year of recompense for the judgment of Zion.* Surely then he is speaking of one and the same *year* and one and the same *day*, during which "the poor will have good news preached to them,"[22] and those who "mourn over Zion will be comforted"[23] at the coming of the Christ. And those who were "wealthy women"[24] are called to lamentation, and the things that were said in the preceding verses about Zion were about to happen. And all these things about the coming of our Savior Jesus Christ were fulfilled, and it was then that those who indeed believed in him and who received the grace that comes through him enjoyed the benefit of those most auspicious good tidings. They set themselves in an unfavorable position, and falling away from every good hope of grace itself, they sank under the threats of the darkest doom.

[34:9-10] And the present prophecy foretells the sort of things that their august and royal city would suffer when it says: And its ravines shall be turned into a burning pitch night and day, and it shall not be quenched forever, and its smoke shall go up above; for its generations shall be made desolate; indeed for a long time it shall be made desolate. And according to Symmachus, the text reads: *Its land shall be turned into a blazing pitch, and night and day it shall not be quenched forever; its smoke shall go up from generation to generation; it shall be made desolate from the battle of battles.* In these verses the Word clearly presents that the place and the nation will be overtaken, even the furthest desert, for he continues on to say: *There will be no one to march through it and there will be no one to pass through it.* And he prophesies in these things that no longer will any Jew pass through that place, and already it was fulfilled in the Roman laws and edicts when the Jews were disallowed from setting foot in this place.

[34:11-15] On the one hand *there will be no one to march through it*, but on the other hand the text says that certain *birds and hedgehogs and ibises and ravens shall live in it*, by which he alludes to unclean souls. The kinds of animals following them in the passage are those idolaters from other tribes and those from other nations and races who will *live* in the place. And not only does he say that these animals shall *live* in the place instead of the former inhabitants, but even *donkey-centaurs* and *sirens* and *ostriches*, by which he alludes to certain demons who lurk in the exquisite designs of their idolatrous images. For this reason he continues on to say next: *Demons shall meet with donkey-centaurs and call one to another*, but he says also that *a measuring line of desolation shall be cast over* the place. But instead, Symmachus translated the verse: *And a measure of destruction will be stretched out on it.* But all of these things [225] will come on the former inhabitants who had been driven out and delivered over to destruction. Therefore he continues on to say: *Its rulers shall not*

---

[19]Is 32:10. [20]Cf. Is 32:10. [21]Cf. Is 61:1-3. [22]Mt 11:5. [23]Cf. Is 61:2. [24]Cf. Is 32:9.

be, *for the kings and its nobles shall be destroyed.*
And whenever you will see their synagogues
outside of Jerusalem, listen to the sort of
things that he proclaims about them when he
says: *Thorn trees shall grow up in their cities,*
clearly referring to their fruitless doctrines.
For this reason also, it is clear from the above
statements that their "vineyard" had been
overgrown with "thorns": "I waited in order
that it might produce a cluster of grapes, but it
produced thorns."[25] Then, concerning the
furthest desert, which was in their souls, and
concerning their land, which was full of
thorns, he rightly foretells that the unclean
spirits will be put to rest among them: *There
donkey-centaurs shall repose, for they have found
for themselves a place to rest. There has the
hedgehog made a nest and rescued his offspring,*
or, according to Symmachus: *And rescued and
hatched and gathered together his offspring.*

Therefore, because their *ravines* represent
their souls, since they are found down in the
crevices and chasms, he says that their *ravines
will be turned into pitch* and *into sulfur* and that
their *land shall burn like pitch day and night,
and it shall not be quenched forever.* For their
eternal chastisement will be unquenchable,
and the *smoke* of their fire *will go up above,* and
the ascending *sulfur* of their retribution in the
depths will allow them to see the evil that lies
below them, the dark, black *pitch* that will be
all around them. We see what sort of evils in
the desert of Zion will next come on them
during "the year of their recompense"[26] when
he says: *There deer met and beheld each other's
faces.* And the Holy Scripture is aware that
deer are "clean"[27] animals, and it teaches many
lovely things about *deer,* for example when it
says: "Just as the doe longs for the springs of
water, so my soul longs for you, O God,"[28] and
again: "The Lord's voice, as he prepares deer,"[29]
and once more: "Let the fawn of your love and

the foal of favors consort with you,"[30] and in
the book of Job: "Did you protect the months
of pregnancy of the *deer*; will you send away
their birth pangs?"[31] And the "kinsman" of the
bride is compared with a *deer* in the Song of
Songs, when we read in this book: "My
kinsman is like the gazelle or a fawn of stags
on the mountains of spices."[32] Therefore, when
even "the bridegroom" himself is compared
with a *deer,* how could anyone deny [226] that
many *deer* represent his disciples and apostles?
And there is also a serpent-killing animal
counted among the "clean" animals. [33] Therefore, the present word teaches that the *deer*
from the desert of the Jewish nation that
passed by were the disciples of our Savior. For
there deer met and saw each other's faces. For
they knew themselves, and those who were
"according to the image of God"[34] recognized
the character of their souls.

[34:16-17] And yet, they *passed by* that place,
and thus they separated themselves. Therefore
the text reads: *They have passed by in number,
and not one of them has perished.* Then, after
that, not one remained in the city, but they ran
about every place and proclaimed the gospel.
Because of this it has been said: *They did not
seek each other, because the Lord has commanded them, and his Spirit has gathered them.*
For he who told them to "go and make disciples of all nations in my name"[35] commanded
them not to spend their lives as they always
had done but to run about everywhere and to
lay with foresight the foundation of his church.

He will himself cast lots for them; his hand
has distributed food for them to eat. You will
inherit the land forever. Therefore, he provided
strength and aid for them in addition to lots
for generations of generations, so that they
would rest in their own lots. This verse is
clearly referring to the nations whose remem-

---

[25]Is 5:4. [26]Cf. Is 34:8. [27]Deut 14:5. [28]Ps 42:1. [29]Ps 29:9. The KJV preserves the sense of a deer ("hind") in this verse, as do multiple foreign language translations. [30]Prov 5:19. [31]Job 39:1, 3. [32]Song 2:9. [33]Deut 14:5. [34]Gen 1:27. [35]Mt 28:19.

brance was allotted to be rekindled for generations of generations in the churches that were established within them.

You see that he is prophesying these things about the *deer*, because it is perfectly clear that it was not possible that these promises should be fulfilled in the aforementioned desert of Zion, since he says that *hedgehogs* and *donkey-centaurs* and *demons will live in it*. For this reason the land of the *deer* might refer to other things, for it is in this land that the Lord *himself cast lots for the deer, and his hand* gave them *food to eat forever*. And therefore it is this land that was allotted to the *deer*, this land which the Word presents when he says in the Psalms: "The voice of the Lord restores the deer, and he will uncover the forests."[36] Therefore, he apportioned *lots* for them in the forests, clearly referring to those among the nations. And therefore often the forests were assigned to foreign nations and overrun with *deer*, and these deer were paid in return according to *lots* and quotas and were received into another land, in alignment with the command of God. And now you know what the psalm is saying when the text reads: "The voice of the Lord restores the *deer*" and "uncovers forests."[37] The word is teaching that through the *deer* which were "restored" by the Lord, certain "forests," [227] fields and woodlands "were bared" of the beasts and reptiles in them by these *deer*. And it is clear through this discussion of the "forests" that these deer will drive away the other tribes and the nations that were enemies of God.

[35:1-2] Therefore, after the aforementioned things "about the deer," the prophecy preaches about this *wilderness* in the passage at hand when it says: *Rejoice, O thirsty wilderness!* And many other things are spoken concerning this *wilderness*, as for example we find in the passage later on in the prophecy, when we read: "Rejoice, O barren one who does not bear; break forth, and shout, you who are not in labor! Because more are the children of the desolate[1] woman than of her that has a husband."[2] Therefore, one might say that this *wilderness* is not the aforementioned Zion, in which we read that "hedgehogs and ibises and ravens"[3] and "demons and donkey-centaurs live,"[4] and the "ravines" shall be full of "pitch and sulfur."[5] And a portion of these statements have been delivered concerning Zion and concerning Jerusalem, and another portion are meant to be understood as about another *wilderness*. And this *wilderness* was the forest "of the deer"[6] and the land of the foreign nations. Here the word proclaims that the Lord apportioned "the lots" "to the deer"[7] that were returned when it says: *Rejoice, O thirsty wilderness! Let the wilderness be glad, and let it blossom like a lily.* For this *wilderness* was formerly *thirsty* and barren due to the absence of the running water of heaven, but the Word commands it to be glad and *rejoice* because, as the Word continues on to say, it will *blossom like a lily*, just as we read: "We are the aroma of Christ to God in every place."[8]

But it says the young shoots *will also bloom* and produce graceful "flowers," as was spoken of in the Song of Songs: "The flowers have appeared on the earth";[9] "the mandrakes have given forth fragrance."[10] And he states precisely what sort of *wilderness* he is giving an account of when he says: *And the deserted places of the Jordan shall be glad.* This account is recorded in the Gospels, for it was "in the river Jordan"[11] that John first preached the kingdom of heaven. And when the worship prescribed according to the law of Moses—a "baptism of repentance"[12] and "the washing of regeneration"[13]—was no

---

[36]Ps 29:9. [37]Ps 29:9. **Chapter Thirty-Five** [1]The adjective here translated "desolate" is a substantival adjective and could also be translated "wilderness." [2]Is 54:1. [3]Is 34:11. [4]Is 34:14. [5]Is 33:9. [6]Is 34:15. [7]Is 34:17. [8]2 Cor 2:15. [9]Song 2:12. [10]Song 7:13. [11]Mt 3:6. [12]Mk 1:4. [13]Tit 3:5.

longer in operation in Jerusalem, the prophet allowed himself to be baptized "in the river Jordan."[14] Our Savior and Lord Jesus, the Christ of God, sanctioned the preaching of John when he was "baptized in the Jordan"[15] by him, confirming in himself the mystery of regeneration. And again, the *wilderness* was without water and without fruit: I am speaking about the church of God, bringing about the kingdom of God [228] through the cleansing "of the washing of regeneration"[16] in baptizing as well as preaching. The church, which was once the *wilderness* of God, keeps this practice throughout the whole world. It is for this reason that the Word encourages it to *rejoice* and *be glad* and to *blossom* like a fragrant *lily*. In this way the *glory of Lebanon and the honor of Carmel has been given*. Therefore, in the passage above, *Lebanon* represents the altar and the temple, where "the sacrifices with frankincense"[17] and the worship according to the law was performed with offerings. But *Carmel* refers to the people of the uncircumcision, as it has often been observed. Therefore, the *honor* of the former people and the *glory* of the temple in Jerusalem, the city that was once a *wilderness*—it is prophesied that all this *will be given* to the church from the nations. And then the text continues on to say: *And my people*, no longer Israel, but he says that his *people shall see the glory of the Lord*. The Word offers this promise to the new people, inasmuch as they welcomed the first coming of the Savior. Therefore, they shall *see* his second and glorious appearance, and they will behold his *loftiness*.

[35:3-4] In the next verses, he proclaims that they will be released from the sufferings of the soul through the illumination of the Savior when he says: *Be strong, you weak hands and feeble knees! Give comfort, you who are faint of heart and mind!* But according to Symmachus,

the text reads: *Be strengthened, you weak hands and frail knees! Be powerful and say to the senseless, Be strong, do not fear!* And, very similarly, Aquila and Theodotion translate the word that our Savior calls out to the disciples and the apostles, that is, *to strengthen* the souls among the nations who have been *passed by* and *to establish the knees* of those who have become weak, and to say to those who were once *faint of heart: Be strong, do not fear!* For even if those who threaten you should pursue and attempt to produce fear in you, even applying torments and tortures, the text says that you who were once *fainthearted* will be transformed in strength and power and will not *fear*, since you have your God who accompanies you through everything. Therefore, according to Symmachus, the text reads: *Do not fear! Behold, your God shall come and bring vengeance and retribution. The Lord himself shall come and save you.* For this reason, after you have been taught these things, you who were once *fainthearted* will be *strong* and will *not fear*.

[35:5-6] After prophesying about this and clearly announcing the coming of God, the Word introduces signs and tokens of his virtuous actions when he says next: *Then the eyes of the blind shall be opened, and the ears of the deaf shall hear; then the lame shall leap like a deer, and the tongue of stammerers shall be clear.* And these things were distinctly fulfilled during the advent of our Savior, Jesus Christ, when each of these statements found [229] fulfillment, for in his divine and rejuvenating power he healed every sickness and infirmity. He healed not only the sufferings of their bodies with the word of his teaching but also of their souls. Still, even now throughout the whole world, among all the nations, there are those who, in their crippledness and blindness of soul, were once astounded at the lifeless and

---

[14]Mt 3:6. [15]Mt 3:13. [16]Tit 3:5. [17]Eusebius here draws Lev 6:15 into the discussion because the Greek word for Lebanon (λίβανος) is also the spelling of the word for "frankincense."

motionless statues. Illuminated by his light, the eyes of their souls are enabled to see what kind of gods these statues are, and so they eschew the superstition handed down to them from their ancestors and instead make known the one and only true God. And the dumb and those who were at first deaf to the divine words, through his grace they have now become versed in listening to the inspired words, and those who passed by the steps of the soul leaped up like "deer"[18] and became like their teachers, whom the prophecy called 'deer' a little earlier. And the *tongue of stammerers*, which "Satan bound"[19] so that it would not acknowledge the true God, this *tongue* has learned to utter *clear* and articulate sounds. And one would not be incorrect to say that the *stammerers* are none other than "the wise men of this age,"[20] who scarcely ever dare to think or say anything correct about God.

He says in all these things in the prophecy that is here foretold, *water has broken forth in the* place that was once a *wilderness*, and a *gully* was found in which a life-giving spring appeared. But according to Symmachus, the text reads: *Torrents have broken forth in a thirsty land*. Therefore, the *water* here spoken about was the water from the Jordan, concerning which it was said a little earlier: "And the deserted places of the Jordan shall be glad,"[21] by which "the washing of regeneration"[22] and the mystery of the new covenant are foreshadowed. And when he says *streams*, he is talking about the gospel words of our Savior.

[35:7-8] And yet, along with these things, there is in the aforementioned wilderness the *joy of birds* and *a bed of flocks*,[23] by which phrases he is speaking about winged and elevated souls, as well as other tame and gentle animals that are cared for by good shepherds, so that they are able to say: "The Lord shep-

herds me, and I shall lack nothing." [24] Therefore, above we read that "ibises, hedgehogs, ravens, donkey-centaurs and demons shall live"[25] in the wilderness of Zion, but in the passage at hand the word announces good tidings for the wilderness. And what was said about the "pitch, sulfur and fire"[26] will be fulfilled, and so will this saying about the *springs* and *streams* and *torrents of water*.

And he then says *there shall be a pure way, and it shall be called a holy way*. And one could say that this way leads to the thrice-blest destination "of the heavenly city of God,"[27] and the Savior spoke of this way when he said: "I am the *way*."[28] Therefore, the saving [230] word directs those who go to the Father and into the kingdom of heaven through him. It is prophesied that only the saints will be permitted to travel the *way* established in the wilderness, and it is evident that *no one* who is *unclean shall pass* through this *way*. But he also says *those who have been dispersed shall walk on it*. And who are these if not the ones who were once scattered abroad by God and who had wandered far from the truth? For they shall run back again and, after finding the straight and steady *way, they shall walk in it*.

[35:9-10] And he says *and no lion shall be there*, and this means in the path to which the text has already referred, *nor shall any of the evil beasts come up on it or go there*. For in view of the saying "I am the way," how could any sort of evil creatures *be found* there? According to Solomon, it is not possible to find the "ways of a snake on a rock."[29] *But*, he says, *the redeemed shall walk on it*, clearly referring to those whom he *redeemed* "with his own precious blood"[30] *and those gathered together through the Lord*—not through the prophet or through any human effort. *Through* him and *through the Lord, those who have been redeemed*

---

[18]Cf. Is 34:15. [19]Lk 13:16. [20]1 Cor 1:20. [21]Is 35:2. [22]Tit 3:5. [23]Here Eusebius has "flocks" instead of "marshlands." [24]Ps 23:1. [25]Cf. Is 34:11, 14. [26]Cf. Is 34:9. [27]Heb 12:22. [28]Jn 14:6. [29]Prov 30:19. [30]1 Pet 1:19.

and gathered together shall walk the aforementioned path, and it is on this path that they shall arrive on the thrice-blest destination "of the heavenly Zion." The apostle says about this: "We have come to Mount Zion and to the city of the living God, the heavenly Jerusalem."[31] For this reason the text says: *And they shall come to Zion with joy.* For then it is not possible to interpret *Zion* in this context as the same place concerning which it has been said: "A year of recompense for the judgment of Zion, and its ravines shall be turned into pitch,"[32] and the rest. Therefore, one should know that those who speak of Zion do not all use the name in the same way. On the one hand, there is the earthly city to which the threats are addressed, but on the other hand there is the "heavenly"[33] to which it is said that *the redeemed and those gathered by the Lord shall come,* and concerning which it has also been said: *Everlasting joy shall be above their head.* For those who are shown to be victors in the great contest will be crowned with a crown *of joy,* and we see that the divine apostle Paul spoke of this too when he said: "Henceforth there is laid up for me the crown of righteousness."[34] For this reason the text reads: *Everlasting joy shall be above their head,* and again: *For on their head shall be praise and gladness, and joy shall take hold of them,* clearly referring to those who proceed unswervingly along the path of salvation and who through it arrive upon the thrice-blest destination. And those who are rewarded with the crown of eternal life will enjoy their reward in the kingdom of heaven, where *pain and sorrow and sighing will have fled away.*

[36:1-3] [231] Indeed, the story presented above is also a marvelous narrative of the events that happened during the time of Hezekiah. It has been included with the other accounts in the fourth book of Kings[1] and in the second book of Chronicles.[2] Nevertheless, it has also been documented in the prophecy or book at hand, inasmuch as an account is recorded in the prophecy at the end of the story concerning the certain great and incredible deed that was fulfilled during the time of Hezekiah. And one must note that it was "in the sixth year of Hezekiah's reign"[3] that "the king of Assyria," that is, Sennacherib, stood up against Samaria and demolished Israel's authority in the region. He summoned all the people of Israel and deported them to the land of Assyria. And during the seven intervening years, "in the fourteenth year of Hezekiah,"[4] he set up the strongest fortifications against the Jewish cities and finally took the city, for he had already set his hand to take Jerusalem. And the Scripture recounts in the book of Chronicles the greatest and most worthy of Hezekiah's accomplishments when it says that "he did what was right before the Lord, just as his father David had done."[5] We also read that "he opened the doors of the Lord's house and repaired them,"[6] for the doors had been disfigured during the time of Ahaz his father when he deposed the temple and the priests who performed their duties in it. And Scripture testifies that he also celebrated the Passover feast, for "from the days of Solomon son of David king of Israel there has not been such a feast in Jerusalem."[7] And "he cut down the groves and completely dismantled the high places and altars,"[8] and in the face of every form of idolatry that was prevalent in former times throughout the whole of Judea, "he did what was good and true before the Lord his God. And in every task with which he began in the word in the Lord's house and in the law and in the ordinances, he sought out his God with his whole soul and acted and succeeded."[9] And there are countless other passages that

---

[31]Heb 12:22. [32]Is 34:8-9. [33]Heb 12:22. [34]2 Tim 4:8 RSV. **Chapter Thirty-Six** [1]Cf. 2 Kings 18–20. [2]Cf. 2 Chron 29–32. [3]Cf. 2 Kings 18:9. [4]2 Kings 18:13. [5]2 Chron 29:2. [6]2 Chron 29:3. [7]2 Chron 30:26. [8]2 Chron 31:1. [9]2 Chron 31:20-21.

speak of these things, for example, when the Scriptures continue on and testify concerning him: "And after these matters and this faithful dealing, Sennacherib, king of the Assyrians, came into Judea and encamped against the walled cities and said that he would take possession of them."[10]

Then the Scripture teaches that Hezekiah trusted in God so that he in fact had no concern for the security of these places. For this reason, he strategically "sealed up the springs outside the city, so that" the enemy "could not find them"[11] and interrupt the "water" supply in that place. He fortified "the wall"[12] around Jerusalem, and outside this he made "another external wall," and he took precautions to fashion "weapons" and every instrument of warfare. Then, after taking such precautions, he called together a great crowd, and he addressed them with words of conviction and told them that no one should fear the enemy. Then he said: "With us there are more than with [232] them."[13] "For," he says, "with Assyria there are physical armaments, but with us is the Lord, our God, to save us and to fight our war for us."[14] And the text continues on to say: "And the people took heart at the words of Hezekiah, king of Judah. And after this, Sennacherib, king of the Assyrians, sent his servants from Lachish to Jerusalem to speak to Hezekiah, king of Judah, and to all the people in Jerusalem,"[15] and the rest. Therefore, along with Hezekiah's other accomplishments, God exhibited an indication of the exercise of virtue and great reverence in him through his opposition to the enemy, for on the one hand he demonstrated himself to be militarily prepared against the enemy, but on the other hand he had everything dedicated to God. And he commended religious instruction to the multitudes as well. But such was not Ahaz his father, who at one time enslaved himself to Babylon and all the people with him, and at another time he was conquered by the Syrians who lived in Damascus. Therefore, God provided a demonstration of virtue in the person of Hezekiah by allowing the Assyrians to approach Jerusalem. One should note that earlier "in the vision concerning the ravine of Zion,"[16] the prophet makes mention of the men who are named among them, I am speaking about *Eliakim* and *Shebna*. For there the text reads: "Go into the priestly chamber, to *Shebna* the treasurer," and the rest, [17] "and I will call my servant *Eliakim* the son of Hilkiah."[18]

And it was a necessary observation for us to interpret the words that were borne in that prophecy in reference to the story laid out above. And the text says that this *Shebna* and the children of the Hebrews came of their own volition to Assyria, surrendering to their king at last along with the others because of their fear of him. And it is because of this that the things which were prophesied above concerning him have been said.

[36:4-5] And the text reports the extent to which the adversary was filled with arrogance and madness when he said: *Thus says the great king, the king of the Assyrians*. For just as there was a certain opposing power in the prophetic word which said: *Thus says the Lord*, so even this one cries: *Thus says the great king, the king of the Assyrians*.

At that time, the adversaries did not fail to understand that Hezekiah and those with him prevailed through prayers and words of godliness, and the commander of Assyria reproached him precisely for these things, as he said while Hezekiah was present: *In whom are you trusting? Does marshaling take place through counsel and by words of the lips?* Then he was called for the engagement of the weapons of war, and it may be that Hezekiah

---

[10]2 Chron 32:1. [11]Cf. 2 Chron 32:3. [12]Cf. 2 Chron 32:5. [13]2 Chron 32:7. [14]2 Chron 32:8. [15]2 Chron 32:8-9. [16]Cf. Is 22:1. [17]Is 22:15. [18]Is 22:20.

and those with him said to him: "These call on chariots, and those on horses, but we will call on the name of the Lord, our God."[19] But according to Symmachus's version, instead of *In whom are you trusting?* [233] the text reads as follows: *I said: Why are you confident and courageous? In a word from my lips is council and authority for battle.*

[36:6-7] And because the enemy was a denouncer, he spoke falsely to Hezekiah when he said: *See, you are trusting in Egypt and in Pharaoh, the king of Egypt*, who was a cruel enemy of everyone who opposed him as well as those who put their trust in him, and he did not care to keep the treaties that he had made with those who sought his protection. For this reason, he is likened simultaneously to a *reed* and a *rod*, for he was both cracked in nature and gave splinters to those who pushed against him. And he advanced against the alliance of the Egyptians, remembering that it was nothing compared with the help that comes from God, by which Hezekiah and the whole company of men with him had prevailed even against them, since they did not know that the God of Israel was the God over all of them. And the victory over the error of idolaters that he thought was because of Hezekiah was in fact because of the God of the universe. Therefore, it was in vain that he said that he had put his trust in the God "who brought down his high places and altars,"[20] for he had been deceived and did not know that the things that had been demolished by Hezekiah were hostile to God.

[36:8] Then, next, concerning the Jewish cavalry, he said that even if he would *give* them *two thousand horses*, Hezekiah would not *be able* to set *riders* on them. And, indeed, this was a reasonable statement, for the God-fearing king lived in accordance with the principle that is written in the law of Moses concerning

the one who reigns in a godly fashion, "He shall not multiply cavalry for himself, and he shall not multiply wives for himself,"[21] and so there is a law against expanding the cavalry sector. And then Assyria says: you would not wish to supply *riders* for the *horses* that we would deliver to you, because it would be a boundless line of *horses* arranged for battle.

[36:9] *How then are you able to turn to the face of our governors?* But instead of *and how then are you able to turn to the face of the governors*, Symmachus writes: *And how might he set the face of one ruler of the least of the servants of my Lord?* And he says that because you do not have your own force of horsemen, *you trust in riders* and the *horses* of the *Egyptians*, although you know that the Egyptians themselves are our *house servants*. So then, at first there were many who put their trust in those who speak nothing true; for it was not that they placed their confidence in the *Egyptians* but that they were careless about keeping the divine law concerning the preparation of *horses*.

[36:10] Then, after what had been done against Samaria and Damascus and against the greatest of all the other nations had also been done in Assyria, he concluded that he was also thinking about Assyria when he said: *Is it without the Lord* that I captured all these things? For I did not ever conquer such as these, nor did the one who has authority over everything and who delivered them into my hands, so that by the command of God I should be a servant and come up on your land. *For*, he says, *the Lord said to me: Go up* [234] *onto this land and utterly destroy it.* And he says that it was a visible sign according to the command of God that Samaria was captured and all Israel led away captive. For "as I took" those who were your brothers, so it will not be any different when "I take"[22] you also; it will

---

[19]Ps 20:7. [20]Cf. 2 Kings 18:22. [21]Deut 17:16-17. [22]Cf. Is 10:10.

be again as God wills and with his approval. And the text does not state whether he said these things as though aiming to rule over the people that style themselves the people of God—I am speaking of Israel—or whether he in fact truly perceived that God had decreed that he should come up against the country of the Jews because of the transgressions that they had committed.

[36:11-20] For at first *Rabsaces said* these things, and then at the end of his speech used *promises* to urge the multitude that stood there along the *walls* and in the towers to deliver the city over to him, and after he had made these agreements, he cried aloud to everyone and attempted to reproach the godliness of Hezekiah before all the people and said: *Do not let Hezekiah deceive you when he says, "God will rescue us."* And above he said: *"Who removed his high places and his altars."*[23] For he was not ignorant that the multitude delighted in these things in the time before this during the reign of Ahaz. Therefore, because he was still well disposed toward these things, he reproached Hezekiah, accusing him of providing one of the greatest testimonies of godliness that exists. And it is good when your enemy accuses you of things like this, for someone who lives according to God's standards would be proud of such an accusation. Then he continued on to say: *Have the gods of the nations delivered each one his own country?* And he continues on: *Where is the god of Hamath and Arphad? And where is the god of the city of Epharouem?*[24] *Have they been able to deliver Samaria out of my hands?* In these statements he presents the reason why Samaria and Israel had been delivered over to him, and this was because they had turned to many gods in disobedience to the law of their ancestors. Then, inferring from the fact that *the gods of the nations* were incapable of

protecting them and that peoples who were related to them were destroyed, he says that the *God of Jerusalem* will also not be able to preserve them in the city, since he thought there was no difference between the God who was revered in Jerusalem and the idols that were erroneously believed to be gods among the other nations.

[36:21] In the face of such boasting and blasphemy on the part of *Rabsaces*, those who listened answered nothing but kept silence in accordance with the royal decree, *because the king had ordered this.* In ordering the people not to answer such overly bold accusations, Hezekiah was an example of great sagacity and godliness. For there is nothing more to say when one utters such things against God, and he who is discreet does not converse with a blasphemous person, lest he be provoked and fall into further blasphemies. For this reason, we read elsewhere: "Do not stoke a sinner's coals." [25] It is not sanctioned to enter into discourse with people like this, and neither should we anticipate that anything will help those whose souls are plagued with an incurable disease. But rather we are merely to safeguard our own position [235] and secure ourselves from all quarters with the weapon of silence, since the true words do not reside in us anyway, and we await the judgment that will come from God against the blasphemers. The leaders from among the multitude obeyed what the king wisely commanded, and this is precisely what we must do in times of persecution or in public debates with godless and blasphemous people.

[36:22] We will say nothing of the obvious interpretation that such a story so often requires so that those who had heard the blasphemies against God *ripped* their *tunics asunder,* seeing that King Hezekiah himself

---

[23]Is 36:7. [24]Eusebius preserves an alternate spelling for this city name. [25]Sir 8:10.

had also heard the profane sayings. After they had communicated the report that God had been blasphemed because of them, they understood that they themselves were responsible. For it was not permitted for the enemy to enter into their gates of the city of God and do such rebellious things as these. And even if they themselves were not responsible for these things, yet they were anxious because they certainly did not want to suffer the same fate that Samaria and its people suffered because of their own wickedness.

[37:1-3] Instead of donning his royal raiment, *Hezekiah* put on *sackcloth* as a sign of his misery and distress, and with this appearance he went out through the middle of the city from the royal palaces to the temple of God. And because he showed himself to be humble before God with this appearance, he was found to be worthy of compassion and mercy. And he sent others of the priests of God wearing *sackcloth* instead of their priestly robes and commanded them to say to the prophet Isaiah: *This is what Hezekiah says*, not adding "the king." For time did not leave it to him to say this, since he had been humbled because of the present misfortune. Then, because of the present circumstances, he says that it is a *day of rebuke* and a day to be convicted of our sins, but it is also a *day of wrath*, and those who have committed crimes worthy of *wrath* will be put to shame. And now, we have been taught that the situation is analogous to a *woman in travail*, who is about to give birth and is exhausted from persevering through the *pangs*. For we are not those who say: "From fear of you, Lord, we conceived and *travailed* and gave birth to the breath of your salvation."[1] It was because of this that we sent the man of God through you, so that your God who helps would be present in time because of those who supplicate for you. And we do not dare to

name this God as our own, but we understand that he is precisely your Lord and God. Therefore, we beseech this very one neither to look on our trespasses nor to remember our sins but to act against the godless voices of the enemy who speak in such insolence and pride and who do what they please whether allowed or deserving prosecution.

[37:4-7] And you indeed, O prophet of God, you reminded us that there was a multitude of our people, captured and already in Assyria, who prayed [236] to God on behalf of those of us who were left behind that their courage might not fail. For we believe and are convinced that great things will work together for our salvation because of your petitions on our behalf. The king ordered them to say these things to the prophet.

And as soon as they appeared, Isaiah anticipated their words and commanded them to announce the prophecy that he had delivered, and he said that he would *put a spirit in him*, and after he is deceived by this *spirit*, he will come back to his own land, and there a sword will end his life. And the Word makes this first prophecy about the above story.

[37:8-13] And as we read above, the prophet foretold that after he caused a great deal of trouble, *Rabsaces* would withdraw from the siege completely unsuccessful. And then he hurried to meet with the king of Assyria, and God drove him out of his mind. And after *Lachish*, the king of Assyria *besieged* another city of the Jews, *Libnah*, and while the foreboding announcement according to the word of God agitated him, he pressed on to the Ethiopians. Not overlooking the threat of the Jews, *he sent messengers* and ordered that a document be read before Hezekiah, a document that contained everything that he had said earlier, and they delivered this letter. Therefore, with

---

Chapter Thirty-Seven [1]Is 26:18.

such great deeds and with these words and promises, he raised himself up and was not ignorant of his deceit. And again that profane person was boasting and let loose slanderous utterances against God, and he recounted how the domestic gods of the nations that had come under his hand had never come to their aid. And the prophet made clear this boasting of Assyria through what he said above, and calling aloud future events "before they happened"[2] he said: "Woe to the Assyrians! The rod of my wrath and anger is in their hands" and the rest. "But he himself did not plan thus, nor has he reasoned thus in his soul."[3] But he said: "As I did to Samaria and to the works of her hands, thus will I do also to Jerusalem and to its idols."[4] And he added further warnings to these here. And although these things were spoken a long time ago, they were only now fulfilled in the present times.

[37:14-20] And, indeed, just has Hezekiah had hurried earlier, so now he ran "into the house of God"[5] and brought the letter before God alone. And the text says that he offered up a petition through prayer while he was with *God alone* and there was no one else around. And since he *alone* created the *heavens and earth* and the entire universe, there is no one who shares in this divine power with him; he is the living God, the God over the inanimate things and the dead. He *alone* possesses life without beginning and unbegotten life; he is to be credited as the cause of the life of all who share in life. And now, he had confidence that God is alive and is present in every kingdom in the whole world, and he listens to the voice of those who are worthy and who declare that he is *God alone*, for he protects those who place their trust in him. [237] And now the king addressed the many great attributes of God through the prayer of self-surrender, although he did not vow when he at first went up "into

the house of God"[6] and had "sackcloth" as a covering because of his extreme piety. And then he dared to raise up his mouth against God. For this reason, he sent the prophet and asked him to offer petitions to God on their behalf. And now, he in turn prayed to God, confidently trusting in the prophet's sacred pronouncements and predictions against the enemy as recorded in the passage at hand, and he sent up the pious prayer above that contained such rich theology.

[37:21] In times then far distant, the prophets of God foretold events that were yet to happen, but at that time they had no proof for the populace that they were indeed prophets. For although the prophets were not unaware of the accomplishment of what they said, they themselves preceded the fulfillments. And the people assumed that the test of the prophet's truthfulness was the immediate outcome of the event, and they believed in the predictions about these future events. Therefore, Samuel prophesied to Saul "concerning the donkeys,"[7] or another time when the king was sick[8] or again when he foretold the death of the king of Israel.[9] This was so that the people would not be drawn away into longing and lusting for foreknowledge and idolatrous divinations and oracles. For it was not through their lifeless images but through the prophets of God that the people had significant knowledge of future events, and not a word came from an outside source. For then also, in the passage at hand we read that the God-loving King Hezekiah "went up into the house of God"[10] and offered up the petition recorded above, and God answered him by sending his prophet Isaiah to him. And he delivered this second response to him to let him know that he had heard the words of his prayer.

[37:22] So then, he delivered such a word to Assyria because they were boasting and

---

[2]Is 10:5. [3]Is 10:7. [4]Is 10:11. [5]Is 37:1. [6]Cf. Is 37:1. [7]1 Sam 9:20. [8]2 Kings 20:1-11. [9]2 Kings 1:2-17. [10]Is 37:1.

threatening the people of that place. You threatened me like a tyrant and said that you would bring such things about, because you thought that threats would be the way to make me afraid. But the city of God is incorruptible and for this reason is compared with a *virgin*. The people in her are called *daughter of Zion* and *daughter of Jerusalem*, and she is compared with a *virgin* because of the fact that she has kept herself pure from all idolatry. Confident in her purity and that God would come to her aid, *she distained and mocked* your arrogant arguments and threats as entirely invalid. For this reason, the text reads according to Symmachus: *Daughter of Zion set you at naught and disdained you, daughter of Jerusalem has shaken her head behind your back.* For she gave you no answer when you called out in a blasphemous voice, but she went around behind you and there the aforementioned *daughter of Jerusalem* and *virgin daughter of Zion has shaken her head at you*. And thus she [238] no longer kept silence when she did this but then offered a reply. Therefore the text says that *she has shaken her head at you*.

[37:23-29] And the reply was as follows: *Whom have you reviled and provoked* (the other Greek translations render this word *blasphemed* instead)? *Or against whom have you raised your voice?* You neither looked to heaven nor have been mindful of the highest God, nor have you considered that it was the *Holy One of Israel* whom *you have reviled*, ridiculing and scoffing at him as though he were one of the many gods who are under your hand. For you believed in your heart that in your own power and *with the multitude of your chariots*, you would mount up *to the heights of the mountains and to the utmost limits of Lebanon*, and there you would *cut down* the beauty of the many *cedar* and *cypress* trees. And in this verse he is speaking about the elevated and flourishing kingdoms among the other nations. For the great multitude of Lebanon lives among the tallest *cedar* and *cypress* trees—or *juniper* trees according to Symmachus, or *silver fir* trees according to Aquila—and from these images we should understand that these nations are flourishing. But instead of *into the height of its forest region*, Symmachus translated this phrase: *Into the height of its peak in the forest of Carmel*. And in speaking of a *forest* the word is alluding to the fruitless wood of those nations that do not know God, and the king of Assyria thought in his heart that he would place these nations under his hand when he said: *I have gone up to the height of the mountains and to the utmost limits of Lebanon, and I cut down the height of its cedar and the beauty of its cypress, and I entered into the height of its forest region.*

And still he spoke boldly when he said: *And I built a bridge and desolated the waters and wherever waters gathered*, or according to Symmachus: *I dug and I drank water and laid waste, stopping up all rivers with my footprint.* You see how also in these things the Word calls to mind the *waters* and *rivers* that were obliterated by Assyria, and I think that these things signify the multitudes among the nations and their boasts concerning their gods, whom they thought supported their lives. And, indeed, he was proud of the fact that his very *footprint* had created a desert. He boasts in nothing positive but rather in turning regions into desert by setting foot on them, and he boasts in the destruction of what the text refers to as the *beauties of Lebanon*.

And you did think these things, reasoning in your own mind that you brought such things about *with the multitude of* your *chariots*, but I say to you: "Do not deceive yourself!" For it was not in your own strength that you overcame all of these nations, but it was I who ordained these things against them, in case you did not know or in case you have not *heard* my counsel from ancient times. For from of old and *from ancient days*, I myself have determined that these things should be accomplished through you against the godless and wicked nations.

And now I *exhibited* my counsel through action, raising you up for the ruin of those who were worthy of vengeance. And I used you *to make the nations desolate* and to drive away those **[239]** who *live in strong cities*, the cities that I formerly defended and preserved.

And when they were acting profanely, not knowing their own Savior, *I weakened* my own *hands* and delivered myself to them for punishment. And immediately they became deserts, since they were deprived of my oversight. For this reason at once *they have withered, and they have become like dry grass on housetops and like wild grass*. Therefore, this was the cause of their destruction: they did not bear any good fruit of godliness. This is why they are compared with neither a grapevine nor an olive tree nor any of the fruitful garden plants but with *dry grass* and *wild grass*, and then they were most deservedly delivered over to your hand. But you did not understand any of these things, O ruler of the Assyrians, but reasoning in a godless and wicked way you thought that you would take the city dedicated to my God just as you had taken those that did not know God. But I know your ideas *and the going out and coming in* of your reasonings, and thus I say to you that your *wrath* has not escaped my notice. And this wrath has been used against those who style themselves my people, *and your bitterness has come up to me*, or according to Symmachus, *your boastfulness has come up to my ear*. Therefore, because such things have been dared against him, then listen to the rest of what was said next: *I will put a muzzle* on your *mouth*, so that even your *nose* will be constrained, and you will suffocate and no longer be able to say such things. But according to Symmachus, the text reads: *And I will put a ring in your nostril and a bit on your lip*, in order that you might not go wherever you please but trail along behind even when you do not wish. For you will be *turned back* by an entreaty *in the way*, the way down which you had already journeyed.

[37:30-32] Therefore, these things were spoken as though to the ruler of Assyria, and even though he was not present in body it was nonetheless to be announced to everyone. And since the prayers which you offered, Hezekiah, and which were answered were necessary, take then this word for yourself. You heard what was spoken concerning the ruler of Assyria, but if you are nevertheless in need of a *sign* for the confirmation of my words, know that you are to use as food the plants that spring up of themselves during the current *year*, but you shall not be able to approach the growing fields as usual because of the advance of the enemies. For this reason *this year eat what you have sown*. But instead of *what you have sown*, all the other Greek translations render this phrase *of themselves*. And, again, in the coming *year, eat the plants that have been left from the year before*. But instead of *in the second year what is left*, Aquila renders this phrase: *And in the second year that which is wild grown*, and Symmachus: *And in the second year from trees*, and Theodotion: *And in the second year that which is wild grown*. And, again, these two years will be difficult because they will not be able to approach the growing fields. But *in the third year* you will experience complete prosperity. And, therefore, *sow, reap, and plant vineyards, and eat their fruit*, knowing well that you will bring *those who remain in Judea* after the captivity of the **[240]** multitudes in Samaria to a peaceful end, if in accordance with my will they shoot out steady *roots* of godliness in their souls and if they look up to me and yield the holy fruit of my field. Therefore, in this way *they who have been left in Jerusalem shall be preserved*, if they are fruitful for me and "bear worthy fruit."[11] For because the Lord is "jealous"[12] for his city that is dedicated to him and

---

[11]Lk 3:8. [12]Zech 1:14; 8:2.

---

for his people who style themselves his people, all these things will be done.

[37:33-35] And neither the king of Assyria nor anyone else will advance against the city, nor will anyone be capable of mounting an attack against it. For I myself will *shield* my *city*, and *I will save her* as well as the inhabitants. For it is like me to do this because I am God. Therefore, I will do these things *for my own sake*, not because those whom I aided were worthy. And the men of the city need to respect the fact that it was clearly God who guarded the city *for the sake of my servant David*, or, according to the other Greek translations, *my slave*. I will keep the city for the sake of the founder of the city and the former king of those who lived there, so that others will learn how worthy of honor it is before me to be a God-loving man, and so that they will be zealous admirers and imitators of his godliness.

[37:36-38] And so, the words of God were reported through the prophet Isaiah in this manner to King Hezekiah. Not long after these words, in fact immediately after the prophecy, a certain fearful and divine deed followed: countless masses of men were found *dead*. They were cast down not by a human means but by the hand of one *angel*. For it was to serve the judgment of God that such a great number of the enemy were killed, and the king of the enemy received a severe trial, because he had spoken profanely against God. And, therefore, because of this, although such a great number were destroyed, the king did not perish with them, so that his godless tongue would be bridled when he witnessed what was done. For this reason, then, the text records that God said: "So I will put a muzzle on your nose and a bit on your lips,"[13] so that he would never again dare to speak such things. And

although the reason stated above did not benefit the multitude at all, it was the same with Pharaoh, who was kept alive to watch the rest of the Egyptians receive retribution. Even while he was in his own territory, he watched his own servants slay themselves.

[38:1-3] For it was God who said: "I will kill, and I will make alive; I will strike, and I will heal,"[1] and he struck the enemies with a righteous judgment through one *angel*, and he healed [241] and restored to life the God-loving king, "rescuing him from death."[2] This verse in fact fits in very well with what we then read: *At that time Hezekiah became sick to the point of death*, or according to Aquila: *To the point of dying*, or according to the other Greek translations: *Sick to death*. For *at that time*, when the Assyrians suffered the aforementioned things, the time of *death* came near to Hezekiah. And because God willed to save him publicly, the text does not fail to mention the end of his sickness. Therefore, because he pleaded with him for salvation, the end of the ailment was plainly stated for him through the prophet, so that he would *pray* and after praying he might receive an addition to his life past the time of his appointed death. And so the Word teaches us that the time of death that has been appointed for everyone is not something that determines the allotted human life, nor is it something that cannot be turned back. But God holds power over all things, and he is the cause of life and death, and therefore he knows that the life of everyone alive will expire at such and such a time, lasting until such and such a year and coming to such and such an end. And what happened among us is possible for him alone, for he alone can summon us from "the gates of death."[3] And now, indeed, Hezekiah was preserved from a deadly ailment, and an addition of life was given to him of a whole *fifteen years*. And the divine Scriptures

---

[13]Is 37:29. **Chapter Thirty-Eight** [1]Deut 32:39. [2]Cf. Is 33:19. [3]Cf. Ps 9:13.

tells us that others after they had died came to life again. So all those words concerning Hezekiah's allotted years have been recorded in order to demonstrate that God has power over fate and all being and nature and everything.

When Hezekiah saw that his body was clean, he quickly went to the temple of God, and there he called on his God who had also been the Savior of the people and of the city. And after he had done this, the sickness departed from his presence, and from the very bedding he sent up the prayer to the God who is present everywhere and who listens and acts on the prayer of the righteous. Then it was only after he had remembered that he had lived pleasingly before him and with great courage that he no longer imposed a petition of death and no longer demanded his life. Knowing that God arbitrates all reasoning according to his own thoughts, he committed his prayer to God and added also a *great weeping*, on which the worthy mind will focus attention. For it was necessary to record the good hope after death that the God-fearing man declared, especially since he had called on God in good conscience as a witness to the fact that he had lived pleasingly before him *with truth and with a true heart.*

[38:4-8] Therefore, continuing on, the text teaches us the cause of the *weeping*, and no sooner had the king prayed than the prophet was sent a second time from God and said: *Thus says the Lord,*[4] *the God of your father David.* And God called David his *father*, thus affording the very highest witness [242] of his worthiness, and he was compared with his God-loving father by virtue of the likeness of his actions. For this reason also in the histories it is recorded that "he did right according to all David had done."[5] Therefore, God said through the prophet: *I have heard your prayer*

and have seen your tears. Since the *prayer* was not comprised of "many words"[6] but rather was worthy of the hearing of God, and since the affair about the *tears* came at a fair and necessary moment, he drew the watching eyes of God to him and moved to pity God's love of humankind. For this reason also he promises to him and in fact delivers an addition of life, because death has not been ordained indeterminately for people or by a causation that cannot be altered by prayer.

And God promised him not only additional time but also that it would go well for him during this time and that he would have a tranquil and peaceful life. And he will take it on himself to *rescue* him as well as the people together with him and *the city from the hand* of the enemies. And he gave him a *sign*, another wonder assuring him that the things that he had said would happen. Therefore he said: *This is the sign to you from the Lord, that God will do this thing: behold, I will turn the shadow of the steps on which the sun has gone down—the ten steps of the house of your father—I will turn back the sun those ten steps.* But according to Symmachus, the text reads: *Behold, I will run the shadow of the steps backwards ten degrees on which the sun has gone down on the sundial of Ahaz your father.* And how the *house* could be said to belong to the *father* of Hezekiah—I am speaking about that idolatrous man Ahaz— the house which still even now can be seen in Jerusalem around the area of the temple courts, which still even now they refer to as the house of Hezekiah, I cannot say. Therefore, we should note that in the translation of Symmachus, the place is not called the *house* of Ahaz but the *sundial of Ahaz.* And perhaps Ahaz had constructed the *degrees* on the face of the *sundial* in that place, the face of the sundial on which and customarily the hours of the day were indicated by the rays of the sun. But

---

[4]NETS translates τάδε λέγει κύριος as "This is what the Lord says," but the translator opts to translate this phrase "Thus says the Lord" in light of the fact that Eusebius understands the phrase to sound authoritative and definite.   [5]Cf. 2 Kings 18:3.   [6]Mt 6:7.

according to Aquila, the text reads: *On the degrees of Ahaz*, and according to Theodotion: *On the steps of Ahaz*, and thus according to none of the translations is the place claimed to be the *house of Ahaz* but either a *sundial* or a *degree*.[7] Perhaps Ahaz used this courtyard as an entrance, and there he advanced on foot following the rotation of the sun in the sky as, incredibly, it returned from the west to the east and ran a second time, the hours elapsing in reverse. And, indeed, the *sign* was marvelous, and Hezekiah's life *ran back again* a second time from the west where the sun sets.

[**38:9**] And the time of that day doubled and recovered the length of hours. And after the wonder that God had promised, the king expressed his gratitude [**243**] and composed this word. Therefore, the text reads according to Aquila: *The writing of Hezekiah, king of Judah, when he had been unwell. And he lived after his sickness*, and according to Theodotion: *The writing of Hezekiah, king of Judah*. And in none of the other translations is it called a *prayer*.

[**38:10-11**] Therefore, coming to the word of gratitude, the *writing* that we have before us says: *I said: At the height of my days, I will come to the gates of Hades*, or, *I said: In the fullness of my days*, according to Aquila, or, *I said: When I was unwell*, according to Theodotion, and according to Symmachus: *I said: When my days were put to silence*. For seeing myself "in the gates of death,"[8] at that moment I came near to despairing and giving up any hope for my life in this world. For this reason *I said: I shall leave behind my remaining years*. But, *I said*, also to myself: being deprived of life, *I shall certainly not see the salvation of God in the land of the living*. But according to Symmachus, the text reads: *I shall not see the Lord in the land of the living*. And while I reflected on

these things, I said to myself: may I never be found unworthy of life with God after death and of the portion of the *living* who abide with him and thereafter *the salvation of God*. For he was, of course, familiar with the verse in the Psalms: "Return, O my soul, to your rest, because the Lord acted as your benefactor,"[9] "I will be well pleasing to the Lord in the country of the *living*,"[10] and once again: "I will be well pleasing to the Lord in the light of the *living*."[11] Therefore, since he had seen another "country of the *living*" than this present life, and since he had seen another "rest of the soul"[12] which is in the presence of God, understanding the "light" not to be that of the sun but the "light of the *living* before God,"[13] he then took thought so that he might never be deprived of these or fall away from *the salvation of God*, although Christ had been his. In the same way, after he stands in the assembly after the departure from this life, he will indeed remember the God of his righteousness. And in *weeping*, he pleads not to fall away "from the country of the *living*."[14] And he was greatly distressed, lest after death *he not see a man* of God and lest he not rest with the blessed and God-loving souls.

[**38:12-13**] And still, in addition to the things that have been said above, it grieved Hezekiah that there was no one from his offspring to take his place in the succession, for he had no child, at least at the time when he said these things. Therefore, he was then about to die childless and leave behind no one to take his place in the succession, the succession from which *salvation* among people had been awaited. He was thus cut off, separated from the generation of Christ and from the "seed of David,"[15] and the text says that he then said to himself: *My spirit has gone out and departed from me like one who pitches a tent* and then

---

[7]It would seem that Eusebius conceives here of an alternative instrument which measures the angle of the sun to keep time. [8]Cf. Ps 9:13. [9]Ps 116:7. [10]Ps 116:9. [11]Ps 56:13. [12]Cf. Mt 11:29. [13]Cf. Ps 56:13. [14]Cf. Ps 116:9. [15]Rom 1:3.

takes down the tent. And he is speaking about the body when he says *tent,* as also the divine apostle called his body a "tent" **[244]** when he said: "For while we are still in this *tent,* we sigh with anxiety."[16] And in the deliverance from the *tent* he is speaking about the putting aside of the body, for the *spirit takes down* the tent and leaves the body behind. But also *as a web of a weaver,* after *severing* the woven robe—the things of my life and of every life—he pushed away the *severed* web in the end. And therefore, each one of the saints is *weaving* a robe and adorns his soul through his deeds. It is for this reason that he said he was *as a web of a weaver,* and then he added *who approaches to cut it off* because of the death that drew near to him. Then he says: *I was given over as to a* man-eating *lion,* and indeed, so long as the ailment had been placed on him, this lion *broke all my bones all night and day long* and almost swallowed me whole. And, therefore, in all this I did not perish, nor did I withdraw from my God, but I was restored in faith and good hope, in weeping and wailing, and I *delivered* myself over to prayer.

[38:14-15] Then *like a swallow I cried out* in lamentation, and *like a dove I muttered* in brokenness. And while praying I said over and over, as I lay in surrender before God, *my eyes have failed from looking to the height of heaven, toward the Lord.* And the one who seemed not to care, *he rescued me and took away the pain of my soul.* In a single night he proved the very word that he promised to his saints when he said: "While you are still speaking, I will say, 'Here I am.'"[17]

[38:16-18] And, therefore, "he rescued my soul from death."[18] *For I was told concerning this,* and I beseeched you concerning this through prayer. For it was destined that my soul would not be swallowed by death, but you

heard and *revived me, O Lord, and I, comforted, came to life!* But according to Symmachus, the text reads: *You made me to flourish again, and you enlivened me,* and you changed my *bitterness into peace,* and *you have chosen my soul—* you snatched it from them, "from the gates of death"[19]—*so that my soul may not perish* in destruction. And you did not do this because I was worthy of these things. For I myself was full of many sins, but in your mercy and in your love of humanity you performed these things. Therefore, *you have cast all my sins behind me* and far away. And you deemed me worthy of these things, "rescuing my soul from death"[20] *so that it may not perish* and be deprived "of the country of the living in your presence,"[21] being pulled down to the depths of Hades and being laid down together with the souls of the ungodly.

For those who are in Hades will not praise you, nor will those who are in Hades hope for your mercy. For this is the place of the ungodly. Therefore, my soul **[245]** was set free from it, and rejoicing, I gave thanks to God. "And the country of the living" is "in the presence of God," and he welcomes those who *praise* him. And, then, I believe that in the end you will give your grace to me.

[38:19-20] And even if the succession "from my kindred"[22] had at first been abandoned, I will now be of good courage and believe in your mercy, *because from today I will produce children, who will declare your righteousness,* and for this reason *I will not cease praising you all the days of my life.* And I will do this *before the house of God,* attending you through everything and not allowing anyone to separate me from your holiness. Indeed, "the writing of Hezekiah"[23] contained these things, and after seven years passed, a son named Manasseh was born to him. And this was clearly during the "fifteen years which were added"[24] to his life

---

[16]2 Cor 5:4. [17]Is 58:9. [18]Cf. Ps 56:13. [19]Cf. Ps 9:13. [20]Cf. Ps 33:19. [21]Cf. Ps 116:9. [22]Is 38:12. [23]Is 38:9. [24]Is 38:5.

after the ailment. And after Hezekiah had died, his son succeeded him when he was eight years old, as the book of Kings records.[25]

[38:21-22] And after this, it seems that another incident happened to Hezekiah's body. And the *wound* was special, but because he asked for all things, even the smallest things, from God, the prophet counseled him to use a *cake of figs* and told him to *apply it to the wound*, so that no one would ever think that what was applied would be used for healing the body. And one should note among the details that the prophet exhorted him to do this. And the other Greek translations all call what was healed through the application of the *cake* a *wound*, but at first it was not called a *wound* but an ailment and a "sickness to the point of death."[26] And it was for this reason that tears and prayers for the visitation of God were undertaken. And there was a bodily healing for the special *wound*, which the prophet had prescribed. But the king did not want the *cake* to be a *sign* of healing for him, and so he said: *This* will be a *sign* of salvation for me: *I will go up to the house of God.* For it was enough for me to be able to go up and to worship my Savior and to be within *his house.* For this will be better to me than any other good, and the *wound* would make no difference, so long as I am not hindered from going up *to the house of God.*

[39:1-2] And searching out and examining these events in the light of the following passages, the teacher of the Jews said that Hezekiah would have remained sick had he not sung a song of thanks to God at the downfall of the Assyrians, as Moses had sung at the destruction of the Egyptians and Deborah at the destruction of Sisera and Hannah at the birth of Samuel—although Hezekiah did not compose the song when the sickness befell him. And Babylonia knew the severity of his

sickness and dispatched to him men who were not idle, but when that day had come to an end, the *sign* of the *sun* running backward made duplicate [246] hours. For this did not escape the notice of the Babylonians, since they were prodigious observers of the stars. And then they witnessed that the sun, which they considered to be a deity, was drawn back to where it had been by a superior power. Because this happened, they asked after its cause. And so, since they were so inquisitive, they learned that the God of the Hebrews is great and that he is the creator of the whole world. And after King Hezekiah's sickness, the king of Babylon wanted to affirm his friendship with Hezekiah, that God-loving man, because of the miracle that occurred after the wound had been plastered over and dressed. These things are recorded according to the Hebrew text.

And I see that all of this happened in one and the same year; I am speaking about the attack of Assyria and the plague against Judea and against the Assyrians through the angel of God, and the escape of Sennacherib and the insurrection of his servants, and the silent destruction of his son who would have been his successor. I suppose that all of this made Merodachbaladan think soberly about rushing in and ruling other races outside of the Babylonian and Chaldean empire. Probably because he knew how Hezekiah had been helped, he no longer greeted the God-loving king with hostility or adversity but rather as a friend, for he knew that the miracle of his recovery from his sickness had been from God. And because all of this happened and was accomplished during one and the same season, you will learn and understand that the attack of Assyria was in the "fourteenth year"[1] of the reign of Hezekiah. And "he reigned twenty-nine years"[2] and achieved all these things, and "fifteen" of these "years were added"[3] to him after the sickness. Therefore, he had been sick

---

[25]Cf. 2 Kings 21:1. [26]Cf. Is 38:1. **Chapter Thirty-Nine** [1]Cf. 2 Kings 18:13. [2]Cf. 2 Kings 18:2. [3]2 Kings 20:6.

in his fourteenth year, and all the other things had been accomplished during the time before the sickness. Then, therefore, as soon as the king of Babylon heard all these things, he made a gesture of friendship with Hezekiah and *sent him gifts and ambassadors and letters.*

Hezekiah *rejoiced* over these and over their presentation, being affected as a human would, and in an extraordinary flash of ambition, he gave the emissaries a tour of his riches and *the house of treasure,*[4] although Aquila and Symmachus render this phrase *the house of spices.* But he showed them *even the silver and the gold and the spices and the expensive perfume and all the storehouses of his vessels,* as Symmachus translates this passage.

[39:3-8] Then, because it had not been necessary for him to reveal his wealth to these foreign men, but he had rashly and thoughtlessly revealed it to them, the prophet understood what was going on and advised that the time would come when the Babylonians would *take everything* and carry it away into their land. And then he added, they will take some *from your sons* who have not yet been born but who are about to be, and they will castrate them and they will become *eunuchs,* and they will present them to their kings. When Hezekiah had heard this [247], he reverently and piously confessed that every *word* that God would say is *good,* even if it would seem to be distressing for those to whom it was addressed. And the things that had been threatened were not to take place during the time of his worthy life, but *peace and righteousness* would be *in his days,* or, according to the other Greek translations, *peace and truth.*

[40:1-2] And the Hebrew text again goes on to say that God did not approve of Hezekiah's attitude. For he certainly cared about his own

problems, but for the people he did absolutely nothing, and this appeared to be blameworthy to God. For this reason the prophet went on to say next: *Comfort, O comfort my people, says God.* For Hezekiah had spoken, thinking only of himself, and he did not even mention the people, but God was concerned to *comfort* his own *people,* and he encourages them to do precisely this.

We do not find the phrase *O priests, comfort the people* either in the Hebrew text or in the other Greek translations, and therefore this phrase is marked with obeli in the Septuagint.[1] And therefore, according to Symmachus, the text reads: *Console, O console my people, says your God. Encourage the heart of Jerusalem.* The other Greek translations are equivalent to this. And there are certain individuals whom the Word does find worthy to appoint *to comfort the people.* And when he says the *heart of Jerusalem,* one should know that he is talking about Jerusalem, just as any living being has a heart. For the Word depicts the city as alive and clearly rational when he says: *Speak to the heart of Jerusalem.* When he says to speak to Jerusalem, he is speaking about the people who dwell in the city, for we often speak of the city instead of the inhabitants, but here the Word even mentions the *people* when he says: *Comfort my people.* And then he specifically adds: *Speak to the heart of Jerusalem.* Therefore, one finds three groups to examine: there are those individuals who are appointed *to comfort, the people* who are *comforted* and *the heart of Jerusalem.* Indeed therefore those who *comfort* are perhaps those who have received the comforting Spirit—that is, the apostles and disciples of our Savior, and the evangelists and others such as these—to whom the Savior said: "And I will pray the Father, and he will give you another Counselor, to be with you for ever, even the Spirit of

---

[4]The LXX simply transliterates the Hebrew word, resulting in the Greek word νεχωθά. **Chapter Forty** [1]The obelus also appears in the Hexapla and in early Christian manuscripts as a text-critical marker. Again, see Jerome's discussion in *Adv. Rufin.,* 2.225, 27.

truth,"[2] and again: "But when the Counselor comes, the Holy Spirit, whom my Father will send in my name, he will teach you all things,"[3] and again: "But when the Counselor comes, whom I shall send to you from the Father, even the Spirit of truth, who proceeds from the Father, he will bear witness to me,"[4] and again: "It is to your advantage that I go away, for if I do not go away, the Counselor would not come to you."[5] Therefore all those who have received the comforting Spirit are appointed *to comfort* **[248]** *the people* of God but neither Israel nor Jacob nor Judah. And who were the people of God if not the nation of the Jews, as Zechariah the prophet teaches when he says: "Rejoice, and be glad, O daughter of Zion. For behold, I am coming and will tent in your midst, says the Lord. And many nations shall flee to the Lord for refuge on that day and shall become a people to him, and they will tent in your midst. And you shall recognize that the Lord Almighty has sent me to you."[6] And therefore it is clear that "many nations" will be called the *people* of God. And the Lord says these things after he had been sent by another Lord, and he foretells his coming into humanity. And just as *the people* have been declared to be the people of God, so also *the heart of Jerusalem* will be understood to be the innermost constituency of the *people*. For as the heart is sovereign over all in the body, so also in the body of the church the constituency that is sovereign over all can rightly be said to be the *heart*, and he will conclude that it is the constituency of those who are more intellectual and who are different in their thinking and reasoning. Therefore, perhaps this is why he said: *Speak to the heart of Jerusalem*. And thus one should understand the clear word which he said: *speak* to those who are intelligent and reason-

able among the people of God. Therefore, he commands *the priests to speak* to them and *to comfort* the rest of *the people*, for they need comfort and consolation.

Therefore, after the prophecy concluded the theme of the story of Hezekiah, the evangelical word begins a new section and addresses those who have received the comforting Spirit of Christ, crying out: *Comfort, O comfort my people, says God*. For he commands them *to comfort* everyone who is worthy to be called his people, "whom he has chosen out from all the nations."[7] Paul teaches us what also the apostles then did when he says: "Blessed be the God and Father of our Lord Jesus Christ, the Father of mercies and God of all comfort, who *comforts* us in all our affliction, so that we may be able *to comfort* those who are in any affliction, with the comfort with which we ourselves are *comforted* by God. For as we share abundantly in Christ's sufferings, so through Christ we share abundantly in comfort too. If we are afflicted, it is for your comfort and salvation; and if we are comforted, it is for your comfort, which you experience when you patiently endure the same sufferings that we suffer. Our hope for you is unshaken; for we know that as you share in our sufferings, you will also share in our comfort."[8] You see then how often he referred to the word of comfort in other passages, and as if obeying the prophetic exhortation, he cries out and says: "We beseech[9] you on behalf of Christ to be reconciled to God,"[10] and again: "And, a prisoner for Jesus Christ, I beseech you."[11] In the same way, the rest of the disciples of Christ were also comforters, comforting the people of God. And they were also *speaking to the heart of Jerusalem*. One may either understand this according to the deeper sense—I am speaking

---

[2]Jn 14:16-17a RSV. [3]Jn 14:26. [4]Jn 15:26. [5]Jn 16:7. [6]Zech 2:10-11. [7]Cf. Deut 14:2. [8]2 Cor 1:3-7 RSV. [9]The word translated "beseech" here is the same word in Greek that is elsewhere translated "to comfort" (παρακαλέω). Eusebius is thus gathering up the various passages where παρακαλέω appears in the Pauline epistles. [10]2 Cor 5:20. [11]Eph 4:1.

about the innermost constituency of the *people*—or according to the other sense, in which case we are to understand the more intellectual **[249]** of the inhabitants of Jerusalem. For the rest of the multitude are fleshly and represent the more dull parts of the body, but those who distinguish themselves by their intelligence and thought and understanding, they could perhaps be rightly interpreted to be the *heart of Jerusalem*. And it is to these individuals that he wants those who have received the spirit of comfort *to speak,* and he wants them also *to comfort* those who are the *heart of Jerusalem* by preaching the forgiveness of sins to them. We know this because of the prophecy adduced next and concerning the coming of Christ. Accordingly, he wants those who were indicated *to speak* in secret to the *heart of Jerusalem* and to persuade them *that her humiliation has ceased and her sin has been done away with.* For she endured a *double* punishment, even beyond what her sin deserved. And finally it happened that she was comforted and consoled because the appearance of the Savior shone freely on the life of all humanity. And you might say that the *double* punishment came on the *heart of Jerusalem*. According to history, when they had driven away evil from the multitude, those indicated, because they had been humiliated by other foreign nations, punished themselves, according to the deeper sense, because of the loss of the multitude, mourning and weeping for the fall and calamity of many. But Jerusalem was besieged a second time when the temple in the city was demolished to its foundations and endured a *double* retribution for the profane acts that had been dared in it.

[40:3] And nevertheless, the appearance of the Savior is next announced, and he provided a portion of this comfort to the intelligent, whom he called the *heart*. And he states what

that comfort is when he says next: *A voice of one crying out in the wilderness: "Prepare the way of the Lord; make straight the paths of our God."* And he adds on to this verse: *And all flesh shall see the salvation of God,* that is, the evangelical preaching. And this is the comfort: the prophecy that *the salvation of God* will be known among all. Indeed, Moses once led the people of the Jews through "the wilderness,"[12] but now the text draws our attention to another wilderness and to a certain man who *cried out* in it, or, according to Aquila: *A voice calling out in the wilderness.* And who was the one *crying out in the wilderness,* and what sort of wilderness was it, about which the text says: *Prepare the way of the Lord; make straight his paths?* And it seemed that those who listened to these things would live and await the accomplishment of the prophecy, and they would see the prophesied *salvation of God* through prayer. For this reason, when these things were about to happen, those who carefully examined the prophetic words awaited for those who had been sent by the chief priests and teachers of the people to inquire of John, to ask who he might be and "if he were not the Christ or Elijah or the prophet."[13] Indeed, he said that he was none of them, and so they then asked him and said: "Therefore tell us, 'Who are you? Give us an answer for those who sent us. What do you say about yourself?'"[14] This is the answer that he gave: "I am the voice of one crying in the wilderness, 'Prepare the way of the Lord,' as **[250]** the prophet Isaiah said."[15] For it was enough for them to hear him say, "I am the voice of one crying in the wilderness,"[16] as though they knew the prophecy perfectly well and were awaiting its accomplishment. For he was teaching that the prophecy had been fulfilled in himself, and indeed he presents himself to be the one *crying* in the *wilderness* and shows the desert to be none other than the one in which Moses spent his life. And he

---

12Ps 136:16. 13Jn 1:20. 14Jn 1:22. 15Jn 1:23. 16Jn 1:23.

signals that *the salvation of God* is now at "the very gates,"[17] and according to the prophecy it is about to be made known to all flesh. As the prophecy says: *A voice of one crying out in the wilderness: "Prepare the way of the Lord,"* that is, the evangelical preaching, or this new comfort, this *salvation of God* which seeks to be known among all.

He states clearly that the prophesied events will not take place in Jerusalem but in the *desert*; I am speaking about the verse: the *glory of the Lord shall appear* and *the salvation of God* will be known *to all flesh*. And these things were fulfilled in word and deed when John the Baptist preached the *saving* theophany[18] *in the wilderness* of the Jordan, where the *salvation of God appeared*. Christ himself and his glory were made known to all; when he was being baptized "the heavens were opened"[19] and "the Holy Spirit descended in the form of a dove," and "it remained on him."[20] And a fatherly "voice" sounded, witnessing to the Son: "This is my beloved Son; listen to him."[21] All these signs of the *saving glory* happened in the *desert* of the Jordan. And the things that were attested by John the Baptist refer to the church of the Gentiles, a place that according to the deeper sense had formerly been a *desert* of God, and yet still today the same *voice cries out*, proclaiming *the salvation of God* and preparing those present who will listen for the reception of the *glory* of the Word of God that "was in the beginning with God."[22] The text does not call him *one crying out in the wilderness* as a comparison or as an analogy, but for a time the *voice crying out* prepared the souls of people for the coming *appearing* of the final word. And so, now it is necessary *to prepare the way of the Lord* and *to make straight the paths of our God*. But according to Symmachus, the *voice in the wilderness* said: *Get the way of the Lord ready, level the inaccessible way of our God.*

For he said these things when the eternal God was coming to reside in the *wilderness* and in the *inaccessible way*. And a knowledge of God was about to come to all the righteous of God and to the prophetic men in all the desolate and out-of-the-way nations. For this reason, the *voice* exhorts them *to get the way ready* for the Word of God and to make the *inaccessible* and rough places *level*, in order that *our God* might set foot here and come to stay. Note the addition of the word *our*, for the text reads *make straight the paths of our God*. As though addressing others, *the one crying out in the wilderness* says [251] these things. For those present at the Jordon baptism were a countless multitude, and there were even those who were from foreign nations, and the evangelical word in the church addresses these things to the nations throughout the whole world.

[40:4-5] Then he rouses the souls that have been humiliated in the depths of evil when he continues on to say: *Every ravine shall be filled up*. And he teaches that the arrogant and those who raise themselves up against the knowledge of God will have the opposite done to them when he says: *And every mountain and hill shall be made low*. And he says that *even the crooked ways shall be straight*, and he commands the *rough* soul to be *level*, so that it be worthy for God to set his foot on it. He exhorts that all these things be done because of the reason that he next sets forth and presents when he says: *Then the glory of the Lord shall appear*, or according to the other Greek translations: *Then it shall be revealed*. And to whom *it shall be revealed* he indicates clearly when he adds: *And all flesh shall see the salvation of God*. And they were *flesh*, as all people are in and of themselves only "carnal"[23] and not at all "partakers of the Holy Spirit,"[24] whom Moses also presents when he recorded that God said:

---

[17]Mt 24:33. [18]The Greek word Eusebius here uses is θεοφάνεια, an important word in Eusebius's theological vocabulary. [19]Mt 3:16. [20]Jn 1:32. [21]Mt 17:5; 3:17. [22]Jn 1:1. [23]Rom 7:14. [24]Heb 6:4.

"My Spirit shall not abide in these humans, because they are flesh."[25] And this was because *all flesh* was about to make known *the salvation of God*. And through the Old Testament preaching *the voice in the wilderness cried out* and delivered instruction. "For the one who promised never lies."[26]

[40:6-8] The disobedience and faithlessness of the Jewish people certainly did not escape the notice of the prophetic Spirit. Therefore, the same voice *cried out* a second proclamation and said: *All flesh is grass; all the glory of man is like the flower of grass.* And therefore this is the nature of *all flesh* and of the one who bears "the image of the man of dust,"[27] but I am speaking about those who love the body and "live according to the flesh."[28] Therefore, as the *grass* of the earth and the seasonable *flowers* blossom and bloom for a while, not long afterward they wither away because of the fluctuation and constant change in nature, precisely as the Scripture teaches when it says: *The grass has withered, and the flower has fallen.* And here the prophecy teaches these things in a generic fashion, but the Hebrew text definitely makes mention of the Jewish people when it continues on to say: *Truly, the people are grass. The grass has withered, the flower has fallen.* But instead of *but the word of our God remains forever,* Symmachus says: *But the word*[29] *of our God will stand forever.* "The voice in the wilderness"[30] foretold this concerning the Word of God. I am speaking about the voice of John, who taught that Christ alone would *stand forever.* And he will keep those who have stood with him and held steadfast to him, those who have received *salvation* from him.

[40:9] After what he had said concerning "the voice crying out in the wilderness,"[31] at the right time he speaks of the evangelists in the deeper sense of the aforesaid things [252], and he announces the good news of the coming of God among people. For in the prophecy, the part about John the Baptist was followed by the word concerning the evangelists of the Savior, and this is the explanation of his prophecy. But according to the other Greek translations, instead of *the one* [masculine] *who brings good news,* the text read: *the one* [feminine] *who brings good news.* For this reason Symmachus says: *Go up on a high mountain, you* [feminine] *who bring good news to Zion, and lift up your voice high, you* [feminine] *who bring good news to Jerusalem, lift it up; do not fear.* And through these things we see that the Word considers Zion and Jerusalem to be animate and living. And therefore he urges her to *go up on a high mountain* and to *lift up* her *voice and bring good news* of the coming of God. And therefore who is this one who went up *on a high mountain* if not *Zion* herself? For this *mountain* was Zion, as the Scripture makes clear when it says: "This Mount Zion, whereon you encamped."[32] And the apostle says: "You have come to Mount Zion,"[33] which is perhaps the place called the "heart of Jerusalem"[34] in the verse above. No one would imagine that he is not speaking about the apostolic band which was chosen from out of the people who were once of the circumcision, would he? For this is *Zion,* and *Jerusalem* has been recognized to be "the salvation of God."[35] For what was elevated he compares with the mountain of God and his only-begotten Word, and he commands to go up *to the mountain* and *to proclaim* the saving word. And so the evangelical band and the sanctified and elevated souls who are approved in spirit are called *Zion* and *Jerusalem,* and they are ordered to go up *on the high* divine *mountain* of

---

[25]Gen 6:3. [26]Tit 1:2. [27]1 Cor 15:49. [28]Rom 8:12. [29]Whereas in the line above the English word translated "word" was represented by the Greek word ῥῆμα, the word translated "word" here is from the Greek word λόγος. [30]Is 40:3. [31]Is 40:3. [32]Ps 74:2. [33]Heb 12:22. [34]Is 40:2. [35]Is 40:5.

the only-begotten Son of God and there from on high *to bring good news* and to preach to all the coming of the Christ of God to earth.

Then, when many had stood up, he went on to say: *lift it up; do not fear.* And then he commands them to announce to the former *cities of Judah*—I am speaking about the Jewish synagogues—that the one whom the prophets of old preached has come, the one they said would come and live among people, who is very God and Lord and who has been long awaited by them!

[40:10-11] But also he will come once again, and at his second coming he will exercise great *strength*, and *his arm* will come *with authority*, with complete and absolute authority, just as he said. And he continues on to say: *See, his reward is with him, and he has his work before him.* Indeed, this is about the second coming of Christ, when he will come "in glory and repay each one according to his works."[36] He will then do this *with strength* as master and Lord and with the authority called his *arm*.

[253] The next verse reads: *He will tend his flock like a shepherd,* and this was fulfilled during his first sojourn, when "he emptied himself, taking the form of a servant, and was found in human form."[37] He clothed himself in sheep's clothing, as shepherds do, and after donning a human body, *he tended his flock,* or according to Symmachus: *He fed his herd.* For not as a Lord *with strength* and with an *arm of due authority* and power, but, he says, *he will tend his flock as a shepherd.* And Jesus testified to this when he said in the Gospels: "I am the good shepherd; I know my own and my own know me, and I lay down my life for the sheep."[38] He says *and he will gather the lambs in his arms.* And *his arms* belong to the one living in the body of divinity that appeared, and by which it has been said that *he will gather lambs*

and comfort those that are with young. And when he speaks of *lambs,* he is referring to those who are "newborn"[39] and those who "have been born anew"[40] in Christ. And he says that *those that are with young* are those who once conceived and travailed because of the hope of his coming, whom the text says he *comforted* through his coming. Therefore, the text reads: *And he will comfort those that are with young.* And it seems that the apostles were they who conceived and gave birth to those who were born anew in Christ, and the apostles indeed had the Comforter. You will perceive this analogy from the one who said: "My little children, with whom I am again in travail until Christ be formed in you!"[41] You see how Paul travailed on behalf of those whom he discipled. And the rest of the apostles were like mothers as well. They were *with young* and conceived those who were to be born anew in Christ through them. And they travailed, and they were in extreme distress lest anyone might become an untimely birth and be miscarried from the process of being shaped and developed in Christ. For this reason the text said above that the *shepherd will comfort* them.

[40:12-14] The verse about "the wise men of this age"[42] refers to those who subscribe to the philosophy that everything happens by itself and that every natural occurrence has been decreed by fate and necessity, but the present word states that the things which exist did not simply appear "but all things by measure and number"[43] are appointed by the Lord. For, indeed, what was wet and what many suppose to be an immeasurable sea, and streams, rivers and torrents, he measures in their greatness and abundance. And he says that he supplies the amount needed at each moment so that there is neither an overabundance of water nor

[36]Mt 16:27. [37]Phil 2:7. [38]Jn 10:14-15. [39]1 Pet 2:2. [40]1 Pet 1:23. [41]Gal 4:19. [42]1 Cor 1:20. [43]Cf. Wis 11:20.

a lack of what is needful. And the immensity of the heavens and the boundlessness of the vault of the sky he measured with the very *span* of his hand, neither was it too much for him to span the indescribable compass of the universe nor was it too small for him to join in as the one who came into the world. And this verse should be understood figuratively, for it uses dimensions that we are accustomed to so that we might arrive on the meaning of the teaching by way of the things with which we are acquainted and the names we use **[254]** when discussing things. Then, because "from the greatness and beauty of created things comes a corresponding perception of the creator,"[44] he rightly sees that things which appear large to us are small in comparison with the higher thing, summoning in one's mind the one who orders the entire universe. And, therefore, he says that the heaven which is so great and encompasses the entire world is small before God, and it can be supposed to be comparable to the measure of a *span* of his hand. In this same way, every element of the earth is infinitesimal before him and comparable to a *handful* of dust crowded together. But instead of *who has measured the water with his hand*, Aquila says: *Who measured out the water with his lesser span?*[45] He thus compares the ease with which God in his power measured so great a vastness with the ease of measuring something with the lesser span and the smallest finger. And the text says concerning these things that if anyone claims to understand apart from a certain word the things on the *mountains* of the earth and *the hills* and *the forests*, let him know that has been deceived, for nothing is simple among the things that he laid as a foundation. And, therefore, the greatness and the excellence of the mountains of the entire earth and their height and depth

and length came into existence all in a moment at the command of the wisdom of God. And, likewise, the elevation and the weight of the *hills* have words that are applicable and appropriate to the proportion of everything, so that he weighs out in a pair of balances the weight of everything fairly and in proportion to everything. But instead of *and the forests with a balance*, the other Greek translations render this phrase *and the hills*.

He continues on: *Who has known the mind of the Lord, and who has been his counselor?* And the Word answers the one who asked the question: *Who has measured the water with his hand and heaven with a span and all the earth by a handful? Who has weighed the mountains with a scale and the forests with a balance?* For when it was asked who had undertaken these things and who had established these things with a *measure* and a *scale*, he then answered that no one other than the one alone whose *mind* is incomprehensible to all. Therefore, he continues on to say: *Who has known the mind of the Lord*, the mind that has thought out everything that has been spoken into being?[46] He has no need of a *counselor*, neither does he receive knowledge from anyone. But in his wisdom and unspeakable power, he "created what is from what did not exist,"[47] from what simply and absolutely did not exist.

[40:15-17] Next he teaches all those who have been called out from the nations to the evangelical grace, to whom also "the voice crying in the wilderness"[48] proclaimed "the salvation of God"[49] through the above statements, that "all the nations who do not know God" are nothing. For this reason, there is a countless multitude of rational spirits, divine powers and angels who minister before God who patrol the entire kingdom in the sky and

---

[44]Cf. Wis 13:5. [45]The lesser span represented the space between the forefinger and thumb and was an even smaller and mundane measurement than the span of the hand. [46]Literally, "the mind that has thought out everything that has been spoken." [47]Cf. 2 Macc 7:28; Wis 1:14. [48]Is 40:3. [49]Is 40:5.

in the atmosphere and even beyond. And he says that the "nations" of the earth "that do not know God"[50] are like the smallest *drops* flowing from the fullness of the divine reason, and they are like the smallest *balance* that leans and *sinks* slightly to one side because [255] of the weight of evil and godless sin drawing it down. They are also like *spittle* that is spit out on the earth and mixes so that it is no different from the ground. For on the one hand those who are rational suffered from this *spittle*, but on the other hand they are mixed up with those who "have no knowledge of God"[51] and with all ungodliness.

Therefore, he teaches that even in all their service of blood and sacrifices, there is nothing fit for a god. For even *if all the four-footed animals of the earth* were offered, and even if he would use all the wood of the trees of *Lebanon* for *whole burnt offerings* of sacrifices, it would still be nothing worthy of God. And then he adds: *And all the nations are as nothing, and they have been accounted as nothing.* And who could they be except the nations "that do not know God"[52] and who cling to the deception of idolatry? And the text says that *they will be accounted as a drop from a jar and as the sinking of a balance and as spittle.*

[40:18-20] And after these things he reproves them when he says: *To whom have you likened the Lord, or with what likeness have you likened him? Has an artisan made an image, or has a goldsmith, after casting gold, gilded it*, and the rest. And immediately after providing the theological discourse about Christ, he went on to preach to the nations how great was "the one who has measured the water with his hand and heaven with a span and all the earth by handful" and "who established the mountains with a scale and the forests with a balance."[53] And, therefore, in these statements he force-fully objects to the error that so preoccupies the nations, at once turning them from their error and calling them up to the knowledge of the theological discourse. Then the prophetic Spirit levels the souls of the nations with the evangelical preaching, covering them and cleansing them from the superstition of their ancestors.

[40:21-24] Then, after unmasking the deception of those who believe in lifeless images among the nations, he calls aloud to all who will listen to him: *Will you not know? Will you not hear? Has it not been declared to you from the beginning?* Although you were not taught this by your ancestors, you were now chastened and derived profit from it; you learned who is *able to hold the foundations of the earth.* For, since you were not able to lift up your thoughts to heaven above, he says you fixed them on the earth, where you held your discourses. And you sought after that on which your thoughts settled, but who is this one who supports such great elements unmoved and unshaken? And those who study nature inform us that the shape of the earth is spherical.[54] For this reason, he called the earth a *circle* when he said: *It is he who holds the circle of the earth.* He even orders them to know the Word of God who supports the entire universe, who holds together the great elements of the earth with everything else so that its position does not fall away nor is it moved. And who, he asks, [256] is the one who scattered such great nations over the earth so that they are compared with *grasshoppers* because of the smallness of their bodies? Then, once more, he ascends in word from the earth to the heavenly vault, and that the hemisphere is suspended above the earth like a *vault* should cause all to wonder and to reflect on the incredible power that erected the heavens. And one could not suppose that the

---

[50]Cf. 1 Thess 4:5. [51]Cf. 1 Cor 15:34. [52]Cf. 1 Thess 4:5. [53]Is 40:12. [54]Those who still think the ancients held to the idea of a flat earth will obviously find no support in Eusebius.

one who supports it is idle, but like a *tent* he has unfolded it on the inside of all heaven, and he has spread out a divine dwelling place on the far side of heaven. And, as he spoke as one who studies nature and called the element of the earth the *circle of the earth*, thus also he called the hemisphere in the arch of the heavenly *vault* the expanse of heaven and compared it with a *tent* that had been stretched out. And just as he attended the *tent*, so also he looked after those who live inside the *tent*.

Therefore, during various times and seasons, he has set up *rulers* for those people who live out their lives in the earth, taking care to set up *rulers* appropriate for those who are to be ruled. Therefore, he continues on to say: *He appointed rulers to rule for naught.* And it may be that he is calling the mortal life *naught*, or it could be *the earth*, since he teaches it to be *nothing* when he says next: *And he has made the earth nothing.* Then he adds to these statements: *For they will not plant, nor will they sow, neither will their root take root in the earth.* All these things have been said about those who ruled and who were in positions of absolute power over the earth during their times, for such an end will come on them.

[40:25-26] He says such things, and he says *to whom did you liken me*, the God of all, *and to whom will I be made equal? said the Holy One. Look up on high with your eyes, and see: who has exhibited all these?* For it is neither possible to recount them nor even to tell them in part. All we can do is to see with our eyes "the great and the beautiful things"[55] and the harmony and motion of all things. From contemplating these, we marvel at "the Creator of everything,"[56] and we know and make known the one who *brings forward* in order and *by number his ornamentation*, or according to the other

Greek translations: *his armies.* For this reason, he has been called the *Lord of hosts*,[57] although here it has been translated *Lord of armies*.[58] For the angelic *armies* have been subjected under a great king who controls the whole *world*,[59] and no one but he alone knows what each is called, and he has honored them with natural and appropriate names.[60] Therefore, the names of the divine spirits and of the archangels and of God's incorporeal ministering powers beyond the heavens are appropriate for each one, but they are incomprehensible and unknowable to us. Therefore, those who are *called by name* by him submit to him alone, and *because of* his *abundant glory* and surpassing *strength*, not one of those who are *called* refuses compliance, and all will be provided for by his direction.

[40:27-29] [257] After the above theological discussion, the Word reproves those who suppose that God does not watch over their deeds, and this is what many among the former people assumed. Therefore, he inveighs against them when he says: why do you consider these things among yourselves and dare to say that *your way has escaped the notice of God?* Are you not under *judgment* because you have failed to know him and because of what you have done? Then, *have you not heard* the aforementioned theological discussion and that *nothing escapes* his *notice*, therefore it was just said: "Because of abundant glory and by might of strength, nothing has escaped you."[61] Why therefore do you deceive yourself when you say: *My way was hidden from God, and my God has taken away my judgment and has withdrawn?* Therefore, listen to these things now, since you did not listen formerly and *you have not known*, neither have you understood these things even though they have been told often to you. And now,

---

[55]Cf. Wis 13:5. [56]Wis 13:5. [57]κύριος σαβαώθ. [58]κύριος στρατιῶν. [59]This is the same Greek word translated "ornamentation" above: κόσμος. [60]Eusebius's antiquated cosmology is again showing through here: he maintains that the stars are angels. He subscribes to the view that the heavenly hosts (i.e., the stars) are an angelic army. [61]Is 40:26.

therefore, learn that *God everlasting* encompasses all things, and he has power over not only the things in heaven but also the things on earth. And he *prepared the ends of the earth*. Therefore, you will not be able to *escape* his *notice* doing such things, as the impious and godless suppose. But instead of *he will not hunger or grow weary*, Symmachus renders this phrase: *He did not faint, neither did he hunger*, and the other Greek versions translate it similarly. Therefore, just as there is no weakness or human failing in him, so too *there is no searching of his knowledge*. And the wisdom that exists in him is incomprehensible and unattainable, and through it he "orders all things."[62] And, therefore, just as he is concerned about everything and every part of everything, so he watches over the universe and determines the deeds of people with his divine word, and he appropriates to each the life that has been allotted to him. So, on the one hand, he often supplies *strength to those who hunger* for a lack of food and physical strength for the body, but on the other hand, to those who do not hunger and to those who abound in riches, there is anxiety and grief—grief that corrects their wantonness.

[40:30-31] According to the same word, then, it seems that the *youths* and the *young* and those who have arrived at manhood are able to work through weakness, although surrounded by various calamities and diseases, but myriads who were vigorous and swift in their youth he prepared to put to death. And he did not fall to the depths of old age, although driven to extreme poverty so that he could not even find daily food. But once again he did away once and for all with the others who had boasted in riches and glory among people. But then again, those who *wait for God* during the period of their persecutions, although they are weak and pitiful according to the standards of this present life, they are deemed worthy of divine transformation, so that they are not only calm and free, but *they shall grow wings* like *eagles*, and they will fly away and be lifted up high and soar through the air, and finally set out on their journey into the heavens. For the nature of eagles is fallen from heaven, but they alone are able to drink in the light of the sun. And, therefore, it is in these flashings that *those who wait for God* are comparable to eagles, although from a human standpoint they were homeless and with no place to rest and hopeless and distressed by anxiety during the times of their persecution in this mortal life. And, therefore, after [258] being deemed worthy by God of the visitation of exceeding afflictions, they lived their lives in peace and *grew wings* like *eagles*, and they were raised up into the heights. And if it shall happen that just as those who contend and overcome in their testimony to godliness are made perfect, how much more appropriate for them is the promise that says: *But those who wait for God shall renew their strength*. And, therefore, exchanging mortal life for the angelic life and preparing themselves for the heavenly journey, *they shall grow wings like eagles; they shall run and not be weary; they shall walk and not hunger*, or according to the other Greek translations, *they shall not faint*. Therefore, if he shall grant such transformations to *those who wait for* him, he will also repay those who do the opposite with punishments, partially during the present life but to the fullest during the time of judgment. How dare you then—you who are called "Jacob" and "Israel"[63] and who have been instructed in the divine words—how dare you say among yourselves that "your way was hidden from God, and your judgment has been taken away, and he has withdrawn"?[64]

[41:1] Therefore, O Jacob, how can you think such things? For when he proclaimed the salva-

---

[62]Cf. Wis 8:1.   [63]Cf. Is 40:27.   [64]Is 40:27.

tion of humanity among you, the Savior of the universe then discussed things with you very clearly, but to the other nations he said similar things, summoning all of them to come immediately to acknowledge him. Therefore, he says: *Be dedicated to me, O islands, for the rulers will renew their strength*. But Symmachus says instead: *Serve me, O islands, and let the nations renew their strength*. And according to Aquila and Theodotion, the text reads: *Keep silence before me*. He thus commands the *islands to keep silence and be still*, so that they hear the divine instructions and preaching of salvation. And he repeatedly calls the churches from all nations *islands* because just as *islands* are surrounded by the sea, so the churches are surrounded by a salty and evil culture. Then, above he said, "those who wait for God shall renew their strength,"[1] and in this verse he says: *For the rulers will renew their strength*, or according to Symmachus: *And let the nations renew their strength*. For what was promised above "to those who wait for" him, he appoints also to the *islands* and to the *nations* when he says: *And let the nations renew their strength*. He says this so that they might change their ways and exchange the worse for the better. Then he says next: *Let them approach and speak together*, and it is clear that he is saying to that the nations: *Let them approach* God and *let them speak* his words *among themselves*, and it is clear that this should be done in his church. And next he teaches that it is proper for them to *speak* to those who are summoned when he says: *Then let them declare judgment*. For he wills that the *nations* learn the word of *judgment* and *announce* it to others.

[41:2-3] [259] And he even commands them to learn and to know this: *Who has roused righteousness from the east?* For the work of *righteousness* was that not only the Jews, but the rest of the nations too were called to the knowledge of God. Who therefore is the one who *raised* this *righteousness from* the light of *the east* and who *called* him to follow after him? And who has *placed it before* all the *nations* so that the *kings of the nations were astonished* with his command and their officials were confused? And pursuits were attempted and wars incited according to the word of *righteousness*, and they were conquered by the God of *righteousness*, who fights on behalf of those who have welcomed *righteousness*. He indeed did away with the hostility of the enemies of *righteousness* as though they were *brushwood*, and he smoothed away for himself a path so that *his feet passed through it in peace*.

[41:4-6] Who therefore is the one who achieved all these things if not the God of all? For this reason, the text continues on to say: *The one calling her from the beginning of generations, I, God, am first, and for the things that are coming, I am*. But instead of this, Symmachus translates this phrase: *I, the Lord, am first, and I am also present in the last times*. For he is the one who was known to those who were highly favored from ages past, and it is in him the church now believes after the first people. Therefore, he continues on to say: *The nations saw and became afraid*. And the Word testifies to the advantage that is lacking among the nations, for if they would turn from their former blindness and polytheism, they would perceive the truth of what has been said: *I, God, am first, and for the things that are coming, I am*. And after they *saw, they were afraid*, thus arriving at the "beginning of wisdom." "For the fear of the Lord is the beginning of wisdom."[2] But also the *ends of the earth were amazed*. For the wonder was this, that even the barbaric tribes and those who settled in the lands away farthest from the country of the Jews—although it was thought that God revealed

---

Chapter Forty-One [1]Is 40:31. [2]Ps 111:10.

himself only in ancient times—even they acquired knowledge of godliness and were *amazed* at the righteousness of God. Thus grace rushed in and came to the aid of the one who preached: "Let them approach and speak together."[3] And there they were encouraged *to speak* everything—clearly, that is, to glorify God—but here the word says: *They drew near and came together, each deciding to help his neighbor.* For those who had been summoned *came* not only to save themselves but also their *neighbors,* in accordance with the principles of the love of fellowman. Therefore, they wanted to heal their *neighbors* as well as their own *brothers* and relatives, and they were saying these things to those who were still caught up in wickedness.

[41:7] There was a time, then, when we too were *the artisan outdoing himself* in fashioning idolatry *and the smith beating out with the hammer* [260] his own gods. But now we have learned that those idols were nothing, and we have condemned the error that we inherited from our ancestors, and since you have learned this it has been an advantage to you. And the evidence of the weakness of those whom we once supposed to be gods is that they are not able to stand, if not fastened with various bolts and *nails.* And then they are able to stand only because they are stood up by others. But the proof of their lifelessness is that they are not able to *move* at all. This is what they are like; they neither stand by themselves, nor are they able to *move* when they are stood up by others. However he says that they are considered gods by their neighbors, when the Word prophesies to the nations, since the nations had been ordered above not only to "draw near" to God but also to "speak." For he said: "Let them approach and speak together."[4] It is correct to say through the prophecy, then, that they "drew near" and that after coming they discussed certain things with their relatives.

[41:8] Indeed, in the above, God censured Jacob and Israel when he said: "My way was hidden from God, and God has taken away my judgment and has withdrawn." But in the verse at hand he calls *Israel* his *servant* and says that *Jacob* is the one who has been *chosen.* Clearly, the Word is describing two kinds of people of the circumcision—the one he is accusing and condemning, and to the other he makes the present promises. Therefore, the first kind are those who have fallen from God because of their disbelief, and the other kind are those who obeyed in faith and so were accounted worthy of the grace of the Savior, and these are the disciples and apostles of our Savior and all the rest who have believed in him from the people of the circumcision; and these are Israel and Jacob. Therefore, consequently, it is to the choice of the apostles and disciples of our Savior that the message concerning the nations refers. Therefore, the prophecy says to their face: *But you, Israel, my servant, Jacob, whom I have chosen, the offspring of Abram, whom I have loved.* First he calls the one who was reared among rulers and yet in fear of bondage, *servant,* and thereafter *chosen* and then *loved.* Such was the apostolic band, for their first life was "under a custodian"[5]—the law. And this is whom he calls *chosen,* the one who ever progresses in the calling of the Savior, the one who has been counted worthy of selection. And the *offspring of Abram* is another rank from among the *chosen* ones, and who might they be other than the multitude of the Jews to whom the Savior said when conversing with them: "I know that you are descendants of Abraham"?[6] But there were others alongside "Abraham's children," and he taught concerning these when he said: "If you were Abraham's children, you would do what Abraham did."[7]

---

[3]Is 41:1. [4]Is 40:1. [5]Gal 3:24-25. [6]Jn 8:31. [7]Jn 8:39.

Indeed, *Abram* was *beloved* of God and his *friend*. For this reason, it has been written: *The offspring of Abram, whom I loved*; or according to Symmachus: *The offspring of Abram my friend*; and according to Aquila: *The offspring of Abram my beloved*. [261] And it has been said that his *offspring* was not *loved* like Abram. But, nevertheless, he calls the *offspring of Abram* through his chosen ones when he said to them: "Go to the lost sheep of the house of Israel."[8]

[41:9] And because these *offspring of Abram* were scattered abroad into all the earth, he continues on to say next: *You whom I took hold of from the ends of the earth, and I called you from its mountain peaks*, or according to Symmachus: *And from its bends I called you*. And through these things he signifies those in the diaspora of the Jewish people, those who were first deemed worthy of his calling. Therefore, just as the apostle Paul stood by the Jews when he said: "It was necessary for the word to be preached to you first, but since you turned away we will go to the Gentiles,"[9] therefore he says to those among the Jews who heard the call and to those who welcomed the evangelical word: *You whom I took hold of from the ends of the earth, and I called you from its mountain peaks*. For there were many Jews who welcomed the word of Christ during the apostolic times, not only in the land of Judea but also in the other nations. But, remembering that they are the *offspring of Abram*, he returns to the chosen of the apostolic band, and he says to them: *You are my child*,[10] or according to the other Greek translations: *You are my servant; I chose you, and I did not abandon you*. Therefore, even the divine apostle confesses himself to be a "servant,"[11] proud of the great honor of being in the service of the Savior. And the Word proceeds to confirm this when he says: "It is a great thing for you to be called my child."[12] And again, he teaches that he was first a *servant* and then chosen when he says: *You are my child*, or, *you are my servant, and I have chosen you and not forsaken you*.

[41:10-12] He encourages this chosen fellowship to preach the gospel without fear to all nations, and the Savior himself gave these instructions in the Gospels when he said: "Behold, I am with you always, to the very end of the age."[13] Then he continues on to say: *Do not fear, for I am with you; but do not wander off*, he says, *for I am your God who has strengthened you, and I have helped you, and I have made you secure with my righteous hand*. For he says, behold, lest you should think that in your own strength you were able to minister such a great message. For you would have been nothing and unable to do anything unless I was *with you* and traveled along beside you among all the nations. But *I strengthened you* and gave you endurance and perseverance and power, *and I have made you secure with my righteous right hand*, so that there was no impediment in your way for you to preach the gospel to everyone.

[262] And there may be certain individuals who *oppose* the word of the gospel that you preach and who attempt to be a hindrance to you, but have no fear of those who look disdainfully, because *all who oppose you shall be ashamed and disgraced, for they shall be as though they were not, and all your adversaries shall perish. You shall seek them, but you shall not find the people who shall treat you violently, for they shall be as though they were not, and those who are against you shall no longer exist*. For certain people thought you were of no significance during the time when they were *warring* against you and persecuting you. But you will endure

---

[8]Mt 10:6. [9]Acts 13:46. [10]The word translated "servant" here (παῖς) primarily means "child," but it was translated correctly above as "servant" too. [11]E.g., Rom 1:1. [12]Is 49:6. [13]Mt 28:20.

and see their destruction, but *they shall not be,* and their lives will quickly vanish.

[41:13-18] For this reason, it is right for you to bear patiently and to endure the afflictions that they bring on, since you have in view the end that is in store for them and have confidence in my promise that I already proclaimed to you really and truly: *Because I am the Lord your God, and I will hold your right hand, who says to you, "Do not fear; I have helped you."* This is not how the text reads in the Septuagint: *I have helped you; do not fear, Jacob, you worm,* and the text reads this way in the other Greek translations too. And this one, who above was called "chosen" in the phrase "Jacob, whom I have chosen,"[14] now is called a *worm,* because as a *worm* he creeps down into the cities of the unbelieving nations and into all their polytheistic error and demonic activity. He corrupts the minds of people at the deepest level and thus makes it impossible for them to understand the simple and uncomplicated message of the apostolic preaching. Even the Savior himself calls himself a *worm* when he says: "But as for me, I am a worm and not human, a reproach of humankind and despised by people."[15] Then, since the number of the disciples of our Savior was small—the apostles being "twelve,"[16] and the ones who came after them were only "seventy"[17]—because of this he continues on to say: *O small Israel,* or according to Symmachus, *number of Israel,* or according to Aquila, *Israel who died,* and according to Theodotion the text reads, *dead of Israel.* Nevertheless, after calling them *worms* and saying that they were *small,* he continues on to say: *Do not fear, I have helped you, says God who redeems you, the Holy One of Israel.*

And he adds: *Look, I made you as the threshing wheels of a cart, new and saw-shaped.* For in this way the power of the one who "strengthened"[18] them was demonstrated,

when they were no different from a *worm,* and when they were *small* and *dead* and when they represented those who *died from Israel.* Nevertheless, such as they were, as one severs straw when *threshing* by the *wheels of a cart,* so they sawed asunder the demonic idol industry of the Philistines and the godless nation. [263] Therefore, he continues on to say: *And you shall thresh mountains and grind hills to powder,* and by *mountains and hills* he alludes to the opposing powers that were once raised up against the knowledge of God. Accordingly, these powers were likened to high *mountains,* and concerning the evil spirits that descended like *hills,* he says that *you shall grind* them *to powder, and you shall thresh and winnow* them, *and a wind shall take them, and a tempest shall scatter them.* And so the demonic error will no longer be established among the nations. And when the abovementioned *mountains* and *hills* are disappearing, "you," "my chosen servant"[19] who successfully accomplished these things, *you shall rejoice in the Lord, and you shall praise the Holy One of Israel.* But instead of *they shall be in the holy things of Israel,* Aquila translates this phrase: *You shall boast in the Holy One of Israel* and, Symmachus: *You shall praise the Holy One of Israel.*

After prophesying this about the apostles, the Word begins a new paragraph and continues on to address the conversion of the Gentiles: *And the poor and needy shall be glad; they shall seek water, and there will be none; their tongue has been dried up from thirst.* But they believed these things of old, and now he says: *I the Lord God, I the God of Israel will listen to them, and I will not forsake them. But I will open rivers on the mountains and fountains in the midst of the plains; I will make the wilderness into marshlands of water and the thirsty land as watercourses.* And you will see that these things came to pass and still even now they are being carried out in the churches of

---

[14]Is 41:8. [15]Ps 22:6. [16]Mt 10:2. [17]Lk 10:1. [18]Cf. Is 41:10. [19]Cf. Is 41:8; 42:1.

God that the apostles of our Savior founded everywhere. And, therefore, those souls who formerly lived as beggars among the nations and lacked the knowledge of God could not get even a drop from the living stream, and so their tongue and the word their tongue proclaimed dried up. Although they were not partakers in any of the moisture of the saving word, yet an amazing kindness of heavenly grace occurred so that they were filled with *springs* and *rivers* and all sorts of living waters. And they took advantage of the water, as it has been said above: "And they will drink water from the *springs* of salvation."[20] And they drank "from the *springs* of Israel," which the Word mentioned when he said: "Bless God in the assemblies, the Lord from Israel's *springs*."[21] And these were ever the Holy Spirit who springs up in the church of God and pours forth living water, sometimes from the old covenant and sometimes from the new and evangelical teaching. But, also, ever-flowing *rivers* run and flood the place that was once a *wilderness*, and the source of these *rivers* is the great river, concerning which it has been said: "The strong currents of the *river* make glad the city of God,"[22] and: "The *river* of God was filled with water."[23]

[41:19] [264] And *in the* once *dry land*, one can see the church of God and souls flourishing from such waters. And these souls soar to a great height and in this way are analogous to trees, plunging roots down to the plentiful waters. And the Septuagint tells us what sort of trees they are: *A cedar and a box tree and a myrtle, a cypress-wood as well as a white poplar.* But according to Symmachus, they are *a cedar and a smokeless olive tree, a cypress-wood and a wild boar tree*[24] *and a boxwood and similar trees.* And all these are nourished by means of the plentiful waters and grow as these trees,

and being surrounded by the flourishing souls in the church of God, the great quantity of the divine and spiritual waters caused them to soar to the heights. And when indeed the Word wants to speak of the fruits of the church, he uses the image of an "olive tree"[25] or a "palm tree"[26] or a "grapevine."[27] But when they are now flourishing and soaring to the heights and youthful and blooming—clearly referring to the ones who prosper in the church—then they are declared to be in the image of the aforementioned trees. These trees, in fact, did not grow in a firm and fertile land filled with water, but instead—and here is the amazing part—he promises that there will be an abundance of water in the formerly *dry* and parched and thirsty land, and it has been foretold that such plants would shoot forth there instead. And so it will be in the *land* that was once a *wilderness* and *dry*, among those who were once foreign and godless nations. For he prophesies that such will be the change among them, and it will be for a demonstration of his saving work.

[41:20] Therefore, he continues on to say: *So that together they may see and know and consider and understand that the hand of the Lord has done these things, and the Holy One of Israel has exhibited them.* For if it was not God and *the hand of the Lord* through his apostles who effected such a change among the nations, how would the churches of God ever establish themselves in such desolate places as these nations, and how would the spiritual waters in these places abound everywhere on the earth, so that the nations that were once desolate and without water are cultivated with the word of godliness? And how else would they produce shoots that rise high into the air, at once rooted firmly in the ground (i.e., in the mortal and human life) and at the same time

---

[20]Cf. Is 12:3. [21]Ps 68:26. [22]Ps 46:4. [23]Ps 65:9. [24]The Greek word πτελέα means "wild boar," but it is to be understood that Eusebius is speaking of some sort of tree. [25]Ps 52:8. [26]Ps 92:12. [27]Ps 128:3.

lifted up above in the heights so that they extend to the kingdom of heaven and set their hopes on another world? For this reason, they are compared with fragrant plants that soar to the heights.

[41:21-23] And after the Word filled the place that was once a fruitless and *dry wilderness*—and the transformation into fruitfulness alludes to the change from the worse to the better in the church of God—he turns to address those who remain in the former error of idolatry. For this reason, it is as though speaking to them that he inveighs against them and says: *Your judgment draws near, says God.* He says "for you are without excuse,"[28] speaking to those who remained in the error of polytheism and who did not reflect on [265] the magnificent grace that has achieved such great things. And so, it was truly "the hand of the Lord"[29] that achieved such great things and that testified that these things would occur even "before they happened."[30] And these things happened "so that they may see and know and consider and understand that the hand of the Lord has done all these things."[31] Therefore, the Word then threatens those who did not understand and recognize and consider these things when he says: *Your judgment draws near, says the Lord God.* For condemnation is immediately brought forward against those who "are without excuse."[32] For this reason, he continues on to say: *Your counsels have drawn near.* But Symmachus says instead: *Draw near your forces,* and Theodotion says: *Draw near your strength,* and Aquila says: *Marshal your troops.* For they said gather together into your midst what you suppose to be *your strength* and *forces*—more plainly said, your gods—carry them into your midst, *let them draw near and declare to you.* Or according to Symmachus: *Let them approach and*

report to you the things that will happen or speak of the former things, what they were, and we will apply our mind and know the last things—and tell us the things that are coming. Declare the things that are coming at the end, and we will know that you are gods.

For truly it is to be despised as the listlessness of demons who formerly pretended to divine things and constantly used to predict what would happen, although nothing they divined and predicted ever turned out to be correct. But when the Christ of God shall come and dwell among humanity, he will abolish their practice of fabricating idols, and the temples that have been erected in all of their cities will be abandoned, and their divination and soothsaying will be exposed as false. For these things were accomplished at the end of days through the coming of our Savior. We need not fail to understand that it was the evil demons who pretended to divine things and to see what was about to happen. And, therefore, they prognosticated and prophesied these things, since there really was a certain divine power among them. For this reason the Word says to them: *Tell us what the last things will be and what the coming things will be. Declare the things that are coming at the end, and we will know that you are gods.* Indeed, the prophets of God shared in the inspired Spirit and predicted the last things and foretold in detail the change for the better that would take place in the arid and infertile and unfruitful land of the Gentiles and the coming of the Christ and the preaching of his apostles and the other great things that are contained in the prophecies. And in these prophecies it was made known that God truly existed, for God prophesied these things among them and through them. But the evil demons were able to know the determination and resolution of the God of the universe and

---

[28]Rom 1:20; 2:1. [29]Is 41:20. [30]Is 46:10. [31]Is 41:20. [32]Rom 1:20; 2:1.

he things that he ordained concerning the
oming of the Christ and concerning their
overthrow and destruction. Therefore, they
knew neither *the things that are coming* nor the
hings that will *happen* in the *last* times
oncerning the calling of the Gentiles and of
heir wilderness. And so too, they neither
knew about *the former things*, since none of
hem has been able **[266]** to dictate these
hings among those prophets whose prophe-
ies were deemed worthy by the Spirit of God
o be transmitted in the Scripture. One of the
prophets was Moses, who recorded *the former
hings* when he wrote: "In the beginning God
made the heaven and the earth. Yet the earth
was invisible and unformed."[33] For these
hings and the things like these were *the
ormer things*, and *the last things* are the things
oncerning the conversion of the Gentiles, and
he disproof of the demonic error and the
hings concerning "the close of the age";[34] and
fter these things "God's righteous judgment"[35] will be established. Therefore, since
hey are not able to know or announce *the last
hings*, how then can they be *gods*? Then he
urns to another refutation when he says: *Do
ood, and do harm, and we will see as well as
wonder.* And even if you are evil demons and
lo extreme deeds of *harm*, that would still be
no sign of divine activity. Therefore, it is first
necessary for us to demonstrate what is
unique to God—I am talking about how he
loes good—and thereafter you declared
righteous judgment and avenged those who
were worthy of punishment. But now you
welcomed uncritically anyone who belonged to
your false religion, and you announced
lluring promises to everyone in an indistinct
voice and obfuscating arrangement of words in
order to conceal your ignorance behind a
curtain of ambiguity. And now, by means of
lisreputable men and licentious women, you

produced oracles that cannot be confirmed
claiming that you are *gods*.

[41:24-26] This is why he then next asks:
*Because whence are you and whence is your
work?* And he set forth the substance of
disproving their claims when he answered:
*From the earth. They have chosen you as an
abomination.* For even if the idols are made of
gold or silver, iron, copper or stone, all these
are of the *earth* and merely natural elements.
Those things, then, which were used for the
fabrication of idols became an *abomination* not
because they were so by nature (since, after all,
every work of God is good) but rather because
of the false artifice of evil people, who use
these things for befouled and abominable and
despicable purposes of atheism. And these
things are lifeless, neither able *to do good* nor *to
do evil*, so that the things which are thought to
be the cosmic forces that present the oracles of
people are in fact the deceits of sorcerers and
the folly of the many pretenders.

After the Word said these things and
proclaimed to those who remained in idolatry,
he sets forth their error: *But I stirred up the
one who is from the north* (or according to
Symmachus, *I will awaken the one who is from
the north), and the one who is from the rising of
the sun*, whom he says *will be called by my
name.* In speaking about *the one who is from the
rising of the sun*, he signifies the Christ and his
"righteousness."[36] For this was already made
clear from what had been said previously in the
verse: "Who has roused righteousness from the
east?"[37] and one might add that this verse
clearly addresses the Gentiles. And *the one who
is from the north* concerns the people from the
Gentiles, for they were formerly in the *north*,
as we read in the verse: "From the face of the
north evil shall flare up against all the inhabitants of the land."[38] Therefore, he says, *I will*

---

[33]Gen 1:1-2. [34]Mt 13:39. [35]Rom 2:5. [36]Is 41:2. [37]Is 42:1. [38]Jer 1:14.

awaken this Gentile people [267] *from the north*, in order that they might no longer be among the heathen, and I will also call *the one who is from the rising of the sun*, clearly speaking of the Christ of God. And he adds on to these things: *They shall be called by my name.* And he explains who they were when he continues on to say: *Let rulers come.* Here he is either speaking of those angels who guard over his kingdom, through whom he says the overthrow of the godless error had been accomplished, or else he is speaking of the *rulers* and the leaders of his church. Therefore, when the people *from the north* and *from the rising of the sun* shall be gathered together and the indicated *rulers* shall also be there, he continues on to say what will then take place: *And like potter's clay—even as a potter treading clay—so shall you be trodden down.* When he says *you*, he is clearly again speaking to those whom he addressed: *Because whence are you and whence is your work? From the earth. They have chosen you as an abomination.*

Therefore, he again speaks out as against them and says: *For who shall declare the things that were from the beginning so that we might know them, and the former things, and we will say that they are true?* After saying this to those indicated above and offering the same proof of their false claims, he then adds: *There is none who foretells or any who hears your words.* Again the Word identifies two things here: the final destruction of the oracles and the renewed sobriety of those people who were themselves once deceived. And the phrase *there is none who hears your words* has a double meaning: those to whom the word was spoken are neither able to perceive nor to know the word, and neither did anyone listen to those who once persisted in the error of polytheism. And the reason why those who have been aided by the word of truth no longer listen to them is that they recognize that polytheism is an ancient deception.

[41:27-29] He further adds: *I will give dominion to Zion, and I will comfort Jerusalem on the way.* And what he is saying is this: know, O people, that to my church, which is called *Zion* and *Jerusalem* above, I myself *will give dominion* over everything, and *I will comfort* my church and I will place it *on the way.* For among the *nations* that remained in disbelief, *no one* found God, *and from among their idols, there was none who declared.* And therefore their idols were put to shame, since they were proven to be nothing and were unable to do anything. Therefore, *if I should ask them where they come from*, none of them will give an answer. For it is clear that their fabricators and artisans are mere mortals, since all "the idols of the nations are the works of human hands."[39] Therefore, all those who *led you astray are vain.* For this reason, I want you to know that *I myself will give dominion* over everything to my church, and I will present authority over my kingdom to my *Zion*, and *I will comfort* my *Jerusalem.* I will place it *on the way*, because all who journey with it are on their way to the thrice-blessed and holy destination—to the God of the universe and his heavenly kingdom.

[42:1] [268] After he refutes the idols, he then compares and contrasts the prophecy concerning the Christ and the call from the nations that accompanies this prophecy. But it is worth noting in our consideration of these texts that neither the name of *Jacob* nor that of *Israel* was found in the prophecy that was exposited above. For this reason, neither the other Greek translations nor the Hebrew text mentions Jacob and Israel; instead, Symmachus renders the text as follows: *Behold my servant; I will support him. He is my chosen one, in whom my soul is well pleased*, and Aquila: *Behold my servant; I will lay hold of him.* Therefore, in the passage discussed earlier, the apostolic band

---

[39]Ps 115:4.

was called *Jacob* and *Israel* where the text reads: "But you, Jacob, my servant, Israel, whom I have chosen, the offspring of Abram, whom I loved."[1] And in the passage at hand, a superior person is introduced, so one should never suppose that the text is speaking of him in the statements about the one who is called *Jacob* or *Israel* or *offspring of Abram*; rather, clearly these statements have been said concerning the Christ of God, even as the evangelist witnesses: *I have put my spirit on him, and he will bring forth judgment to the nations.* And after all these things, *the nations will hope on his name*, those that had not already accommodated themselves to the message of the apostolic band. It was therefore right then that the names *Jacob* and *Israel* were not mentioned in the prophecy discussed above. Therefore, there is here another one who is spoken of as the *servant* of God and of his *chosen one*. For this reason, the following statement is then added: *My soul has accepted him.* For this one alone was the *chosen one* of God, the one *accepted* by him who is referred to as the *soul* of God. Usually, the one to whom the name *soul* is applied in the divine Scriptures is God, although God is also presented in a more human form as having feet and hands and fingers and eyes. *I have put my spirit on him; he will bring forth judgment to the nations.* And you will find that these things are in harmony with what has been prophesied above concerning the one who will come "from the root of Jesse."[2] But the *chosen one* cannot be referring to the apostles, since it has been said to the *chosen one* alone: "Whom my *soul* has chosen,"[3] and: "The *Spirit* of God descended on him alone."[4] "For in him the whole fullness of deity dwelt bodily."[5] And the *Spirit* that was given to the one who came "from the root of Jesse"[6] was the only-begotten Word of God, as also the apostle Paul made clear when he said: "Now the Lord is the Spirit."[7] Therefore, he alone

understands the Spirit of the Father, and he accomplishes everything that is mentioned next when he announces the universal *judgment* among the *nations* so that all might be prepared for the coming *judgment* of God. For this reason, the text reads: *He will bring forth judgment to the nations.*

[42:2-3] He journeyed through his human life gently and softly, so as not to give himself away to those whom he healed or to make himself manifest to all. Because of this, the text reads: *He will not cry out or send forth his voice, nor will his voice be heard outside*, and *neither will he break a bruised reed.* [269] For he will pass through his life among people so silently and peacefully that he will not vex even the most humble and weak of all those with whom he comes into contact; and they are called *reeds* because of their weakness. And *neither will he quench a smoking wick*, or according to Symmachus: *Neither will he quench a glimmering wick*, or according to Aquila: *And he will not quench a glimmering wick*, and according to Theodotion: *And a glimmering flax he will not quench.* And you could say that the smoldering *wick* is the one who in his fleshly nature and in his mind has become accustomed to being proud and deluded, and then the text would be saying that the one whose coming is prophesied will neither extinguish nor do away with their vanity. And the Christ of God did fulfill these prophecies in his actions when he lived in this mortal world. Therefore, he did not vex those who were humble and weak among people, and neither did he seek to punish the proud and the arrogant. Rather, to all he was "gentle and humble in heart."[8]

[42:4] He truly and boldly commanded what concerned the judgment of God among all, and he did not stop until he had *shown forth* as

---

Chapter Forty-Two [1]Is 41:8. [2]Is 11:1. [3]Mt 12:18. [4]Cf. Is 11:2. [5]Col 2:9. [6]Is 11:1. [7]2 Cor 3:17 RSV. [8]Mt 11:29.

light in the resurrection from the dead, to which the prophetic word alluded when it said: *He will blaze up and not be overwhelmed.* For, indeed, those who plotted his death attempted to *overwhelm* and *extinguish* him. And although this entire mortal generation is disposed by nature to be *overwhelmed* in death, he was not *overwhelmed.* Rather, this one alone was shown to be greater than anyone from this age of death. This has been rightly testified in the prophecy that says: *He will blaze up and not be overwhelmed.* And then it continues on: *Until he has established judgment on the earth, and nations will hope in his name.* Therefore, also after his resurrection from the dead, he *shown forth* as light into the whole world, and he did not stop until he had established the administration of his church on the earth and *judgment* as well, which he handed over to his disciples.

[42:5] And he goes on to speak of the disciples when he says: *Thus says the Lord God, who created heaven and established it, who bolstered the earth and the things that are in it and who gave breath to the people on it and spirit to those who tread on it.* And see how the text mentions *the one who has established it,* since in the creation account of Moses it is said that he appointed the formation of the waters. But this is not what the Greek philosophers[9] say. They maintain that the atmosphere and the *heavens* are in fact made of fire, and they believe that *the earth has been established* in proper order so that the center of the universe is unmoved, although the text does not say that he set *the heavens* in order. However, instead of *And the things that are in it,* Symmachus says: *You established the earth and the things coming from it.* And that these things have happened he shows plainly when he says next: *The one who gave breath to the people on it and spirit to those who tread on it.*

For it is necessary for you to learn from a certain person what was said concerning the Christ, for the prophetic word tied everything together when it said at the beginning: "Jacob [270] is my servant; I will lay hold of him; Israel is my chosen; my soul has accepted him; I have put my spirit on him."[10] And the text has not yet stated who the one who said these things is, but it does plainly show in the present passage who the one who has prophesied these things is. Therefore, he continues on to say: *Thus said the Lord God.* For he himself was the one who said the prior as well as the additional things that were said. For he says that you were not the sort of people who would fail to see the invisible and incorporeal presence of God. But, looking up into the greatness of such *heavens,* you considered the greatness of the one who made it all. But even if you looked around the *earth,* such as it now stands, you would see that the entire universe has been immovably positioned and firmly fixed and founded so that it is absolutely impossible for it to be moved. And you would reflect on how great the ineffable power is that *established* it and that caused it to be fertile and bring forth fruit so that it would support so many animals and plants. Therefore, then, the one who fashioned such good and great things is the Lord and God of all, and it was he who delivered the prophecy above concerning his Christ.

And afterwards, then, the text says that *he gave breath*[11] to those over whom he kept watch and *to the people* on the earth, that is, to all the people whose lot it is to live on the earth. And then, at the first creation of man, "God breathed into his face a *breath* of life, and the man became a living being,"[12] so that from that moment all people shared in life and were no longer mere *spirit.* For the text says that *spirit* was *given* only to those who *tread* on the earth.

---

[9] φυσιόλογος.   [10] Is 42:1.   [11] In the following paragraph, Eusebius uses the Greek word πνεῦμα to express the ideas of either "spirit" or "breath."   [12] Gen 2:7.

And one could say that those who *tread* about with an earthly mind refers to every kind of rational and irrational creature on the earth in the above passage.

[42:6-7] And to what has already been said, the *Lord* and *God* says these additional things to his Christ: *I, the Lord God, have called you in righteousness, and I will take hold of your hand and strengthen you.* And he addresses these things to him whom he called his "servant" above, to him whom he said "I will give my spirit." [13] First, the creator *will call* him *in righteousness* according to his worthy calling and according to his most righteous standing. Then, *he will take hold of his hand* and *strengthen* him. And, third, he promises that he will graciously grant him as a gift, as a great *light* to the *nations*, when he says: *I have given you as a covenant to a race, as a light to nations.* Therefore, the old covenant was given through Moses to the Jewish people a long time ago. But here we read that the prophesied one will be given *as a covenant to a race* of people and *as a light to nations.* Therefore, the Christ of God was the *covenant*, not the Scriptures or scrolls that Moses delivered. For he himself was the *covenant*, inasmuch as he was first "mediator between God and people." [14] And *he was given as a light to nations*, and in him *the eyes* of those souls that were once *blind were opened* and enlightened. **[271]** They will receive sight, and once they see clearly the knowledge of God, they will no longer render the honor of God to stones and sticks and inanimate matter.

And these very individuals "are bound fast by the ropes of their own sin," [15] and they have been shackled in darkness by evil. But they will be deemed worthy of the forgiveness of sins through the grace of Christ, and they will be released from prison and set free and delivered from the dungeon of the devil. Because of this, the text next adds: *to bring out from bonds those who are bound and from the prison house those who sit in darkness.* And God in his munificence promises that *he will give* all of these things through his Christ not to Israel or to the nation of the Jews but to all the *nations* together.

[42:8] The text continues on to say: *I am the Lord God; this is my name; my glory I will not give to another.* And one should note that the other Greek translations and the Hebrew text read: *My glory I will not give to another.* "The sayings of the Lord are tried by fire," [16] and therefore one should not consult them superficially. But it is worth noting that the text does not read: *My glory I will give to no one at all.* For had he said *to no one at all* he would have excluded everyone, but in saying that he *will not give to another* he indicates his consent to give his glory only to one—clearly, to the one who is being addressed. And this is the one to whom it was said: *I have called you in righteousness, and I will take hold of your hand and strengthen you; I have given you as a covenant to a race, as a light to nations.* Therefore, because he said to you *I have given my glory*, one may conclude that he will not *give it to another* besides you. And what the *glory* of the one who said these things is has already been taught when he said: *I am the Lord God; this is my name.* Therefore, the *name*, by which he was magnified as the *Lord* and *God* of all, he says *I will not give to another* except to you alone, you whom I presented *as a light to nations.* And in accordance with the promise, the Christ of God was designated as *Lord* and *God* among the *nations* by the Father who freely gave this *glory* to him alone. The text goes on to say: *My virtues I will not give to the graven images*, or according to Aquila: *And my worship I will not give to the graven images*, and according to Symmachus: *My praise I will not give to the graven images.* I suppose that in these words all the nations are instructed not to praise the

---

[13]Is 42:1. [14]1 Tim 2:5. [15]Prov 5:22. [16]Ps 18:30.

idols that they used to revere as gods but God alone and to glorify the Christ of God and "the Father who sent him"[17] alone. And through the Father the Christ alone is worshiped, and therefore the God of all gave his *glory* and his *virtues* to him alone and not to any another.

[**42:9**] After these things the text then reads: *As for the things that were from the beginning, see, they have come; also new things, which I myself will declare; before they are announced publicly, they were made plain to you.* But according to Symmachus, [**272**] the text reads: *As for the first things, see, they arrived, and I will declare new things; before they were announced publicly, I will make them to be known to you.* For *the first things* that I said were in fact fulfilled; and as I promised Abraham concerning his "offspring,"[18] so I also did. And all that was foretold by Moses and the other prophets also happened. And so now, he says, I promise to all that even *before they were announced publicly* these things will become clear through this prophecy, because *I made them to be known to you.* And what these things are he explains in detail in what he says next.

[**42:10**] He predicted that he would do *new things* in the verse above, and what these *new things* are he teaches in the preceding passage. Then he commands them *to sing to the Lord a new song,* or according to the other Greek translations, *to chant a new chant.* And it is necessary for everyone to do this, since he says *his dominion* and royal authority are *glorified* in all the earth. *He glorified his name until the ends of the earth,* and so the whole world is now full of Christians, those who derive their name from the Christ. But according to Symmachus we read, *Sing his praise from the ends of the earth.* He exhorts them to *sing the new chant*

and the *new song to the Lord.* And he teaches to whom the preaching is addressed when he says next: *The ones who go down to the sea and sail in it,* thereby clearly signifying the apostles of our Savior. For they were the ones "while passing by the sea he saw casting a net into the sea; for they were fishermen,"[19] and so with the rest of the apostles. Therefore, the prophetic Spirit says to them: *Sing to the Lord a new song, you who go down to the sea and sail in it.* And according to us, they are the ones who *sail around in the sea,* at one time preaching the gospel among the *islands*[20] and at another time crossing over beyond Italy to Spain,[21] so that in a short period of time even the capital city of the empire had been filled with the teaching of the Christ.[22] Otherwise, the verse is speaking about those who *sail in the sea* of human life and preach the gospel among all nations and among the *islands.* And then they proclaimed the *new song* to all, preaching and teaching in the midst of the churches. For this reason, he then commands them *to sing* the *new song* among the *islands,* and clearly this is among the churches of God, among those who are surrounded by the aforementioned sea and among those who are blown on every side by the winds from the outside. For this reason he continues on to say: *The islands and those who inhabit them,* speaking about those who are assembled in the churches.

[**42:11-12**] Then, again to the *wilderness,* which has been mentioned numerous times in the passages discussed above,[23] he brings good news when he says: *Rejoice, O wilderness and its villages,* or according to the other Greek translations: *And its cities.* For many *cities* [**273**] are planned according to the different forms of administration in the church of God, as is shown "in the vision concerning Egypt"[24]

---

[17]Jn 7:18. [18]Gen 12:7. [19]Mt 4:18. [20]This may be a reference to Paul's first missionary journey on the island of Cyprus. [21]Cf. Rom 15:24. [22]Eusebius shares the enthusiasm of the author of the Acts of the Apostles for the achievement of reaching Rome with the gospel. [23]Cf. Is 35:1; 40:3; 41:18. [24]Is 19:1.

n which it was said that "there will be five cities in Egypt speaking the Canaanite language and swearing in the name of the Lord of hosts."[25] He also promises that the *homesteads and those who inhabit Kedar and those who inhabit Petra will rejoice*. And *Kedar* lies beyond Arabia in the furthest wilderness, where he says the Saracen race dwells. In speaking of all those who inhabit the wildernesses and the remote places on the earth, the Word intends to indicate the spiritual rejoicing in God for the grace of Christ that extends even to us. And *Petra* is a certain city in Palestine where superstitious people are submerged in a great and demonic deception, but he says that even the inhabitants of this city will share in the grace, for *those who inhabit Petra will rejoice*. The fulfillment of these words in actuality confirmed the truth that this prophecy is about the churches of Christ and about the city of those who dwell on the rock, and they are found in the wildernesses of the Saracens and all around us. *Kedar* translates into Greek as "darkness," since these people were transformed from darkness to the aforementioned "light to the nations."[26] So too, the Word says that those *who inhabit Petra will rejoice*. "And the *rock*[27] was Christ."[28] All these entities the prophecy counts as being in the heights and in the elevated words of God and as though standing on high mountains. Thus, the Word prophesies that they will sing to God and *give him glory* when he says: *They will call from the top of the mountains, and they will give glory to God*. And therefore also the text reads above: "Go up on a high mountain, you who bring good tidings to Zion; lift up your voice with strength, you who bring good tidings to Jerusalem."[29]

[42:13] But these things were to take place in the *wilderness* and among the *islands* and in the *Kedar*, and admittedly then these places do not refer to the nation of the Jews. And so the Word proclaimed in this passage continues on and then signifies the jettisoning of Israel when it says: *The Lord God of the powers will go forth and crush the war*, and according to Symmachus: *The Lord will go forth as a powerful warrior*. You see how he says that the Lord himself will appear in the figure of a *man* and as a *man of war*, and will do battle with his enemies. Then the text continues on to say: *He will stir up jealousy*, and Moses also taught this when he said concerning the nation of the Jews: "They made me jealous with what is no god, provoked me with their idols. So I will make them jealous with what is no nation, provoke them with a nation lacking understanding."[30] Therefore, he says that *he will stir up* this *jealousy* by adopting and appropriating for his own *Kedar* and the *islands* and the other foreign nations, shaking off and thrusting away from himself [274] the Jewish people, and doing so with a reasonable and prudent defense. Therefore, the text continues on to say: *And he will shout against his foes with strength*.

[42:14] For it is not without reason that he will make war against them, and he will make this reason clear and shout it out with a mighty shout, as he also taught when he said: *I have been silent. Shall I even always be silent and hold back?* For when they transgressed and acted profanely, he was *silent*, being longsuffering and bearing with them in his patience and not immediately bringing forth wrath on them. Also during the time of his passion he endured false charges and was "silent,"[31] and, although falsely accused, "he made no answer."[32] But, indeed, he says *I have been silent*, not *and I shall always be silent*. And then *I endured like a woman in labor*, but now

---

[25]Is 19:18. [26]Is 42:6. [27]The Greek word πέτρα is both the city name Petra as well as the word *rock*. [28]1 Cor 10:4. [29]Is 40:9. [30]Deut 32:21. [31]Mt 26:63. [32]Mt 27:12.

is the "time of recompense,"[33] and therefore *I will amaze and wither at once*, or according to Symmachus: *I will both draw a breath and blow forth.*

[42:15] The text continues on according to the Hebrew reading and the other Greek translations: *I will lay waste to mountains and hills, and I will dry up all their grass.* In speaking of *mountains and hills*, he alludes to the rulers of the people, and the *grass* refers to their sin.[34] He threatens to raze to the ground their vanity and the arrogance of those who rule over them and to *dry up their grass.* Because these things are said concerning them, the Word advances and displays that these things are not far away. And concerning the *rivers* among them—that is, the teachings that were once abundantly supplied to them like *rivers*—he says *I will turn into islands.* And yet also there will be areas among them that become stagnant for lack of spiritual water,[35] so that they become comparable to *marshlands*, and he says *I will dry up* these places.

[42:16-17] Then, after threatening these things concerning them, he again turns to speak of the grace that will be given to the Gentiles. Therefore, he continues on: *And I will lead the blind by a road they have not known.* And did he not teach who these blind were in the verses above when he said in the person of Christ: "I have given you as a covenant to my race, as a light to nations, to open the eyes of the blind"?[36] Therefore they themselves, then, were once *blind* among the Gentiles, and he promises to make them walk *by a road they have not known.* For how have we come *to know the way* to God except through his divine grace? Since all the translations read

unanimously, *and I will lead the blind by a road they had not known*, we remember that the Savior said these things when he said, "I am the way."[37] And seeing that we did not at first believe in Christ and his saving word, he directs his promise to us who were *blind.* When he speaks also concerning the *paths of which they had no knowledge*, he clearly indicates that we will understand the prophetic Scriptures by living lives in accord with the divine teachings. *He will turn the darkness into light* for us *and the crooked places into a straight path.* For the ignorance of God which once abounded in our souls he changed *into the light* of knowledge, and the *places* that were once *crooked* to us, that is, the sayings from Scripture that we thought were obscure, he promises *to make* these [275] plain. And he continues on to say: *I will do these things*[38] *for them*, and to be perfectly accurate, he did not promise that he would speak *the words* to them but that he would *do* them. For, indeed, these things were said of old among the prophets, and he has taken it on himself to accomplish them in deed; and, he says, *I will not forsake them.*

Then, after saying these things concerning those who were once *blind*, he turns again to the word addressed to those who were once close to God. And he says: *After they were turned back*, alluding to those of the circumcision, concerning whom he says: *But they turned back.* Then, as the conversion of the Gentiles had been displayed to them, and they turned from their error and came *into the light* from the darkness, he continues on to say reproachfully to those idolaters: *Be ashamed with shame, you who trust in the graven images, who say to the molten images, "You are our gods."* For truly those of the idolatrous Gentiles were formerly *ashamed* before they turned to fear the God of

---

[33]Is 34:8; 61:2. [34]It may be that Eusebius has in mind that our unworthy works are likened to hay in 1 Cor 3:12. [35]Through the Gospels, one encounters the expression "living water" or "running water," as the underlying Greek is the same. It may be that Eusebius assumes that "spiritual water" would be running water, and therefore his analogy concerning stagnation through a lack of spiritual water makes sense. [36]Is 42:6-7. [37]Jn 14:6. [38]The Greek word is ῥήματα, a word that could be either translated "things" or "words."

he Jews; and therefore he was prophesying these things during the time when they were devoted to idolatry. But now, they have stopped being *ashamed* because of the conversion of the Gentiles. And this was prophetically foretold when he said: *They will be ashamed of their shame.* For he says that those who were once *blind* see, since they then turned *into the light,* and *they will be ashamed* and stop *saying to the cast images,* "*You are our gods."*

[42:18-19] After the Word has said these things, he shouts to those whose ears are *deaf* and cries out: *Hear, you that are deaf, and you that are blind, look up to see!* In order that no one should suppose that these things have been said concerning the Gentiles who were once *blind* and *deaf,* he then makes his meaning quite clear and interprets the sense of the text when he continues on to say: *And who is blind but my servants, and deaf but they who lord it over them?* Then, according to Symmachus, he adds: *Who is blind like the perfect one?* And he expounds the word still more clearly when he says: *Even God's slaves have become blind,* but according to Symmachus the text reads: *Receive again sight, O you who are blind, and hear, O you who are deaf. Who is blind if not my servant and deaf like my messenger whom I sent? Who is blind like the perfect one and deaf like my servant?* This is equivalent to what the other translations say. He says that his *servant* is someone other than the people of the circumcision, and he identifies him as the same person as his *messenger* and the *perfect one* and the *servant of the Lord* in his judgment. And in these things he is saying, "I wanted them to be my *servant* and *perfect one* and *messenger,* but *they were blind."*

[42:20-22] And how they became *blind* and *deaf* he continues on to explain: *You have often seen but not observed; your ears have been*

opened, but you have not heard. And this is also what had been said before in the verse: "*You will listen by listening, but you will not understand, and looking you will look, but you will not perceive. For this people's heart has grown fat."*[39] But according to Symmachus, the text says: *You saw many things, but you did not observe them; your*[40] *ears have been opened, but you will not hear anything. The Lord* [276] *wanted to justify him and to make him greatly admired and a marvel. But the people were in fact spoiled and carried away captive.* You see that all these things were said concerning the people of the circumcision. But on the one hand *the Lord has willed to justify him and to magnify praise.* And their souls were surrendered to their enemies, and they have become a *people spoiled and plundered. For the snare was within the secret rooms* of their souls *as well as in their houses.* For in the very schemes that those who wanted to do something against Christ were *hiding,* even in these schemes there was a snare also against them, *and there was no one to rescue* them, no *one to deliver* them, or anyone to say, "*Restore!"*

[42:23-25] Then, afterwards, he addressed the *deaf,* and turning to his audience he said: *Who is there among you who will give ear to these things, and who is there who will listen for the things to come?* For, he says, the accomplishment of these deeds has not yet arrived, but they will be fulfilled presently. *Who* then will there be who will understand these things *among you?* Who will look into the reason for the plundering of the people so as to ask: *Who gave Jacob for spoil and Israel to those who plunder him?* And if anyone should look into who did these things, he would find that the one who *gave them for spoil* was none other than the one *against whom they have sinned, and they would not walk in his ways.* For those who were called to the evangelical ways did not

---

[39]Is 6:9-10. [40]The Greek has a third person singular personal pronoun ("his ears").

listen, neither were they willing *to hear the law* of the new covenant. For this reason *he brought on them the anger of his wrath, and war over-powered them.* For once before they had been attacked and were able to recover themselves, so that Jerusalem and the palace in it were secured. But now *war overpowered them,* and not only the war from without, but also the war that besieges their souls from within. For this reason the text says: *Those who were burning them all around,* as well as those who suffered these things, *did not understand, neither did they take it to heart.* Here we read the reason these evils had overtaken them.

[**43:1-2**] If we remember the things that were just said concerning the people of the circum-cision—whom the Word denounced as "blind" and "deaf" when he said "and who is blind but my servants, and deaf but they who lord it over them? Even God's slaves have become blind,"[1] and again, "and the people were plundered and spoiled"[2] and the following lines in which he threatened "to bring on them anger and wrath and war"[3]—we will conclude that the present things are no longer said concerning them. Therefore, the Word turns to the superior rank of those from among the people who received the saving word, and it is these he addresses when he says: *But now thus says the Lord God, he who made you, O Jacob, he who formed you, O Israel.* And even if there cer-tainly were those among you who were un-faithful and "blind" and "deaf," [**277**] who after doing such things were delivered over to the anger of God, yet now you listen. But I say you were the ones "who failed to know your own maker and creator,"[4] although you ob-served the saving and sound image in which you had been created. For this reason, the creator addressed you as truly Jacob and as the one worthy of the name Israel in the verse

above, and he said these things to you. Indeed, many are those who are deprived of your salvation and those who are hindered from having the evangelical word that you preach set before them, but I encourage you *not to fear* these things. For even *I am the Lord God who made you and who formed you*; indeed, he made the soul when "he made it according to the image of God,"[5] and he *formed* the body when he took "from the earth"[6] and formed it. I gave my own blood as a "ransom"[7] for your salva-tion; *I ransomed you, and I have called you.* Also, I made you my possession, so that "you were my people, and I was your God."[8] And, therefore, you were commanded to be coura-geous, since I deemed you worthy of such things, and to walk in the way in which you were instructed, and you were courageous and "preached the evangelical word everywhere to all the nations of the earth."[9] For although he said that the *fire* burns and the *waters* and *rivers overflow*, none of these things will harm you because I will be with you everywhere. For truthfully I promised: "Behold, I am with you always, to the close of the age."[10]

[**43:3-4**] And, look here, just as I "redeemed"[11] you my people and gave "my precious blood"[12] for your salvation, so also you are the *exchange* for the other nations. And I say that nations will be saved through you, the *Egyptians* and *Ethiopians* and those who dwell in *Soene,* or as the other translations render the text, *and Sheba.* And Symmachus says: *I gave Egypt and Ethiopia and Sheba as a ransom in your place.* For thus *you have become precious* to me and so *you have been glorified before me,* and so *I have loved you,* and in this way God brings the news of salvation through you to all people and to the very ends of the earth. And of all the people who were deemed worthy to be called through you, the Egyptians are the most superstitious.

Chapter Forty-Three [1]Is 42:19. [2]Is 42:22. [3]Is 42:25. [4]Cf. Wis 15:11. [5]Cf. Gen 1:27. [6]Cf. Gen 2:7. [7]Cf. Mt 20:28. [8]Cf. Jer 31:1. [9]Gf. Mk 10:13. [10]Mt 28:20. [11]Is 43:1. [12]1 Pet 1:19.

Therefore, on the one hand, through the *Egyptians* he alludes to all those who are superstitious and idolatrous, and on the other hand, through the *Ethiopians* and the people of *Soene* he alludes to those who dwell in the furthest extremities away from us. And if the text mentions *Sheba*, one should know that this is the nation of the Sabateans, where the "queen of Sheba"[13] lived during the times of Solomon. Therefore, **[278]** the text says I acquired all these nations *in your place* or *on your behalf*, and I will give over to destruction those who war against you because of the word you announced.

[43:5-6] For this reason, I exhort you to be courageous, because I will be with you through everything, and the *offspring* that you engendered throughout the whole world and the many children to whom you gave birth according to God I will gather into "my heavenly city."[14] I will raise them up high in the air so that they will soar like winged birds on the winds, that is, like the angelic hosts. And, indeed, I will receive them *from the north* and *from the southwest*, or according to the other translations, *from the south*. For I will command the corners of the earth to give them up because they are my *sons* and *daughters*, those whom you scattered and who were born again in my church.

[43:7] And should it be necessary to identify them by name, I have already made them known to all, for they are the ones *who will be called by my name*. And where does the name Christian come from if not from the name of Christ? And it was he who predicted these things through the prophet. Instead of *for I prepared him in my glory*, the other translations say: *I created him in my glory*. For this new people *I created for glory*, so that I would be glorified among the people, *and I formed them* when they were unformed in their ways.

[43:8-11] He says: *And I have brought forth* a people that was in darkness at first and a *blind people*. For although they appeared to have *eyes* in their souls and common sense, all in all they were blind in regards to the error of idolatry. Next, after these things, the text reads: *All the nations have gathered together, and rulers will be gathered from among them*. And the accomplishment of this word is the fulfillment of these deeds. For those who were once *blind* and *deaf* were transformed through the apostolic offspring, and *they were gathered* into the church of God. And the *rulers from among* the nations opposed the people of God. After saying these things, the prophet predicted that something of astonishment and consternation would befall them when he addressed them and said: *Who will declare these things? Or who will declare to you the things that were from the beginning? Let them bring their witnesses, and let them be justified and speak truths*. Then he says who it will be who will see with his eyes the fulfillment of all these words. Let the witnesses of these events come, and *let* those who have testified *be justified*, since *even I God* will be their *witness, and the servant whom I have chosen*, concerning whom he said above: "Behold, my servant whom I have appointed, my chosen one, my soul receives him favorably."[15]

Therefore, *God* himself is *even this servant, my chosen one*, as the Savior made clear in the Gospels when he said: "Whoever acknowledges me before **[279]** men, I also will acknowledge him before my Father who is in heaven."[16] I will serve as a witness for my witnesses, *so that you may know and believe and understand that I am. Before me there was no other god, nor shall there be any after me*. For the reason for the coming of Christ and for the witness of his apostles to every nation was nothing other than the preaching of the knowledge of God to everyone, and faith in him and understanding concerning him to those who were formerly

---

[13]1 Kings 10:1. [14]Heb 12:22. [15]Mt 12:18; Is 42:1. [16]Mt 10:32.

void of understanding and to those who were faithless and disbelieving and to those who were ignorant concerning him, because the eyes of their minds were blinded and closed because of the godless error of idolatry. For this reason, he shines forth: *Be my witnesses; I too am a witness, says the Lord God, and the servant whom I have chosen.* And he continues on to say: *So that you may know and believe and understand that I am. Before me there was no other god, nor shall there be any after me.* For if one is from the beginning, this one must be divine, as the theology concerning his one and only Son counsels.

Continuing on with delivering his instruction, the Word says: *I am God, and besides me there is none who saves.* And he affirmed this when he proclaimed above: *Even I, the Lord God, am the servant whom I have chosen*, and so he does not fail to connect the present passage with the theological discussion above concerning the *servant, whom he has chosen. I am God, and besides me there is none who saves, and I am the servant whom I have chosen.* For he said that he was a *witness, and the servant whom he has chosen*, and so we conclude that this *God who saves* is *also the servant, whom he has chosen.* And although the text says: *Besides me there is none who saves*, it is not denying that the *servant whom he has chosen* is indeed a Savior. For the present prophet viewed him as a "Savior," as we see in the following verse: "And the Lord will send them a Savior who will save them—judging he will save them."[17] But even if the text says that *the servant whom I have chosen* is the "Savior" who saves, yet it does not say that *he saves besides me* but rather with my judgment and by my direction. For apart from my will and *besides me there is none who saves.*

[43:12] The text says: *I declared in advance that I myself am God* through my prophets, and according to my words *I saved* those worthy of

salvation through my servant. But instead of *reproached*, all the other translations read: *And I made to hear.* For, anticipating the things that I made to be heard, the God who is among you came neither as a *stranger* nor an exile. And *you are witnesses* that nothing was unusual or *strange among you* when my prophets predicted these things. And I was a *witness, even I the Lord God and the servant whom I have chosen.* I was with him when he predicted these things—these things were **[280]** from him and with him, the *servant whom I have chosen*, witnessed through the prophets.

[43:13] It is certainly true that the Word existed prior to the incarnation and that Christ was then in union with the Father, but when the text says *from the beginning* it affirms that God has ordained his will to stand, and there is no one who is able to deter or divert his will. For "there is no other God,"[18] and clearly there *is no one* who is able *to rescue from my hands, no one* who is able to overturn the things that I have appointed. Now on the one hand these things were said about Jacob and Israel, but on the other hand they refer to the apostolic band. And the Word discusses all the generations of the Jews who received the Christ of God.

[43:14-18] The meaning of the above statements is as follows. Indeed, once my bountiful kindness were with the Jewish nation, but it became necessary to discipline and chasten them, and so I delivered them over to the Babylonians. But not long afterwards I set them free from their captivity *in Babylon*, for God is the Lord of all. And I decimated the Babylonians who came up against Jerusalem, and the *Chaldeans* among them were set to flight, and they were placed in chains and taken aboard *ships* of the sea by certain other enemy powers who were stronger than them. *I, God*, accomplished *these things*, and thus I

---

[17]Is 19:20. [18]Cf. Is 45:5.

showed forth my kingdom to people. But instead of *the one who exhibited Israel as your king*, Symmachus says: *I am the Lord, your holy One, the restorer of Israel your king.*

And God says that he accomplished these things among the Babylonians and the Chaldeans. He spoke prophetically through Isaiah about events that had not yet happened and were yet about to be as though they were already fulfilled. But also, he says that during those ancient times he made his divine power manifest among those in Egypt. For he carried his people away across the Red *Sea*, making a way *in the mighty water* and a dry *path* through the very *sea*. "The chariots of Pharaoh and his host he threw into the sea,"[19] and thus *they have lain down* and "sank into the deep,"[20] and *they will* no longer *rise*. And they who were once like a burning fire *have been quenched like a wick*. Indeed, these are the things that I performed and that have been remembered from very ancient times, and these are the stories that have been passed on from generation to generation from very long ago, but now, in the present time, I encourage you no longer to wonder at the things that were done in Babylon and in Egypt. For this reason, the text reads: *Do not remember the former things or consider the things of old*, or according to Symmachus: *Do not reflect on.*

[43:19-21] For this reason, I did not want you to wonder at those things in the future, but there are certain newer wonders that are in no way inferior to the wonders done in old times, and like a light they *shine forth* among all, and *you will know* these things when they happen. [281] And what does he mean when he says: *I will make a way in the wilderness?* Clearly he is speaking again about the church that he established among the nations, which was then a *wilderness* concerning the knowledge of God

before the Christ came to dwell, who said: "I am the way."[21] And he says *I will make a way* in that place that was once a *wilderness*, just as I once made a way through the Red Sea. *Rivers* of divine words will flow from the teaching of the Holy Spirit *into the dry land*, just as *rivers* "gushed out"[22] *in the wilderness* for Moses. But, indeed, the water that flowed was physical and perishable, but the water that now flows is from the inspired abundant supply of the rational and spiritual water.

Then he made a *way in the wilderness* and the *rivers* of his springs inundated the dry country. Concerning these "springs" it was said above: "And you will drink water from the springs of salvation."[23] At that time, *the wild animals of the field*—that is, the souls that have become wild—will change from a savage state by the force of the river, so that they who were once *wild animals will praise him*, although they did not always do so. But it is not stated when this change in the people happened, whether it was during the time in Egypt or the exodus from Egypt or the captivity in Babylon. And even if also there were certain *sirens* who beguiled human souls with pleasures and demonic lyrics, adorned in eloquent illusory words, even these too *will praise me* after they are changed. Yet there are also *daughters of ostriches*, or according to the other Greek translations: *Also ostriches*,[24] an animal that lives in the wilderness and uninhabited areas, and it too was tamed and taught *to praise God*. And the reason for these things is that I gave *water in the wilderness* and provided the force of the *rivers* flowing *in the wilderness*. Then the *animals of the field* and *the sirens* and the *ostriches* will drink my water, and their nature will be changed so that they are tame and rational. *My people* and *my chosen race* will learn to *set forth my virtues*, or according to Symmachus, *my hymn.*

---

[19]Ex 15:4. [20]Ex 15:5. [21]Jn 14:6. [22]Cf. Ps 78:20; 105:41. [23]Is 12:3. [24]Here Eusebius uses a synonym. Both words mean "ostrich." The second word Eusebius uses portrays the ostrich as a bird with a camel-like neck.

[43:22-24] Incredibly, these things were indeed accomplished. And you should see, *O Jacob*, that at that time you were not worthy of my calling, or according to Symmachus: *Neither did you call on me, O Jacob*. But according to Aquila and Theodotion, the text reads: *And you did not call on me, Jacob*. For, indeed, *the animals of the field* and *the sirens* and *the daughters of the ostriches will praise me*. But you, *O Jacob*, you did no such thing, nor were you worthy to call on me; but according to Symmachus the text says *you were wearied by me*; Aquila and Theodotion, respectively, read: *Because* [282] *you wearied me*, and I *did not do anything but you wearied me*. Therefore, what seemed to be burdens to you, I already asked for when I said earlier: "What to me is the multitude of your sacrifices? says the Lord; I am full of whole burnt offerings of rams, and I do not want the fat of lambs or the blood of bulls and goats."[25]

But *neither incense nor frankincense nor sacrifices*. I asked for no such things from you in the laws of the new covenant, which I ordained "through my servant whom I have chosen,"[26] and neither did you bring these things to me. And truly it is necessary to say, you did things other than those you were supposed to do. *For in your sins I have stood before you*, or according to the other translations, *in your sins and in your iniquities you called me*. You see how in the verse above he speaks of the "wilderness" and the "wild animals"[27] and voices his expectation that they would do good, but now he rebukes the people of the circumcision for their ungodliness, sometimes calling them *Jacob* and sometimes *Israel*. Thus he refers to them with austere names and addresses them neither as his "servant" nor as his "chosen,"[28] although he had granted them a superior status.

[43:25-28] Therefore, after procuring a conviction for those whom he accused, he urges them to turn around, and those who turned around will admit their failures. For this reason, he says: *I am the one who blots out your sins, and I will not remember them at all*. And *remember* what you once were. For the remembrance of former sins is declared through confession. For this reason, he continues on to say: *State your sins first*, for when you do this *you shall be justified*, because "the righteous accuses himself at the beginning of his speech."[29]

Do not be like the *fathers* who were sinful and your *rulers* who at that time *acted profanely against me*. But instead of *and your rulers acted lawlessly against me*, Aquila and Symmachus render the phrase: *And your interpreters*. Then he says: *And the rulers defiled my holy things*. And there are three ranks present in this verse: *Fathers*, *interpreters* and *rulers*. The *rulers* clearly refer to those who instruct the nation, the *interpreters* are those who interpret the Holy Scriptures, and the *fathers* are those who are aged and in their later years. He says that they all *acted profanely*, and he affirms that they were worthy of the destruction of Jacob. For because of them he says: *I gave Jacob to destroy and Israel for a reproach*, or according to the other Greek translations, *for defamation*.

[44:1-4] Here again, he addressed without qualification as *Jacob* and *Israel* those who were accused, and those who were attacked he no longer addressed in the same manner but with the customary qualification. Therefore, he continues on to say: *But now hear, O Jacob my servant and Israel whom I have chosen*, and in this verse he is once again referring to the apostolic band, whom he addresses when he says: *Thus says the Lord God who* [283] *made you and who formed you from the womb, you will still be helped*, but according to Symmachus: *The one who formed you from the womb helps you still*. It is he who says to them: *Do not fear*,

---

[25]Is 1:11.   [26]Cf. Is 43:10.   [27]Is 43:20.   [28]Is 42:1.   [29]Prov 18:17a.

O Jacob my servant and the beloved Israel whom I have chosen, because I will provide water for their thirst to those who walk in a dry land. And he makes it clear that it is he who speaks when he says: *I will put my spirit on your offspring and my blessings on your children.* For through his Holy Spirit, he will provide an abundant supply of intellectual, life-giving and spiritual water in the *dry land* and in the *wilderness*. And the *offspring* of the apostles are the churches of God, and their *children* are those who are "reborn through the Holy Spirit"[1] everywhere across the face of the earth and among all the nations. He says, *they will also spring up like grass in the midst of water*, but according to Symmachus: *And they will spring up like willows in the midst of green grass by flowing water*, and according to Theodotion the text also reads: *In the midst of green grass by flowing water*. And, because it is an ever-blooming and youthful plant, he here compares the *willow* with the presence of an abundance of intellectual waters flowing in the church.

[44:5] So great is the advance and success of godliness of those who once inhabited the "dry land" and the "wilderness"[2] that they all ran toward God. Then, as though in a competition, they snatched at the grace of God and *said "I am God's."* And *another was inscribed with the name of Jacob*, although he was not from Jacob but from the "wilderness" and the "dry land." But he was encouraged *to call out the name* of those who once styled themselves the people of God. Therefore, he said: *This one will say, "I am God's," and this one will call out in the name of Jacob*, or according to Symmachus: *He will be called by the name Jacob, and another will write with his hand, "I am God's,"* and again, *another will call out in the name of Israel*; he exalts himself saying that he is *Israel*. And the power of the prophetic words is truly wonderful and astounding, so that we

ascertain the fulfillment of the prophecy in fact. And, therefore, in the persecutions against us, we witnessed many of the pagan nations claiming for themselves titles of holy men, so that one calls himself *Jacob* and another *Israel*, and yet another Jeremiah and another Isaiah and another Daniel. And, therefore, they passed on so many *names inscribed* to the witness of God with great courage and boldness. And this is what the prophecy is signifying when it says: *This one will say, "I am God's," and this one will call out in the name of Jacob, and another will inscribe with his hand, "I am God's," yet another will call out in the name of Israel.*

[44:6] [284] The Word concludes the former subject, which was about the gospel in that it foretold the illumination of the chosen one of God among people and announced a future for the places among the nations that were once *dry land* and *wilderness*. The Word then starts a new section about the idolatries of the Jewish nation, saying: *Thus says God, the king of Israel.* He clearly identifies who the *king of Israel* is when he continues on to say: *And the one who delivered him, the God of hosts*, thus teaching that only *the one who delivers Israel* is *king*, and not those who are accused of idolatry. And this is what he says to those who are humble and dismayed in their hearts, but then he applies a rebuke concerning the error of idolatry, exhorting the people and teaching them that there is no other *God* to lead them but him alone, and there is none other, neither will there be any after him. Therefore, he says: *I am first, and I am after these things; besides me there is no god.* Then, again, it pertains to explain and add on a comment about the following verse: "And the servant whom I have chosen."[3] For at once, when the Word spoke through the above verse, it is necessary for us who remembered it to consult this very word

Chapter Forty-Four   [1]Jn 3:5. [2]Is 43:20. [3]Is 43:10.

221

in subsequent theological discussions. For the verse also testifies that God spoke truthfully, and what has been said truthfully is necessarily true everywhere. Who was "the servant whom I have chosen"[4] or him concerning whom it has been said: "Behold, my servant whom I have chosen, my elect; my soul receives him; he will bring forth justice to the Gentiles, and the Gentiles will hope in his name,"[5] and the rest? Is it not clear that the Word is speaking of the Christ of God? The Word appealed to various expressions in the verses above, but through them all the present word delivers this teaching to those who remain in the error of idolatry and accept many gods and commands: *Besides one there is no other god.* For that which is unbegotten is one, and the monarchical authority over all is one. And the word of God also includes in this theological discourse a reference to the Father, for "In the beginning was the Word, and the Word was with God, and the Word was God."[6] But it was not the right time to unveil the mystery concerning the only-begotten Son of God to those who were still distracted by images and statues and inanimate wood. For this reason, indeed, he oversees the coming of his Son and the grace that was given through him to all who no longer practice idolatry and to those who are not still deceived by the doctrine of polytheism and who do not believe in inanimate statues and all kinds of images as gods. But such were the Jews, according to the prophet.

[44:7-11] Afterwards, the Word adds a rebuke and says: *Who is like me? Let him stand; let him call, and let him proclaim, and let him make ready for me, inasmuch as I have made man forever.* For if anyone else is God, let him speak. And he demonstrates that he alone is God through the works he performs in this universe. For if the world is one and its nature is everywhere consistent, then the maker of this world should also be one. [285] For "from the greatness and beauty of created things comes a perception of the creator"[7] of all things. And if anyone introduces another creator, let him show forth and display another world such as this one. But no other world exists alongside the world that we see, and "then there is no other god."[8] And if there is another god, first of all, the text says *let him stand,* and I say let him prove that he really exists. But God—because he is being in his very substance and because he exists in and of himself—remains. Then, the text says, *let him declare* and emit a distinct voice fitting for God and tell us what will happen in this life in the future or what existed from the very beginning, from which I created man and placed him on the earth until the present time. For by this we will know that the word of God is in him.

But what I want to say is "do not be conformed"[9] to those who, although they see, place a veil over their eyes: *For you did not give ear,* neither did you know anything of these things *from the beginning.* But I proclaimed and *announced in advance* through my prophets, and I displayed in this world miracles of divine power. And *you are witnesses* of these miracles, and I delivered explicit instructions too, so that you learned from Moses that even if you do not want to, you are to confess that *besides me there is no god.* And at that time, I permitted you to see my divine "virtues,"[10] which I exhibited in Egypt, and in the Red Sea and in the wilderness, where I displayed countless wonders. No one from these times was present with me nor yet earlier, for he says, they were not *from the beginning,* that is, before the times of the flood; the artisan who fashioned their inanimate images did not exist then. And *you are witnesses* that *they did not previously exist.* What I mean is that from the very beginning of the inception of the history of humanity, there were not found among

---

[4]Is 43:10. [5]Mt 12:18, 21. [6]Jn 1:1. [7]Wis 13:5. [8]Cf. Is 44:6. [9]Rom 12:2. [10]Is 43:21,

people *those who fashion and carve gods*, neither by engraving nor by the art of sculpting. But then, after much time had passed, a great number of such artisans sprung up, *but they will all be put to shame*, and they will then cease, and they will blush and hide themselves because of their idolatrous error. But if they remain in their error, they will be delivered over to destruction during the time of vengeance. The present passage is about you, and the present word is for you.

[44:12-20] Why, then, did you never reason among yourselves and ask what is the nature of those "godmakers" who fashion inanimate statues for you? For is it not plain for all to see that the gods are the works of "artisans"?[11] They have been fabricated with *axes* and *augurs* and such tools. They are the contrivances of poor day laborers, who, because of their need for food in order to pursue their work, promote the business of idolatry for the *bread* of leisure. And why did you not ask what is the nature of God, and whether God needs food, and whether *he will become hungry* if you do not offer sacrifices, and whether [286] God *will also become weak* if he is not nourished, or according to Symmachus: *He will become hungry and weak and exhausted, and he will not drink water*. And why does he say *he will not drink water*, unless he had actually been in need of water? And if he will neither eat nor drink, is he not in fact worse off than an irrational animal? How, then, have you been deceived, O *vain* people, when such a state of reality proves the impotence of the statues?

[44:21-22] Passing on to the idolatry of the Jewish nation, he continues on to say: *Remember these things, O Jacob and Israel*. And he says this because they forget and need reminding of these things because of the dullness of their minds. Then he reminds Israel and says: *For you are my servant; I formed you* to be *my servant*. This is why you should remember your value and not insult the image of God, as those who reverence inanimate wood that has been formed by the hands of artisans and those who make gods for themselves. Then, urging them to hurry to repentance, he promises them that if they turn, he will grant them forgiveness for their earlier faults. Therefore, he says: *I have blotted out*—instead of *I will blot out*—*your acts of lawlessness like a cloud and your sins like darkness*. Then he adds: *Return to me, and I will redeem you*, instead of abandoning you and surrendering you to your enemies.

[44:23] After saying this, the prophet then foresees that many of them will obey the prophetic word, and anticipating this he salutes the *heavens*—that is, he addresses the heavenly powers at work for their salvation—and says: *Rejoice, O heavens, because God has had mercy on Israel*. For "there will be joy in heaven over those who are about to come to repentance"[12] from the evil deeds they used to do. He also says: *trumpet, O foundations of the earth*, or according to the other Greek translations: *Shout aloud, O deepest places in the earth*. And if there are certain divine forces that support the earth itself, let them ascribe shouts of praise and songs to God. But it would seem that in this passage the prophets and all the righteous and God-loving people are referred to as the *foundations of the earth*. And the apostle Paul taught this when he spoke of the church as "built upon the *foundation* of the apostles and prophets."[13] He also says: *Shout for joy, O mountains*, and let *the hills and all the trees that are in them* send forth their voices as well; let them glorify God for the repentance of those mentioned above and for their salvation. The *mountains* represent those whose souls are elevated and soar above, and the *hills* are those whose souls are higher

---

[11]Cf. Hos 13:2; Jer 10:3. [12]Lk 15:7. [13]Eph 2:20 RSV.

than average, and the *trees* are those whose souls are fruitful. He even enjoins the universe and everything in it to praise God when he says: *Because God has redeemed Jacob, and Israel will be glorified!* Or according to the other Greek translations: *And he will be glorified in Israel!* This in fact was fulfilled in the prophetic words of instruction delivered among the first people [287], and they listened to these words and converted from the error of idolatry to the worship of God.

[44:24] After setting forth a rebuke of idolatry in the above verses, the Word affirms that those who listen to the announcement of the prophetic teaching and return from the Babylonian captivity will cease from idolatry. For since they committed idolatry, they were delivered over to the Babylonians, and Jerusalem itself had survived the siege and absolute destruction that came to pass during the time of the Assyrians because of the deeds that had been dared by the inhabitants of Jerusalem. And he prophesies release from their troubles for those who suffered these things, if they ceased from their idolatrous error. This was fulfilled during the times of Cyrus, the first king of Persia. And it is absolutely extraordinary that he mentions him by name, "Cyrus,"[14] because it was nearly two hundred years later that the Jews were released from their captivity, and it was he who ordered the people to rebuild the temple.

For this reason, because of such a promise of blessings in the verse above, he calls out to the *heavens* and to the *foundations of the earth* and to the *mountains* and to the *hills* and to *all the trees* to sing songs of praise and glorify God. In the passage at hand, he continues on to say to them: *Thus says the Lord, who redeems you, who forms you from the womb.* And the book of Jeremiah will teach us who *the one who forms you in the womb* is in the

passage where it is written: "And a word of the Lord came to him, saying, 'Before I formed you in the belly, I knew you, and before you came forth from the womb, I had consecrated you.'"[15] The prophet clearly understood this to be the word of the Lord, and it teaches that the Lord is the sculptor of those who are being carried bodily in the womb. Then, afterwards, he alludes to their return from captivity when he called him favorably *the one who redeems.* And since those to whom these things were said were physically-minded people, it was right that he remind them then that it was he *who formed* them *from the womb.* He goes on to say: *I am the Lord, who accomplishes all things,* or according to the other Greek translations: *The maker of all things.* And first he says, *I alone stretched out heaven,* and then, *I bolstered the earth.* For "all things were made through him, and without him was not anything made."[16] *He alone stretched out heaven, and he bolstered the earth* in the sanction and will of the Father. "For he it was that spoke, and they came to be; he it was that commanded, and they were created."[17] Therefore, it has been written in the book of Proverbs as from his own mouth: "When he prepared the sky, I was present with him."[18] For on the one hand the Father "prepared" the sky through willing and commanding him "to be present," but on the other hand, he brought forth and accomplished the deeds that had been ordained by the Father. For this reason, he says: *I alone stretched out heaven, and I bolstered the earth.* For, indeed, the *earth* is solid and firmly established, and this entire present world has been unalterably established, and so it has been said rightly [288] that the earth has been *bolstered.* And the *heaven,* as if unfolding throughout the whole world, is *stretched out.* Therefore, also, in another passage it has been said: "He who stretched out the sky like a tent."[19]

---

[14]Is 44:28; 45:1. [15]Jer 1:4-5. [16]Jn 1:3. [17]Ps 32:9. [18]Prov 8:27. [19]Ps 104:2.

[44:25-26] What is it that the Lord teaches when he continues on to say next: *Who else will scatter the signs given by ventriloquists and the divinations from the heart?* And he declares what will happen in the period after this, when in his power *he will scatter* all the *divinations*, and *he will scatter* the oracles of those who were once supposed to be gods. He also says: *I will turn backwards* that which is supposed to be the counsel "of this age,"[20] and I will prove to be "foolish"[21] that which is supposed to be "their wisdom." This is how I will handle these things. And I say that the one referred to as "my beloved and elect servant"[22] is Christ and the great things said above are all about him. The text says: *I will establish the words of my messengers*—the text is speaking of the apostles and disciples and evangelists—and *I will vindicate their counsel*. Therefore, I, the one who is about to do these things—I predict and I promise now that I will reestablish and renew *Jerusalem* after the former destruction of the Babylonians; *the cities of Judea will be inhabited*, and the *deserted places* in them will again be established "as at the beginning."[23]

[44:27-28] And I will establish even the *deserted place* that is supposed to be the *deep* and evil, and *I will completely dry up the rivers* of the great cities as well, so that Babylon will no longer be established, nor its *rivers* which had endured even in many different circumstances. And I will do all these things for my servant, and I announced that the one who would reign over them would be a man of Persian descent. And if it is necessary to prophesy his name—*Cyrus* is the name of the one who is prophesied. I will establish the *wise* servant of my words, and I who speak the truth informed him that I will *do everything in my mind*, and I will command *Jerusalem to be rebuilt* and the temple in it *to be restored*. Or

according to Symmachus: *Who tells Cyrus to be my shepherd, and he will fulfill all my will, and who says to Jerusalem, "Let it be built," and the foundations of the temple will be laid.*

[45:1] For after I arranged and willed these things, Cyrus, the king of the Persians, completed them in deed, and for this reason *I called him the anointed one*, because I advanced him to the kingdom. For *the anointed ones* among the Hebrews were all those who were led forward by God and anointed as kings. And afterwards I found the good servant "of my plan,"[1] the one who was revealed as a "man." Therefore, I now promise that *I will grasp his* [289] *right hand*, and he will neither be turned aside nor conquered by anyone greater. And I will subject many nations under him, and he will rule over them. Through him *I will break the strength* of every power among the nations. After making everything smooth and level for his feet, I will now deliver over into his hands city gates and even entire cities, so that nothing will be able to oppose him.

[45:2-7] Because he is considered worthy, let him hear—even *Cyrus* himself—the predictions that are spoken about him. It is about you, therefore, that I said: *I will go before you and level mountains; and I will break in pieces doors of bronze.*[2] But to those who are broken and who have been shut out by *bars of iron* and to those who were once kings, I will display the riches inside my secret and *unseen treasures*. And so you will know these deeds, and you will know that I am the one who engraved your name in my prophetic Scriptures so many years earlier as an everlasting monument. I am *the God of Israel*, who has come and you were not unaware, O Cyrus! For I will graciously grant to you everything that has been predicted, not for any other reason than *for the sake of* my "people,"[3]

---

[20]Lk 16:8. [21]Cf. 1 Cor 1:20. [22]Cf. Is 42:1. [23]Cf. Is 1:26. **Chapter Forty-Five** [1]Is 46:11, [2]There is a lacuna at this point in the text that makes the following sentence difficult to interpret. [3]Deut 14:2.

whom "I have chosen out of all the nations" for myself out of respect for their ancestors. And, therefore, *I called you by name*, and I designated you as *the anointed one*, and I received you as my own family, although *you did not know me*. Instead, you turned to "other gods,"[4] whom you inherited from your ancestors, and offered up sacrifices to them, not knowing that *there is no other god besides me*. But even if you did not know this beforehand, now therefore learn from what I will accomplish, and all those who dwell in the entire world *will know that there is no other god besides me*. For they will learn this from what would happen to them. For, indeed, it became necessary to bring painful things on my people for correction and instruction, and so I delivered them over to their adversaries and to the darkness and wrath of the impious because of their disobedience. But after the rest turned around and received aid, he arose, and then the *light of peace* and of all good rose on him. For he abundantly supplies me with the light and all things pertaining to *peace*, and those pertaining to wrath are also brought forward for my judgment. This is why you should learn this lesson from me: I myself am therefore the creator of *light* and the patron of *peace* as well as of *darkness* and what is thought to be disaster. Although the majority of people believe that *evil* exists, I conclude that the creator brings on everyone what they deserve in righteous judgment. Therefore, *I am God, and there is no other besides me; I am the one who does all these things*. And even if one should imagine that the things God does are evil, yet they are not evil in their nature. God brings about even the things that I think are terribly *evil* **[290]** for the profit and salvation of those who are thereby returned to their senses.

[45:8] These things happened just as the Word proclaimed and prophesied, for the people returned from captivity during the time of Cyrus. And, again, the Word continues on to speak to the heavenly powers: *Let heaven rejoice from above, and let the clouds shower down righteousness*. For just as it was during the time "when I commanded the *clouds* to send no rain"[5] to the vineyard, so now at this time I will command "my *clouds*," which are spiritual, not to send physical water but in fact to sprinkle *righteousness from* the heights *above* on those who dwell on the earth. And let the *earth* be revived, although once barren because of the sins of the people, and let it *shoot forth* fruits of godliness and produce *mercy and righteousness*. And when I say *earth*, I am speaking of those who dwell on the earth. And he says all these things will happen, since *I am the Lord who created you*, and I ordered these things to be. For I established you "out of what did not exist,"[6] and I led into the light what once had not been. And I will bring about all the other predictions in my creative power, renewing you and *recreating you* as you were at the beginning. Then, through all these things, the prophetic word is present, making rousing appeals to the people to turn from the error of polytheism altogether and granting to those who are there foreknowledge about what will happen. And so, from the present Scripture, Cyrus had confidence and eagerly performed the things that had been narrated and communicated about him, for God anticipated his life and said these things concerning him. For there was nothing remarkable about this book, preserved by the Jews in Babylon, but it revealed the prophecy about King Cyrus, who then began to show kindness to the people at the admonition of God. Josephus testifies to this word in his *Jewish Antiquities*, writing in his characteristic style. Thus says King Cyrus: "Since God almighty appointed me to be king over the earth, I believe that he is the one that the nation of the Israelites worships; for he foretold my name through the prophets and that I should

---

[4]Ex 20:3. [5]Is 5:6. [6]Cf. 2 Macc 7:28.

build him a temple at Jerusalem in the country of Judea."[7] Cyrus knew these things because he had read the book in which Isaiah had written down his prophecy two hundred and ten years prior. And these things have been recorded in the eleventh book of the *Antiquities*.

[45:9] But instead of *what better thing have I formed* and the obscure statements that follow in the Septuagint translation, Symmachus renders the meaning more lucidly when he writes: *Woe to the one who contradicts the one who formed him, a vessel among vessels of the earth. Shall the clay say to the one who forms it, "What are you doing?" and to your work, "Are they not their hands?"* But [291] according to Aquila, the text reads in this manner: *Woe to you, you who accuse the one who formed you, you earthenware jar who accuse your craftsman; shall the clay say to the one who forms it, "What are you doing?" even against your work which does not have hands?* And according to Theodotion, the text reads: *Woe to the one who stands in judgment of the one who formed him, the one who plows those who plow the earth; shall the clay say to the potter, "What are you doing?" and how are you doing your work, since you do not have hands?* It seems to me that in these statements, the Word is warning those who—after the kindnesses that he provided in the return from captivity and in the restoration of the temple in Jerusalem—neither ran to God nor confessed him as the God over all who should instruct his own people whenever he wishes, his people whom he received again and whom he led back into their own land, when he decided that this should happen. For to those who speak against his foreknowledge of all that he will administer, he says: *Woe to the one who speaks against the one who formed him.* For when indeed there was need of instruction and conversion, even I shattered Jerusalem as an earthen vessel, and I delivered over the

people to their enemies and adversaries. And then, again, after sufficient chastening, it was necessary to display deeds of benevolence, and then *I prepared better things* than had existed earlier when I transformed and renewed as *potter's clay* the temple and the city that had formerly been shattered. And in the book of Jeremiah things similar to these have been written: "And I went down to the potter's house, and behold, he was doing a job on the stones. And the vessel he was making crumbled in his hands, and again he made it into another vessel, as seemed good to him to do. And a word of the Lord came to me, saying: Shall I not have the power to do with you, O house of Israel, just as this potter did?"[8]

And it is for this reason that he says in the present passage: *I have formed something better from the clay,* from the people who were once shattered. But instead of *shall the plowman plow the earth,* Theodotion renders the text in this way: *He plows those who plow the earth.* For I myself am God, and I till those who dwell on the earth as with the plow of my word, and I myself *plowed* and *formed like potter's clay* the people and the temple, thereby completing a *better* work than the first. Therefore, the *clay* is not able to tell *the potter* what to do or to speak against its fashioner or to find fault with him and say: *"What are you doing," or "Why are you not working or have hands?"* But just as *the clay* would never say these things *to the potter,* so it is not right to find fault with the maker of all and with the creator God, to whom we are all reckoned as *clay.* Therefore, let him instruct everyone, he who clad himself in a body of dust, taken "from the earth."[9] Although he was not at all different from *clay* in comparison to the one who created him, yet he did not dare in the administration of God to contradict nor to find fault with the words of providence. For *woe to the one who contradicts the one who formed him.*

---

[7]Josephus, *Jewish Antiquities* 11.1.3-4. [8]Jer 18:3-5. [9]Gen 2:7.

[45:10] **[292]** And let especially the people dedicated to God and claiming him as *father*— let them keep guard over their mouths and not speak rashly. For *woe to the one who says to his father, "What will you beget?" and to his mother, "With what are you in labor?"* But according to Symmachus: *"What did you beget?" and to the woman, "With what are you in labor?"* For many are those who are fond of faultfinding, those who are accustomed to accusing others and those who ask why the beginning of life had to pass, and why these things will thus happen and why there was need of such things. And it was necessary for these things to happen and for *woes* to have been laid up for them.

[45:11] Next, the *Lord, the Holy One of Israel* himself, goes on to say: *Ask me about my sons and command me concerning the works of my hands,* as if anyone would ever counsel me *about my sons or concerning the works of my hands.* For the *sons* clearly allude to the intellectual and spiritual beings that he created, and *the works of his hands* are the material parts of creation. And the text says that if anyone has a word of correction to deliver, let him step into the center and speak. But if he has nothing to teach, let him seek to listen, if he wishes, and to ask me *about my sons and concerning the works of my hands.* And let him learn about the way in which I manage and administer everything, providing for and caring for all who live on the earth, for I especially provide for those *works of my hands* who have been considered worthy to be called *my sons,* concerning whom I spared no care. If you are ignorant of these things, learn from me by consulting my prophets.

[45:12] After saying this, he next continues on to deliver a pious doctrine about his manifest providence: *I made the earth and humankind on it; I bolstered heaven with my hand; I com-* *manded all the stars.* Therefore, who could find fault with God for doing these things? And what kind of beauty does not exult, or what kind of greatness does not protect? And who will not ascribe these qualities to the present order and to the well-lived human life? For, indeed, *I made the earth* neither a desert nor inarable but rather as a dwelling place for people. Therefore, I also prepared the rest of the animals and plants for the use and service of people, and *I bolstered heaven,* and I adorned it with *stars,* and *I commanded* their movements to be orderly and harmonious. And so they "give light on the earth"[10] and are "for signs and for seasons and for days and months and years."[11]

[45:13] Therefore, *I,* the maker of such grand and beautiful works, I accomplished this because of my people, and *I raised the king with righteousness.* But what is this I have made? This one will be called "Cyrus"[12] the king of the Persians, whom also the word calls to remembrance in the verse above when it says concerning him: *And all his paths shall be straight,* or according to Symmachus: **[293]** *And I shall straighten all his paths. And he shall build my city.* For, in effect, he was the one who *built the city* of Jerusalem in allowing those who wanted to go up from Babylon to go and rebuild the place. But the text also says: *And he shall turn back the captivity of my people, not with a ransom or with gifts, said the Lord God.* This was fulfilled according to the history of the king of Persia. But someone else could say that these things refer to Zerubbabel, who stemmed from the royal family and from the tribe of Judah and the succession of David. For he led the people in the return from Babylon, as they ascended to Judea, and he built the temple of which the prophets Haggai and Zechariah spoke, and so it has been said concerning him: "The hands of Zerubbabel laid the foundation of this house; his hands

---

[10]Gen 1:15. [11]Gen 1:14. [12]Is 44:28; 45:1.

shall also complete it."[13] In another instance in the verse above, he refers to the Christ of God, "whom the Father raised from the dead,"[14] "having loosed the pangs of death"[15] and whom he established as *king with righteousness*, when he correctly asserted: "But I was established king by him, on Zion, his holy mountain."[16] But truly it was only for Christ that *all his paths shall be straight*, and he *built* the true *city* of God concerning which the promise had been made: "On the rock *I will build* my church, and the gates of Hades shall not prevail against it."[17] For this *city* has truly been built "from living stones,"[18] and the *city* of God has stood "from the sun's rising to its setting,"[19] reaching every nation and supplying them with God-fearing administration. And the Christ of God alone rescued our souls from the *captivity* of the demonic error, setting us free from slavery. He did this *not with ransom or with gifts*, which is what the apostle teaches when he says: "By grace we have been saved."[20] And someone could say that these things were spoken about Zerubbabel or about Cyrus, since they are precise archetypes and symbols of what came to pass, but these things are fulfilled spiritually in the true Lord and the true Christ of God. And the word indeed speaks truly about him when it says: "Thus says the Lord to my anointed,[21] Cyrus."[22] For, according to the passage at hand, the king of the Persians was not the Christ of God who appears and *builds* Jerusalem, for the construction of the city was not completed during his lifetime. For he only laid the foundations during his lifetime, but when he abandoned the work, the place remained a desert until the time of King Darius. But what is said next should be applied to the Christ [294] of God rather than to the king of Persia, and to our Savior rather than to Zerubbabel.

[45:14-17] For the text reads: *Thus says the Lord of hosts; Egypt has toiled, and the merchandise of the Ethiopians, and the proud Sabean men, will be transferred over to you, and they shall be your slaves; and they shall follow behind you bound in handcuffs.* And he says, *Egypt has toiled* at the error of idolatry because the devil and the evil demons around it reduced them to slavery. Nevertheless, he promises that *Egypt* will be allowed to rest awhile from its labor, and through Egypt he is alluding to every race of idolaters. And he says, *and the merchandise of the Ethiopians and the proud Sabean men shall be transferred over to you*, the prophesied king, *and they shall be your slaves*. It appears that he is speaking here of certain savage barbarians and nations that live in the outermost regions of the earth, prophesying then that they will serve Christ. Therefore, he continues on to say: *They shall follow behind you bound in handcuffs, and they will bow down to you. Sheba* is the nation of Ethiopia from which the "queen of Sheba"[23] descended, "who listened to Solomon's wisdom."[24] And he promises them a good end: *They will bow down* to the prophesied one and *they will pray* in him, inasmuch as God was in him and because God dwelled in him, and he was God.

But *those who bowed down* to him long ago *did not know* that he was God, and yet they had knowledge and profited from their knowledge of great things. For he was the very *Savior of Israel*, and therefore the name Jesus is translated as *savior*. Whenever, therefore, the souls of the idolaters and those enslaved by savage and barbaric people *may have bowed down* to him, the Christ of God, *they bowed down to him* knowing him to be God because of the one who dwelled in him. Then he writes: *All who oppose him shall be ashamed and disgraced, and they shall go in shame.* And so,

---

[13]Zech 4:9a. [14]Acts 3:15; Rom 10:9. [15]Acts 2:24. [16]Ps 2:6. [17]Mt 16:18. [18]1 Pet 2:5. [19]Ps 113:3. [20]Eph 2:5, 8. [21]The Greek word for "anointed" is the same as the word for "Christ." Thus, Eusebius can conclude that this verse unambiguously refers to Christ. [22]Is 45:1. [23]1 Kings 10:1-13. [24]Mt 12:42.

all who oppose Christ at the present time *will be put to shame and disgraced*, and those of the circumcision and of the nations, and all those who instigated persecutions against his churches, the evidence stands through works rather than words. But instead of *because God is in you, and there is no God besides you*, according to Theodotion the text reads in this manner: *Strength is in you alone, and there is no strength but his.* For *there is no other* God but the one who dwells in you. But instead of *for you are God, and we did not know it*, Symmachus writes: *You are really God, although concealed*; and Aquila writes: *Then you are strong, although hidden from view*; and Theodotion writes: *On account of this you are strong, although concealed*, **[295]** indicating that because he is ineffable he calls him the *concealed God* in his invoking of the divine Christ.

Next, he continues on with these things: *Dedicate yourselves to me, you islands! Israel is being saved by the Lord with everlasting salvation; they shall not be ashamed or disgraced forever.* And he subsequently adds on what concerns the apostles and disciples and evangelists of our Savior. For they were the *Israel who is being saved*, and through them the *islands* which are referred to many times in the above verses *were revived*. And these were the churches of God, surrounded by an evil way of life as though surrounded by the sea. Therefore he says that these islands are to *dedicate themselves* to him and to return through the calling of his apostles, who were the *Israel who is being saved by the Lord with everlasting salvation*. And the phrase *they shall not be ashamed or disgraced forever* clearly applies to the work of witnessing that was accomplished by them throughout the whole world through the churches of God.

[45:18-19] It seems to me that the above verses teach how greatly the human race has

been honored by the God who made everything. This is why he deemed them worthy even of the call to salvation and of all the things that are promised in the present prophecy. For, he says, just as I of necessity established the heaven to serve as the place where angels and sacred spirits reside, as the place where the world and the universe meet, in the same manner so I did not cultivate the elements of the earth to lie fallow and unprofitable. And I constructed the dwelling place and the very space for those who lived rationally, for those who had seen God and who were living in a godly manner, inasmuch as they were created "according to the image of God."[25] And, therefore, although the "messengers and ministers of God"[26] are in heaven, the people who take an interest in God are on the earth. If, therefore, I deemed the human race worthy of so great an honor, so as to establish the entire earth for them, it is right that I should have the evangelical preaching plainly proclaimed to all people, so that not only the Jews but even all the nations of the earth might arrive at salvation through me. Therefore, the text continues on to say: *I am the Lord, and there is no other. I have not spoken in secret or in a dark place of the earth.* For "the whole earth and" all the people "in it are mine";[27] because of this, he says, I did not permit my word to be hidden or forgotten as in darkness, but after bringing it into the light for all to see, I opened it "so that the saving gospel might be preached to all nations."[28] Therefore "the voice" of my apostles "went out into all the earth and their words **[296]** to the ends of the world."[29] And then he immediately concludes these things with the statement: *Dedicate yourselves to me, you islands! Israel is being saved by the Lord with everlasting salvation; they shall not be ashamed or disgraced forever.*[30] In this passage, the Word calls to mind the churches of God and the apostles of

---

[25]Gen 1:27. [26]Ps 104:4. [27]Ps 50:12. [28]Mk 13:10. [29]Ps 19:4. [30]Is 45:16b-17.

our Savior when he then brings forward this verse: *I have not spoken in secret or in a dark place of the earth*, and according to Symmachus, the text says: *I did not speak in secret or in a dark place of the earth.*

And these things correspond well only with the evangelical preaching. For if anyone wants to examine this closely, he will find that the oracles of Moses *have been spoken in secret*, in the Hebrew language and with peculiar letters that are not known among all. And if one should reflect on the phrase "in a dry and weary land where there is no water,"[31] in which the law of Moses is referred to, one will find that *it has been spoken in a dark place of the earth.* And this is certainly not the case with the gospel of Christ. Therefore, "the voice" of his apostles "went out to all the earth and their words to the ends of the world."[32] They have been delivered to every nation in every kind of language and dialect and idiom, so that they are famous among all nations. Therefore, even if something besides this has also been cried aloud miraculously and auspiciously, still I say: *I have not spoken in secret or in a dark place of the earth.* After this statement, he continues on and says: *I did not say to the offspring of Jacob, "Seek a vain thing."* But according to Symmachus, the text reads: *I did not say to the offspring of Jacob, "Seek me in vain,"* or according to Aquila and Theodotion: *I did not say to the offspring of Jacob, "Seek me to no end."* For, indeed, he says I called them first through the evangelical preaching, and I promised to them first the kingdom of heaven as a reward for faith in me, promising them this lest they conclude that they worship God *in vain.* Therefore, I promised them eternal life and good things, "what no eye has seen, nor ear heard, nor the heart of man conceived."[33] For *I am God, speaking righteousness and declaring truth*, according to the word *of righteousness* with all those whom I called to myself.

[45:20-21] From here, I now preach to everyone, saying: *Assemble yourselves, and come; take counsel together, you who are being saved from among the nations!* But instead of *take counsel together*, Symmachus says: *Draw near to me, you who are escaping from the nations!* You see how he calls those whom he wishes *to save from among the nations.* And because they were neither about to listen to the preaching nor to receive the grace of the call, but rather to remain in their godless error, after the record of these things he says in addition: *They did not know* [297]—*those who lift up the wood, their graven image, and pray to gods that do not save them.* And if anyone might have anything to say in defense of the household gods, let them come to and *draw near* to me. For those who draw near "will come to know the true God,"[34] the great evidence for whose divinity was expounded through the prophets and was *reported from the beginning* in your hearing. Therefore, he says: *Who made from the beginning these things that are to be heard. Then it was declared to you.* But instead of this, Symmachus says: *From the first, then, I said these things.* For if you suppose that anyone else is God, tell me who besides God knew and predicted these things? And who reported events that were still in the future? No one else knew and no one else predicted, since there is no *other* God, but I alone foretold these things. Therefore, I say: *I am the Lord God, and there is no other besides me. And I prophesied and predicted because I am righteous and a savior.* Therefore, according to the word of the righteous one, I will call all the nations to salvation in my presence.

[45:22-23] After these things, he continues on: *Turn to me, and you shall be saved, you who are from the end of the earth!* Or according to Symmachus: *Turn around to me and be saved, all you boundaries of the earth!* You see how he

---

[31]Ps 63:1. [32]Ps 19:4. [33]1 Cor 2:9a RSV. [34]Cf. Jn 17:3.

proclaims the universal preaching to all nations. And he adds: *I am God, and there is no other. By myself I swear, "Verily righteousness shall go forth from my mouth."* And, again, hold on to *righteousness* with the traditional oath "for the confirmation of the promise,"[35] "so that," as the divinely appointed apostle says, "through two unchangeable things, in which it is impossible that God should prove false, we might have strong encouragement."[36] And through the *righteousness* that comes from him, salvation is promised to everyone. And he says that these, *my words, shall not be turned back.* But what sort of words are these, or through whom did he say: *Turn to me, and you shall be saved, you who are from the end of the earth?*

He continues: *Because to me every knee shall bow and every tongue shall acknowledge God,* or according to the other Greek translations, *every tongue shall swear to God.* In this verse he prophesies that *every knee shall bow* to him, not only of the Jews but also of all the other nations, than whom there could be no one more blessed. And the fulfillment of this prophecy was accomplished in the coming of our Savior Jesus Christ, for now afterward, the people in his church throughout the whole world are taught and are well disciplined in bending the knee to God in prayer, and yet the Jews do not know to do this. For this reason, it has been written: *Because to me every knee shall bow.* For neither any longer to other gods nor in the error of idolatry, but he says *to me every knee shall bow,* to the God **[298]** who declared these things beforehand, *and to me every tongue shall swear.* Although it was to be expected. For those among all the nations who acknowledge me as God through all sorts of *tongues* and speech, "both through barbarian languages and Greek,"[37] "those who establish their faith will receive"[38] me as a witness "in their oaths."[39]

[45:24] And they themselves will say: *Righteousness and glory shall come to him,* or according to Symmachus: *Righteousness and strength will come to him.* Every virtue among people will have the same end, and every strength of those people who contend on behalf of godliness *will come to him,* and they will receive the fruit of their toil and the reward for their virtue, *but those who distance themselves from him shall be ashamed.* Therefore it has been said in another verse: "All who bow down to carved images *shall be put to shame,* those who make their boast in their idols."[40] And they *shall be put to shame* now or whenever *every knee shall bow to God and every tongue shall acknowledge him.*

[45:25] Next, after these things, the text reads: *They shall be justified, and all the offspring of the sons of Israel shall be glorified in God.* Note the exactness of the Word. For he neither said *Israel* nor *the offspring of Israel,* but *the offspring of the sons of Israel.* And the *sons of Israel* perhaps represent the first preachers of the saving gospel, whose *offspring* and posterity it has been said *shall be justified* and *glorified.* In the beginning of the prophecy concerning them, we read: "If the Lord of hosts had not left us *offspring,* we would have become like Sodom and been made similar to Gomorrah."[41]

[46:1-2] After concluding the discussion concerning the conversion of the nations and the election of *the offspring of the sons of Israel,* the prophecy again addresses a word to the Jews and points toward the complete dissolution of idolatry when it says: *Bel has fallen; Dagon has been crushed; their graven images have gone to the beasts and cattle. Bel* was an idol, although the Greeks call him "El,"[1] thus interpreting him as the one whom they call Kronos. They were once so terrified of him

---

[35]Cf. Heb 6:16; Rom 4:16; 15:8. [36]Heb 6:18. [37]Rom 1:14. [38]Col 2:6-7. [39]Heb 6:16. [40]Ps 97:7. [41]Is 1:9. **Chapter Forty-Six** [1]ἤλ; see *Praeparatio Evangelica* 1.10.16, in which passage Eusebius again identifies El and Kronos.

hat they slaughtered their nearest and dearest for him and everywhere offered countless human sacrifices. *Dagon* is the name of the wooden idol whom the foreign tribes who dwell in Ashkelon and Gaza worship. And, therefore, especially with these idols in mind but also generally concerning all who are everywhere worshiped as gods, the word next continues on: *Their graven images have gone to the beasts and cattle.* This is completely true of Egypt, where they are accustomed to revering all kinds of *beasts* and *cattle* as gods. But according to Symmachus: *Their idols have become handed over to the wild animals*, inasmuch as they have been cast out and occupy every wilderness. Then, we read next: *You carry them bound as a burden for the weary*, and according to Symmachus: *And on your beasts* [299] *of burden, the load is borne for delivery. They were weighed down; they swayed to and fro; they were not able to balance their burden.* These things were in fact fulfilled according to the letter during our own times, and, according to the allegorical sense, the heavy and unbearable and diabolical *burden* of the error of idolatry had been laid on them long ago. For this reason, the text says that, as a *burden* placed on a *hungry* person who no longer has *strength* and is *feeble* from lack of nourishment, so are the heavy demonic burdens on those who are desperate and have been enslaved by their error. They were not *saved from* the one who captured their souls in *war*, but, as a punishment, after they had been put in diabolical collars and chains, *they were led away as captives.* For this reason, the text says: *Who will not be able to be saved from war, but themselves have been led captive.*

[46:3] The Word teaches these things to the nation of the Jews so that they may turn away from the idolatry that oppresses them, and he directly addresses them when he says next:

Hear me, O house of Jacob, and everyone who is left in Israel. But he neither calls them *Jacob* nor refers to them as *Israel*, but only the *house of Jacob* because of their kindred relationship according to the flesh. They are what is left remaining, as if the refuse and dregs of Israel. He then reproaches them for having tender nails and a thorough knowledge of the divine readings, which, although they learned *as children*, "they contemplate in vain"[2] into their *old age*, and because of this it has been said: "And peoples contemplate vain things."[3] They are a great example of paying attention to the divine Scriptures "in vain and to no purpose,"[4] still then committing idolatry and failing to follow the prophetic words reproaching their error and calling them to turn away. But even if you say such things, *I am* God, the one who exists in and of himself, and I will not stop rushing *to save you.*

[46:6] He addresses these things still to the people of the circumcision, whom he neither any longer calls "his servant"[5] nor his "chosen and beloved Israel."[6] For these quotations from the verse above indicate their election. Therefore he says to them: Indeed, you are the ones who *as children* and *from the* very *womb* learned Scripture—as the text says, you were *brought up* in the divine sayings and *grew old* with them—yet you reaped nothing to the advantage of the soul from them. And even *I*, after such a falling away as yours, yet even now *I bear with you* and call you to repentance, since you are my workmanship. For *I have made; therefore even I set free.* I also promise to grant forgiveness for those who have sinned among you, if you will turn around. For this reason, I say: *Even I will set free*, and again, *I will take you up*, and *I will save you.*

[46:5-7] As for my part, I promise these things as an exhortation, but as for your part, consider

---

[2]Ps 2:1. [3]Ps 2:1. [4]Cf. Is 30:7; 49:4. [5]Is 41:8; 42:1; 45:4. [6]Is 41:8.

what sort of rebellion and ungodliness into which you have fallen, daring *to liken me* to nonexistent beings and failing to affirm my divinity. And you considered me as equal in honor to [300] lifeless material, which you forged: soldering together *gold* and *silver* and casting an image through the skill of human hands, you are not ashamed *to bow down* to idols who are able neither to walk nor *to move*. Their idols are carried about *on their shoulders* or carted around, and they are able neither *to hear* nor *to save* them. And you consider me to be like these idols, O you who are defective in soul!

[46:8-9] But, after seeing clearly for a short while, you reflected and fell headlong into such a depth of ungodliness. And *after remembering* these very things, *repent* and *turn* to correct arguments for the conception of my divinity, and reflect among yourselves that from infinite ages past and before all time had been invented, *I am, and there is no other God besides me.*

[46:10-11] And I made a presentation to the people through my prophets, foretelling what was about to happen and predicting what would be in times yet far off from now, which I accomplished in fact and will once again perform in the present day. *And all the things I have planned* and ordained will happen one after another, in fulfillment of my words. And *I plan* to call my servants who fly through the air like birds and winged creatures—I am speaking about the angelic powers and "the ministering spirits, sent forth to serve for the sake of those who are to obtain salvation."[7] And, therefore, the text reads: *Calling a bird* (or according to Symmachus, *a flying creature*) *from the east and from a far country* those sacred powers that serve me. Although *I spoke* through my prophets in former times, I will in reality accomplish these things through them. According to Symmachus and the other Greek

translations, he says: *My whole will I will do, calling a flying creature from the east, a man of my plan from a far country. And I will bring it; I spoke, and I will do it.* And who would you say is the *man of* his *plan*, if not his Christ whom he says he summoned *from the east*, clearly from the innermost parts of Hades? Everything that I promised beforehand, *I will do*, and in reality it will happen through him.

[46:12-13] And yet, these things are addressed to the people of the circumcision, and it is appropriate that he should add on to what has been said above when the Word prophesied to them and said: "Hear me, O house of Jacob and you who are left of the house of Israel,"[8] and he continued on: "To whom have you likened me? See, act with cunning, you who are going astray!"[9] And there he called them "you who are going astray," and here he says: *Hear me, you who have ruined your heart,* or as Symmachus translates this phrase: *You who are hard of heart.* And then he adds: *You who are far from righteousness,* and, indeed, he says that *you distanced* yourselves from my *righteousness.* But I did not act as you deserved but according to kindness, and, as a good and righteous God, *I brought near* [301] *my righteousness, and I will not delay the salvation that comes from me.* And I will do this, neither procrastinating nor *delaying,* but from here on now *I will give salvation in Zion and glory to Israel.* Symmachus translates this verse in this way: *I will give deliverance in Zion and glory to Israel.* Therefore, acting in my kindness, *I will give* these things *in Zion and to Israel,* and I will display *my righteousness* while proceeding against those who besieged them.

[47:1] Those who besieged them were the Chaldeans and the Babylonians, to whom he turns and refers when he prophesies the destruction of the kingdom and the abasement

---

[7]Heb 1:14.   [8]Is 46:3.   [9]Is 46:5.

of the lofty, for they had boasted that they would rule over the nations for years to come. And he identifies their kingdom, naming it the *daughter of Babylon*. He calls her a *virgin* because she was adorned and groomed like a *virgin*, wanting to appear youthful and pass off as a maiden. Then, as to one who is seated in grandeur, he commands her to stand up and *come down* from her throne, *and to seat herself down on the ground*; to do her best to try to hide the disgrace that she will suffer in the change for the worse. And this is what he is talking about when he says: *Enter the darkness*. Then, identifying the kingdom as a *virgin*, he says: *She will no longer be called tender and delicate*.

[47:2-4] You once were this way; when you formerly treated your subjects with contempt, such names then suited you. Therefore, since that luxurious kingdom has been set aside, prepare yourself to serve your masters after the manner of a miserable female slave or a maid of the mill. *Taking a millstone* and *grinding* with it clearly represents receiving this bitter and painful servitude in exchange for the former luxuriousness. And as for *your covering*, although you had covered your head with gold and precious stones and had adorned yourself with all the other frivolous embellishments, they were stripped away from you. After a great deal of time, you decayed and grew old while ruling as a tyrant over the nations, but you concealed your agedness and decrepitude from view, *veiling* your *gray hairs* in a garb of worldliness, so that you were still regarded as a *tender and delicate virgin*. Now, listen, you who are put to shame, because you are fated to *bare the gray hairs* on your head and to show your agedness to everyone. But according to Symmachus, the text reads: *Cover up your ears and uncover your legs; come to the rivers; let your shame be uncovered, for even your reproach shall come to light; I will take vengeance on you, and*

no man shall stand against me. This is how Symmachus translates these lines, and, in this passage, using the word picture of an enslaved woman, the Word speaks about the leading away of the people into a foreign land and the captivity imposed by her enemies and opposing forces. And the interpretation is determined by the juxtaposition used in the passage and by the public reading of the text. For instead of *I will take from you what is right; I will no longer deliver you over to men*, Symmachus writes: *I will take vengeance, and no man shall stand against me*. And instead of *he who delivered you—the Lord of hosts*, Aquila writes: *The Lord, the one who is near[1] to us*, and Symmachus: *The Lord, the redeemer of our powers*, and [302] Theodotion: *The Lord, the one who redeems us from the powers, the Holy One of Israel is his name*.

[47:5-6] For, he says, our Lord, "the one who redeems us,"[2] the one who sets us free from our bondage under you, has appointed these things against you. Therefore, he says: *Sit distressed*, or according to Symmachus: *Keep silent*. The one who was formerly exalted and boastful, the one who ordered around other nations as though household slaves feels repentance for her wrongdoings and is *distressed* in soul. *Sit on the very ground*, humiliated, or, if you are able to do so, hide yourself and deliver yourself over to *darkness* in order that you might not experience further disgrace. Then, according to Symmachus, the text reads: *For no longer shall you be called the mistress of kingdoms. I was angry with my people; I profaned my heritage*. And on the one hand, in accordance with justice and for the sake of their correction and conversion, I delivered my people into your hands in an attempt to call them to their senses. But you, on the other hand, although it was useless it was still necessary, did no further kindness nor showed compassion on them.

Chapter Forty-Seven   [1]This verb literally means to be next of kin to someone. The Lord, then, is next of kin to us.   [2]Is 43:14.

[47:7-10] These verses are clearly about the arrogance of the kingdom of the Chaldeans. They describe the boastfulness of the men who ruled among them and record how they thought they would have a rule of immortal and unconquerable power. But, he says, at one and the same time, loss of husband and the death of children *shall come on you*; the husband representing the one who rules among you and your children representing your subjects. These things *shall come on you* all at once, and you shall be presented as both a *widow* and *childless*. And these things shall happen to you not only because of the prophecies but also *on account of the abundance of your witchcraft and your enchantments*. For you placed your hope in them, and you were not only insolent but even said: *I am, and there is no other*. But instead of *know, the understanding of these things shall be*, Symmachus says: *And your knowledge deceived you; therefore you said in your heart: I am, and no one shall exist after me*.

[47:11-15] But the wrath of God shall come on you to apprehend *the enchantments and witchcraft* from which you had been used to procuring aid for yourself. For these were your lessons *which you learned* from ancient times and *from your youth*. We know from the book of Daniel how there were certain "magicians" and "enchanters" and "sorcerers"[3] who lived in Babylon and who were prominent among the Chaldeans, and they were skillful and knowledgeable about such things. They were highly esteemed by the king, and he believed that they assured the success of the kingdom. They devoted themselves not only to *witchcraft and enchantments* but also to astronomical observation. In their presumption, they claimed to understand the heavens and the movements of the stars and their effects on human destiny and on the events of the present time, as though you could discover the things that were

about to happen to you. But by observation alone, no one is able to tell what is about to happen. For, above all, retribution "through fire"[4] will overtake those who were highminded among them. **[303]** And when "every city" is "burned with fire,"[5] then they will be put to shame, and no one will be able to come to their aid. This end—I am speaking about *being burned in coals* and *fire*—awaits all of you. And, then, the *coals* of your former affluence will be more valuable to you, for they will be glowing warm and useful. The phrase *they will be a help to you* does not appear in the other Greek translations. In saying this, he says that you will be surrounded in the end, O you Chaldea! Since ancient times you bound yourself in deceit, and so the text reads: *From your youth you have labored in your traffic*. Or according to the other Greek translations: *Your merchants from your youth all wandered away by themselves; from among them no one is found as a savior for you*, or according to Symmachus: *There is therefore no one who saves you*.

[48:1-2] After announcing in advance what would happen to Babylon and to its inhabitants and kings, the Word vindicates the Jewish people through what he says above: because it is right in my sight, I will bring forward these things against the Chaldeans, but certainly not because you are worthy of help. Anticipating these very things, he predicted events "before they happened,"[1] prophesying in divine foreknowledge, in order that when these things happen precisely as stated and the prophecies against the Chaldeans become reality, you will not ascribe the credit to your gods or claim as your own the gods to whom the idolaters devote their service. They have received this retribution from their enemies, and I had already prophesied that these things would happen and promised through my prophets that I would bring the aforesaid things on the

---

[3]Dan 2:2. [4]1 Cor 3:15. [5]Cf. Is 1:7. **Chapter Forty-Eight** [1]Is 46:10.

236

kingdom of the Babylonians. When these things shall become reality even as I commanded, it will be absolutely compulsory that you confess that I am God alone, the one who has proved his words to be true. And he calls them *house of Jacob*, since they are not worthy to bear the name of their forefather, and he also says: *Who are called by the name of Israel.* Although they are not *Israel* and the appellation is not appropriate for them, nevertheless he calls them thus. Then, he continues on: *And who came from out of the seed[2] of Judah.* For they were not worthy of the soul of the patriarch, even though they came *from his seed* and from his bodily sperm. They were merely bodily and fleshly sons, and not true children of his soul. And when he says the *seed of Judah*, he is speaking about the "royal race"[3] from the succession of David and from the tribe of Judah, who continued to live in Jerusalem during the times of the prophets. And just as they are falsely styled *Jacob* and *Israel* and *Judah* and are now accused of not being truly worthy of these names, so too they *swear by the name of the Lord* and call the *God of Israel* to remembrance, but it is only with their lips and mouth that they do these things. It was certainly *not with truth* according to their oaths that they acted, and although they appear to *cling* to *the city* that is dedicated to God and to *lean on God*, they are hypocrites.

[48:3] [304] After announcing these things to the people of the Jews, he next commands them, saying: do not suppose that I prophesy in vain about future events. For all of this happened so that from the fulfillment of the events, the faithless among you might learn that the words of my prophets are not human words! For it is not from human nature that the prophets possess knowledge of future events. But I am God, the one who prophesies these things, and

who prophesied these things already during the former times! I predicted certain things, and certain words *came through the mouths* of my other prophets, so that the predictions came to the hearing of many, and the events that followed are in accord with the predictions.

[48:4] Nevertheless, since you, the people of the Jews, seem to have an unbending and *iron neck* and are even now impudent, one could say without fear of error that you have a *brass forehead.*

[48:5-7] Because of this, even now *I declared to you beforehand* the things that would happen, lest from the terrible events that came on the people of the Jews you should ever suppose that those who are falsely believed to be gods *did* these things. But even the fact that you will derive no profit from these words does not escape the attention of my foreknowledge. But, nevertheless, persisting in my benevolence, even now I testify and describe for you the things that will happen in Babylon and among the Chaldeans, who are about to wage war against you. For, behold, I declared these things beforehand so that you might know the destruction that will befall them. And so, when your enemies who come up against you from Babylon arrive, you might make known the God who prophesied these things to you and call for his aid. For this reason, the end has been declared beforehand and clearly communicated to them. And they were only able to know these things from my words to you, and you did not receive any of your information from any source other than my words. Do not deceive yourself, or say that you knew these things before my prophecy. For can it be that I was somehow not present with you to make these things known? But I am persuaded that you will derive no profit from these words.

---

[2]Here Eusebius uses the Greek word for "water" to mean sperm or seed. This is significant, as some scholars have contended that the Greek word does not contain sperm within its semantic range. [3]Dan 1:3.

[48:8] For I know, and I knew before this, that *betraying, you would betray*; therefore, before you were born, you had been called *lawless* and violent in my presence and in the presence of God who is prescient of all. Therefore, according to Symmachus, the text reads: *And you were called faithless from the womb.* Nevertheless, it was not because of you but because of my own benevolence that I then predicted and showed to you what was about to take place when ruin would come on your enemies, for I was endeavoring through every pretense to save you.

[48:9-10] Therefore, when I delivered you over to your enemies, it was *not for silver that I sold you*, but it was to help you, and I did this so as to chasten you in this way, because you would not receive instruction through words and exhortation. And it was *not for silver that I sold you* to your enemies but because of your sins and impiety. "For your sins you were sold."[4] Nevertheless, I will not permit you to serve your enemies forever, but [305] I will ransom you again; and as *from the furnace of poverty*, I will liberate you again from your oppression under the Babylonians.

[48:11] And *I will do* all these things *on account of my name*, since your enemies have taken inappropriate liberties and have spoken irreverently about my divinity. And I did not want to deliver you over to them, since they were conceited and arrogant, assuming me to be nothing, and they glorified their gods, claiming them to be the causes of their victories over you. For this reason, I will not surrender *my glory*, nor will I concede my divinity *to another*, which establishes the righteousness that is extended to all.

[48:12] Even now, the Word inveighs against them and says these things concerning them:

Hear me, O Jacob, and Israel, whom I call, or according to Symmachus: *My called one*, and according to Aquila: *O my called one.* He summons those who are upright, although in the verses above he had addressed those who had been cast aside, but now he converses with those who are more excellent, whom he names as his *called ones.* For from that class there were "many called, but few chosen,"[5] except that those here are clearly not *chosen* but only *called.* And he reminds them of the theology about him when he says that he is the *first* and the *last.* For this reason, according to the other Greek translations, the text reads: *I am the first and the last.* And it has been written elsewhere "concerning the only-begotten of God"[6] that he is "the first and the last"[7] and "the Alpha and the Omega."[8] And he shows plainly how he is the *first* and the *last* when he next says: "The living one, although I died."[9] On the one hand, he is the beginning of life, because "he was the life,"[10] and on the other hand, again, he is the *last*, since "he emptied himself, taking the form of a servant, and he humbled himself and became obedient to the Father unto death, even death on a cross."[11]

[48:13-16] Then he presents his exceedingly great power when he says next: *My hand laid the foundation of the earth.* For this reason, it has been said in the book of Proverbs: "God by wisdom founded the earth."[12] And he says: *And my right hand bolstered heaven* (or according to the other Greek translations, *the heavens*), clearly referring to the supernatural and heavenly powers. He continues on: *I will call them, and they will stand together.* For the aforesaid powers will obey as though obeying a commanding master, and after being *gathered* to the same place, they stood *hearing* his words. This was plainly revealed to you even at the beginning of the book when the Word

---

[4]Is 50:1. [5]Mt 22:14. [6]Jn 3:18. [7]Rev 1:17; 2:8; 22:13. [8]Rev 1:8; 21:6; 22:13. [9]Rev 1:18. [10]Jn 1:4. [11]Phil 2:7-8. [12]Prov 3:19.

said: "Hear, O heaven, and give ear, O earth, for the Lord has spoken."[13] In the verse above, he puts to shame those whom he addresses. For if the divine powers render such obedience and reverence to the master of the universe, how will you who are mere mortals not regain a sense of godly fear? But instead of *who has declared these things?* Symmachus translates this verse: *Who has declared these things to them?* [306] *The one whom the Lord loved, he will perform his will.* And when was this made known to people, that even those who are called heavenly powers obeyed, and even those who listen to the counsel of God were carried away? If you long to know, then learn that the Lord himself *declared* and made this manifest to you because he *loved you.* But according to Aquila, the text reads as follows: *Who among people declared these things? The Lord loved him.* Likewise, in Symmachus we read: *Who among them declared these things, whom the Lord loved?* Therefore, this one himself, *whom the Lord loved*, he made these things to be heard *among people.* And this one himself, *whom the Lord loved*, he will accomplish "the will of the Father,"[14] what has been stated in the verses above, against Babylon. And he will lead his people on and call them back from the land of the enemy. *He will restore* them to the household, and he will lead him *on his way.* Therefore, I will do these things in the time that is coming, and because you have known these things before, *they have not been spoken in secret,* but they have been announced with boldness to you. You have come seeking me eagerly. For when the Father planned these things, *I was* with him, *and now the Lord* himself, who is God over all, *sent me his Spirit* of holiness in order that I might accomplish once and for all the things that he has ordained.

[48:17-19] Hear, O Israel, whatever *the Lord who delivered you* teaches you. And in the middle of every word, remember that *I am your God*, "and there is no other."[15] For *I have shown you* all these things so that *you might find the* "way of salvation."[16] Therefore, if from the beginning you had listened to me, you would not ever have been handed over to your enemies. And so great is the "abundance of peace"[17] that has been stored up for you that it may be likened to the current of a *river*, a great "abundance of *peace*" that flows to you from me. And *your* renowned righteousness *has become like a wave of the sea*, sounding forth for all to hear. And in these phrases he expresses the idea of an "abundance of peace" in the image of a *river* and a *wave of the sea*, or an *ocean flood*, according to the other Greek translations.[18] He is speaking of the *righteousness* of the people; if only it had turned out to be true! In other passages, we could suppose that these terms refer to the literal *sea* and to literal *rivers*, but this is not possible in the present context. For he says that *your offspring* has been multiplied into an innumerable multitude, and so it is compared with *sand*, and the descendents *of your womb* he expresses as *the dust of the earth* because of their multitude. He says that all these things would have been true if you had kept his *commandments*! But instead of *as the dust of the earth*, the other Greek translations say *as the grains of the earth.* If, therefore, anyone might understand these things literally as referring to those who are physically and literally Jews, one would answer that the promise was addressed exclusively to the great multitude of children, since they do not reflect on anything revered or awesome. And if you despise the promise of God and the reputation of the one who speaks, know that my *offspring* from Israel are those who have

---

[13]Is 1:2. [14]Mt 7:21. [15]Cf. Is 45:5. [16]Acts 16:17. [17]Cf. Ps 37:11. [18]In fact, Eusebius presents merely an alternate spelling for the Greek word for "wave." Both "wave of the sea" and "ocean flood" are fair translations of Eusebius's Greek, but his reason for turning to the other Greek translations is to point out that some translators spelled the Greek word for "wave" slightly differently.

been indicated above in the verse: "If the Lord of hosts had not left us offspring, we would have become like Sodom,"[19] in which context is indicated the apostolic band and all who would become disciples of our Savior from among the Jews. The fathers established the churches of the world and the multitude of those in them who have been reborn [307] according to God, "who were born, not of blood nor of the will of the flesh nor of the will of man, but of God."[20]

But these things, he says, would have been true of you *if you had heard his commandments*. And, if anyone should say that these promises apply to the Jews, although they did not pay any attention and did not keep the *commandments* but in fact committed idolatry and "killed the prophets,"[21] he propagates a false reading of the text.[22] Therefore, the Word delivers this remarkable promise with a reservation when he says: if you had done these things, *your peace would have become like a river, and your righteousness like waves of the sea, and your offspring and your descendants*. Therefore, it is sufficient for the multitude if they act justly to them, and "the abundance of peace"[23] and abundance of children were present among this one, and there is nothing else to say. Because they practiced *peace* poorly, that peace "has withdrawn far,"[24] and now they are still enslaved to their enemies, and the place that was once sacred and holy has become to them "desolate and trackless."[25] Their customs and kingdom have been destroyed. Because they practiced peace poorly, they continue to multiply, but their offspring are like worms. It would appear difficult to interpret the meaning of the prophecy in any other way than has been explained to us. But even now he says, although you did not keep the *commandments*, nevertheless because of my benevolence, *you*[26] *will not be utterly destroyed*,

nor will your name be wiped out before me, or according to Symmachus, *from before me*.

[48:20-22] Therefore, since I have already promised that *you will not be utterly destroyed, nor will your name be wiped out*, I now say to you *to go out from Babylon*, released and free from the fear of enemies. And since you have received permission to return to your estates, make the journey in all eagerness, not in a relaxed or sluggish way. For a *voice of joy* will meet you, and in fact you can already hear it, and all who hear my words will rejoice at your salvation. And they will shout aloud so that the news will be made known to all those who live *at the ends of the earth*, and they will *say*, *"The Lord has delivered his slave Jacob!" Even if they are thirsty, he will lead them through the wilderness; he will bring forth water for them out of a rock; a rock will be split, and water will flow, and my people will drink. "There is no rejoicing," says the Lord, "for the impious."* On the one hand, in a historical sense, these things were not fulfilled during the time that those who had been set free by the Persian kings Cyrus and Darius returned from Babylon. But on the other hand, in a deeper sense, because we do not find that *water* literally flowed from a *rock* during the return journey of the people, we will say that they were set free from a spiritual captivity, concerning whom the Christ of God said: "He has sent me to preach good news to the poor, to proclaim release to the captives,"[27] to prove the gospel true. For to these, spiritual water will pour out from the true *rock*, "and the rock was Christ,"[28] according to the [308] apostle. Our very Savior also states this when he says: "Whoever drinks of the water that I shall give him, out of his heart shall flow rivers of living water, welling up to eternal life."[29] And such are the promises of

---

[19]Is 1:9, [20]Jn 1:13 rsv. [21]Cf. Mt 23:31. [22]Literally, "he multiplies the things of the procreation of children according to the flesh." [23]Cf. Ps 37:11. [24]Cf. Is 59:11. [25]Cf. Ps 63:1. [26]Eusebius has changed the second person singular verb in the lxx to a second person plural. [27]Lk 4:18. [28]1 Cor 10:4. [29]Jn 4:14; 7:38.

God. But since the Word had seen that many who heard the prophecy were unworthy of the promises, lest the children of the Jews uncritically interpret the things above as spoken concerning them, it was necessary to add to the promises: *"There is no rejoicing," says the Lord, "for the impious."* For every delight from God and joy and pleasure and all that he promised is presented to those who live piously, but to those who live impiously, there is no word about anything being promised.

[49:1] After discussing at length the things that pertain to the Jewish people, the Word again begins afresh and turns to address the calling of the Gentiles, as well as prophesying about the advent of our Savior among people. Therefore, we recall those who rule the churches of God, which are situated everywhere on the earth among the unbelieving nations, who are surrounded on all sides, as though by the sea, by the salty waves of evil. It is for this reason that he calls them *islands* and says: *Hear me, O islands.* But, lest anyone should falsely criticize our interpretation as an incorrect explanation, the Word clearly states his meaning when he continues on and says: *Pay attention, O nations!* The Word expresses himself perfectly clearly that the present text does not allude to the Jews, and neither is it about literal *islands* but rather refers to the *nations* and the churches of God that are interspersed throughout the nations. According to Symmachus, the text reads as follows: *Hear me, O islands, and listen, O nations.* He goes on to say what he wants to teach his churches: *After a long time it shall stand, says the Lord.* And one should first note that these things are spoken from the mouth of the Lord, as well as the things that are said afterwards, where the Lord himself begins the passage as though it is concerning someone else. But in it he acknowledges that he has been born, and he

calls himself a *slave*, and other things too he states in the subsequent verses.

Therefore, one should be attentive to what the Lord teaches when he calls to the *islands* and to the *nations.* He says that he will not pass through these things in detail now but that you should expect to see the full completion of these words. For the time is far off in the future, the time when the things that have been prophesied will in fact happen. But instead of *after a long time it shall stand,* the other Greek translations say *far away,* adding on *far away* to the thought above. And so Symmachus translates this phrase: *Listen, O nations, even you who are far away.* Then he continues on: *The Lord called me from infancy, and from my mother's womb remembered my name.* For you were taught this, O nations, and you too, O islands. And what could this mean except that the Lord, the master of the universe, even before he appeared among people, was called while still being carried in the womb, [309] and that his very *name* was presented to me? It is known only to him. But in time even to you yourselves, I say, even to all the *nations,* it will be clearly known.

[49:2] *And he who is God and Father made my mouth like a sharp sword,* which cuts so as to divide and determine those who are worthy of God from those who are not. He already confirmed this in the Gospels when he said: "Do not think that I have come to bring peace on earth; I have not come to bring peace, but a sword."[1] And so he also says: *And he made my mouth like a sharp sword.* He continues: *And under the shelter of his hand he hid me,* here adumbrating the secret administration of his incarnate coming, an administration that escaped the notice of many. And as he called his tongue a *sharp sword,* so he also says that *he had been made a chosen arrow* by the Father, in order that when he wishes he

---

Chapter Forty-Nine [1]Mt 10:34 RSV.

should wound those who are worthy of his piercing. Such are the souls who say, "I am sick with love."[2] In addition, he who is God and Father *hid* also this *arrow* as *in a quiver* or as in a sheath of arrows, in order that no one should see it or be aware of its presence except those who are worthy. And he uses the term *arrow* and the word *quiver* in succession. And you would not miss the mark[3] in saying that the *quiver* or the case for arrows represents the flesh which God the Word took up while residing among people.

[49:3-5] After equipping him in such a way, the Lord says: my God and Father *said to me, "You are my slave, Israel, and in you I will be glorified."* For you then came forth *from* your *mother's womb,* and you submitted to be born among the children of Israel. And you did not ordain your incarnation in another race or among other nations, but it was in Israel that you "descended from David according to the flesh"[4] and "from the tribe of Judah."[5] And so you style yourself Israel and a *slave,* since you took up the "form of a servant"[6] and yet were the "only Son."[7] In a similar fashion to the verses above, the divine master[8] conceals the actual name of the Son, and he applies the title *slave* to the Son, speaking to his coming and to the grace which was revealed through him among people. Although he had in no way ever been a *slave,* yet he says that this will come about through you: *In you I will be glorified.*

Therefore, he who is God and Father says these things. But I the Lord, after hearing these words, answered and said: and how "will you be glorified in me, O Father?"[9] And then, after laboring over these things and enduring untold suffering for the salvation of people, I accomplished nothing. For many of them "persisted in unbelief,"[10] as did the nation of

the Jews earlier. For this reason, I say: *I have labored vainly; I have given my strength in vain and for nothing.* Then he adds: *Therefore my judgment is* [310] *with the Lord, and my toil before my God,* or according to Symmachus: *My verdict is with the Lord, and my work is with my God.* For if they are not worthy of the toil that I endured on their account, it would be better if they did not even exist. But after doing my things *before my God,* I accomplished the Father's will.

Therefore, I first preached the Father's grace to them who are of the circumcision. For it is the will of him *who formed me from the womb to be his own slave* and who "prepared a body for me"[11] from Israel that I should first preach to them his grace and *to gather Jacob to him and Israel.* Therefore, he instructed the disciples in a similar fashion when he said: "Go nowhere among the Gentiles, and enter no town of the Samaritans, but go rather to the lost sheep of the house of Israel."[12] Therefore, the text states that the Father was well pleased to send me among people in order that I should *gather Jacob and Israel* when we read: *In you I will be glorified.*

And when *I* had seen the "unbelief and hardness of heart"[13] of Israel, *I said* already then that *I labored vainly; I have given my strength in vain and for nothing.* And he says the same thing in other verses too: "What profit is there in my blood, when I go down to corruption?"[14] But now I say that although there are many people who disbelieve and remain in their hardness of heart, *I will be gathered before the Lord, and my God shall become my strength.* For only the glory from him keeps me, and he *is my strength.* Therefore, the wonderful and incredible works that were done through me were in fact a display of his power.

---

[2]Song 2:5; 5:8. [3]Eusebius here uses the Greek verb ἁμαρτάνω, a verb that can mean either "to sin" or "to miss the mark." [4]Rom 1:3. [5]Rev 5:5. [6]Phil 2:7. [7]Jn 3:16. [8]Eusebius chooses the term ταμιευόμενος, a title that could also be translated "treasurer," "paymaster" or "controller." [9]Jn 13:31. [10]Rom 11:23. [11]Heb 10:5. [12]Mt 10:5b-6. [13]Cf. Mk 16:14. [14]Ps 30:9.

[49:6] Then he continues on: *And he said to me, "It is a great thing for you to be called my servant* (or according to the other Greek translations, *my slave*) *so that you may set up the tribes of Jacob and turn back the dispersion of Israel."* For it was truly a great work for our salvation that he took up the "form of a servant"[15] and submitted to be born among people. It is for this reason that he says to him: *It is a great thing for you to be called my servant,* or according to the other Greek translations, *my slave.* And he tells us the reason why the Savior was born as a *slave* when he says: *So that you may set up the tribes of Jacob and turn back the dispersions of Israel.* Therefore, to them first "he proclaimed liberty" to those whose souls are "captive" and "recovery of sight" to those who are "blind."[16] And because they did not receive grace, he subsequently says: *See, I have made you a light of nations, that you may be for salvation to the end of the earth.*

[49:7] The prophetic Spirit then addresses the nations and says: *Thus says the Lord.* But because they did not understand that it was the Lord who was speaking, he then adds: [311] *The one who delivered Israel,* or according to Symmachus: *The one who redeemed Israel,* or according to Aquila and Theodotion: *The one who is near to Israel.* The one who once *delivered Israel* "from the hand of the Egyptians"[17] speaks, and he addresses these things to you nations and commands you: *Sanctify him who despises his own soul.* You give him glory because "he humbled himself unto death, even death on a cross,"[18] but *he is abhorred by the* unbelieving *nations* who serve "the rulers of this age."[19] And I should say, they rather serve evil demons, to whom they are enslaved when they blaspheme and *abhor* the Christ of God, ridiculing and scoffing and *despising* his death. But for you to whom the Word calls, *sanctify* him and give him glory,

because "every knee will bow to him, in heaven and on earth and under the earth, and every tongue confess that Jesus Christ is Lord, to the glory of God the Father."[20] At that time, *kings shall see him, and rulers shall stand up and bow down to him* "when he comes in the glory of the Father with his angels and will sit on his glorious throne,"[21] "judging the living and the dead."[22] For then all *will bow down to him for the sake of the Lord,* his Father, *because the Holy One of Israel is faithful, the one who has chosen him.* But instead of *and I have chosen you,* Symmachus says: *Who chose you.*

[49:8] Therefore, the statements above have been delivered to the nations, but the following verses are prophesied from the mouth of the Savior. The prophetic Spirit says to him from the mouth of the Savior: *In an acceptable time I have listened to you, on a day of salvation I have helped you; and I formed you, and I gave you as a covenant to nations.* It is extremely important to note that the text reads: *In an acceptable time I have listened to you,* for this was the time of his resurrection. For it was during the time of suffering that the Savior "cried out" and said: "'Eli, Eli, lama sabachthani?' That is, 'My God, my God, why have you forsaken me?'"[23] But also he prayed and said: "Father, if possible, let this cup pass from me."[24] Then, when he saw that the Father had denied his request, he continued: "Father, if it cannot pass, your will be done."[25] Therefore, the Father accepted this prayer, and, although it was after suffering and after the descent into hell, he looks forward to the time of his resurrection and says to him: *In an acceptable time I have listened to you, on a day of salvation I have helped you.* But instead of: *And I formed you,* the other Greek translations say: *And I kept you.* And he adumbrates his resurrection when he adds: *I gave you as a covenant to nations,* for [312] he calls to mind the time of the new

---

[15]Phil 2:7. [16]Cf. Is 61:1. [17]Ex 3:8. [18]Phil 2:8. [19]1 Cor 2:6. [20]Phil 2:10. [21]Mt 25:31. [22]2 Tim 4:1. [23]Mt 27:46. [24]Mt 26:39. [25]Mt 26:42.

covenant. Then he clarifies when he says: *To establish the land and to inherit the wilderness heritages.* Therefore, he said earlier, before the suffering and before those of the circumcision had laid hands on him: *So that you may set up the tribes of Jacob and turn back the dispersions of Israel.* But since they did not receive grace, nor in fact do they even remember those times any longer, he says, then, concerning the nations: *And I gave you as a covenant to nations, to establish the land and to inherit the wilderness heritages,* or according to Symmachus: *To encourage the land and to distribute the parcels of land that had been forgotten.* And such were the souls of the godless and polytheistic nations—*wildernesses* without God—and truly they had been completely *forgotten.*

[49:9] He says *to those who are in bonds, "Come out!"* These are the ones who are "bound fast by the ropes of their own sins,"[26] to whom he preached release and to whom he in fact delivered over the way of regeneration. For he said *to those who are in bonds, "Come out," and to those who are in darkness that they be revealed.* For "we were all children of wrath,"[27] and "we were once *darkness,* but now we are light in the Lord."[28] Then he preaches to those who were set free from their former *bonds* and former *darkness* when he says: *And they shall feed in all ways, and all the paths shall be their pasture.* The ancient people of God traveled these *ways* and *paths,* which are the God-breathed Scriptures. As they fed and attained the promises, enjoying the inspired and spiritual nourishment, they found good pasture and said: "The Lord shepherds me, and I shall lack nothing. In a verdant place, there he made me encamp; by the water of rest he reared me."[29]

[49:10] Then, because they are nourished spiritually, *they shall not hunger or thirst,*

neither shall burning heat nor sun strike them down. The flame of mortal existence and the transient pleasures of this life, which people suppose is light, he calls the *burning sun.* And he says that not even these things will assail them, *but he who has mercy on them will comfort them and will lead them through springs of water.* And there are many "fountains of Israel"[30] and "fountains of the Savior"—fountains of the Old Testament and fountains of the New Testament.

[49:11] He says: *And I will turn every mountain into a road,* so that they might not encounter anything that is impassible and rough. And, again, he promises that *he will turn every path into a pasture for them.* As already said previously, there are three ways to interpret Zion and Jerusalem. There is the lower and Jewish way, and there is another, in which it is interpreted as every religious government in which the decrees of the soul are present. There is also a higher way, in which it is interpreted as the angelic city in heaven, concerning which the apostle said: "But the Jerusalem above is free, and she is our **[313]** mother,"[31] and: "You have come to Mount Zion and to the city of the living God, the heavenly Jerusalem."[32] The present word has the meaning of a religious government, which indeed once existed among the Jews but has since been demolished. And the place where their government fell has been turned into a place for the church of the nations, as the verses above prophesied.

[49:12] He makes it clear to whom he is preaching all these things when he says next: *Behold, these have come from far away; these from the north and the sea, and others from the land of the Persians.* He therefore specifies one of the four regions of the earth in saying: *Behold, these have come from far away,* or

---

[26]Prov 5:22. [27]Eph 2:3. [28]Eph 5:8. [29]Ps 23:1-2. [30]Ps 68:26. [31]Gal 4:26 RSV. [32]Heb 12:22 RSV.

according to the other Greek translations: *Behold, these have come from afar.* Although he does not mention the name of the area, he states the remaining three regions. For he clearly indicates *north* and west and east when he says: *These from the north and the sea, and others from the land of the Persians.* And if he mentions those *from the north,* and those *from the sea* (clearly referring to the western parts) *and others from the land of the Persians* (indicating the eastern parts), then it is logical that those whom he said earlier were from the land *far away* are to be interpreted as from the southern parts. The southern land—the land that lies in the southernmost parts of the world—is uncharted, and so he says that *they have come from far away.* And *they have come* to God from all sides and from all four directions, and the Word prophesies that the aforesaid promises will be received.

[49:13] Then he sings aloud about the salvation that is common to all people: *Rejoice, O heavens.* For "there is joy in *heaven* even over one sinner who repents."[33] *And,* he says, *let the earth be glad,* as a mother rejoices over the salvation of her children. But instead of *let the mountains break forth with joy,* Symmachus says: *Mountains will exult over everything,* and Aquila and Theodotion say: *O you mountains, shout aloud praise!* As spiritual beings, then, he commands even the *mountains* to rejoice and *be glad* over the salvation of people. And it may be that the *mountains* are souls that live on the earth, who are said to be elevated to an exceeding height because of their outstanding moral example, or perhaps they are divine and heavenly powers. But he exhorts them *to rejoice* because *God has had mercy on his people and has comforted the humble of his people.* And who

are these people other than those who were earlier identified as those who were summoned from the four regions of the earth?

[49:14-16] Therefore, after speaking concerning the calling of the nations, addressing them as islands and nations, he then continues on in the present passage to say that even if the *Zion* among the Jews has been destroyed, that is, the religious government which was once present among them, it is not to say: *The Lord has forsaken me, and God has forgotten me.* For it is not possible that God should be forgetful concerning a religious government among people.[34] And this principle can be understood through an earthly example. As it is impossible for a *mother* to forget her own child, and as it is not possible for her who has given birth **[314]** *not to have mercy on the descendants of her womb,* so also it is impossible for me *to forget* the spiritual souls among people and the child of the religious government among people. For this reason, *Zion* is not to say: *The Lord has forsaken me, and God has forgotten me.* For a *mother* will sooner *forget* her children than I will forget the race of humankind, although it is no doubt necessary to add: "Whether from the Jews or whether from the Greeks,"[35] or whether from any other nation.

And it is extremely important to investigate the interpretation of the verse: *See, I have painted your walls on my hands, and you are continually before me.* In this verse, he states outright that the true Zion is undefeated and invincible, remaining always and forever established. And so, if anyone longs to be in contemplation of it, let him not look around here below, nor let him search for it in the land of Palestine, but let him listen to God when he says to it: *See, I have painted your walls on my*

---

[33]Lk 15:7. [34]Here is the tension in Eusebius's exegesis. His exegesis is quite supercessionist: Israel is God's people no more, and the church inherits the promises of God. At the same time, however, Eusebius struggles to understand all of the condemning or judging sayings in Isaiah, because technically these would now be directed against the church. In the statement above, it is clear that Eusebius is thinking of Constantine's reign—God could not be forgetful of the reign of his Christian church. [35]1 Cor 12:13.

hands, and you are continually before me. For it is truly the *hands* of God that build such a city and construct it and paint it in diverse colors. And as one etches in writing on a tablet, so God establishes the position and impression of his government in the souls of people. The Word of God clearly teaches then that he is the builder of his own city when the text says: "On the rock I will build my church, and the gates of Hades shall not prevail against it."[36] For the religious government is interpreted as the invincible and unconquerable city of God which is called *Zion* by those who erected it among the ancient Jews and by those who are prominent in the church of God. For this reason it has been said to it: Do not say *the Lord has forsaken me, and God has forgotten me. For I will not forget you, said the Lord. See, I have painted your walls on my hands, and you are continually before me.*

[49:17] Then, since in a short time the church of the nations came about after the disappearance of the religious government that had been present among the Jews, he continues on to say: *And soon you will be built by those by whom you were destroyed.* For just as the Jews were responsible for its destruction, so again they became the builders of the new structure—the apostles of our Savior and the disciples and evangelists, through whom the church of God was raised up from the nations. And these are in fact the ones who demolished the Jewish self-chosen form of worship (as the apostle teaches when he says: "But if I build up again those things which I tore down"[37]) who constructed the new Zion according to the government of the gospel. But, there are others besides them, whom the text identifies as *those who made Zion desolate*, and they certainly did not build it up, and so the text says concerning them: *And those who made you desolate will go forth from you.* One should not be amazed that

the word was fulfilled in a spiritual and historical sense when, after the formation of the church of the nations, the entire nation of the Jews and the physical city situated in Palestine were cast aside, and so their religious government came to nothing.

[49:18] [315] After these things, he paints a word picture and introduces a certain *young wife* who is awaiting many children, and so he addresses her: *Lift up your eyes all around, and see them all; look, they have gathered and have come to you. I live, says the Lord; he will clothe himself with all of them like an ornament.* But he does not say who the *all* are in this context, because he had already said this beforehand and explained who they were and where they came from when he said: "Behold, these have come from far away, these from the north and the sea but others from the land of the Persians."[38] These, he says, *all have gathered and have come to you. I live, says the Lord; you will clothe yourself with all of them as an ornament and put them on like a bride's ornament.* And, therefore, it is the *bride* of the Lord who is adorned with spiritual ornaments, and it is the church that is exalted and cleansed—beautified with the multitude of virtues and gifts of the Holy Spirit that have been freely bestowed on her.

[49:19] Then he says: *And your desolate and destroyed and fallen places will now be crowded on account of your inhabitants.* For a great multitude of churches throughout the whole world and from every nation has replaced the people of the circumcision. And he says that *those who swallowed you up and were far away from you* have been brought near. He tells us what sort of people they were, they who once held power among the people of the circumcision—the false prophets and Pharisees and Sadducees: "Those who swallow down the people with open mouth."[39] And he foretells

---

[36]Mt 16:18. [37]Gal 2:18. [38]Is 49:12. [39]Is 9:12.

that he will drive them away and remove them far way from the new and freshly established city of God. He prophesies that the multitude of those present in the aforementioned city will be so large that the buildings will need to be more expansive and greater.

[49:20-21] The same, then, is set forth in this verse: *For the sons whom you lost will say in your ears: "The place is too narrow for me; make a place for me so that I may settle."* For these individuals who now run to the government of God through the grace of the Savior were once in destruction, and the church of God is amazed by them when she says: *Who has begotten me these?* But while she was yet unaware of the calling of the nations, in a moment of fear she confessed the barrenness that had come over her from the nation of the Jews. Therefore she says: *But I was childless and a widow, so who has reared these for me? But I was left all alone, so from where have these come to me?*

[49:22] Then, since he had looked on her, God answered and said: *Look, I am lifting up my hand to the nations, and I will lift my signal to the islands, and they shall bring your sons in their bosom, and your daughters shall they lift on their shoulders.* He thus teaches her that he will gather her *sons* and *daughters* (concerning whom she had asked: *From where have these come to me?*) from the elect of the nations to her. And when he says: *I will lift up my hand to the nations and to the islands,* he is clearly speaking about the *signal* [316] of the church. And what could this refer to except the suffering of the Savior, his resurrection from the dead and the evangelical preaching, for he says *they will bring your sons* and carry them *in their arms.* For Aquila and Theodotion translate this verse as follows. The former says: *And they shall bring your sons in their arms,* and the latter says: *And they will bear your sons in their arms, and they shall lift your daughters on their shoulders.* And who will do this, if not those who lead others by the hand and introduce them into the church of God, instructing them in their infancy? Such was Paul when he said to the Corinthians: "I fed you with milk."[40]

[49:23] He then states that *kings* will be the *foster fathers* of the church of God, and he says that the *women who rule* them will be her *nurses.* And we saw with our own eyes this literally fulfilled among them, for those who bear authority in the abovementioned position have carried the church of God as *foster fathers.* And the *women who rule* over them (here the text is clearly referring to those who are served as the "principalities and powers"[41] over each nation and each district in the abovementioned kingdom) will provide for those of the church who are in need as *nurses,* supplying them with an abundant allowance by royal sanction. For this reason, they are called *nurses,* or, according to Symmachus, *wet nurses,* for he translates this phrase: *And the women who rule over them will be your wet nurses.* And whoever has seen with his own eyes the aforementioned "principalities and powers"[42] in the church of God bending their knees and pressing their foreheads to the ground, how could he not confess that he has witnessed the literal and historical fulfillment of this exact prophecy, which says: *On the face of the earth they shall bow down to you, and they shall lick the dust of your feet.* Then he says that when these things actually turn out, then *you will know that I am the Lord, and those who submit to me will not be put to shame.* It is good neither to esteem lightly nor to despair of the hope of those things that God has promised would happen. For *those who submit* to him *will not be put to shame.*

---

⁴⁰1 Cor 3:2. ⁴¹Eph 3:10. ⁴²Eph 3:10.

[49:24-26] After relating this, he next teaches about the nations that were under the hand of the devil but have since been set free from him through the power of our Savior. For he says: *Will anyone take spoils from a mighty one?* And the *mighty one* refers to the devil and his adversarial power. Therefore, does not the text say in this verse that the *mighty one* is able to stand against and to trouble one who is equally strong? If someone might attempt *to take* such a person *captive*, is it *just*[43] to assume that *he shall he be safe?* Will he not place his safety in peril and perhaps be conquered by the *mighty one* who is stronger than him? But instead of *unjustly*, the Hebrew text contains the meaning *justly*. For *the one who takes a mighty one captive* and strips him of his arms would probably be doing this *justly*. Accordingly, [317] Aquila and Theodotion translate this term *justly*. For it would in fact be *just* to strip a tyrant of his arms and to take *captive* anyone who exercises authority *unjustly* over others. The text tells us who among people is *able* to stand against such a person and *to be saved* from him when it says: "What is impossible with people is possible with God."[44] *Thus says the Lord*: even a *mighty one* will be stripped of his arms, and the one who strips him *will be saved*. And so, according to Symmachus, the text reads: *But even the body of captives of the strong will be captured, and the seizure of the fearful will be preserved.* He then immediately presents who it is who will accomplish these things when he says: *And I will judge my cause, and I will rescue my sons.* And so he clearly teaches that he alone is the one who is *able* to take the *spoils* of the devil.

He next explains that the *spoils* are his sons when he continues on to say: *I will rescue my sons.* And they who had taken from them who were *rescued* and abused them *will eat their own flesh and drink their own blood like wine.* For they will no longer be able *to eat the flesh* of others, and so *they will eat* their own. And neither will they still be able to *drink up* the *blood* of human souls, and so *they will drink their own blood*, and *they will be drunk* from it. And *all flesh* will perceive the accomplishment of these things. That is, all people and all who are still fleshly will perceive *that I am the Lord who rescues and assists you.* All these things were spoken to you, or my city, which is interpreted as Zion. Therefore, he says that *they will know* and all confess in one accord that the accomplishment of the salvation of the nations was not from mortal nature but from the power of God, and this was the power that *rescued* his own sons from the aforementioned *mighty one* and his minions. According to another interpretation, this verse refers to those who once persecuted the church of God, and in describing their ruin says that *they will eat their own flesh and drink their own blood.* And so *they will know* and all confess that the power that *rescued* the church of God was not a mortal power, but it was the *God of Jacob who assisted* it. But instead of *God of Jacob*, the other Greek translations render this phrase as *strength of Jacob.* At just the right moment, the word mentions the *God of Jacob* or the *strength of Jacob*, referring to the God who appeared in the figure of a man to the patriarch Jacob, whom one should suppose to be none other than the Son of God.

The divine is incorporeal, immaterial, intangible and indivisible. And there is no one who has done anything like what he has done in taking on a corporeal appearance. But the sacred letter concerning him is articulated to us in a human way. For it was not otherwise possible for us in these dull bodies to understand, except that these things be conveyed to us by way of examples. And so we succeed in understanding in part the things concerning his divine being from visible and perceivable realities.

---

[43]This term could also be translated "reasonable." The translator has used the term *just* to maintain Eusebius's intended reference to the LXX text of Is 49:24b. [44]Mt 19:26.

[50:1] [318] After going through in detail the evangelical preaching, the calling of the nations through the gospel, the rise of the religious government and the fall of the aforementioned *mighty one*, the Word turns to persuade and reason with the people of the circumcision. After considering all the nations, he concluded that they were to be given over to them. Therefore, he says to their face: let none of you find fault with me as though I have neglected you, for once I was anxious to save you. Let none of you claim that the woman who once held the position of my wife and to whom I gave a *bill of divorce* was *your mother*. And do not let anyone suppose that I was forced *to sell you* in order to repay a debt to a *creditor*. For none of these things is true. The truth is: you *sold* yourself *for your sins*. Because the case so stands, even you yourselves will confess that although I am God and Lord of the universe, I did not hesitate to descend from the grandeur of heaven in order to make my presence even among you.

[50:2-3] Then, *I came* and lived among you, and I resided with you as a man, and *I called* you all to myself, and I did all these things because of my surpassing benevolence. But there *was no one* to meet me, and no one *answered* when I summoned you all to myself. But yet you have endured instruction to which the others would not listen. And at that time, I endured these things patiently, although I was able neither to endure completely nor to endure enough to reverse these things. Or do you not remember that I once ordained "the Red Sea" to be "dry,"[1] and when I wanted to lead your ancestors through it and "to the Jordan River,"[2] the current ran backwards, and I led them by my power, and they crossed over as though on dry land. And no doubt you do not know about the ten plagues against the Egyptians, when I caused *the dark heaven* to be clothed in *sackcloth* for three days.

[50:4-5] Therefore, why is it that the one who revealed such things to our ancestors was not one such as I was and now am? And why did I deliver the bodily instrument that was taken out of your hands because of its humanity? But since this seems to refer to the most glorious Lord of all, who also is my Lord and Father, for this reason then I also call him *Lord* and say: *The Lord, the Lord gives me the tongue of instruction that I may know when it is necessary to speak a word*. In the same way, "when he was accused"[3] "he was silent,"[4] and when you had falsely witnessed against him, "he made no answer."[5] He acted in this way at the command of the Father, because it was necessary "for him to become obedient unto death."[6] It was because of this that I kept silence and suffered insolence on your behalf, because I knew well that there would be a time when "I will no longer be silent,"[7] and when I receive a *tongue of instruction* from the Father, I will proclaim at the proper time, *when it is necessary to speak a word*. And this may be the time when I will establish my churches throughout the entire civilized world. For then I will no longer remain in silence, but I will cry aloud so that, if they listen, all nations might come to know the Father. At the aforementioned time, he will grant me attentive *ears* that are able to understand the meaning of my [319] teaching, and as they listen in the early hours of the morning they will convey my instruction. For it is my Lord himself who *will open my ears* so that they will be attentive and ready to learn. For this reason I say: *He assigned it to me in the morning*, or according to Symmachus: *He assigned it to me at dawn*, or according to Aquila: *He raised me in the morning; in the morning he raised up my ear to hear*. For although he *called* you, you did not *answer*.

Chapter Fifty [1]Ex 14:16. [2]Josh 3:17. [3]Mt 27:12a. [4]Mt 26:63. [5]Mt 27:12b. [6]Phil 2:8. [7]Cf. Is 62:1.

Therefore, I said: *Why was it that I came and no one was there? I called, and there was none to answer?* But there is a time coming when, in the grace of the Father, I will instruct the disciples whom the Father will grant me. And then a word of explanation and a *tongue of instruction* will be given to me, and my disciples will be given *ears* in order that they might be able to understand the *instruction* of my words. Therefore, I know that these things will happen at that time, at the precise moment when I will make my dwelling with you.[8] For "I was seeking"[9] those among you who wanted "to be saved." Although I called all of you, you did not answer. And the Father appointed the time of your daring deed, and he willed that, although falsely accused, I should remain silent and answer nothing.

[50:6-7] Therefore, I offered at once *my back* to those who wanted to strike me. I offered *my cheeks* to those who struck my *face* and shamefully mistreated me, and *I did not turn away my face* from being covered with your spit. But I remained resolute and offered my given human body to all sorts of abuse and insolence, defending myself from nothing that anyone threw at me. For the Father's will was enough for me. And when "I became obedient"[10] to him, I was sustained through everything, knowing that the one who rules over the universe, *the Lord*, has become *a helper for me*. For this reason, I presented *my face like solid rock* because I have become convinced that obedience to the Father does not bring me any shame. And the Father stood close by me, and just like a judge at the games, after he watched me endure through everything, he justified me. If anyone has an accusation against me, and it even seems right that I should be put to death for certain faults, let

him show publicly what the reason or pretext for such an accusation against me is.

[50:8] If anyone wants *to contend with me* and to defend a certain position, *let him draw near me, let him stand* in the middle of everyone, and let him question me. But no one has a complaint to bring forward, neither about my teaching nor about the deeds that I have done, and so the *Lord* has become a *helper for me*. For, he says, he who is God and Father will come to my aid, and he will remove all my abuse, and he will establish my glory. And who among you is able to oppose the undefeatable decree and to afflict the one who is helped by God? Therefore, if the scribes and Pharisees had been sensible, they would have kept themselves far from the schemes [320] and attempts against him, since they would have known through the holy prophets that they would never have been able to do wrong to the Christ, who is God and Lord and true Son of the Father.

[50:9] And *all of you will become old like a garment, and a moth will devour you*, or according to Symmachus, *mold*, or according to Aquila, *decay*. In this verse he is speaking about the obsolescence of their physical worship. "And everything that is becoming obsolete and growing old is ready to vanish away."[11] Like a worm eating at the soul, so this *moth* eats at the consciences of those who committed the daring deed against him. For after seeing the conversion of the nations to God and their own downfall, which they suffered because of their own ungodliness, they slay and devour by their complicity. For this reason, at the end of the present book, he prophesies concerning them and says: "Their worm shall not die, and the fire shall not be quenched, and it shall become a spectacle to all flesh."[12]

---

[8]Eusebius uses a past tense verb for the second half of this sentence, but the translator has chosen to make it a future tense verb so that it is parallel with the first half of the clause. It is clear that Eusebius is speaking from the time of Isaiah, and therefore he speaks of the time of the first advent of the Savior as still in the future. [9]Lk 19:10. [10]Phil 2:8. [11]Heb 8:13. [12]Is 66:24.

[50:10] After going over what happened during his suffering, the Lord himself continues on and addresses them: *and now, if there is anyone among you who fears the Lord, let him listen to his servant.* He says that he interprets himself as the *servant* of God when he says he became a man and is the true Son of God and of the Father. And the phrase about *hearing the voice of his servant* does not refer to the "transgression of the law"[13] but speaks about the confirmation of the law through the impression and engraving recording the truth, which is God and his prophecies. For "I do not will the death of the sinner but his repentance."[14] And yet even now, I call you again while you are in the darkness of ignorance, and I say: *Those who walk in darkness and have no light; trust in the name of the Lord and lean on God.* Only come and listen to the promise and have faith that this salvation is for you!

[50:11] But it seems to me that on the one hand, you shut out every good hope for yourselves, and on the other hand, you heap up *fire* for yourselves and *make the flame stronger* against yourselves, because you "persist in unbelief"[15] and in blasphemies against me, and so you kindle a greater *fire* of "eternal punishment"[16] awaiting you. It is for this reason that *you shall lie down in sorrow*, or according to Symmachus: *You shall lie down in pain*, or according to Aquila: *You shall lie down all worn out.*

[51:1-2] But in order that you might not suffer these things, I exhort you still even now to return to me and to *hear* my words. *Hear, O you who pretend to honor the Lord but do what is contrary to the will of the Lord, driving away what is righteous* and making an enemy of the truth itself. And because of their excessive stupidity, those districts of the Jews who had seen the one only-begotten Word of God in an appearance like ours—that is, as one who had become a man—not only did they not understand the **[321]** mystery about him, but also, failing to understand, they were swift to vex and profane him in insolent voices. Precisely as I said, he made his auspicious glory and power visible to them, and he anticipates certain individuals who want to think less of him when he says: "Trust in the Lord."[1] Therefore, he then says that he who was made visible is himself Lord and God, anticipating as I said those who want to think and speak about him in an earthly way. *What then do I say? Look at the solid rock that you hewed and to the hole of the pit that you dug.* But instead of *and to the hole*, Symmachus says: *To the cleft*, and Aquila says: *To an incision.* And it seems that in this verse, the word foreshadows that very "rock"[2] that welcomed the body of the Savior, in which "Joseph" *dug* the grave "for his own new tomb."

Then he turns to the example of *Abraham* and *Sarah*, who were like infertile and barren and childless *rocks* even into old age. Although they were barren, they produced children "as the stars of heaven for multitude."[3] Therefore, it says: *Because he was but one, then I called him and loved him and multiplied him.* Therefore, because of what I have done for *Abraham*, you should not give up hope that from this *rock*, which you yourselves *hewed*, there will come a prospect of salvation for all people. And this prospect is in no way inferior to the promise that was spoken to *Abraham*, and I will give this prospect to all nations because of the grace of the aforesaid *rock*. And so then, the *rock* represents the grave "that Joseph had *hewn* for a tomb"[4] as well as the Christ himself, whom the divine apostle knew to call a *rock* when he said: "And the rock was Christ."[5] And those who plotted his death and laid hands on him mutilated the body of Christ during his passion, and so the text says: *Look to the solid*

---

[13]Rom 2:23. [14]Ezek 18:23. [15]Rom 11:23. [16]Mt 25:46. **Chapter Fifty-One** [1]Ps 4:5. [2]Mt 27:60. [3]Ex 32:13. [4]Mt 27:60. [5]1 Cor 10:4.

rock that you hewed and to the hole of the pit that you dug. The Savior himself teaches this in the Psalms when he says: "They dug a hole in my hands and my feet; they counted all my bones."[6] And perhaps the *hole of the pit* is an allusion to the wounded "side" of his body, "from which came out blood and water."[7]

[51:3] As it was for *Abraham* and *Sarah*—who although they were physically infertile and childless and barren, yet by incredible and divine power they produced children "as the stars of the heaven for multitude"[8]—so also now it will be for the *rock* that was *hewn* and *dug* by you. For through the rock came *Zion*— I am speaking of the religious government, and I am speaking of the *Zion* for which we had given up hope. *And I will comfort you now,* [322] *Zion,* clearly indicating that *he will comfort* the religious government that he established in the wilderness for your benefit. But I myself will take its wilderness, and *I will make its desolate places as a garden and its desolate places in the west as a garden of the Lord.* And so, by way of comparison with a woman who once had a husband, the church of the nations is now again called *desolate.* This is also what the prophet himself foretells when he says: "Rejoice, O barren one who does not bear; break forth, and shout, you who are not in labor! Because more are the children of the desolate woman than of her that has a husband."[9] And who is the *woman who had a husband* if not she who was given a "bill of divorce"?[10] He also says that in the *desolate place,* there will be a *garden* like *the garden of God,* which Moses records was "planted"[11] in the creation. Therefore, the text reads: *As a garden of the Lord,* and he says that this *garden* will be *in the west.* "For to those who sit in darkness and in the shadow of death, the light" of salvation "has arisen"![12] And *the garden of God* has been filled with the gifts of the Holy Spirit, and so he says that *they will find gladness and joy* and *confession and a voice of praise.* Those who prosper will release a *voice of praise,* and those who turn from their former sins will be cleansed through *confession.*

[51:4] After passing on from the accusation against the people of the Jews and the refutation of their impiety against the Christ and the evil things he received in turn from them and they dared to do against him, he then prophesies concerning the once desolate church and its conversion to a superior way. He prophesies that there will be a *garden of God* in it and *that* those who are *in it will find gladness and joy, confession, and a voice of praise.* After prophesying these things, he then summons no longer the nation of the Jews, that is customarily called Israel, to listen to his words but clearly summons the *people* that has come to him from the nations, and the *kings* of the nations with these precise words: *Hear me; hear me, my people, and you kings, give ear to me, because a law will go out from me, and my judgment for a light to nations.* And one would not be senseless to suppose that in this verse, those who are referred to as his *people* are also those to whom he said: "Look, for your sins you were sold, and for your acts of lawlessness I sent away your mother."[13] And the *people* from the *nations* in this passage are those who "have been saved by the grace of God."[14] Accordingly, he addresses them in the passage at hand when he says: *Hear me; hear me, my people.* And he wills that the *kings* should pay attention to what has been said, as well as the rulers of the *nations* and the kingdoms of the earth. For he makes this clear when he names the kingdoms in this manner. He sets forth a teaching that parallels this phrase when he says: *Because a law will go out from me,* and the other Greek translations render this phrase similarly. It was necessary

---

[6]Ps 22:16-17. [7]Jn 19:34. [8]Ex 32:13. [9]Is 54:1. [10]Is 50:1. [11]Gen 2:8. [12]Is 9:1. [13]Is 51:4. [14]Eph 2:8.

that the new *people* that has come out from the *nations* [323] be given a new *law*. For the *law* that was given through Moses that prescribed every detail of the sacrificial worship in Jerusalem was unsuitable for the government of the nations. Therefore, he certainly adumbrates the new covenant and the evangelical preaching when he says: *Because a law will go out from me, and my judgment for a light to nations.* And, here again, when he promises a *light* for the *nations*, he is certainly not saying for Israel. But instead of *and my judgment*, the other Greek translations all render this phrase: *My decree.*[15] For, he says, I have judged, and I have laid down a *decree* that my *law* and my *decree* will be a *light* for the *nations*.

[51:5-7] He says that these things will not be in a far-off time, but *my righteousness draws near swiftly*, and according to Symmachus: *I will act in a moment; righteousness is near.* For *righteousness* has been fulfilled, and grace has been given equally to all nations. And this was the Christ of God, whom "Simeon took in his arms,"[16] as is recorded when he said: "Lord, now let your servant depart in peace, for my eyes have seen your salvation,"[17] and so on, the prophecy signaling the divinity of the Word. For as he indicated his humanity through the reference to *salvation*, so he also alluded to his divinity in the same way. *Do not fear the reproach of people, and do not be dismayed by their contempt*, because he says: "Those who desire to live a godly life in Christ will be persecuted"[18] and reproached and disparaged by *people*, and they will suffer persecution and all sorts of trials. And then, because he has already fortified them from all around, he encourages them and says: *Do not fear the reproach of people, and do not be dismayed by their contempt.*

[51:8] He says that it is necessary rather to look toward the end that they will receive, which then he also describes when he says: *For just as a garment it will be devoured by time, and like wool it will be devoured by a moth.* And so, clearly they will be delivered over to ruin and perdition. Therefore it is necessary to fear nothing and to be confident in their salvation. And, as he already taught them, this salvation is immortal and ageless and eternal and powerful. And he repeats and ratifies this theological principle in the passage at hand when he says: *But my righteousness will be forever and my salvation for generations of generations.*

[51:9-10] The addition *Jerusalem* is present neither in the Hebrew text nor in the other Greek translations, but Aquila says: *Awake, awake, put on might, arm of the Lord*, and Theodotion says precisely the same: *Awake, awake, put on might, arm of the Lord.*[19] Therefore, according to all the Greek translations, and even according to the Hebrew [324] text, the Word does not address *Jerusalem* but the *arm of the Lord*. And it follows that the Word delivered the address in order to raise you up to the *arm of the Lord*, as it has been written above: *And the nations will hope in my arm.* And we said that the divinity of the Word was signaled in this manner: after he exhorted the people *not to fear the reproach of people and not to be dismayed by their contempt*, the people sent up a prayer of supplication from their mouths to the *arm of the God*, entreating him to *wake up* and fight on behalf of his own people. For, he says, we are nothing unless you cover us with your shield and you fight on our behalf, and unless you, the *arm of the Lord, awake, awake, and put on* your *strength* and your *might*. And he says *awake* as though he meant the imperative to apply to times past. For this reason, according to

---

[15]The difference is in a slightly different word for "judgment," although both terms are both primarily translated with the English term *judgment.* [16]Lk 2:28. [17]Lk 2:29-30. [18]2 Tim 3:12. [19]Theodotion's text is identical to Aquila's, as presented by Eusebius.

Symmachus, the text reads: *Be awakened in days gone by, for ages of generations.* For you were the one who slew "the great dragon,"[20] whose corpse is in Egypt and who destroyed his false pretension when you threw "the chariots of Pharaoh and his host into the sea."[21] And now, *awake, arm of the Lord*, and work similar things among us, and carry us across safe from every trial. Therefore, according to Aquila, the text reads: *Are you not the one who cut down my indignation,* or *pride,* according to Symmachus. The text also reads: *Are you not the one who wounded the dragon,* or according to Theodotion: *Are you not the one who made the sea desolate, the water of the deep, the one who made a way to pass through the depths of the sea for those who were delivered and ransomed by the Lord?*

[51:11] Therefore, discuss with us these things that have been done by the *arm of the Lord* in times past. For the adversaries and enemies of your people will suffer a similar fate at the hand of ancient tyrants, but your attendants and relatives *will come to Zion with joy*. Here he is clearly speaking about "your heavenly city,"[22] and when they arrive, it will be *with joy and everlasting gladness*, and like the winners at the games, they will be crowned with wreathes by you. And therefore *praise* will be *on their head*, which will be placed around their heads instead of a crown, *and joy shall take hold of them*. And when they will be free of all fear, they will no longer keep an eye out for adversaries and enemies. For in "the heavenly Zion,"[23] *pain and sorrow and sighing will have fled away*.

[51:12] The new people and the church of the nations pray these things by the prophetic Spirit, and the one who is called the *arm of the Lord* answers and says: *I am he who comforts you.* "For he is our atoning sacrifice"[24] and "the one who *comforts* the downcast."[25] Then, at the right time, he reminds the reader of the spiritual being that "has been made according to the image of God"[26] when he says: *Acknowledge the one of whom you were* [325] *afraid.* For I have deemed you worthy of a great honor: that I should *comfort* you. For this reason I say: *I am he who comforts you.* And I do not know how, forgetting your own worth, you were subject to timidity and *you were afraid of a mortal man and a son of man.* And he says these things to those who were more timid and less strong in the church. For those who were made perfect and who were adorned with martyrs' crowns attained glory from him. And because we are "all in one body,"[27] "when one member suffers, all members suffer together."[28] And so it is reasonable that, while calling them to repentance, he brings comfort and healing to those who were more timid and less strong and limped a little during the times of the persecutions. For this reason he says: *Acknowledge the one of whom you were afraid, a mortal man and a son of man, who have dried up like grass.* For you should strive to be fearless and undisturbed, because when my people look to the end of the mortal nature of humanity, they will see the coming ruin that those *you were afraid* of will receive.

[51:13-14] And *you were afraid* of them, *and you have forgotten God who made you, who made heaven and laid the foundations of the earth. And always, all the days, you feared the face of the fury of the one who was oppressing you, of the one who had planned to get rid of you.* But if *you were afraid* because of your own frailty, then understand their end and the destruction of humanity, and reflect in your own mind and consider how the *fury of the one who oppressed you* and of whom *you were afraid* has been extinguished. *For when you are saved, they will not stand,*[29]

---

[20]Cf. Ezek 29:3. [21]Ex 15:4. [22]Heb 12:22. [23]Heb 12:22. [24]1 Jn 2:2. [25]2 Cor 7:6. [26]Gen 1:26. [27]1 Cor 12:13. [28]1 Cor 12:26. [29]By changing the number of the verb from singular to plural, it becomes clear that for Eusebius the referent is not God (as in the LXX) but the wicked who "will not stand" (i.e., they will perish in the judgment).

neither will they who were once your adversaries be around any more. And, although you have been humbled for a little while, you will rise from the depths to which you had fallen.

[51:15-16] These things will happen around you because *I am your God*, who once delivered over "Pharaoh to the depths of the sea" and rescued my people, and thereby forever displayed the excellence of my divinity. For a little while I wish to rouse up the *sea*, and I allow its *waves to sound forth and be stirred up*, but then I restrain them and make them mild, and I bring about calm. And so I permit and allow the persecutions against my church to be a test for my champions. For *I am the one who stirs up the sea and makes its waves to sound*, but, when I wish, all things are restrained again and peaceful.

But when the *sea is stirred up* and its *waves are roused up*, *I will put my words in your mouth and shelter you under the shadow of my hand*. So that you will not suffer anything from your adversaries, and so that you might be all the more bold and firm and secure, [326] know that I promise *to shelter you* with my *hand*, the very *hand by which I established heaven and laid the foundations of the earth*, and with my *hand* I brought the whole world "into existence from what did not exist."[30] Therefore, why should you be anxious or be afraid in human fear? You should rather run under my *shadow* and not withdraw from under it, and always bear *my words* in your *mouth*. And the phrase *I will put your words in my mouth* is perhaps similar to what our Savior said to his disciples: "When they bring you into court, do not be anxious how you are to speak or what you are to say; for the word that you are to say will be given to you in that hour; for it is not you who speak, but the Spirit of my Father speaking through you."[31] And by my *hand*, by which *I established heaven and laid the founda-*

tions of the earth, I revealed to people what I *said* to Zion—that is, to my people—to take courage and not to be anxious or *afraid of mortal man*. Therefore, according to Symmachus, the text reads: *And in the shadow of my hand I will shelter you, by which I set up heaven and laid the foundations of the earth, because I said to Zion, "You are my people."* But according to Aquila, the text reads: *And I said to Zion, "You are my people."* And therefore one could correctly call every *people* of God *Zion*, for *Zion* is nothing other than the *people* of God. The entire passage is in fact addressed to the people of the nations, as I argue in the previous sentence.

[51:17] The Word prophesied concerning the call of the nations in the verse above: "Hear me; hear me, my people, and you kings, give ear to me, because a law will go out from me, and my judgment for a light to nations."[32] In this verse, the Word turns to another subject and addresses fallen *Jerusalem* and exhorts it to rise up from its ruin. It seems that he here indicates its final fall, which it suffered after the daring deed had been done against our Savior, and it was for this reason also that it experienced the anger of God. But since the Word is kind and benevolent and does "not will the death of the sinner but rather his repentance,"[33] he encourages Jerusalem to come quickly to repentance, describing its good hope if it should repent. For this reason, he says: *Awake, awake! Stand up, O Jerusalem, you who have drunk from the hand of the Lord the cup of his wrath.* Therefore, *Jerusalem* is *the one who has drunk the cup of anger*. And there is another *Jerusalem*, the supreme *Jerusalem* of which the prophet speaks, and for this very reason one ought neither to allow nor to acknowledge anything adverse to be said about it. For, indeed, it is in heaven, and it is the city over which God is said to reign, that neither *anger*

---

[30]Cf. 2 Macc 7:28. [31]Mt 10:19-20. [32]Is 51:4. [33]Ezek 18:23.

nor *wrath* touches. For "pain and sorrow and sighing have fled away"[34] from it. And it is the city that God established on the earth, and we therefore prove that it represents the religious government among people. But, aside from the heavenly city, there is also the city that has been tested [327] by the *wrath* of God because of the transgressions of its inhabitants. But instead of *the cup of ruin, the goblet of my wrath,* Symmachus renders this phrase: *He drank and wiped out the cup of his anger, the mixing bowl of agony, and there is none to console it.* And when one drinks the *cup of wrath and ruin* and *wipes it out after drinking,* this refers to when all the vengeance and chastisement is settled, which had been administered for the offenses that one had done. As the servants of physicians apply bitter antidotes to those who are unwell in order to purge the preexisting illness from the body of the patient, so also it has been said concerning God: "There is a cup in the Lord's hand, of pure wine, full of a mixture, and he tipped it from side to side, but its dregs were not emptied out; all the sinners of the earth shall drink."[35] For in an analogous way, the physician of souls applies vengeance to the soul as a curative antidote for the purging out of the preexistent disease.

[51:18-19] Therefore, this passage is about *Jerusalem,* and he teaches about the people who live in the city. He says that *no one* from among its *sons* who live in the city was found who was able *to comfort* it and deliver it from its diseases. And this was fulfilled precisely at the time when, after the suffering of our Savior, there was neither prophet nor priest nor any God-loving person found in the city, since they had driven away from their midst the disciples of our Savior and apostles and evangelists. On the one hand they killed them, and on the other they abused them with beatings and chased them as far away from them as possible. For during the times of the Babylonians, when the city was besieged and the people were taken captive, still there remained among them just people and prophets who were able *to comfort* them. But now, the prophecy says: *There was no one who comforted you from among your children whom you have borne.* But instead of *these two things are set against you,* Symmachus says: *There are these things that conspire against you: who will grieve for you?—hardship and ruin and famine and dagger—who will console you?*

[51:20] He continues on, according to Symmachus: *Your sons are the ones who are led; they were driven to the opening of a net, like a pickaxe*[36] *in a net.* According to the other Greek translations, instead of *like a half-cooked beet,* the text reads: *Like a great fish caught with a net* or *seized.* And there is a species of bird called the *pickaxe,* and it is with this bird that he compares the sons of Jerusalem, ensnared as they are in the *net* of the devil. For this reason, they were delivered over to wrath. And so Symmachus continues on: *Who are full of the wrath of the Lord, the censure of God.*

[51:21-23] He continues on: *Therefore hear, you who are afflicted, who are drunk, but not with wine.* And he continues on, according to Symmachus: *Then says* [328] *your master and your God, who will fight on behalf of his people: see, I removed from your hand the cup of agony, the mixing bowl, the cup of wrath; you shall not continue to drink it any longer.* And the Word promises Jerusalem that *he will take the cup of wrath* from it, if it repents. For instead of *I will take,* the text reads: *See, I removed.* This is if you do what I commanded you and if you obey what the Word said to you: "Awake, awake! Stand up, O Jerusalem."[37] For the aforesaid

---

[34]Cf. Is 35:10. [35]Ps 75:8. [36]The term literally means "pickaxe." As Eusebius is about to conclude, the "pickaxe" may be a name for a certain kind of bird. [37]Is 51:17.

promises were said under the condition that it "awakened" and rose up. But if it does not obey and does not rise up and stand up from its fall, but rather remains disobedient and inattentive, then it alone will be responsible that the promises did not happen. And these things were said to the entire nation of the Jews, for they were not addressed to the stones and structures of the place, neither to the soil nor to the dust of the earth there. And you will understand that the message of the Word even from another prophet among them was said to them: "He that falls, does he not rise up? And he that turns away, does he not return? Why do you turn away in a shameless turning away, says the Lord."[38] Therefore, he promises that it will rise up and *no longer drink the cup of wrath*. For it will be given to its adversaries. Therefore, according to Symmachus, the text reads: *And I will place it in the hands of those who carried you away from home, of those who said to your soul, "Bow down, that we may pass by." And you put down your back as the ground and as a pathway for those traveling by.*

[52:1] It seems that this was said concerning the opposing powers, and it is to these powers that every soul that keeps itself away from God submits. For the soul that is present with God stands erect, looking above and being drawn up to him. But the soul that joins itself with those evil demons who work sin is forced "to bow down." And such was "the woman" in the Gospel "who was completely bent over and could not stand upright,"[1] concerning whom the Savior said: "This woman was a daughter of Abraham, whom Satan bound for eighteen years."[2] Therefore, since the entire city of *Jerusalem* fell completely to the ground and was razed to the earth and trampled by those who *humbled* it, he commanded it to rise up, and a second time the Word addresses it and says: *Awake, awake, O Zion! Put on your strength, O*

Zion. For the rational soul has great power and strength, and it has great glory, seeing that it was "made according to the image of God."[3] And he wishes to raise it up again so that it would be a *holy city* and the *uncircumcised* and *unclean* would no longer stride through it. And through the reference to the *uncircumcised*, he alludes to those of another race and of another tribe, and through the reference to the *unclean*, he alludes to the idolater. Therefore, if you obey his commandment and rise up and become the *holy city* of God, the Word promises you that neither idolater nor anyone of another race will stride through you.

[52:2-3] [329] He exhorts it to do something further when he says: *Shake off the dust, and rise up, O Jerusalem.* For it was supposed to clean off the *dust* that had been cast around it, and to rise up from the fall that had happened among it and *to break off the bond* that had been placed around its *neck*, and with such a snare, the adversarial powers bind the soul fast with "ropes of sin."[4] He shows plainly that these things have been spoken neither to the buildings nor to the physical city but to the unbelieving people when he adds on and says: *Break off the bond from your neck, O captive daughter Zion!* For when he says *captive*, he is clearly speaking about none other than the people that had been completely taken *captive* by the diabolical power. For this reason, he clearly addresses the same people and says: *You were sold for nothing*, and above he also said to the people: "Behold, for your sins you were sold, and for your acts of lawlessness I sent away your mother, because I came and no man was there; I called, and there was none to answer."[5] And in this verse the Word directly refers to the pathway of the Lord for people, departing from which "they were sold" for their sins"[6] *for nothing*, receiving their own destruction in exchange for nothing. But after such things, the

---

[38]Jer 8:4-5. **Chapter Fifty-Two** [1]Lk 13:11. [2]Lk 13:16. [3]Gen 1:26. [4]Prov 5:22. [5]Is 50:1-2. [6]Is 50:1.

Word calls them to salvation and promises that they *shall be redeemed*, if they are willing to approach him and receive the grace of Christ. And *not with money shall they be redeemed*, for their captivity was not physical, and so they shall not attain their freedom through physical ransom money, although their souls were truly *sold*. Therefore, he explains that *not with money shall they be redeemed*, "but with the precious blood of Christ."[7]

[52:4-5] After these things, he then denounces the *people* of the Jews who had once *gone down into Egypt* and *sojourned there*, and after these things *they were led away by force* and coercion *to the Assyrians*. But instead of *led by force*, Symmachus says: *And Assyria led the people astray for no reason*. And he said earlier that they were subjected to the *Egyptians* and then to the *Assyrians*, but now in this verse, which also comes from God, the text reads: *They were sold for nothing*.[8] For this reason, he continues on: *And now, why will he be here?* Or according to the other Greek translations: *And now, why is he here with me?* For, he says, I find nothing *here* among them, and his meaning is clarified above when he said: "Because I came and no one was there; I called, and there was none to answer."[9] And once they were enslaved *by force* and coercion, first by the *Egyptians* and then by the *Assyrians*, and they were delivered over because of their sins. But now *they were carried away for nothing* "like a pickaxe[10] in a net,"[11] ensnared in the "nets" of vice by the hunter of souls. For this reason, he continues on: *Because my people were taken for nothing, you marvel and howl*. But Symmachus says: *Those who exercise authority over him howl*, and Aquila says: *Those who exercise authority over him weep*, and Theodotion says:

Those who rule over him howl. And so, [330] when *those who rule* and preside over the people are delivered over to punishment, as the cause of the downfall of the people, *they howl*. For they were the ones who "stirred up the multitude"[12] and denounced our Savior with godless voices. And this was indicated in the earlier verse: "The Lord himself will enter into judgment with the elders of the people and with their rulers. But you, why have you burned my vineyard, and why is the spoil of the poor in your houses?"[13] Then the Word resumes a prior subject and says: *This is what the Lord says, Because of you, my name is continually blasphemed among the nations*, or according to Symmachus: *My name is continually blasphemed all day long*. And the phrase *among the nations* is present neither in the Hebrew text nor in the other Greek translations. In this verse, the prophecy alludes to their blasphemies against the Christ, which *the rulers* of the nation of the Jews do every *day* always and *continually*.

[52:6] But, he says, you are such people, but there is another *people* from the nations who joined me, and it is concerning them that the text says: *They shall know my name*, the *name* that *you blaspheme* "because you do not know its power."[14] And *my people shall know my name*, coming to know it in the very experience of sharing in the saving and divine power. These things will happen *in that day*. And to which *day* is he referring, if not when *I myself*—the one who now utters these things through the prophets—I will make my presence among people? According to Symmachus, the text reads: *Therefore, my people shall know my name in that day, because I myself am the one who speaks: behold, I am*.[15] It is as he said

---

[7]1 Pet 1:19. [8]Eusebius's observation is that while the text said earlier that the people were sold to the Egyptians and Assyrians, the text here seems to say that the people were sold to nothing or for nothing. [9]Is 50:2. [10]See footnote above on Is 51:20. [11]Is 51:20. [12]Mk 15:11. [13]Is 3:14. [14]Mt 22:29. [15]Eusebius's allusion is faint, but it seems that he has changed the Greek verb here in order to allude to Ex 3:14. That is, the one who speaks in this passage is the "I am."

clearly before: *I myself am the one who speaks these things now through the prophet, and because I am the one who revealed myself to people, I can say: Because I myself am the one who speaks. I am here.*

[52:7] After prophesying about his advent among people, "speaking through the prophets in the past,"[16] he then adds a comment about the evangelical preaching, which was spread abroad to all the nations through his apostles, whom he mentions in the preceding passages. Perceiving the deeper sense of this verse, the inspired apostle paraphrased it in the Epistle to the Romans in this way: "How beautiful are the feet of those who preach good news, of those who preach peace!"[17] And Symmachus translated this verse as follows: *How splendid on the mountains are the feet of the one who brings glad tidings, who announces a report of peace, who brings glad tidings of good things, who announces a message of salvation.* Where the Greek text reads *salvation*, the Hebrew word we find is *Jesus*,[18] so that without changing anything, nothing would have prevented the translators who carefully preserve the Hebrew text from saying: *The one who proclaims Jesus.* But according to Aquila, the text says: *How they are beautiful, on the mountains, the feet of the one who brings glad tidings of good things, who proclaims* [331] *salvation,* and according to Theodotion: *Like splendid things on the mountains are the feet of the one who brings glad tidings of good things.* In this verse, the prophetic Spirit marvels at the *feet* of those who preach the gospel, on which they have completed their course, encircling all the nations. And their *feet* were *in season* and clean because the Savior "washed"[19] them. The text says that they were running *on the mountains* because of the prominence and highness of

preaching the gospel. And they proclaimed *peace* to people, *preaching peace* with God— even this very *peace was preached* "to those that are far and to those that are near."[20] This verse clearly refers to the Christ of God, "who has made us both one, and has broken down the dividing wall of hostility in his flesh."[21] It is for this reason that Paul sends "grace and peace"[22] when he writes. And *they preached good* things—things that are truly *good*—proclaiming the blessed announcement that the Savior delivered through the evangelical teaching. The phrase: *He spoke* the proclamation *to Zion,* clearly refers to the godly government and to the apostolic band: *Your God shall reign.* For this reason they proclaimed the kingdom of heaven to all people.

[52:8] But instead of *the voice of those who watch over you was lifted up,* Symmachus writes: *The voice of those who guard you raised up their voice.* He continues on: *In the same way they will rejoice; for they shall look with their eyes when the Lord will turn Zion around,* and here again the godly government is called *Zion.* According to Aquila, the text reads: *The voice of those who guard you raised up their voice, and in the same way rejoiced exceedingly, because they shall see eye to eye.* And according to Theodotion, the text reads: *The voice of those who guard you raised up their voice, and the reason why they will rejoice is because they will see eye to eye.* And here the Word calls the disciples and apostles of our Savior *guardians.* For just as those who were prophets among the people of the circumcision were called *guardians,* so also now the apostles of our Savior have become *guardians* and keepers of the temple and the new Zion—clearly referring to the church of God and the godly government. And those who *with their eyes* became the eyewitnesses and

---

[16]Heb 1:1. [17]Rom 10:15. [18]Technically, Eusebius does not here present the Greek word for Jesus, Ἰησοῦς, but ἰησουὰ, a transliteration of the Hebrew verb "to save." Of course, Jesus' name means the "one who saves" in Hebrew (Mt 1:21). [19]Jn 13:1-17. [20]Is 57:19. [21]Eph 2:14. [22]E.g., Rom 1:7.

earwitnesses of the Savior *lifted up* their own *voice* so that it came to be heard among all the nations. They were filled with every spiritual joy when God had compassion on us and restored Zion to us and saved its once desolate places through the saving redemption.

[52:9] But instead of *let the desolate places of Jerusalem break forth together in joy*, Symmachus writes: *Rejoice and be glad together, you desolate places of Jerusalem*. Jerusalem is to be understood as the city of God—I am speaking about the godly government—and the Word now preaches the gospel to the *places* that were once *desolate*, and they are full of gladness and joy because of the mercy of God.

[52:10] **[332]** He then continues on and presents the things that were said to Jerusalem: *The Lord shall reveal his holy arm before all the nations*, and according to Symmachus, the text reads: *The Lord revealed his holy arm before all the nations, and all the boundaries of the earth will see the saving power of our God.* You see how the evangelical preaching promises that the things that have been announced in this verse are for the nations. For he says that God *shall reveal his holy arm*—and that is God the Word—*to all the nations*, and *all the ends of the earth shall see the salvation that comes from our God*. Therefore, when he addresses *Zion* and *Jerusalem*, he refers to the calling of the nations. For the godly government—whether, as at one time, it is among the Jews, or, whether, as now, it is among the Gentiles—he calls *Zion* and *Jerusalem*. And, therefore, there is always such a city of God established among people. And so there is no difference whether the chosen city that is set apart to God among people is called *Zion* or *Jerusalem*.

[52:11] And perhaps the statements concerning the godly government have been spoken to us, but the prophetic Spirit then speaks directly to the band of the apostles: *Depart, depart, go out from there*—clearly referring to the unbelieving people—*and touch no unclean thing; go out from the midst of it and be separated, you who carry the vessels of the Lord.* And the *vessels of the Lord* are their bodies, chosen by the Lord and *separated* to God "in holiness and honor."[23] Or perhaps the *vessels of the Lord* are the Gospels of the New Testament, which he commands to be brought out with them and delivered from the disbelief of the people of the Jews and *separated* from them.

[52:12] He continues on: *Because you shall not go out with confusion, nor shall you go in flight.* It was not as though they went out because they had been driven out to their circuit around the nations. But it was in all eagerness and deliberation and free choice that they were driven on "to make disciples of all nations in his name."[24] Therefore, it is concerning them that the text reads: *Because you shall not go out with confusion.* And, therefore, they made their journeys with all peace, since they carried with them the promise that he had made to them: "Behold, I am with you always, to the very end of the age."[25] This is what the present passage signifies when it says: *For the Lord will go before you, and the Lord, the God of Israel, is the one who gathers you together.*

[52:13] *Behold, my servant shall understand, and he shall be exalted and* **[333]** *glorified and raised up exceedingly.* For because "he humbled himself and became obedient unto death, even death on a cross, because of this, God has highly exalted him and bestowed on him the name which is above every name."[26] Therefore, the present prophecy indicates the same thing when it says: *Behold, my servant shall understand, and he shall be exalted and glorified and raised up*, for in this verse it is

---

[23]1 Thess 4:4. [24]Mt 28:19. [25]Mt 28:20. [26]Phil 2:8-9.

speaking about his resurrection after death and ascension into the heavens and glorification. After these things, we then read about his humiliation "unto death"[27] when the text states: "We saw him, and he had no form or beauty. But his form was without honor, failing beyond the sons of men,"[28] and again: "He was dishonored and not esteemed. This one bears our sins and suffers pain for us,"[29] and once more: "Like a sheep he was led to the slaughter, and as a lamb is silent before the one shearing it, so he does not open his mouth. In his humiliation his judgment was taken away. Who will describe his generation? Because his life is being taken from the earth, he was led to death because of the acts of lawlessness of my people."[30] Therefore, although the prophetic Spirit here presents verses concerning "his humiliation"[31] and "his death,"[32] he prophesied earlier concerning his glorification after death, speaking first about the more auspicious things before the sullen. And so he says: *See, my servant shall understand*, or according to Aquila: *See, my slave shall be made wise*. He rightly calls him a *slave* "because of the form of a *slave*,[33] which he assumed."[34] For God the Word, "though he was in the form of God, emptied *himself*,"[35] the one who, according to the holy apostle "took the form of a servant and was found in appearance as a man."[36] But this *servant* or *slave* of God, who was "filled" with all "wisdom"[37] and understanding, contained God the Word in himself.[38] Therefore, the text says: *See, he shall be made wise, and he shall be exalted and glorified and raised up.* And all these things were fulfilled in the man who is our Savior because of his union with God the Word.[39]

[52:14-15] The text continues on: *Just as many shall be astonished at you*—but according to Theodotion, the text reads: *Just as many marveled at him*—*so shall your appearance be without glory from the sons of men.* For this one who exceedingly *astonished many* also caused them to be perplexed; I am speaking about his abased and inglorious appearance among people. And, therefore, the word concerning him still even now produces astonishment and perplexity and befuddlement in many. On the one hand, the phrase *many nations marveled at him* speaks about those who believe in him and worship his divinity, and on the other hand, it speaks about those who, although *marveling* at his power, "persist in unbelief,"[40] even though his power is higher and stronger than those who attempt to fight against it. After uttering [334] many blasphemous and godless and profane words against him and persecuting his church, *kings closed their mouths* and submitted to his teaching, since they were not able to bring about an end to their meaningless sufferings. For at various times and seasons, their spirits were broken, and they were driven on by the scourges of destiny. And we who record these things have had the same experience. Some of them *closed their mouths*, but others were encouraged and sang a recantation of the laws and ordinances and offered up prayers for the home and practiced the rituals of the church. And he explains why *kings* were excited about him when he continues on to say: *Because those who were not informed about him shall see, and those who did not hear shall understand.* For this was what excited the *kings*—I am speaking about the fact that his evangelical word spread to the farthest nations. And the Word gently and indirectly convicts

---

[27]Phil 2:8. [28]Is 53:2b-3a. [29]Is 53:3b-4a. [30]Is 53:7b-8. [31]Cf. Is 53:8. [32]Cf. Is 53:9. [33]The word choice of *servant* or *slave* here is between παῖς and δοῦλος. The Greek word translated here is δοῦλος and could mean either "servant" or "slave." The word here has been translated "slave" in this context in order to differentiate it from Eusebius's citation of Is 52:13, in which he reproduces the term παῖς as it appears in the LXX. [34]Phil 2:7. [35]Phil 2:6-7. [36]Phil 2:7. [37]Lk 2:40. [38]This is an important christological statement. Eusebius does not say that the servant *is* God the Word but that he contained (χωρήσας) God the Word. [39]This sentence, also an important christological statement, is loaded with prepositions. It seems that Eusebius is appealing to the preposition πρός in conscious allusion to Jn 1:1. [40]Rom 11:23.

the nation of the Jews for their ignorance concerning him. Although they were *informed* first concerning the prophesied one, and although they learned the prophecies concerning him by heart from their childhood, they certainly did not understand until after he came. For this reason, he says that they *shall not see* or *understand*, but on the contrary *those who were not informed about him* and who have never learned anything of his sayings *shall see and understand*. For, he says, they *shall see* him with the eyes of their souls, and they *shall understand* his teaching. And these things were prophesied in words long ago, but they were fulfilled in deed at the appearance of our Savior among people. Although the children of the Jews saw his appearance with their eyes, and although they heard his voice, they neither *understood* nor yielded their hearing to the one summoning them. And so the prophecy above was fulfilled among them, which says: "You will listen by listening, but you will not *understand*; and looking you will look, but you will not perceive."[41] They neither *saw* nor *understood*, but according to the very voice of the Savior: "Blessed are those who have not seen and yet believe."[42] These people from all the nations—although they never learned about him or knew the Scriptures concerning him—nevertheless *they have seen* him and *understood*, and they accepted the knowledge of his divinity.

[53:1-4] He expresses wonder and consternation at those who have contemplated these things from of old by the prophetic Spirit. Therefore, he continues on to say: *Lord, who has believed our report?* For the prophets of God said these things as they looked on in astonishment at the unbelief of the nation of the Jews and as they contemplated the conversion and obedience of the Gentiles. But he says, *And to whom has the arm of the Lord been revealed?* The prophecy before this one taught *to whom the arm of the Lord has been revealed* in the verse: "And the Lord God *shall reveal* his holy *arm* before all the nations."[1] And we have demonstrated many times that his "only-begotten Son"[2] is referred to as the *arm* of God, who was made known to all nations who believe in him after listening to the prophetic voices. For after the prophets of God marveled at these things, they then prophesy in detail concerning the appearance among people of the one who was above addressed as the "servant" or [335] the "slave" of God: *We announce that he grew up before him like a child,*[3] *like a root in a thirsty land,* but according to Aquila, the text says: *And he will go up like one planted before his face and like a root from desolate ground.* For he says that *before his face*—I am speaking about the prophesied *arm*—*it will shoot up like a root.* This refers to him who was born of the virgin, concerning whom it has been said above: "Behold, the virgin shall conceive and bear a son, and you shall name him Emmanuel."[4] That this *root* was the one who grew up before the face *of the arm of God,* the Word next shows plainly when he says: *Like a root from desolate ground.* The *desolate ground* alludes to the virgin, which no one had approached, and the *root* is the one concerning whom it has been said: "A rod shall come out of the root of Jesse, and a blossom shall come up out of his root."[5] And the text says *he will go up,* but there it says "from the root of Jesse" and here it says *from desolate ground.* And according to Symmachus, the text reads: *And he went up like a branch before him, and like a root from thirsty ground,* which the Word here calls *desolate, thirsty ground.* And according to Theodotion, the text reads: *And he will go up like a suckling before*

---

[41]Is 6:9. [42]Jn 20:29 RSV. **Chapter Fifty-Three** [1]Is 52:10. [2]Jn 3:16. [3]This is the same word translated "servant" in the line preceding. It seems that the Greek reader would understand this word as "child" in the present context, given that the reference is to growing up. [4]Is 7:14. [5]Is 11:1.

him—clearly referring to *the arm of God*—and like *a root in a thirsty land*. And this one, whom the Septuagint translation here calls a *child* when it says, *He grew up before him like a child*, it is this very one concerning whom we read in the passages above: "For before the child knows good or bad, he defies evil,"[6] and again: "For before the child knows how to call father or mother, it will receive the power of Damascus,"[7] and once more: "Because a child was born for us, a son also given to us, whose sovereignty was on his shoulder."[8] And we have demonstrated in the appropriate contexts that these verses refer to the Christ of God. After foretelling the birth of the prophesied one among people—a birth which was *from desolate or from thirsty ground*—he next recounts his sojourn among people and says: *He has no form or glory* (instead of *he had no glorious form*) *and we saw him, and he had no form or beauty. But his form was without honor, failing beyond the sons of men.*

The prophet speaks of the Savior himself as common, and he says that because of his benevolence he was counted among those who were *not esteemed*. And we too, *we did not esteem him*; we neither professed nor supposed him to be anyone at all. But he was the very Savior, who heals our souls and cleanses every sin! Therefore, he continues on: *This one bears our sins and suffers pain for us, and we accounted him to be in trouble and calamity and ill treatment.* But according to Symmachus, the text reads: *Truly he assumed our diseases, and he endured our sufferings, and we esteemed him as one stricken by God with the plague and humiliated.* But Aquila writes: **[336]** *And we esteemed him as one who had been wounded and stricken by God and humiliated.*

[53:5-6] Even as children we had this view concerning him—that he suffered all these things because of us in order that he might set

us free from all retribution. Therefore, he continues on: *But he was wounded because of our sins and has been weakened because of our sins.* But Aquila says: *But he has been profaned by our lawlessness, crushed by our lawless acts.* For he was truly *profaned* when "he became a curse for us"[9] and when *he was wounded* and *profaned* and endured all these terrible things, not because of certain of his own *sins* but because of ours! And *the discipline of our peace was on him.* For, although we should have suffered and been disciplined because of our *sins*, they fell on him for our *peace* with God. And the text says, *by his bruise we were healed*, since he surely bore *bruises* and wounds in his body, since he had been beaten and "scourged"[10] and "slapped"[11] in the face, and they "struck him on the head with a reed."[12] But these *bruises* were our salvation.[13] For *by his bruise we were healed*. And to whom does the *we* refer if not to those who had once *gone astray* and who *did not acknowledge him* and did not understand who he was? And so *all we like sheep have gone astray; a man has strayed in his own way.* For holding different and contrary opinions concerning him, each went in another *way* of error. And it was not without the aid of God that these things came to pass. For *the Lord* himself *gave him over to our sins*, in order that he might be our substitute[14] and "ransom."[15] For thus also he was the "lamb of God who takes away" and purges away "the sins of the world."[16] For this reason, according to Symmachus, the text reads: *And the Lord made the lawlessness of us all to fall on him.*

[53:7] Then, instead of *and he, because he has been ill-treated, does not open his mouth*, Symmachus writes: *He was led, and he obeyed.* And to whom *was he led* other than "to Pilate"?[17] "And although he was accused," "he was silent,"[18] and although they testified falsely

[6]Is 7:16. [7]Is 8:4. [8]Is 9:6. [9]Gal 3:13. [10]Jn 19:1. [11]Mt 26:6. [12]Mt 27:30. [13]Literally, "saviors." [14]ἀντίψυχος means literally "something given in exchange for one's life." [15]1 Tim 2:6. [16]Jn 1:29. [17]Mt 27:12-13. [18]Mt 26:63.

against him, "he made no answer." For this reason, the text reads according to Symmachus: *And he did not open his mouth.*

[**53:8**] After recounting his sufferings, for those listening to the deeper meaning, he continues on and refers to the appearance of his birth: *Who will describe his generation?* For, then, who will find a greater wonder than the endurance of such things, when contemplating that it was he who, as the one "born of God,"[19] "the only-begotten [**337**] Son," caused all these things to exist. For this reason, according to Aquila, the text reads: *Who will keep company with his generation? Because his life is being taken from the earth.* But Symmachus writes: *For he was cut off from the land of the living, and on account of the unrighteousness of my people there was a blow for them.* And Theodotion writes: *Because he was cut off from the land of the living, and because of the faithlessness of my people, he touched them.* Rather, *he appealed*[20] to them, and *there was a great blow for them* that has become his death. And, therefore, after these things, immediately an unrelenting wrath came upon them, and a *blow touched* them. And it is clear that in this verse the prophet prophesied these things concerning neither himself nor the people, as one can conclude because he says: *Because of the lawlessness of my people he was led to death.*

[**53:9-10**] Instead of *and I will give the wicked for his burial and the rich for his death,* Symmachus writes: *And I will give the ungodly for his burial.* And who is the one who *will give* if not the judge of the universe? And whom *will he give* if not those who have done the aforementioned deeds? These he will deliver over immediately and not in a far distant time to their enemies and adversaries and those who besiege them. And, again, he says that he would deliver *the rich for his death,* those who had taken advantage of others. And then, at this very moment, he added that his "legacy had vanished from among people,"[21] from among those who were very powerful among the Jews—the Pharisees and scribes and Sadducees, priests as well as high priests and those who have been honored with royal dignity. They are the ones who were called *rich* above, on whom "the wrath of God came not in a far distant time,"[22] because, although the Christ of God was faultless, they subjected him to such punishment. For this reason, he continues on: *Because he committed no sin, nor was deceit found in his mouth.* And this is the extraordinary thing about our supernatural and most excellent salvation—I am speaking about the fact that he was faultless and blameless in word and deed throughout the whole course of his life. "Therefore, no one has been pure from filth, not even if his life was but one day or he was alone."[23] Therefore "he died for all," in order that he might cleanse and "take away the sin of the world."[24] Therefore, also his God and Father judged him *to cleanse him from his blow*—that is, from the suffering that was laid on him—or according to Aquila: *And the Lord desired to inflame his illness,* and according to Symmachus: *The Lord wished to crush him in wounding.* After these things, the text reads: *If you give an offering for sin, your soul shall see a long-lived offspring.* And what he says here has a deeper meaning. After all the things that have been said above, if anyone who has acted profanely against him wants to offer up a sacrifice for his sin—that is, to display confession and repentance from the sins he has committed—he will not fail to attain good

---

[19]1 Jn 3:9. [20]Καθάπτω, the word here translated "appealed," is a compound version of the verb translated "touched" above, ἅπτω. [21]Cf. Job 2:9 LXX; see also 1 Macc 12:53. This verse appears in the LXX but not in the MT. The LXX here records a tradition that Job's wife did not say "curse God and die" but rather delivered an extended, less drastic speech at this point in the book. [22]Cf. Eph 5:6; Col 3:6. [23]Job 14:4-5. [24]Jn 1:29.

hope in him. For the text certainly reads: *Because I will give the wicked for his* [338] *burial and the rich for his death*; nevertheless *if you*—you who have dared to do such things—*give an offering for sin*, you will receive forgiveness and *your soul* will be saved, and not only will it be saved, but also *it shall see a long-lived seed*.[25] And this is what he scattered among people and what he was talking about when he taught "in parables"[26] and said: "A sower went out to sow," and again: "The kingdom of heaven is like a man who sowed good seed in his own field."[27] Therefore, *if you give an offering for sin, your soul shall see* this rational and heavenly *seed*. Instead of *and the Lord wishes to take away from the pain of his soul*, Symmachus writes: *And the will of the Lord shall succeed in his hand*, and according to Aquila: *And the purpose of the Lord is in his hand*. It is appropriate that this be said only about our Savior. For *the will* of the Father *shall succeed* forever *in his hand*.

[53:11-12] He also gave him *light* in order that those who are justified through him might be enlightened, and he presented him with *understanding*. For "the spirit of wisdom and *understanding* rested on him"[28] in order that the intelligent might be perfected and the worthy might be justified because he justifies them.[29] He continues on to say who these are: *And he himself shall bear their sins*, or according to Symmachus: *And he himself bore their impieties*. Taking on himself the *impieties* of those who were formerly sinners and ungodly, he stripped them of the garment of sin and perfected them as righteous. For this reason, he continues on to say: *Therefore he shall inherit many*. For it was because *he* assumed on himself *the sins of many* that he also has been able to make everyone his inheritance. If there

had been no one to forgive sins, they would have continued on in their faults and never attained salvation. And now, after *he assumed their sins*, he then because of this also received them as an inheritance from the Father. He himself teaches this when he says: "The Lord said to me, 'you are my son; today I have begotten you. Ask of me, and I will give you nations as your heritage.'"[30] And *he divided the spoils of the strong*—clearly, the adversarial powers and the evil demons who captured the souls who had been enslaved by them—and made them *spoils* for himself, and he distributed these *spoils* to his disciples when he established different churches through them. For this reason, the text reads above: "And they will also rejoice before you like those who rejoice at the harvest and in the same way as those who divide *spoils*."[31] He is able to do all these things, and he will do them. *Because his soul was given over to death*, he received these things as a reward from the Father—I am speaking about the fact that because he forgave the sins of those who had sinned formerly, [339] he brought them under his inheritance. *His soul was given over to death, and he was reckoned among the lawless; he assumed the sins of many, and because of their lawlessnesses he was given over. Because of this, he shall inherit many, and he shall divide the spoils of the strong*. The Gospel teaches how *he was reckoned among the lawless* when "they crucified" him between two "robbers," thus fulfilling what the prophecy said. The text reads in Mark: "And with him they crucified two robbers, one on the right and one on the left. And the Scripture was fulfilled which says: *And he was reckoned with the lawless*."[32]

[54:1] After the prophecy concerning our Savior—which described his birth among

---

[25]This term is translated "offspring" in NETS, as above. However, Eusebius uses the term to mean "seed" in the following sentences. [26]Mt 13:3. [27]Mt 13:24. [28]Cf. Is 11:2. [29]Note Eusebius's language concerning justification in connection with the sufferings of Christ. [30]Ps 2:7-8. [31]Is 9:2b. [32]Mk 15:27-28.

people and his life afterwards and his death and the reason for his death—the Word preaches that the church, although now established by him throughout the whole world, was formerly *desolate* and infertile and fruitless, and therefore he calls it a *barren* woman, since such souls as comprise the church came from the unbelieving nations. But now, preaching to them a change for the better, the Word exhorts the formerly *barren* woman to *rejoice*. Because she has received seed and conceived and is about to *bear* the saving and good progeny, he continues on: *Break forth and shout, you who* formerly *did not bear*. Or according to Aquila, instead of *break forth and shout*, the text reads: *Shout praise and roar, you who are not in labor*, but Symmachus writes: *Exult in great joy and roar, you who do not bear*, and Theodotion writes: *Break forth in joy and be glad, you who are not in labor*. He continues on: *Because more are the children of the desolate woman than of her that has a husband*, and according to Symmachus: *For more are the children of the woman who had been rejected than the children of the married woman*. For at first the church of the nations was *rejected* and *desolate*, inasmuch as she was not yet married to the heavenly bridegroom. But much fruitfulness and many children are promised to her, in fact more than *of her who has a husband*. And who was this woman other than the nation of the Jews and Jerusalem, the city that had formerly been honored as God's own. She *who has a husband*—the husband being the heavenly Word—was disgraced because she gave him a "bill of divorce"[1] and committed fornication away from him, as the text reads above: "How the faithful city Zion has become a whore! She that was full of justice, wherein righteousness lodged—but now murders!"[2] Therefore, the Word preaches to her that the one who was formerly married to a husband will be comparable to the one who was *desolate*

of God among the nations, who at first had only an auspicious promise to go on but was later deemed worthy of an abundance of children and descendents; thus the people [340] of the circumcision are compared with the multiple children of this woman. Therefore, it has been said: *Because more are the children of the desolate woman than of her that has a husband.*

[54:2-3] Then he addresses her and says: *Enlarge the site of your tent and of your curtains; make it firm; do not hold back; lengthen your cords, and strengthen your stakes.* These things have been said in reference to "the tabernacle"[3] that was constructed by Moses. For, after appealing to that image, the Word addresses the church of the nations and urges it not to be small-minded concerning its borders but to *enlarge* its tent and stretch it out to an untold "length"[4] and "breadth." For indeed, the "length" of the tabernacle that was constructed by Moses was "one hundred" cubits and the "breadth fifty." Then the text reads: *Do not hold back* from this, neither allow yourself to be confined by any limits, but extend and *lengthen* and *strengthen* yourself, *because you must spread out* further *to the right and to the left.* And I am sure that the length and breadth and magnitude of this new tabernacle—which a mortal did not pitch but the Lord—on the one hand brings to mind the dimensions of the tabernacle constructed by Moses and on the other hand the temple in Jerusalem, which was "sixty cubits long and twenty wide."[5] And so, if the temple in one city situated in Palestine was worthy of wonder, how much more for their multitude and magnitude and beauty are the churches of God that have been erected throughout every region! He clearly states that these things are prophesied concerning the church from the Gentiles when he continues on to say: *And*

Chapter Fifty-Four [1]E.g., Deut 24:1. [2]Is 1:21. [3]E.g., Ex 27:9. [4]Ex 27:18. [5]1 Kings 6:2.

your offspring will inherit the nations and will inhabit the cities that have become desolate. And would not the *offspring* of the church of God be the evangelical word, concerning which it has been said: "A sower went out to sow,"[6] and: "Didn't you sow good *seed*[7] in the field?"[8] These same *offspring* occupied the *cities that have become desolate.* And according to Symmachus, the text reads: *And your offspring will inherit the nations, and they will inhabit cities that have disappeared.* It is also possible that the *offspring* of the church is the succession of the apostles and disciples of our Savior, because of whom the godly citizens occupied the churches that had formerly disappeared and had been abandoned by God.

[54:4-5] After these verses, he continues on to say next: *Do not fear because you were put to shame, neither feel disgraced because you were reproached.* For when she was *barren* and *one who does not bear,* neither *one who is in labor* nor *one who has a husband,* she was disgraced and full of shame. But now he says to her: Then you were doing things worthy of *shame* and *reproach,* but now you are confident, *because you will forget your ancient shame, and the reproach of your widowhood you will not remember.* And here he calls barrenness from the Word, the bridegroom, *widowhood,* which he says *you will not remember because the Lord of powers* [341] is the one who makes you. For your formation has not been from people neither through a man but through the Lord himself. Therefore also the Savior himself promises when he said: "On the rock I will build my church, and the powers of death shall not prevail against it."[9] Therefore, *the Lord of powers himself is the one who makes you,* and he who was once the *God of Israel* alone is now known *in all the earth.* Therefore, according to Symmachus, the text reads: *He will be called God of the entire earth.*

[54:6-8] As the Word continues to discuss the promises to the desolate woman, he says: *The Lord has not called you as a forsaken and faint-hearted woman, or as a woman hated from youth, your God has said.* But according to Symmachus, the text reads: *For the Lord called you in the Spirit as a woman in great suffering and abandoned and a woman driven away from youth, God has said. I abandoned you for a little while, but I will gather you together in great compassion; in a flash of anger I hid my face for a moment from you, but with everlasting mercy I had pity on you.*

[54:9-10] Then he continues: *Just as I swore to Noah* that I would never again destroy those on earth in a flood, so now also I swear to you, and I guarantee my people that *I will no longer be angry at you; for the mountains will be shaken and the hills will be troubled, and my mercy shall not be turned away from you, nor shall the covenant of my peace be pushed away,* the Lord who has compassion on you has said. For *the mountains will be removed* from their proper positions *and the hills will be troubled* sooner than my *mercy will be moved away.* And the Word promises these things to the godly citizenry, which once resided among the Jews but, after falling away from them, passed over to the church of the Gentiles. And he promises a *covenant of peace* when he says: *Nor shall the covenant of my peace be removed.*

[54:11-12] Then he reminds the reader of the kind of godly citizenry that once resided among the Jews and the change for the worse that would befall them. Therefore, he says: *O humbled and unsteady one.* For the physical religion among the Jews was *humbled* in the circumcision of the body and in animal sacrifice and in many other things like these that could be enumerated, and therefore he calls them *humbled and unsteady.* Then he

---

[6]Mt 13:3. [7]The word σπέρμα can mean "seed" or "offspring," as translated above. [8]Mt 13:27. [9]Mt 16:18.

continues: *You have not been comforted.* For there was no one among the prophets or God-loving people who could restore and revive them. But the text does not say that anyone did things to you, but rather: *See, I myself am preparing for you charcoal as your stone.* But instead of this, Symmachus writes: *See, I set forth a black powder*[10] *for your stones,* and Theodotion writes: *See, I will throw your stones in* [342] *black powder.* For just as a woman who adorns herself "applies black powder to her eyes,"[11] so he says: *I myself will arrange the stones* of your house in exceptional refinement and ornamentation. But according to the Septuagint, the text reads: *He will prepare a* precious *charcoal stone* for her. Perhaps the reference to *charcoal* signifies the cleansing of the soul, since also "one of the seraphim cleansed the lips of the prophet Isaiah with a *charcoal* from the altar."[12] When he says that he has cleansed every such *stone* from your house, he clearly is saying that he will prepare them so that no *stone* of the house will be unclean—*and I will lay your foundations* from the stone *lapis lazuli.* Therefore, according to the other Greek translations, the text reads: *And I will found you in lapis lazuli.*

But also I will build *your battlements* from *jasper* stone, or according to Symmachus: *And I will make your houses out of Carthaginian stone and your gates out of carved stones,* and according to the Septuagint: *And your gates of crystal stones and your enclosure of precious stones.* We understand that all these stones are the precious and costly souls out of which God promised to build godly citizens. He compares them with *lapis lazuli* because *lapis lazuli* resembles the color of heaven.[13] And their government is heavenly and angelic, as Paul teaches when he says: "But our common-

wealth is in heaven."[14] And there is the verse in the prophet Ezekiel that says: "Under the throne of God, as *lapis lazuli.*"[15] Therefore, "all the prophets and the apostles"[16] were the "*foundation*" of the godly commonwealth, firm and "steadfast,"[17] and portrayed as *lapis lazuli* because they administer the "government of heaven" and because they "bear the image of the man of heaven."[18] For this reason, the text reads: *And I will lay your foundations in lapis lazuli.* And the *battlements* of this temple and of the new Jerusalem are of *jasper* stone or *Carthaginian* stone, according to Symmachus, and this stone is special and translucent. Such were those in the church who defended the faith with spiritual armaments, standing as champions of the godly commonwealth and able "to demolish every proud obstacle to the knowledge of God"[19] and to expose every false word spoken against the truth. For just as the *battlements* in the walls are the front line of defense and are prepared to be the first armament against the adversaries, so also are those in the church who, mighty in word and wisdom, could rightly be called *battlements.* With these, he founded others whom he portrays as *crystal stones,* through whom he prophesies that the *gates* of the city will be established. And so he points to the radiance and purity of the wholesome faith of those who believed the early and elementary and introductory teaching. He promises them that *he will make* the *enclosure* of the temple of the city of God out of [343] *precious stones.* And those who fortify the church all around and who secure every defense through prayer to God are these precious stones who fortify the entire structure of the city, including its grand, extravagant and highly valued buildings.

---

[10]The Greek noun here, στίμμι, appears to be a reference to antimony. It was used as make-up for the eyelids. [11]Cf. Ezek 23:40. [12]Is 6:6. [13]Eusebius is saying that the redeemed are likened to lapis lazuli because this gem is the color of the sky, and he finds it fitting that those who are destined for heaven would be likened to a stone of the color of the sky. [14]Phil 3:20. [15]Cf. Ezek 1:26. [16]Eph 2:20. [17]Col 1:23. [18]1 Cor 15:49. [19]2 Cor 10:5.

[54:13] He says many other things concerning those who will inhabit the above-mentioned city. For instance, they will claim God himself as their teacher. He presents this teaching when he says: *And I will make all your sons taught by God.* He said this in the Gospels: "Do not call anyone on earth your teacher, for you have one teacher in heaven."[20] From the formerly "barren woman"[21] he will produce *sons taught by God,* and her *children* will be *in great peace.* For he promised this to them when he said: "My *peace* I give to you; my *peace* I leave with you."[22]

[54:14-15] After this, he continues: *And in righteousness you shall be built.* To speak with absolute precision, he is the builder of the universe, the wisdom of God who, in setting the "living"[23] and firm "stones" in the building, makes them *battlements,* and lays them down as *foundations,* and arranges them in *enclosures,* and sets them apart for the temple of the city and for the innermost place in the temple and adorns the rest of the city with them as well. Therefore, it has been said: *And in righteousness you shall be built.* He then explains what God had promised his church above when he says: *Keep away from injustice, and you shall not be afraid, and trembling shall not come near you.* What happened earlier to you is by my grace, and even if you were anxious, you never feared an attack from any of your enemies. Be encouraged in my command! If you do this, what I spoke about earlier will not happen to you, but if you do not keep the commandment, you will have no one but yourself to blame when you fall into human dangers. For this reason, I testify to you and say: *Keep away from injustice, and you shall not be afraid, and trembling shall not come near you.* And when you remain with me and serve God, then, according to that very appropriate word, *guests shall approach you,* but not apart from my will. For they *will*

also dwell beside me. And one could say that the *guests,* who appear in the text after the mention of the ordinances of the church, are those who live among the multitude but are neither lawfully nor genetically related to them. He says that *they will dwell beside* but not in the city, and so they are made to be as an entryway into the city proper. Therefore, it has been said to the most beautiful among them: *See, guests shall approach you through me and shall dwell beside you and flee to you for refuge.* For those who need a place of refuge surrender themselves because they need protection and patronage, but there are also those who because of different life circumstances he calls *guests,* and he says rightly that *they will dwell beside* the city in accordance with the resolution of people.

[54:16-17] And he says that *I myself, the Lord,* will do all these things, since [344] I myself am your creator ("I built my church on the rock"[24]), and *I created you* not by any human craft but with divine and unspeakable grace. Therefore, I say: *See, I created you, not as a smith who blows the coals and produces a vessel for work.* For such things are fashioned with human tools and by human effort. Therefore, although all things come to ruin and *destruction,* he has produced my incorruptible *work.* Therefore, I say: *But I have not created you for destruction,* neither *fashioned any vessel that will ruin you.* For nothing will be found against my *work* that will *completely ruin* or destroy it. But, he says, *and every voice that shall rise,* and everyone who devises schemes to pass judgment on you, *they will be defeated.* He continues on: *You will defeat all of them.* After these things, the text reads: *There is a heritage for those who do service to the Lord,* immediately afterward. For after the verses above, it was necessary to mention, too, the *heritage* in the age to come. And what could this be other

---

[20]Mt 23:8. [21]Cf. Is 54:1. [22]Jn 14:27. [23]1 Pet 2:5. [24]Mt 16:18.

than the kingdom of heaven? But the verse in the Septuagint which reads, *and those who are held by you shall be in sorrow,* is present neither in the Hebrew text nor in the other Greek translations. After these things, he then continues: *And you shall be righteous to me, says the Lord,* and this phrase is added on to the above verse in the other Greek translations. Therefore, according to Symmachus, the text reads: *This is my heritage for the servants of the Lord, and their righteousness is from me, says the Lord.*

[**55:1**] The prophecy at hand refers to the very Christ of God when it says: *You who thirst, go to water.* Then he alludes to the grace that was freely given through the Savior to people when he says: *And as many of you as have no money, come, buy and drink without money.* But instead of *and wine and fat without price, in order that you should set a price with money,* Symmachus writes: *And wine and milk with nothing in exchange.* Aquila likewise translates this phrase *wine and milk,* so that this verse promises not only *water* but also *wine and milk* to those *who thirst.* On the one hand, *water* "from the springs of salvation"[1] clearly refers to the evangelical preaching, and *wine and milk,* on the other hand, allude to the mystery of regeneration in Christ. For "those who are born again of water and the Spirit,"[2] "like newborn babes,"[3] are nursed "with spiritual *milk*" and partake of the *wine* of the new covenant. You should not be ignorant of the fact that, in former times, mystical *milk* was administered to those who were born again in Christ along with the body and blood of the new covenant. And they say that this custom is preserved in certain churches still even now. But if this text is not interpreted according to the literal sense, the mystical blood of Christ is administered to those who are deemed worthy of regeneration in Christ instead of *wine* and instead of *milk.* It

could be said that the word *fat,* which one finds in the Septuagint, alludes to the abundance, richness and nourishment of spiritual food in Christ, which again the Savior made clear when he said: [**345**] "Unless you eat my flesh and drink my blood, you have no life in you."[4] What Isaiah called *fat,* Jesus here calls "flesh," and what Jesus calls "blood," Isaiah called *wine;* the words *fat* and *flesh* clearly refer to his incarnate physical existence,[5] and the words *wine* and *blood* signify the mystery of his suffering. Therefore, he promises to supply without reimbursement and to give freely these things to those *who thirst* for salvation in God.

[**55:2**] Why do you dedicate *your labor* and occupy yourselves with things that do not nourish your soul? Why do you attempt to take pleasure in food that *does not satisfy?* Therefore, according to Symmachus, the text reads: *Why do you spend your money on what is not bread and work for what does not satisfy?* And you will perceive who they are who purchase *with money* the *bread* of the soul, and you will understand who they are who charge fees for spiritual teaching, promising to be "the wise of this age,"[6] or those who sell for payment the tradition of Jewish readings to those who would become their disciples. Next, after this, he exhorts them *to incline their ears* in order that they understand and apply the obedient attention of their souls to the things that are being said. Therefore, he says: *Listen, and you shall eat good things, and you soul shall revel in good things.* After this verse, he speaks of the hope of other *good things* and says that an inspired delight has been stored up for the souls of those who listen. For the gift "of the good things to come"[7] is not presented to their bodies but expressly to their souls.

[**55:3**] After this, he adds: *Pay attention with your ears, and follow my ways.* But according to

---

Chapter Fifty-Five [1]Cf. Is 12:3. [2]Jn 3:5. [3]1 Pet 2:2. [4]Jn 6:53. [5]οἰκονομία. [6]1 Cor 1:20. [7]Heb 10:1.

Symmachus, the text reads: *Incline your ears and come to me*, and *obey me, and your soul will live among good things*, and all these he promises to their souls. Then, after persuading them to listen and awakening their hearing, he begins to teach them: *I will make with you an everlasting covenant, the sacred things of David that are sure.* For, indeed, because the old covenant was temporary, it passed away and came to an end. In many places in the Scriptures, promises are made to David that the Christ of God would come from his "offspring,"[8] and so discipline your ears and *hear* the Word concerning these things. For you know well that if you devote your ears to my words, I will produce in you the fruit of obedience. And the promise that I have made to David, I graciously give to you: therefore *I will make with you "the new covenant"*[9] which will not only be for the time of Moses, but will be enduring and *everlasting* and will remain until the consummation of everything. And *the sacred things of David* which I promised to him, I will make *sure*, for I will substantiate my promise.

[55:4-5] Then, because the prophetic Spirit is prescient and can predict the future, he was not unaware of the fact that the Jews would suppress these voices among themselves, and their souls will certainly not profit further. [346] Therefore, he turns to the foreigners and the *nations* of other races, and he professes that he will give these promises to them when he says these words: *See, I have given him as a testimony among the nations, a ruler and commander for the nations. Nations that do not know you shall call on you, and peoples that do not understand you shall flee to you for refuge, for the sake of the Lord your God, the Holy One of Israel, because he has glorified you.* Therefore, in these verses he refers to what happened to the one whom is signified in the verse above, where one reads: "Because those who were not informed about him shall see, and those who did not hear shall understand,"[10] and: "We saw him, and he had no form or beauty."[11] Therefore, he calls that one "him," about whom all these things have been spoken: *I have given him as a testimony among the nations.* For this reason, I preached and exhorted "the barren one who formerly did not bear and who had no husband to stretch out and enlarge her tent."[12] Because of what has been proclaimed concerning the sins of my people, he had to suffer these things. It has been said rightly, then: *I have given him as a testimony* not to the Jewish people but *among all the nations*, and *a ruler and commander for the nations.* For it is clear to my God that all the *nations* will listen to him before the people of the circumcision. And his *testimony* was what was preached about him, just as he taught when he said: "It is necessary for this gospel to be preached throughout the whole world, as a testimony to all nations."[13] Then the Spirit addresses directly the one who is prophesied above and says: *Nations that do not know you shall call on you, and peoples that do not understand you shall flee to you for refuge.* He says that all these things will happen *for the sake of the Lord your God, the Holy One of Israel, because he has glorified you.*

[55:6-7] Next, he encourages them *to seek the Lord*, adding to the command a promise that they would find him. Therefore, he says: *Seek the Lord, and when you find him, call on him.* Then he exhorts them and says: because *you seek him*, he has come to stand near to you, and he has not settled far away, and because you stood before him, your own life prospered. Because he addresses these things to the nations that were formerly godless and impious, he exhorts them immediately afterwards and says: *Whenever the Lord should draw near to you, let the impious forsake his ways, and the lawless person his plans.* For repentance and the

---

[8]2 Sam 7:12. [9]Jer 31:31. [10]Is 52:15b. [11]Is 53:2b. [12]Is 54:1. [13]Mt 24:14.

leaving off of bad things is good. Even if you consider things to be incurable according to your own abilities, and even if they are hopeless among people, things are not incorrigible and incurable with me, for I *abundantly forgive*.

[55:8-11] *For my plans are not like your plans or like your* human *ways, and so also are my judgments and ways, says the Lord. For just as heaven is high above the earth, so my ways will be exalted above your ways and my thoughts above your thoughts. For in the same way as rain and snow comes down from heaven and will not return there but will soak through the earth and cause it to be fruitful and to bud, and the rain will give seed to the sower and bread to the one who eats, so* [347] *shall my Word[14] be, which shall go out from my mouth. It shall not return to me without result but will do whatever I have willed and accomplish whatever I sent it to accomplish.* He clearly stated all these things in order to confirm the promise that had been made to the ungodly and lawless people who converted from the Gentiles, when he said that the "Word"[15] who was "in the beginning" came down from the Father above like *rain* and *snow* and *came down* on people. He waters their souls and causes them to bear fruit. And his return to the Father he has made clear when he says: *It shall not return to me without result but do whatever I have willed and accomplish whatever I commanded it to do.* Once *it has first done these things*, then *it shall return to me.* But if one concludes that the word issues from the mouth of Christ, it is then necessary to add that this is the same significant word that was uttered in our presence, since it would neither be correct to ascribe a physical *mouth* to God nor to conclude that the preordained *thought* should fail. And how can it be that the non-substantial[16] word is different from the one that is sent forth and goes down and *does* and *accomplishes* something and *returns* again to the

one who sent it? For these things clearly agree with the evangelical doctrines in which God the Word is introduced, who was sent from the Father and fulfilled the dispensations among people and ascended again to the Father.

[55:12-13] After this, the prophecy says to those of the nations who belong to the saving Word: *For you shall go out with joy and be taught with happiness.* On the one hand *you shall go out* from the error handed down to you from your ancestors, and on the other hand you shall attain the teaching of the saving gospel which will inspire divine *joy* among you. But Symmachus writes: *You shall go out with joy and be led in peace.* And then: *The mountains and the hills will be distributed before you in exultation, and all the trees of the field will clap their hands.* I suspect that this verse is talking about how the divine powers rejoice with those on earth who repent, which also the Savior taught when he said: "There will be *joy* in heaven over one sinner who repents."[17] And *the trees of the field clapping their branches* are probably the fruitful souls who rejoice with the souls of the lawless who have turned to God. Therefore, they exhibited signs of *joy* through *clapping their branches.* But he says: *And instead of the briar shall come up a cypress, and instead of the nettle shall come up a myrtle.* Allegorically, this verse alludes to the fruitfulness of those souls who turned from inferior things to the superior, who, when they were in godlessness, produced nothing useful, nothing nourishing. And so it was that in that desolate and dry and uncultivated place, only *briars* of useless material and most foul-smelling *nettles* and completely useless weeds grew. But now, because they became partakers of divine grace, they produced most fragrant and lofty *myrtles* and again fragrant *cypresses.* But according to Symmachus, [348] the text

---

[14]Eusebius here has λόγος in place of the LXX's ῥῆμά. [15]Jn 1:1. [16]ἀνυπόστατος. [17]Lk 15:7.

reads: *Instead of a briar shall come up a juniper, and instead of the nettle*[18] *shall come up a myrtle*, as if he were very clearly saying: Instead of depravity, righteousness will come up, and instead of intemperance, self-control, and instead of impudence, manliness, and instead of folly, prudence, and, generally speaking, instead of evil, virtue. And then he promises something else marvelous to the nations who have turned to God: for he says *the Lord shall be for a name* for them *and for an everlasting sign and shall not fail*. Who would not be amazed at the fulfillment of this word, when they see that throughout the whole world Christians are called by the name of the Christ of God? And this *shall be for them an everlasting sign* of salvation in the presence of God, for they are engraved with the *name of the Lord*, and it shall remain forever on them *and shall never fail*. "For the gifts of God happen to be irrevocable."[19]

[56:1-2] Because the people of the Jews practice nothing good neither *keep judgment* nor *do righteousness* but spoke of a single *sabbath* day as though they were granting God some great favor, he says rightly to them: Hear, O people, you neglected to do the important things because you thought that it was necessary *to keep the sabbath* day and that these things are the significant parts of the service of God, but he is concerned that you are not ignorant that it is necessary first of all *to keep judgment and to do righteousness*. For the one who does these things would be worthy of the blessing that comes from God. In addition to these things, it was necessary to keep *the sabbaths so as not to profane them*. And this will happen if *you watch to keep your hands* clean from all wrong practices. If you do not practice these things but spend the *sabbath day* in rest and relaxation, you see that your hands will practice nothing wrong.

[56:3-4] Then he calls to the foreign converts among them as well as those who are *strangers* in race but who have been joined to the people because they have come near to God. The Word urges those who serve God to come and teach the children of the Jews not to think too highly about their race or to be proud of their ancestors. Therefore, according to Symmachus, the text reads: *Let not the son of the stranger who has been faithfully devoted to the Lord say, "Surely the Lord will divide me from his people."* Because the Jews believed that the abundance of children was the blessing of God and interpreted the abundance of offspring as the reward and fruit of the service of God, they removed this glory from them. When they had been deprived of this glory, they were disgraced because they were sterile and not able to produce children because they had been castrated. But the promise that has now been made is that there will be nothing preventing the *eunuchs* from saying that they have attained blessings from God, if they might choose life according to God. Therefore, he gives hope to the [349] *eunuchs* who are like fruitless *trees* because of the childlessness of the body, and he gives the same hope to Israel. For even they, if they *keep* the things said above and abstain from all unrighteousness and partake in the life that is pleasing to God through godly works, and if they *keep* the exact law concerning the *sabbaths*, then he will prepare them for what has been promised. Therefore, he commands them *to keep the sabbaths* exactly, and he says that they should concern themselves to choose what he wants—and he says that he does not want *the sabbaths*. Therefore, at the beginning of the book, he affirms: "Your new moons and sabbaths and great day I cannot endure."[1] He thus exhorts them to allow what he wants and *to hold fast his covenant*, which he indicated when he recently said that it was necessary *to keep judgment and to do righteous-*

---

[18]Eusebius is using here another word for "nettle": κνίδης instead of the LXX's κονύζης. [19]Rom 11:29. **Chapter Fifty-Six** [1]Is 1:13.

ness, and: *Blessed is the one who does these things, the person who holds them fast and watches his hands so as not to do wrong.* For how shall the person who has received such promises not be *blessed?* For these things are what I want, and if the *converts* and *eunuchs* practice them, nothing will ever distress them, and they will *keep the sabbaths* as far as concerns the precepts of the law.

[56:5] Therefore, to the *eunuchs* and to those who keep what was mentioned above but who have no fruit in terms of descendents, he promises that instead of an abundance of offspring, *he will give them an esteemed place in the house and within this wall,* or according to the other Greek translations: *A hand and a name better than sons and daughters,* and, he says: *I will give to them an eternal name that will not be removed.* For just as I gave "the *name* Israel to Jacob"[2] and called him this instead of Jacob—and, in fact, I made him an envoy[3] from God, for "Israel" is translated into the Greek language as "a man who sees God"—so also if those who are without offspring according to the flesh should choose to serve God, I will grant them a *name* which will exceed any abundance of children for them. And according to the saving teaching that "there are *eunuchs* who have made themselves eunuchs for the sake of the kingdom of heaven,"[4] it may be that the following text is to be read concerning them: *I will give to them, in my house and within my wall, an esteemed place.* For "there are many rooms with the Father,"[5] and "the city of God, the heavenly Jerusalem,"[6] is a *place* for them within the *house* of God, "in the many rooms."[7] A place will be given to them *within the wall* "of the heavenly city of God."[8] A *name* will be given to them *better than sons and daughters,* or according to Aquila: *And a name superior to sons and daughters, an eternal name*

I will give to them. In this verse, I suppose that the Word refutes the glory of the Jews, since [350] they thought that they were highly favored by God because they had abundant offspring. For they assumed that this demonstrated the blessing of God.

[56:6-7] To the converts from the Gentiles, he promises that if *they might keep* the aforementioned things, and not only *be subject* to God but also purpose in their hearts to *love* him *and to hold fast* his *covenant,* then *he will bring* them *into* his *holy mountain,* and *he will make them joyful* and will accept their *sacrifices,* even if they are regarded as *aliens* and strangers. For his *house* did not belong to one nation or another but has been opened *for all the nations* because of his superabundant benevolence, so that even *eunuchs* and converts are admitted. In the verse above, he says that he will assuredly accept their *sacrifices* through prayers and praises.

[56:8-9] If someone says that he has not sinned in offering physical sacrifices, these things were said to those who were governed according to the law of Moses before the new covenant. And the God who is about *to gather the dispersed* (or according to Aquila, *the exiled*) *of Israel* promises all of this. I suppose that the literal sense of this verse refers to the return of the people from Babylon during the time of Cyrus and Darius and Artaxerxes, when God said that he would *gather the dispersed of Israel.* For during that time, the kings of the Persians allowed the people of Israel to return from their captivity, as has been recorded in the history of Esdras.[9] During that time, the multitude of the people sojourned like one of the foreign nations, and because of their foreign lifestyle and race and because of their wild manner of living, the Word called them *wild animals of the fields.*

---

[2]Gen 32:29. [3]θεωρὸν; this Greek word means "envoy" but comes from the root word "to see." [4]Mt 19:12 RSV. [5]Jn 14:2. [6]Heb 12:22.
[7]Jn 14:2. [8]Heb 12:22. [9]2 Esd 2:8.

And he says that these animals *will be gathered with Israel*, and Israel was *gathered* from the dispersion, which, according to the deeper sense, may refer to the prophetic band and all those who lived a godly life among the first people. These are the evangelists, disciples and apostles of our Savior, all those from Israel who received the Christ of God. The Savior himself taught about them when he confirmed and quoted the prophecy of Isaiah: "The Spirit of the Lord is upon me, because he has anointed me to preach good news to the poor. He has sent me to proclaim release to the captives and recovering of sight to the blind."[10] The *animals* that are *gathered* with Israel are perhaps those from the Gentiles who are present in the word, whom he summons next when he says: *All you wild animals of the forest, come here; eat!* We have noted that the multitude of the foreign nations is often referred to as a *forest*. Therefore, he deems these *animals* worthy of the calling of God and summons them to a feast. Thus, according to Aquila, instead of *all the animals*, the text reads: *Every one of his creatures*, and again: *All his creatures*. And to whom does *his* refer if not God? Therefore, he does not call all the *animals*, but only *his own*. Then, after he mentioned **[351]** the foreign nations as the *animals of the forest*, he perceived in the Spirit that they would obey the call, while the multitude of the Jews "remains in unbelief,"[11] and, turning to them again, he censures them as blind. For the *animals* and the *creatures of the forest* were about to turn to the godly life, but they were perishing in their own wickedness.

[56:10-12] The things that are brought against them are said reasonably, and he continues on to say: *Observe that all have become totally blind*, and Symmachus writes: *His guardians are blind, they are all senseless, they are all dumb dogs that are not able to bark*. The rulers of the

nation of the Jews are said to be *blind guardians* and *senseless* and *silent dogs that are not able to bark*. For it is necessary that they come to the aid of the sheep of God and, as hunting *dogs*, drive away the wolves from the nurslings. But as *silent dogs*, they did not even think *to bark* but, differing in nothing from a sleeping state, they were intent only on fantasies as though *dreaming*. Therefore, according to Symmachus, the text reads: *Visionaries, sleepers, loving to slumber*, and according to Aquila: *Ones who imagine things, loving to slumber*. Such were the rulers of the Jews to those outside, to those enemies against whom it was necessary to be awake and sober and *to bark*. But to those inside they acted *shamelessly* and "devoured the sheep"[12] that they were supposed to shepherd. For this reason, he continues on to say next: *The dogs are shameless in their soul, not knowing satisfaction. They are evil, not knowing understanding. They have all followed their own ways*, not *the ways* of God but their own, because they lived out their own thoughts.

[57:1-2] After mentioning the *blind guardians* and denouncing them as *dogs*—for on the one hand they *slumbered* and did not know how *to bark*, and on the other hand they acted *shamelessly* and were evil and committed bold deeds against the righteous and God-loving people among them, voicing threats against the prophets—he says: *Observe how the righteous is being taken away, and no one takes it to heart; righteous people are being taken away, and no one takes notice*. For how could those who were *blind* ever *notice* these souls? They did not understand, and although they had seen the *righteous one*, they did not perceive the plan about him. Instead, they were *blind* and *shameless dogs*, and they dared to do such things against the *righteous ones*, but they were received by God *in peace*. And *his burial has been taken away from their midst*. Someone

---

[10]Lk 4:18 RSV. [11]Rom 11:23. [12]Cf. Jer 5:17.

might say that these things could apply to the Savior and to his disciples, against whom the nation of the Jews schemed. This saying also alludes to the resurrection of our Savior. His death is addressed in the mention of his *burial*, and his resurrection is addressed in the phrase: *His burial has been taken away from their midst.* But *he has been taken from the midst of unrighteousness*, and he now dwells *in peace*, and *his burial* has disappeared [352] *from their midst*, because he did not stay in the place of his *burial*. And so "the angel standing there said to the women: 'Whom do you seek? Jesus? He is not here. Come, see his place.'"[1]

[57:3-4] But *you* who formerly dared to do such things to the prophets of God—you who are truly "blind and silent dogs and shameless"[2]—*draw near here* (or, *come near here*, according to the other Greek translations), *you lawless children and offspring of adulterers and of a whore.* For you are not worthy to be called "children of Abraham and Sarah."[3] "If you were Abraham's children, you would do what Abraham did."[4] But the Word knows to call the ones who formerly committed idolatry *adulterers.* It has been said about them: "They committed adultery with a tree and a stone."[5] The *whore* was Jerusalem, as the present prophet clearly states in the verse above: "How the faithful city Zion has become a whore!"[6] Therefore, according to Symmachus, the text reads: *Offspring of adulterers and of her who committed fornication,* so that the text does not say that the children of the Jews commit idolatry at present but rather that they are *offspring of adulterers and of a whore.* Therefore, the Word says to them: *Offspring of adulterers and of a whore, draw near here* and, when you have come close, say: *In what have you indulged,* or according to Symmachus: *In what have you reveled, and against whom have you opened your mouth and stuck out your* tongue? For he strongly accused their *tongue* and *mouth,* because they raised their voices against the Savior and still even now blaspheme him. Therefore he says: *Against whom have you opened your mouth wide? And against whom have you let loose your tongue? Are you not children of destruction?* For *he has been taken away from the midst of unrighteousness,* and he now dwells *in peace,* and *his burial has been taken away from their midst.* And you were then *children of destruction and lawless offspring.*

[57:5-8] *You are the ones who call on their idols under thick trees, slaughtering their children in the ravines, among the rocks. That is your portion; this is your lot, and to them you have poured out libations, and to them you have brought a sacrifice,* or according to Symmachus: *Slaughtering their descendents under every blossoming tree, in the ravines, under the clefts of the rocks.* He says that you were worthy of these things, for *that is your portion and this is your lot.* Therefore, this verse clearly shows that the present prophecy applies to the idolatries that were committed during the times of Isaiah the prophet, and, recording their transgressions, he continues on: Therefore, then, is it not right that I should release my anger against you *for these things,* since in fact *on a high and lofty mountain, there was your bed, and there you brought up your sacrifice, and behind the posts of the door you have set up your memorials?* He says that when you practiced these things, you did not conceal your sacrilegious actions but performed them openly. [353] *On their highest mountains* they fulfilled their demonic *sacrifices.* Even now, *behind your doors,* instead of a phylactery there are the *memorials* of your idolatry, clearly referring to lifeless statues. You practiced these things because you thought that you would find *something greater* in my absence. These things have been spoken

---

Chapter Fifty-Seven   [1]Mt. 28:5-6.   [2]Cf. Is 56:10.   [3]1 Pet 3:6.   [4]Jn 8:39 RSV.   [5]Jer 3:9.   [6]Is 1:21.

to "the blind guardians"[7] and "the silent dogs," and what he says next he speaks to Jerusalem itself and the synagogue of the people of the Jews: *You have loved those who lay with you,* but according to Symmachus and the other Greek translations: *You have loved their bed.* And who are *they* if not "your" aforementioned "guardians" and "the shameless dogs"?[8]

[57:9-10] *And you have multiplied your fornication with them.* Therefore, it has been said concerning them: "Dreaming in bed, loving to slumber."[9] These were they who "dream in beds" and "love to slumber," but in the verse above they were accused, and he listened and welcomed the charge: *You have loved those who lay with you and multiplied your fornication with them,* and *you have made many those who were far from you.* For *many* fled Jerusalem—people who were dedicated to God—because of the godless deeds that had been perpetrated in it. Therefore, it has been said: *And you have made many those who were far from you,* and he also says: *And you have sent ambassadors beyond your borders,* or according to Symmachus: *And you have multiplied your ointments; you have sent your hostages far away.* He dramatizes all these things as though addressing an adorned prostitute who would do anything for the pleasure of those who were present with her. For this reason he says: *You were humbled even to Hades; you grew weary with your long journeys.* For you did not travel along the one "King's Highway,"[10] but you followed many wandering roads. Therefore, *you grew weary* and could not stand, but *you did not say, "I will stop in order to regain strength,"* but as though you were *strong* and youthful, *you accomplished* worse things than these, continuing on in your habitual obscenities. Therefore, you neither turned around, nor *did you entreat me,* or according to Aquila, *you did not pray to* attain forgiveness.

[57:11] And you kept on going forever in fearlessness and irreverence. If you ever resolved to serve God, you lied when you made any such promise. Before this he says: *You did not remember me, nor did you take me into your thought or into your heart.* Therefore, it is fitting that he says *I will disregard you,* and because of these things I will leave you desolate. For still even now you lack any fear of God.

[57:12-14] Therefore, learn about what awaits you and what these things are. The avenging anger of God will overtake you for all the things you have dared to do, and then your *evils* will be exposed, and when his anger comes on you no one will be present with you, nor will those whom you imagine to be gods attend to your voice. But instead of *let them deliver you in your affliction,* Symmachus writes: **[354]** *Let your synagogues deliver you.* The Word baldly and clearly teaches that their *synagogues will not help* them at all. Then he continues: *For the wind will take all of these, and a tempest will carry them away. But those who cling to me shall possess the earth and inherit my holy mountain. And they shall say, "Cleanse the ways before him, and remove the obstructions from my people's way."* Therefore, he says that *the wind will take all* those who are convicted, *and a tempest will carry them away.* And such an end *will take* those who were accused in the verses above. But those "who have chosen the good portion"[11]—clearly, those who have chosen me as God—and those who *cling* to me genuinely and purely will receive repayment from me. For *they shall possess the earth* that I have promised to them *and inherit my holy mountain.* They will then be teachers of others, exhorting them to level *the people's ways* in making the teaching for the people pure and plain, so that in it "there is nothing twisted or crooked."[12] And, as I said above, the *earth* and the *holy mountain* are probably

---

[7]Is 56:10. [8]Is 56:11. [9]Is 56:10. [10]Num 20:17. [11]Lk 10:42. [12]Prov 8:8.

Jerusalem and Mount Zion respectively. The region of Judea could also be interpreted as the *holy mountain* according to the true reading of the text, for in the verses above, the *holy mountain* is frequently presented as "the heavenly Jerusalem."[13] The *earth* could be interpreted both as the heavenly way of life and as the entirely heavenly region, and there *those who cling* to God will receive a worthy calling. But according to Symmachus, the text reads: *But the one who speaks openly concerning me shall inherit my holy mountain. And he shall say, "Clear the way! Attend to the way! Remove all obstacles from the way of my people!"* For the one who lives before God will take thought not only for his own salvation, but also he will make himself useful for the *people* of God, commanding that the *way* of godliness be leveled for them and that the things that appear to be *obstacles* to the divine reading be removed through the interpretation of the clearer passages.

[57:15] The Word addressed the prophecy above to the rulers of the nation of the Jews, whom he called "silent dogs"[14] and "blind guardians" and "lawless sons and offspring of adulterers and of a whore,"[15] and he prophesied appropriate events for the people under them in the above verses. But he announces comfort and reassurance for those among them who are prudent and possess a fear of God and who are repentant for their sins,[16] for those whom the present passage calls *broken of heart and faint-hearted*. For there were some among them—one assumes very few in number—but nevertheless there were some people who were devoted to God, not only the prophets but also their followers and those who had learned from the prophets and studied their teachings. Those who had been spared from the destruc-

tion of the multitude spent their lives in humiliation and oppression—"destitute, afflicted, ill-treated, [355] wandering in deserts and mountains, and in dens and caves of the earth."[17] There were again others who had been spared from their own evils, who humbled themselves and disciplined their lives in the areas where they had sinned. For this reason, the present word calls them *broken of heart and faint-hearted*, or according to Symmachus: *Crushed and humble in spirit*. And he introduces the God who is over all, the one who is beyond the universe, the one who is *most high and who dwells forever in lofty places, the holy one, the one who rests among the holy ones*, and says that he is the one who speaks to the *humble* and *faint-hearted*. Even though he is *most high* and has his abode *in lofty places*, nevertheless he does not overlook the *humble*, but "he gives grace to them,"[18] and he brings their humiliation to an end when he raises them up high. For this reason, it has been said: "God resists the arrogant, but he gives grace to the humble,"[19] "and he who humbles himself will be exalted."[20] And, therefore, "he exalted the *humble*,"[21] and *he will dwell* among them. Because he is *most high*, *he dwells forever in lofty places*. Therefore, he concerns himself with the *humble* that he might exalt them by coming to *dwell* with them. And so, because he is *holy*, he chooses the holy ones among people and *rests* among them. Therefore, the text reads: *The holy one rests among the holy ones*. But because he is also patient, he regards the human weakness of those who are subdued in this mortal life because of their godliness, and with their afflictions *he gives patience to the faint-hearted* so that they can endure their afflictions vigorously and resolutely. And yet, for them, God himself is "life,"[22] and his presence is a "fountain of life"[23] *to those who*

---

[13]Heb 12:22. [14]Is 56:10. [15]Cf. Is 57:3. [16]Eusebius's Greek phrase here (ἐφ᾽ οἷς ἥμαρτον) is notably parallel to Paul's disputed phrase in Rom 5:12b (ἐφ᾽ ᾧ πάντες ἥμαρτον). Eusebius's testimony here lends credence to the interpretation that Paul should be read "because all sinned" and not "in whom all sinned." [17]Heb 11:37-38. [18]Cf. Prov 3:34. [19]Prov 3:34. [20]Lk 14:11. [21]Cf. Lk 1:52. [22]Jn 11:25. [23]Jer 2:13.

are broken of heart, for "sacrifice to God is a *broken* spirit; and a *broken* and humbled *heart* God will not hold in contempt."[24] From his eternal and immortal life, therefore, God freely grants such good things to the *humble* and *faint-hearted*. And then, addressing them, he says that he will *rest* among them.

[57:16] *I will not punish you forever*. For I will not always unceasingly take vengeance for sins that have been committed among you. Because you are only human beings, you need vengeance merely for a little while. But because you also participated in the sins of the people and were led away with the multitude, you were delivered over to your proper punishment because of the sins of the others. Therefore, you ought to know that although all the others and those of the people who are truly ungodly and sinners will receive eternal anger, *you I will not punish forever, nor will I always be angry with you*. For you are a concern to me and my *Spirit*, who *went forth from me* and dwelled among you. I am the maker of *every breath* that is able "to praise" me, as the verse reads: "Let every *breath* praise the Lord."[25] And God "breathed into"[26] his creation "a breath of life, and the man [356] became a living being." The next line of the text reads: *I have made every breath*. Job also teaches this when he says: "It is the Spirit of the Lord that has made me and the Almighty's breath that teaches me."[27] Accordingly then, with those who keep *my Sprit, with which I also made breath*—through which "the man became a living being"[28]—*I will not always be angry*.

[57:17-19] For *a little while*, because of those *sins* that came in because of human weakness, *I grieved and struck* those who sinned, because "a father disciplines his sons."[29] "For whom the Lord loves, he disciplines, and he punishes every son he accepts."[30] But once you felt my discipline, "you were grieved with a godly grief,"[31] *and*, after you repented, *you went on sullen*. Because of your conversion and repentance, after I had seen the deeds that followed and *the ways* of life, *I healed and comforted* you and *gave true comfort*. For everything from me that I supply to my own is *true*. Therefore, to those who were chastened by my discipline *I gave true comfort* and *peace*, not a superficial or transient *peace* but one that multiplies, so that those who are *near* as well as those who have settled at a distance and *far away* will possess it. The Lord who is known to be God promises these things and continues on to say: *I will heal them*, and he promises his healing for the souls and hearts who have been afflicted. He brought about this outcome for those who have received the benefit of the discipline of God.

[57:20-21] But, he says, such individuals shall not remain: *The unrighteous and impious shall be tossed like waves and shall not be able to rest*. Then, because those who have been alienated from God do not have a nature that can share in joy, he adds the following verse: *There is no rejoicing for the impious, says the Lord*. But according to Symmachus, the text reads: *But the impious will be cast about as the sea, for they will not be able to find calm, and mud and mire will be cast about in its waters. There is no peace, says my God, for the impious*. Here again, one should note that he compared the multitude of the *impious* with a *sea that is cast about* and with a "surging"[32] and troubled "sea." For this reason, he says that as a *sea that is cast about, they will not be able to find calm*, and he says that the *waters* of such a sea are like *downtrodden mire*. The translation of Aquila reads similarly: *And the impious are like a sea that is cast about, because they will not be able to find calm, and its waters are cast about like mud and mire*. And so, if anyone is discussing a passage about the *sea of Egypt* or certain *waters*, it is

---

[24]Ps 51:17. [25]Ps 150:6. [26]Gen 2:7. [27]Job 33:4. [28]Gen 2:7. [29]Prov 3:12. [30]Heb 12:6. [31]2 Cor 7:9. [32]Cf. Is. 5:30.

important to remember the verses above, for they are useful for interpretating such things.

[58:1] [357] After prophesying about the "humble and brokenhearted,"[1] the Word turns again to the command to the *impious* among them, against whom he addressed the above statement: "There is no rejoicing for the impious, said God."[2] For it was necessary for us to learn who these *impious* were and what they had done that led to the statement against them. Therefore, he commands the prophet to bring these things out into the open with all boldness and with a strong *voice* and not to draw back from or keep hidden the preaching of God, despite the fear of death or any other human threats. Therefore, he commands him *to cry out* and to declare the words of God like a *trumpet*—the loudest of all musical instruments—so that those he convicts can hear him. Thus, in the verse above, the saving word is spoken to the evangelists: "Go up on a high mountain, you who bring good tidings to Jerusalem; lift it up; do not fear."[3] But in this verse, the prophet is ordered not "to go up on a high mountain." For those to whom he was to address his message were not up high. He was only *to cry aloud with strength and not to hold back*, and because he spoke to deaf ears, he was commanded *to lift up his voice* like a *trumpet*. And a *trumpet* is a signal for war. He orders him to issue a *shout* in addressing the impious and sinful adversary, so that he might assail the mind of his listeners and conquer it with the most overpowering word. Then he says: *And declare to my people their sins*, thus calling his sinful people into judgment, whom, he says, I adopted and whom I did not deem unworthy to be called my *people*. But because they had been delivered over to their own evils, they kept themselves at a distance from me.

[58:2] In vain and to no use they pretend *to seek me* each day, says God; they are zealous to meet in their synagogues, and in vain they present what they want to hear in the divine readings. They act as though they wish *to know my ways*, and they seem to set about these things busily, as though they successfully accomplished everything required of them and fulfilled in deed all the fruits according to *righteousness*. And yet, they are convicted by their own practices, for *they have forsaken the judgment of God* because of the excessive senselessness of their own evils. And so, while they are placed on trial and judged by me, at the same time *they ask* me for compensation for their good conduct. *They demand righteous judgment* from me, as if they *desire* to live in a godly way and be near me, but they do not want me, and they turn away from me to the most unrighteous activities.

[58:3-4] Therefore, they complain and accuse saying, "*Why is it that we have fasted, but you did not see, humbled our souls, but you did not know?*" Thus, because they dare to say such things without any shame, you, my prophet, respond to them and convict them with a loud cry, because *they have forsaken my judgment*, and everything that they say they cannot truly confirm. Well then, since they have become so proud of their fasting, it would have been far better for them had they cultivated a love of fine food [358] rather than to have dared to say such things! It is for this reason that the text reads at the beginning of the prophecy: "Your fasting and holidays and feasts my soul hates."[4] And, therefore, presently they claim that they are *fasting*, and they say that they are *humbling* their *souls* during the *day of* their *fast*, but convict them one and all whether this is what they do, and prove them in this. Speak to them in this way and show them that during these days, which they are so proud of and call *days of fasts*, they do not seek my *wishes* but their own pleasures, and they dedicate their

---

Chapter Fifty-Eight [1]Ps 34:18. [2]Is 57:21. [3]Is 40:9. [4]Is 1:13-14.

time to their own evil deeds. *You strike those under you*, and so you have been quite worn out by *fights* and disputes with one another, and you who have been struck by them let out *voices* of weeping and an unbecoming *clamor*.

[58:5-6] Therefore, he says: *This is not the fast that I have chosen*, nor is this such a *day of humbling*, not even if they should *bend* their *necks like a ring* and bow down low in order to show their humility, or if they should put *sackcloth* on their own flesh in order to bring suffering and misery on themselves because of the roughness of *sackcloth* or if they should punish themselves by *spreading ashes* on their body. For all these things would be an empty gesture if accompanied by the sins described above. If anyone should wish to learn how to perform a *fast* that is truly pleasing to me, God, let him do these things: "Put on a cheerful face and anoint your head with oil,"[5] according to the exhortation in the Gospel, and keep your *fast* "in secret,"[6] and show the abasement of your soul only to "the Father who sees secrets." Let them present the spiritual fruits of reverence in a visible and tangible fashion for all to see, in order that they might *loose every bond of injustice*. For if there are any among you who have established beforehand affairs and contracts and commercial dealings—even if these deals have been contracted during a time of worship through a fast—it is right that they be *undone* and that *the knots of contracts made by force* be shaken off. In fact, the saying delivered by the Savior completes this verse: "If you are offering your gift, and there remember that your brother has something against you, leave your gift there and go; first be reconciled to your brother, and then come and offer your gift."[7] Proclaim the forgiveness of debt to those who have been crushed by loans, *and tear up every unjust note*. On the other hand, if there are not any among

you who have contracted such *knots* and you have purified yourselves from such sins, still it is necessary for you who wish to be acceptable to God to do this: you are to keep his *fasts*.

[58:7] Your own *bread*, which if you had not regularly *fasted* you would have eaten, *break with the ones who are hungry*. For there is no shortage of those who lack food among humanity. And so, while it appears that your abstaining from food is of no advantage to you, you will nourish [359] your soul with another kind of bread as you revive the one who desperately needs to eat. He does not stop here but rather welcomes *into your* very *house* those who are not wealthy and those who are not able to repay you the same day, *poor* people— those who are found to be in truly life-threatening situations, those who are outcasts and who do not know how to find shelter. You were a shelter to them, receiving them *into your house*, and so you satisfied the requirements of a good and God-pleasing *fast*. If you see someone *naked*, do not pass by on the opposite side of the street or regard him as a stranger. For the God of the universe supplies food and goods to some, but he allows others to experience need and penury. He does this in order to test both the rich and the poor, so that some should attain the fruit of their prosperity through supporting those in need, and that others should be exercised in poverty instead of a position of abundance and experience the generosity of those who are prosperous, as has been said above. *And you shall not neglect any of the relatives of our seed*. For it is proper that we ungrudgingly share basic necessities with everyone, but we are to impart special privilege "to those who are of the household of faith."[8] The apostolic rule encourages us to be kind "to all people, and especially to those who are of the household of faith."[9] But these statements are what you kept for your laws: *Do not humble*

---

[5]Mt 6:17. [6]Mt 6:18. [7]Mt 5:23-24. [8]Gal 6:10. [9]Gal 6:10.

your soul, *neither bend your neck like a ring nor spread under you sackcloth and ashes*. But looking cheerfully to God above, receive repayment from him.

[58:8] And learn now what this repayment will be. For just as there is a complete change from night and darkness to the *light* that appears during the day, which shining forth shows the brilliant gleaming of the sun, so also in the same way all at once a heavenly and divine *light shall break forth early in the morning* for you. And this *light* comes against the darkness that formerly hung over our souls and drives it far away, so that we now live in the day of God and in the *light* of knowledge and truth. *The healings* of your soul *shall rise* with this very *light*, so that your soul will be free of every disease and sickness and every impurity. Even now, such a *light* will appear among others. For *your righteousness shall go before you* in glorious deeds, and many will see those deeds shining forth. Your fruits will speak for you. And *the glory of God* will adorn your soul in abundance as a crown, just as Jesus was glorified "both among people and among God himself."[10]

[58:9] In addition to all this, you will have this special privilege: as soon as you *cry out* to God, you will have his attention. Not only when you raise your voice but even when you utter a syllable *he will say, Here am I*. And all these things will be yours *if you* avoid the aforesaid things and *remove from you* the *shackles* of your sins. For it cannot hurt anything to mention to them again a second time: *If you remove from you a bond* of sin, and the *stretching of the hands* to unrighteousness, and your *words* of complaining and *murmurings* against God.

[58:10-12] [360] And so, as it has been said before: *Give to one who is hungry your bread,* and in so doing be one who gives to himself

even greater things. In the same way, if *you satisfy* from your prosperity the *soul that has been humbled* by poverty, the Word will again make the same promises to you: *Your light shall rise in the darkness, and your darkness shall shine forth like noonday. And your God will be with you continually, and he will satisfy you exactly as your soul desires.* He promises for you nourishment of the soul and the benefit of good things in his presence, and he says that *your bones*—clearly, the inner strength of the soul—*shall be enriched* by spiritual and inspired nourishment. And *there will be a "spring of living water"*[11] in you and a *garden* that is always in bloom and producing the fruits of the Holy Spirit.

The places of your soul that were once *deserts shall be built* and restored through the learning of divine words. You acted as your own *builder* in the inspired teachings, *building* arguments in your mind. Now you will set up a *fence* around your soul, *fencing* it in from all around and fortifying it from all trouble outside. These things have been spoken in the face of all the people—to everyone who will listen. For if you—the people who censure your former ways—will do these things, the things that have been promised will be yours. *Your light shall rise in the darkness, and your darkness shall be like noonday. And your God will be with you continually, and you shall be satisfied exactly as your soul desires, and your bones shall be enriched.* One could say that the *bones* of the people is the inner strength that props up the whole body. And *there shall be* among you a place *like a soaked garden and like a spring whose water has never failed. And ancient deserts shall be built for you.* The places that have long since become *desolate* because of sin, they *shall be built. And your foundations shall be everlasting, for generations of generations.* You will understand what *the foundations* are if you are attentive to the apostolic Scrip-

---

[10]Lk 2:52. [11]Cf. Jer 2:13.

ture that says: "Built on the foundation of the apostles and prophets."[12] *And you shall be called a builder of fences.* The *builder of fences* erects *fences* and walls—church doctrines all around with philosophical arguments. The one who removes apparent obstacles to faith from the divine readings in order to clarify what the text really says—this one is he who removes the stones from *the paths between them.*

[58:13] After this, he says to everyone: *If you turn your foot away from the sabbaths, so as not to do the things you wish on the holy day, and you call the sabbaths delightful, holy to God, and you lift not your foot for work or speak a word in anger out* [361] *of your mouth; then shall you trust in the Lord.* For if you keep the *sabbaths* with all the other requirements, then, as the Word implies, these necessary things will also be yours. And the Word submits that you are not to do *the things you wish,* devoting yourself to "drunkenness and dissipation,"[13] but rather spend your life in holiness and purity. And so you are to sanctify the *day* and keep it *delightful* and free from toil because of the rest that God has prescribed, not even moving your *foot* to attend to other affairs or defiling your lips with a *word.* But you are to devote yourself only to the study of divine things throughout the entire day.

[58:14] All at once, then, these things will happen, and he will prepare a sabbath that will not be unprofitable for you, and he will make "the fast acceptable"[14] for you. And so *you shall trust in the Lord,* being confident in the life to come and maintaining his promises to be unerring. And in these promises he professes that he will give them life—I am speaking about the life that is unlike the manner of life that we now know, for then, as it has been said above, the *earth will bring up* fruit to you and yield *good things* for you "what no eye has seen, nor ear heard, nor the heart of man conceived,

what God has prepared for those who love him."[15] *And he shall feed you* provisions in that place, and he will give to you *the heritage* that he promised to *your father Jacob.* The heavenly and spiritual promises were made to the fathers. Therefore, even though these things have been spoken through a man, they were not human words, but God was the one who uttered these things through the prophet. For this reason he continues on to say to everyone: *For the mouth of the Lord has spoken these things.* One could understand the verse about the *earth* and its *good things* in a Jewish way, since everything that has been said to the people of the circumcision has been shown to be addressed to them.

[59:1-2] In the passage above, it seems that the Word gave orders expressly to the people of the Jews, on the one hand making appropriate promises to those who accomplished the orders, but on the other hand threatening proper vengeance for those who chose to do the contrary. In the verses above, he brings the accusation against them that they have chosen to do what is contrary to the will of God and in this way have fallen from grace into evil practices. Therefore, he says to them: it was not too difficult for me, God, to lift up you who were perishing, *neither was my hand powerless to save* you who were unworthy. And my *ear,* which hears everything, was not hard of hearing so that I could not *listen* to you crying out. But *rather your sinful acts* keep you from me, because you heap up evil deeds and erect a "dividing wall"[1] *between God and you.* It is neither right nor expedient for you to save people like this. And the apostle Paul says somewhere concerning the Savior: "He has made us both one, and has broken down the dividing wall [362] of hostility in his flesh."[2] He says that the Savior "has broken down the dividing wall" by the forgiveness of sins. The

---

[12]Eph 2:20. [13]Lk 21:34. [14]Is 58:5. [15]1 Cor 2:9 RSV. **Chapter Fifty-Nine** [1]Eph 2:14. [2]Eph 2:14.

present prophet teaches that the *sins* of each one that have come *between God* and humanity damn the soul that sins far away from God, because it is an impossible scenario that sin could stand before God. Therefore, he continues on: *And because of your sins I have turned my face away from you.* Your lawless life does not allow you to benefit from divine intention, because your sin is so abominable, foul, shameful and dishonorable.

[**59:3**] Therefore, he teaches that the reason the people have fallen away and been jettisoned so far from God is nothing other than their sins. He recounts their situation when he says next: *Your hands have been defiled with blood and your fingers with sins, and your lips have spoken lawlessness.* One can see clearly that he does not find fault with them for idolatry or some other lawless practice but rather for the murder of their *hands* and the lawlessness of their mouths, by which he alludes to their uprising against the Savior and their scheme against righteous people. And he spoke about these righteous people when he said in the verse above: "Observe how the righteous person is being taken away, and no one takes notices; righteous people are being taken away, and no takes it to heart. For the righteous person has been taken away from the presence of lawlessness. His burial will be in peace; he has been taken away from their midst."[3] They themselves may not have been the murderers of the Savior, but they demanded that "his blood be on them and on their children."[4] And they proclaimed with godless cries that they indeed had *hands that had been defiled with blood*, and *lips that had spoken lawlessness* and *a tongue that had plotted unrighteousness.*

[**59:4-5**] Thus the prophet says: *No one speaks righteous things, nor is there true judgment.*

Then, because they deceived themselves and expect another human Christ and tell mythic tales about him, he continues on to say: *They trust in vanities, and they speak empty words.* Therefore, the divine apostle admonishes "not to give heed to Jewish myths or to commands of men who reject the truth."[5] But these very ones, devising ingenious arguments and contriving from their own minds blasphemous words against Christ and God, *conceive trouble and give birth to lawlessness.* For they could not say: "From the fear of you, O Lord, we conceived and travailed and *gave birth* to a wind of salvation."[6] And the things that *they conceived* have been described in another passage: "Look, he was in travail with injustice; he conceived *trouble* and *gave birth to lawlessness.* A pit he dug and cleaned it out, and he shall fall into the hole he made."[7] Inventing ingenious arguments from his own mind, everyone fashions impious and godless doctrines.

[**363**] Such individuals, *conceiving* the offspring of the opposing powers in themselves, *broke the eggs of asps.* Therefore it has been said to their evil and wicked sons: "You serpents, you brood of vipers."[8] As he had referred to the divine seed above, he now calls the seed of the opposing powers *eggs*, appealing to the analogy of the offspring of serpents. *Asps* and snakes and such creatures are oviparous. And in such an evil way, although they promise teachings from the divine Scriptures, they delve into "silly myths"[9] and into "traditions of people,"[10] which contain nothing sound or beneficial. He continues on rightly: *And they weave the web of a spider;* so unsound and dishonorable is their endeavor that he compares it with *the web of a spider. And,* he says, *the one who intended to eat their eggs, on breaking them found a wind, and in it was a basilisk.*[11] What kind of *eggs* they were, the verse above explains: *They broke the eggs of*

---

[3]Is 57:1-2. [4]Mt 27:25. [5]Tit 1:14. [6]Is 26:17b-18. [7]Ps 7:14-15. [8]Mt 23:33. [9]1 Tim 4:7. [10]Mk 7:8. [11]The Greek word refers to a kind of snake, perhaps an Egyptian cobra.

asps. Therefore, those who are fully developed in wickedness *break* these *eggs* and catch the creatures that are developing in them, but those who are not fully developed die before they are able to *break* these eggs and eat them. For this reason, according to the other Greek translations, the text reads: *The one who eats their eggs will die.* And if anyone should be found to be a person of understanding—one who is able *to break* them with a penetrating word of refutation—such a person *will find* that there is nothing in them but vanity and *wind*, a foul and destructive *wind* that slithers everywhere yet conceals itself from every creature and whose very glance is deadly. I am speaking about the *basilisk*. According to Aquila, the text reads: *And the viper hatched and shattered out*, but according to Symmachus: *And the asp coils up and strikes*, and according to Theodotion: *The asp hatched and broke out.* Such are the *eggs*, as has been made clear above, *because they conceive trouble and give birth to lawlessness.*

[59:6-8] He had said before *and they weave the web of a spider*, but now he expounds the idea in fuller detail when he says: *Their web shall not become a garment, nor shall they be clothed with their works, for their works are works of lawlessness.* We learn what the *web* is from the prophet Isaiah himself when he says in an earlier verse: "This people honors me with their lips, while their heart is far from me, and in vain do they worship me, teaching doctrines and human precepts."[12] For they treat with respect "the traditions of the elders"[13] but disregard the law of God, *weaving* and stringing together "commandments of people"[14] who have abandoned the truth. For this reason he says: *Their web shall not become a garment, nor shall they be clothed with their works, for their works are works of lawlessness.* On the one hand, those who "interpret spiritual truths to

those who possess the Spirit"[15] *weave* [364] a divine tunic out of the divine words that have been spoken by the Holy Spirit. On the other hand, those who waste their time "in Jewish mythologies"[16] pursue nothing more than the *web of a spider*, so that they may prey on easy souls and ensnare them in their mythologies. The text next reads: *For their works are works of lawlessness. And their feet run to wickedness, swift to shed blood, and their reasonings are reasonings of fools.* They *weave* all these things for themselves through their own *web*, copying the *spider*, and *they run to evil* and are *swift to shed innocent blood*, according to the other Greek translations. For this reason, he also said above concerning them: "For your hands have been defiled with *blood* and your fingers with *sins*, and your lips have spoken *lawlessness*, and your tongue plots unrighteousness,"[17] and he says further: *Destruction and wretchedness are in their ways, and a way of peace they do not know.* For this reason, the Savior also wept aloud for them when he said to Jerusalem: "If only you had known the things that make for your peace. For the days shall come on you when your enemies will erect an embankment about you and encircle you, and dash your children to the ground."[18] Therefore, *they did not know a way of peace*, and neither was *judgment* found *in their ways*, but rather every kind of misjudgment and unrighteousness, and all *their paths* were *crooked, and they* did *not know peace.* They did not welcome the magistrate of peace, concerning whom it has been said: "For he is our peace."[19] Therefore, he presented this peace to his disciples when he said: "My *peace* I give to you; my *peace* I leave with you."[20]

[59:9] Because of all of this, he says: *Their judgment has departed from them, and righteousness will not catch up with them.* In this verse he says *judgment*, and about this he also said above:

---

[12]Is 29:13. [13]Mt 15:2. [14]Mt 15:9. [15]1 Cor 2:13. [16]Tit 1:14. [17]Is 59:3. [18]Lk 19:42-44. [19]Eph 2:14. [20]Jn 14:27.

"Behold, my servant whom I have chosen, my beloved whom my soul loved. He will bring forth *judgment* to the nations."[21] Accordingly, this *judgment* has *departed from them* and been given to the Gentiles, and *righteousness* has abandoned them and withdrawn and been presented to the Gentiles through the saving grace. Then, because they were expecting that the Christ of God would be preached to them through the prophetic words—"he came, but they did not welcome him"[22]—subsequent to this the text reads: *Having awaited light, darkness came to them; having waited for sunlight, they walked in midnight.*

[59:10] Although *they grope for* the divine Scriptures, they do not understand the meaning that has been concealed in the deeper sense of the words of the text. They are occupied only with the literal sense, and so it is as though *they grope* for a *wall*. Because of this, the text continues on to say: *They will grope like blind people for a wall, and like those who have no eyes they will grope.* Then he adds: *They will fall at noon* [365] *as at midnight like dying people.* But during the time of the *noon* light for the nations, in which the saving and evangelical sunlight shines on the church of God, those "whose sin is mortal"[23] alone have fallen, and they live their lives *in midnight.*

[59:11-12] And he says: *And they will groan like a bear and like a dove, and they will walk together.* If their groaning had been comprehensible and had occurred because of what they had dared to do against the Savior, it would have been beneficial. For they needed to mourn and *to groan* and to lament and to weep for the sins which they had allowed to overcome them. But, because they did not even pretend to do this, they wept over the perceptible city—I am

speaking about Jerusalem—and *groaned* incomprehensibly over its downfall; thus they have been compared with a wild animal. Therefore, the text reads: *They will groan like a bear*, and another passage says: "As a *bear* robbed of her young."[24] Therefore, they are called a *bear* because a *bear* is a man-eating beast, and they devoured people and committed murder, "killing the prophets."[25] They have been compared with a "*bear* robbed of her young" because of the destruction of her children.

Instead of *and like a dove they will walk together*, Symmachus and Theodotion write: *And we will exercise as a dove exercises*, and Aquila writes: *And we vocalize our voice as doves do.* Even after all that has happened, they still even now attempt to *exercise* themselves in the divine Scriptures, but this alone is all that remains for them to learn and *to exercise* in confessing: that they coo with their voice and seem to be no different from an irrational *dove* in what they do, for they utter a *voice* but certainly do not render an intelligible word. Therefore, Aquila renders the Hebrew text in its proper sense[26] when he says: *And we will vocalize our voice as doves.* The other Greek translations set forth all the things that have been added as though it came from the mouth of the accused. For this reason, according to Symmachus, the text reads: *On account of this, judgment was far from us, and it will not catch up with us. For we expected righteousness in the daylight but behold the darkness; we expected moonlight, but we walk in gloom. We will grope like blind people for a wall, and like those who have no eyes we will grope.* And the next verse, which is spoken as though from the mouth of the people, is also different from the Septuagint: *We were awaiting judgment, but it did not come. Salvation has withdrawn far from us. For our lawlessness is great before you.* And the

---

[21]Is 42:1; Mt 12:18. [22]Jn 1:11. [23]1 Jn 5:16. [24]2 Sam 17:8. [25]Cf. Mt 23:31. [26]The Greek word κυριολεκτέω means "to use words in their proper or literal sense," but for the church fathers, the pun "to use words in their lordly sense [i.e., as pertaining to the Lord or in their christological sense]" seems to have been clear.

prophet speaks these things as though from the mouth of the people, thereby teaching them to confess their sins to God and to denounce themselves, so that their souls might be stricken with terror and they might recant and turn around and repent. *They were awaiting judgment, but it did not come* because they did not find the *judgment* that had been announced [366] to the Gentiles, as has been said before. For *judgment has departed far* from them, and they themselves explain why when they say: *For our lawlessness was great before you, and our sins have risen up against us; for our acts of lawlessness are in us, and we realized our wrongs.*

[59:13] They explain again what all these things are of which they accuse themselves when they say: *We were impious and lied,* or according to Symmachus, the text reads: *We knew how to do wrong and to lie against the Lord,* or according to Aquila: *We knew how to deny the Lord*—clearly, the denial that they here describe—*and we turned our backs on our God. We spoke blackmail.* You see that he does not accuse them anywhere of idolatry but rather of *blackmail* and *lying words* and things such as these. He says: *And we disobeyed, and we conceived and rehearsed unrighteous words from our heart,* or according to Aquila: *They spoke blackmail and revolt, and they conceived lying words from their heart,* or according to Symmachus: *They spoke blackmail and moral decline; they conceived and exercised themselves in lying words from their heart.*

[59:14-18] Then the text reads: *And we turned back judgment.* For he does not say that *judgment* abandoned us but that we *turned it back, and righteousness withdrew far away, because truth was consumed in their ways, and they could not travel through a straight path,* or according to Symmachus: *Because truth was weak in the street, and uprightness was not able*

to come, and truth was deficient. He is diligent in denouncing those who deny the *truth,* and he convicts those whom he finds anywhere to have *lying* arguments among them. Next, he leads on: *The Lord saw it, and it did not please him that there was no judgment. And he saw, and there was no man.* Above, the text reads: "Why was it that I came and no man was there? I called, and there was none to answer?"[27] But in this context he again says: *And he saw, and there was no man, and he took notice, and there was none who helped; so he defended them with his own arm, and with his compassion he upheld them,* or according to the other Greek translations, *and with righteousness he supported them. And he placed a helmet of salvation on his head, and he put on righteousness like a breastplate, and he clothed himself with a garment of vengeance and with his cloak, as one about to render retribution, a reproach to his enemies.* This is the end of the present accusation against the people of the Jews, in which he openly declares the war of God that arose against them and punished them and that they in fact suffered in the final siege during the time of the Romans.

[59:19] After describing in detail in the above verses the impieties that the people of the Jews committed against the Savior and all the accusations against them and after noting that God himself will become their enemy, the prophetic word turns [367] again to the subject of the calling of the Gentiles, and he speaks, too, of the coming of Christ. For it was right that grace should be included in the prophecy concerning Christ that was introduced through him to the nations. And, therefore, he begins by saying: *And those from the west shall fear the name of the Lord.* "And the fear of the Lord is the beginning of wisdom."[28] Therefore, he prophesies that Israel will not partake in this wisdom but those *from the west*—clearly, those

---

[27]Is 50:2. [28]Ps 111:10.

who have been assigned to live in the western regions—*and those from the rising of the sun.* Likewise, *they shall fear his glorious name.* And the text reads above: "Behold, these will come from far away, these *from the west* and these from the north, and others from the land of the Persians. Rejoice, O heavens!"[29] He says many things concerning "those who *fear* the Lord,"[30] such as: "Blessed is the one who *fears* the Lord,"[31] and: "Those who *fear* him have no want,"[32] and: "The *fear* of the Lord is discipline and wisdom,"[33] and: "The *fear* of the Lord adds days."[34] Therefore, the prophet proclaims all these things to the Gentiles when he says: *And those from the west shall fear the name of the Lord, and those from the rising of the sun, his glorious name.* Next he presents the reason for such a salvation for the Gentiles when he says: *For the anger of the Lord will come like a rushing river—it will come with wrath.* But the Hebrew reading does not mention either *anger* or *wrath*, and the other Greek translations do not either. For it does not use the words *wrath* or *anger of God* in these promises for good things.

Therefore, according to Aquila, the text reads: *Because the Spirit of the Lord will come as a river—a sign for himself*; but according to Symmachus: *The Spirit of the Lord will come as a turbulent river; he presses onward and he will come*; and according to Theodotion: *For the Spirit of the Lord will come as an overpowering river; he thus interpreted the sign in himself.* But nowhere in this verse does the text say either *anger of the Lord* or *wrath.* So then, *the Spirit of the Lord will come as a rushing river, in order that those from the west and those from the rising of the sun should fear* him. This is why the text says that *the Spirit of the Lord will come.* And we should note that the text says that *he will come as a rushing river*, for we see the fulfillment of the word in the Acts of the Apostles, when they were gathered together in the same place: "Suddenly a sound came from heaven

like a *rushing* wind, and it filled all the house where they were sitting. And there appeared to them tongues as of fire, distributed and resting on each one of them. And they were all filled with the Holy Spirit."[35] Therefore, the text reads that *the Spirit of the Lord will come as a rushing river*, and he also says: *As a sign for himself.* This was the *sign* of the ascension of our Savior, just as he taught when he said: "If I do not go away, the Counselor will not come,"[36] and again: "When I go away, I will send to you the *Spirit* of truth."[37]

[59:20] The text then reads next: *And the one who delivers will come for the sake of Zion*, but according to Symmachus: *And the one who is the next of kin will come to Zion*, and according to Aquila: *And the one who is the next of kin will enter into Zion.* The Savior himself indicated this [368] when he said: "I came only to the lost sheep of the house of Israel."[38] And, again in this context, the godly commonwealth is signified in the word *Zion*, which elsewhere was demonstrated to be the church of God. Therefore, the text says that *the one who delivers* or *the next of kin will come* for the sake of the city of God. And why will he do this? He will forgive unrighteousness for those who belong to him. Therefore, the text reads: *He will turn impiety away from Jacob*—that is to say, for those who *convert from Jacob.* If they do not convert, they can only blame themselves that they did not also partake of grace as did the Gentiles, although they had been called first.

[59:21] *And*, he says, *this will be the covenant to them from me.* What sort of covenant this will be he continues on to say: *My spirit that is on you.* This *spirit* in fact was *the covenant.* For this reason, when our Savior and Lord Jesus, the Christ of God, gave the *Spirit* to his disciples, he said: "Receive the Holy Spirit. If

---

[29]Is 49:12-13. [30]Ps 112:1. [31]Ps 112:1. [32]Ps 33:10. [33]Prov 15:33. [34]Prov 10:27. [35]Acts 2:2-4. [36]Jn 16:7. [37]Jn 15:26. [38]Mt 15:24.

you forgive the sins of anyone, he is forgiven."[39] And so the Holy *Spirit* is a key part of the mystery and the new *covenant*. Therefore it has been said: *And this is the covenant to them from me, said the Lord, my spirit that is on you.* And he addresses these things to the *next of kin* and to the *one who delivers* and forgives sins. Therefore, then, he transmitted this *Spirit* to his disciples so that they would transmit it to the saints. *And*, he says, *my words that I have put in your mouth*—the things that will be delivered through the new *covenant*—they in fact are my *covenant*. For *my spirit and the words that I have put in your mouth are* your *covenant*, which *shall not fail out of your mouth or out of your offspring, said the Lord, from now on and forever.* His *words* will endure *forever* and ever, as the Savior himself taught when he said in the Gospels: "Heaven and earth will pass away, but my words will not pass away."[40]

[60:1-2] After announcing the coming of Christ, the prophet for the first time encourages *Jerusalem*—clearly referring to the entire nation of the Jews that once dwelled in Jerusalem—to partake of the *light*. Accordingly, because the Christ of God himself "was the *light*"[1] and "the truth and the life"[2] and "the *light* that enlightens every one coming into the world,"[3] it is only reasonable that the Word would tell *Jerusalem* to profit from this coming and say: *Shine, shine, O Jerusalem, for your light has come.* He says that the *light* is Jerusalem's because it was in the city that the prophets preached the promises concerning the Christ. And if it had obeyed the message and shared in the *light* and received the Christ of God, it would have remained in peace until the end. For, he says, [369] it was previously announced to you that *light* has now come. Therefore, do not delay but *shine, shine* and partake of grace! For you will be *enlightened* immediately. And all the things that I spoke against them would

have perhaps scarcely been fulfilled, at least in a literal way, if they had been obedient to the command and received the Christ of God who dwelled among them. But, now, in a single moment, they deprive themselves of the *light* by denying Christ and all at once forfeit everything that had been promised through the prophets. This is how the text would be interpreted according to the mere letter, but it would be interpreted differently according to the deeper meaning, because in the other Greek translations the name *Jerusalem* is not present. For Aquila translates this verse as follows: *Arise, shine, because your light has arrived*, and Symmachus writes: *Arise, shine, for your light has come. Jerusalem* is not mentioned in the Hebrew reading, and so it is reasonable to understand that these things have been said to those who would receive the promised "redeemer or next of kin."[4] These were the ones about whom it was said: "And those from the west shall fear the name of the Lord, and those from sunrise, his glorious name."[5]

And the godly commonwealth has been restored to us many times in the souls of godly people, and it is called the city of God and Jerusalem. Once, a godly commonwealth did exist among the Jews, when the prophets and righteous people flourished among them and there were many pious and God-loving persons; and now, truly, the city of God and the service of God according to God's will is ours while theirs has come to an end. But all those who had been made perfect "waited for the coming"[6] of Christ that the prophets announced, and they departed from life hoping "until death"[7] that he would come down for their salvation. It is because of this that the Word promises those who "sit in darkness"[8] the coming of the *light*: *Shine, O Jerusalem, for your light has come.* These things were partially but not entirely fulfilled at the first coming of our Savior, but they will happen completely at his second and

---

[39]Jn 20:22-23. [40]Mt 24:35. **Chapter Sixty** [1]Jn 1:9. [2]Jn 14:6. [3]Jn 1:9. [4]Cf. Is 59:20. [5]Is 59:19. [6]2 Pet 3:12. [7]Phil 2:8. [8]Is 9:2.

glorious theophany. At that time there will no longer be "sun"[9] or "moon" or stars but the very Christ of God—"the true *light*"[10] and "the sun of righteousness."[11] He will be sufficient for the illumination of those souls who are deemed worthy of his kingdom. According to the holy apostle Paul: "The Lord himself will come down from heaven with a loud command and with the voice of the archangel, and the dead in Christ will rise first. Then we who are left shall be caught up together with them in a cloud to meet the Lord in the air; and so we shall always be with the Lord."[12]

Whenever his glorious coming shall be, it will be at that time that the Word will address the saints and say: *Shine, shine, O Jerusalem, for your light has come*, or according to the other Greek translations: *Arise, be enlightened,* [370] *for your light has arrived.* And see if he did not clearly prophesy the resurrection from the dead when he said: *Arise!* The cause of the resurrection from the dead was the coming of the *light*. For the souls of the saints who have already passed away will be rekindled in the life-possessing rays of his *light*. Therefore, according to the Apostle Paul: "The Lord himself will come down from heaven with a loud command and with the voice of the archangel; then the dead in Christ shall arise."[13] Then, after they arise, they will see his *glory*. Therefore, the text continues on: *And the glory of the Lord has risen on you. It has risen* not on all but only on the saints. For he will not receive such individuals, but he has threatened "outer *darkness*"[14] and "eternal fire"[15] and such things for the ungodly. But, he says, *the glory of the Lord has risen on you*, the city of God, the new Jerusalem, and once you have partaken of this glory, *shine! Darkness* is reserved for those who have not known the Lord or paid any attention to his arrival which

happened before their very eyes, as he then indicates when he says: *Look, darkness shall cover the earth and gloom on the nations, but the Lord will appear to you*, or according to the other Greek translations: *The Lord will arise on you; his glory will be seen on you.* And they needed to see the *glory* of his *light* and rising first, so that, as those who had witnessed "the *glory* of the only-begotten God,"[16] they should be able to stand in the day of divine *light*.

[60:3] Then he says: *Nations shall walk by your light and kings by your brightness.*[17] It seems to me that in this verse, there are two commands for those who are being saved: the first command is for the company of those who have walked uprightly among the nation of the Jews. For there were prophets and patriarchs and priests and God-loving people and high priests, men as well as countless women, who were saved from among those among whom the godly commonwealth formerly resided, so that they would be not a small part of the city of God, those who, according to the holy apostle, "although being made perfect through faith, all these did not receive the promises, since God had foreseen something better for us, that apart from us they should not be made perfect."[18] Therefore, they were confined to the regions of death because they expected the coming of Christ immediately. John the Baptist taught this when he inquired of the Christ and said: "Are you he who is to come, or shall we look for another?"[19] Because all the saints who have fallen asleep first were waiting for him, it is right that the present word should promise their souls that the Savior would descend among them, as he clearly affirms when he says: *Arise, shine, for your light has arrived.* And so this first command is for those of the former people who are being saved. The second

---

[9]Is 60:19. [10]Jn 1:9. [11]Mal 4:2. [12]1 Thess 4:16. [13]1 Thess 4:16. [14]Mt 8:12. [15]Mt 18:8. [16]Jn 1:14. [17]Eusebius reverses the order of "nations" and "kings" in his statement here from the LXX order, but he then proceeds to follow the LXX order in his exegesis below. [18]Heb 11:39. [19]Mt 11:3.

command is for the church of the Gentiles, called through the grace of Christ, concerning whom he then adds: *And nations shall walk by your light.* For it was this *light* that you announced before, and it was by this *light* that the prophets and patriarchs and all those among the Jews who lived as citizens of the godly commonwealth had the eyes of their souls *enlightened,* and it is by this *light* that the *Gentiles,* foreigners and people of other races will be *enlightened.* The text also speaks of *brightness,* for you announced that the city has been wiped and scrubbed and brightened [371] and cleansed from every filth and every stain by the divine words. And foreign *kings* will be cleansed by this *brightness* and scrubbed in the power of the divine mysteries.

[60:4] One has to marvel and be amazed at the fulfillment of the oracle, how it was fulfilled during our times when the above *kings* were deemed worthy of the grace "by washing."[20] Then, because he mentioned *kings of nations*— and *nations* come after the former city of God—he teaches that all those from the nations who belong to the godly commonwealth will lead the way for their own *children.* Therefore, he says: *Lift up your eyes round about, and see your children gathered together; all your sons have come from far away, and your daughters shall be carried on shoulders.* Therefore, all those from the *nations* who have believed in God through Christ and have taken hold of the promise will rest "in the bosom of Abraham"[21] and Isaac and Jacob—this the Savior himself has taught. And in many other verses, the church of the nations is proclaimed to be the daughter of Zion and the daughter of Jerusalem. Accordingly, the mother of the new Jerusalem that is composed of the nations is she who in times past walked uprightly among the former people, and we are all her *children.* Therefore, it has been said: *All your sons have come from far away.* For we were

very *far away* "from the commonwealth of Israel, and strangers to the covenants of promise, having no hope and without God in the world,"[22] but, he says, "you who once were far off have been brought near."[23] For this reason, it has been said: *All your sons have come from far away, and your daughters shall be carried on shoulders.* For since they are tender souls and still infants, "longing for the spiritual and pure milk like newborn babes,"[24] and since they are *"children* of Abraham"[25] through rebirth in Christ, they are borne along and *carried on shoulders* and lifted up by their teachers who lead them by the hand. Paul was such a teacher, who said: "Like a nurse taking care of her children, so we longed to be with you and were delighted to share with you not only the gospel of Christ but our lives as well."[26]

[60:5-7] After the mother mentioned above saw these things, she was filled with joy: *Then you shall see and rejoice and be afraid and be amazed in your heart.* The phrase *and you shall be afraid* is not present in the other Greek translations. For if "there will be joy in heaven over one sinner who repents,"[27] how will the souls of the saints who have passed away and who practiced her righteous ways and who were made perfect in her, how shall they not *rejoice* over the nations that repent? Even now such people *will rejoice when they see the wealth of the sea* and of the *nations and of the peoples* of all races *turned over to* her. Therefore, according to Symmachus, the text reads: *When the multitude of the sea, the power of nations,* [372] *will be converted to you.* And one should note that he here likens the tremendous number of those who are being saved to the *multitude of the sea.* And the *power of nations* perhaps represents those who walk uprightly and who are never too tired for the strain of the godly life but are strong enough to say: "I can do all things in Christ Jesus who strengthens me."[28]

[20]Tit 3:5. [21]Lk 16:22. [22]Eph 2:12. [23]Eph 2:13. [24]1 Pet 2:2. [25]Jn 8:39. [26]1 Thess 2:7-8. [27]Lk 15:7. [28]Phil 4:13.

Therefore, *they shall rejoice* in the first place over the *power* of them. But after these things, *he shall see* the remaining *multitudes* of those who are imperfect and irrational in their faith, whom he likens, after a fashion, to *herds of camels* when he says: *And there shall come to you herds of camels, and the camels of Madiam and Gaiphar shall cover you. All those from Bashan shall come, bringing gold, and they shall bring frankincense.* I suppose that in this verse he is alluding to those in the church who are well off and abounding in much wealth. The Savior also compared the rich person with a *camel* when he said: "It is easier for a *camel* to pass through the eye of a needle than for a rich person to come into the kingdom of heaven."[29] Indeed, this is a miracle, for "with people this is impossible, but it is possible for God."[30] Therefore, Jerusalem is amazed and filled with joy at seeing those souls who have been compared with *camels* convert and, as it were, pass "through the eye of a needle"[31] and through "the narrow and hard way enter into eternal life."[32] These souls do not arrive without cargo, but they bear gifts for God as "ransoms for their souls."[33]

Camels from Saba shall come from foreign nations. Through the one nation of the Sabateans, all the other foreign nations are signified, because they were intelligent like *camels*. One should pay careful attention to what the text says concerning these *camels: There shall come to you herds of camels, and the camels of Madiam and Gaiphar shall cover you. All those from Bashan shall come, bringing gold, and they shall bring frankincense and announce the good news of the salvation of the Lord.* Therefore, *camels shall announce the good news of the salvation of the Lord,* after they present the aforementioned gifts: *frankincense* representing the spiritual fragrance of the worship of God, and *gold* representing physical abundance. And *Madiam and Gaiphar* are foreign regions where *camels* are bred, as is *Saba* which lies above Arabia,

where *camels* are very plentiful. It is for this reason that the Word appeals to this metaphor.

Nevertheless, it is quite a paradox that the animal-like and irrational souls of those who are rich according to this world will convert—those who have been compared with *camels* because they bear burdens and are very temperamental[34] and curved[35] animals—so that they would attain the privilege of *announcing the good news of the salvation of the Lord.* Christ himself was this *salvation,* but he also says that *the sheep of Kedar shall be gathered, and the rams of Nabaioth shall come, and they will be offered on the* **[373]** *altar* of God. And it seems to me that in this verse the Word charms and coaxes the childish and bodily-minded Jews, dragging them on and urging them forward to strive after their godly citizenship. And even if they were not at all like godly citizens, they are still like young children in their desire for the promises of God, clamoring for attention. He promises the things that we think are special and pleasant during childhood in order to encourage those whom he wants to instruct as children. For in the same way, I think that the Word reveals mystical and divine concepts to those who have been enlightened, conversing secretly with the souls and hearts of the people of the Jews as with children and offering the promises to his acquaintances with the same words and tones. But perhaps all these things would not have been literally fulfilled among them if they had received our Savior and Lord Jesus Christ, as has already been said to us. And, therefore, after exhorting them to be enlightened, the Word is willing to introduce the next subject, if they are willing to be illuminated by the light of saving grace.

When they did not share in the light that shone among those who were earlier, it happened too that they neither enjoyed the benefit of the events that were to happen next. This is why they failed, because they expected him to

---

[29]Mt 19:24. [30]Mt 19:26. [31]Mt 19:24. [32]Mt 7:14. [33]Mt 20:28. [34]πολύτομον. [35]The allusion would seem to be to the camel's hump.

be among them, but God, fulfilling his unerring promises, presents them in their deeper sense, the promises having been suitably secured by divine assurance. Because the divine Scriptures know that the rational souls are the simple among people, he presents them as *sheep*, even as we hear from the evangelical voice that says: "Go to the lost *sheep* of the house of Israel."[36] For this reason, he continues on: *And all the sheep of Kedar shall be gathered to you, and the rams of Nabaioth shall come. Kedar* is translated as "darkness." It is said that around the desert there are foreigners called Saracens. It may be, too, that *Nabaioth* represents another region of the land of Israel. Therefore, just as he said that the foreign and strange *camels* will come from *Madiam* and *Gaiphar* and from *Saba*, so also the *sheep* and *rams* will come from *Kedar* and *Nabaioth*, thereby alluding to the nations of other races and tribes. Therefore, *camels* represent those who are well off and wealthy among people, and *sheep* represent the tame and simple, and *rams* represent royalty from the nations that have converted, whom the Word says *shall offer gifts on the altar* of God. And the oracle has been fulfilled before our eyes, when one saw such souls from the conversion of the Gentiles dedicating themselves to the word of godliness and to the worship of the altar that is in the service of God. For the church of God is glorified through the conversion and salvation of such as these. Thus, the text then reads: *And my house of prayer shall be glorified.* These things were once [374] promised to Jerusalem, to the mother of the new city, which he said was composed of those who walked uprightly among the former people—prophets and patriarchs, righteous and God-loving people—to whom the Word first proclaimed the coming of the Christ.

[60:8-9] Next, the text reads as though speaking from their very mouths: *Who are these that fly to me like clouds and like doves with their young?* We who have paid attention to the instructive voice of Paul will know that "we who are alive, who are left for the coming of Christ, shall be caught up in the *clouds* to meet the Lord in the air; and so we shall always be with the Lord"[37]—clearly those who have joined in and identified with the band of those who walked uprightly among the former people. Therefore, marveling at the grace of Christ that has been poured out on humanity and on the multitude of those who are being saved from the Gentiles, and at their ascension into heaven after their departure from life, he says: *Who are these that fly to me like clouds, and like doves with their young? The islands waited for me.* In the previous chapters, the Word frequently alluded to the churches as *islands*. Since the churches of God spend their time awaiting the promises that had been made to the fathers and are found in the prophecies, it is right that he says: *The islands waited for me, and the ships of Tarsus were among the first to bring your children.* And *ships of Tarsus* foreshadow the bodies into which souls floated during this mortal life. *Tarsus* again was a territory of the foreign peoples. For this reason, somewhere the text reads concerning the unbelieving foreign peoples: "With a violent blast you will shatter the ships of *Tarsus*."[38] Indeed "he shattered" them, but here the *children* of the former Jerusalem who will be added to her from the Gentiles will come on *ships from far away*—that is, in the bodies of those who have been changed for the better. "For the perishable nature must put on the imperishable, and the mortal nature must put on immortality."[39] The aforementioned will come in bodies, bringing with them deeds which, because of their excellence, are called *silver* and *gold*. The apostle Paul uses the terminology of *gold* and *silver* for deeds too.[40] Therefore, it has been said: *Their silver and their gold with them, and the holy name of the Lord will be glorified.*

---

[36]Mt 10:6. [37]1 Thess 4:17. [38]Ps 48:7. [39]1 Cor 15:53. [40]1 Cor 3:12.

[60:10-12] After this, the text reads: *And aliens shall build up your walls.* You will see this accomplished in fact if you note in your mind that it has been the leading people from among the *aliens* and foreign nations of the church of God who have defended the spiritual teachings. It was they who safeguarded the word of godliness with certain enclosures and *walls* in order that those who are hostile to the faith **[375]** should neither worm their way into nor attain a place for their schemes against the doctrines of the truth. And he says: *And their kings*—clearly, the *kings* of the *alien nations*—*shall attend to you*, and this also happened for your eyes to see. And so the rulers of the Roman legions and the terror of the conquering kings contributed to the overthrow of those who attempted to scheme against the church of God. For this reason, it has been said: *And their kings shall attend you.* He goes on to say: *For because of my wrath I struck you down, but because of my mercy I loved you.* For, he says, although you professed to be serving God in the holy city, because of the multitude of those who were not serving God among you, *I struck* you and delivered you over to your enemies and to captivity, so that even prophets and teachers suffered under the wrath against the ungodly. As that happened earlier, so now because of those who walk uprightly you will be deemed worthy of my "love,"[41] "the fruits" of which are "great courage and peace."[42]

Therefore, it has been said: *And your gates shall always be opened—day and night they shall not be shut.* And who are the *gates* of the city of God except the teachers who instruct in elementary and introductory doctrine, whom the text says are *opened night and day* to all so as to admit all who have been elected from all the nations to serve God? Therefore, the text says: *To bring to you the power of nations*, and he promises to admit even the *kings* of their *nations* into the aforementioned *gates*. For the *powers of*

nations are the ones who are able to say: "I can do all things in him who strengthens me,"[43] and their *kings* are the chosen ones who are worthy of the kingdom of heaven. Since we have now seen literal *kings*—Roman emperors—run through the *gates* of the church of God and be deemed worthy of the mysteries within these *gates*, how could anyone not testify to the truth of the prophecy? Therefore, the *gates* shall admit them even to the kingdom of heaven. But what sort of end the *nations* that "remained on in unbelief"[44] and their rulers and *kings* who died in idolatry will have, the Word states next when he says: *For the nations and kings that will not be subject to you shall perish.* It is necessary *to be subject* to the saving and most beautiful service in the city of God—I am speaking about the church and the godly commonwealth, where those who are worthy of salvation dwell. But those who act profanely toward this service will be delivered over to destruction.

[60:13] But the most beautiful and highest of the trees in *Lebanon* will be recovered for you, the church of God and its godly commonwealth, in order that through you *my holy place might be glorified.* But, again, *Lebanon* is a mountain in foreign lands, where the trees that are highest and greatest and most serviceable for construction grow. Perhaps these are the people of the Gentiles who are eloquent and have been schooled in the **[376]** "wisdom of this age"[45] and are prominent in the church of God, who adorn it with carefully prepared sermons from the Word. When you read the text according to the law of allegory, you would not be wrong to say that they are the trees of *Lebanon, cypress, pines and cedars*, through whom *the holy place* of God *is glorified, the place of* his *feet*—clearly, the church.

[60:14] After all these things, because many envied the people of God but were not able to

---

[41]Gal 5:22.   [42]2 Cor 3:12.   [43]Phil 4:13 RSV.   [44]Rom 11:23.   [45]1 Cor 2:6.

buy this right for their souls at any price, they were humbled and degraded, and though they pretended to honor and to accept the saving word, in fact they spoke about it with derision. The prophet does not pass over their memory but says: *The children of those who humbled and provoked you shall come to you with dread.* But we have known many who once blasphemed the church and *provoked* and persecuted it but who have converted and come to *worship* God in it. And then he says: *You shall be called the city of the Lord.* For, truly, when "the full number of the Gentiles comes in,"[46] then "all Israel will be saved."[47] After the band of the former saints has been unified in the people that has been formed from the Gentiles through Christ, and after he has made them "one body,"[48] he will fashion one *city.* Therefore, the "body" united from all nations *shall be called the city of the Lord, Zion of the Holy One of Israel.*

[60:15] He continues on: *Because you have become forsaken and hated, and there was none who helped.* For "when a member suffers, all suffer together."[49] Because the former people transgressed, "the natural branches were cut off from the cultivated olive tree,"[50] and they became *forsaken and hated, and there was none who helped them.* But now, instead of "the branches that have been cut off" and introduced again, those "from the wild olive tree" have filled up the part that was lacking from the place of those who had been cast off. And thus it is in the power of the Savior that the fullness of those who are being saved and the entire band of God is united from two peoples into one, and from two companies into one *city,* which is called the *Zion of God.* And it is in this *city* that all that has been promised below is fulfilled: *And I will make you an*

everlasting gladness and a joy for generations and generations.

[60:16] Again, he prophesies that the *milk of nations* will be delivered over to it when he says: *And you shall suck the milk of nations.* What might the *milk of nations* be if not the new mystery of the evangelical teaching and the elementary teaching of the new covenant, of which those who have been regenerated have partaken in Christ? And he promises the *wealth of kings* to the people indicated above. Again, one should understand *kings* in this context as none other than those who are worthy of the Beatitudes, to whom the Savior promised "the kingdom of heaven."[51] Anyone who has seen the gracious provision of the rulers [377] for the church[52] and the gifts and opulent sacred spaces[53] that have been presented to the church would say that all these things have been confirmed literally from all the verses above, for he says: *You shall know that I am the Lord who saves you and rescues you, the God of Jacob.*

[60:17] In addition to the things that have been expounded above, learn these things, because there is no longer any demand for useless *wood.* For such wood serves only as fuel for the fire, and neither will you have any need for *stones*—that is, for foolish[54] souls. Therefore, instead of these things, *I will bring you* more valuable things. Those people of *iron* who were once as obstinate as *bronze* and harsher and harder than anything have been changed into *gold* and *silver,* and they will be likened to "God's own building."[55] And those who are as foolish and senseless as dry *wood* will be changed from *bronze* and *iron* so that they will be useful for you. Indeed, they will

---

[46]Rom 11:25. [47]Rom 11:26. [48]1 Cor 10:17. [49]1 Cor 12:26. [50]Rom 11:21ff. [51]Mt 5:3. [52]This would seem to be a clear allusion to Constantine's particular generosity to the church. Eusebius's reference to anyone who has seen these things would seem to be a clear statement of his amazement and satisfaction as an eyewitness of the conversion of the empire under Constantine. [53]ἀναθήματα πλούσια; I interpret this as a reference to Constantine's lavish construction projects for the church. [54]Eusebius is punning here: the word for "stone" (λίθων) is cognate to the word for "foolish" (ἠλιθίων). [55]1 Cor 3:9.

become better than the first ones and even more useful "in God's building," for their value has been exchanged from that of *bronze* and *iron* to that of *gold* and *silver*. After *your rulers* advance in *peace*, they shall spend the rest of their life presiding over and leading the church of God. And because he had prophetic foreknowledge in the Lord, he applied the title *overseers* to them, and so God now calls them when he said: *I will ordain your rulers in peace and your overseers in righteousness.*

[**60:18**] He continues on to say: *And injustice shall no longer be heard in your land*—that is, in your way of life—and *neither destruction nor wretchedness within your borders.* Therefore, no enemy or adversary shall remain, and neither shall there then be any remembrance of evil, for "pain and sorrow and sighing have fled away."[56] Then he says: *Your walls shall be called salvation.* But instead of *salvation,* the Hebrew reading presents the very letters and characters of the name Jesus, and so this refers to our Savior. Thus, the very power of our Savior Jesus stands as an enclosure and a solid *wall* for those who are worthy of these things. On the one hand, these things are already here for us to see, but on the other hand, they will happen in the new age after the consummation of the present one. Then he says: *And your gates shall be called sculpture,* or according to Aquila: *And your gates shall be called a hymn,* or according to Symmachus, *praise.* You see how the word turns us away from a literal interpretation, so that we do not fall into the ordinary and Jewish interpretations. It is for this reason that he calls the *gates* of the new Jerusalem *hymn* and *praise.* For the entrances of the godly commonwealth are established through these things—through the singing of hymns and praises to God and the instructing of those who enter.

[**60:19-20**] And *the sun shall no longer produce the day for you, nor shall the moon give you light through the night,* because those who will be deemed worthy of the new age will neither be in *night* nor in perceptible and literal *light.* For, superior to any [**378**] *sun,* they will have *the Lord* himself *as an everlasting light and God as their glory.* Therefore, the prophecy next says: *And the days of your mourning shall be fulfilled.* The blessed one will in fact be confirmed, who says: "Blessed are those who mourn, for they shall be comforted."[57]

[**60:21**] *And the people shall all be righteous,* and he says that no unrighteous one will then appear or be found among the people. For this reason, the chosen one *will inherit the land* that has been promised to him. The Savior also taught this when he said: "Blessed are the meek, for *they shall inherit the earth,*"[58] and he here alludes to the heavenly way of life in "the city of God, which is the heavenly and true Jerusalem,"[59] "and she is our mother,"[60] as the apostle says. But instead of *guarding their plant, the works of their hands,* Symmachus writes: *A blossom of my plant, in order that the works of my hands may be glorified.* For such a people is the *blossom* of my *plant:* for "every *plant* which my heavenly Father has not planted will be rooted up."[61] But the *blossom* is of the *planting* of God and the *works of his hands; they shall inherit* the promised *land* when they are *glorified* with such good things.

[**60:22**] And then *the smallest one* in the present life *shall become thousands,* according to the saving promises. In this verse, he promises that "he will appoint them rulers"[62] and then say to them: "You shall have authority over five cities,"[63] and: "You shall have authority over ten cities."[64]

Therefore, they shall become *thousands,* as a commander over a thousand of those who will

---

[56]Is 35:10. [57]Mt 5:4 RSV. [58]Mt 5:5 RSV. [59]Heb 12:22. [60]Gal 4:26. [61]Mt 15:13 RSV. [62]Cf. Ps 45:16. [63]Lk 19:19. [64]Lk 19:17.

be saved. And the one who is now *the least shall be a great nation* then. This is similar to the pattern of what Paul says: "But, although I am the very *least* of all the saints, this grace was given to me."[65] Then they will be rulers of a heavenly nation that will be considered great before God. And he says that all these things will happen when *I the Lord will father them in due time, in the time* that I have appointed. For the promises have not yet been realized, but the time that I have appointed will come, and then all these things will happen at my gathering: "For then he will send out his angels, and *they will gather* to him all the saints from one end of heaven to the other."[66]

[61:1-3] After the evangelical promises, he says in the passage above at the end of the oracle: *I, the Lord, will gather them in due time.* Thereafter, he cries aloud and says: *The Spirit of the Lord is on me, because he has anointed me.* And so he teaches how the gathering will be done when he says: *The Lord will gather them in due time,* and then he added: *The Spirit of the Lord is on me, because he has anointed me.* This verse is clearly directed at those who suppose that the Christ of God was neither a real man nor a fleshless and bodiless Word or who believe that he never partook of mortal nature. But they say that he was both God and man. He is God according to the verse which states that he is "the only-begotten God, who is in the bosom of the Father,"[1] and [379] he is considered to be man according to the verse, "who was descended from David, according to the flesh."[2] Therefore, God the Word has spoken in a proper sense[3] in the prophecy, and along with the other promises that he has made, he adds this and says: *I, the Lord, will gather them in due time.*

Then he states which man he is referring to when he continues on and says: *The Spirit of the Lord is on me, because he has anointed me.* It has often been demonstrated in the verses above that "the *Spirit* of God" has rested on the one from the root of Jesse "and the spirit of wisdom and understanding and the spirit of counsel and might and the spirit of knowledge and godliness."[4] Therefore, this was fulfilled when our Savior and Lord Jesus Christ taught the prophecy, as it has been recorded in the Gospel of Luke: "He came to Nazareth, where he had grown up; and he went to the synagogue, as his custom was, on the Sabbath day. And he stood up to read; and there was given to him the book of the prophet Isaiah, and after he opened it he found where it says: 'The Spirit of the Lord is on me, because he has anointed me to preach good news to the poor. He has sent me to proclaim release to the captives and recovery of sight to the blind, to set at liberty those who are oppressed, to proclaim the acceptable year of the Lord.' When he closed the book and gave it back to the attendant, he sat down; and the eyes of all in the synagogue were fixed on him. And he began to say to them, 'Today this Scripture has been fulfilled in your hearing.' And all spoke well of him, and wondered at the gracious words which proceeded out of his mouth."[5] If you pay attention to the time referred to in the phrase "today this Scripture has been fulfilled,"[6] you will find that it refers to the time when "after he had been baptized in the Jordan, the *Holy* Spirit descended in the form of a dove"[7] and "remained on him."[8] Then "he was led up into the wilderness to be tempted by the devil."[9] Then, "after he came to Nazareth, he read"[10] the aforementioned prophecy. For this reason, he continued on to say accurately: "Today this Scripture has been fulfilled in your hearing."[11]

---

[65]Eph 3:8. [66]Mt 24:31. **Chapter Sixty-One** [1]Jn 1:18. [2]Rom 1:3. [3]κυριολεκτέω is the Greek term here. The primary sense of the term is "to use words in their proper or literal sense," but to Christian exegetes, it also came to mean "to speak with reference to the Lord," that is, "to interpret a phrase in light of christological fulfillment." [4]Is 11:2. [5]Lk 4:16-22. [6]Lk 4:21. [7]Mt 3:16. [8]Jn 1:32. [9]Mt 4:1. [10]Lk 4:16. [11]Lk 4:16.

For surely it was at the same time when "the Holy *Spirit* came down on him in the form of a dove"[12] that the prophecy was fulfilled which he spoke with his own mouth: *The Spirit of the Lord is on me, because he has anointed me.* For this was not a physical anointing, as in old times, that led him to say *I have been anointed.* And he would not have had any special honor if he had been *anointed* by other people.

But now the anointing receives a special honor above all others because it comes from the Holy *Spirit,* and our Savior is revealed to be the only-begotten Christ of God. The phrase *he has sent me to bring good news to the poor* was fulfilled at that time when "he preached the kingdom of heaven"[13] and pronounced blessings on his disciples and said, "Blessed are the poor in spirit, for theirs is the kingdom of heaven."[14] But he also *healed the brokenhearted,* healing them with promises when he said: "Blessed are those who *mourn,* for they *shall be comforted,*" **[380]** and "Blessed are those who weep, for they shall laugh."[15] And now, to the nations whose souls had been taken captive by invisible and spiritual adversaries, *he proclaimed release,* and he exhorted his disciples to preach the same when he said: "Go and make disciples of all nations, baptizing them in the name of the Father and of the Son and of the Holy Spirit."[16] And the *release* of which he spoke is the *forgiveness*[17] of former profane acts. Therefore, *he proclaimed release to the captives,* and *he proclaimed recovery of sight* to those who suffered blindness and were enslaved in the error of polytheism. *He spoke the acceptable year of the Lord,* and this *year* represented all the time that he sojourned among people and granted the light of day to those who came near to him. But perhaps he alludes to the age that will come after the consummation of the present age when he says: *To summon the acceptable year of the Lord and*

the day of retribution of our God, or according to the other Greek translations: *A year of good will.* For in the mind of the Lord, that time and age may be the same age as the *day of retribution.* He will render compensation at that time to those who have labored in this present life.

Therefore, it has been said: *To summon the acceptable year of the Lord and the day of retribution of our God* and *to comfort all who mourn.* For he said: "Blessed are those who *mourn,* for they *shall be comforted.*"[18] He promised them comfort, and during the *day of retribution* he will revive and *comfort* them with his words, and *to those who mourn for Zion he will give glory and oil of joy instead of ashes.* And Paul "mourned"[19] over Zion, and there were many like him who wept over the fall of the Jewish nation and of the godly commonwealth that had been among them. It is to these, therefore, that *he will give glory instead of mourning and instead of ashes,* which the distressed had placed on their heads as a demonstration of their penitent attitude before God on behalf of the people, and *he will give the oil of joy instead of a spirit of weariness.* But because they had worn out their *garment of glory* and because of his abounding benevolence, he promised that he would *give* them these things during his first coming, and the Savior promised that he would do this on the *day of retribution.* And so he continued on to read the part of the prophecy that says: "Today this Scripture has been fulfilled in your hearing."[20] Then, after these things, the text reads: *And they will be called generations of righteousness, a plant of the Lord for glory.* But who and when will *be called,* if not the ones who will be deemed worthy of the *acceptable year* and the *day of retribution?* But according to Symmachus, the text reads: *And they will be called strong ones of righteousness, a plant of the Lord to be glorified.*

---

[12]Mt 3:16. [13]Mt 4:23. [14]Mt 5:3. [15]Lk 6:21. [16]Mt 28:19. [17]The Greek term ἄφεσις can mean either "release" or "forgiveness." [18]Mt 5:4. [19]2 Cor 12:21. [20]Lk 4:21.

[61:4] *They shall build up the desolate places of old*—clearly, the souls of the nations that were formerly *desolate*. Therefore, he continues on to say: *They shall raise up the former devastated places; they shall renew the desolate cities, places devastated for generations.* In all of this, the Word prophesies a change from the worse for the better.

[61:5-6] [381] Then he continues on to say: *And aliens shall come, feeding your sheep.* The prophecy promises that pastoral care will be provided by *aliens*. And he says that *allophyles will be plowmen and vinedressers for you.* And, therefore, *strangers* and *aliens will shepherd the sheep* of God, and certain *foreigners* shall be *vinedressers* in the vineyard, or the church. *Aliens* shall tend the vineyard—they who were once idolaters and "separated from the covenant of God and *strangers* of the promises, having no hope and without God in the world."[21] Then he addresses them and says: *But you shall be called priests of the Lord, ministers of your God.* And to whom does *you* refer if not the *plowmen* of the church and the *vinedressers* and the shepherds? But they *shall devour the strength of nations*, or according to Aquila: *You have eaten the wealth of nations.* For there will be no such food for the *priests* of God and the shepherds of the church and the *vinedressers* and *plowmen* that corresponds to the *strength* of the *nations* whom they save. And you should understand that the *strength of nations* refers to the martyrs of God throughout the entire empire, since we see the strength and unconquerable endurance of those who "strove for the truth"[22] among all the nations. But he also says: *With wealth you shall be admired.* You will understand what the *wealth of nations* refers to from the testimony of Paul, who wrote in his Scriptures to the Corinthians: "I give thanks to God through Jesus Christ, that in every way you were enriched in him, with all speech and all knowledge, even as the testimony to God was confirmed among you, so that you are not lacking in any spiritual gift."[23]

[61:7] But they *inherited the land a second time,* and they even *inherited* the entire empire,[24] concerning which it has been said in the Psalms: "The Lord said to me, 'My son you are; today I have begotten you. Ask of me, and I will give you nations as your heritage, and as your possession the ends of the earth.'"[25] Therefore, those who presided over his church *inherited* this inheritance from the Savior, and this is the *everlasting joy above their head.* The prophet apprehended all these things in part during his lifetime, but he refers to the fulfillment of the promise in the hope of the coming age.

[61:8] And he says that these things will happen because *I am the Lord, who loves righteousness and hates spoils obtained by injustice.* For indeed the adversarial powers and evil demons enslaved the souls of people, and they did this by force and unjustly. For this reason, *I hate these spoils* but *I love righteousness,* and I poured out my grace not on the Jews only but also on all nations. And, he says, *I will give them their hard work righteously.* And who are *they* if not they who *inherit the land a second time?* But instead of *righteously,* all the other Greek translations say *in truth.* Therefore, they will not be cheated out of *their hard work,* but it will be kept for them *in truth.* **[382]** *And I will make an everlasting covenant with them;* I will no longer give them the temporary commands of Moses but the mystery of the new *covenant,* which will be enduring and *everlasting.*

[61:9] Then, after this verse, the text reads: *And their offspring and their descendants shall be known among the nations and in the midst of*

---

[21]Eph 2:12. [22]Sir 4:28. [23]1 Cor 1:4-7a. [24]This seems to be an allusion to the coming of Constantine. [25]Ps 2:7-8.

the people; *everyone who sees them shall acknowledge them, because these are an offspring blessed by the Lord.* And who would not confess that this ecclesiastical *offspring* has truly prevailed by the blessing of God, so that they are indeed known throughout the entire empire? We understand their *offspring* to be either the word and the evangelical teaching or those who are genuinely instructed by them in word and life, and so it is clear that they are an *offspring blessed by God.*

[**61:10-11**] After the above promises, which the Son of God himself made at his first coming, the Word then speaks of the church of God as one who received good things and expressed thanks for them, because she had suffered for them. Having received an appropriate portion in the fullness of those who are saved, he speaks of her as a becoming *bride* with a gracefully composed body who puts on the *ornaments of the bridegroom* given by himself. *Let my soul be glad in the Lord.* He states why when he says: *For he has clothed me with a garment of salvation.* And the *resurrection body*, which is here referred to as the *garment of salvation*, shall be as a pillar of divine light flashing forth. For we shall no longer dwell in a "body of death,"[26] as Paul clearly stated when he said: "Who will deliver me from this body of death?"[27] His soul will be clothed in *salvation*—the *garment of salvation* and the *tunic of joy.* For each one *will be clothed with an ornament* for his deeds and for the things that he has done in righteousness. And because "they have attained to mature manhood and the measure of the stature,"[28] and they have been made like his *bridegroom* and have become "mature" according to the image of the *bridegroom*, he will say: *He has put on me a mitre as on a bridegroom.* To those who stand in the second rank of excellence, he will say: *And he adorned me with ornaments like a*

bride. After the *bride* receives the seed of the *bridegroom*—that is, the word—she produces flowering fruits in season. For this reason, he says: *And as the earth makes its flowers grow, and as a garden will cause its seeds to spring up.* Then, after this, so that the children of the Jews would not appropriate these things for themselves, the Word states clearly and says: *So the Lord will cause righteousness and gladness to spring up before all the nations.*

[**62:1-2**] After prophesying these things and setting forth what has been said, the prophet then calls aloud and says: *Because of Zion I will not be silent, and because of Jerusalem I will not slacken*—or according to the other Greek translations: *And because of Jerusalem I will not* [**383**] *keep quiet*—*until its righteousness goes forth like light and its salvation shall burn like a torch*, or according to Aquila: *And its salvation shall be kindled like a torch.* For, he says, I will not be able to be still and to keep silent; rather, it is necessary for me to cry aloud night and day and to devote myself to prayers and petitions. I will see with my own eyes the fulfillment of the things that have been said when the *righteousness of Jerusalem* and her *salvation* shall shine forth like *light* to all people. For it is not in her alone that these things will happen and that *light* will shine forth to her alone, but rather he will share his own sparkling light with all nations. Therefore, he continues on: *And nations shall see your righteousness and all the kings of the earth your glory.* And, again, the godly commonwealth was formerly situated among the Jews, and the band of those righteous and God-loving people who were prominent among them and all the prophets who were worthy of salvation he calls *Zion and Jerusalem.* He promises that the *light*, which is brighter than every *torch*, will shine forth to all the nations, so that *all kings*—clearly referring in this way

---

[26]Rom 7:24. [27]Rom 7:24. [28]Eph 4:13.

to the kingdoms of the earth—*shall see* their glory. Then he continues on: *And you shall call it the new name, which the Lord will name.* For the name of the Lord adorns his church.

[62:3-4] Then he says: *And you shall be a crown of beauty in the hand of the* Lord—which he says he shall receive when "I have fought the good fight, I have finished the race, I have kept the faith. Henceforth there is laid up for me the crown of righteousness"[1]—*and a royal diadem in the hand of your God.* For all who win the victory through him truly are the *crown* of Christ, *and* the holy martyrs who have wrestled in the contest for him are his *royal diadem.* The Father chose them with his *hand* and placed them on the Son, crowning him with a kingly *diadem* and honoring him with a great number of those who have been saved by him and through him. When these things are fulfilled, *it shall no longer be called Forsaken* or *Desolate Land,* but it shall receive a *new name.* Although it was once such, he says now it has been deemed worthy of such good things and so *it shall be called My Will*—that is, it shall be named according to *my will, and your land* shall be named *Inhabited.*

[62:5-6] In the new age of the kingdom of Christ, it shall be that she shall have only inhabitants who have been deemed worthy of the promises of God, and they shall spend their time in rejoicing and gladness. They shall be like a *holy young man* who lives with a pure *virgin* who has in no way spoiled her virginity but who rejoices in her maidenly chastity and in her pure lifestyle and community. And *so your sons shall rejoice,* and the Lord himself shall receive **[384]** his *bride* and establish the holy church from the mature members of the former people and from the new people of the Gentiles. *A bridegroom shall rejoice over a bride, and he will post sentinels*—clearly, divine

angels and holy powers who shall keep and guard the *walls* and the fortifications of this new *Jerusalem*—and so the ruler shall live in peace forever. He says that the aforementioned *sentinels* shall not stop to sleep *all day* and *all night* but shall sing praises to the one who is responsible for such good things and shall rejoice over their salvation.

[62:7] But instead of *for you have none like him, if he should restore Jerusalem and make it a boast on the earth,* Symmachus says: *Do not keep quiet or allow him to rest until he prepares Jerusalem and places it as a place of praise in the earth.* And to whom have these things been said if not to those who said above: "Because of Zion *I will not be silent, and because of Jerusalem I will not slacken until her righteousness goes forth like light*"?[2] For the Holy Spirit said these things concerning the prophetic band, encouraging and impelling them to continue on in prayer for those who have been mentioned. For this reason, he says: *Do not keep quiet nor allow him to rest*—clearly speaking to the Lord who promised these things—*until he prepares Jerusalem and places it as a place of praise in the earth.* In this verse, he commands those who are able from all the people to pray and *not to be silent or keep quiet.* For they are not *to allow* God *rest* but are to awaken him with cries and relentless shouts, so that he should keep the promises to the end.

[62:8-9] To those who cry aloud and do not acquiesce, he promises that they will be lifted up to the Lord and says: "While you are still speaking, I will say, 'Here am I,'"[3] for he will deem them worthy of an answer. Therefore, he continues on to say next: *The Lord has sworn by his glory and by his mighty arm: I will not again give your grain and your food to your enemies, and not again shall foreign sons drink your wine, for which you have labored.* For it

---

Chapter Sixty-Two [1] 2 Tim 4:7-8a. [2] Is 62:1. [3] Is 58:9.

used to be so, that they handed over their crop as *food* for the *enemies* of God and acted so that their deeds were the provision of demons. But now, to those who have been deemed worthy of the new age and prepared for the promises, the Lord swears an oath that he will no longer *give* their crops *to enemies*; instead, they shall enjoy them. For those who succeed in living a virtuous life and spend their time in God-fearing and righteous activities shall enjoy their own crops, even as the verse says: "The labors of your crops *you shall eat*."[4] And he says, *they shall eat and drink in my holy courts.* Perhaps the *courts*—or according to the other Greek translations, *chambers*—that he then mentions are the **[385]** "many rooms by the Father,"[5] and he afterwards mentions the temple.

[62:10-11] Therefore, he continues on to say next: *Go, go through my gates, and make a way for my people, and cast the stones out of the way.* This verse seems to refer to "the heavenly city of God"[6] and its *gates* and the *chambers* within the city. All these things will then be displayed to those who are worthy in the promised age, and he will say: *Go, go through my gates.* Then, he says, let no hindrance or impediment or any ill will or envy or pretense or demon or evil spirit or adversarial power prevent my people from entering into the kingdom of heaven. And he said these things to the angelic powers. He continues on to say: *Raise up a signal for the nations. For see, the Lord has made it to be heard to the end of the earth.* For, he says, let not anyone suppose that these things have been said concerning the Jewish people, for he commands *a signal to be raised for* all *the nations*, and he proclaims his message for all *until the ends of the earth.* Then he clearly teaches that the *daughter of Zion*—the church—is to expect her Savior when he says: *Say to the daughter of Zion.* And he called the new church of God, who received a new name,

daughter of Zion, because she is the daughter of the godly commonwealth that was formerly among the Jews. It is she whom he addresses when he says: *See, your Savior has come to you, having his own reward.* And one should note that this verse repeats an earlier verse: "See, the Lord comes with strength; see, *his reward* is with him *and his work* is before him";[7] and now: *Say to the daughter of Zion, "See, your Savior has come to you, having with him his own reward and his work before him."* Therefore, this verse refers to the Savior during his first coming long ago, when he worked and suffered on behalf of the race of humankind and secured salvation from God for those who believe in him—in him who "was called Jesus,"[8] according to the testimony of the angel. But the verse also refers to his second advent, for the Word introduces him as the judge and giver of rewards.

[62:12] *And he shall call it a holy people, redeemed by the Lord.* But instead of *And he shall call it,* the text in the other Greek translations reads: *and they shall call them,* clearly speaking about those who will be saved. They, therefore, *shall be called a holy people, redeemed by the Lord, and you the city* of God, and it is to them that it has been said: *You shall be called "A City Sought After" and "Not Forsaken."* Jerusalem had been *forsaken* **[386]** and had been *called* so, but it is concerning this city that the Word says it will be *sought after and not forsaken.* "For the one who came *to seek* and to save the lost"[9] found it and saved it and granted that it would never again be destroyed.

[63:1] Just as it was said to those who walk in godliness that the Savior would come *having his own reward* and that he should recompense and award the prize of the above titles to those who contended for godliness, so also it is prophesied that the terrible avenger will come

---

[4]Ps 128:2. [5]Jn 14:2. [6]Heb 12:22. [7]Is 40:10. [8]Mt 1:21. [9]Lk 10:19.

to the ungodly and those who went the opposite way. For it was said above: "And it shall be that as a bridegroom shall rejoice over a bride, so shall the Lord rejoice over you,"[1] and everything else that the Word promised to those who walk uprightly. But the passage above also describes the judgment of the ungodly, in which judgment "he will put all enemies under his feet."[2] This is what the divine apostle teaches when he says: "Then comes the end, when he destroys every rule and every authority and power. For he must reign until he has put all his enemies under his feet. The last enemy to be destroyed is death."[3] And, therefore, the present prophecy signals the demolition of these adversarial powers and rulers and authorities. The Word poses questions as though from the perspective of one who sees the Christ of God approaching in military array and his clothing stained with blood, and they are amazed at the strangeness of his appearance and say to one another: *"Who is this that comes from Edom, a redness of garments from Bosor, so beautiful in his apparel, in might, with strength?"* But according to Symmachus, the text reads: *"Who is this one who comes from Edom, whose clothing from Bosor is dyed red, so stylish in his apparel, marching forward in his strength?"* Because *Edom* and *Bosor* were lands of foreigners who had always been enemies of Israel, it was appropriate that he should allude to the adversarial powers in these names, which they say have been destroyed and whose *clothing* has been stained with blood as though slaughtered. Because they had seen him act far differently in avenging the ungodly, they did not seem to know that he was cheerful and peaceful and gentle. For this reason, they inquire and say: *"Who is this that comes?"* He answers them and says: *"I discourse about righteousness and judgment of salvation."* But according to Symmachus, the text reads: *I speak in right-*

eousness, fighting in order to save. For he *fights* for those who are unjustly subdued by the adversarial powers, pursuing the enemies and saving and setting free those under the domination of the enemies.

[63:2-3] [387] After this answer, they ask him a second question and say: *"Why are your garments red, and your clothes as if from a trodden wine press, completely trampled?"* But according to Symmachus, the text reads: *"Why have your clothes and your garments become fiery red as a trodden wine press?"* And he does not refuse to teach that this happened. Therefore, according to Symmachus, the text continues on to say: *I alone trod on the wine press, and from the people there is not one with me, and I trod on them in my wrath, and I trod them down in my anger, and their triumph was sprinkled on my garments, and I stained all my clothes.* Note that the text reads: *I alone have trampled the wine press.* For it was to him alone that "the Father has given judgment,"[4] and it is usual to refer to the extraction of sins as a *wine press.* Therefore, Jeremiah writes in Lamentations: "The Lord *trod the wine vat* for his virgin daughter Judah. For these things I weep."[5] But just as the chastisement of sins and the dishonor that comes from them and the extraction and retribution for sins is called a *wine press,* so also God-loving people and those who are pleasing to God are *wine presses* because of the good fruits that they have gathered in from the good vine, concerning whom the "hymns over the wine vats"[6] have been written in the Psalms. But the text says that he *alone trod the wine press* and no one joined in with him, and he put under his feet all his enemies during the time of the vengeance, "when he destroyed every rule and every authority and power. For he must reign until he has put all enemies under his feet."[7] And, therefore, after subduing his enemies and

---

Chapter Sixty-Three [1]Is 62:5. [2]Ps 110:1. [3]1 Cor 15:24-26. [4]Jn 5:22. [5]Lam 1:15. [6]Cf. Ps 8:1. [7]1 Cor 15:24b-25.

crushing to bits their descendents so that nothing at all remains of the enemy or of the devil or of demons or of evil or of sin, he will bring before the Father those who will reign in the new age, "when he will deliver the kingdom to God the Father,"[8] according to the apostle. It is said expressively in a word picture that *he stains* his *clothes* so that they are *red*. And this is the *blood* of his enemies, concerning which he says: *And brought down their blood to the earth*. But if one understands that this *blood* from the adversarial powers is not physical, then is not one to admit that these things are to be understood figuratively?

[63:4] Then he again mentions *a day of retribution* and *a year of ransom*, as it has been said above in that auspicious passage: "To proclaim the acceptable *year* of the Lord and the *day of retribution* for our God."[9] For the new age as a whole is called the *acceptable year of the Lord*, and in the new age "the Lord will be as an everlasting light."[10] And he is called the *day of retribution*, as the text reads: *A day of retribution has come to them, and a year of ransom is here*. For here we see that he will ransom his own, but [388] "he will repay" his enemies, according to the verse in the book of Moses: "And I will repay my enemies with a sentence, and those who hate me I will repay."[11]

[63:5-6] Then he says: *And I looked, but there was no one helping, and I observed, but no one was assisting; so my own arm delivered them*. We will apprehend what the Word is saying if we understand that he alone "emptied himself, taking the form of a servant and humbled himself and became obedient unto death, even death on a cross."[12] For he alone took on himself on behalf of our salvation what no mortal or angel or divine power had ever conceived, and therefore to him alone the Father "bestowed the name which is above every

name"[13] and put into his hands the judgment of all. And he received from the Father authority to *deliver* those who are worthy of salvation and to put to flight his adversaries and enemies. For this reason, the text reads: *And my wrath was present, and I trampled them down, and I brought down their blood to the earth*. Instead of *their blood*, the other Greek translations render this phrase as: *their victory*. For, although they once seemed as though they were unbreakable and would surrender the victory to no one, he rightly alludes to their defeat and humiliation when he says that *their victory has been brought down to the earth*.

[63:7-8] The prophecy above delineates the second coming of Christ, but the Word now begins another subject in which he declares the kindness of God to the people of the Jews. And he voices his accusation as from the mouth of the people, presenting through his statement the abandonment and final desolation of Jerusalem that has happened in the righteous judgment of God. Therefore, he says: *I called to mind the mercy of the Lord*, and he continues on: *The virtues of the Lord I shall recall*. And I shall surely never let the incredible kindness of his *mercy* slip into forgetfulness, but *I shall always call to mind* his *mercy* and the marvelous deeds that he showed to us. We may be saddened to know that the nation and the city of Jerusalem came under the anger of God in the end, when its temple was delivered over to be destroyed to the very foundations. But instead of *in all the things which he rewards us*, Symmachus says: *Concerning all the things in which he showed us kindness*. And, again, instead of *the Lord is a good judge to the house of Israel*, and so on, Symmachus says: *The Lord showed an abundance of goodness to the house of Israel, who showed them kindness according to his compassion*. Therefore, he says *I shall recall all these things and enumerate the abundance*

---

[8]1 Cor 15:24. [9]Is 61:2. [10]Cf. Is 60:19. [11]Deut 32:43. [12]Phil 2:7-8. [13]Phil 2:9.

of his goodness, whereby he granted them vast grace and deemed the people worthy to be called "his *children*" if "they do not *reject* his grace."[14] Therefore, [389] according to Symmachus, the text reads: *Nevertheless they are my people, although they have not acted faithfully.* He convicted them at the beginning of the prophecy when he said: "I begat *sons* and exalted them, but they *rejected* me."[15]

[63:9] Therefore, he begins anew and presses on to the salvation of his people, bringing the news himself and announcing to them the abundance of his goodness himself and not through others. For this reason, he says: *It was no ambassador or angel but he himself saved them, because he loved them and spared them,* and so on. But they presented themselves as unworthy of such benevolence and of his kindness, and they tried to cast him as their enemy. And so the one who had freely offered such good things to them declared himself to be their enemy, reminding them that the situation had not always been as it is now. But even from the beginning of his advent, they had always been cruel and insensitive to the kindness of God.

[63:10-14] Therefore, although they had been deemed worthy of witnessing the innumerable acts of incredible kindness performed by Moses, they did not at all reflect on who it was who was showing them kindness,[16] neither did they reason among themselves who it was who displayed such wonders to them. But "they made a calf"[17] and committed idolatry and committed countless other acts of ungodliness in the wilderness, while it never crossed their minds that *he led them through* the Red *Sea,* and he set *Moses* as the *shepherd of the sheep* over them, whom he demonstrated to be his great "prophet"[18] and "servant"[19] and whom he

filled with his own *Spirit.* But instead of *he overcame water from before him,* Symmachus says: *The one who struck the waters before them to make among them an everlasting name.* Therefore, although he *split* the *waters* of the Red *Sea like a horse through a wilderness and led them as cattle through a plain* because he had dried up the *waters,* they did not remember these things, and it is concerning them that the Word says *they disobeyed and provoked his Holy Spirit.* It is for this reason that he says: *Therefore he turned to them in enmity, and he himself warred against them.*

[63:15-16] The one who had once defended them judged them with an upright word and in righteousness, but because God is in his nature benevolent and good, we should not become insensitive or despair of receiving salvation from him. For it is possible that if we devote ourselves to supplications and confessions we will procure atonement. Therefore, all together—I the prophet say these things as do you who have been chosen to live godly lives among the people—we earnestly entreat and plead with carefully prepared requests: *Turn from heaven, and see from your holy house and glory.* And if we demonstrate to him a change from the worse to the better, we say: *and see, O Lord, and remember that* [390] you often acted graciously toward us, not because of anything we have done but because of your *zeal,* and even though we are unworthy yet you offer your *mercy.* Therefore, *where is your zeal and your strength and the abundance of your mercy?* Now and then, because we had often sinned, *you held back from us,* and no wonder, since you had deemed us worthy to say about us: "My people are my children, and my people are my sons."[20] Therefore, as our *father* once *held back* from his children, so also now again *you held back.* For *Abraham* was not *our father,*

---

[14]Cf. Gal 2:21. [15]Is 1:2. [16]Literally, "they did not at all place before their eyes the one who showed kindness." [17]Cf. Acts 7:41. [18]Cf. Hos 12:14; Wis 11:1. [19]Cf. Num 12:7; Heb 3:5. [20]Cf. Is 63:8.

and even though it seems that our race stems from him according to the flesh, in the true sense *you are our father*, inasmuch as you are "the *Father* of all spirits"[21] and of all souls that have been "made according to your image."[22] Therefore, we beg you *to deliver* us, because we claim for ourselves *your name*. For this reason, show kindness "to your *name*, lest it be blasphemed among the nations,"[23] and deem us worthy of your *mercy*.

[63:17-18] In the passage above, the prophet spoke in his own voice and in the voice of the pious from among the people, but then he continues to speak in the voice of those from among the people who love to accuse and who love to find fault with others and many times who do not even hesitate to blame God himself. Therefore, he says: *Why, O Lord, did you make us stray from your way, and harden our hearts so that we would not fear you?* He speaks these things from the voice of the people. For, he says, as *you hardened* "Pharaoh's heart"[24] then, so now judge us worthy to fear you. And you yourself *caused us to stray*, O Lord, so that we did not know *your way*. But even if we acted in such a way, nevertheless, because you are God, we beseech you *on account of your servants*, and because we acted in such a way along with all the people, *turn back*. Because we were deemed worthy to be called your portion, we beseech you: *Turn back on account of your servants and on account of the tribes of your inheritance.* We beseech you in order that, because we are *your servants and the tribes of your inheritance*, even we might be found to be worthy of a *little* part of the *holy mountain* that you promised. Although now we have completely fallen away, because *our adversaries have trampled down your holy precinct.*

[63:19] And they did this because you abandoned us. And so, since we have been deprived

of your presence we have now become desolate, even as *we were at the beginning*. For this was the time when we had "neither prophets nor priests nor kings"[25] nor any of your graces, so also now we find ourselves in [391] that same desolate state. And such was our condition during the many years we passed in Egypt before Moses had been set over us. For at that time you had neither adorned us with *your name* nor called us "your people"[26] or "the portion of your inheritance,"[27] but now we have circled around to the same end. It seems that all these things refer to the time after the coming of our Savior, when they were completely abandoned because of the things that they dared to do against our Savior. For truly *we have become such ones as at the beginning, when God did not rule* them.

[64:1-3] But instead of *if you should open heaven, trembling from you would seize the mountains*, and so on, Symmachus translated the text in this way: *We have become as from an age over whom you would not exercise authority, nor was your name called on among them, nor did you come down after striking the mountains. The mountains collapsed before your face; the sea melted as burning fire; the waters were terrified.* And he says that we have become such as those who never experienced your wonders and to whom you did not show the wonderful works you performed through Moses. But according to the Septuagint, the text reads: *We have become as we were before you ruled us.* Nevertheless, we know most definitely and are persuaded that if you want *to open heaven*, because you are God and able to do all things, *trembling from you would seize the mountains*—clearly, the adversarial powers that raise themselves up against your knowledge—*and they would melt as wax from the fire, and fire would consume the adversaries* of your divinity. In fact, the power of your *name* will be displayed before all your

---

[21]Cf. Heb 12:9. [22]Gen 1:26. [23]Cf. Is 52:5. [24]Ex 7:3. [25]Cf. Hos 3:4; Ez 7:26; Lam 2:9. [26]Cf. Ex 3:7. [27]Cf. Ps 15:5; see also Sir 24:12.

enemies and "the nations that do not know God."[1] If you are willing simply to *lay open* your *heaven* and visit those on the earth, *they shall be terrified*, and *trembling from you would seize* the aforementioned *mountains*.

[64:4] Such power is at your command as *from ages past we have not heard*. We are not able to say truthfully that there is any other God, nor have *our eyes* seen any other creator of such works, nor do we know of another God *besides you* who performs divine works. And the works that you performed *for those who wait* on you to see, we considered to have been done by another. Therefore, it is established that God has been seen, since the prophetic word introduces him as such when it speaks in the voice of the people: *Nor have our eyes seen any God besides you*. And yet, because "no one has ever seen God,"[2] and "no one shall see my face and live,"[3] it seems that this verse is alluding to the Christ of God and to the one who conversed with Moses in the wilderness, who was seen by all the people in the glory [392] that appeared to all, concerning which it has been said: "And all the people saw the glory of the Lord."[4]

[64:5-6] After these things, the text continues on: *Look, you were angry, and we sinned*—this could be said more clearly, because *we sinned, you were angry*—and he also says: *We went astray, and we have all become like unclean people*. If anyone thought that there were righteousness and righteous deeds found among us, our righteousness has been discovered to be filthy and exposed as dishonorable. For this reason, we have become like a fruitless tree that has cast off its fruit, and *we have all fallen off like leaves*, and we have been scattered abroad "like dust before the *wind*."[5]

[64:7-12] He says that there is no one among us

who calls on your name and who is able to plead with you through prayers. There is no one who clings to you or remembers the help that you gave. Therefore, it is with good reason that he says: *You have turned your face away from us*. And yet we know that *you are our Father*, and we know well that we also are nothing but *clay*, of which *you* alone are the sculptor, and we are a fragile earthenware vessel, good for nothing but to be broken apart and shattered. Therefore, looking to you in the impotence of our weakness, we plead with you to pardon those who have sinned, reminding you that we once called ourselves your *people* and your *city*, which is now a *wilderness*, and your sanctuary, which has now been demolished. And we remind you that *the house of your holiness* has been turned into *a curse*, and the place *blessed by our ancestors* has been delivered over to *fire*. But according to Symmachus, the text reads: *Jerusalem has become a wilderness; our house of holiness where our ancestors praised you has been destined for destruction and burning fire, and everything that we held in esteem has been destined for disgrace. You did not intervene in these things, Lord, but you were silent and humiliated us terribly.*

[65:1] To the statements set forth above—which were spoken in the voice of the people and which related supplications and confessions and even censure, as in the verse: "You have made us stray from your way and hardened our hearts so that we would not fear you"[1]—the prophetic Spirit gives the following answer. How can you say this of me, who "does not wish the death of the sinner but the repentance"[2] of those who pray such things and confess to have overlooked my commands? And how is it possible for me, the one who wills all people to turn from error to the truth and the one who calls "those who fall to rise up"[3]—how is it possible for me to cause you

---

Chapter Sixty-Four   [1]Cf. Jer 10:25; 1 Thess 4:5.   [2]Jn 1:18.   [3]Ex 33:20.   [4]Cf. Ex 20:18; Lev 9:23.   [5]Cf. Ps 18:42; 35:5.   **Chapter Sixty-Five**   [1]Is 63:17.   [2]Ezek 33:11.   [3]Cf. Jer 8:4.

"to stray from my way" or "to harden your hearts so that they would not fear me"?[4] And, certainly, if anyone wants to reflect on my benevolence in an evenhanded manner, he will find that I extend my kindness [393] even to those who have removed my knowledge far away from them. And, therefore, *to those who* never *inquired about me* I have now made myself *visible* because of my abounding benevolence, in order that the foreign races and foreign tribes should receive my knowledge, although they aided nothing in this process. I shared my grace with *those who did not seek* it, and I extended consolation to others. Before you prayed and before you beseeched me, *I said*, *"Here I am."*

[65:2] Therefore, why is it that to those who were strangers to my knowledge, I became gentle and kind, but to you I appeared fierce and hard and most unjust? And, certainly, I initiated in giving you my grace, and *I stretched out my hands* to you first, and I took you in my arms as my legitimate children. But although you *disobeyed*, you continue to call and demand that I hasten to bring my salvation.

[65:3-4] You traveled in the opposite direction, multiplying your evil deeds. Do you not continually *provoke me* when you abandon the temple that has been dedicated to me, or when you give yourselves up to idolatry and the error of polytheism and *sacrifice in the gardens* and *burn incense* to unclean spirits and evil *demons* on the brick altars that you have prepared or when you *sleep in the tombs and in the caves?* And you somehow imagined the things that are supposed to represent the supernatural power of the gods to be oracles. And why would this be except that they are compared with Gentiles without the law who gorge themselves on pigs' *flesh* and who do not hesitate to *defile all the vessels* with abominable sacrifices?

[65:5] But this is the worst sin, and it especially fills God with anger and vexes him, because they are proud of their good deeds and think of themselves as more pure than all other people, so that that they do not even want to associate with those around them, nor do they deem their neighbors worthy of their attention. Instead, they *say* to those present: *Do not come near me, for I am clean.* Therefore, then, because their deeds are not more righteous, will not the aforesaid *wrath* of God be stirred up against them—clearly, the avenging power—and a *fire* kindled against them?

[65:6-7] For it is *recorded before me* that these things shall not happen until they repay vengeance on their behalf—and not vengeance on their behalf alone, but also on behalf of *their ancestors* who acted in an ungodly manner, *burning incense on the mountains* and committing idolatry *on the hills* and scoffing at my laws—until the time when *it shall be repaid into their bosom.*

[65:8-9] These things have been spoken against the ungodly among the people, but it may be that among the multitude someone is found who has hope of salvation, and he is free of the things that have been said above. For we remember that "the vineyard of the Lord Sabaoth is the house of Israel,"[5] and "instead of grapes [394] it produced thorns,"[6] and "instead of justice it produced lawlessness, and not righteousness but a cry."[7] Because of the absence of these good things, it has been determined that it should be absolutely destroyed, but if some wholesome and desirable *grape should be found as in a* dry *cluster* destined for destruction, this one shall not fall away in my judgment, neither shall he perish along with those who are destroyed, because he shares in the *blessing.* And so it shall be with this worthy and rare *grape* before me. In accord

---

[4]Cf. Is 63:17. [5]Is 5:7. [6]Is 5:2. [7]Is 5:7.

with this example, so shall I do to every nation, if any *should be found* worthy of salvation among them. For this reason, *I will not destroy them all*, but *I will bring forth the one who is subject to me* among them and separate him from the ones who are to be destroyed. And this one shall be an *offspring from Jacob, an offspring* and a useful spark, who shall be able to be useful and bear fruit for others. And this is the one concerning whom the following verse speaks: "And if the Lord Sabaoth had not left us *offspring*."[8] This good and wholesome *offspring*—clearly, the apostolic band that was separated from the multitude of those who were destroyed—*will inherit my holy mountain*. And this is what they claimed to make known when they said: "We have come to *Mount* Zion and to the city of the living God, the heavenly Jerusalem."[9] In this verse he says *my chosen ones and my slaves* shall receive a heavenly inheritance and *shall dwell there*. And, again, in another context, the *chosen ones* and *slaves* refer to his apostles who *have been found grapes*, which he selected while sorting through the others and called a "holy *offspring*" and *chosen*.

[65:10] He says that the next things to be fulfilled are these: *And there shall be in the forest folds of flocks*. The Scripture is accustomed to calling the multitude of foreign tribes and foreign nations a *forest*, among which he prophesies that *there shall be folds of flocks*, alluding to the churches of the sheep of God. And the *Ravine of Achor* has become a depository for stones, as the account of Joshua in the books of Moses records.[10] For *Achor*,[11] along with his whole family, was put to death in the *ravine* by stoning because of the transgression that he committed, and he was accursed. And so the land of the godless has become a depository for stones—clearly, the nations of the foreign tribes. This land *shall become a resting place of herds for my people for those who*

have sought me. And the *people who have sought* him were the *grape* and the *offspring* spoken of above, his *chosen slaves*, through whom he calls aloud and prophesies that the *herds* and *flocks* shall be settled neither in Israel nor in the land of the Jews but *in the forest* and in the aforementioned *Ravine of Achor*.

[65:11-12] Therefore, he says these things to them, but again the Word inveighs against the Jewish people and says: *But as for you who forsake me and forget my holy mountain*, an expression which has often indicated us. Those [395] of the nations who engage in idolatry and who dedicate offerings *for Fortune* among them and who set the *table for the demon*—the *demon* who lurks in the aforementioned image of *Fortune*, to whom *mixed drinks* are offered—listen to what awaits you: *You shall all be delivered over to a* hostile *dagger*. And if any of you should inquire as to the reason why, I answer: In order that I may pass by the rest, because I myself deemed you worthy of my coming, and *I called you* first of my own initiative, but *you did not answer*. Is this not what I said earlier when I accused: "Because I came and no one was there; I called, and there was none to answer"?[12] Now again I say: *Because I called you and you did not answer, I spoke and you misheard, and you did what was evil before me and chose the things I did not desire*. Therefore, *I called you* first, and I first extended to you the offer of my grace, but you were inattentive and disobedient, even disparaging and blaming and accusing and daring to say: "You made us stray from your way, O Lord."[13] Therefore, I refuted this impious voice when I said earlier: "I became visible to those who were not inquiring about me, and I was found by those who were not seeking me," and: " 'Behold,' I said to those who did not call on my name, 'Here I am.'"[14] On the contrary, although you were being called and addressed,

---

[8]Is 1:9. [9]Heb 12:22. [10]Josh 7:24-26. [11]It seems that Eusebius means Achan here. [12]Is 50:2. [13]Is 63:17. [14]Is 65:1.

you absolutely did not *answer* but insulted the grace that I once imparted to you.

[65:13-14] The Word proclaims that the nations will be chosen from the Jews, and, like good seed, they will be kept for planting and fruitfulness among others. These very nations shall establish "folds of flocks in the forest,"[15] and "in the Ravine of Achor" that was referred to above they shall make "resting places of herds." Then the Word pronounces anew what are set forth next to the multitude of those who will be destroyed. He makes the above accusations against them and teaches that the God of righteousness, who does all things judiciously, will certainly not overlook where those who are *subject* to him have come from and among which nations they may be. For he will receive absolutely every one of those who are *subject* to him, and to them he will supply heavenly food—the saving Word who said: "I am the bread which came down from heaven."[16] On the one hand, therefore, they shall be nourished and satisfied with the one who was called "bread," but on the other hand, he says that *you* who do not receive my grace, *you shall be famished* and lack spiritual food. And, again, those who are *subject to me* shall be filled with a drink of immortal life, concerning which it has been said: "Whoever drinks of the water that I shall give him, it shall become in him a spring of water welling up to eternal life."[17] *But you* who "reject"[18] my "grace," inasmuch as "they abandoned the fountain of life,"[19] *you shall be thirsty.* And, again, *those who are subject* [396] *to me* shall be deemed worthy to partake of the inspired joy of the drink and food, *but you* who spit on my grace *shall be put to shame* because you shall be deprived of these things. And *those who are subject to me shall be glad with joy*, rightly rejoicing in their souls, inasmuch as they are deemed worthy of such good things, *but you*, when you see them

enjoying these things, *you shall cry out* from *the pain* of your soul, *and you shall wail for crushing of spirit.* For the *pain* of the body is a small thing compared with the *pain* of the *heart*, and therefore it is not the *pain* of the body but the *pain* of the *heart* that you shall experience, suffering and sending forth screams and cries for those who destroyed themselves.

[65:15-16] But instead of *for you shall leave your name for fullness*, the other Greek translations render the text in a way that makes better sense: *For an oath.* It is often the case that those who suffer terrible things swear an oath. We certainly shall not suffer things equal to what they have suffered, and just as *your name* shall be *an oath to my chosen ones*, so *your name* shall be shunned because of what shall happen to you, and so *your name* and the memory of your evil deeds shall be *to my chosen ones for an oath.* But, finally, your evil deeds shall overtake you, and death shall suddenly come on you and separate you from God himself. This will not be a separation of the soul from the body but a loss of immortal life and God himself. These things therefore will await you, *but to those who are subject to me* the promises shall be granted, regardless of the nation from which they come. If you are curious and wish to learn who these who will be *subject to me* are and what their *name* is, you know that God does not yet wish to bring their name out into the open. All that he indicates is that they shall neither be called Israel nor Jacob nor Jews nor anything other than people as generally understood.

For some *new*, fresh and foreign *name* shall be given to them, a name such as has never been heard, *which shall be blessed on the earth*, exalted and magnified above every physical blessing. For there is no more magnificent and creative blessing from God than that the *name* shall be given *to those who are subject to me.*

---

[15]Is 65:10. [16]Jn 6:41. [17]Jn 4:14. [18]Cf. Gal 2:21. [19]Cf. Jer 2:13.

Therefore, let no one be inquisitive at present before the fulfillment of these events, but let those who are said to be *blessed* continue *blessing the true God.*

And instead of *the true God,* Aquila says: *And he shall call his slaves another name, by which the blessed one shall surely be blessed in the earth.* And Symmachus says: *But he shall call his servants another name, by which the blessed one on the earth shall be blessed by God. Amen.* For just as they say *they shall bless the true God,* so *they shall surely be blessed,* or according to Symmachus: *Amen. And those who swear on the earth*—those who shall be *subject to me*—*they shall swear by the true God.* And they shall no longer be deceived by those that are thought to be gods, but, learning from the Savior, **[397]** they shall come to know "the only true God, and the Lord Jesus Christ whom he sent."[20] The ones who shall be *subject* to him *shall forget the first affliction*—the *affliction* to which they were once subjected, since they had been subdued by the evil demons. *And* the distress of the error of idolatry *shall not come up into their heart,* and because they have turned from darkness to light, they shall erase their memories of the former condition.

[65:17-18] And so, for them *heaven will be new and the earth will be new.* For, although they once looked to *heaven* and "worshiped the creature rather than the creator"[21] and likewise deified the *earth* and the fruits that it brought forth, when they shall see the *new heaven* and the *new earth* they shall confess that these things are "works of God's hands"[22] and no longer suppose them to be gods. Therefore, he continues on: *They shall not remember the former things, nor shall they come on their heart, but they shall find joy and gladness,* sharing in the fountain of good things. And then *I myself*—the God who is able to do all things—*I shall make Jerusalem as*

gladness for them. For this *gladness* and this *joy* along with pure godliness shall all be theirs from God. I will set *Jerusalem and my people in joy,* and it is to that *new people* that I promised to give a *new name.*

[65:19-20] And *I myself, God, will be glad over Jerusalem*—clearly, I will behold the godly commonwealth of those who will be "subject to me,"[23] and I will judge it in my presence to be far superior to the bodily Jerusalem. Therefore, *I will be glad* over it *and rejoice over my people.* The godly polity "of those who are subject to me"[24] shall practice such things, and so the works and deeds of *weeping* and *crying shall no more be heard among them, neither shall there be one who dies untimely or an old person there.* For everyone there shall have experienced the resurrection in my presence during the time of the promises, and everyone shall have souls "to mature manhood, to the measure of the stature."[25] Everyone shall be in the prime of life, so that there shall be found among them neither an *untimely* infant who has not grown up nor one who is spent and who has grown old. But all shall be equal in age, because all shall come into existence at one time in the resurrection, and all shall share in one rebirth. Therefore, the *young person* who is saved shall be mature and at the prime of life at, as it were, *a hundred years old,* and the *sinner* who is destroyed shall be of the same age. They shall come to life again at the same time and shall be equal in age, since they will experience the resurrection "of eternal life"[26] at the same time. But those who shall be subject "to the second death"[27] shall be delivered over to "punishment"[28] and vengeance against their souls. And, surprisingly, just as he says that the *young person* who is saved shall be *a hundred years old,* so likewise he says the *sinner* shall be *a hundred years old,* and so he states that they will experience the resurrec-

---

[20]Jn 17:3. [21]Rom 1:25. [22]Cf. Ps 102:25. [23]Cf. Is 65:13. [24]Cf. Is 65:13. [25]Eph 4:13. [26]Mt 25:46. [27]Rev 2:11. [28]Mt 25:46.

tion of the dead [398] at the same time. Therefore, the *sinner shall* also *be a hundred years old, and he shall be accursed*, and he shall die in the prime of life, when his evil sin is mature. Again a *young person shall be a hundred years old*, and when he is mature he shall at last be welcomed into salvation.

[65:21-22] And these *shall build houses, and they themselves shall inhabit them*. For by their works and their own deeds they shall secure for themselves "the rooms in the presence of the Father,"[29] and "the *labors* of their crops *they shall eat*."[30] Therefore, they shall farm such things, and they shall harvest and acquire and be nourished from these things, no longer anxious that anyone will seize their *labors*. For this reason, the text reads: *They shall not build and others inhabit; they shall not plant and others eat*, but they shall live in an endless age of immortal bliss. Therefore, it has been said: *For according to the days of the tree of life shall the days of my people be*, and: "They have been planted in the paradise of God."[31] Therefore, they demonstrate that the promises do not apply outside of the paradise of God. He is clearly speaking about eternal and immortal *life* when he says: *For according to the days of the tree of life shall the days of my people be*. Elsewhere Solomon teaches that the wisdom of God is a *tree of life* when he says: "It is a tree of life to all those who lay claim to it, and it is steadfast to those who lean on it, as on the Lord."[32] But as the wisdom of God is everlasting and "an eternal fountain *of life*,"[33] so, the Word promises, shall be the *days* of the *people*. Why else would he prophesy above such happiness for them? And, he says, I shall do these things for my people, "and I shall rejoice over my people."[34] *For according to the days of the tree of life shall the days of my people be*. In this verse, he clearly introduces for himself another people

than the nation of the Jews. And he says: *They shall make old the works of their labors*. For they shall not *become old*, neither will those who will then cease from their *labors* in life leave to others their *fruit*, but they shall receive for themselves *the works of their labors*, and they shall delight in their own fruits.

[65:23] God promises all these things neither to those who are special nor "to the called." "For many are called, but few are chosen."[35] For this reason, he announced beforehand to the *chosen* and said: *My chosen ones shall not labor in vain or bear children for a curse*. For there shall be some sort of saving and good and pleasurable work during the time of the promises—perhaps such as which the angelic order performs—but their business shall not be in vain. [399] For they have treasured up "deserved wages"[36] for themselves. Their *descendents* shall not be *for a curse*—and here we should understand *descendents* to signify the spiritual fruits of the soul and intellect—and while others shall be worthy of a *curse*, he prophesies that they shall be worthy of a blessing. And *their offspring is blessed by God*. It is possible to interpret these things as concerning the present life. For as from the beginning so again the Word alludes to the apostolic band in the verse: *My chosen ones shall not labor in vain or bear children for a curse*. One needs only to open one's eyes to see that the labors of the apostles have not been *in vain*, for the church that they established can be found throughout the whole world. And we understand that their children are those who have been born again in Christ "through the washing of regeneration."[37] We understand that they have not been born *for a curse*, although they had been placed under the *curse* in Adam, and it had been said to the woman: "With pains you will bring forth children. And your recourse will be to your husband."[38] Our first parents *bore* according to

---

[29]Jn 14:2. [30]Cf. Ps 128:2. [31]Rev 2:7. [32]Prov 3:18. [33]Jn 4:14. [34]Is 65:19. [35]Mt 22:14. [36]Cf. Lk 10:7; see also 1 Tim 5:18. [37]Tit 3:5.
[38]Gen 3:16.

the flesh, and their children were not *the chosen ones* of God. But the evangelical *offspring* which they bore among all the churches of God have become *blessed* among them—clearly, among the *chosen ones* of God, the apostles and disciples and evangelists of our Savior.[39]

[65:24-25] He promises something else and says: *And it shall be that before they have cried out I will listen to them; while they are yet speaking I will say, "What is it?"* These things were then fulfilled in the deeds of the apostles. For God displayed "many signs and wonders"[40] through them, and they performed such things, and then came the conversion of the foreign nations. Those who used to be rapacious and savage so as to be compared with *wolves* changed and became as tame as *lambs* and *oxen*, and they flocked together as one and partook of the same spiritual food of the divine reading.

Those who used to live no differently than *lions*, carnivorous beasts who consumed raw flesh, became like *oxen* and ate the grass of the inspired teaching. And the person who used to be like a snake, full of venom and spitting out the evil that resided in him, *shall eat bread*, living off of spiritual food fit for humans, instead of the *earth* which he used to eat. And thus these beasts shall be tamed so that they shall *do* nothing *wrong* or *destroy* anything *in the mountain* of God, in which also they shall spend their lives because of the change in their way of life. It is fitting for the Jews that these things shall come in a physical sense [**400**] to Jerusalem. They expect to say first that nothing good concerning them will be remembered, but only reproaches and insults with accusations of their ungodliness. Why then is it necessary that there should be *lions* and *wolves* and *snakes in the holy mountain* and in Jerusalem itself? The reason is that it demonstrates the validity of the promise of God, that *in the holy mountain* of God *snakes* and *lions* and *wolves* should spend their lives together in blessedness. Clearly these animals refer to different kinds of people.

[66:1-3] Then he mentions his *holy mountain*, adding on forcefully: *Thus says the Lord: Heaven is my throne, and the earth is the footstool of my feet; what kind of house will you build for me, says the Lord, or of what kind will be the place of my rest? For all these things my hand has made, and all these things are mine, says the Lord.* In this verse, he clearly refers to the Jerusalem on earth, indicating that it will not be on the physical mountain where the promises will be rendered to those who are worthy. As the verse above says: "For heaven will be new, and they shall not remember the former things, nor shall they come on their heart."[1] Then "heaven will be new and earth will be new,"[2] and there will no longer be remembrance "of the former things," and there will be remembrance neither of the physical mountain nor of the earthly Jerusalem. Then, speaking to the refutation of the Jewish prejudice, he adds: *What kind of house will you build for me? says the Lord, or of what kind will be the place of my rest? For all these things my hand has made, and all these things are mine.* What should we expect the house of God on earth to be, or what should we interpret the Jerusalem below to be? For if "*heaven* will be new, and the *earth* will be new,"[3] it follows, too, that such a Jerusalem will appear, and so there will no longer be any remembrance of all the "former things." The word before us then clearly introduces a "new heaven" and a "new earth" and a "new people" and a "new name"[4] and Jerusalem, and likewise it states that new doors will be constructed. It is after this verse that it continues on to say: "And they shall not remember the former things, nor shall it come on their heart."[5]

---

[39]In this last bit of exegesis, Eusebius is dealing with the phrase καὶ τὰ ἔκγονα αὐτῶν μετ' αὐτῶν ἔσονται, a phrase that is not translated in the NETS edition of the Septuagint. The phrase could be rendered: "And their descendents shall be with them."   [40]Acts 2:43.
Chapter Sixty-Six [1]Is 65:17. [2]Cf. Is 65:17. [3]Is 65:17. [4]Cf. Is 62:2. [5]Is 65:17.

And then he leads the children of the Jews into a sustained reflection on the offering of sacrifices and the slaughter of animals. God shakes off and turns aside from these things, but he says that he will receive without qualification the reverent and *humble* soul and the one who is dedicated to him. But he will turn away from libations and sacrifices. For this reason, he says: *To whom will I look but to the one who is humble and quiet and trembles at my words? But the lawless who sacrifices a calf is like one who kills a dog.* But according to the Hebrew reading and the other Greek translations, the text does not contain *but the lawless*, and when this phrase is removed the text simply continues on: *The one who slaughters a calf is like one who beats a man, and one who sacrifices out of the sheep is like one who cuts the throat of a dog, the one who offers revenue is like one offering the blood of a young pig, the one who makes mention of frankincense is like one who gives praise to wrongdoing.* Afterwards he adds: *What kind of house will you build for me, or of what kind will be the place of my rest?* [401] For the one who abolishes the *house* on earth also abolishes the activities that are performed in it. And so he continues: *And they have chosen their own ways and their abominations, which their soul wanted.*

[66:4] But, these abominations are not my will, neither are they "my ways," but they are ways of their own choosing. *So I will choose mockeries for them,* or according to the other Greek translations: *Mockery for them.*[6] They will be mocked and delivered over to those who will chastise them, *and I will repay them their sins.* But he reminds them again that these things will come on them because, as he says, *I called them and they did not answer, but they did what was evil in my sight and chose the things I did not desire.* One should note that this is already the second time that this has been said in the prophecy, since the

text says only a few verses above: "Since *I called* you and *you did not answer* me, and I spoke and you misheard, and *you did what was evil before me and chose the things I did not desire.*"[7] But when did *they not answer the one calling them* or not understand the one conversing with them, or when did he who dwelled among them call: "Come to me all, all who labor and are heavy laden, and I will give you rest"?[8] But, because they did not submit themselves to the *one calling,* because of this he will restore the promises to the worthy and they will enjoy them, but the others he will deliver over to their sins.

[66:5-6] After prophesying that all things will be new during the time of the promises, the Word then addresses those who in the verses above already learned these things during the present life and says: *Hear the word of the Lord, you who tremble at his word.* But who are these concerning whom he taught above and said: "On whom will I look but to the one who is humble and quiet and *trembles at my words?*" Therefore, he calls to those who exhibit a pious and godly manner of life in *trembling at his word* and says: *Hear the word of the Lord, you who tremble at his word; speak, our brothers, to those who hate and abominate you.* Then he delivers to them an evangelical precept that is no different from the verse: "Love your enemies, do good to those who hate you, pray for those who abusively threaten and persecute you, so that you may be children of your Father who is in heaven."[9] And so the prophecy prescribes what the Gospel also teaches. For it is not enough *to tremble* at the divine sayings and to be disposed to them in all godliness, but we must receive them and act according to the highest virtue and go to the greatest lengths of forbearance so that we call our enemies [402] *who hate us brothers,* and we do not look on those who *abominate* us as adver-

---

[6]The difference between the Greek translations that Eusebius is trying to point out is between a neuter plural and a masculine plural: ἐμπαίγματα versus ἐμπαιγμούς. [7]Is 65:12. [8]Mt 11:28. [9]Mt 5:44-45.

saries but show affection for them and love them as genuine friends. "For so you will be,"[10] says the Savior, "children of your Father who is in heaven, who makes his sun to rise on the righteous and the unrighteous and sends rain on the evil and good."[11] And the prophecy says these things: Do this, *so that the name of the Lord may be glorified and seen in their joy*, or according to Symmachus: *And we will look into your joy*. If you practice these things, your *joy* will be manifest to all when you receive your reward. But when *those ones* see their end and in fact learn of their destruction during "the righteous judgment of God,"[12] *they shall be put to shame*. For "the day of *retribution*"[13] has not yet come, when all kinds of *voices* of those who are punished will be heard—voices of the inhabitants *from* the *city* crying out, and voices of the priests and the other ministers *from* his *temple* who are removed. But at that time, the *voice* of his judge will be heard, *rendering retribution to his adversaries*. Therefore, these things are stored up for *those who hate you* and *those who abominate you*, and because of this, bear patiently the hatred and insolence that comes against you in the present life, and *speak, our brothers, to those who hate you*, and "love your enemies and do good to *those who hate* you."[14] The prophetic word seems to say these things from the perspective of the apostles of our Savior, at the moment when they were driven away by the Jews and especially by the inhabitants of Jerusalem. The promise was fulfilled when the apostles established the churches of God throughout the whole world. But the wrath of God without delay overcame those who *hated* and *abominated* them. And so, all in the *city* send up *voices* of mourning, and those who attend the *shrine* send up additional shouts because of the adversaries who surround them when God brings *retribution* on them. Therefore, it has been said: *A voice of crying from the city! A voice from the shrine! The voice of the Lord, rendering retribution to those who oppose him.*

[**66:7-9**] These things have been said to the adversaries, but the godly commonwealth and the new and renewed Zion—clearly, the church of God which will be established through you—will all at once then bear a multitude of people, so that he who hears of it shall be amazed. For as if a pregnant woman who carries a child in her womb should have no *pangs* and then suddenly bear a *male* child, so in the same manner the renewed Zion *shall give birth* to a new people and a whole *nation* suddenly, *all at once*. This is most contrary to what was expected and has never been heard of before. For the nation of the Jews and Israel [**403**] were not established in a moment, but first came their forefather and his "twelve children."[15] Then, from each one of these children came sons and daughters, and your sons and offspring and descendants were born. And so their nation came into being over the course of many years and through the succession of generations and various families. One would find that other nations also progressed in the same way and over the course of many years. But the people of the church of God filled the farthest corners of the world suddenly and in a single day. Such an astonishing event and wonder has never happened before, "neither has eye *seen* nor ear ever heard."[16] And the Lord says that he is responsible for these things, the author of incredible works, who already at that time *gave* to you *this expectation*, who reports the events that will be in the future through my prophecies, in order that when the fulfillment of the events occurs you might steadfastly believe in my words. I foretold all of this for your salvation, but *you*— the people with whom I conversed—*did not remember me*, and although you saw with your eyes you did not believe.

---

[10]Mt 5:45. [11]Mt 5:45. [12]Cf. Rom 2:5. [13]Cf. Is 61:2. [14]Mt 5:44. [15]Gen 35:22. [16]1 Cor 2:9.

The verse *you did not remember me, said the Lord* does not appear in the other Greek translations. But according to Symmachus, the text reads as follows: *Am I not the one who causes women to give birth, and do I not cause them to bring forth children, said the Lord? Am I not the one who stays beside you in birth and keeps you secure, said your God?* For, he says, how *shall a nation be born* on the earth, if not through my power? For I am the one who *causes* women to conceive in their wombs and *to give birth*, and I am the one who is responsible for the fact that they bring forth a man into the light and bring what did not formerly exist "into being."[17] Therefore, am I not the one who performs these things in physical birth, and will I not be the one who performs the future birth of an entire nation? By whom will the nation be *caused* to be born all at once if not by me, and who else could bring about this divine birth immediately, safely and without pain? Is it *not I the Lord* who am the one who continually *causes to bring forth* what is born and who *keeps* pregnancies *secure* so that the baby remains concealed in the womb?

[66:10-11] How then is it possible for me to do these things—I who establish by my divine and saving power all those who come "into being from nonexistence"[18] through physical generation? For in the verse that follows, he does not say that some of those who hear these things should *rejoice* and be full of gladness at the new Jerusalem but *all* who hear. And we should no longer understand Jerusalem as the city of lifeless stones but rather as the city built from the souls of the saints, and we *rejoice and celebrate* the feast *together* not outside of it but *in it.* And, he says, *rejoice over it, all* of you who see it—the new and renewed city—and *all* of you who once *mourned* from afar over the punishment it had received. For, as Paul says:

"While we are in this tent we groan and are burdened"[19] "and long to put on our heavenly dwelling."[20] But now, because you have received that over which you once groaned and mourned and that for which you once longed, "rejoice and be glad"[21] because you are about *to be satisfied* **[404]** with her milk. For she is the one who afterward all at once gave birth to a *male* people for God, and her children were satisfied and nourished by her milk. And, "spiritual milk"[22] shall flow from her two breasts—clearly, from the Old and New Testaments. From both of her breasts "spiritual milk" shall flow, as it said in the Song of Songs: "Your breasts are better than wine."[23] For they nourish her children with "pure and spiritual milk"[24] that turns them into mature people. For this reason, the comforting and consoling words for the immature souls are properly called "milk,"[25] but the "solid food"[26] lies in reflecting on mystical doctrines and in contemplating the divine Scriptures. But you, children of the New Jerusalem and "newborn babes,"[27] *rejoice*—you who hear these things—because you will soon enjoy and be nourished in the promises of God.

[66:12-13] The text then reads: *Because this is what the Lord says: See, I myself turn to them like a river of peace and like a wadi overflowing the glory of nations.* Again, in this verse, he adds the phrase *glory of nations* to the new Zion and new Jerusalem spoken of above, and he compares the *peace* that will be given to the nations with a *rushing river.* The text speaks of this *river* in other passages: "The *river* of God was filled with water,"[28] and: "The *river's* strong currents make glad the city of God."[29] And the text says that a deep *peace* will flow over the church of God like a river or a powerful stream, for *their children shall be carried on shoulders and comforted on knees.*

And these things were stated in the prom-

---

[17]Cf. 2 Macc 7:28; Wis 1:14. [18]Cf. 2 Macc 7:28; Wis 1:14. [19]2 Cor 5:4. [20]2 Cor 5:2b. [21]Mt 5:12. [22]1 Pet 2:2. [23]Song 1:2. [24]1 Pet 2:2. [25]Heb 5:12. [26]Heb. 5:12, 14. [27]1 Pet 2:2. [28]Ps 65:9. [29]Ps 46:4.

ises above, indicating that "foster fathers"[30] would support those in the church who are still infants and are nourished with milk. These "foster fathers" are perhaps teachers or those who legitimately preside over the church of God or perhaps divine and heavenly angels. For our Savior clearly stated this when he said: "Do not despise one of these little ones"[31] in my church, "for their angels always behold the face of my Father who is in heaven." Therefore, the mighty will lift up the weak *on shoulders, and they shall comfort them on knees.* As a *mother will comfort* her children, *so even I* myself, the Lord, because I am the Father of all, *I will comfort* the comforters of the downtrodden.

[66:14] And so, he says, *you shall see* this fulfilled, *and your heart shall rejoice.* And what *shall you see* if not clearly God? *And your bones* [405] *shall grow like grass,* or according to Symmachus: *They shall flourish like fresh grass, and the hand of the Lord will be known to those who fear him.* This will be the end result of the promises: "*You shall see* God." For this reason, the Savior pronounced them blessed when he said: "Blessed are the pure in heart, for *they shall see* God."[32] And so *it will be known* to all that it was neither the hand of people nor a human power that accomplished these great things, but it was truly the *hand of God,* and *it shall be known to those who fear him.* For those who have "fear" receive the "wisdom" of God, "for the fear of the Lord is the beginning of wisdom."[33]

They will understand that although his great and amazing grace reached humanity, God will not always be easy to reach. Therefore, some will have knowledge of these things, but the Word *threatens* the others in the following verses.

[66:15] To those discussed above he promises the aforesaid blessings, but he says that *he shall threaten* those who have walked in a perverse

manner. Then he teaches the form of the threat when he presents the second and glorious coming of the Savior, when he will come "with the glory of the Father and with his angels"[34] "to judge the living and the dead."[35] Therefore, he says: *See, the Lord will come like fire.* But instead of *he will come like fire,* all the other Greek translations render this phrase: *He will come in fire. And his chariots will come like a tempest. His chariots* are the angels and powers that surround him, and the text says that those who are worthy of punishment will experience them like a *tempest.* And the text says that *he will come* because of the ungodly, and he will let his *wrath* loose on them. His *wrath* is commonly called the corrective and avenging powers. And he will release *his rebuke with a flame of fire* against them. But instead of *and rebuke,* the other Greek translations render this phrase: *His contempt.* Therefore, according to this verse, this is how the *wrath* will be. But, as the text has frequently and clearly stated above, to those who are worthy of his kingdom, he will show "the glory" of his kingdom "to his elders."[36] And he will act as a "bridegroom" and will welcome "his bride,"[37] but these things are for those whom the Word proclaimed would partake of the promises.

[66:16] Then he threatens them when he says: *And by the fire of the Lord shall all the earth be judged, and all flesh by his sword; many shall be wounded by the Lord.* He appeals to the physical terms *sword* as well as *wound,* because the Jews were not otherwise able to understand and follow the deeper meaning of the words. And the apostle speaks clearly of the message of the verse when he says: "But by your hard and [406] impenitent heart you are storing up wrath for yourself on the day of wrath when God's righteous judgment will be revealed. For he will render to every man according to his works."[38]

---

[30]Cf. Is 49:23. [31]Mt. 18:10. [32]Mt. 5:8. [33]Ps 111:10. [34]Mt 16:27. [35]2 Tim 4:1. [36]Cf. Is 24:23. [37]Is 61:10. [38]Rom 2:5-6 RSV.

[66:17] The prophet next leads into a refutation of the Jews who acted in an ungodly fashion during the same time when he says: *Those who sanctify and purify themselves for the gardens and who in the porches eat swine's flesh, the abominations and the mouse shall be consumed together, said the Lord.* In this verse, the Word does not accuse those who *eat the flesh of swine* but those who practice the things to which he alludes when he says *eating the flesh of swine publicly*, and so on. For those who live among the nations and those who live as citizens among the Gentiles differ in no way from the Jews in their manner of life. For this reason, he says that those whom he has delivered over will perish in the same punishment as the Gentiles. But he said that they *purify themselves for the gardens*, because they no longer *purify themselves* "with ashes of a heifer and with the instruments of sprinkling for seven days"[39] and with the purifications of animal sacrifices, according to the law that Moses delivered. Instead they wandered through the gardens, supposing that the cleansing of water would be sufficient for them if they washed themselves in the water *in the gardens*, and they thought that then they would have left nothing undone that is required by the law. And so they committed defiled and unclean deeds and acted unlawfully and shamelessly, and they thought that they could *purify* their souls with mere water!

[66:18-20] Therefore, he continues on: *I am coming to gather their works and their reasonings.*[40] The Word then turns to the theme of the universal judgment and says: *I am coming to gather all the nations and tongues, and they shall come and shall see my glory. And I will leave a sign on them, and from them I will send forth those who are saved.* The Savior clearly taught these things in the Gospels when he said:

"When the Son of man comes in the *glory* of his Father, and all the angels with him, and *they will gather all the nations* before him, and he will separate them, as a shepherd separates the sheep from the goats, and he will place the sheep on the right and the goats on the left."[41] To those on the right he will say one thing, but to those on the left he will say another. And this is what the prophecy states in the verse: *And I am coming to gather their works and their reasonings, all the nations and tongues, and they shall come and see my glory.* Again he promises the *nations* that those who are deemed worthy will see his *glory*. But, in order that this might happen and that the promises might come to a good end among the nations, he says that he will select certain ones *from them*. But certain ones of *them* will clearly be destroyed, concerning whom it has been said: *They shall be consumed together.* For it is *from them* that those who remain shall receive my *sign* and the call of the nations who are about [407] to *see my glory*. For this reason, the text reads: *I will leave a sign on them, and from them I will send forth those who are saved.*

And these are "the remnant chosen by grace,"[42] concerning whom it has been said: "If the Lord Sabaoth had not left us offspring."[43] This, then, is "the offspring," and he says *from them*—from those who have been *preserved* from destruction—*I will send forth to the nations*, to the peoples of other races and tribes, *to Tharsis and Phoud and Loud and Mosoch and Thobel and to Greece and to the islands far away*—those who have not heard my name or seen my glory. In the verses above, he said: "Because those who were not informed about him *shall see*, and those who did not *hear* shall understand,"[44] and again: "I became visible to those who were not inquiring about me; I was found by those who were not seeking me. I said, 'Here am I,' to those who did not call on my name."[45] In a passage related to the one

---

[39]Num 19:9. [40]It seems that Eusebius has inadvertently dropped part of the original text, forcing the English translator to conflate the first two thoughts in the LXX version of Is 66:18. [41]Mt 25:31-33. [42]Rom 11:5. [43]Is 1:9. [44]Is 52:15. [45]Is 65:1.

quoted above, he promises *to send* his apostles to *nations* foreign to Israel and *far beyond* Judea and to the *islands*, where no one has ever *heard* the *name* of a prophet, and he says that his apostles will bear a *sign* with them and will live among them. And what is this *sign* if not the saving *sign* of "the *glory* of the only-begotten of God"[46] that they fearlessly *announced* to all the *nations*? And they will *bring* their very brothers—those who had formerly been enslaved in the error of idolatry but who have now been set free—to God and bear them as a *gift*. They will do these things at the time of the completion of "the city of God and the heavenly Jerusalem."[47] At that time *they shall bring* them and achieve a good end, when they shall be taken up like "Elijah" and flash with heavenly light as they are borne on angelic "*chariots*."[48]

Therefore, the text reads: *With horses and chariots, in mule-drawn litters with sunshades, into the holy city Jerusalem, and they shall bring your kindred from all the nations.* You will understand what the *horses* and the angelic *chariots* are when you reflect on the prophecy of Zechariah, when the Word alludes to angelic powers in the phrase "dapple-gray *horses* and various shades of white *horses* and *chariots*."[49] The *mule-drawn litters* seem to signify our resurrection bodies, in which our souls will mount up and be received into the heavenly city. And *litters* is an appropriate word picture, because of the glory that will shine forth from our resurrection bodies. But instead of *mule-drawn litters with sunshades*, Symmachus translates this phrase: *On horses and chariots and litters and carriages and sedans.* All these things were spoken in a coarse and literal fashion, as was appropriate for the Jewish audience. But according to the deeper meaning, this phrase signifies their journey [408] up through the air and on into heaven, as one would interpret it in light of the clear teaching of the divine apostle: "We shall be caught up

together with them in the clouds to meet the Lord in the air; and so we shall always be with the Lord."[50] And so they shall enter into the heavenly city of God, and so those who have been saved from every nation shall come to the heavenly Jerusalem, just as *the sons of Israel* ascended and were bringing *their sacrifices* up on the earth. This is what he means when he says: *So that the sons of Israel may bring to me their sacrifices with music into the house of the Lord.* But according to Symmachus, the text reads: *Even as the sons of Israel were bringing the offering in a clean vessel into the house of the Lord.* Therefore, just as those who prescribed the worship in the earthly Jerusalem according to the bodily law then practiced these things, so in accord with the earthly example shall those who ascend into the heavenly Jerusalem come with their own fruits. And each will offer the most excellent fruit-bearing gifts in his life.

[66:21-22] He continues on: *And I will take some of them.* He says that he will make some *of them* his own, from the nations whom he named a little earlier: "Tharsis and Phoud and Loud and Mosoch and Thobel and to Greece and to the islands far away—those who have not heard my name or seen my glory."[51] *From them,* he says, *I will take priests and Levites, said the Lord.* And the Word advances a reasonable argument when he explains: *For as the new heaven and the new earth, which I am making, remain before me, says the Lord, so shall your offspring and your name stand.* For if *heaven* will be *new* and the earth *new* and Jerusalem *new*, it follows that the *priests and Levites* will also be *new*. For this reason, the text reads in the verse above: "They shall not remember the former things, nor shall they come up on their heart."[52] Therefore, *I will take some of them* whom I earlier called *priests and Levites.* For it is not convincing that he would say *I will take priests and Levites* to the Jewish people, as they

---

[46]Jn 1:14. [47]Heb 12:22. [48]Cf. 2 Kings 2:11. [49]Zech 6:3. [50]1 Thess 4:17. [51]Is 66:19. [52]Is 65:17.

suppose these things to be addressed to them. For he neither says *I will take Levites* from the *Levites* nor *priests* from *priests*, because only *priests* from the tribe of *Levi* are *Levites*. But the passage promises that he would do this in the calling of the Gentiles. And these things will occur when *the new heaven and the new earth* will arrive, *which I am causing to remain.* "For the former things remained no longer."[53] Therefore, the text reads: "*Heaven* and earth will pass away,"[54] and again: "*Heaven* shall roll up like a scroll,"[55] and: "The earth shall be ruined with ruin"[56] in the coming age when "Christ the firstfruits shall come, and then those who belong to Christ at his coming."[57] Then shall come *the new heaven and the new earth*, concerning which he said in the Beatitudes: "Blessed" are these, "for theirs is the kingdom [409] of heaven,"[58] and: "Blessed are the meek, for they shall inherit the earth."[59] Therefore, this *new heaven* and *new earth* of the new age shall *remain* and last for a boundless and endless age. It seems to me that he reflects on the different rooms in the kingdom: "For they are many in my Father's house."[60] There are some rooms on earth that lead to heaven, but there are some that lead in the opposite direction and are shut to the glory of heaven and descend below. And there are things that shall *remain* forever and never pass away. "For the things that are seen are transient, but the things that are unseen are eternal."[61] For this reason, he says: *Which I am making to remain before me, and your name*, and so it shall endure forever *before me*. In speaking of *forever*, he alludes to eternal, immortal and boundless life.

[66:23] Then he continues on to say: *And it shall be that month after month and sabbath after sabbath all flesh shall come before me to bow down in Jerusalem, said the Lord.* The words *in Jerusalem* neither appear in the other Greek translations nor in the Hebrew text. But it is not problematic that the phrase does appear in the Septuagint, for it is clear that it refers to the heavenly Jerusalem and introduces the kingdom of our Savior. And if rooms and symbols and images of the heavenly realms had been ordained by Moses, it follows that we could learn something about the feasts in heaven and the true *sabbaths* and *months*. For "about this we have much to say that is hard to explain."[62] The subject would require a great deal of study time to address properly. But just as in the Jerusalem below, when a great multitude of different nations inhabited the city and yet it was chosen as a place of holiness where those who lived in another country came and "performed the ritual duties of God,"[63] so also in the designated heavenly city and chosen place of holiness, it is accessible to no one except "only the high priest"[64]—clearly the Son of God. And it is his right alone to approach the divinity of the Father and to enter the very presence of the Father. And because they will dwell in the "many" heavenly "rooms"[65] at the appointed times, it is necessary to understand what sort of times and years there will be there. One of the prophets understood this and said: "And years of long ago I remembered and meditated."[66] For they will enter the chosen celestial city and place set apart in the kingdom of God, and they will experience the very height of blessedness, of which they will never be deprived and which will never fail them.

As certain sojourners they will reach the heavenly feasts, and they will partake of a never-ending and inspired joy and have the benefit of unspeakably good things, concerning which it has been said: "What no eye has seen, nor ear heard, nor the heart of man conceived, what God has prepared for those who love him."[67] [410] When they have been filled with these things, they will return to their own

---

[53]Rev 21:4. [54]Mt 24:35. [55]Is 34:4. [56]Is 24:3. [57]1 Cor 15:23. [58]Mt 5:3. [59]Mt 5:5. [60]Jn 14:2. [61]2 Cor 4:18. [62]Heb 5:11. [63]Cf. Heb 9:6. [64]Cf. Heb 9:7. [65]Jn 14:2. [66]Ps 75:5. [67]1 Cor 2:9.

rooms and resume spending time as is proper and appropriate for each one. And then the true "sabbath rest"[68] and the perfect and true "rest of souls"[69] will be rendered to those who are worthy of these things. For this reason, it has been said: *And it shall be that month after month and sabbath after sabbath all flesh shall come before me to bow down in Jerusalem, said the Lord.* In saying *all flesh,* he thus indicates all nations. And this is how we should interpret the verse above: "*All flesh* shall see the salvation of God,"[70] and elsewhere: "I will pour out my spirit on *all flesh,* and they shall prophesy."[71] And, lest the Jews suppose that these things were said concerning them, he forcefully explains that the verse applies universally to *all flesh,* thus clearly indicating the entire human race. But *they shall come* at that time, and the citizens of Jerusalem are "myriads of angels,"[72] even as the apostle taught: "And the assembly of the firstborn who are enrolled in heaven."[73] *They shall* not *come* from distances, but they shall forever dwell in the city and live as citizens, serving as "ministers"[74] and "priests" under a "high priest" to the Son of God, forever enjoying good things. And *they shall* all *see* the destruction of the ungodly and reflect on the good things of which the ungodly were deprived.

[66:24] Therefore, the text reads: *And they shall go forth and see the limbs of the people who have transgressed against me,* or according to Symmachus: *And they shall see the end of the people who rejected me.* Who these were, he clearly states at the beginning of the prophecy: "I begat sons and exalted them, but *they rejected* me."[75] Therefore, he alludes to those of the Jewish nation who "*rejected*"[76] the saving "grace." Those who are far from them and *shall go forth* from Jerusalem *shall see* them, and they shall depart to their own rooms. The Word states this when he says: *And they shall go forth*

and see the limbs of the people who have rejected me, whose worm shall not die and whose fire shall not be quenched, yet they shall become a spectacle to all flesh. Therefore, this is the worst of all punishments, because their *worm* will be endlessly among them. Thus he calls their righteous conscience a *worm,* because it eats away at them, and their consciences convict them of their evil deeds when their souls repent, because they acted in an ungodly way, imagining that they had been chosen because of their good deeds. Therefore, each one of them will confess and become his own accuser, recounting all that he did in his mortal life and being stung by his conscience. And thus their *worm* persists endlessly. For, then, he is not speaking concerning a physical *worm* when he says that these things will be and "their *fire*"[77] shall be "unquenchable." Our Savior delineated the end of the ungodly when in the Gospels he said to those who will stand [411] "on his left": "Depart into the eternal fire prepared for the devil and his angels."[78] Therefore, although he speaks of "eternal" *fire* in the preceding verse and "unquenchable" *fire* in this verse, yet both of these Scriptures are speaking of one and the same thing. *And,* because they will be in such punishment, *they shall become a spectacle to all flesh.* To whom does the word *flesh* refer? Certainly not to those who will be punished but to those who will be deemed worthy of the view from heaven, concerning whom the text reads above: "*All flesh* shall come before me to bow down, said the Lord,"[79] *and they shall go forth and see.* Therefore, those to whom the word *flesh* refers shall be deemed worthy to *see* the end of those who will be surpassingly punished. But those who will be delivered over "to eternal *fire*"[80] shall carry their *worm* in their soul endlessly, and they shall be exposed to the view of those who will be deemed worthy of the inspired bliss.

---

[68]Heb 4:9. [69]Mt 11:29. [70]Is 40:5. [71]Joel 2:28. [72]Heb 12:22. [73]Heb 12:23. [74]Cf. Is 61:6. [75]Is 1:2. [76]Cf. Gal 2:21. [77]Mt 3:12. [78]Mt 25:41. [79]Is 66:23. [80]Mt 25:41.

Subject Index

Scripture Index